CW01102921

WHS

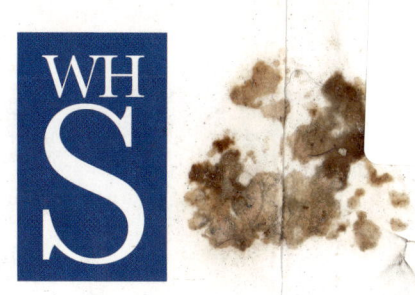

Study and Revise

GCSE
Science: Double Award

Eileen Ramsden, David Applin
and Jim Breithaupt

KEY TO SYMBOLS

As you read through this book you will notice the following symbols. They will help you find your way around the book more quickly.

 shows a handy hint to help you remember something

 shows you some key facts

 means remember!!!

 says 'Did you know this?' – interesting points to note

 gives worked examples to help you with calculations and equations

 points you to other parts of the book where related topics are explained

 shows a sequence of linked processes

 refers you from a diagram to a checklist of related points

Acknowledgements

Copyright photographs have been used, with permission, from the following sources:
Planet Earth Pictures **p. 17**; Science Photo Library **pp. 34, 97**

Copyright © Eileen Ramsden, Jim Breithaupt, David Applin 1997, 2004

First published in this edition 2004
exclusively for WHSmith by
Hodder & Stoughton Educational
338 Euston Road
London NW1 3BH

All rights reserved. Apart from any use permitted under UK copyright law, no part of this publication may be reproduced or transmitted in any form or by any means, electronic or mechanical, including photocopying, recording or any information storage and retrieval system, without permission in writing from the Publisher.

Impression number   10 9 8 7 6 5 4 3
Year   2010 2009 2008 2007 2006 2005

Illustrations: Peter Bull, Simon Cooke, Chris Etheridge, Ian Law, Joe Little, Andrea Norton, Mike Parsons, John Plumb, Dave Poole, Chris Rothero, Anthony Warne

Prepared by Starfish, London

Printed and bound in the UK by Scotprint

A CIP record for this book is available from the British Library

ISBN 0 340 85859 1

GCSE Science: Double Award and
this Study and Revise book   iv

Life processes and living things   1

1   Introducing biology   2
2   Organisms in the environment   9
3   Cell activity   27
4   Green plants as organisms   45
5   Humans as organisms   56
6   Inheritance and evolution   90
Answers   108

Materials and their properties   115

1   Matter and the kinetic theory   116
2   Elements, compounds and
    equations   119
3   The structure of the atom   124
4   Electrolysis   128
5   The chemical bond   135
6   The periodic table   140
7   Acids, bases and salts   145
8   Air   153
9   Water   165
10 Planet Earth   169
11 Metals and alloys   177
12 Reaction speeds   186
13 Tackling chemical calculations   190
14 Fuels   196
15 Alkenes and plastics   202
Periodic table   207
Answers   208

Physical processes   218

1   Beyond the Earth   219
2   Energy resources and energy
    transfer   227
3   Radioactivity   235
4   Waves   244
5   Sound waves and seismic
    waves   249
6   Light   254
7   The electromagnetic spectrum   261
8   Force and motion   267
9   Forces in balance   275
10 Electric charge   283
11 Electric circuits   290
12 Electromagnetism   297
Equations and symbols you
should know   304
Answers   305

Index   315

GCSE Science: Double Award and this Study and Revise book

Tailor-made for Science: Double Award

This *Study and Revise GCSE Science: Double Award* book covers all the syllabuses for GCSE Science: Double Award for the different Examining Groups. It is not intended to replace your school textbooks. As tests and examinations approach, however, many students feel the need to revise from something a good deal shorter than their usual textbook. This book is intended to fill that need.

Getting the most out of the guide

We have tried to depart from the textbook style by presenting material in the form of charts, tables and concept maps.

Each chapter begins with a set of Test yourself questions to give you an idea of how well you have already grasped the topic. You should work through the questions again after you have revised the topic. The improvement should be encouraging. There is a set of Round up questions at the end of each chapter. You can work out your improvement index from your score on the Round up questions compared with your first score on the Test yourself questions.

Revision tips

Here is some important advice for each stage of your revision:

- **Leading up to the exam**, make a timetable for homework and revision and stick to it. Be realistic and make sure you include all your subjects, and leave time for leisure activities. Planned use of time and concentrated study will give you time for recreation as well as revision.

- **When the exam arrives,** make sure you have everything you need the night before, such as your pen, spare cartridge, pencils, rubber and calculator (in working order). Decide what to wear and get everything ready. Avoid last minute dithering. Be optimistic and be confident. Don't sit up late at night trying to cram.
- **In the examination room**, read the instructions on the front of the paper before you set pen to paper. Don't spend more time than you should on a question. Attempt all the questions you are supposed to answer and make sure you turn every page over. If you suffer a panic attack, breathe deeply and slowly to get lots of oxygen into your system to clear your thoughts. Above all, keep your examination in perspective – it is not a matter of life or death! Finally, don't agonise over an examination afterwards.

We hope our book leads you to success.

Eileen Ramsden, Jim Breithaupt, David Applin

Life processes and living things

1	**Introducing biology**	**2**
1.1	Living on Earth	2
1.2	Characteristics of life	3
1.3	Grouping living things	3
1.4	Identifying living things	6
2	**Organisms in the environment**	**9**
2.1	Introducing ecology	9
2.2	Food chains and webs	11
2.3	Ecological pyramids	14
2.4	Distribution of organisms	16
2.5	Population size	18
2.6	Food production	20
3	**Cell activity**	**27**
3.1	Cells at work	27
3.2	Into and out of cells	28
3.3	Cell division	32
3.4	Cells, tissues and organs	33
3.5	Chemicals in living things	39
4	**Green plants as organisms**	**45**
4.1	Photosynthesis and mineral nutrients	45
4.2	Transport in plants	49
4.3	Plant responses	50

5	**Humans as organisms**	**56**
5.1	Food and diet	56
5.2	The digestive system	58
5.3	Breathing, gaseous exchange and respiration	62
5.4	Blood and the circulatory system	65
5.5	Senses and the nervous system	70
5.6	Sense organs	73
5.7	Hormones	77
5.8	Maintaining the internal environment	80
5.9	Health and disease	81
6	**Inheritance and evolution**	**90**
6.1	Reproduction	90
6.2	Asexual reproduction in plants	92
6.3	Monohybrid inheritance	93
6.4	Biotechnology	99
6.5	Variation	101
6.6	Evolution	102
Answers		**108**
Index		**315**

Chapter 1   Introducing biology

How much do you already know? Work out your score on page 108.

Test yourself

1. What would happen to ground temperature if Earth were **a)** nearer to the Sun **b)** further from the Sun? [2]

2. **a)** List the processes which tell you that something is living. [7 × ½]

   b) Put a tick (✓) next to the processes which you think apply to animals. [7 × ½]

   c) Put a cross (✗) next to the processes which you think apply to plants. [6 × ½]

   d) Do plants and animals have the same characteristics? If not, how are they different? [1]

3. Using the forget-me-not and oak tree as examples, explain the meaning of the words 'annual' and 'perennial'. [3]

4. **a)** What is a biological key used for? [1]

   b) Why are features like exact colour, size and mass not suitable for including in a biological key? [3]

5. List the physical features of soil which make it a suitable place for earthworms to live. [4]

1.1 Living on Earth

PREVIEW

At the end of this section you will:
- understand why Earth is a suitable place for living things (organisms)
- know that soil, air and water are the physical environments in which organisms live.

Why the Earth can support life

Earth is a planet in orbit round a star we call the Sun. It is the only planet we know of that supports life.

★ Earth is close enough to the Sun for its surface temperature to be in the range in which life can exist. The temperature at the Earth's surface varies between −70 °C and 55 °C.

★ Earth is massive enough to have sufficient gravity to hold down an atmosphere of different gases essential for living organisms.

★ The layer of ozone which surrounds Earth reduces the amount of ultraviolet light from the Sun reaching the planet's surface. Too much ultraviolet light destroys living things.

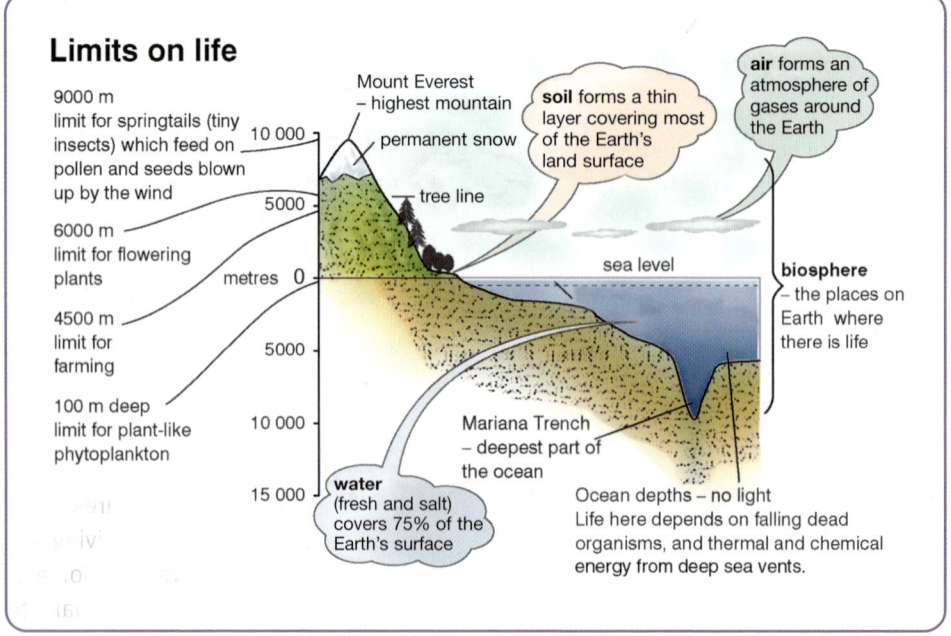

Earth's physical environment

Introducing biology

The diagram on the opposite page shows that soil, air and water form Earth's environment.

★ **Soil** is formed when the weather, the roots of plants and the different activities of animals break down rocks into small particles.

★ **Air** consists of: 78% nitrogen; 21% oxygen; 0.035% carbon dioxide; and less than 1% water vapour, argon, xenon and other gases.

★ **Water** fills the seas, oceans, rivers and lakes. About 2% of the Earth's water is locked up as ice, in the soil, in the bodies of living things or is vapour in the atmosphere.

1.2 Characteristics of life

PREVIEW

At the end of this section you will know the characteristics of life:
- Movement
- Respiration
- Sensitivity
- Growth
- Reproduction
- Excretion
- Nutrition

Handy hint

The memory aid **Mrs Gren** will help you remember the characteristics of living things.

More about MRS GREN

The characteristics of life are the features that are common to all living things.

★ **Movement**: animals are able to move from place to place because of the action of **muscles** which pull on the **skeleton**. Plants do not usually move from place to place; they move mainly by **growing**.

★ **Respiration** occurs in cells, and releases energy from food for life's activities. **Aerobic** respiration uses oxygen to release energy from food. **Anaerobic** respiration releases energy from food without using oxygen.

★ **Sensitivity** allows living things to detect changes in their surroundings and respond to them.

★ **Growth** leads to an increase in size. **Development** occurs as the young change and become adult in appearance.

★ **Reproduction** produces new individuals.

★ **Excretion** removes the waste substances produced by the chemical reactions (called **metabolism**) taking place in cells.

★ **Nutrition** makes food (usually by the process of photosynthesis) or takes in food for use in the body.

Fact file

Respiration is sometimes compared to combustion, but there is a vital difference. When fuel is burnt, energy is quickly released. If cells were to release energy from food as suddenly, the sharp rise in temperature would kill them. Respiration releases energy from food gradually.

Remember

- **Respiration** releases energy from food.
- **Gaseous exchange** takes in oxygen for respiration and removes carbon dioxide produced by respiration.
- **Excretion** removes wastes produced by metabolism.
- **Defecation** (or egestion) removes the undigested remains of food.

1.3 Grouping living things

PREVIEW

At the end of this section you will:
- understand that groups of living things are named according to Linnaeus' system of classification
- know the major groups of plants and animals
- understand binomial names.

Classification

Living things which have features in common are grouped together. Organising living things into groups is called **classification**. Some characteristics are unique to the group; other characteristics are

Introducing biology

Arachnids
- The body is made up of two parts.
- There are **eight legs**.
- Scorpions, mites and harvestmen are close relatives of spiders.

Cnidarians
- The body has no front or rear. Its parts are arranged evenly in the round.
- Tentacles surround an opening which is both mouth and anus.
- Stinging cells are used to capture prey.

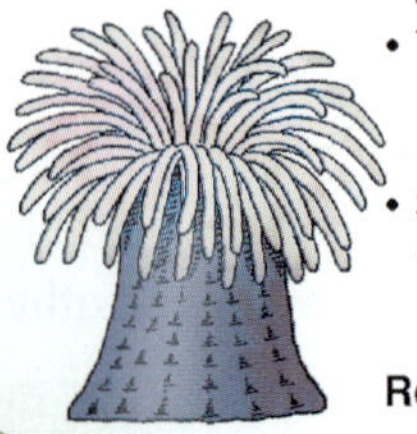

Crustaceans
- The body is made up of two parts.
- There are 14 legs.
- Woodlice are the only crustaceans that live on land.
- Crabs, lobsters and prawns are close relatives of woodlice.

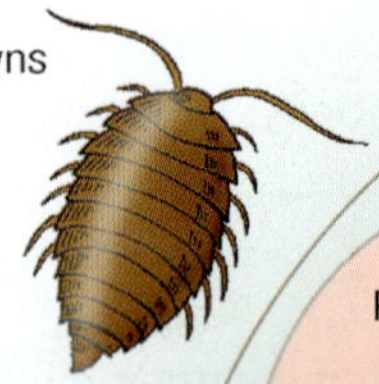

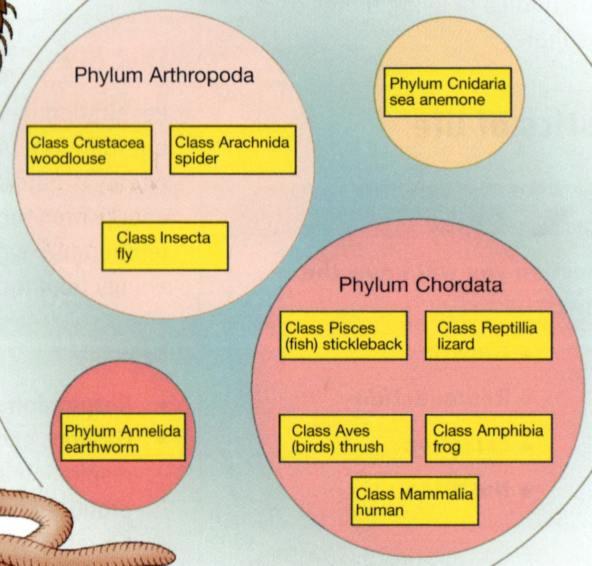

Reptiles
- Skin is dry and covered with scales that restrict water loss from the body.
- As a result, reptiles can live in dry environments.
- Lay eggs, each protected by a hard shell.
- As a result, water is not necessary for breeding.

Insects
- The body is made up of three parts: head, thorax and abdomen.
- There are six legs.
- There are usually two pairs of wings, but flies have one pair.

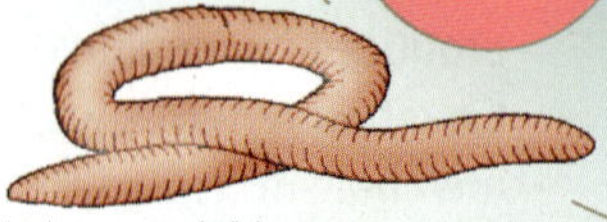

ANIMAL KINGDOM

- Phylum Arthropoda
  - Class Crustacea — woodlouse
  - Class Arachnida — spider
  - Class Insecta — fly
- Phylum Cnidaria — sea anemone
- Phylum Annelida — earthworm
- Phylum Chordata
  - Class Pisces (fish) — stickleback
  - Class Reptilia — lizard
  - Class Aves (birds) — thrush
  - Class Amphibia — frog
  - Class Mammalia — human

Worms
- The body is long and thin.
- The body is made up of many segments.

Birds
- The body is covered with feathers which:
  > make flying possible
  > keep in heat
  > keep out water.
- The beak is specialised (adapted) differently in different species to deal with different foods.
- Birds lay eggs, protected by a hard shell.

Amphibians
- Live on land but breed in water.
- Development of the young into adults is called a metamorphosis.
- Soft skin is a surface for gaseous exchange. The gases are in solution.
- As a result the skin loses water easily in dry air.
- As a result amphibians are restricted to living in damp places when on land.

Fish
- The body is covered with scales.
- Fins control the position of the body in water.
- Gills are surfaces for gaseous exchange. They are exposed to the environment. The gases exchanged are in solution.
- As a result gills lose water easily in dry air.
- As a result fish are restricted to living in water.

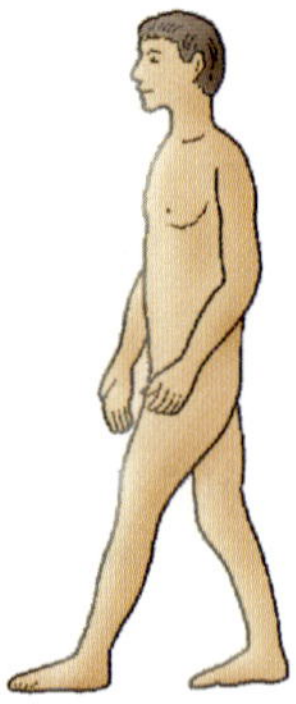

Mammals
- Hair helps conserve body heat.
- Young feed on milk produced by the female's breasts (mammary glands)
- Have a small tail bone called the coccyx.

Groups within groups – the major groups of the Animal kingdom and the Plant kingdom are listed with an example of each. Each major group of plants is called a Division rather than a Phylum.

Introducing biology

Mosses
- Mosses quickly lose water in dry air.
- As a result, mosses live in damp places.
- Roots are absent.
- As a result, water is soaked up by capillary movement over the leaves.
- Stalks grow from moss plants, each carrying a spore capsule filled with spores.
- Each spore is able to develop into a new plant.

REPRODUCE BY MEANS OF SPORES

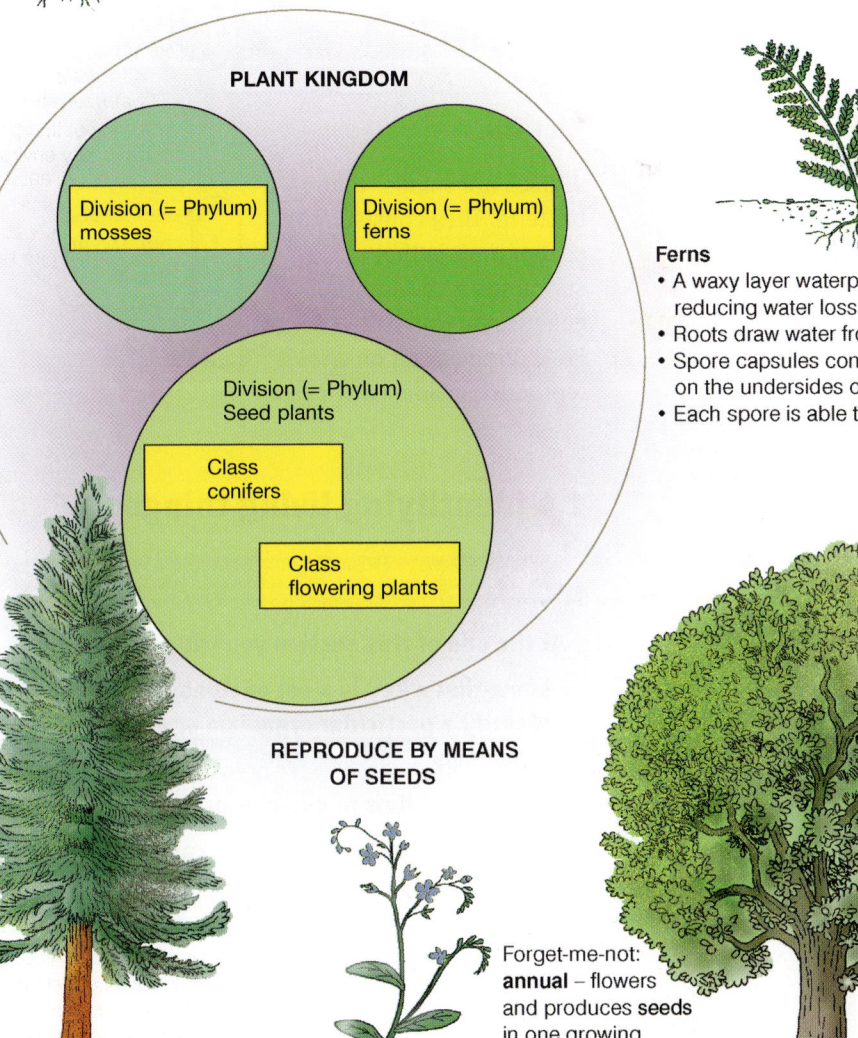

Ferns
- A waxy layer waterproofs the plant's surfaces, reducing water loss in a dry atmosphere.
- Roots draw water from the soil.
- Spore capsules containing spores grow in patches on the undersides of leaves.
- Each spore is able to grow into a new fern plant.

REPRODUCE BY MEANS OF SEEDS

Forget-me-not: **annual** – flowers and produces **seeds** in one growing season. The plant then dies.

Oak tree: **perennial** – produces seeds year after year. The plant survives for many years.

Conifers
- Seeds are contained in cones.
- Covered with leaves all year round ('evergreens').
- Roots draw water from the soil.
- Waxy layer waterproofs plant surfaces.

Flowering plants
- Seeds are contained in fruits.
- Leaves of trees/shrubs fall once a year ('deciduous').
- Roots draw water from the soil.
- Waxy layer waterproofs plant surfaces.

Introducing biology

shared with other groups. Groups therefore combine to form larger groups. The largest group of all is the **kingdom**. Each:
- kingdom contains a number of **phyla**
- phyl**um** (singular) contains a number of **classes**
- class contains a number of **orders**
- order contains a number of **families**
- family contains a number of **genera**
- gen**us** (singular) contains one or more **species**.

The genus and the species identify the individual living thing, rather like your first name and family name identify you. For example, humans belong to the genus *Homo* and have the species name *sapiens*; barn owls are called *Tyto alba*.

Since the name of each living thing is in two parts, the method of naming is called the **binomial system**. Notice that the genus name begins with a capital letter, the species name begins with a small letter, and the whole name is printed in italics.

The Swedish naturalist Carolus Linnaeus (the Latin version of his name) published *Systema Naturae* in 1735. The book established the system of naming organisms that we use today.

The five kingdoms

There are five kingdoms. Living things in each kingdom obtain food in different ways. Their structure and body chemistry are different. Each kingdom, therefore, represents a way of life which all its members share. Pages 4–5 show the major groups in the Animal kingdom and Plant kingdom. The other kingdoms are:

Kingdom Fungi – organisms made up of cells that form thread-like structures called **hyphae**.

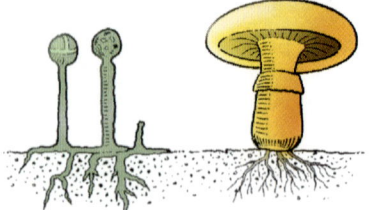
(not to scale)

Kingdom Protista – single-celled organisms. The cell body contains a distinct nucleus within which is the genetic material (DNA).

 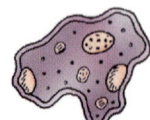
(not to scale)

Kingdom Bacteria – single-celled organisms. The cell body is simple in structure compared with the cell body of protists. The cell body does not contain a distinct nucleus. The genetic material (DNA) lies in the cytoplasm.

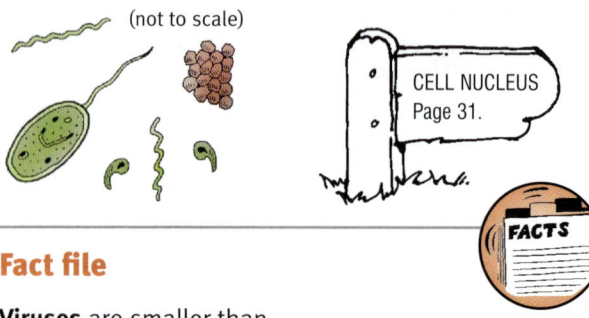
(not to scale)

CELL NUCLEUS Page 31.

Fact file

Viruses are smaller than bacteria. They consist of a coat of protein that surrounds a strand of genetic material (DNA or RNA). Viruses can only reproduce inside living cells.

DNA AND RNA Page 41.

1.4 Identifying living things

PREVIEW

At the end of this section you will:
- know that a key is a set of clues that help identify a particular organism or group of organisms
- understand how to use a dichotomous key
- know that a dichotomous key can be written in different ways.

What is a key?

A **key** is a means of identifying an unfamiliar organism from a selection of specimens. A key consists of a set of descriptions. Each description is a clue that helps in the identification. A set of clues makes the key.

Introducing biology

The easiest type of key to use is called a **dichotomous** key. 'Dichotomous' means branching into two. Each time the key branches, you have to choose between alternative statements. The alternative statements may be presented diagrammatically as a chart, or written in pairs or **couplets**. For example, a key to amphibians would begin:

	yes	no
1a The animal has a tail.	**newts**	go to **2**
2b The animal has no tail.	**frogs and toads**	go to **3**
and so on …		

By comparing the pairs of statements with the organism in front of you, you will eventually find one that fits. This identifies the organism. A key is therefore the route to a name. Different keys are used to name different living things.

When making a key, it is important to choose features that are characteristic of the type of organism rather than of the individual itself. For example, shape or proportions and patterns of colour are fairly constant in a type of organism and are therefore useful clues in a key. Size and shades of colour vary from individual to individual and are of limited use.

Does the specimen have …?

- a tail → NEWTS
  - a rough warty skin which is dark brown with dark spots on top and a blotched yellow or orange belly — **GREAT CRESTED (WARTY) NEWT**
  - a smooth skin which is green or brownish with or without dark spots. The belly is yellow or orange and may be spotted — **SMOOTH OR PALMATE NEWT**
    - the throat is whitish and spotted — **SMOOTH NEWT**
    - the throat is pinkish and not spotted — **PALMATE NEWT**
- no tail → FROGS AND TOADS
  - a warty skin and no dark flash behind the eye — **TOADS**
    - a yellow strip running down its back — **NATTERJACK TOAD**
    - no yellow strip running down its back — **COMMON TOAD**
  - a smooth moist skin and a dark flash behind the eye — **COMMON FROG**

Different ways of writing a key to amphibians

Introducing biology

ROUND UP

How much have you improved? Work out your improvement index on page 108.

1. What would happen to Earth's water if Earth were **a)** nearer to **b)** further from the Sun? [2]

2. **a)** Which gas is used during aerobic respiration to release energy from food? [1]
   b) Which gas is produced during aerobic respiration? [1]

3. **a)** Distinguish between respiration and gaseous exchange. [3]
   b) Distinguish between excretion and defecation. [2]

4. In the 1890s, when people saw cars for the first time, many thought that the cars were alive. Imagine that you are a reporter writing a short article for the local newspaper reassuring people that although cars seem to move under their own steam, they are not alive. [8]

5. Match each characteristic of life in column **A** with its description in column **B**.

A characteristics	B descriptions
movement	making or obtaining food
respiration	responding to stimuli
sensitivity	removing waste substances produced by cells
growth	producing new individuals
reproduction	releasing energy from food
excretion	changing position
nutrition	increasing in size [7]

6. Different types of animal are listed in column **A**. Match each type with the correct description in column **B**.

A animals	B descriptions
insect	no legs
worm	eight legs
spider	two legs
bird	six legs [4]

7. Briefly describe how a biological key is used. [4]

8. Briefly explain how the binomial system of biological names works. [4]

9. A key can be written in couplets. What are 'couplets'? [1]

Organisms in the environment — Chapter 2

How much do you already know? Work out your score on pages 108–9.

Test yourself

1. Match each term in column **A** with the correct description in column **B**.

A terms	B descriptions
biosphere	the place where a group of organisms lives
community	all the ecosystems of the world
habitat	a group of individuals of the same species
population	all the organisms that live in a particular ecosystem [4]

2. a) Why is a food web a more accurate description of feeding in a community than a food chain? [2]
   b) Why do food chains and food webs nearly always begin with plants? [4]

3. a) Why is the pyramid of biomass usually a better description of a community than the pyramid of numbers? [2]
   b) Why is the pyramid of energy the best description of the feeding relationships within a community? [3]

4. Give reasons for the rapid increase in the human population. [4]

5. Weigh up the benefits in food production of intensive farming against the costs to the environment. [5]

2.1 Introducing ecology

PREVIEW

At the end of this section you will understand that:

- an ecosystem is a self-contained part of the biosphere, such as a pond or an oak wood
- the community consists of the organisms that live in a particular ecosystem
- the habitat is the place where a group of organisms live
- a niche is the role each species has in its habitat
- a population is a group of organisms of the same species living in the same place at the same time.

Some ecological terms

Ecology involves studying the relationships between organisms and between organisms and the environment.

The diagram on page 11 shows that all the places on Earth where there is life form the **biosphere**. Each organism is suited (**adapted**) to the place where it lives. This place consists of:

- an **environment** of air, soil or water
- a living **community** of plants, animals, fungi and microorganisms.

Environment and community together form an **ecosystem**, which is a more or less self-contained part of the biosphere. 'Self-contained' means that each ecosystem has its own characteristic organisms not usually found in other ecosystems. These organisms are the living (**biotic**) community of the ecosystem. The physical environment is the non-living (**abiotic**) part, consisting of air, soil or water. The diagram on page 10 shows the different components of an oak wood ecosystem.

Fact file

Polar bears are adapted to survive Arctic cold. Their thick fur coat is easily shaken dry and its hairs stay erect, trapping a layer of air, which helps to insulate the body from heat loss because air is a poor conductor of heat. A thick layer of fat (also a poor conductor of heat) under the skin insulates the body from heat loss as well. A polar bear's fur is white, camouflaging it in the landscape of snow and ice. The camouflage makes it difficult for seals, the bear's main food source, to see when danger (the bear) threatens.

Camels are adapted to survive in hot deserts. Fat insulates the body's surfaces exposed to the Sun, in this case restricting heat flow into the body.

Organisms in the environment

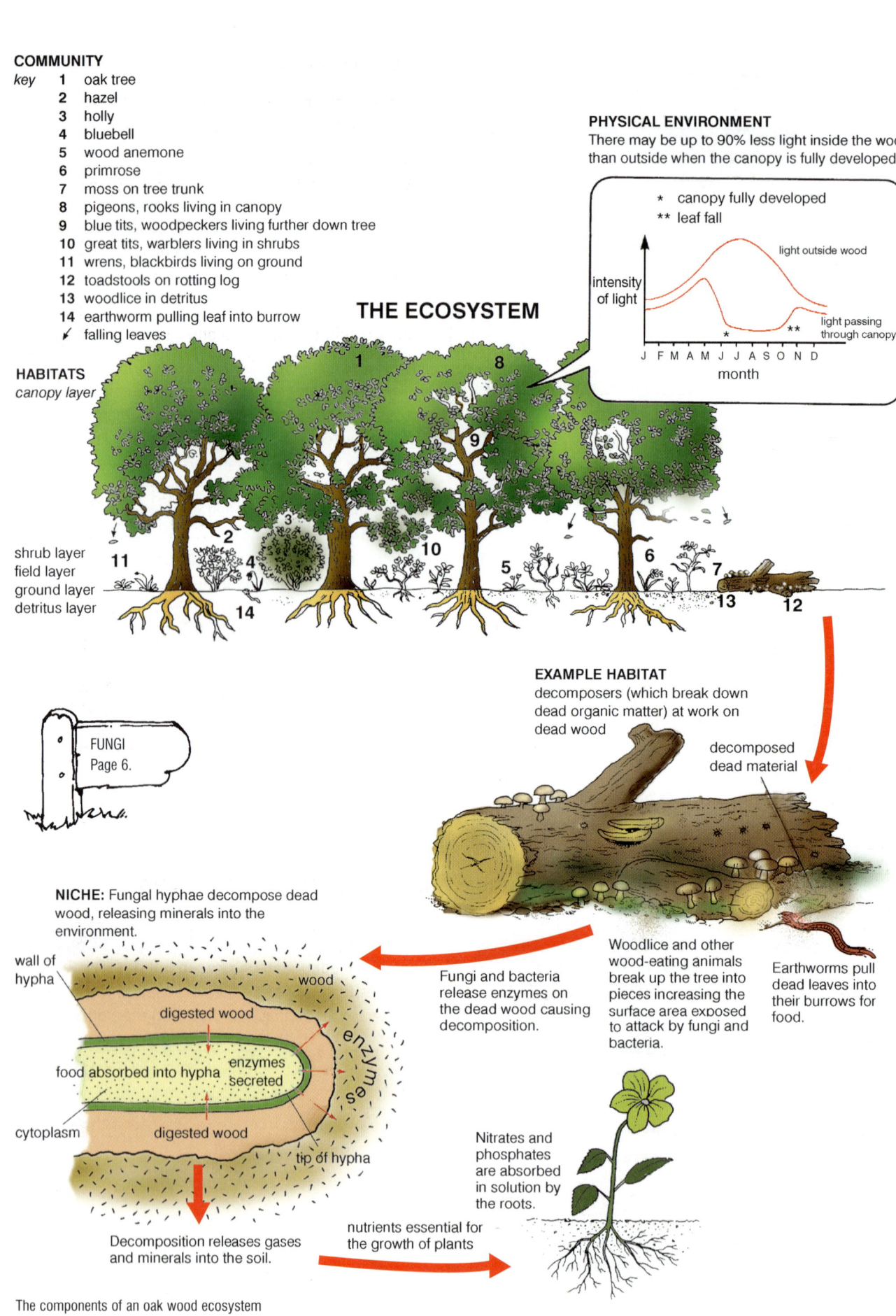

The components of an oak wood ecosystem

Organisms in the environment

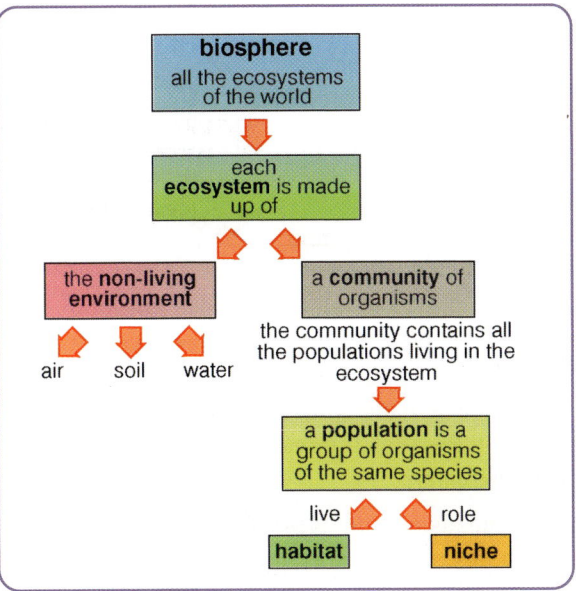

The flow chart above shows the hierarchy of ecological terms.

Decomposition

Notice in the diagram of an oak wood ecosystem that bacteria and fungi release enzymes on to dead organic material, digesting it. The products of digestion are absorbed by the bacteria and fungi and are a source of energy for their growth. Their activities are the cause of **decomposition**. Mineral nutrients are released into the soil. The nutrients are absorbed in solution by the roots of plants. In this way, plants obtain the substances essential for their growth. Animals obtain nutrients by eating plants and/or other animals.

Nitrates are nutrients used by living things to make **protein**. The element **nitrogen** is present in nitrates (e.g. calcium nitrate). Decomposition recycles it from living things to the air, soil and water and back again. Other elements essential for life (such as carbon) are also recycled between organisms and the environment.

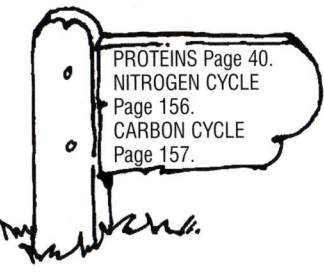

PROTEINS Page 40.
NITROGEN CYCLE Page 156.
CARBON CYCLE Page 157.

Artificial fertiliser and untreated sewage entering streams, rivers and the sea cause the water to become richer and richer in nutrients. The process is called **eutrophication**.

★ Water plants increase and grow.

★ Algae increase in number, clouding the water in a greenish scum – an algal **bloom**.

★ When the plant material and algae die, bacteria decompose the organic matter and multiply.

As a result, the bacteria use up the oxygen in the water.

As a result, wildlife dies through lack of oxygen.

As a result, the water becomes black and unable to support wildlife.

The sequence runs:

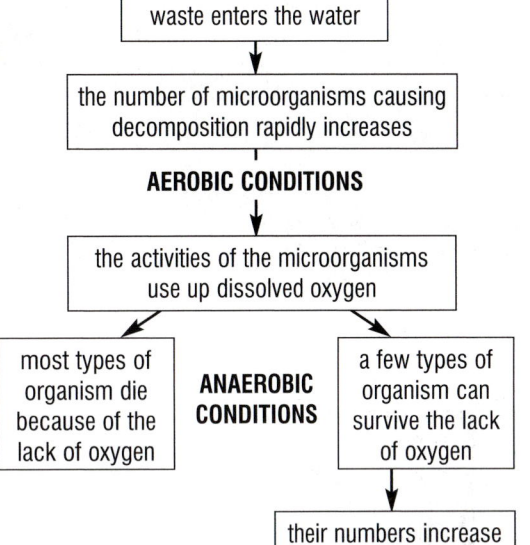

2.2 Food chains and webs

> **PREVIEW**
>
> At the end of this section you will:
> - know the meaning of the terms producer, herbivore, carnivore and omnivore
> - understand that energy is transferred along food chains
> - be able to interpret diagrams of food chains and food webs.

Organisms in the environment

Who eats whom?

Finding out 'who eats whom' is one way of describing how a community works. Looking at:
- animals' teeth or mouthparts
- what is in the intestine
- animals feeding
- what food an animal likes best (a **food preference test**)

helps find out what animals feed on.

The working community

Animals fall into three categories according to what they eat.

★ **Herbivores** eat plants.

★ **Carnivores** eat meat.

★ **Omnivores** eat both plants and meat. (Most human beings are omnivorous.)

Most carnivores are **predators** – they catch and eat other animals. The animals caught are their **prey**, and are often herbivores.

Scavengers are carnivores that feed on the remains of prey left by predators, or on the bodies of animals that have died for other reasons such as disease or old age.

A **food chain** shows the links between plants, prey, predators and scavengers. Some examples of food chains are shown opposite.

Notice in each example that:
- the arrows represent the transfer of food (and therefore food energy) between different organisms
- the arrows point from the organism eaten to the organism which eats it
- the number of links in a food chain is usually four or less.

A **food web** is usually a more accurate description of feeding relationships in a community because most animals eat more than one type of plant or other animal. Some examples of food webs are shown on page 13.

Notice in each example that:
- several food chains link up to form a food web
- plants and algae produce food by photosynthesis
- different types of animal eat the same type of food.

Producers

Plants, algae and some bacteria (see page 6) are called **producers** because they use sunlight to produce food by photosynthesis.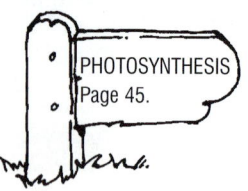
This is why food chains and food webs mostly begin with plants (or algae or photosynthetic bacteria). Animals use this food when they eat plants. Even when they eat other animals, predators depend on plant food indirectly since somewhere along the line the prey has been a plant eater. Because they eat food, animals are called **consumers**.

No light means no photosynthesis, but communities of organisms flourish in the dark of the ocean depths around openings in the sea floor called **vents**. Larva, hydrogen sulphide (H_2S) and other gases escaping from the vents provide substances which different types of bacteria can use to make sugars. The bacteria are the producers upon which the food web of the vent community depends.

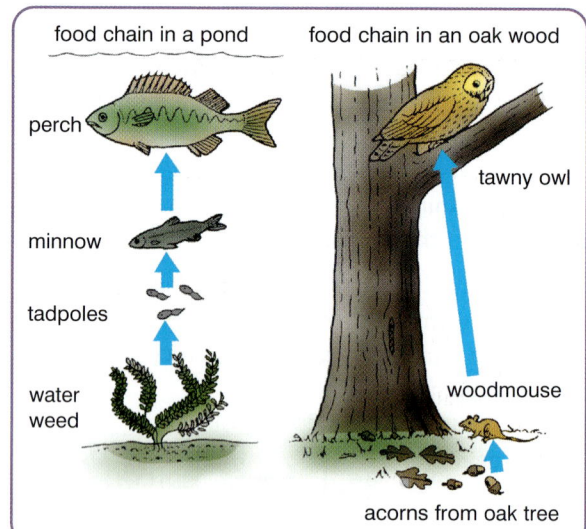

Food chains

Organisms in the environment

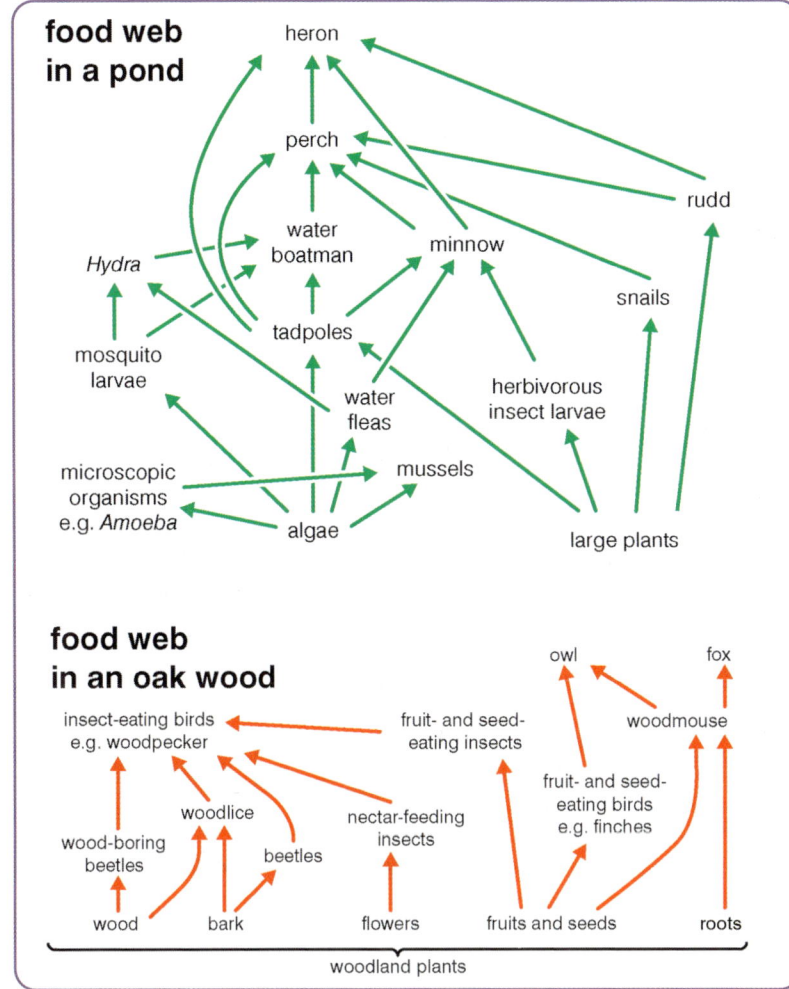

Food webs

Energy flow

Sunlight underpins life on Earth. Without sunlight, and the photosynthesis which depends on it, most communities would cease to exist.

Through photosynthesis, plants convert light energy into the chemical energy of food. A food chain represents one pathway of food energy through the community of an ecosystem. A food web represents many pathways. The diagram below shows the idea.

At each link in the food chain, energy is lost in the waste products produced by organisms and as a result of the metabolism (chemical reactions taking place in cells) of each living thing. Much of the energy lost is in the form of heat.

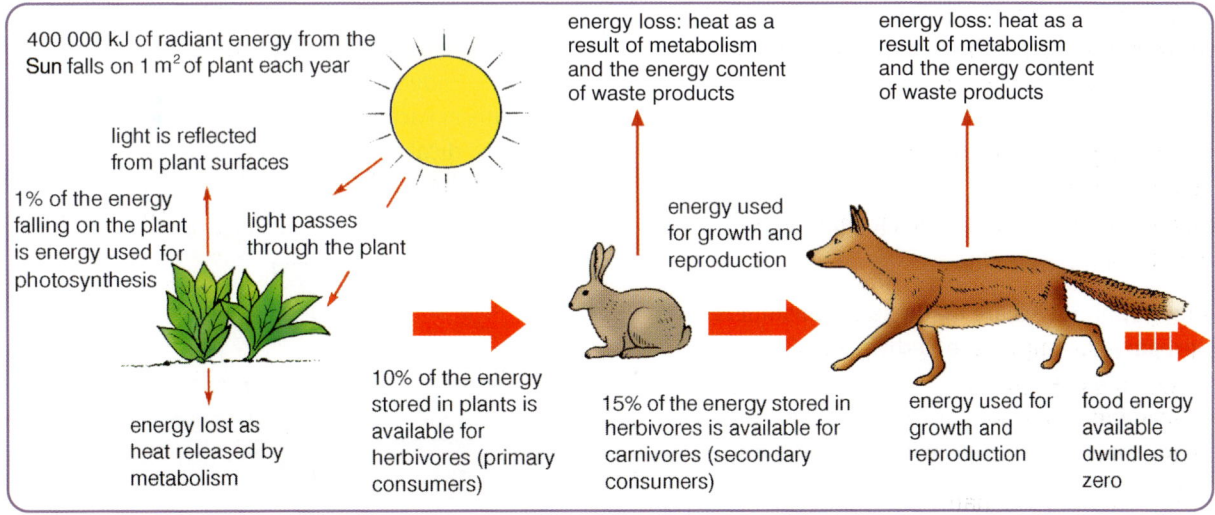

The flow of energy through a food chain. Notice that only a small proportion of the Sun's radiant (light) energy is used in photosynthesis

Organisms in the environment

2.3 Ecological pyramids

PREVIEW

At the end of this section you will:
- understand the term trophic level
- know how to build a pyramid of numbers
- be able to interpret pyramids of numbers and pyramids of biomass
- understand that the pyramid of energy gives the best picture of the relationships between producers and consumers.

Food chains and **food webs** describe the feeding relationships within a community. However, they do not tell us about the numbers of individuals involved. Many plants support a limited number of herbivores which in turn support fewer carnivores.

Trophic levels

Below is a diagram of an ecological pyramid.

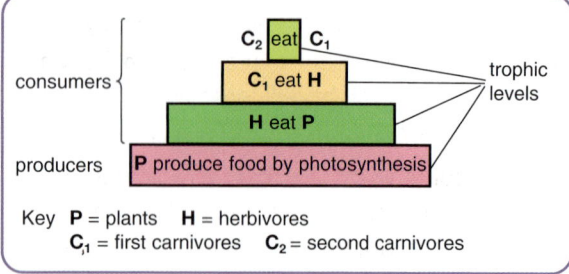

Ecological pyramid

- ★ The pyramid has several feeding levels called **trophic levels**.
- ★ Producers (plants/algae/some bacteria) occupy the base of the pyramid.
- ★ Other trophic levels are made up of consumers:
  - **primary** consumers are herbivores (H) that feed on plants
  - **secondary** consumers or first/primary carnivores (C_1) are carnivores that feed on herbivores
  - **tertiary** consumers or second/secondary carnivores (C_2) are carnivores which feed on first/primary carnivores.

Each trophic level groups together organisms that have similar types of food. For example, a snail and a sheep are herbivores. Both belong to the second (H) trophic level.

The group of organisms in each trophic level is smaller than the one below it. This gives the shape of a pyramid.

Pyramids of numbers

Pyramids of numbers show the *number of organisms* in each trophic level. The table below shows the numbers of insects and spiders collected from grass with a sweep net.

sample	number of insects	number of spiders
1	135	5
2	150	10
3	110	10
4	115	5
5	120	15
	630	45
	average = $\frac{630}{5}$ = 126 insects in each sample	average = $\frac{45}{5}$ = 9 spiders in each sample

Samples of insects and spiders collected with a sweep net. Each sample was collected with ten sweeps while walking around an area of $10\,m^2$.

Data like those in the table can be used to plot a pyramid of numbers, as shown below. Half the number of organisms in each trophic level is plotted on one side of the vertical line, the other half is plotted on the other side of the vertical line.

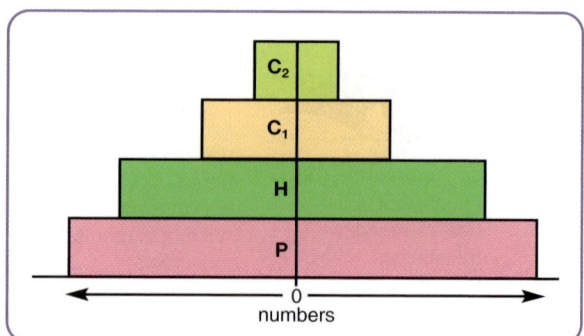

How to plot a pyramid of numbers

Organisms in the environment

In grassland, the producers (grasses) and consumers (mainly insects and spiders) are small and numerous. A lot of plants support many herbivores (mostly insects), which in turn support fewer carnivores (mostly spiders). Plotting the number of organisms in each trophic level of the grassland community gives the shape of a pyramid.

Problems with numbers ...

Example 1: the pyramid of numbers for a woodland community (shown below) has a point at the bottom as well as the top. This is because relatively few producers (trees) support a large number of herbivores and carnivores. You might think that woodland consumers are in danger of starvation! However, each tree is large and can meet the food needs of many different organisms.

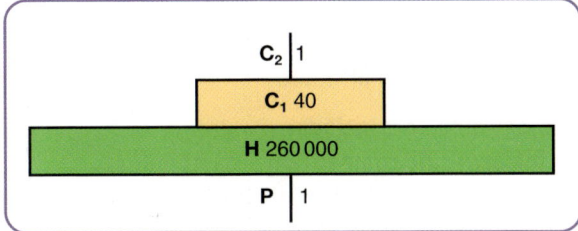

Pyramid of numbers for a woodland community

Example 2: pyramids of numbers including parasites appear top-heavy, as shown below. Many parasites feed on fewer secondary consumers.

In both these examples, number pyramids are not an accurate description of the feeding relationships in the different communities. Why? Because each number pyramid does not take into account differences in size of the different producers and consumers.

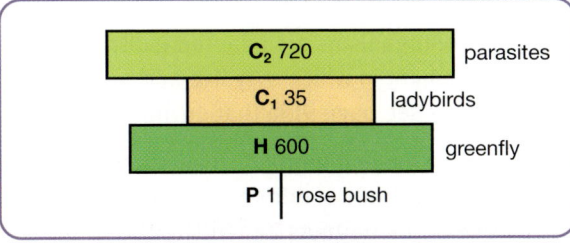

Pyramid of numbers including parasites of the secondary consumers (ladybirds)

... and the solution

A **pyramid of biomass** allows for differences in the size of organisms, because the pyramid shows the *amount of organic material* in each trophic level.

- A representative sample of the organisms at each trophic level is weighed.
- The mass is then multiplied by the estimated number of organisms in the community.

In practice, dry mass is used because fresh mass varies greatly as organisms contain different amounts of water. The sample is dried out in a warm oven until there is no further change in mass. The dry mass data are plotted as kilograms of dry mass per unit area (m^2) of the community.

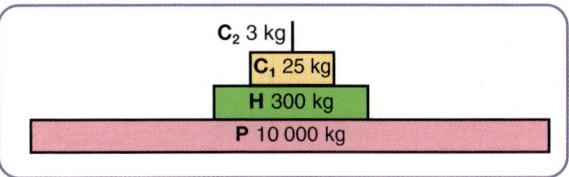

Pyramid of biomass for a woodland community

Problems with biomass ...

Example 1: the biomass of an organism can vary during the year. For example, an oak tree in full leaf during the summer will have a much greater biomass than in winter without its leaves.

Example 2: some organisms reproduce so quickly that sampling misses the rapid fluctuations in population. For example, below is an upside-down pyramid of biomass for the English Channel. Microscopic algae (producers) only live for a few days but reproduce millions of offspring very quickly. Collecting them over a short period misses this rapid turnover of living material and results in a pyramid which suggests that the biomass of herbivores (H) is greater than that of the producers (P) they feed on.

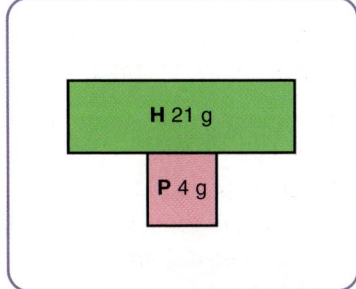

Pyramid of biomass for the English Channel, grams per unit volume (m^3) of water

Organisms in the environment

... and the solution

A **pyramid of energy** gives information about the *amount of energy* at each trophic level over a certain period of time. In other words, the energy pyramid shows the amount of food being produced and consumed in a given time. Its shape therefore is not affected by differences in size, or changes in numbers of individuals.

The food energy in each trophic level is measured by incinerating samples of organisms in a **bomb calorimeter**. The heat given off is a measure of the energy value of the samples and is therefore representative of the food energy in the trophic level to which the sample of organisms belongs. The diagram below shows you the idea.

Notice that:
- feeding transfers food energy from one trophic level to the next (energy flows)
- energy is lost from each trophic level

through life's activities, mostly in the form of heat released by the metabolism of cells.

METABOLISM Page 57.
BOMB CALORIMETER Page 57.

As a result, the amount of food energy in a trophic level is less than the one below it.

As a result, the amount of living material (biomass) in a trophic level is less than the one below it.

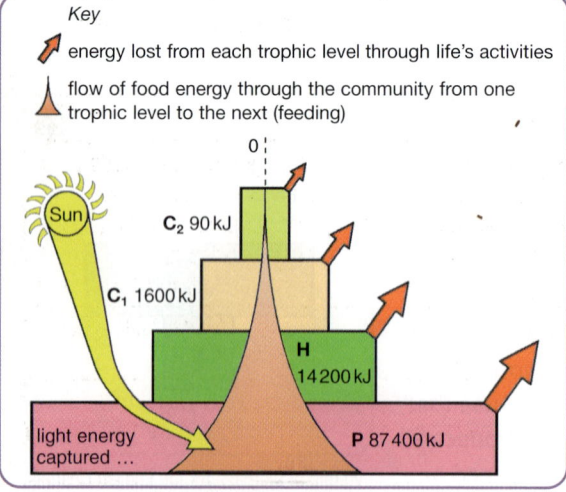

Pyramid of energy for a stream in kJ/m²/year

2.4 Distribution of organisms

PREVIEW

At the end of this section you will:
- understand the effect of environmental factors on the distribution of plants
- know that competition affects the distribution of organisms
- understand that different adaptations enable plants and animals to survive.

Competition between organisms

The distribution of organisms (where living things are found in the environment) is affected by different factors.

★ Physical factors include:
  - the amount of light
  - the abundance of water.

★ Biological factors include:
  - **intraspecific competition** – competition between individuals of the same species
  - **interspecific competition** – competition between individuals of different species
  - **interactions** between predators and prey
  - **adaptations** which increase the chances of survival of organisms in different environments.

Fact file

★ **Competition:** in nature, organisms that are rivals for something that is in limited supply are competitors. The 'something' is a resource like water, light, space, food or mates.

★ **Adaptation:** organisms are adapted (suited) to the environment in which they live and to their role (niche – see page 9) in that environment.

★ **Symbiosis:** a general term for close associations between individuals of different species where either one of the partners benefits to the detriment of the other (**parasitism**) or both benefit (**mutualism**). Where one member of the partnership is found, so too is the other, each affecting the distribution of the partner.

Organisms in the environment

Examples of different factors affecting the distribution of organisms follow below.

Example 1: intraspecific competition for light

In a wood, the branches of full-grown trees spread in all directions. They touch the branches of neighbouring trees, forming a continuous layer. This is the **canopy** which shades out plants beneath. When a tree is blown over, light floods through the gap in the canopy, stimulating vigorous plant growth on the woodland floor. This sunlit clearing becomes an arena for intense competition between tree seedlings which sprout from seeds that may have lain dormant for years, and then grow into saplings (young trees). Many competitors start out but there is limited space for spreading branches, which also overshadow slower-growing rivals. Many young trees perish along the way. Only the one that grows the fastest will fill the gap in the canopy, finally cutting off the sunlight that signalled the start of the race many years previously.

Which sapling will survive to fill the gap? The length of the branches sets the distance between neighbouring trees, producing a continuous canopy and a regular pattern of tree trunks. The sunlit clearing caused by the fallen tree breaks the pattern and provides opportunities for new plant growth and competition between saplings to complete the canopy once more.

Example 2: intraspecific competition for water

The cacti in the photograph at the top of the next column are widely spaced apart, and look as if they have been planted out in a regular arrangement. The pattern appears because the roots of the cacti spread out underground, setting the distance between neighbouring plants. Although many cactus seedlings sprout in a particular area, there is only enough water for some of them to grow into mature plants. Growing cacti are the competitors and water is the resource in short supply.

Cacti in the Arizona Desert, south-western United States, where rainfall is erratic and infrequent

Example 3: interspecific competition

Competition between different species is usually greatest among individuals that occupy the same trophic level. This competition for the same resource often leads to one species replacing another (called **competitive exclusion**). For example, when two species of clover (both producers) were grown separately, they grew well. However, when grown together one species eventually replaced the other. The reason was that the successful species grew slightly taller than its competitor and overshadowed it. The unsuccessful species received less light. Its rate of photosynthesis and therefore its rate of growth were less than its successful competitors.

Example 4: predator and prey

Predators are adapted to catch prey, and prey are adapted to escape predators. The table below summarises their different strategies.

predator	prey
eats a variety of prey species, reducing the risk of starvation should one prey species decline in numbers	large groups (e.g. herds of antelope, shoals of fish) distract predators from concentrating on a particular individual
catches young, old and sick prey	stings and bitter taste deter predators
catches large prey which provides more food per kill	warning coloration tells predators to avoid particular prey
moves to areas where prey is plentiful	camouflage conceals prey
predator tries to run/swim/fly faster than prey	prey tries to run/swim/fly faster than pursuing predator
	shock tactics startle predators

Strategies for predator success and prey survival

Organisms in the environment

2.5 Population size

> **PREVIEW**
>
> At the end of this section you will:
> - know how populations increase in size
> - understand that the impact of human activity on the environment is related to population size
> - be able to identify specific effects of human activity on the environment.

The size of a population

★ A **population** is a group of individuals of the same species living in the same place at the same time.

★ **Births** and **immigration** increase the size of a population.

★ **Deaths** and **emigration** decrease the size of a population.

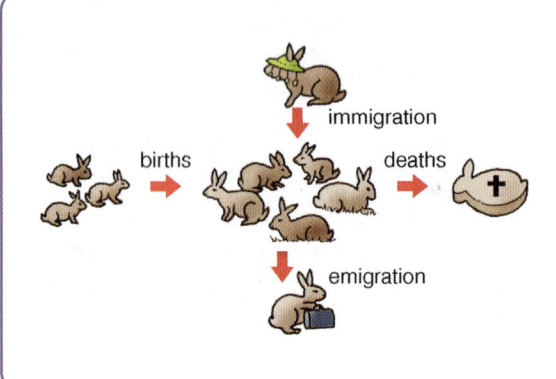

Factors affecting the size of a population

Population growth

The following graph shows that populations grow in a particular way. **Limiting factors** stop populations from growing indefinitely. They include:

shortages of
- food
- water
- oxygen
- light
- shelter

build-up of
- poisonous wastes
- predators
- disease
- social factors.

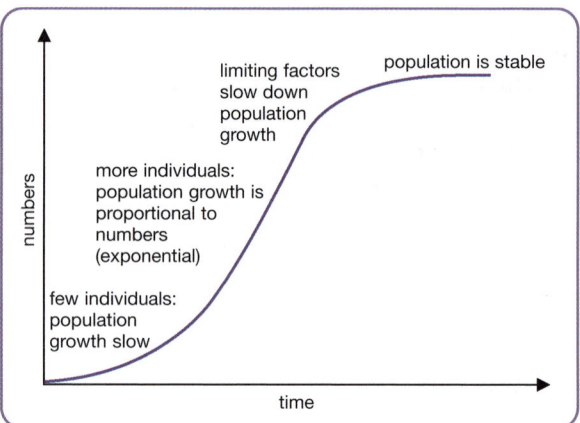

Population growth curve

Predator and prey populations

Predation affects the number of the prey population. The number of prey affects the predator population: if prey is scarce, then some of the predators will starve. The graph below shows the relationships between the numbers of predators and prey.

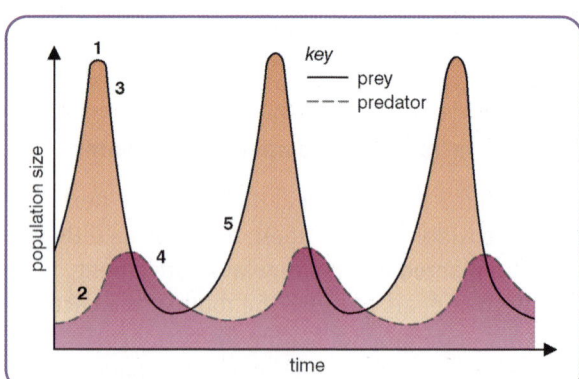

Predator–prey relationships

1. Prey breed and increase in numbers if conditions are favourable (e.g. food is abundant).
2. Predators breed and increase in numbers in response to the abundance of prey.
3. Predation pressure increases and the number of prey declines.
4. Predator numbers decline in response to the shortage of food.
5. Predation pressure decreases and so prey numbers increase ... and so on.

Notice that:
- fluctuations in predator numbers are *smaller* than fluctuations in prey numbers
- fluctuations in predator numbers *lag* behind fluctuations in prey numbers.

Why is this? There are fewer predators than prey, and predators tend to reproduce more slowly than prey.

The human population

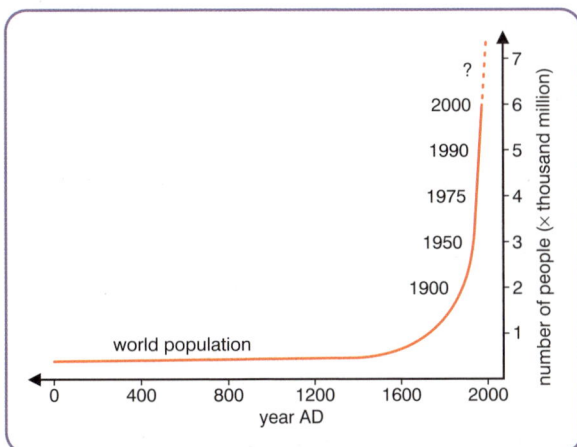

World population growth over the past 2000 years showing predicted future increase based on present trends

This graph shows that the human population has grown dramatically since the beginning of the nineteenth century. Although the populations of Europe, North America and Japan (countries with developed economies) are levelling off, the populations of some countries with developing economies are still growing rapidly as a result of:
- improvements in food production
- more drugs for the treatment of disease
- improved medical care
- improved public health.

The rate of population growth is affected by the number of young people in the population, particularly women of child-bearing age. The table below summarises the problem.

A large proportion of the world's population is young so the problems listed in the table are global. The problems are particularly acute in developing countries.

problem	result
present birth rate high	adding to the rate of population increase
future birth rate high	as children in the population 'bulge' grow older and have their own children, adding further to the rate of population increase
social services inadequate	large numbers of children put strain on the educational system, medical services and housing

Problems of a young population

In Britain (and other countries with developed economies) the problems are more to do with a population that has an increasing proportion of old people. The diseases of old age (cancer, arthritis, dementia) take up an increasing proportion of the resources available for medical care.

Human impact on the environment

1.5 million years ago: early humans probably moved from place to place in search of food. They hunted animals and gathered plants. Their impact on the environment was no more than that of other medium-sized animals.

10 000 years ago: about 12 million people lived in the world. In the Middle East they harvested wild wheat and other grains. When the grain was ripe, a family could probably gather over a year's supply in just a few weeks. People had little impact on the environment beyond their village.

Organisms in the environment

2000 years ago: people had started to farm. Skills in crafts and tool-making developed. Villages became larger and some grew into towns. People had a much greater impact on the environment – farming the land, using raw materials.

Today: about 6.2 billion (thousand million) people live in the world. In countries with developed economies, food is produced by relatively few people. Industry and technology use raw materials, often obtained from countries with developing economies where environments may be stripped of resources. Pages 22–3 show the impact of human activities on today's environment.

Conservation

Our well-being depends on keeping a balance between using and protecting environments. Conservation aims to:

- use renewable resources in a **sustainable** way and reduce the exploitation of non-renewable resources through **recycling** and the discovery of **alternative** materials for the production of goods
- use land so that **conflicting interests** between human needs and the impact of these needs on the survival of wildlife and their environments are reduced
- reduce **pollution** by the development of more efficient industrial processes, which produce less waste and use less energy, and the introduction of more environmentally friendly methods of farming.

Different initiatives attempt to protect wildlife in danger of extinction (**endangered species**) because of human activities.

★ **Convention on International Trade in Endangered Species** (CITES) aims to control the trade in, and products from, endangered species.

★ **Sites of Special Scientific Interest** (SSSIs) have been established as protected habitats for rare and endangered species.

★ **Captive breeding programmes** have saved species from extinction. Rare species are captured and individuals held in zoos where they breed. When numbers have been built up, some individuals are released back into the wild under close supervision.

★ **National Parks** have been established to conserve areas of outstanding beauty and scientific interest.

★ **Seed banks** are cold stores of seeds. Species of plant threatened with extinction are conserved as seeds in store with a view to building up numbers and conserving genetic material for future breeding programmes.

2.6 Food production

> **PREVIEW**
>
> At the end of this section you will:
> - understand why a short food chain makes more food energy available to the consumer than a long food chain
> - know that intensive farming produces food in great quantities.

Fact file

★ **Intensive farming** means that farmers use different methods to produce as much food as possible from the land available for raising crops (**arable** farming) and the land available for raising animals (**livestock** farming). The methods impose a duty on farmers to limit the damage on natural ecosystems and to treat intensively farmed animals humanely. New laws are being introduced to improve the welfare of farm animals.

★ **Productivity** means the amount of food produced (crops or livestock) per unit area of land (e.g. per hectare [ha]).

Energy and farming

Farms are ecosystems with people as consumers in a food chain of crops and livestock. The amount of food a farm produces depends on:
- the amount of energy entering the farm ecosystem
- the efficiency with which energy is converted into plant and animal tissue.

The energy that enters the system is the **input**. The energy content of the food produced is the **output**.

Shortening the food chain

The inefficiency of energy transfer between trophic levels affects the amount of food available for human consumption. The *fewer* the trophic levels (links in a food chain), the *less* food energy is lost and so the *more* food is available to consumers. **Vegetarianism** shortens the food chain and reduces the loss of food energy between trophic levels. Output therefore increases.

Energy transfer between producers and consumers is inefficient because:
- some of the plant material is not digested and passes out of the herbivore's body as faeces
- the herbivore uses energy to stay alive
- when the herbivore dies, its body represents 'locked up' energy, some of which transfers to decomposers.

Eating meat is therefore wasteful in terms of food energy. The diagram in the next column illustrates the point. What percentage (%) of the food energy eaten by the cow in a year is available to the consumer as milk and meat?

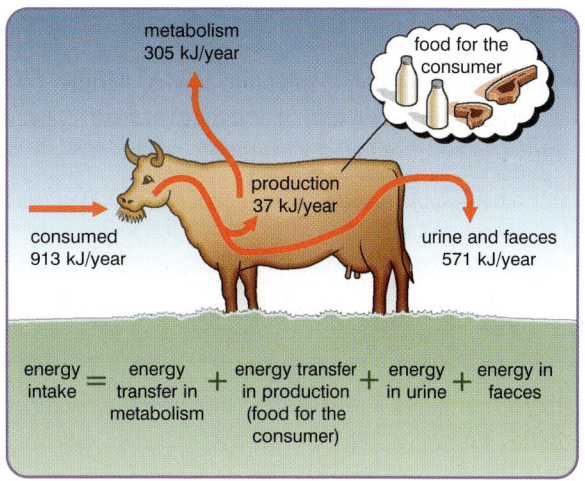

Wasting energy

Farming

The concept map for **food production** on page 25 shows different technologies at work on the modern intensive farm. The checklist points on page 24 summarise the benefits for food production but also highlight the impact on the environment and the possible risks to human health.

Organisms in the environment

Resources are the raw materials needed to satisfy human demands for food, homes, hospitals, schools and manufactured goods.
- **Renewable resources** are replaced as fast as plants and animals can reproduce and grow. If a resource is over-used it will decline. Damage to the environment also limits the production of renewable resources.
- **Non-renewable resources** cannot be replaced when used up. For example, there are only limited amounts of fossil fuels (coal oil, natural gas) and metals.

RESOURCES

CASE STUDY: Fishing in the North Sea

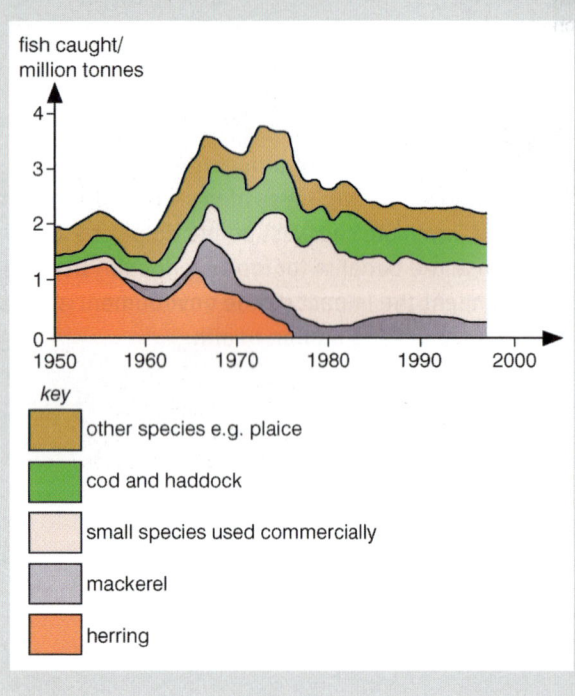

Catches of fish are reduced overall because of:
* **overfishing:** increased efficiency of fishing methods means more fish are caught than are replaced by reproduction
* **pollution:**
  - nutrients (e.g. nitrates and phosphates) from sewage works and surplus artificial fertilisers enter rivers which discharge into the North Sea
  - pesticides used to protect crops enter rivers which discharge into the North Sea
  - metals (e.g. mercury, cadmium, copper) from different industrial processes.

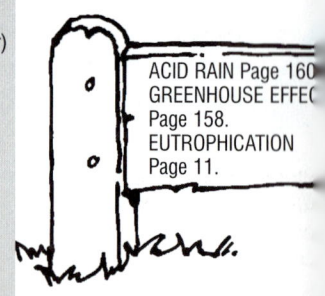

ACID RAIN Page 160
GREENHOUSE EFFECT Page 158.
EUTROPHICATION Page 11.

CASE STUDY World reserves of metals

The table shows estimated world reserves of some metals vital for the manufacture of goods and technological development. Work out how long reserves of each metal will last at present rates of use.

iron ore	annual use	1.6 billion tonnes
	reserves	216.4 billion tonnes
copper	annual use	10 million tonnes
	reserves	570 million tonnes
tin	annual use	226 thousand tonnes
	reserves	4.2 million tonnes

Answers (to the nearest whole number)
Iron ore: 135 years
Copper: 57 years
Tin: 19 years

FARMING Page 25.

How human activities exploit resources and land, and produce pollution

Organisms in the environment

LAND USE → **Land use** destroys habitats, driving thousands of species of plants and animals to the verge of extinction. The pressures are:
- economic development
- growing human populations
- the increasing need for food for the increasing population.

} increase the use of land

CASE STUDY: Land use in the United Kingdom

Out of 24 million hectares of land in the UK:
- 19 million hectares are used for agriculture
- 1.7 million hectares are used for housing.

Quarrying (gravel, limestone, sand and sandstone) for building materials and the disposal of household waste account for some of the rest.

CASE STUDY: Exploiting tropical rainforest

Rainforests girdle the equator covering 14.5 million km² of land. The vegetation recycles carbon dioxide and oxygen through photosynthesis. Moisture absorbed by the forest evaporates back into the atmosphere, to fall as rain thousands of miles away. Rainforest is being cleared at a rate of 100 000 km² each year for:

Beef: about 20 000 km² of Brazilian forest are cleared each year for cattle ranches.

cheap beef is exported to be made into hamburgers

Opencast mining for metals causes much damage to rainforest.

After clearing, nutrients are used up and the soil is soon exhausted. Semi-desert develops: the ranchers move on to clear a new area.

Logging: only 4% of trees are felled for timber, but another 40% are damaged or destroyed in the process.

POLLUTION ↓

Pollution is the result of industry making goods that maintain our standard of living.
Air is polluted by gases, dust and smoke from vehicles and industry.
Water is polluted by wastes from factories and runoff of agrochemicals.
Land is polluted by agrochemicals and the dumping of rubbish and waste.

CASE STUDY: Environmental problems caused by pollution

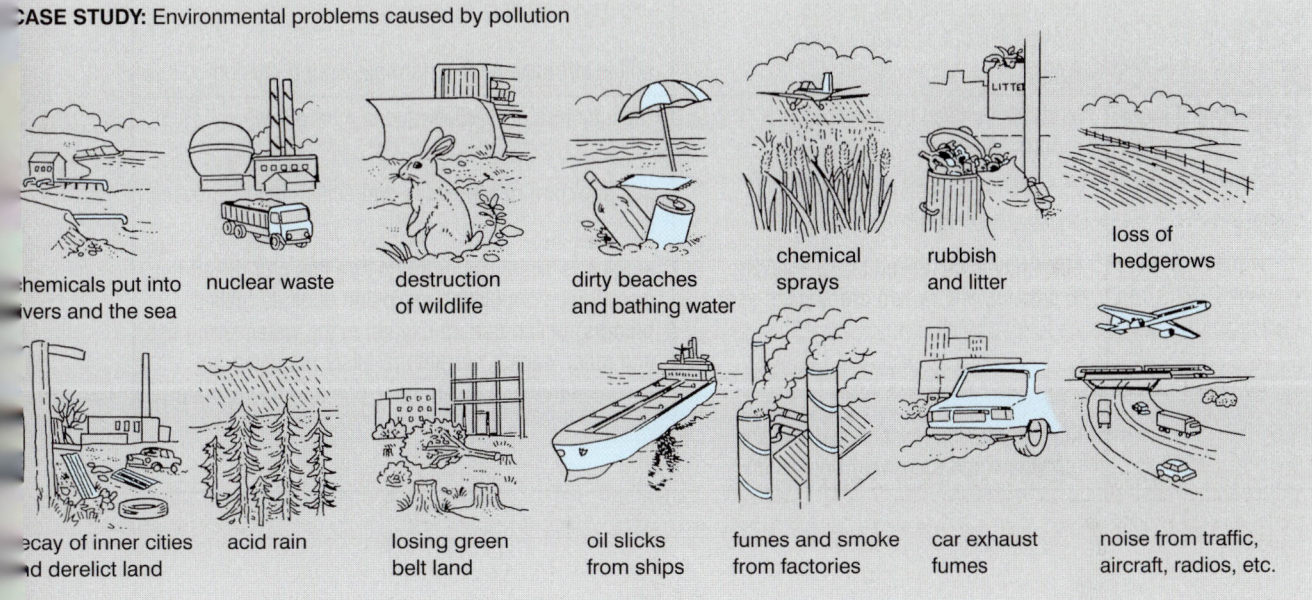

chemicals put into rivers and the sea | nuclear waste | destruction of wildlife | dirty beaches and bathing water | chemical sprays | rubbish and litter | loss of hedgerows

decay of inner cities and derelict land | acid rain | losing green belt land | oil slicks from ships | fumes and smoke from factories | car exhaust fumes | noise from traffic, aircraft, radios, etc.

Organisms in the environment

Checklist for intensive farming

checklist	benefits	impact
1 pesticides	kill pests which damage crops	spray is carried in the wind (**drift**) which can harm wildlife
	food production increases	pesticide **runoff** seeps into groundwater, eventually draining into ponds and river systems, possibly contaminating drinking water and harming wildlife
2 irrigation	brings water to land	**salination**: the Sun's heat evaporates water, increasing the concentration of mineral salts in soil. Eventually land is too 'salty' for crops to grow, reducing crop yields
	food production increases	overwatering: land becomes **waterlogged**, reducing crop yields. In warm countries the threat to human health increases because habitats are created for the spread of water-borne diseases such as malaria and schistosomiasis
3 mechanisation	powerful machinery needs few people to work it, cutting wage costs	land is **cleared** of woods and hedges to make fields larger – large machinery is most efficient in big fields
	more land can be used for farming	habitats are **destroyed** with loss of wildlife
	harvests crop more quickly	soil is **packed**, causing waterlogging
4 manure	spreading manure on land adds humus which improves soil structure	water is needed to **wash manure** into lagoon
		slurry **leaks** from lagoon, seeping into streams and rivers, killing fish and other wildlife
5 monoculture	efficient use of expensive machinery	crop provides **unlimited** food for consumer populations, which increase to pest proportions
	reduces labour costs	costs are **high** because crops must be sprayed with pesticides
	high yields mean farmer can take advantage of selling in bulk to obtain best prices for produce	soil **loses** its nutrients which are replaced with expensive artificial fertilisers
		soil is left **bare** between crops, risking erosion
6 artificial fertilisers	land can be used continuously for growing crops	manufacture of fertilisers **uses** a lot of fuel
	farmers do not need to keep animals for manure	soil structure **deteriorates** and soil erosion increases
	efficiency is increased by specialising in growing one or two crops each year	surplus fertiliser runs off into streams and rivers: this encourages population explosion of algae (called **blooms**) which use up oxygen in the water, killing fish and other wildlife. Surplus fertiliser may also put excess nitrates, a health hazard, into drinking water
	food production is increased, helping feed the world's growing population	

Organisms in the environment

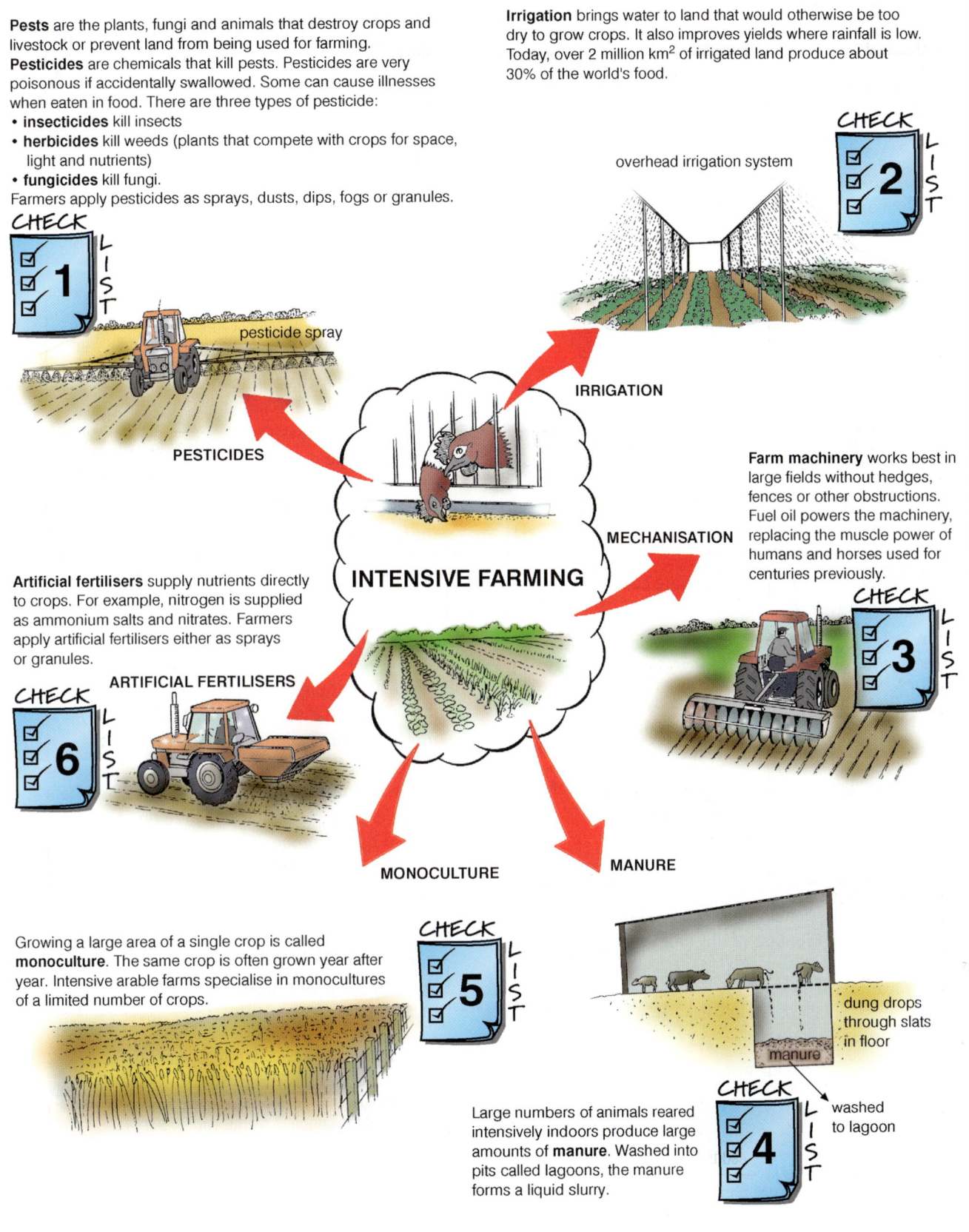

The intensive farm at work (Checklist numbers refer to the checklist on page 24.)

Organisms in the environment

ROUND UP

How much have you improved?
Work out your improvement index on page 109.

1. Look at page 10. List the different components of an ecosystem. [6]
2. a) Explain the meaning of the word 'abiotic'. [1]
   b) Why is the amount of light an important abiotic influence on life inside a wood? [4]
3. Look at the pond food chain on page 12.
   a) How many links are there in the food chain? [1]
   b) Name the producers. [1]
   c) Briefly explain why they are called producers. [1]
   d) Name the herbivores. [1]
   e) Briefly explain why they are called herbivores. [1]
   f) Name the carnivores. [2]
   g) Briefly explain why they are called carnivores. [1]
4. Why is the efficiency of energy conversion in photosynthesis less than 8%? [3]
5. In what circumstances is the pyramid of numbers an accurate description of the feeding relationships in a community? [1]
6. The diagram shows a pyramid of biomass for a rocky seashore.
   a) Name the producers. [1]
   b) Name the secondary consumers. [1]
   c) Severe weather conditions virtually wipe out the periwinkles. What will be the effect on the biomass of dog whelks and saw wrack? [2]

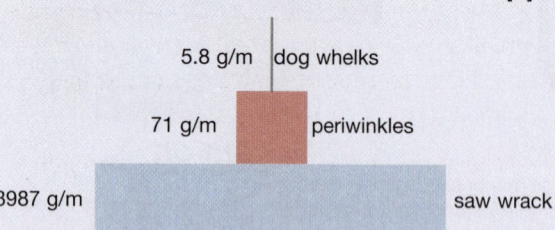

7. Explain the differences between
   a) intraspecific competition and interspecific competition
   b) adaptation and survival
   c) camouflage and warning colouration. [6]

8. The graph shows long-term changes in the numbers of snowshoe hare and its predator the Canadian lynx.

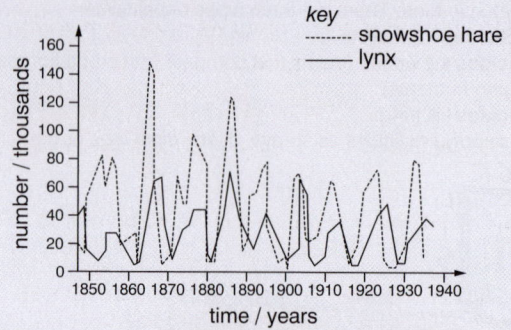

   a) Why do the highs and lows in the numbers of lynx lag behind the highs and lows in the numbers of snowshoe hare? [3]
   b) Although the numbers of snowshoe hare and lynx fluctuated between 1850 and 1940, what do you think is the *overall* trend in the population growth of each species between these years? [1]
   c) In 1890, if disease had virtually wiped out the lynx population, what do you think would have happened to the numbers of snowshoe hare? [1]
   d) If the lynx population had recovered from the effects of disease by 1910, what then do you think would have happened to the numbers of snowshoe hare? [2]
   e) If the lynx population had never recovered from the effects of disease, what then do you think would have happened to the numbers of snowshoe hare? Briefly explain your answer. [2]

9. The terms in column **A** refer to different aspects of intensive farming. Match each term with its correct description in column **B**.

A terms	B descriptions
fertiliser	kills plants
herbicide	an unwanted plant
irrigation	supplies plants with nutrients
monoculture	supplies plants with water
weed	a crop plant grown over a large area [5]

Well done if you've improved. Don't worry if you haven't. Take a break and try again.

Chapter 3 — Cell activity

How much do you already know? Work out your score on pages 109–10.

Test yourself

1. Match each of the structures in column **A** with its function in column **B**.

A structures	B functions
mitochondrion	partially permeable to substances in solution
plasma membrane	where energy is released from the oxidation of glucose
chloroplast	fully permeable to substances in solution
cell wall	contains the chromosomes
nucleus	where light energy is captured [5]

2. Why do you think the process of active transport requires more energy than diffusion? [1]

3. Explain the difference between
   a) a plasmolysed cell and a turgid cell [4]
   b) a fully permeable membrane and a partially permeable membrane. [3]

4. What is a clone? [1]

5. What is formed by the replication of DNA? [2]

6. a) Why do the cells of a tissue undergo mitosis? [3]
   b) In mitosis, what is the relationship between the number and type of chromosomes in the parent cell and in the daughter cells? [2]

7. Briefly explain the meaning of 'haploid' and 'diploid'. [4]

8. Complete the following paragraph using the words below. Each word may be used once, more than once or not at all.

   types   organism   tissues   organs   cells   an organ

   Living things are made of _____. Groups of similar _____ with similar functions form _____ that can work together as _____. A group of _____ working together form _____ system. [6]

9. Cellulose and chitin are important building materials in living things. Give an example of a structure where each may be found. [2]

10. Briefly explain the difference between saturated and unsaturated fats. [2]

11. What is a nucleotide? [4]

3.1 Cells at work

PREVIEW

At the end of this section you will know that:
- all living things are made of cells
- plant cells and animal cells have structures in common but are also different from one another
- mitochondria and chloroplasts are structures in cells which convert energy from one form to another
- different types of cells are each specialised to perform a particular biological task.

Cell functions

The structures that make up a cell are organised in a way that depends on the **functions** of the cell (the way it works).

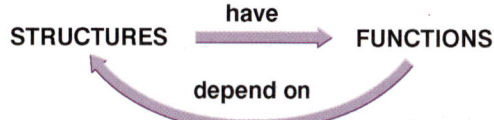

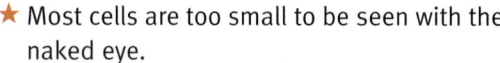

Fact file

★ Most cells are too small to be seen with the naked eye.

★ The light microscope helps us to see the structure of cells.

★ The transmission electron microscope reveals cell structures too small to be seen under the light microscope. It enables us to see the structure of cells in great detail.

★ The human body is made of more than 200 different types of cell.

Cell activity

How cells work

The diagram on pages 30–31 is the concept map for **cells at work**. The numbers on the diagram refer to the checklist of points on page 30.

3.2 Into and out of cells

> **PREVIEW**
>
> At the end of this section you will:
> - understand that there is constant movement of solutions inside and into and out of cells
> - know about diffusion, osmosis and active transport
> - know that solutions move along a concentration gradient.

Moving molecules

Cells need a non-stop supply of water and the substances dissolved in it to stay alive. Substances therefore move inside and into and out of cells.

★ **diffusion** – the movement of a substance through a solution or gas *down* its concentration gradient (that is, from a region of high concentration to a region of low concentration of the substance).

★ **osmosis** – the movement of **water** *down* its concentration gradient through a **partially permeable** membrane.

★ **active transport** – the movement of a substance through a solution *up* (against) its concentration gradient (that is, from a region of low concentration to a region of high concentration of the substance).

Fact file

Why does sugar sprinkled on to strawberries turn pink? Because it makes the juice come out of the strawberries.

In and out of cells

On page 29 is the concept map for **movement into and out of cells**. The numbers on the concept map refer to the checklist of points below.

Checklist for movement in and out of cells

1 ★ The molecules of a substance move at random, but there is a better than even chance that some molecules will spread (diffuse) from where they are highly concentrated to where they are fewer in number.

As a result, there is a net movement of molecules from where the substance is in high concentration to where it is in low concentration.

★ **Diffusion** continues until the concentration of the substance is the same throughout the gas or solution.

★ The greater the difference in concentration between the regions, the steeper the concentration gradient and the faster the substance diffuses.

2 ★ During active transport, the molecules of a substance pass from where they are in low concentration to where they are in higher concentration.

As a result, cells may build up stores of a substance which would otherwise be spread out by diffusion.

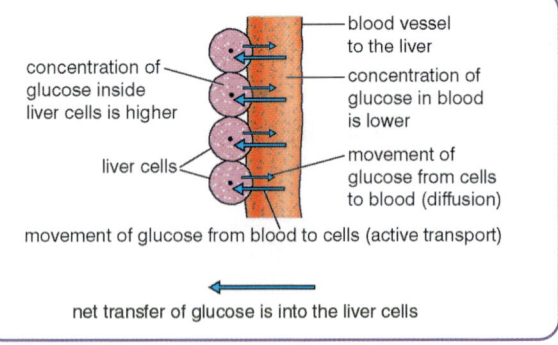

Glucose passes from the blood into the liver by active transport

★ Active transport requires more energy than diffusion.

3 ★ The flow of water from a more dilute solution to a more concentrated solution is called **osmosis**.

Cell activity

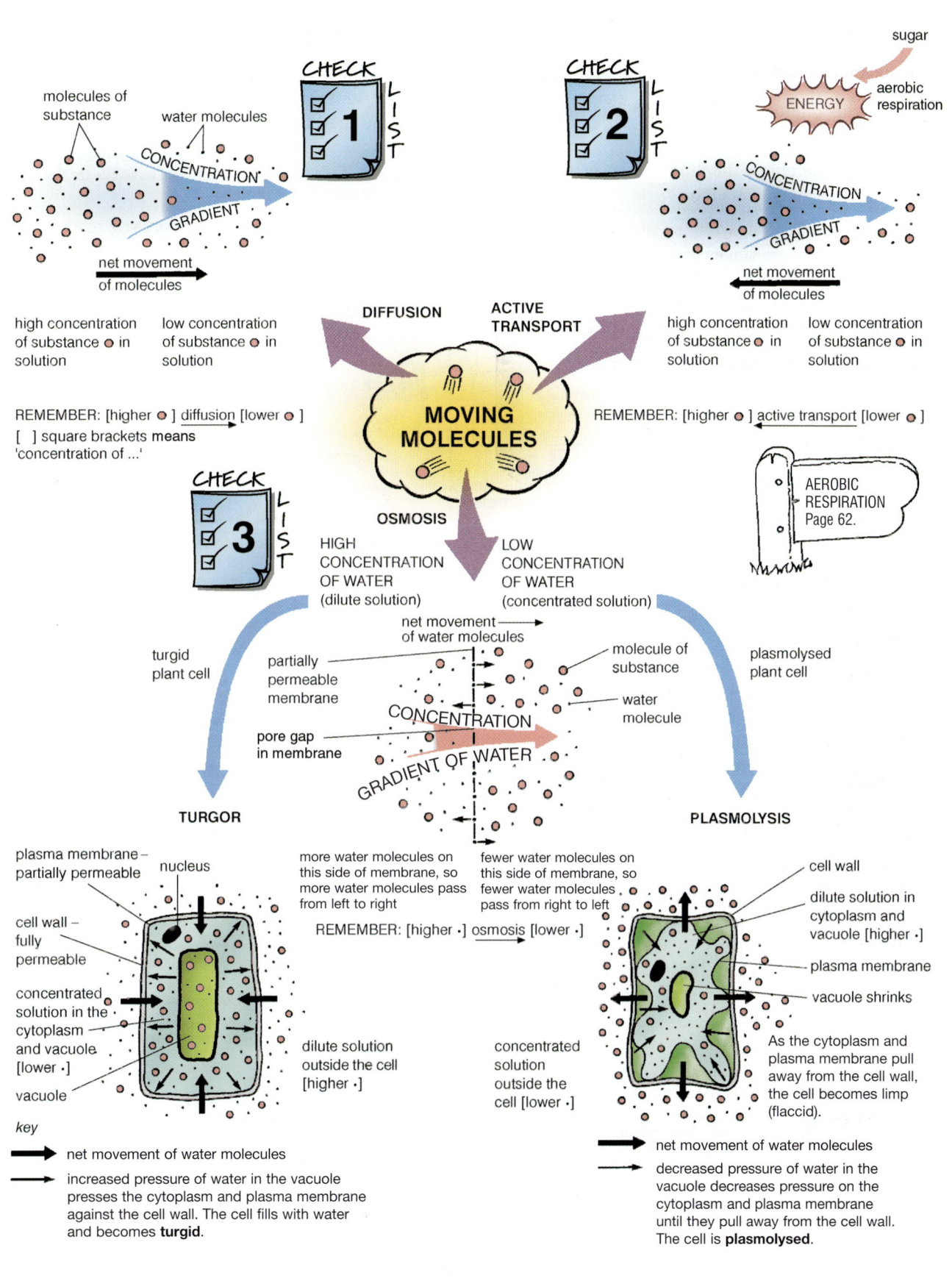

Movement into and out of cells (Checklist opposite on page 28.)

Cell activity

Checklist for cells at work

1 ★ During photosynthesis, oxygen is released into the environment.

★ During aerobic respiration, oxygen is used to release energy from food.

As a result, photosynthesis and aerobic respiration are stages in a cycle, the by-products of one forming the starting point of the other.

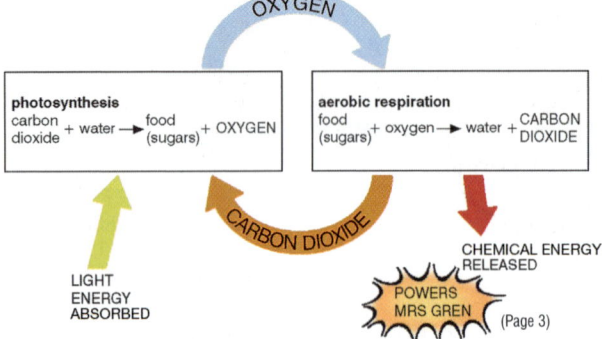

The oxygen–carbon dioxide cycle

The energy released during aerobic respiration enables:
- cells to make (synthesise) larger molecules from the combination of smaller ones
- muscle cells to contract
- mammals (including humans) and birds to maintain a steady body temperature even though the temperature of the surroundings changes.

2 ★ There are different types of cell for different functions.
★ Each type of cell is suited (**adapted**) to carry out its function in the animal body or plant body.
★ A sheet of cells which covers a body surface is called an **epithelium**.
★ Red blood cells do not have nuclei.

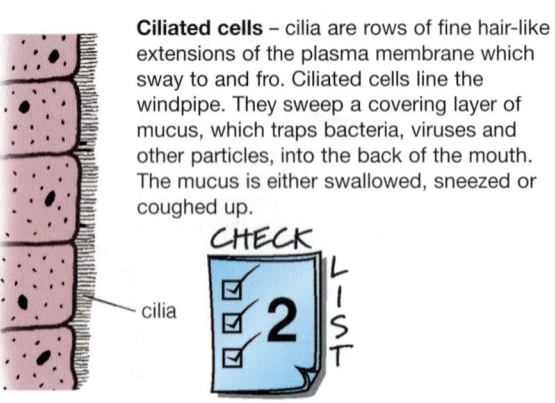

Ciliated cells – cilia are rows of fine hair-like extensions of the plasma membrane which sway to and fro. Ciliated cells line the windpipe. They sweep a covering layer of mucus, which traps bacteria, viruses and other particles, into the back of the mouth. The mucus is either swallowed, sneezed or coughed up.

Cells at work

VARIETY OF CELLS

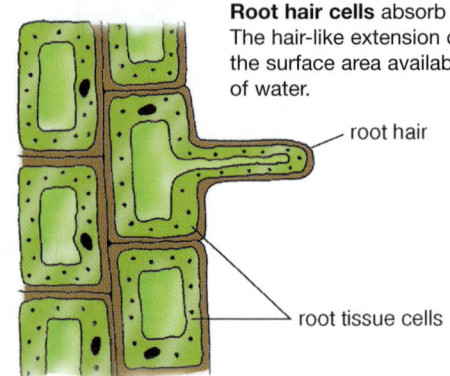

Root hair cells absorb water from the soil. The hair-like extension of each cell increases the surface area available for the absorption of water.
- root hair
- root tissue cells

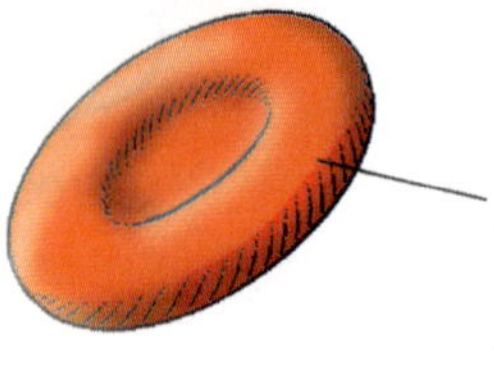

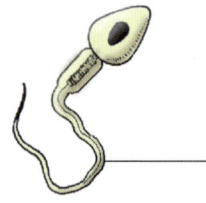

Red blood cells transport oxygen around the body. They contain the pigment haemoglobin which combines with oxygen.
- flattened disc shape increases surface area for the absorption of oxygen

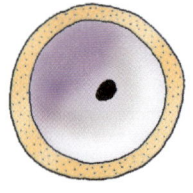

sperm – the male sex cells which swim to the egg
- tail-like flagellum lashes from side to side

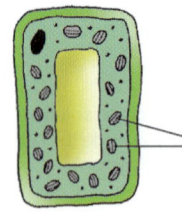

Ovum (egg) – the female sex cell which is fertilised when a sperm fuses with it

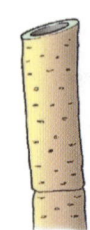

Leaf palisade cells each contain numerous chloroplasts where photosynthesis takes place.
- chloroplasts

Xylem cells form tubes in the stem, roots and leaves, transporting water to all parts of the plant.

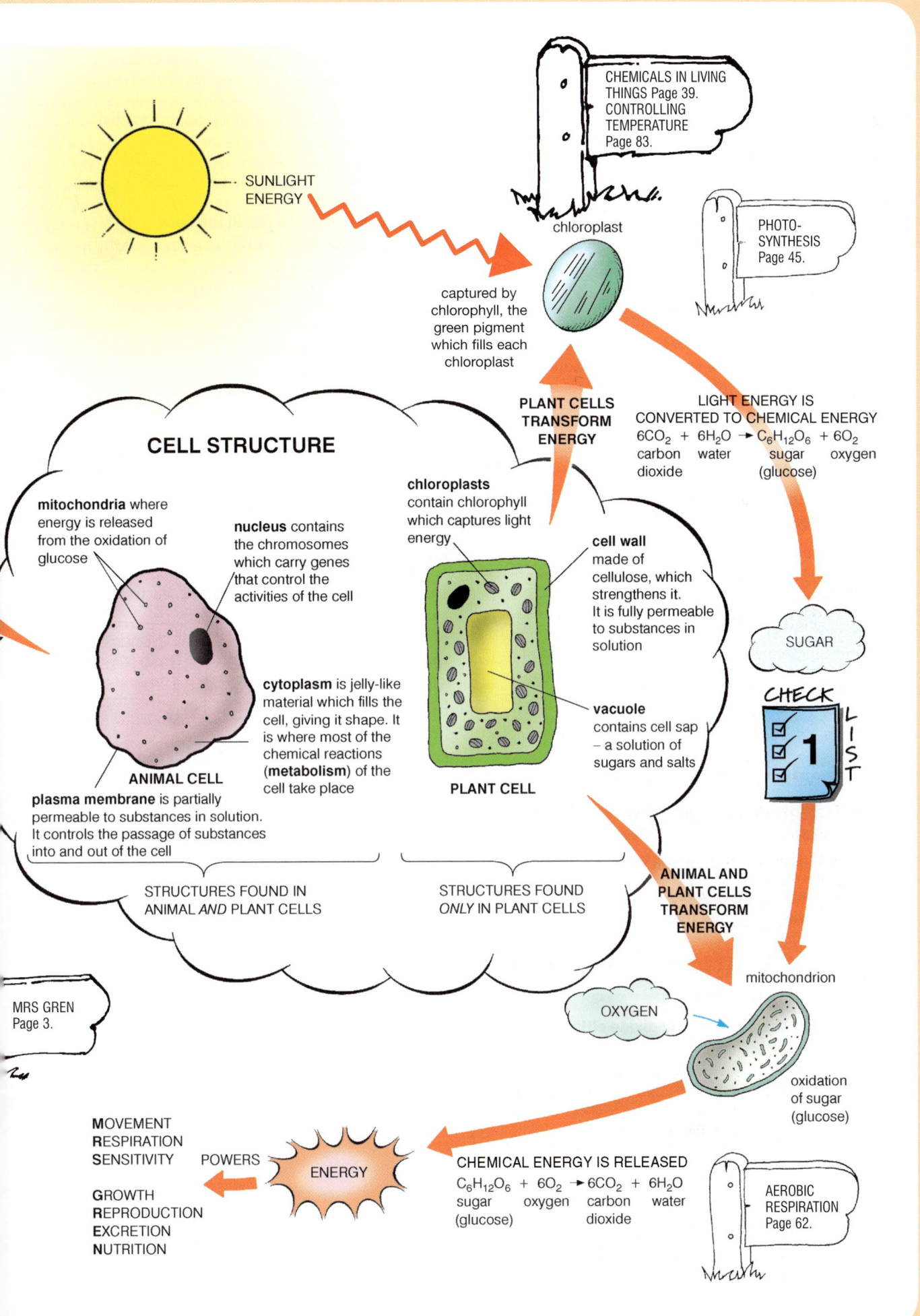

Cell activity

★ A partially permeable membrane is a membrane that allows some substances to pass through but stops 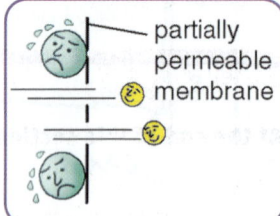 others. The passage of substances across such a membrane depends on the:
- size of the molecules
- size of the membrane pores
- surface area of the cell membrane
- steepness of the concentration gradient
- temperature.

★ The changes happening inside plant cells due to osmosis bring about visible changes in the plant.
- **Plasmolysis** causes a plant to **wilt** through lack of water.
- The plant recovers following watering because the turgor of its cells is restored. **Remember** that a cell filled with water is said to be **turgid**.

★ Osmosis continues until the concentration of water on one side of the membrane, through which the water passes, is equal to the concentration of water on the other side.

3.3 Cell division

> **PREVIEW**
>
> At the end of this section you will:
> - know that new cells (daughter cells) are formed when old cells (parent cells) divide into two
> - understand that the cytoplasm and nucleus divide during cell division
> - know that the nucleus may divide either by mitosis or meiosis.

How cells divide

On pages 34–5 is the concept map for **cell division**. Study it carefully.

Remember

★ The nucleus of each **cell of the body** (except some of the cells of the sex organs) divides by **mitosis**.

★ The nucleus of each of the **cells of the sex organs** that give rise to the sex cells (**gametes**) divides by **meiosis**. Sex cells are produced in the sex organs:
- the **testes** of the male and the **ovaries** of the female in mammals
- the **anthers** (male) and the **carpels** (female) in flowering plants.

SEXUAL REPRODUCTION Pages 90–92.

Mitosis and meiosis

The nucleus contains **chromosomes**, each consisting of a double strand of **deoxyribonucleic acid** (**DNA**) wound round a core of protein. In cell division, the chromosomes are passed from the **parent** cell to the new **daughter** cells. 'Daughter' does not mean that the cells are female. It means that they are the new cells formed as a result of cell division.

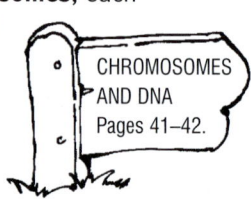

CHROMOSOMES AND DNA Pages 41–42.

Mitosis produces daughter cells with the same number of chromosomes as the parent cell. The daughter cells are described as **diploid** (or **2n**).

Meiosis produces daughter cells with only half the number of chromosomes as the parent cell. The daughter cells are described as **haploid** (or **n**).

The importance of mitosis

The daughter cells each receive an identical full (diploid) set of chromosomes from the parent cell.

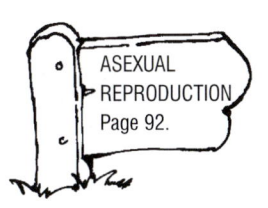

ASEXUAL REPRODUCTION Page 92.

As a result, the parent cell and its daughter cells are genetically identical. They form a **clone**.

As a result, mitosis is the way in which living things:

- **repair damage:** for example, mitosis replaces damaged skin cells with identical new skin cells
- **grow:** for example, the root of a plant grows because root tip cells divide by mitosis to form new root tissue

DEVELOPMENT Page 80.

- **reproduce asexually:** for example, parts of stems can sprout roots and grow into new plants. The new individuals are genetically identical to the parents and are therefore clones.

The importance of meiosis

The daughter cells each receive a half (haploid) set of chromosomes from the parent cell.

As a result, during fertilisation (when sperm and egg join together), the chromosomes from each cell combine.

As a result, the fertilised egg (**zygote**) is diploid but inherits a new combination of genes contributed (50:50) from the parents.

As a result, the new individual inherits characteristics from both parents, not just from one parent as in asexual reproduction.

VARIATION Pages 101–2.

3.4 Cells, tissues and organs

PREVIEW

At the end of this section you will:

- understand that cells are organised into tissues, tissues into organs, and organs into organ systems
- know about the importance of the surface area to volume ratio for living processes
- understand that organ systems are specialised for exchanging materials.

Building an organ system

On pages 36–7 is the concept map which revises **cells**, **tissues** and **organs**.

Plants and animals are **multicellular**: they are made of many types of cells. Each type of cell is specialised, enabling it to carry out a particular biological task.

★ A group of similar cells makes a **tissue**.

VARIETY OF CELLS Page 30.

★ Different tissues together make up an **organ**.

★ Different organs combine to make an **organ system**.

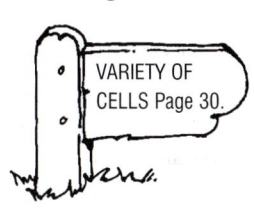

Surface area to volume ratio

All cells (tissues, organs, organisms) exchange gases, food and other materials with their environment. The exchanges occur mostly by diffusion across surfaces. Look at the calculations for surface area (SA), volume (V) and surface area to volume ratio (SA/V) on page 38.

- The SA/V of cube B is half that of cube A.
- The SA/V of cube C is two-thirds that of cube B and one-third that of cube A.

Cell activity

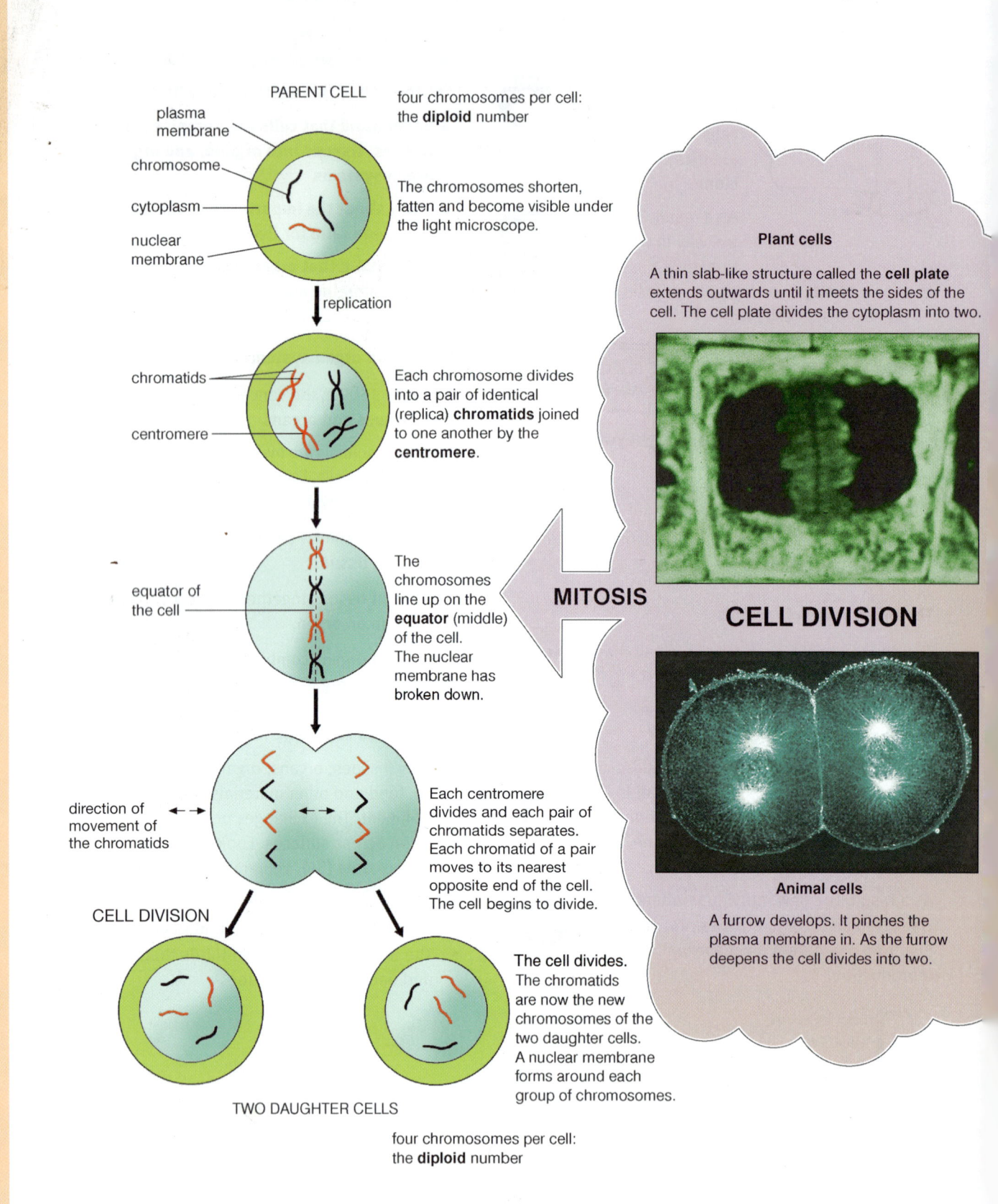

Cell division

PARENT CELL — four chromosomes per cell: the **diploid** number

Labels on parent cell: plasma membrane, chromosome, cytoplasm, nuclear membrane

The chromosomes shorten, fatten and become visible under the light microscope.

↓ replication

Labels: chromatids, centromere

Each chromosome divides into a pair of identical (replica) **chromatids** joined to one another by the **centromere**.

Label: equator of the cell

The chromosomes line up on the **equator** (middle) of the cell. The nuclear membrane has broken down.

Label: direction of movement of the chromatids

Each centromere divides and each pair of chromatids separates. Each chromatid of a pair moves to its nearest opposite end of the cell. The cell begins to divide.

CELL DIVISION

TWO DAUGHTER CELLS

The cell divides. The chromatids are now the new chromosomes of the two daughter cells. A nuclear membrane forms around each group of chromosomes.

four chromosomes per cell: the **diploid** number

MITOSIS — CELL DIVISION

Plant cells

A thin slab-like structure called the **cell plate** extends outwards until it meets the sides of the cell. The cell plate divides the cytoplasm into two.

Animal cells

A furrow develops. It pinches the plasma membrane in. As the furrow deepens the cell divides into two.

Cell activity

PARENT CELL

four chromosomes per cell: the **diploid** number

- plasma membrane
- chromosome
- cytoplasm
- nuclear membrane

The chromosomes shorten, fatten and become visible under the light microscope.

↓ replication

Each chromosome divides into a pair of identical (replica) **chromatids** joined to one another by the **centromere**.

- chromatids
- centromere

Matching chromosomes pair up, forming **homologous pairs**. The nuclear membrane breaks down and homologous pairs of chromosomes line up on the **equator** (middle) of the cell.

- equator of the cell
- homologous pair of chromosomes

Homologous pairs of chromosomes separate, each pair moving to its nearest opposite end of the cell. The cell begins to divide.

↔ direction of movement of chromosomes

MEIOSIS ⟹

CELL DIVISION

A new nuclear membrane forms around each group of chromosomes and the cell divides.

The nuclear membrane breaks down. The chromosomes (still as pairs of chromatids) arrange themselves on the **equator** (middle) of the cell.

— equator of the cell

Each centromere divides and each pair of chromatids separates. Each chromatid of a pair moves to its nearest opposite end of each cell. The chromatids are now new chromosomes. Each cell begins to divide.

↕ direction of movement of chromatids

CELL DIVISION

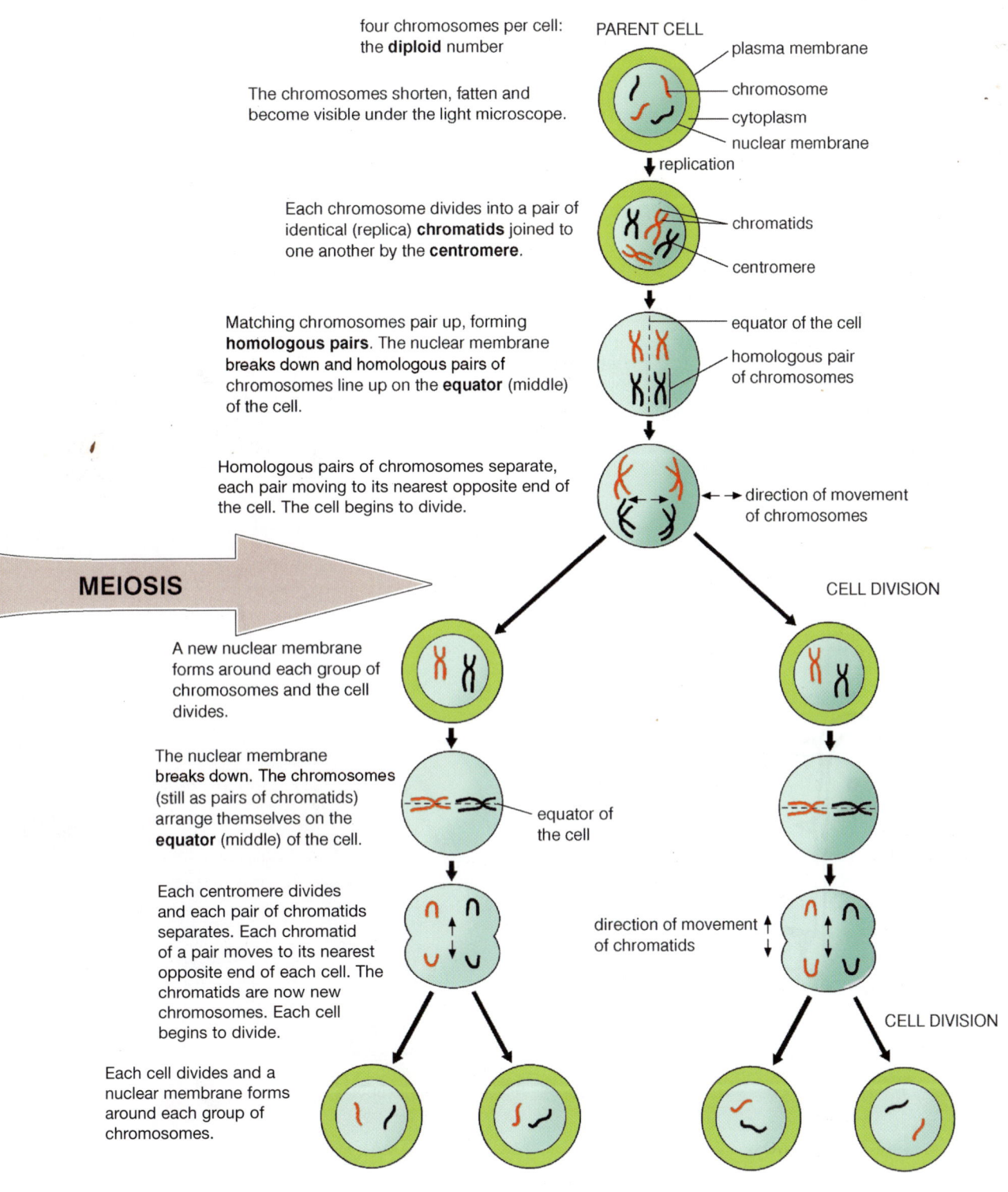

Each cell divides and a nuclear membrane forms around each group of chromosomes.

FOUR DAUGHTER CELLS

two chromosomes per cell: the **haploid** number

Cell activity

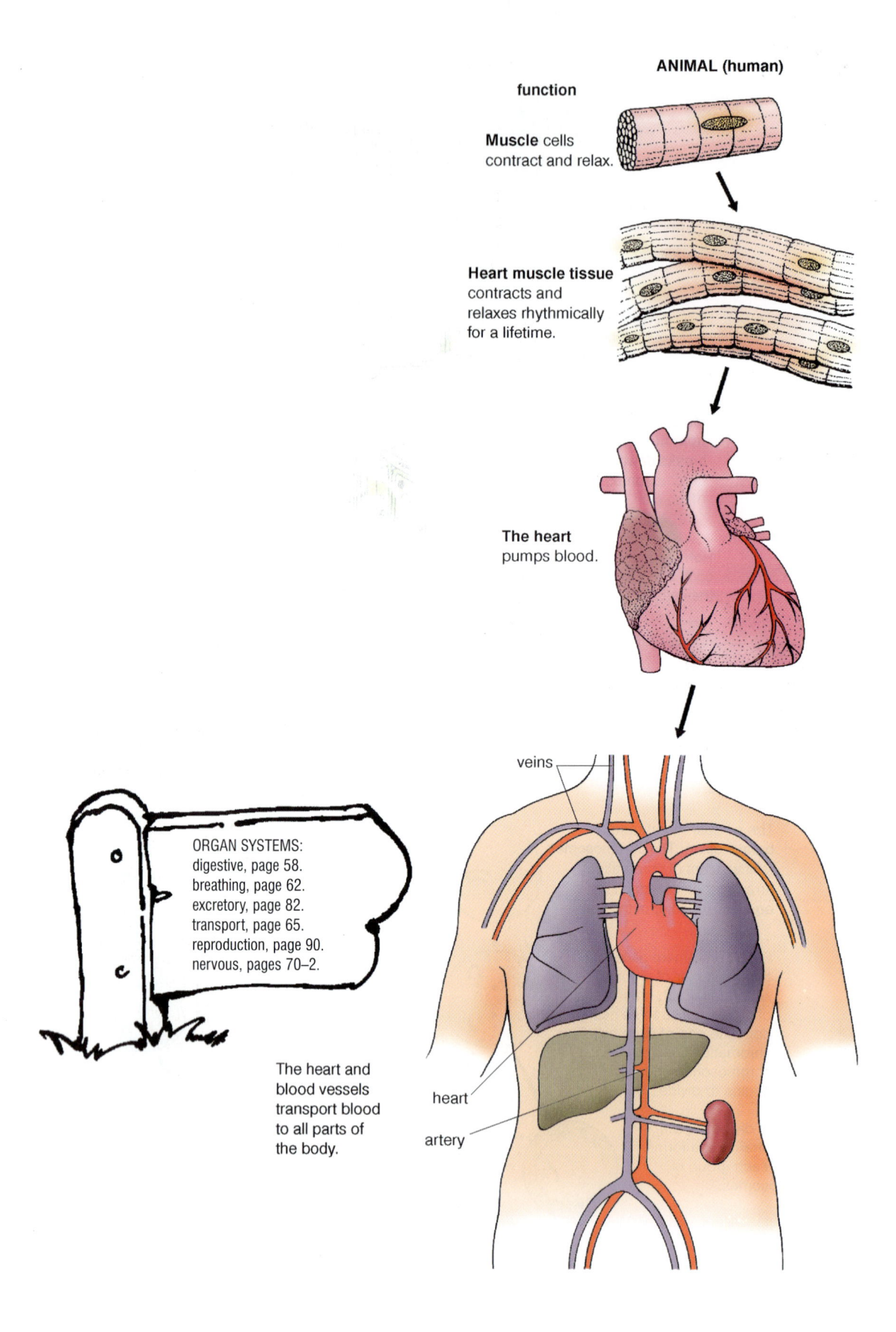

ANIMAL (human)

function

Muscle cells contract and relax.

Heart muscle tissue contracts and relaxes rhythmically for a lifetime.

The heart pumps blood.

ORGAN SYSTEMS:
digestive, page 58.
breathing, page 62.
excretory, page 82.
transport, page 65.
reproduction, page 90.
nervous, pages 70–2.

The heart and blood vessels transport blood to all parts of the body.

veins
heart
artery

Cells to organ systems

Cell activity

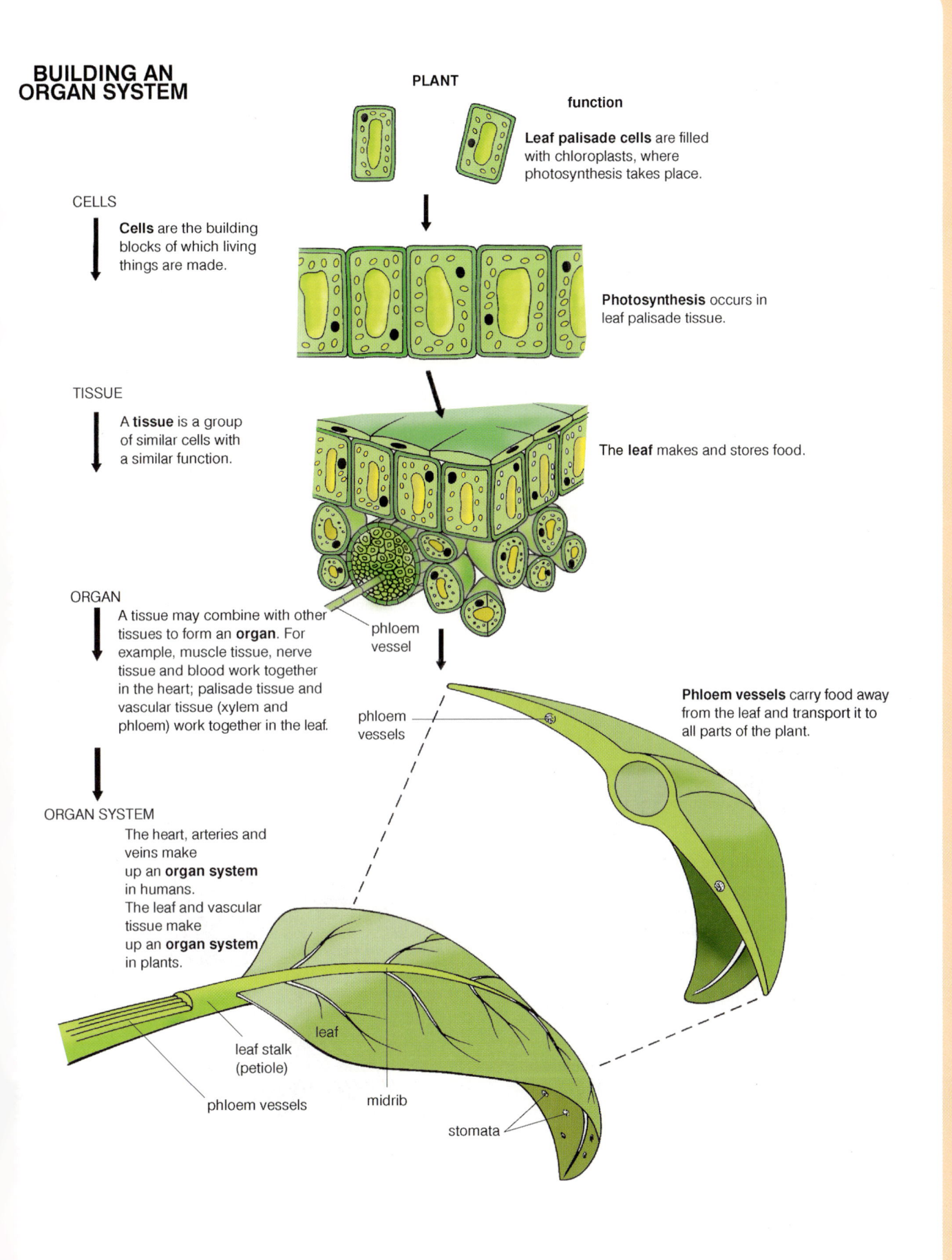

BUILDING AN ORGAN SYSTEM

PLANT

function

CELLS

Cells are the building blocks of which living things are made.

Leaf palisade cells are filled with chloroplasts, where photosynthesis takes place.

Photosynthesis occurs in leaf palisade tissue.

TISSUE

A **tissue** is a group of similar cells with a similar function.

The **leaf** makes and stores food.

ORGAN

A tissue may combine with other tissues to form an **organ**. For example, muscle tissue, nerve tissue and blood work together in the heart; palisade tissue and vascular tissue (xylem and phloem) work together in the leaf.

phloem vessel

Phloem vessels carry food away from the leaf and transport it to all parts of the plant.

phloem vessels

ORGAN SYSTEM

The heart, arteries and veins make up an **organ system** in humans. The leaf and vascular tissue make up an **organ system** in plants.

leaf

leaf stalk (petiole)

midrib

phloem vessels

stomata

37

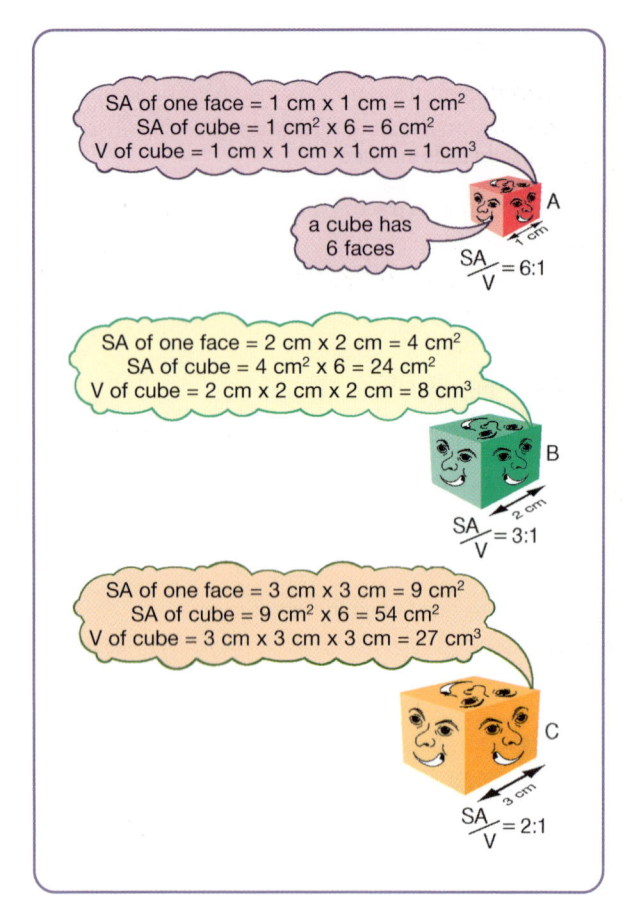

Cell activity

SA of one face = 1 cm x 1 cm = 1 cm²
SA of cube = 1 cm² x 6 = 6 cm²
V of cube = 1 cm x 1 cm x 1 cm = 1 cm³

a cube has 6 faces

A $\frac{SA}{V} = 6:1$

SA of one face = 2 cm x 2 cm = 4 cm²
SA of cube = 4 cm² x 6 = 24 cm²
V of cube = 2 cm x 2 cm x 2 cm = 8 cm³

B $\frac{SA}{V} = 3:1$

SA of one face = 3 cm x 3 cm = 9 cm²
SA of cube = 9 cm² x 6 = 54 cm²
V of cube = 3 cm x 3 cm x 3 cm = 27 cm³

C $\frac{SA}{V} = 2:1$

Cubic arithmetic

Remember

The LARGER the cube becomes, the SMALLER its SA/V.

★ Surface area increases with the **square** (power²) of the side.

★ Volume increases with the **cube** (power³) of the side.

Cells (tissues, organs, organisms) are not cube shaped, but the calculations apply to any shape. For example, as a cell grows it:
• takes in more food and gases
• produces more waste substances.

After the cell reaches a certain size, its surface area becomes proportionally too small to meet the needs of the larger volume of living matter inside.

At this point, the cell divides into two smaller daughter cells. This restores the ratio of surface area to volume because the surface area to volume ratio of each daughter cell is greater than that of the parent cell.

As a result, sufficient food and gases can pass across the cell surface into the cell.

As a result, wastes can pass across the cell surface out of the cell.

Fact file

The SA/V of large animals is less than the SA/V of small animals. Large animals, therefore, lose proportionally less body heat than small animals. However, it takes them longer to warm up.

Organ systems specialised for exchanging materials

We all exchange gases, food and other materials between our body and the environment. The exchange happens by diffusion across body surfaces. Special features of organs and organ systems increase the available surface area for the exchange of materials with their surroundings. These features increase the ratio of surface area to volume of the organs and organ systems in question.

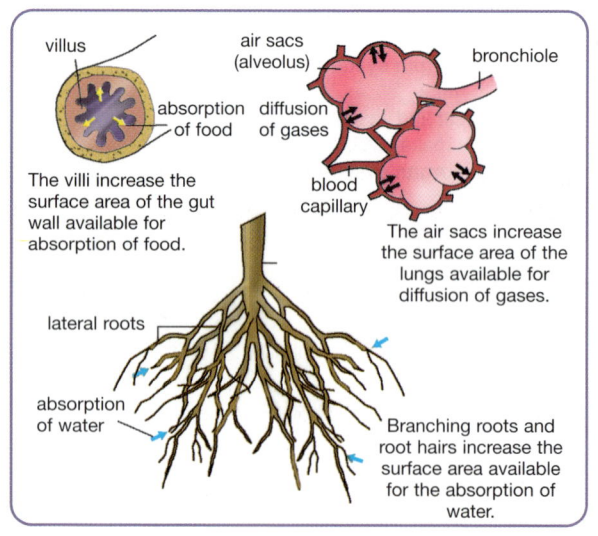

The villi increase the surface area of the gut wall available for absorption of food.

The air sacs increase the surface area of the lungs available for diffusion of gases.

Branching roots and root hairs increase the surface area available for the absorption of water.

Increasing surface area

3.5 Chemicals in living things

PREVIEW

At the end of this section you will:
- understand that living things are made from the same elements as other types of matter
- know that carbohydrates, lipids, proteins and nucleic acids are important chemicals in living things
- understand that atoms of carbon are able to combine to form long chains.

Elements for life

All matter is made of chemical elements. Of these elements, six make up more than 95% by mass of living matter. They are:
- carbon (C)
- hydrogen (H)
- nitrogen (N)
- oxygen (O)
- phosphorus (P)
- sulphur (S).

Handy hint
The symbols of the elements arranged in order of abundance in living matter make the memory aid **CHNOPS**.

Compounds for life

Important categories of compounds in living things are:
- **carbohydrates**: major sources of energy and structural materials
- **lipids**: stores of energy
- **proteins**: for building and repairing bodies
- **nucleic acids**: carry a code which enables cells to make proteins.

Fact file

Carbon is the most common element in the substances that make up living things. Carbon atoms can combine to form long chains. Many of the carbon compounds in living things have large molecules (**macromolecules**) formed by small molecules combining.

Carbohydrates

Carbohydrates are compounds containing the elements carbon, hydrogen and oxygen. There are three categories:

Monosaccharides are simple sugars. Sweet-tasting **fructose** and **glucose** are examples. Both have the molecular formula $C_6H_{12}O_6$. The six carbon atoms form a ring. Sugars (especially glucose) are an important source of energy in all living things.

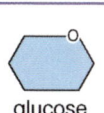

RESPIRATION Page 62.

fructose   glucose

The structural formulae of fructose and glucose in shorthand form. Although the molecular formula of each sugar is the same, the structural formulae are different.

Disaccharides are more complex sugars. They are formed when two monosaccharides combine. For example, two molecules of glucose combine to form one molecule of **maltose**:

$$2 \text{ glucose} \rightarrow \text{maltose} + \text{water}$$

$$2C_6H_{12}O_6 \text{ (aq)} \rightarrow C_{12}H_{22}O_{11} \text{ (aq)} + H_2O \text{ (l)}$$

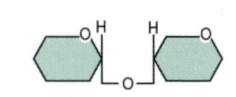

The formula for maltose in shorthand form

A molecule of fructose and a molecule of glucose combine to form one molecule of **sucrose**:

$$\text{glucose} + \text{fructose} \rightarrow \text{sucrose} + \text{water}$$

Polysaccharides are carbohydrates whose molecules contain hundreds of sugar rings. For example, **starch**, **cellulose** and **glycogen** are polysaccharides. Their molecules consist of long chains of glucose rings.

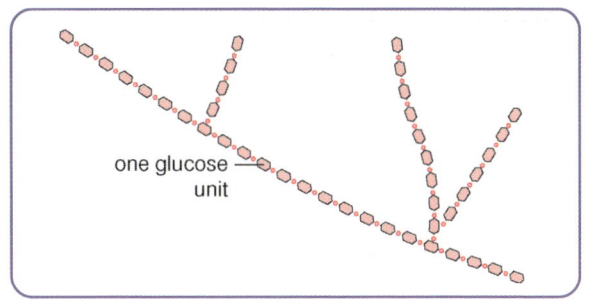

one glucose unit

Part of a starch molecule

Cell activity

Polysaccharides differ in the length and structure of their chains. They are important storage and structural materials in living things.

★ **Starch** is a food substance stored in plants. Starch can be converted into glucose, which is oxidised (respired) in cells. Energy is released.

★ **Glycogen** is a food substance stored in animals. Liver cells convert glycogen into glucose, which is oxidised (respired) in cells. Energy is released.

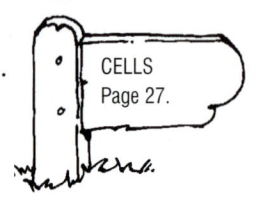

CELLS Page 27.

★ **Cellulose** is an important component of the cell walls of plants.

★ **Chitin** is an important component of the exoskeleton of insects.

Lipids

Lipids are compounds containing the elements carbon, hydrogen and oxygen. There are two types of lipids: **fats**, which are solid at room temperature; and **oils**, which are liquid at room temperature.

Fats and oils are compounds formed by the reactions between **fatty acids** and **glycerol**. A molecule of glycerol can combine with three fatty acid molecules to form a **triglyceride** molecule and three molecules of water. Fats and oils are mixtures of triglycerides.

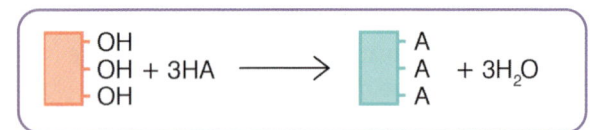

glycerol + fatty acid ⟶ triglyceride + water

$$\begin{matrix} \text{OH} \\ \text{OH} \\ \text{OH} \end{matrix} + 3\text{HA} \longrightarrow \begin{matrix} \text{A} \\ \text{A} \\ \text{A} \end{matrix} + 3\text{H}_2\text{O}$$

Making a triglyceride

Saturated and unsaturated fats and oils

Fatty acids (and therefore the fats and oils of which they are a part) may be:
- **saturated** – the carbon atoms are joined by single bonds, *or*
- **unsaturated** – the carbon atoms have double bonds between them. If there is one double bond in the molecule, the compound is **monounsaturated**. If there is more than one double bond in the molecule, the compound is **polyunsaturated**.

HEART DISEASE Page 69.

Fats and oils are important as:
- components of cell membranes
- sources of energy
- sources of the fat-soluble vitamins A, D and E
- insulation which helps to keep the body warm
- protection for delicate organs.

Proteins

Proteins are compounds containing the elements carbon, hydrogen, oxygen, nitrogen and sometimes sulphur.

Amino acids are the building blocks which combine to make proteins. Two or more amino acids can combine to form a **peptide**, which can combine with more amino acids to form a **protein**.

Fact file

★ **Peptides** have molecules with up to 15 amino acids.

★ **Polypeptides** have molecules with 15–50 amino acids.

★ **Proteins** have still larger molecules.

There are 20 different amino acids that combine to form proteins. The protein made depends on the type and number of amino acids joining together.

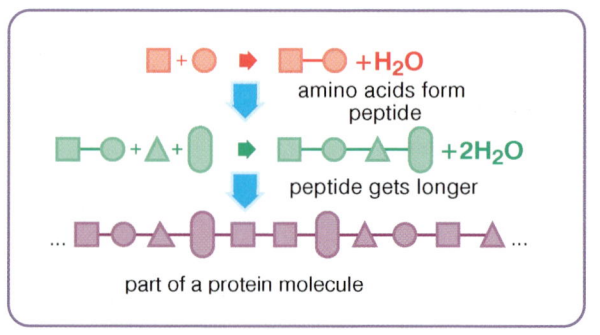

How amino acids combine to form peptides and proteins. Each shape represents a particular type of amino acid.

Cell activity

Proteins are important because:
- they are the materials from which new tissues are made during growth and repair
- most **enzymes** are proteins. Enzymes control the rates of chemical reactions in cells
- some **hormones** are proteins. Hormones control the activities of organisms.

HORMONES Page 77.

CATALYST Pages 187–8.

Enzymes in action

Enzymes are made by living cells. They are **catalysts** which control the speeds of chemical reactions in cells. There are thousands of different enzymes in a cell. Enzymes also speed up the rate of digestion of food in the gut.

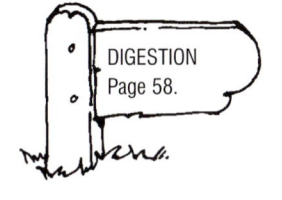

DIGESTION Page 58.

Enzymes are:
- **specific** in their action – each enzyme catalyses a certain chemical reaction or type of chemical reaction
- sensitive to changes in **pH**
- sensitive to changes in **temperature**.

The substance that the enzyme helps to react is called the **substrate**. The substances formed in the reaction are called **products**.

The features of enzymes are shown below.

Nucleic acids

Deoxyribonucleic acid (**DNA**) and **ribonucleic acid** (**RNA**) are nucleic acids.

★ DNA makes up the chromosomes in the nucleus of the cell. The **genes** that carry information from parents to offspring are lengths of DNA. They carry the **genetic code** which enables cells to assemble amino acids in the correct order to make proteins.

★ RNA occurs in the nucleus and cytoplasm of the cell. It transfers the information in the genes to the places in the cell where proteins are made.

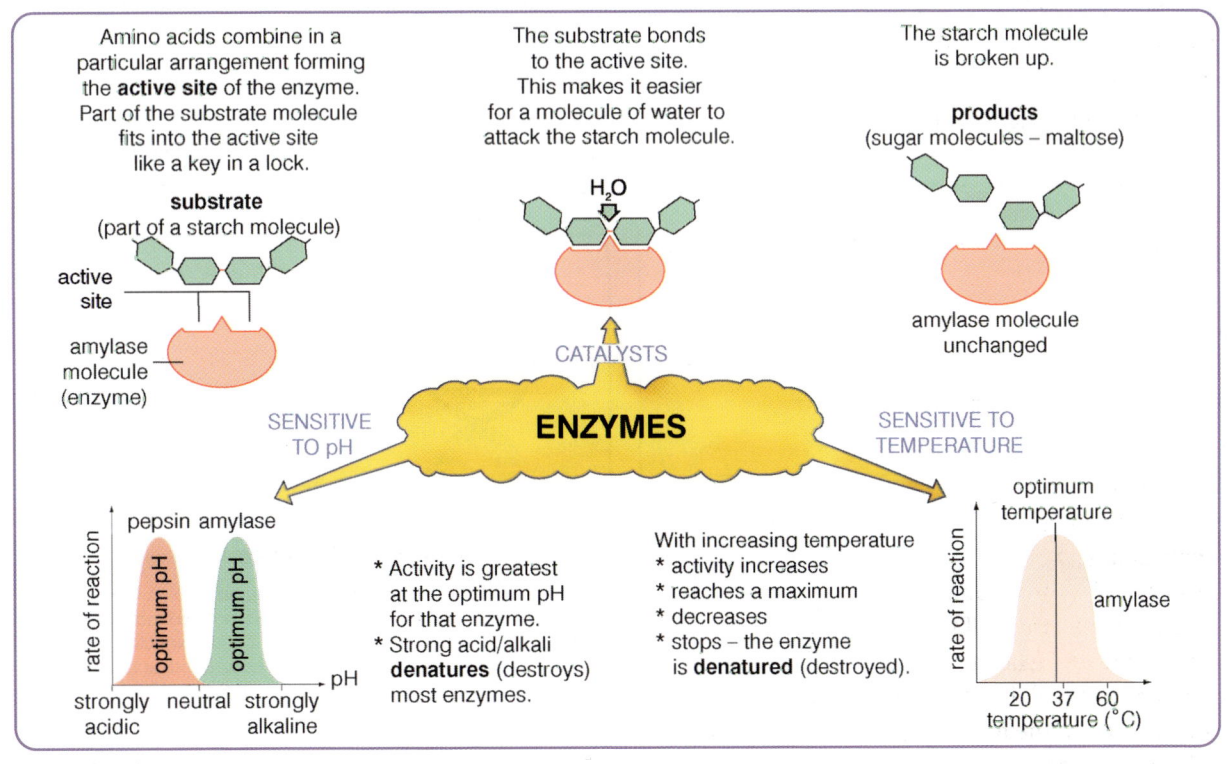

Amino acids combine in a particular arrangement forming the **active site** of the enzyme. Part of the substrate molecule fits into the active site like a key in a lock.

substrate (part of a starch molecule)

active site

amylase molecule (enzyme)

The substrate bonds to the active site. This makes it easier for a molecule of water to attack the starch molecule.

CATALYSTS

The starch molecule is broken up.

products (sugar molecules – maltose)

amylase molecule unchanged

ENZYMES

SENSITIVE TO pH

pepsin amylase
optimum pH optimum pH
rate of reaction
strongly acidic — neutral — strongly alkaline
pH

* Activity is greatest at the optimum pH for that enzyme.
* Strong acid/alkali **denatures** (destroys) most enzymes.

SENSITIVE TO TEMPERATURE

With increasing temperature
* activity increases
* reaches a maximum
* decreases
* stops – the enzyme is **denatured** (destroyed).

optimum temperature
rate of reaction
amylase
20 37 60
temperature (°C)

Enzymes in action

Cell activity

The structure of DNA

DNA and RNA are large complex molecules made from lots of smaller molecules called **nucleotides**.

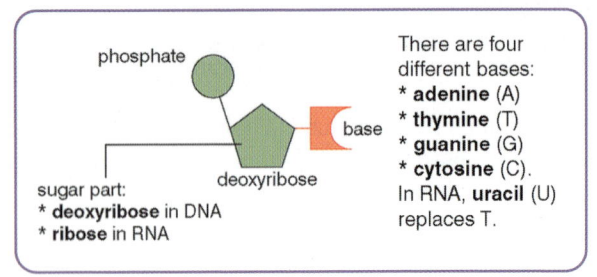

There are four different bases:
* **adenine** (A)
* **thymine** (T)
* **guanine** (G)
* **cytosine** (C).

In RNA, *uracil* (U) replaces T.

sugar part:
* **deoxyribose** in DNA
* **ribose** in RNA

A nucleotide molecule

★ Many nucleotides join together, sugar to phosphate, to form a long strand.

★ Two of these strands link together by **base pairing** to form a molecule of DNA:
  - adenine (A) bonds to thymine (T) or *vice versa*
  - guanine (G) bonds to cytosine (C) or *vice versa*.

★ The double strand twists into a spiral called a **double helix** – two intertwined spiral strands.

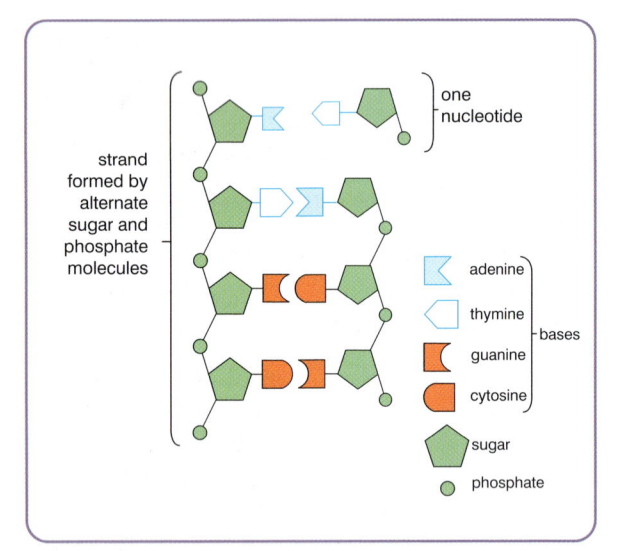

Part of a molecule of DNA

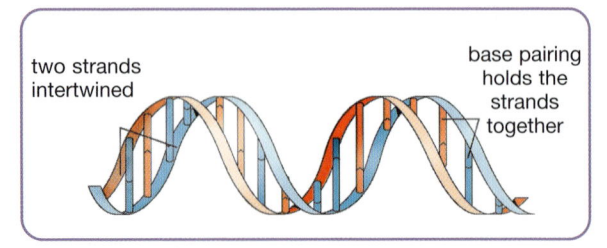

The double helix: two spiral strands connected by their bases

★ A **chromosome** consists of a folded double strand of DNA coiled round a protein core. The DNA part of the structure controls the inheritance of characteristics.

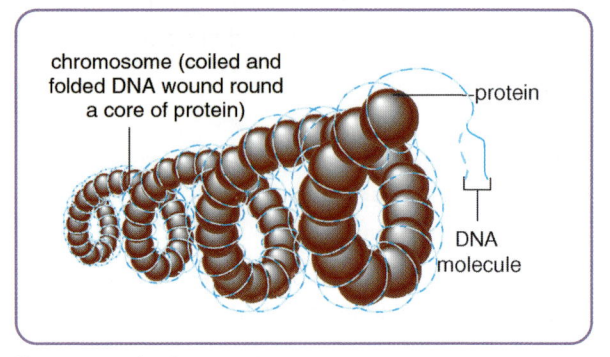

The structure of a chromosome

DNA replication

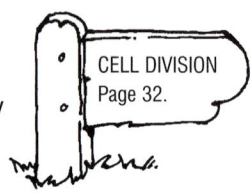

CELL DIVISION
Page 32.

During cell division, the chromosomes **replicate** – they form an identical copy of themselves. This means the DNA molecule must make a copy of itself. The diagram below shows how this happens.

Now you can see why the daughter cells formed by mitosis are genetically identical to each other and to their parent cell. The two new molecules of DNA are each a replica of the original because of the base pairing. A always pairs with T (or vice versa), and G always pairs with C (or vice versa). All the cells in the body that die are replaced by mitosis, so the new cells are identical to the old ones that gave rise to them.

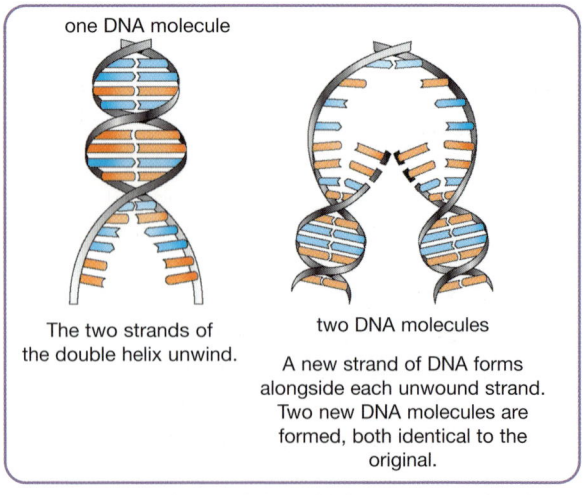

The two strands of the double helix unwind.

two DNA molecules

A new strand of DNA forms alongside each unwound strand. Two new DNA molecules are formed, both identical to the original.

DNA replication. The horizontal shapes joining two strands of DNA represent the bases A, T, G and C shown opposite.

Mutation

Hundreds of thousands of nucleotides a second can be added to the replicating DNA. Occasionally the wrong nucleotide with its base adds by mistake. Then the new DNA formed is slightly different from the original. The change is called a **mutation**.

The genetic code

★ A **codon** is the length of a DNA molecule that codes for one amino acid. It is three nucleotides long.

★ A **gene** is the length of a DNA molecule that codes for one complete protein.

★ A gene, therefore, is a long line of codons in a particular order. The order of the codons controls the order in which amino acids are assembled to produce a particular protein.

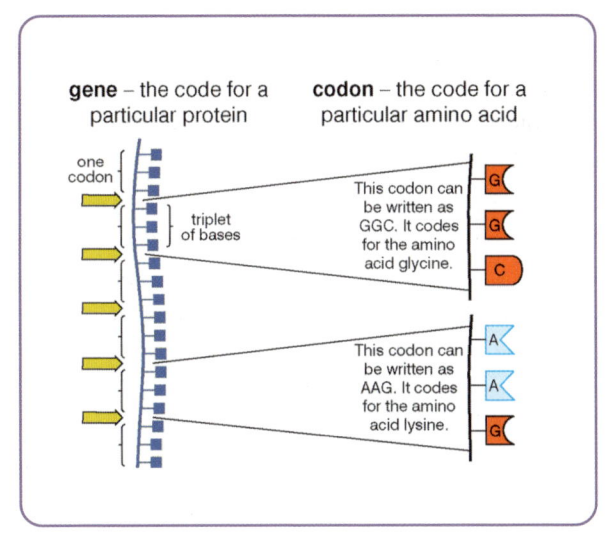

gene – the code for a particular protein

codon – the code for a particular amino acid

This codon can be written as GGC. It codes for the amino acid glycine.

This codon can be written as AAG. It codes for the amino acid lysine.

The genetic code

Remember that:
- one of the five bases – adenine (A), thymine (T), guanine (G), cytosine (C) or uracil (U) – is a component of a nucleotide
- nucleotides whose base is uracil are not components of DNA but are components of RNA
- a length of DNA consists of a sequence of nucleotides (and therefore bases)
- the sequence of bases of a gene is a set of instructions (one part of the genetic code) which enables a cell to make a particular protein.

The human genome

The word **genome** refers to all of the DNA in all of an organism. Scientists working on the human genome:
- have worked out the order (**sequence**) of bases of the lengths of DNA that form our genes
- aim to identify where individual genes are located on chromosomes
- aim to identify the proteins for which the genes are the code.

Nearly all human cells each have about 30–40 thousand genes. These genes determine our vulnerability to disease, patterns of behaviour, appearance and all of the other characteristics we inherit from our parents. Samples of cells (white blood cells and sperm) are taken from anonymous volunteers. The DNA extracted from the cells is analysed and its sequence of bases worked out.

The discovery of the sequence of the bases of the human genome is the key that unlocks the possibilities of new drugs and treatments as a result of our knowing the genetic causes of disease.

Fact file

★ **The Human Genome Organisation** was established in the late 1980s to co-ordinate the research of scientists in the USA, UK and other countries working to discover the sequence of the human genome. The organisation receives money from public funds.

★ **The Institute of Genomic Research** was privately funded and set up soon after its founder Craig Venter had applied in 1991 for **patents** on more than 300 human genes. A patent is a legal document that registers a person's (or organisation's) claim for an invention. In the case of genomic research, the invention refers to the base sequence of the DNA that makes up the human genome.

Cell activity

Issues

The publication of the publicly funded and privately funded working draft of the human genome sequence on 15 February 2001 highlights difficult issues that arise from knowing our genetic make up. Here are a number of points for you to think about.

★ Patents stop other people and organisations from making use of genomic information. Exploiting the genome to improve health care may well depend on paying the owners of the patents large sums of money.

★ If our individual genome is part of our medical records, will organisations that provide life insurance require people to be tested for their risk of developing genetically related disease? An unfavourable genetic profile may also make it difficult for people to obtain a mortgage to buy a house.

★ It is likely that genetic testing for intelligence, eye and hair colour and other characteristics will soon be possible. Should parents be able to choose a 'designer' baby?

These are just a few of the issues that you need to think about. The more accurate finished human genome was announced on 14 April 2003.

ROUND UP

How much have you improved? Work out your improvement index on page 110.

1. Which of the structures listed below are found in a) animal cells and plant cells b) plant cells only?

   nucleus   plasma membrane   cell wall   large vacuole   mitochondria   chloroplasts   cytoplasm   [7]

2. Describe what happens in the cells of a plant deprived of water which is then watered. How will the appearance of the plant change?   [5]

3. Complete the following paragraph using the words below. Each word may be used once, more than once or not at all.

   osmosis   faster   gains   down   slower   partially   energy   against

   The movement of a substance _____ a concentration gradient is called diffusion. The steeper the concentration gradient, the _____ is the rate of diffusion. Active transport occurs _____ a concentration gradient. The process requires more _____ than diffusion. The diffusion of water through a _____ permeable membrane is called _____.   [6]

4. Why is mitosis important for maintaining the health of the tissues of the body?   [1]

5. Compare and contrast the processes of mitosis and meiosis by listing the similarities and the differences in different columns.   [8]

6. Below is a series of words that describe the organisation of living matter. Arrange the words in the correct sequence, beginning with the simplest level of organisation and ending with the most complex.

   organs   cells   organisms   organ systems   tissues   [5]

7. Match each substance in column **A** with its function in column **B**.

A substances	B functions
fat	carries the genetic code
cellulose	insulates the body
DNA	a component of the plant cell wall
polypeptide	a food substance stored in the liver
glycogen	most enzymes are made of this substance
protein	made of about 40 amino acids [6]

8. a) The following is a sequence of bases for a length of DNA. How many codons are there in the sequence, assuming the first codon begins at the left-hand side and there is no overlap?

   T T A G G A C T G A T C

   b) If each codon codes for one amino acid, how many amino acids are coded for in this length of DNA?   [2]

Green plants as organisms — Chapter 4

How much do you already know? Work out your score on page 110.

Test yourself

1. a) Name the inorganic substances that are the raw materials for photosynthesis. [2]
   b) Name the gas given off during photosynthesis. [1]

2. Minerals are needed for healthy growth. Match each substance in column **A** with its function in column **B**.

A substances	B functions
nitrogen	used to make cell membranes
phosphorus	used to make chlorophyll
magnesium	used to make protein

   [3]

3. Complete the following paragraph using the words below. Each word may be used once, more than once or not at all.

   active transport   evaporates   increase translocation   osmotic   stomata   xylem osmosis

   Root hairs _____ the surface area available for the uptake of water. Water passes across the root into the _____ by _____. The uptake of minerals in solution is by _____. Water moves through the _____ tissue in unbroken columns connecting the root with the leaves of the plant. Water is lost from the leaves as it _____ through the _____. [8]

4. Different types of tropisms are listed in column **A**. Match each type with the correct description in column **B**.

A tropisms	B descriptions
phototropism	growth movement in response to gravity
geotropism	growth movement in response to touch
hydrotropism	growth movement in response to light
thigmotropism	growth movement in response to water

   [4]

4.1 Photosynthesis and mineral nutrients

PREVIEW

At the end of this section you will:
- understand that in most plants, photosynthesis takes place in their leaves
- know that limiting factors affect the rate of photosynthesis
- be able to identify the minerals that plants need for healthy growth.

Photosynthesis

Photosynthesis is a chemical process that traps the energy of sunlight. Plant cells use the energy to convert carbon dioxide and water into sugars. A summary of the process is:

$$\text{carbon dioxide} + \text{water} \xrightarrow{\text{catalysed by chlorophyll}} \text{glucose} + \text{oxygen}$$

$$6CO_2(g) + 6H_2O(l) \longrightarrow C_6H_{12}O_6(aq) + 6O_2(g)$$

There are lots of different chemical reactions that make up the process of photosynthesis. The reactions happen inside chloroplasts, in the cells of leaves and other green parts of plants.

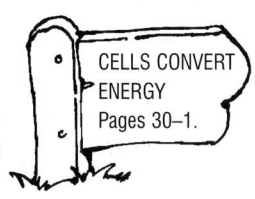

CELLS CONVERT ENERGY Pages 30–1.

Leaves

A leaf is a food-making factory. It is **adapted** for photosynthesis. Carbon dioxide and water circulate within the leaf. Light is captured by the pigment chlorophyll, which is packaged in the chloroplasts that pack the cells of the leaf. On pages 48–9 is the concept map for **photosynthesis**, and its checklist of points is on page 47. The diagram below shows you how the plant uses sugars.

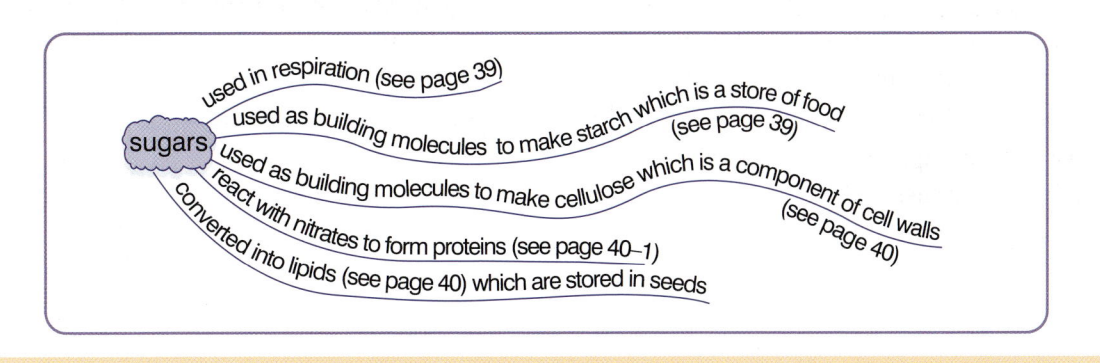

sugars
- used in respiration (see page 39)
- used as building molecules to make starch which is a store of food (see page 39)
- used as building molecules to make cellulose which is a component of cell walls (see page 40)
- react with nitrates to form proteins (see page 40–1)
- converted into lipids (see page 40) which are stored in seeds

Green plants as organisms

Limiting factors

The rate at which plants make sugar by photosynthesis is affected by supplies of **carbon dioxide** and **water**, **temperature** and the **intensity of light**. These factors are called **limiting factors** because if any one of them falls to a low level, photosynthesis slows down or stops, even if the other factors are in plentiful supply. The diagram below illustrates the point. At low concentrations of carbon dioxide, the carbon dioxide limits the rate of photosynthesis, whatever the light level is. Carbon dioxide is the limiting factor. At higher concentrations of carbon dioxide, the rate of photosynthesis increases if the light is bright enough. Light is now the limiting factor.

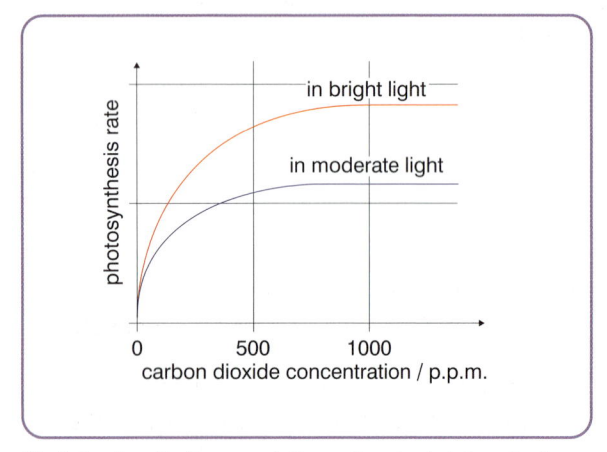

Effect of carbon dioxide concentration on the rate of photosynthesis (carbon dioxide concentration is given in p.p.m., parts per million)

The higher the temperature, the faster the chemical reactions of photosynthesis, within limits. Extreme cold slows the activity of the enzymes which control the chemical reactions of photosynthesis; extreme heat destroys (denatures) them.

Water is a raw material for photosynthesis. However, water is also the solvent in which most of the reactions of metabolism occur within cells. Singling out the direct effect of the availability of water on photosynthesis is therefore very difficult.

In a greenhouse, conditions are controlled so that limiting factors are eliminated. The diagram in the next column shows you this idea.

Fact file

Bottles of 'plant food' sold at garden centres contain solutions of some of the important minerals needed for healthy plant growth.

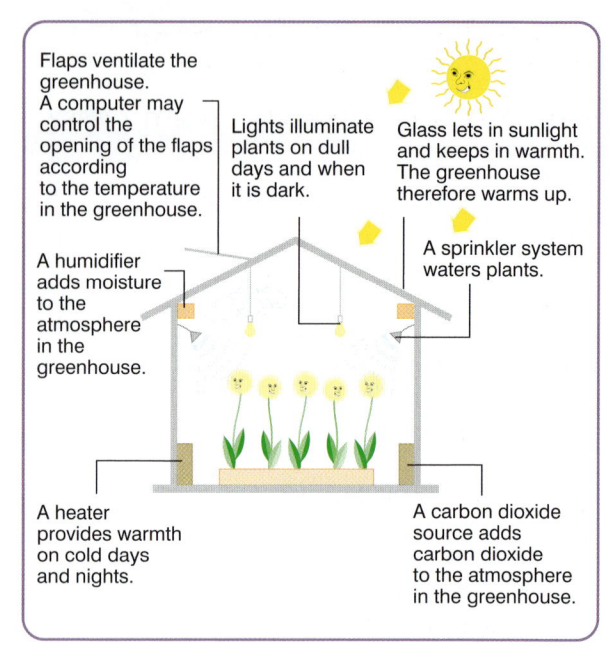

Flaps ventilate the greenhouse. A computer may control the opening of the flaps according to the temperature in the greenhouse.

Lights illuminate plants on dull days and when it is dark.

Glass lets in sunlight and keeps in warmth. The greenhouse therefore warms up.

A humidifier adds moisture to the atmosphere in the greenhouse.

A sprinkler system waters plants.

A heater provides warmth on cold days and nights.

A carbon dioxide source adds carbon dioxide to the atmosphere in the greenhouse.

The maximum-efficiency greenhouse

Mineral nutrients

Plants grow using the food (sugars) they make by photosynthesis. Healthy plant growth also depends on **minerals** which are absorbed from the soil through the roots as solutions of salts.

Major elements are needed in quite large amounts.

★ **Nitrogen (N)** is used by plants to make protein.

★ **Phosphorus (P)** is used by plants to make cell membranes. It is also a component of DNA and has an important role in the chemical reactions of photosynthesis and respiration.

★ **Potassium (K)** promotes the activity of enzymes, which control the chemical reactions of photosynthesis and respiration.

Plants deprived of any of the major elements grow less well. Most artificial fertilisers are NPK fertilisers. Shortage of:
- nitrogen in the form of nitrate ions leads to stunted growth and yellow older leaves
- phosphorus in the form of phosphate ions leads to poor root growth and purple younger leaves
- potassium in the form of potassium ions leads to yellow leaves with dead spots.

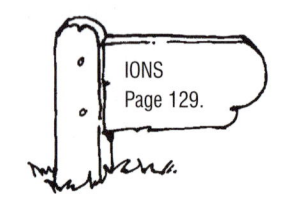

IONS Page 129.

Green plants as organisms

Trace elements (micronutrients) are needed in much smaller amounts than major elements.

★ **Magnesium** (Mg) is a component of the chlorophyll molecule.

★ **Iron** (Fe) is also a component of the chlorophyll molecule.

If magnesium and iron are in short supply then leaves become mottled and pale. **Copper** (Cu), **sodium** (Na) and **manganese** (Mn) are also trace elements. Absence of any one of them from the soil leads to poor plant growth.

Checklist for photosynthesis

1 ★ Leaves are arranged so that the lower ones are not overshadowed by those above. The arrangement is called the **leaf mosaic**.

  As a result, more leaves are exposed to direct sunlight.

  ★ The leaf blade is flat.

  As a result, a large surface area is exposed for the absorption of light.

  ★ The leaf blade is thin.

  As a result, light reaches the lower layers of cells in the leaf.

2 ★ Water moves up to leaves in the **transpiration stream**.

  TRANSPIRATION Page 49.

  ★ Carbon dioxide enters leaves through the **stomata**.

3 ★ The cells of the upper leaf surface do not contain chloroplasts and are transparent.

  ★ **Palisade cells** beneath the upper epidermis are column shaped, tightly packed and filled with chloroplasts.

  As a result, many chloroplasts are exposed to bright light, maximising the rate of photosynthesis.

  ★ **Spongy mesophyll cells** contain fewer chloroplasts and are more loosely packed.

  As a result, there are air spaces between the spongy mesophyll cells.

★ The spaces allow carbon dioxide and water vapour to circulate freely within the leaf, bringing the raw materials for photosynthesis to the leaf cells.

STOMATA Page 50.

★ Each **stoma** is flanked by guard cells which control the size of the opening of the stoma.

  As a result, the rate of diffusion of gases into and out of the leaf through the stomata is controlled.

★ The cells of the lower leaf surface lack chloroplasts, except the guard cells.

4 ★ Chloroplasts pack the inside of each palisade cell.

  ★ Chloroplasts stream in the cytoplasm (**cyclosis**) to the region of the palisade cell where light is brightest.

  As a result, the rate of photosynthesis is maximised.

5 ★ Membranes inside the chloroplasts are covered with the green pigment **chlorophyll**.

  ★ Chlorophyll absorbs light, especially wavelengths in the red and blue parts of the spectrum.

  ★ The membranes are arranged like stacks of pancakes, maximising the surface area of chlorophyll exposed to light.

6 ★ During photosynthesis, light energy is converted into the energy of chemical bonds of glucose (sugar).

  ★ Chlorophyll makes light energy available for the synthesis (making) of sugar.

  ★ The region between membranes contains enzymes which convert water and carbon dioxide into sugar. The energy needed for the conversion comes from the light absorbed by chlorophyll.

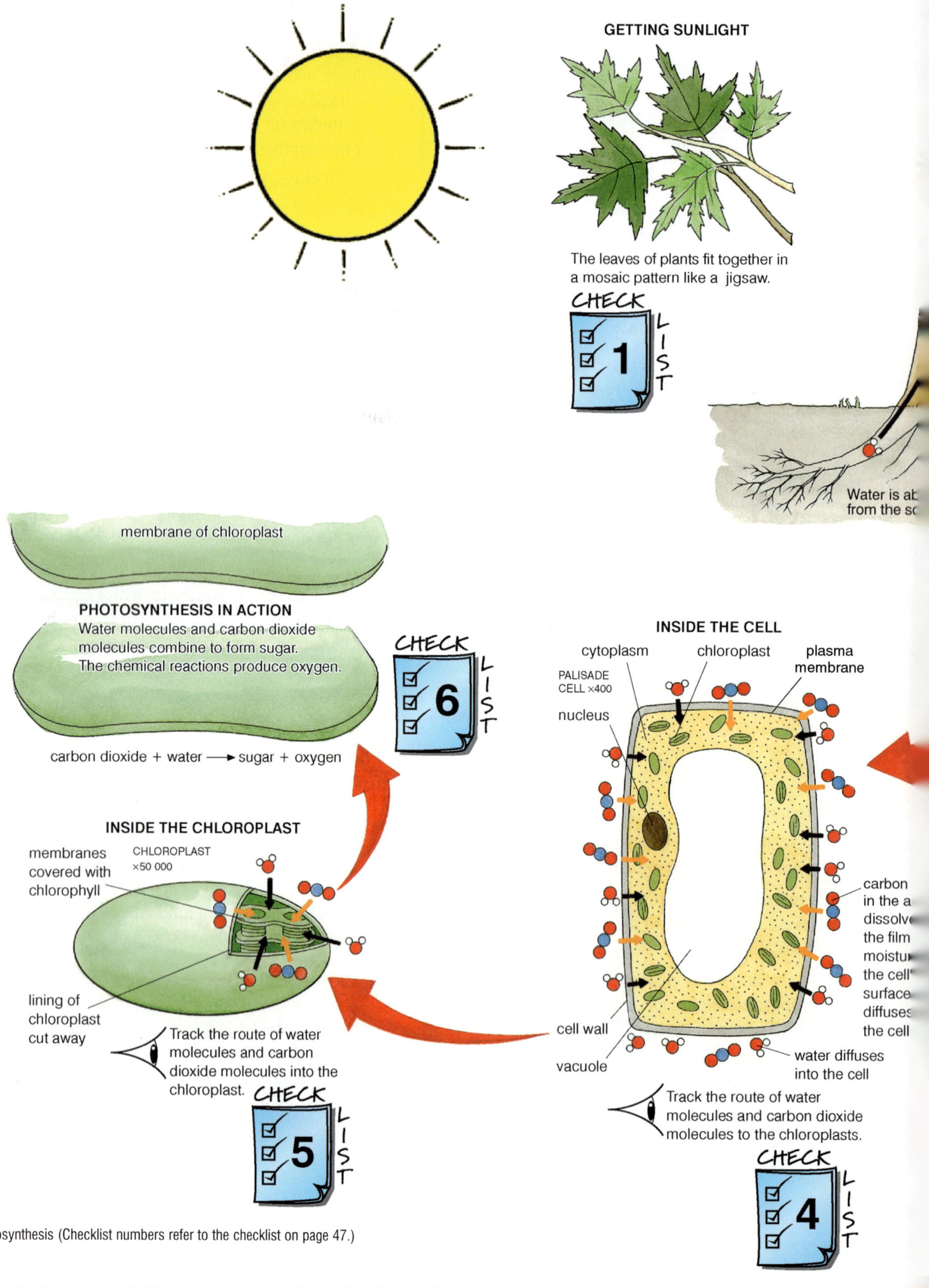

Green plants as organisms

GETTING SUNLIGHT

The leaves of plants fit together in a mosaic pattern like a jigsaw.

CHECK LIST 1

Water is absorbed from the soil

PHOTOSYNTHESIS IN ACTION
Water molecules and carbon dioxide molecules combine to form sugar. The chemical reactions produce oxygen.

membrane of chloroplast

carbon dioxide + water ⟶ sugar + oxygen

CHECK LIST 6

INSIDE THE CELL

PALISADE CELL ×400

- cytoplasm
- chloroplast
- plasma membrane
- nucleus
- cell wall
- vacuole

carbon dioxide in the air dissolves in the film of moisture on the cell's surface and diffuses into the cell

water diffuses into the cell

Track the route of water molecules and carbon dioxide molecules to the chloroplasts.

CHECK LIST 4

INSIDE THE CHLOROPLAST

CHLOROPLAST ×50 000

- membranes covered with chlorophyll
- lining of chloroplast cut away

Track the route of water molecules and carbon dioxide molecules into the chloroplast.

CHECK LIST 5

Photosynthesis (Checklist numbers refer to the checklist on page 47.)

Green plants as organisms

GETTING THE RAW MATERIALS
Water and carbon dioxide are both abundant in the environment.

leaf stalk

pores (stomata) on the underside of the leaf through which carbon dioxide and water vapour are exchanged between the inside of the leaf and the atmosphere

Key
- water molecule
- carbon dioxide molecule
- → movement of water molecules
- → movement of carbon dioxide molecules

Track the route of water molecules and carbon dioxide molecules to the chloroplast.

CHECK LIST 2

INSIDE THE LEAF
- waxy cuticle
- cells of the upper leaf surface (upper epidermis)
- palisade cell
- air space
- spongy mesophyll cells
- cells of the lower leaf surface (lower epidermis)
- stoma
- guard cell

Track the route of water molecules and carbon dioxide molecules to the cells.

CHECK LIST 3

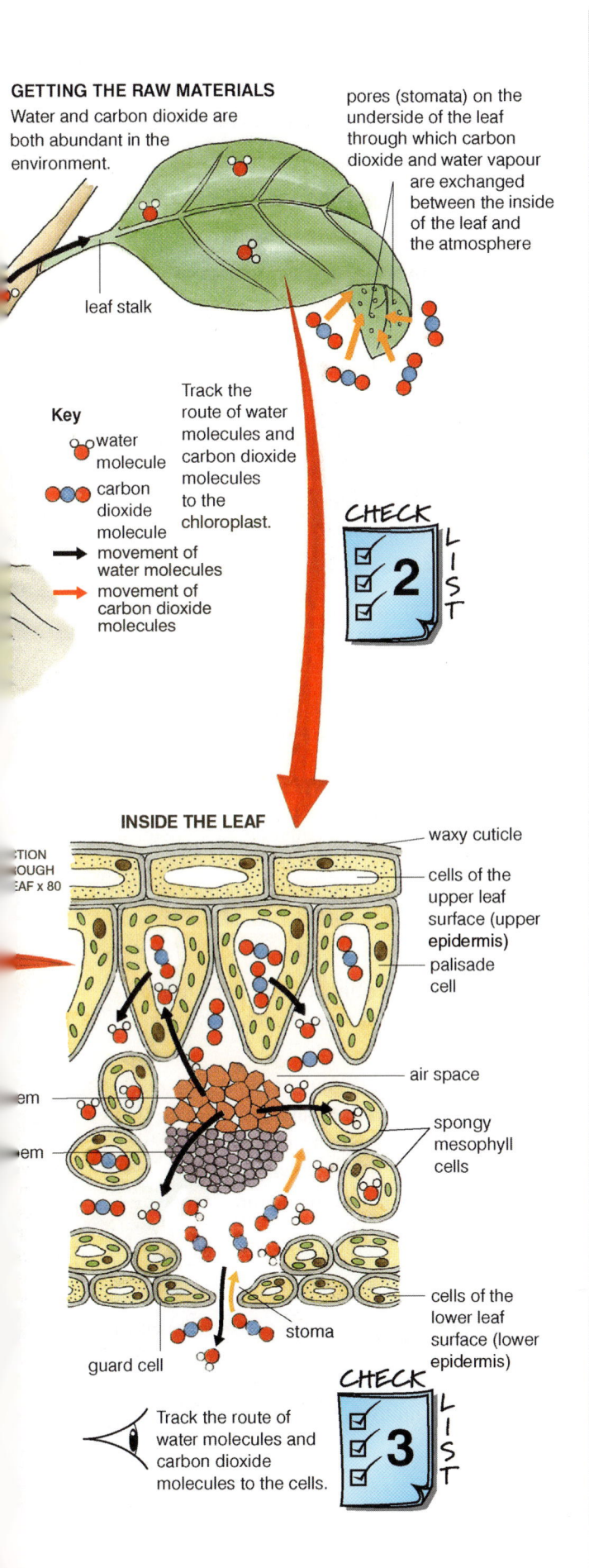

4.2 Transport in plants

PREVIEW

At the end of this section you will:
- know that xylem tissue transports water and that phloem tissue transports food
- understand the processes of transpiration and translocation
- know that xylem tissue and phloem tissue form vascular bundles which pass to all parts of the plant.

Transport systems in plants

On pages 52–3 is the concept map for **transport in plants**, and its checklist. Study them carefully.

Remember that **stomata** are the tiny pores perforating the underside of leaves through which water vapour and carbon dioxide are exchanged between the inside of the leaf and the atmosphere. The loss of water vapour from the leaf is called **transpiration**. Most plants have a waxy layer (**cuticle**) which covers the outer surfaces of the leaf, preventing it from losing too much water. The leaves of plants growing in dry environments are often covered by a cuticle that is thicker than the cuticle covering the leaves of plants growing in wetter conditions.

Factors affecting transpiration

Think of the ways plants lose and gain water.

★ Loss of water is through transpiration.

★ Gain is through the uptake of water by the roots.

If the loss of water is greater than the gain, then the stomata close.

As a result, transpiration is reduced.

If the loss of water is still more than the gain, then the cells of the plant lose turgor and the plant **wilts**.

Remember that the turgor of the cells of a non-woody (**herbaceous**) plant helps to keep it upright.

49

Green plants as organisms

The graphs below show the effect of other factors on the rate of transpiration. Light stimulates the stomata to open wide. The rate of transpiration is therefore greater during the day than at night.

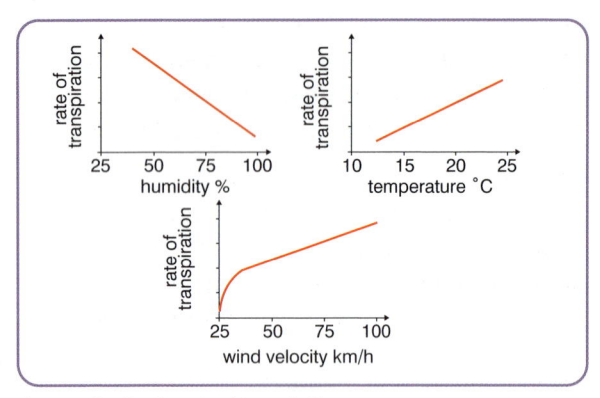

Factors affecting the rate of transpiration

Controlling the size of stomata

Two sausage-shaped **guard cells** surround the opening which forms the stoma. The guard cells contain chloroplasts. Think of the following sequence.

★ During the day, there is an increase in the concentration of potassium ions in the guard cells. There is, therefore, a net flow of water by osmosis into the guard cells making them turgid. The guard cells bow out, opening the stoma.

★ At night, the concentration of potassium ions in the guard cells falls. There is a net outflow of water and the guard cells lose turgor. The guard cells bow in, closing the stoma.

Surviving arid conditions

Losing too much water is a constant threat to plants living in hot, dry (arid) deserts. Different features, which reduce water loss, help the plants to survive. For example, a cactus has:
- leaves that are little more than spines, reducing the area of the surfaces from which water is lost
- a thick, waxy, waterproof cuticle, which covers the plant's surfaces
- shiny surfaces that reflect heat and light
- a thick stem, which stores water
- stomata sunk in hair-fringed pits. Water vapour is trapped in the pits resulting in a humid micro-environment around the stomatal opening.

As a result, the concentration gradient of water between the tissues of the cactus and the micro-environment of the stomatal opening is reduced, reducing the rate of transpiration.

4.3 Plant responses

PREVIEW

At the end of this section you will know that:
- plants grow in response to stimuli
- there are two sorts of growth movement – nastic movements and tropic movements (tropisms)
- plant growth regulators affect the growth of plants
- auxin is an example of a plant growth regulator
- commercial applications of plant growth regulators include weed control and the production of 'seedless' fruits.

Plants move by growing in response to stimuli. One part of the plant grows faster than another. There are two types of growth movement.

★ **Nastic movements** are responses to stimuli that come from all directions. For example, flowers open and close in response to changes in temperature.

★ **Tropic movements** (tropisms) are responses to stimuli which come mainly from one direction. For example, shoots bend towards light.

How plants respond

The diagram opposite and its checklist are your revision guide to **plant responses**. Study them carefully.

Remember that plant responses are the result of growth. **Growth regulators** (sometimes called growth hormones) affect the growth of plants. **Auxin** is an example of a plant growth regulator.

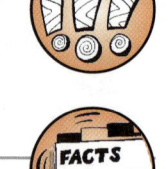

Fact file

Plant growth regulators used to be called plant hormones or plant growth substances. You may come across these terms in other books. In this book, the more up-to-date term is used.

Green plants as organisms

Checklist for plant responses

1 ★ Tropisms are **positive** if the plant grows towards the stimulus and **negative** if it grows away.

As a result of different positive and negative tropisms, the different parts of the plant grow in a way that increases the plant's chances of survival. For example, the roots 'find' water, leaves receive as much light as possible to enable photosynthesis to occur at a maxiumum rate.

★ The growing tips (shoot/root) of a plant are receptors for different stimuli.

2 ★ Auxin makes the cellulose wall of plant cells more elastic.

As a result, the cells elongate rapidly.

As a result, the cells on the shady side of the shoot tip grow *more* rapidly than the cells on the brightly lit side.

As a result, the shoot tip bends towards the light.

3 ★ The effect of the growth regulators produced by the root cap is different from auxin produced by the shoot tip. It *slows down* growth in the underside of the root tip.

As a result, the root bends down and grows into the soil.

Fact file

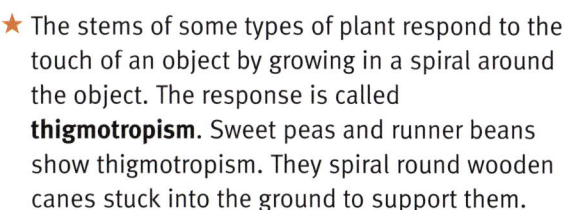

★ The stems of some types of plant respond to the touch of an object by growing in a spiral around the object. The response is called **thigmotropism**. Sweet peas and runner beans show thigmotropism. They spiral round wooden canes stuck into the ground to support them.

★ Does it matter which way up a seed is planted? Positive phototropism means that the shoot will always grow upwards. Positive geotropism means that the roots will always grow downwards. So, no matter which way up a seed is, its shoot and roots will always grow in the right direction.

★ Auxin sometimes prevents growth. It diffuses down the stem and prevents the growth of side shoots. Lopping the top off a plant removes the source of auxin and side branches then develop. This is why a gardener trims a hedge to make it more bushy.

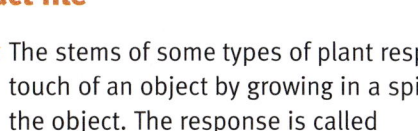

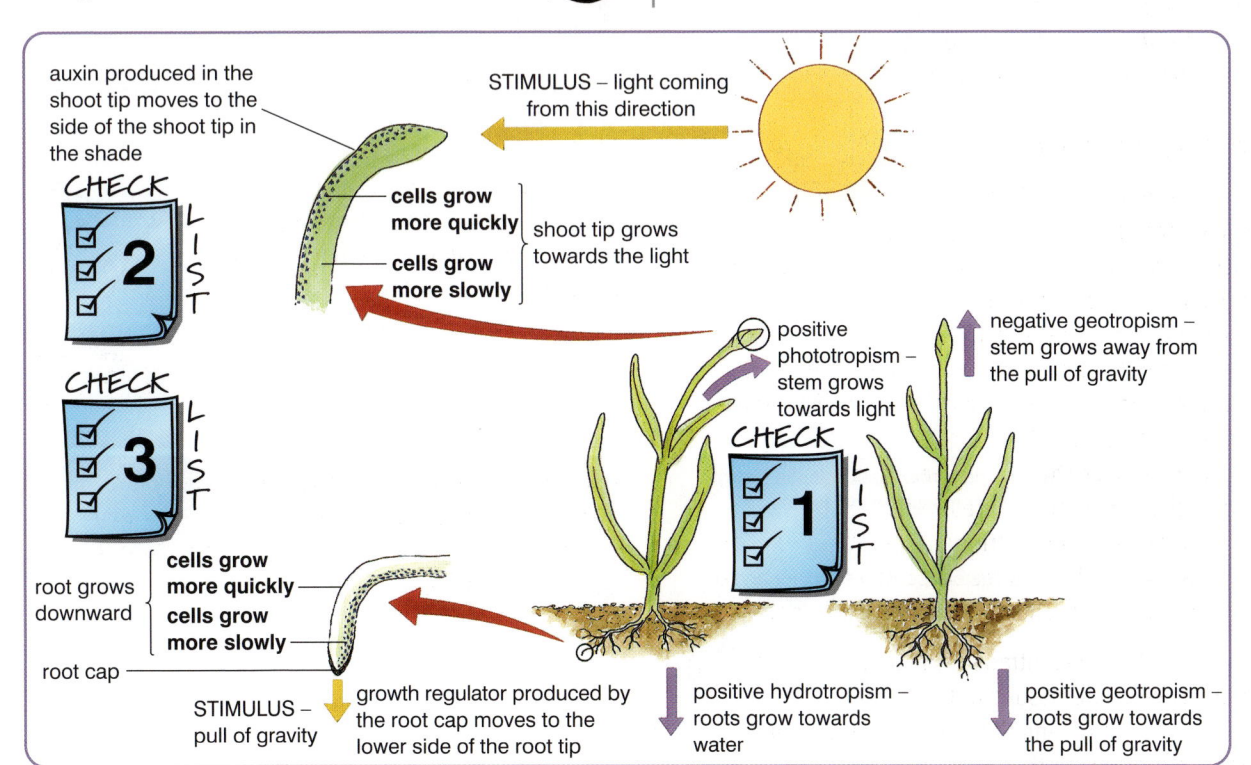

Tropisms – the response of the shoot tip to light and of the root tip to gravity and water

Green plants as organisms

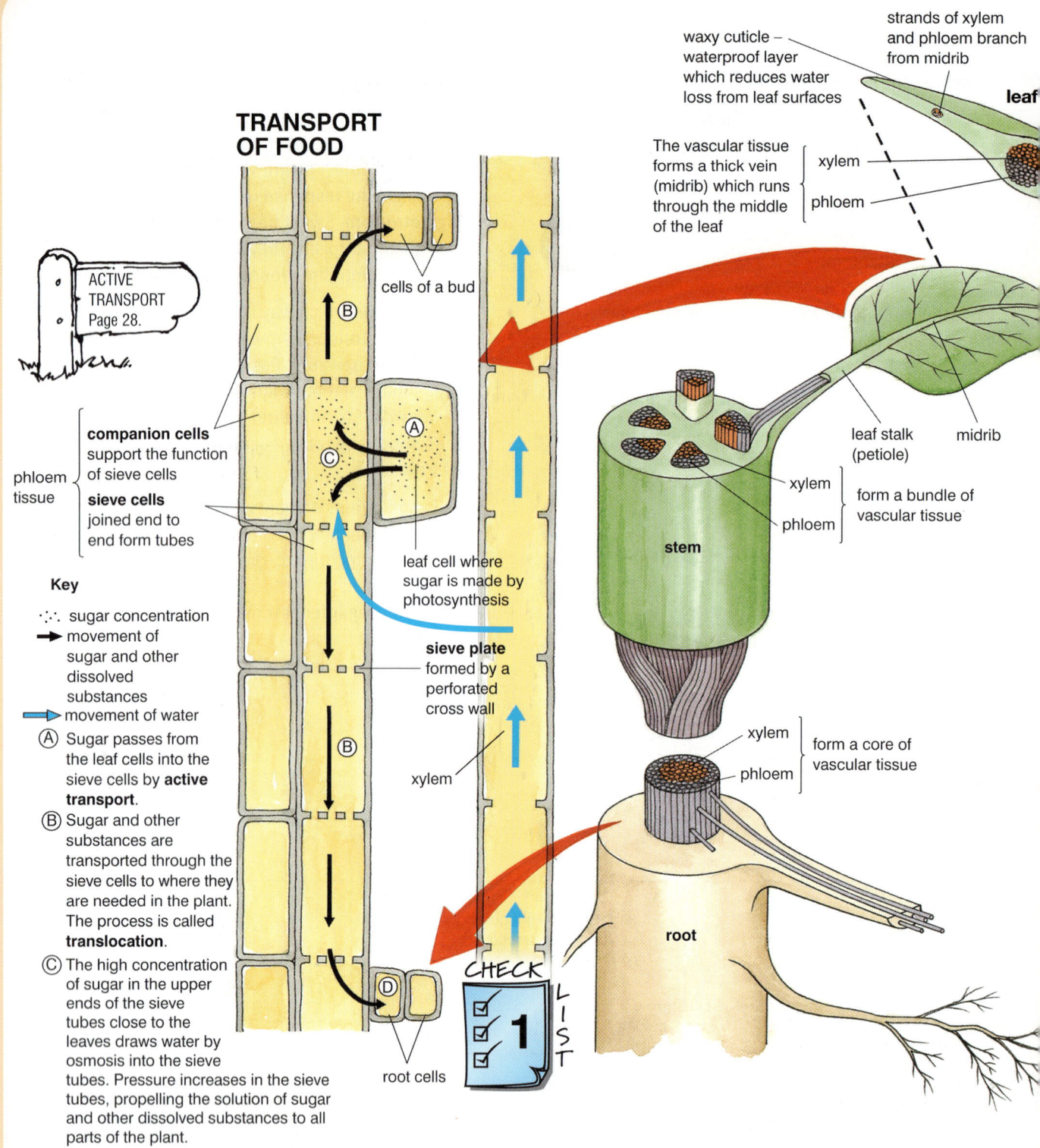

TRANSPORT OF FOOD

ACTIVE TRANSPORT Page 28.

phloem tissue
- **companion cells** support the function of sieve cells
- **sieve cells** joined end to end form tubes

Key
- ∴ sugar concentration
- → movement of sugar and other dissolved substances
- ⇒ movement of water

A. Sugar passes from the leaf cells into the sieve cells by **active transport**.

B. Sugar and other substances are transported through the sieve cells to where they are needed in the plant. The process is called **translocation**.

C. The high concentration of sugar in the upper ends of the sieve tubes close to the leaves draws water by osmosis into the sieve tubes. Pressure increases in the sieve tubes, propelling the solution of sugar and other dissolved substances to all parts of the plant.

D. Root cells convert sugar to starch, which is stored. Sugar is also used in aerobic respiration. Therefore, the concentration of sugar in the lower ends of the sieve tubes is less than in their upper ends. Less water is drawn into them by osmosis, so the pressure within is less.

Translocation depends on the differences in the concentration of sugar in different parts of the plant and, therefore, the differences in pressure within the sieve tubes.

Transport in plants

- cells of a bud
- leaf cell where sugar is made by photosynthesis
- **sieve plate** formed by a perforated cross wall
- xylem
- root cells

- waxy cuticle – waterproof layer which reduces water loss from leaf surfaces
- strands of xylem and phloem branch from midrib
- leaf
- The vascular tissue forms a thick vein (midrib) which runs through the middle of the leaf
  - xylem
  - phloem
- leaf stalk (petiole)
- midrib
- stem
  - xylem
  - phloem
  - form a bundle of vascular tissue
- root
  - xylem
  - phloem
  - form a core of vascular tissue

CHECK LIST 1

Green plants as organisms

TRANSPORT OF WATER

Xylem cells join end to end. Cross walls separating a cell from neighbouring cells are broken down. A continuous tube is formed, rather like a drinking straw.

Key
→ movement of water

A) Root hairs absorb water from the soil by **osmosis**. Mineral ions are **actively transported** into the root.
B) Water passes through the root tissue into the xylem by **osmosis**.
C) Water travels through the xylem of the root and stem in unbroken columns – the **transpiration stream**.
D) Water moves through the xylem of the leaf stalk and veins of the leaf.
E) Water evaporates into the large air spaces within the leaf. The air spaces are saturated with water vapour.
F) The concentration of water vapour in the atmosphere is lower than that in the air spaces. Water vapour therefore diffuses from the leaf through the stomata. The process is called **transpiration**.
G) Water lost by cells through evaporation is replaced with water drawn through the cells by osmosis. Cells next to the xylem draw water from the xylem by osmosis.

Checklist for transport in plants

1 ★ Phloem consists of *living cells*.

★ The concentration of sugar in the leaf is often lower than the concentration of sugar in the upper ends of the sieve tubes.

★ As a result, sugar moves from the leaf into the sieve cells by **active transport**.

★ Osmosis draws water from the xylem and increases the pressure in the sieve tubes.

★ As a result, sugar solution moves to all parts of the plant.

★ Pressure in the sieve tubes drops as cells use sugar or store it as starch.

2 ★ Xylem consists of *dead cells*.

★ The walls of xylem tubes are waterproofed with a substance called **lignin**.

★ As water transpires, more is drawn from the xylem in the leaf.

★ As a result, water is 'sucked' upwards through the xylem of the stem.

★ As a result, more water is supplied to the bottom of the xylem by the roots.

★ As a result, there are unbroken moving columns of water from the roots to the leaves.

Green plants as organisms

The shoot tip

The table below shows the sorts of experiments carried out by scientists investigating the response of plants to light. These experiments suggest that there is a growth regulator (auxin) which:
- is produced in the shoot tip
- diffuses to the region behind the shoot tip
- stimulates growth so that the shoot bends towards light.

Using plant hormones

★ **Ripening** – fruit is quickly ripened in sheds in an atmosphere which contains one part of **ethene** per million parts of air.

★ **Weedkillers** – 2,4-D (2,4 dichlorophenoxyethanoic acid) is a synthetic auxin which kills plants by making them grow too fast. Broad-leaved weed plants like docks, daisies and dandelions are more sensitive to 2,4-D than narrow-leaved crop plants like wheat and barley.

★ **Seedless fruit** – an auxin paste smeared over the carpels (female sex organs) of some crop species produces fruit without fertilisation. Seedless cucumbers and seedless tomatoes are produced in this way.

★ **Rooting** – gardeners use 'rooting powder' which contains auxin that encourages roots to sprout from stem cuttings. The method allows large numbers of identical plants to be grown quickly.

symbol	treatment	response to light	conclusion
	Uncovered intact barley seedling	✔	control, which shows that the shoot tip is sensitive to light
	Uncovered barley seedling with its shoot tip removed	✘	shows that the shoot tip contains a substance which controls the response of the shoot to light
	Intact barley seedling covered with aluminium foil which excludes light	✘	shows that the shoot tip is sensitive to light
	Barley seedling with its tip cut off. The tip is placed on a slip of metal foil and replaced on the rest of the shoot. The metal slip prevents diffusion of chemicals from the shoot tip to the rest of the shoot.	✘	shows that a substance produced in the shoot tip diffuses to the region behind the shoot tip, where it controls the shoot's response to light
	Barley seedling with its tip removed. The tip is placed on an agar block and replaced on the rest of the shoot.	✔	The agar block allows diffusion of a substance produced in the shoot tip to the region behind the shoot tip. Result confirms conclusion from the experiment with a slip of metal foil above.
	Barley seedling with its tip removed. An agar block is placed on the rest of the shoot after it has been soaked in a mash made of the shoot tip.	✔	shows that a substance produced in the shoot tip controls the response of the shoot to the light
	Barley seedling with its tip removed. An agar block is placed on the rest of the shoot after it has been soaked in a solution of auxin.	✔	shows that the substance produced in the shoot tip which controls the response of the shoot to light is auxin
	Barley seedling with its tip removed. An agar block is placed on the remaining part of the shoot.	✘	control for the experiment which shows that auxin, not agar, controls the response of the shoot to light

Response of the shoot tip to light

Green plants as organisms

ROUND UP

How much have you improved? Work out your improvement index on pages 110–11.

1. Name the different cells in the leaf that contain chloroplasts. [3]

2. Briefly explain why most chloroplasts are found in palisade cells lying just beneath the upper surface of the leaf. [4]

3. List the major factors which limit the rate of photosynthesis. Briefly explain how a greenhouse overcomes the effect of limiting factors on the growth of plants. [8]

4. Complete the following paragraph using the words below. Each word may be used once, more than once or not at all.

   **xylem   transport   sugar   translocation
   transpiration   phloem   pressure
   active transport   water**

   Leaves produce _____ by photosynthesis. The concentration of _____ in leaf cells is often less than that in nearby _____ tissue. _____ therefore moves from the leaf cell into the _____ by _____. Osmosis draws _____ into the _____ tissue increasing _____ which helps transport sugar. The transport of sugar is called _____. Storage of _____ as starch in the root cells reduces _____ in the _____. [13]

5. Describe the probable weather on a day when the transpiration rate of a plant is at a maximum. [4]

6. Briefly explain what happens if a plant loses more water through transpiration than it gains through absorption of water by its roots. [3]

7. Compare the characteristics of xylem tissue with those of phloem tissue. List the comparisons in two columns headed 'xylem' and 'phloem' respectively. [5]

8. Complete the following paragraph using the words below. Each word may be used once, more than once or not at all.

   **weedkiller   ripens   growth regulator
   unfertilised   tip   seedless   slowly**

   Auxin is a _____ produced in the _____ of the shoot. Synthetic auxin is used as a _____ to kill unwanted plants. Auxin paste applied to the _____ carpels of some crop species produces _____ fruits. Fruit stored in an atmosphere containing ethene _____ more quickly. [6]

9. The diagram shows an experiment on the shoots of growing seedlings. In experiment A a thin piece of metal was placed between the tip of the shoot and the rest of the stem. In experiment B a thin piece of metal was placed further down, separating the shoot into an upper part and a lower part.

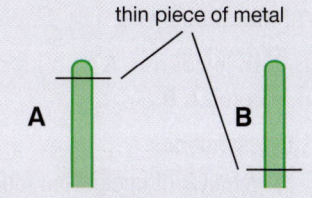

   The growing seedlings were placed in a box which was light-tight except for a slit on one side. The seedlings were illuminated for three days.

   a) What hypothesis was the scientist trying to test? [2]

   b) In each case, what do you think the response of the seedling will be to the light source? (Assume the seedlings survived the treatment for the time of the experiment.) [2]

   Explain your answer. [4]

Well done if you've improved. Don't worry if you haven't. Take a break and try again.

Chapter 5 Humans as organisms

How much do you already know? Work out your score on page 111.

Test yourself

1 The nutrients in food are listed below. Match the nutrients to the following questions.

   carbohydrates   fats   proteins   vitamins   minerals

   a) Which nutrients give food its energy content? [3]
   b) Which nutrient is a source of energy, but is more important for the growth and repair of the body? [1]
   c) Which nutrient releases the most energy per gram? [1]
   d) Which nutrients are needed only in small amounts, but play an important role in the control of metabolism? [2]

2 Match each term in column **A** with its correct description in column **B**.

A terms	B descriptions
ingestion	the removal of undigested food through the anus
digestion	digested food passes into the body
absorption	food is taken into the mouth
egestion	food is broken down [4]

3 Explain the differences between
   a) bronchi and bronchioles [2]
   b) lungs and alveoli [2]
   c) aerobic respiration and anaerobic respiration [4]
   d) breathing and gaseous exchange. [3]

4 Explain how the heart functions as a double pump. [4]

5 The different components of blood are listed in column **A**. Match each component with its correct description in column **B**.

A components	B descriptions
plasma	contain haemoglobin
red blood cells	promote the formation of blood clots
white blood cells	contains dissolved food substances
platelets	produce antibodies [4]

6 The components of the reflex arc are listed as follows: sensory neurone, effector, relay neurone, receptor, motor neurone. Write the components in their correct order. [4]

7 What is the function of each of these parts of the ear?
   a) the eardrum   b) the bones of the middle ear
   c) the pinna   d) the hair cells [8]

8 What are hormones and how are they transported around the body? [2]

9 Distinguish between the roles of the hormones insulin and glucagon in keeping the blood glucose level steady. [2]

10 The structures of the kidney tubule and its blood supply are listed below. Rewrite them in the order in which a molecule of urea passes from the renal artery to the outside of the body.

   tubule   urethra   bladder   glomerulus   Bowman's capsule   ureter   collecting duct [7]

11 Match each body structure in column **A** with its role in the defence of the body against disease in column **B**.

A body structures	B roles
tear gland	produces sebum which kills bacteria and fungi
blood	white cells produce antibodies which destroy antigens
skin	produce hydrochloric acid which kills bacteria
cilia lining the upper respiratory tract	produce the enzyme lysozyme which destroys bacteria
glands in the stomach wall	sweep away mucus containing trapped microorganisms and particles [5]

5.1 Food and diet

PREVIEW

At the end of this section you will:
- understand that different foods contain different amounts of energy
- be able to identify the components of a diet
- know the role of different foods in the body.

Humans as organisms

Nutrients in food

The **nutrients** in food are **carbohydrates, fats, proteins, vitamins** and **minerals**. **Water** and **fibre** are also components of food. Different foods contain nutrients, water and fibre in different proportions. Our **diet** is the food and drink we take in. Remember the sequence:

$$\left.\begin{array}{l}\text{nutrient}\\ +\text{ water}\\ +\text{ fibre}\end{array}\right\} \xrightarrow{\text{components of}} \text{food} \xrightarrow{\text{eaten}} \text{diet}$$

All living things (including us) need food. The nutrients in food are a source of:
- **energy** which powers life's activities
- materials for the **growth** and **repair** of bodies
- substances which control the **metabolism** of cells.

Checklist for food and diet

1 ★ The **energy value** of food is measured using an instrument called a **bomb calorimeter**, shown below.

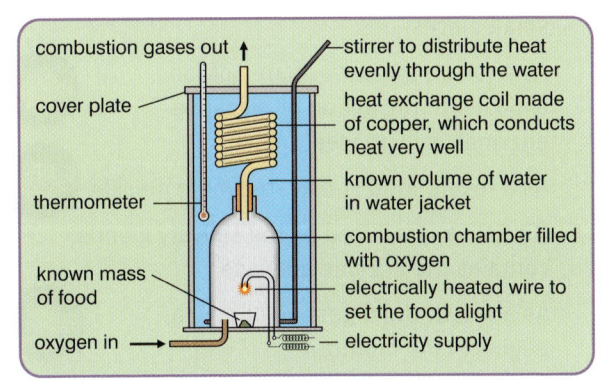

A bomb calorimeter is made to reduce the loss of heat to the surroundings and maximise the transfer of heat from the burning food to the water in the water jacket. In this way the accuracy of the data on the energy values of foods burnt in the calorimeter is improved.

The burning food heats the surrounding water. The change in temperature of the water is used to work out the energy value of the food:

$$\frac{\text{energy released}}{\text{per gram}} = \frac{\text{volume of water in water jacket} \times \text{temperature rise} \times 4.2}{\text{mass of food}}$$

★ The energy released from food depends on the nutrients it contains.
- 17.2 kJ/g for carbohydrate
- 22.2 kJ/g for protein
- 38.5 kJ/g for fat

Although protein can be a source of energy, its most important use in the body is for growth and repair.

★ People have different energy requirements depending on their:
- **age** – on average, young people have greater energy requirements than older people
- **gender** – pregnancy and lactation (milk production) increase the energy requirements of women
- **activities** – any kind of activity increases a person's energy requirements.

★ The rate at which the body uses energy is called the **metabolic rate**. It is lowest (called the **basal metabolic rate**) when the body is at rest.

★ If a person eats more food than is necessary for his/her energy needs, the excess is turned into fat.
As a result, the person puts on weight.

★ To lose weight, a person can:
- take more exercise, which increases energy output
- eat less high-energy food, decreasing energy input.

2 ★ **Additives** are put into food to:
- make it tastier
- make it more attractive
- improve its texture
- prevent it from spoiling.

★ Some additives can make some people unwell.

3 ★ A **balanced diet** is a mixture of foods which together provide sufficient nutrients for healthy living.

★ The 'basic four' food groups help us choose a balanced diet.

4 ★ The amount of **alcohol** people consume is measured in units, as shown below.

Units of alcohol

★ How much alcohol is too much? It depends on a person's age, size, gender (male or female) and metabolic rate.

5 ★ Vitamin C helps cells to join together. It also controls the use of calcium by bones and teeth.

★ Vitamin D helps the body to absorb calcium.

★ Deficiency of iron is a common cause of anaemia.

Humans as organisms

5.2 The digestive system

> **PREVIEW**
>
> At the end of this section you will:
> - know that the digestive system is a muscular tube through which food moves and into which juices produced by the liver and pancreas flow
> - understand that as food moves through the digestive system it is processed (digested) into substances which the cells of the body can absorb and use
> - be able to identify enzymes responsible for digesting food.

Testing your understanding

The terms:

- **gut**
- **intestine**
- **alimentary canal**

all refer to the digestive system.

Digesting food

Food is processed through the digestive system in the following sequence:

- **ingestion** — food is taken into the mouth
- **digestion** — large insoluble molecules of food are broken down into smaller soluble molecules
- **absorption** — the small molecules of digested food pass into the body
- **assimilation** follows the absorption of digested food. It describes the processes in cells that convert digested food materials into living matter.
- **egestion** — undigested food is removed from the body through the anus

---

The digestive system is a muscular tube through which food moves. It processes food.

- ★ **Mechanical processes** break up food and mix it with digestive juices.
- ★ **Chemical processes** digest food using different enzymes in the digestive juices. The body cannot absorb the large insoluble molecules of carbohydrate, protein and fat in food. They are broken down into smaller soluble molecules which the body can absorb.

On pages 60–1 is the concept map for **the digestive system**. The **liver** and **pancreas** are connected by ducts to the digestive system. They play an important role in the digestion of food. The numbers on the concept map refer to the checklist below.

Checklist for the digestive system

(M) = mechanical processes of digestion

(C) = chemical processes of digestion

1 ★ **(M) Teeth** chew food, breaking it into small pieces.

As a result, the surface area of food exposed to the action of digestive enzymes is increased.

As a result, food is digested more quickly.

2 ★ **(C) Saliva**, produced by the salivary glands, contains the enzyme **amylase**.

As a result, the digestion of starch begins in the mouth.

★ **(M)** Saliva moistens the food.

As a result, the food is made slippery for easy swallowing.

3 ★ **(M)** Muscles of the **stomach** wall and **small intestine** mix food thoroughly with different juices containing digestive enzymes.

As a result, a liquid paste called **chyme** is formed.

As a result, food and digestive enzymes are brought into intimate contact.

★ **(C)** Gastric juice, produced by **pits** in the stomach wall, contains **hydrochloric acid** and the enzymes **pepsin** and **renin**.

Hydrochloric acid:
- increases the acidity of the stomach contents.

Humans as organisms

As a result, bacteria in the food are killed.

As a result, the action of salivary amylase is stopped.

Pepsin:
- begins the digestion of protein.

Renin:
- clots milk, making it semi-solid.

As a result, milk stays in the gut long enough to be digested.

4 ★ **(C) Bile**, produced by the **liver**, is a green alkaline liquid which is stored in the gall bladder before release into the small intestine through the bile duct. It:
- neutralises acid from the stomach
- breaks fats and oils into small droplets (**emulsification**).

As a result, the surface area of fats and oils exposed to the action of the enzyme **lipase** is increased.

As a result, fats and oils are digested more quickly.

5 ★ **(C) Pancreatic juice**, produced by the **pancreas**, is released into the small intestine through the pancreatic duct. It contains:
- **sodium carbonate**, which neutralises stomach acid
- **carbohydrases**, **proteases** and **lipases** which digest carbohydrate, protein, fats and oils.

6 ★ **(C) Intestinal juice**, produced by glands in the wall of the **duodenum** and **ileum**, contains:
- **carbohydrases** and **lipases** that complete the digestion of carbohydrates and fats and oils.

Chemistry of digestion

Digestive enzymes catalyse the breakdown of food by **hydrolysis**. Water splits large insoluble molecules of food into smaller soluble molecules which are suitable for absorption into the body. The table below summarises the process described in the checklist on pages 58–9.

What happens to digested food?

Digested food is carried away from the ileum in the blood within the hepatic portal vein and in the fluid of the lymph vessels.

VEINS Page 65.
LYMPH VESSELS Page 60.

★ Blood transports water, sugars, fatty acids, glycerol and amino acids to the liver.

★ Lymph transports fats, oils and fat-soluble vitamins to a vein in the neck where the substances enter the bloodstream.

The **liver** plays a major role in the metabolism of food substances after they have been absorbed into the body.

★ Glucose may be converted to **glycogen** and stored. Glycogen may be hydrolysed to glucose and released back into the blood in response to the body's needs.

★ Iron, obtained from destroyed red blood cells, is stored.

★ Amino acids in excess of the body's needs are broken down (a process called **deamination**). Urea is formed and excreted in urine.

★ Amino acids are converted from one type into another (a process called **transamination**) according to the body's needs.

enzyme group	example	where found	food component	after digestion
carbohydrases (catalyse the digestion of carbohydrates)	amylase	mouth	starch	maltose
	maltase	small intestine	maltose	glucose
proteases (catalyse the digestion of proteins)	pepsin	stomach	protein	polypeptides
	chymotrypsin dipeptidase	small intestine	polypeptides dipeptides	dipeptides amino acids
lipases (catalyse the digestion of fats and oils)	lipase	small intestine	fat and oil	fatty acids + glycerol

Enzymes that digest carbohydrates, proteins and fats

Humans as organisms

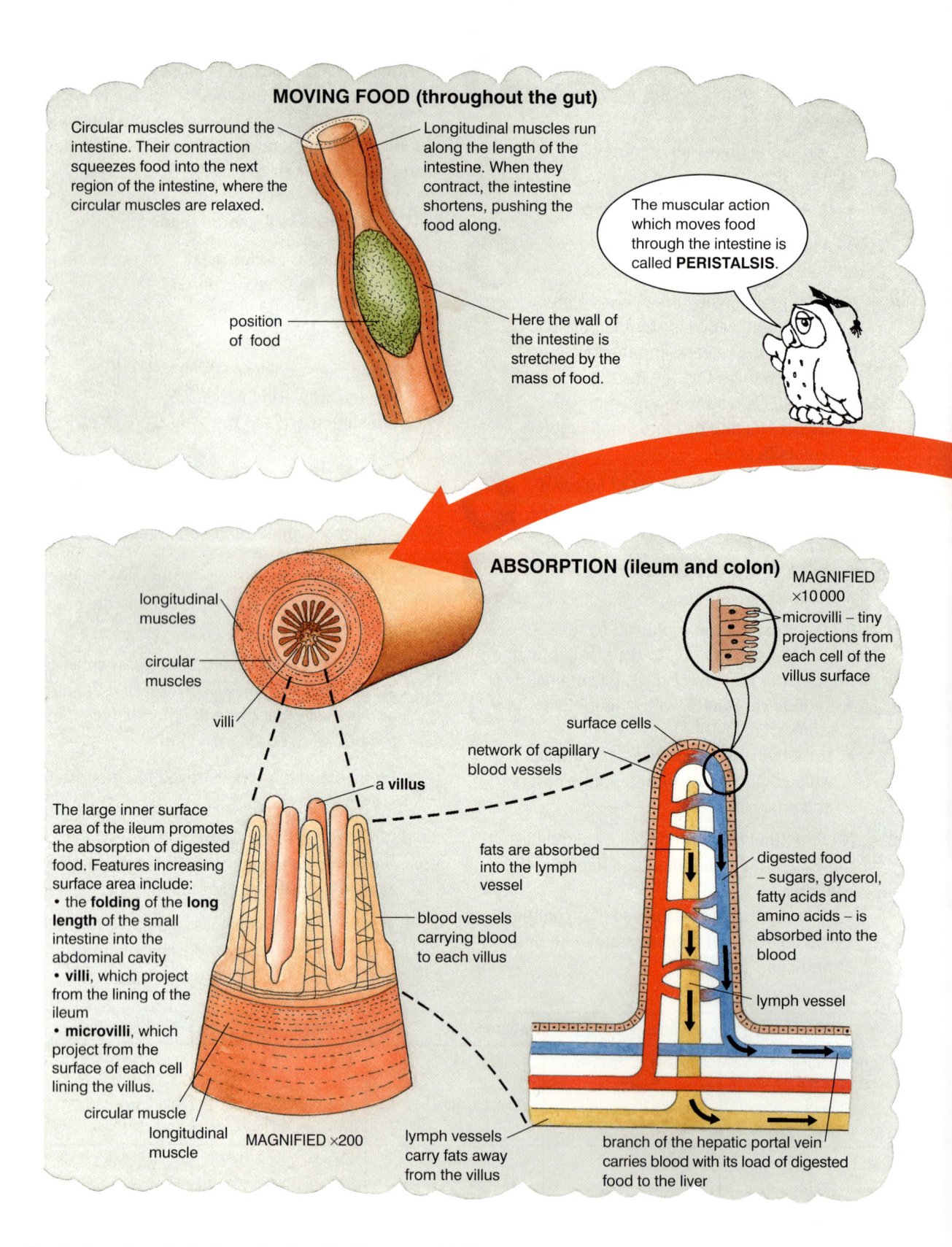

MOVING FOOD (throughout the gut)

Circular muscles surround the intestine. Their contraction squeezes food into the next region of the intestine, where the circular muscles are relaxed.

Longitudinal muscles run along the length of the intestine. When they contract, the intestine shortens, pushing the food along.

position of food

Here the wall of the intestine is stretched by the mass of food.

The muscular action which moves food through the intestine is called **PERISTALSIS**.

ABSORPTION (ileum and colon)

longitudinal muscles
circular muscles
villi

MAGNIFIED ×10 000
microvilli – tiny projections from each cell of the villus surface

a villus

surface cells
network of capillary blood vessels

The large inner surface area of the ileum promotes the absorption of digested food. Features increasing surface area include:
- the **folding of the long length** of the small intestine into the abdominal cavity
- **villi**, which project from the lining of the ileum
- **microvilli**, which project from the surface of each cell lining the villus.

blood vessels carrying blood to each villus

circular muscle
longitudinal muscle

MAGNIFIED ×200

fats are absorbed into the lymph vessel

digested food – sugars, glycerol, fatty acids and amino acids – is absorbed into the blood

lymph vessel

lymph vessels carry fats away from the villus

branch of the hepatic portal vein carries blood with its load of digested food to the liver

The digestive system – its structure and functions (Checklist on pages 58–9.)

Humans as organisms

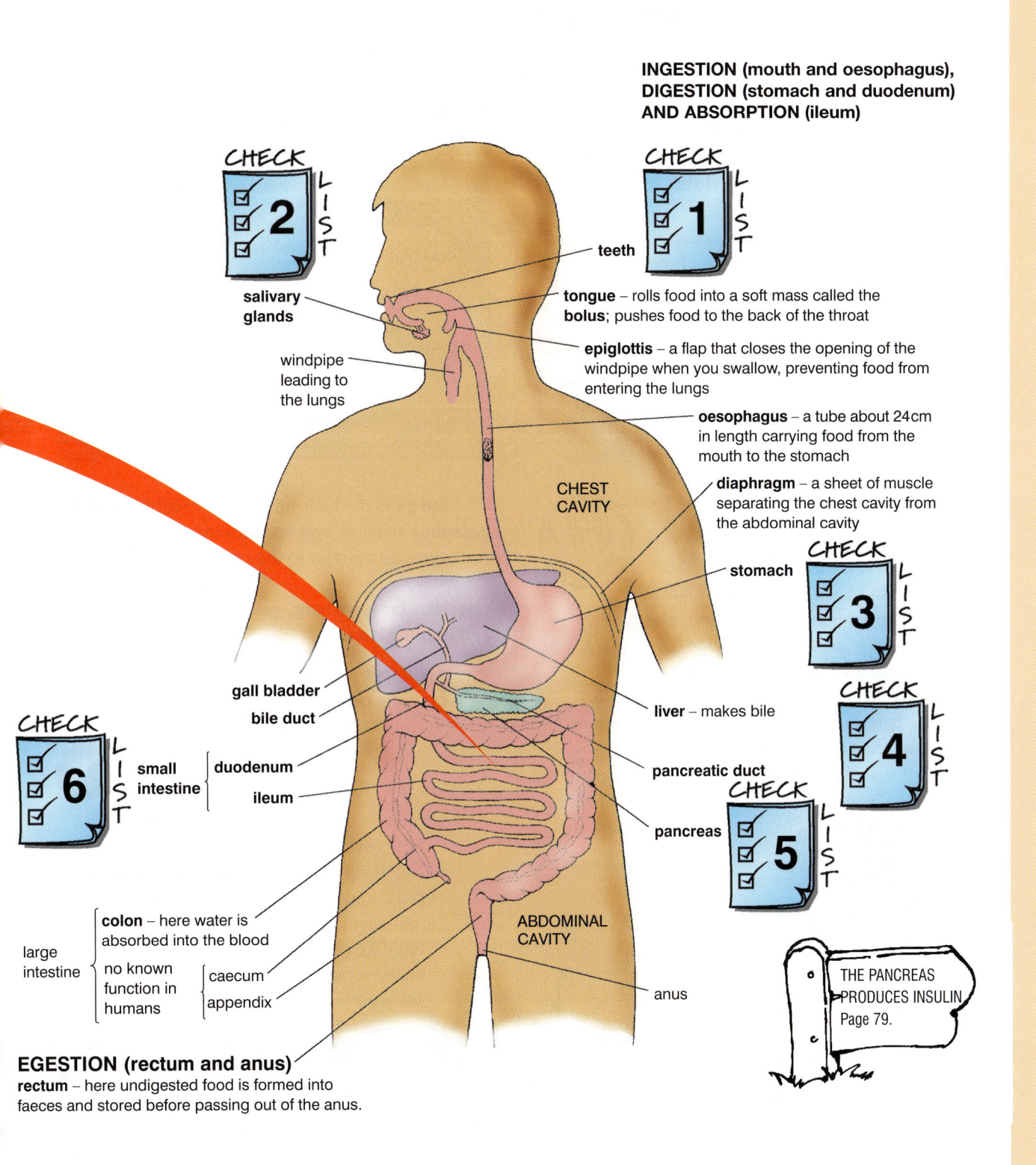

INGESTION (mouth and oesophagus), DIGESTION (stomach and duodenum) AND ABSORPTION (ileum)

CHECK LIST 1
- **teeth**
- **tongue** – rolls food into a soft mass called the **bolus**; pushes food to the back of the throat
- **epiglottis** – a flap that closes the opening of the windpipe when you swallow, preventing food from entering the lungs
- **oesophagus** – a tube about 24cm in length carrying food from the mouth to the stomach
- **diaphragm** – a sheet of muscle separating the chest cavity from the abdominal cavity

CHECK LIST 2
- **salivary glands**

windpipe leading to the lungs

CHEST CAVITY

CHECK LIST 3
- **stomach**

CHECK LIST 4
- **gall bladder**
- **bile duct**
- **liver** – makes bile
- **pancreatic duct**

CHECK LIST 5
- **pancreas**

CHECK LIST 6
- **small intestine**
  - duodenum
  - ileum

large intestine
- **colon** – here water is absorbed into the blood
- no known function in humans
  - caecum
  - appendix

ABDOMINAL CAVITY

anus

THE PANCREAS PRODUCES INSULIN Page 79.

EGESTION (rectum and anus)
rectum – here undigested food is formed into faeces and stored before passing out of the anus.

Humans as organisms

5.3 Breathing, gaseous exchange and respiration

PREVIEW

At the end of this section you will:
- know that breathing in (inhalation) draws air into the lungs and that breathing out (exhalation) pushes air out from the lungs
- be able to describe how breathing movements take place
- know that the exchange of gases (oxygen and carbon dioxide) happens in the lungs, between the gases in the air sacs (alveoli) and the blood of the vessels supplying blood to the alveoli
- understand that the blood transports oxygen to cells which use it for aerobic respiration
- be able to distinguish between aerobic respiration and anaerobic respiration.

Respiration

Remember the distinction between respiration and gaseous exchange. Oxygen is used by cells to oxidise digested food substances (glucose) to release energy. The process is called **aerobic respiration**. The energy released from the oxidation of glucose powers the activities which define the characteristics of life. The table below shows that there is less oxygen in exhaled air than in inhaled air. This is because some of the oxygen is used by cells for aerobic respiration. There is more carbon dioxide in exhaled air than in inhaled air because carbon dioxide is produced by the chemical reactions of aerobic respiration.

gas	amount in inhaled air / %	amount in exhaled air / %
nitrogen	78	78
oxygen	21	16
noble gases	1	1
carbon dioxide	0.03	4
water vapour	0	1

Differences between inhaled and exhaled air

★ How does oxygen reach cells?
★ How does carbon dioxide leave cells?

The answer is by gaseous exchange.

The diagram below shows the links between breathing air, gaseous exchange and aerobic respiration.

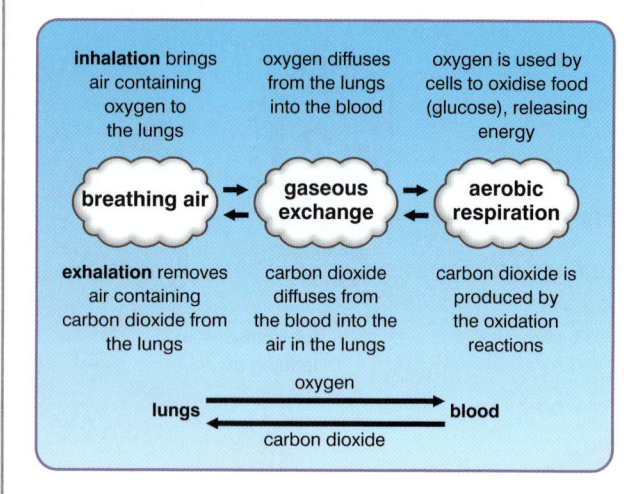

inhalation brings air containing oxygen to the lungs

oxygen diffuses from the lungs into the blood

oxygen is used by cells to oxidise food (glucose), releasing energy

breathing air ⇄ gaseous exchange ⇄ aerobic respiration

exhalation removes air containing carbon dioxide from the lungs

carbon dioxide diffuses from the blood into the air in the lungs

carbon dioxide is produced by the oxidation reactions

lungs ⟵ oxygen ⟶ blood
⟵ carbon dioxide

On page 64 is the concept map for **breathing, gaseous exchange and respiration**. The numbers on the concept map refer to the checklist below.

Checklist for breathing, gaseous exchange and respiration

1 ★ The **upper respiratory tract** consists of tubes from the nostrils and mouth to the lungs.
  • The tubes are well supplied with blood.

  As a result, inhaled air is warmed to body temperature.

  • Hairs in the nasal passage filter out large dust particles.
  • The lining of **mucus**, produced by **goblet** cells, traps bacteria, viruses and dust particles.
  • Hair-like **cilia** sweep the mucus into the **pharynx**, where it is either swallowed, sneezed out or coughed up.

  As a result, the air entering the lungs is cleaned and freed of disease-causing microorganisms.

2 ★ The network of **bronchioles** in the lungs form the **bronchial tree**.
  ★ The millions of **alveoli** in a pair of human lungs form a surface area of about 90 m^2.

  As a result, gaseous exchange is very efficient.

Humans as organisms

3 ★ Oxygen and carbon dioxide diffuse rapidly across the walls of the alveoli because each wall is:
- **thin**, facilitating (making easy) the diffusion of gases
- **moist**; gases diffuse in solution
- **well supplied with blood vessels**; gases are quickly carried away from the alveoli in the bloodstream. The concentration gradient of gases between the blood and air in the alveoli is steep.

MITOCHONDRIA Page 31.

Breathing movements

The **ribs** and **diaphragm** form an elastic cage around the lungs. As they move, the pressure in the lungs changes. This change in pressure causes **inhaling** (breathing in) and **exhaling** (breathing out).

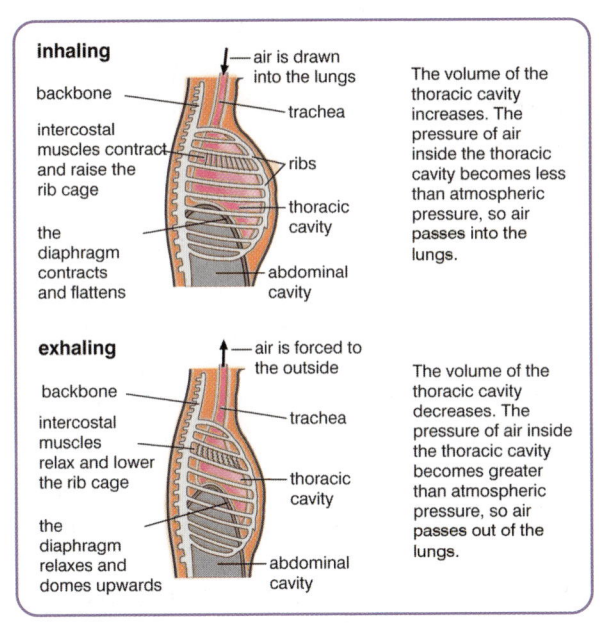

inhaling: air is drawn into the lungs. The volume of the thoracic cavity increases. The pressure of air inside the thoracic cavity becomes less than atmospheric pressure, so air passes into the lungs.
- backbone
- intercostal muscles contract and raise the rib cage
- the diaphragm contracts and flattens
- trachea
- ribs
- thoracic cavity
- abdominal cavity

exhaling: air is forced to the outside. The volume of the thoracic cavity decreases. The pressure of air inside the thoracic cavity becomes greater than atmospheric pressure, so air passes out of the lungs.
- backbone
- intercostal muscles relax and lower the rib cage
- the diaphragm relaxes and domes upwards
- trachea
- thoracic cavity
- abdominal cavity

Inhaling and exhaling

Remember

★ **All** cells respire – animal cells, plant cells and the cells of fungi and single-celled organisms.

★ **Most** cells respire aerobically.

★ **Some** cells, such as muscle cells, the cells of plant roots, yeast cells and some types of bacteria, are able to respire anaerobically when supplies of oxygen are low.

★ **Some** cells, such as the bacterium that causes tetanus, can *only* respire anaerobically.

Mutual friends!

The muscles of the man and dog are working hard. At first, aerobic respiration in their muscle cells gives them a flying start.

EQUATIONS Page 122.

$$\text{glucose} + \text{oxygen} \rightarrow \text{carbon dioxide} + \text{water}$$
$$C_6H_{12}O_6(aq) + 6O_2(g) \rightarrow 6CO_2(g) + 6H_2O(l)$$
$$\text{energy released} = 16.1 \text{ kJ/g glucose}$$

The man and dog are both panting. However, in spite of rapid breathing and strenuous pumping by the heart, oxygen cannot reach the muscles fast enough to supply their needs.

The muscles then switch from **aerobic respiration** to **anaerobic respiration** which does *not* use oxygen. **Lactic acid** is produced, which collects in the muscles (the **oxygen debt**).

$$\text{glucose} \rightarrow \text{lactic acid}$$
$$C_6H_{12}O_6(aq) \quad 2CH_3CHOHCO_2H(aq)$$
$$\text{energy released} = 0.83 \text{ kJ/g glucose}$$

Notice that the energy released per gram of glucose is less than in aerobic respiration. As lactic acid accumulates, the muscles stop working. The man and dog will be unable to run any further until the lactic acid has been removed from their muscles. This removal process uses oxygen. Lactic acid stimulates the body to pant vigorously, bringing a rush of oxygen to the muscles. During the recovery period, the lactic acid is oxidised and the **oxygen debt** is repaid. Aerobic respiration can then start again.

Fact file

Why is there a difference in energy output between aerobic respiration and anaerobic respiration?

★ During aerobic respiration glucose is completely oxidised to carbon dioxide and water, releasing all of the available energy from each glucose molecule.

Humans as organisms

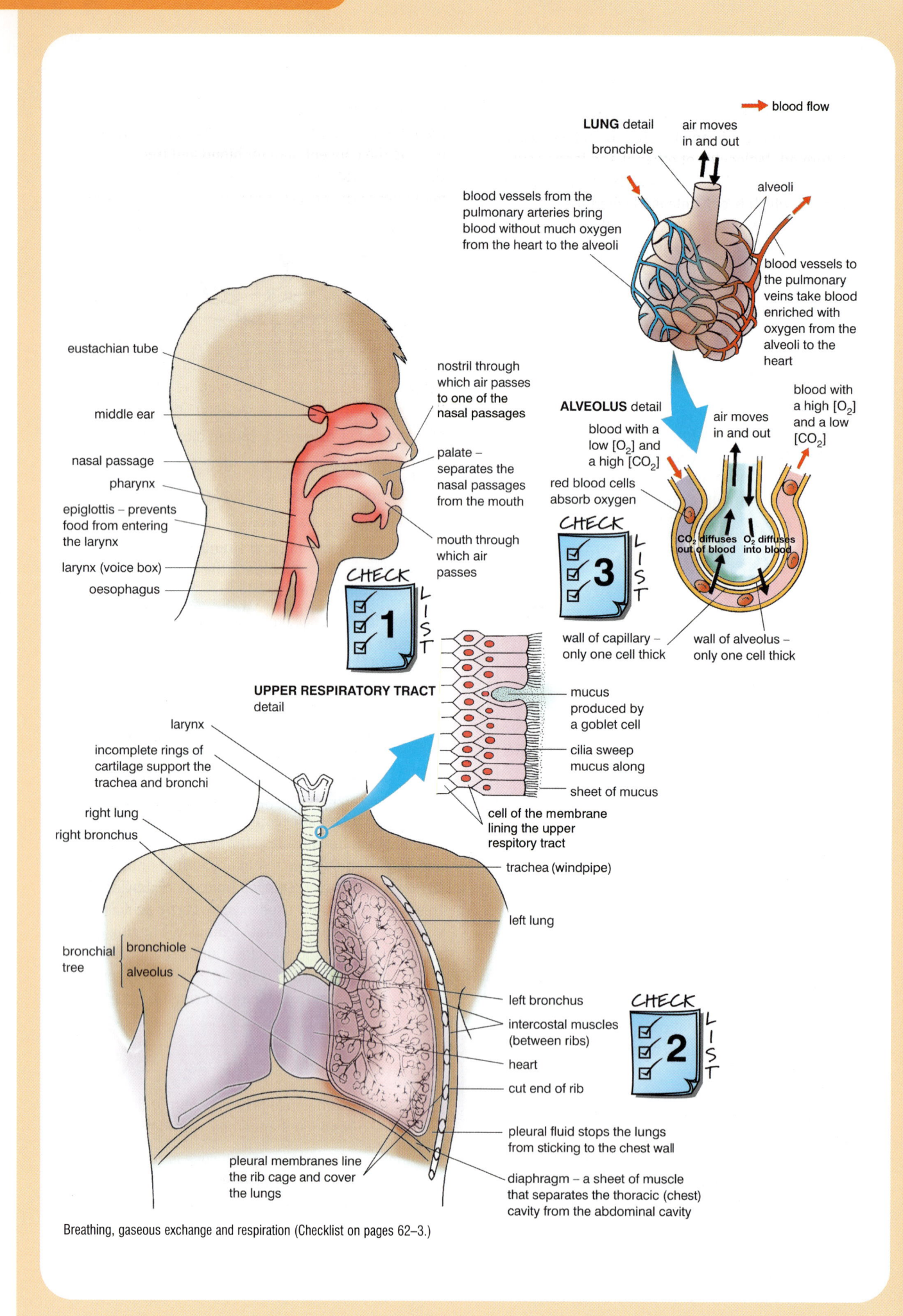

LUNG detail
- bronchiole
- air moves in and out
- alveoli
- blood flow
- blood vessels from the pulmonary arteries bring blood without much oxygen from the heart to the alveoli
- blood vessels to the pulmonary veins take blood enriched with oxygen from the alveoli to the heart

ALVEOLUS detail
- blood with a low [O_2] and a high [CO_2]
- air moves in and out
- blood with a high [O_2] and a low [CO_2]
- red blood cells absorb oxygen
- CO_2 diffuses out of blood
- O_2 diffuses into blood
- wall of capillary – only one cell thick
- wall of alveolus – only one cell thick

CHECK LIST 3

Head/neck diagram labels:
- eustachian tube
- middle ear
- nasal passage
- pharynx
- epiglottis – prevents food from entering the larynx
- larynx (voice box)
- oesophagus
- nostril through which air passes to one of the nasal passages
- palate – separates the nasal passages from the mouth
- mouth through which air passes

CHECK LIST 1

UPPER RESPIRATORY TRACT detail
- mucus produced by a goblet cell
- cilia sweep mucus along
- sheet of mucus
- cell of the membrane lining the upper respitory tract

Thorax diagram labels:
- larynx
- incomplete rings of cartilage support the trachea and bronchi
- right lung
- right bronchus
- bronchial tree { bronchiole, alveolus }
- trachea (windpipe)
- left lung
- left bronchus
- intercostal muscles (between ribs)
- heart
- cut end of rib
- pleural fluid stops the lungs from sticking to the chest wall
- diaphragm – a sheet of muscle that separates the thoracic (chest) cavity from the abdominal cavity
- pleural membranes line the rib cage and cover the lungs

CHECK LIST 2

Breathing, gaseous exchange and respiration (Checklist on pages 62–3.)

Humans as organisms

★ During anaerobic respiration glucose is incompletely oxidised and ethanol or lactic acid is formed. Molecules of ethanol and lactic acid represent a considerable store of chemical bond energy, which is only released when the substances are oxidised aerobically.

The chemical reactions of anaerobic respiration provide us with food, drink and a range of other products.

BIOTECHNOLOGY Pages 99–100.

5.4 Blood and the circulatory system

PREVIEW

At the end of this section you will:
- be able to identify the different components of blood
- understand the functions of blood
- understand why the heart is a double pump
- know that capillary blood vessels link arteries and veins
- understand how different factors (diet, exercise and stress) affect the circulatory system.

Fact file

★ The **heart** is a pump.

★ **Blood** is a liquid containing different cells.

★ **Arteries**, **veins** and **capillaries** are tube-like vessels through which blood flows.

heart $\xrightarrow{\text{pumps}}$ blood $\xrightarrow{\text{through}}$ blood vessels

Moving blood around

The circulatory system consists of tubes (arteries, veins and capillaries) through which blood is pumped by the heart. Blood carries oxygen, digested food, hormones and other substances *to* the tissues and organs of the body that need them. Blood also carries carbon dioxide and other waste substances produced by the metabolism of cells *from* the tissues and organs of the body. On pages 66–7 is the concept map for **blood and the circulatory system**. The numbers on the concept map refer to the checklist below.

Fact file

The English scientist William Harvey (1578–1657) discovered the circulation of blood in 1628. He identified arteries and veins but, in the absence of microscopes, could not see the capillary blood vessels connecting them. However, he predicted the existence of capillaries, a prediction confirmed by Marcello Malpighi in 1661 who observed them through a microscope, which by then had been invented.

Checklist for blood and the circulatory system

1 ★ **Red blood cells** are made in the **marrow** of the limb bones, ribs and vertebrae.

★ Old red blood cells are destroyed in the liver.

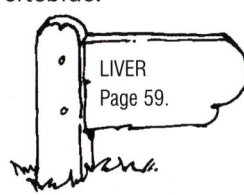

LIVER Page 59.

★ **White blood cells** originate in the **bone marrow** and **spleen**.

★ **Antibodies** produced against a particular **antigen** will attack only that antigen. The antibody is said to be **specific** to that antigen. Antibodies are produced by white blood cells called B-lymphocytes.

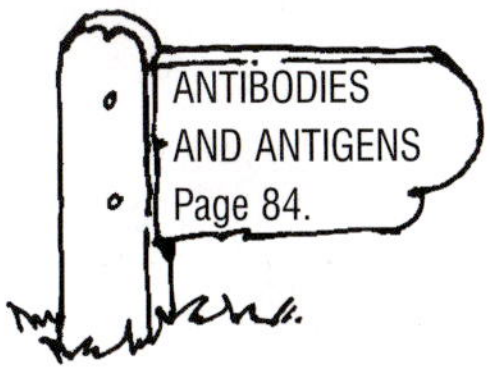

ANTIBODIES AND ANTIGENS Page 84.

2 ★ **Arteries** carry blood *from* the heart.

Veins carry blood *to* the heart.

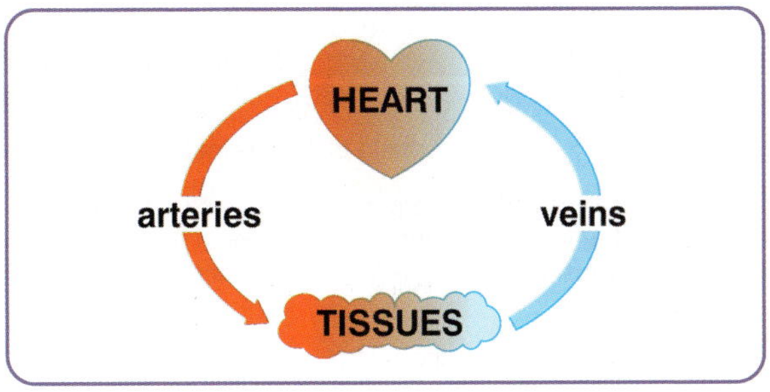

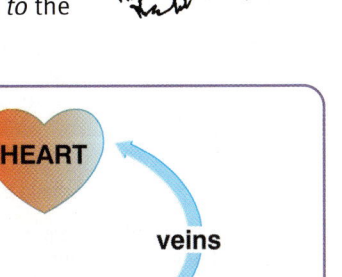

HEART — arteries → TISSUES → veins

continued on page 68

Humans as organisms

Fact file

★ Haemoglobin combines with oxygen to form **oxyhaemoglobin**. This breaks down to release oxygen in tissues where the concentration of oxygen is low.

haemoglobin + oxygen ⇌ oxyhaemoglobin

★ Blood that contains a lot of oxyhaemoglobin is bright red in colour. It is called **oxygenated** blood. Blood with little oxyhaemoglobin looks a deep red-purple. It is called **deoxygenated** blood.

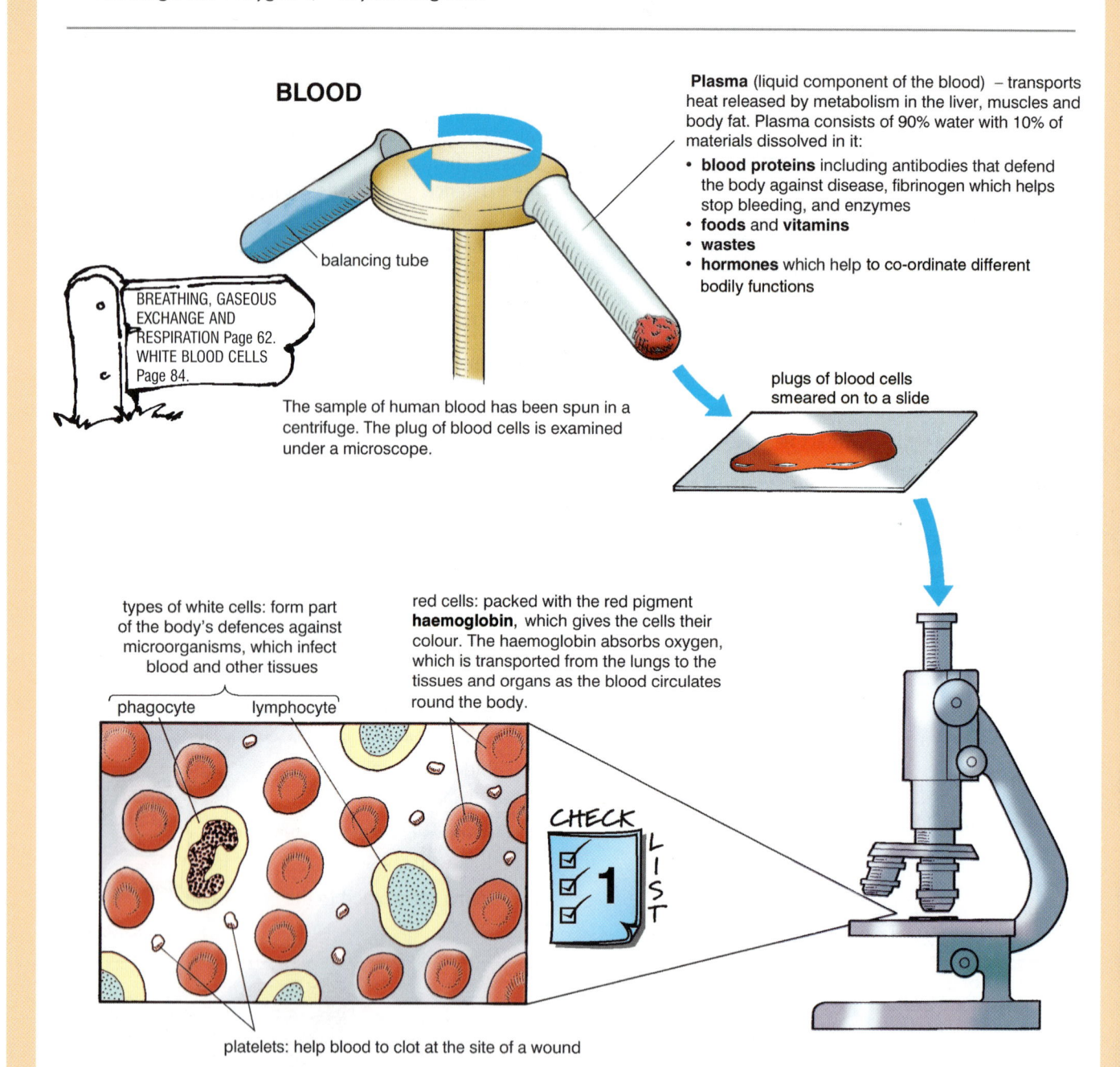

BLOOD

balancing tube

BREATHING, GASEOUS EXCHANGE AND RESPIRATION Page 62. WHITE BLOOD CELLS Page 84.

The sample of human blood has been spun in a centrifuge. The plug of blood cells is examined under a microscope.

Plasma (liquid component of the blood) – transports heat released by metabolism in the liver, muscles and body fat. Plasma consists of 90% water with 10% of materials dissolved in it:
- **blood proteins** including antibodies that defend the body against disease, fibrinogen which helps stop bleeding, and enzymes
- **foods** and **vitamins**
- **wastes**
- **hormones** which help to co-ordinate different bodily functions

plugs of blood cells smeared on to a slide

types of white cells: form part of the body's defences against microorganisms, which infect blood and other tissues

phagocyte   lymphocyte

red cells: packed with the red pigment **haemoglobin**, which gives the cells their colour. The haemoglobin absorbs oxygen, which is transported from the lungs to the tissues and organs as the blood circulates round the body.

CHECK LIST 1

platelets: help blood to clot at the site of a wound

Red blood cells *do not* have a nucleus, but white cells *do*. **Notice** the characteristic shapes of the nuclei of phagocytes and lymphocytes. Platelets look like fragments of red cells.

Blood and the circulatory system (Checklist on pages 65 and 68.)

Humans as organisms

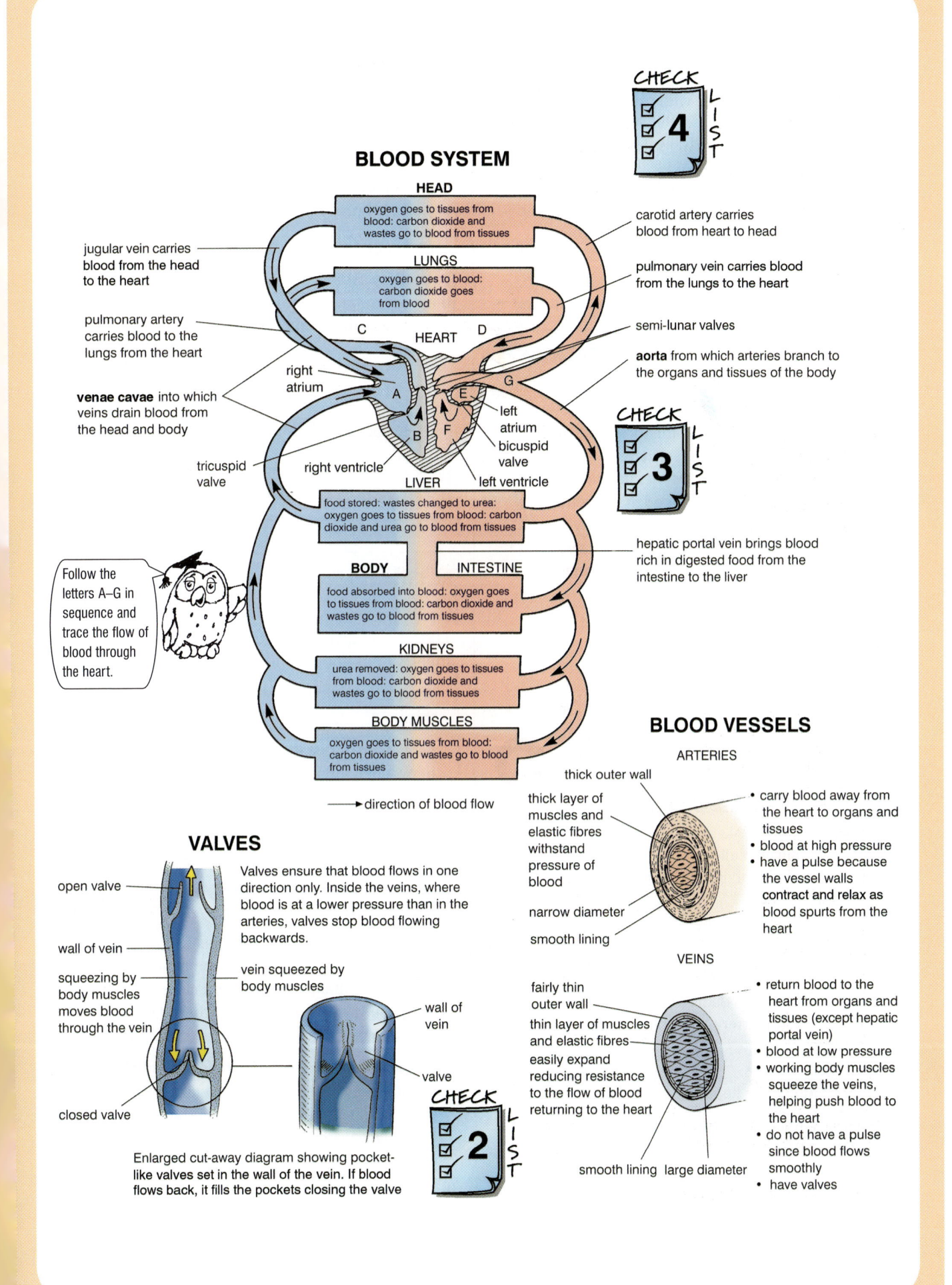

BLOOD SYSTEM

HEAD: oxygen goes to tissues from blood; carbon dioxide and wastes go to blood from tissues

LUNGS: oxygen goes to blood; carbon dioxide goes from blood

HEART

LIVER: food stored; wastes changed to urea; oxygen goes to tissues from blood; carbon dioxide and urea go to blood from tissues

BODY INTESTINE: food absorbed into blood; oxygen goes to tissues from blood; carbon dioxide and wastes go to blood from tissues

KIDNEYS: urea removed; oxygen goes to tissues from blood; carbon dioxide and wastes go to blood from tissues

BODY MUSCLES: oxygen goes to tissues from blood; carbon dioxide and wastes go to blood from tissues

- jugular vein carries blood from the head to the heart
- pulmonary artery carries blood to the lungs from the heart
- **venae cavae** into which veins drain blood from the head and body
- tricuspid valve
- right atrium
- right ventricle
- carotid artery carries blood from heart to head
- pulmonary vein carries blood from the lungs to the heart
- semi-lunar valves
- **aorta** from which arteries branch to the organs and tissues of the body
- left atrium
- bicuspid valve
- left ventricle
- hepatic portal vein brings blood rich in digested food from the intestine to the liver

Follow the letters A–G in sequence and trace the flow of blood through the heart.

→ direction of blood flow

CHECK LIST 4

CHECK LIST 3

VALVES

Valves ensure that blood flows in one direction only. Inside the veins, where blood is at a lower pressure than in the arteries, valves stop blood flowing backwards.

- open valve
- wall of vein
- squeezing by body muscles moves blood through the vein
- closed valve
- vein squeezed by body muscles
- wall of vein
- valve

Enlarged cut-away diagram showing pocket-like valves set in the wall of the vein. If blood flows back, it fills the pockets closing the valve

CHECK LIST 2

BLOOD VESSELS

ARTERIES

- thick outer wall
- thick layer of muscles and elastic fibres withstand pressure of blood
- narrow diameter
- smooth lining

- carry blood away from the heart to organs and tissues
- blood at high pressure
- have a pulse because the vessel walls **contract and relax** as blood spurts from the heart

VEINS

- fairly thin outer wall
- thin layer of muscles and elastic fibres easily expand reducing resistance to the flow of blood returning to the heart
- smooth lining
- large diameter

- return blood to the heart from organs and tissues (except hepatic portal vein)
- blood at low pressure
- working body muscles squeeze the veins, helping push blood to the heart
- do not have a pulse since blood flows smoothly
- have valves

67

Humans as organisms

3 ★ Heart (**cardiac**) muscle contracts and relaxes rhythmically for a lifetime.

★ The heartbeat is a two-tone sound:
- **diastole** – the heart muscles are relaxed
- **systole** – the heart muscles contract. During **auricular (atrial) systole**, contraction of the auricles (atria) forces blood into the ventricles. During **ventricular systole**, contraction of the ventricles forces blood into the pulmonary artery (from the right ventricle) and aorta (from the left ventricle)

★ **Valves** direct the flow of blood through the heart.
- During auricular (atrial) systole, the increase in the pressure of the blood in the auricles forces open the tricuspid valve and bicuspid valve, respectively.
- During ventricular systole, the increase in the pressure of the blood in the ventricles closes the tricuspid and bicuspid valves and forces open the semi-lunar valves guarding the opening of the pulmonary artery and aorta, respectively.

★ A constant blood pressure is needed for the kidneys to work properly.
- The heart is a **double pump**.
- The beating of the heart is controlled by a **pacemaker**.

As a result, the heart beats on average 72 times a minute.

4 ★ The arteries and veins in the human body form two circuits:
- the lung circuit
- the head and body circuit.

Testing your understanding

Examinations test your understanding of ideas and important principles. Be sure you have grasped the arrangement of the **hepatic portal vein** and the role of the **pulmonary artery** and **pulmonary vein** – see page 67.

Understanding the hepatic portal vein

Veins carry blood to the heart. The **hepatic portal vein** is the exception. Notice on page 67 that it carries blood with its load of digested food from the intestine to the liver.

Understanding the pulmonary artery and the pulmonary vein

Arteries are sometimes described as carriers of oxygenated blood (often coloured red on diagrams), and veins as carriers of deoxygenated blood (often coloured blue on diagrams). However, the **pulmonary artery** carries deoxygenated blood from the heart to the lungs. The **pulmonary vein** carries oxygenated blood from the lungs to the heart.

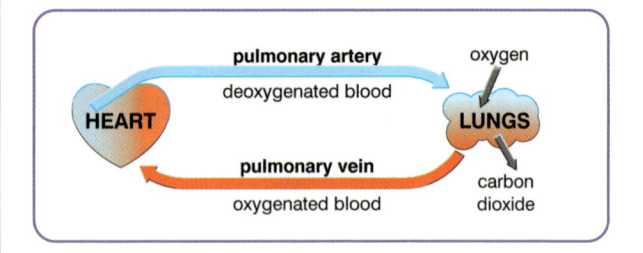

Fact file

Capillaries are tiny blood vessels, 0.001 mm in diameter. They join each artery with its corresponding vein.

★ The walls of capillary blood vessels are one cell thick.

As a result, substances easily diffuse between blood in the capillaries and the surrounding tissues.

★ Capillaries form dense networks called **beds** in the tissues of the body.

As a result, no cell is very far away from a capillary.

★ The blood in capillaries supplies nearby cells with oxygen, food molecules and other substances. It also carries away carbon dioxide and other wastes produced by the cells' metabolism.

★ **Tissue fluid** carries oxygen, food and other substances to the cells. This fluid is blood plasma that has been forced out through the thin capillary walls by the pressure of the blood inside.

★ Red blood cells squeeze through the smallest capillaries in single file.

ABSORPTION OF FOOD Page 60.

Humans as organisms

As a result, the pressure drops as blood passes through the capillaries from the artery to the vein.

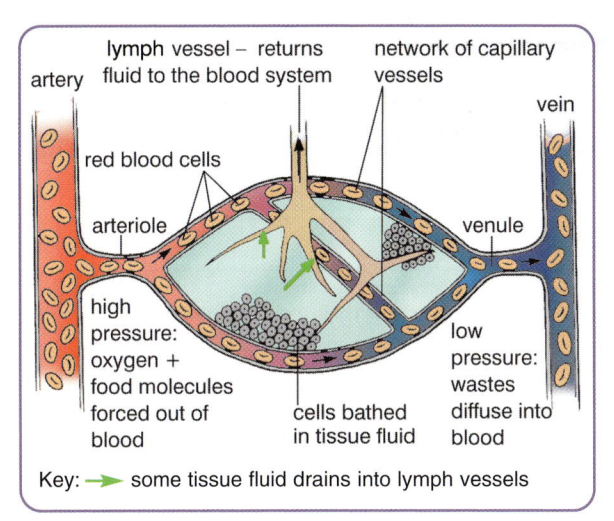

Capillaries at work

Disorders of the blood

★ **Leukaemia** results from the production of abnormal white blood cells.

As a result, there are too few red blood cells.

Treatments of the disorder include using drugs that slow the production of white blood cells, and radiotherapy which kills the abnormal cells.

★ **Haemophilia** is a genetic disease which runs in families. The blood does not clot properly because factor VIII, one of the substances in the blood needed for blood clots to form, is missing.

As a result, **haemophiliacs** (people suffering from haemophilia) lose a lot of blood if they injure themselves.

Treatment is by injections of factor VIII.

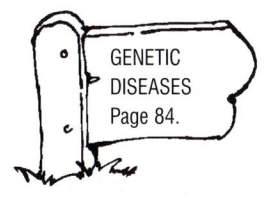

GENETIC DISEASES Page 84.

AIDS

AIDS (**A**cquired **I**mmune **D**eficiency **S**yndrome) is caused by the **H**uman **I**mmunodeficiency **V**irus (**HIV**). The virus attacks a particular type of white blood cell.

As a result, a person infected with HIV has reduced protection from disease-causing microorganisms.

Once HIV has destroyed a number of the white blood cells, the diseases of AIDS develop. Common diseases include:
- pneumonia – a disease of the lungs
- thrush – a fungal infection
- Kaposi's sarcoma – a skin cancer.

Understanding heart disease

The **coronary arteries** supply blood to the heart muscle, as shown in the diagram on page 70. The lining of blood vessels can be damaged and roughened by a fatty deposit called **atheroma**. The build-up of atheroma in the coronary arteries is one cause of **heart disease**. It increases the risk of blood clots forming. A blood clot in the coronary arteries can interrupt the blood supply to the heart, and the person suffers a **heart attack**.

The symptoms are:
- severe pain in the chest, neck and arms
- sweating
- faintness and sickness.

The clot is called a **thrombus**, and the blockage a **thrombosis**.

The diagram on page 70 shows some of the factors affecting the risk of a person developing heart disease.

Humans as organisms

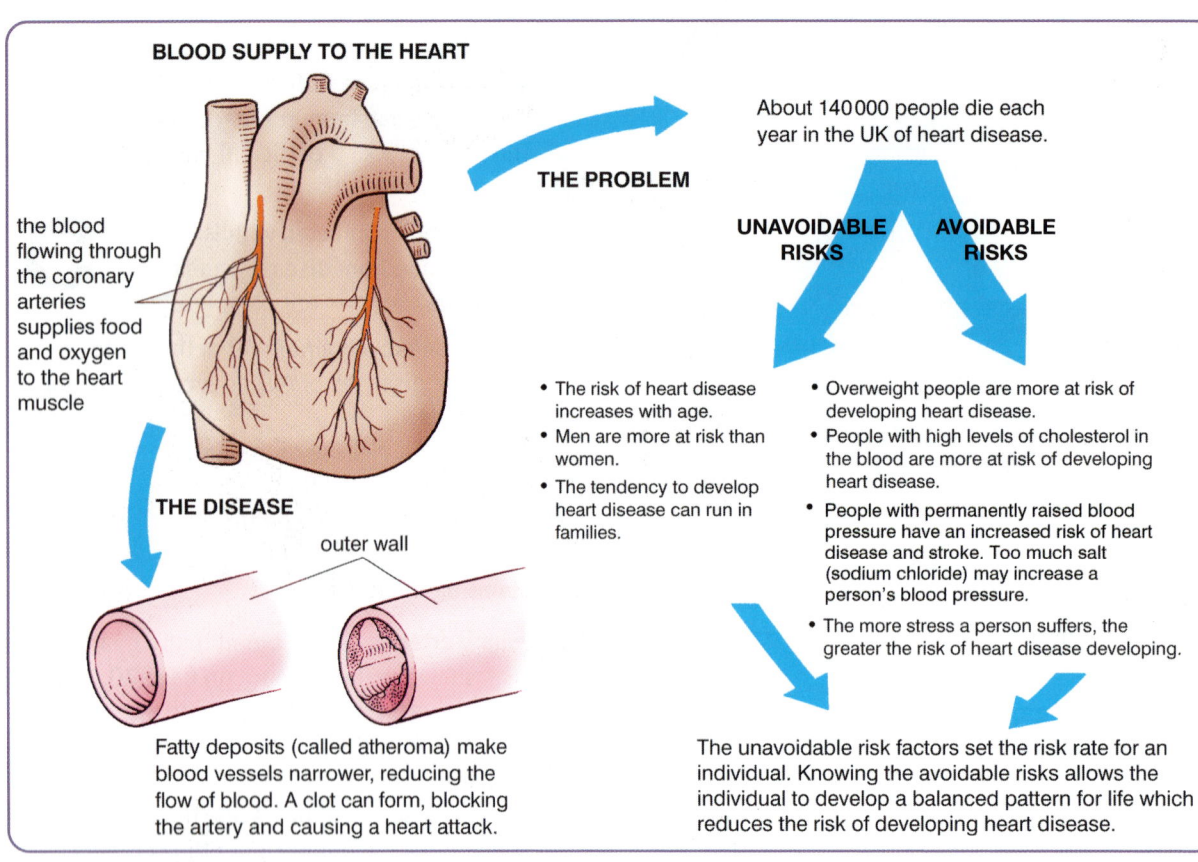

BLOOD SUPPLY TO THE HEART

the blood flowing through the coronary arteries supplies food and oxygen to the heart muscle

THE PROBLEM

About 140 000 people die each year in the UK of heart disease.

UNAVOIDABLE RISKS

- The risk of heart disease increases with age.
- Men are more at risk than women.
- The tendency to develop heart disease can run in families.

AVOIDABLE RISKS

- Overweight people are more at risk of developing heart disease.
- People with high levels of cholesterol in the blood are more at risk of developing heart disease.
- People with permanently raised blood pressure have an increased risk of heart disease and stroke. Too much salt (sodium chloride) may increase a person's blood pressure.
- The more stress a person suffers, the greater the risk of heart disease developing.

THE DISEASE

outer wall

Fatty deposits (called atheroma) make blood vessels narrower, reducing the flow of blood. A clot can form, blocking the artery and causing a heart attack.

The unavoidable risk factors set the risk rate for an individual. Knowing the avoidable risks allows the individual to develop a balanced pattern for life which reduces the risk of developing heart disease.

The risk of heart disease

5.5 Senses and the nervous system

> **PREVIEW**
>
> At the end of this section you will know that:
> - stimuli are converted by receptors into signals called nerve impulses, to which the body can respond
> - neurones (nerve cells) conduct nerve impulses to muscles, which respond by contracting
> - muscles and glands are effectors
> - nerves are formed from bundles of neurones and are the link between stimulus and response.

Stimulus and response

A **stimulus** is a change in the environment which causes a living organism to take action. A **response** is the action that the living organism takes. The **nervous system** links stimuli and responses. The sequence of events is:

★ **Sensory receptor cells** detect stimuli and convert them into **nerve impulses** which transmit information to which the body can respond.

★ Nerve impulses are minute electrical disturbances.

★ **Neurones** (nerve cells) conduct nerve impulses to **effectors** (muscles or glands). Muscles respond to nerve impulses by contracting; glands respond by secreting substances. For example, the adrenal glands respond to nerve impulses by producing the hormone adrenaline, which helps the body cope with sudden stress.

HORMONES Pages 77–80.

The process runs:

stimulus → receptor → nerves → effector → response

Humans as organisms

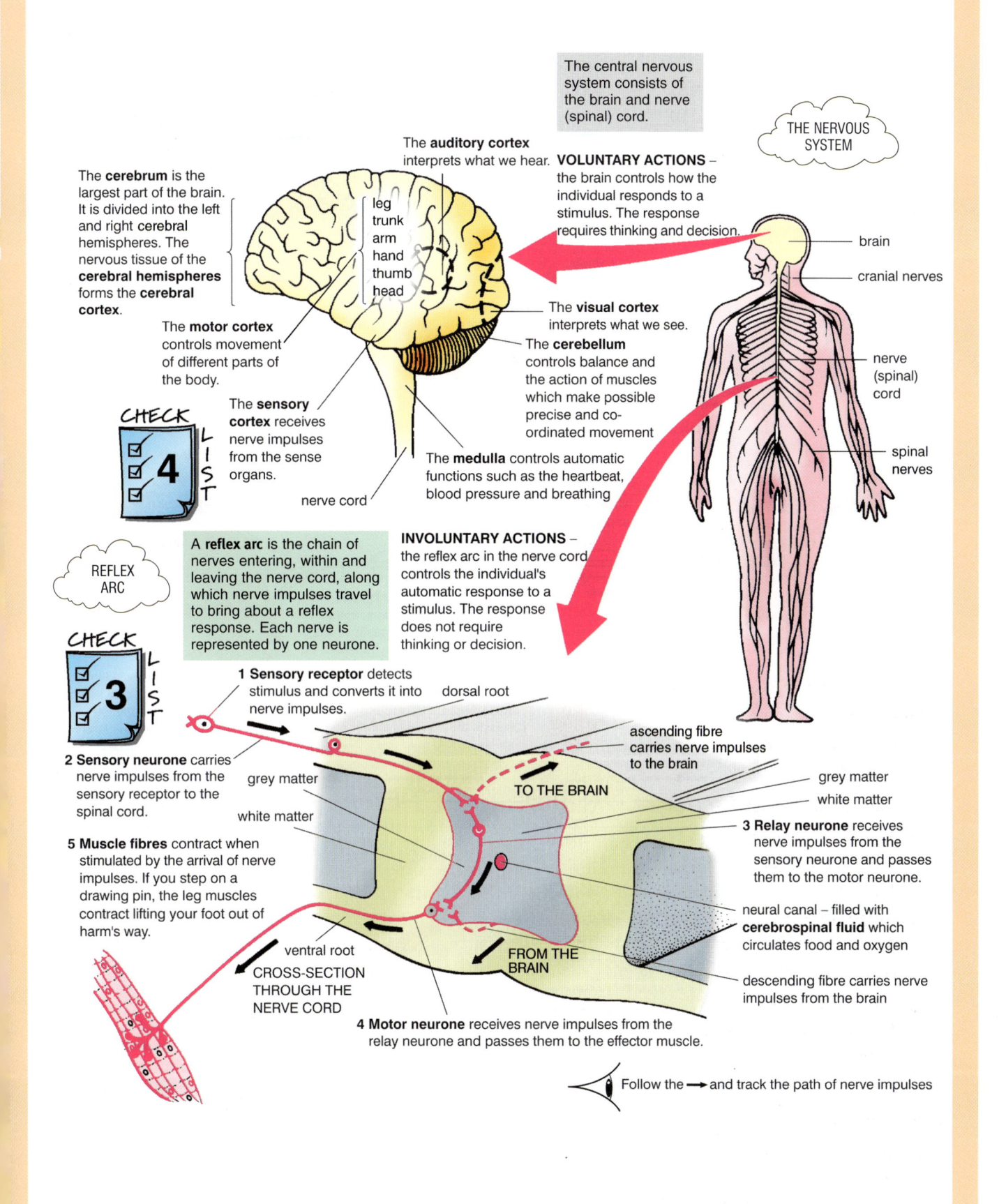

THE NERVOUS SYSTEM

The central nervous system consists of the brain and nerve (spinal) cord.

VOLUNTARY ACTIONS – the brain controls how the individual responds to a stimulus. The response requires thinking and decision.

The **cerebrum** is the largest part of the brain. It is divided into the left and right **cerebral hemispheres**. The nervous tissue of the **cerebral hemispheres** forms the **cerebral cortex**.

The **auditory cortex** interprets what we hear.

leg
trunk
arm
hand
thumb
head

The **motor cortex** controls movement of different parts of the body.

The **sensory cortex** receives nerve impulses from the sense organs.

The **visual cortex** interprets what we see.

The **cerebellum** controls balance and the action of muscles which make possible precise and co-ordinated movement

The **medulla** controls automatic functions such as the heartbeat, blood pressure and breathing

nerve cord

- brain
- cranial nerves
- nerve (spinal) cord
- spinal nerves

CHECK LIST 4

REFLEX ARC

A **reflex arc** is the chain of nerves entering, within and leaving the nerve cord, along which nerve impulses travel to bring about a reflex response. Each nerve is represented by one neurone.

INVOLUNTARY ACTIONS – the reflex arc in the nerve cord controls the individual's automatic response to a stimulus. The response does not require thinking or decision.

CHECK LIST 3

1 **Sensory receptor** detects stimulus and converts it into nerve impulses.

2 **Sensory neurone** carries nerve impulses from the sensory receptor to the spinal cord.

5 **Muscle fibres** contract when stimulated by the arrival of nerve impulses. If you step on a drawing pin, the leg muscles contract lifting your foot out of harm's way.

- dorsal root
- ascending fibre carries nerve impulses to the brain
- TO THE BRAIN
- grey matter
- white matter
- grey matter
- white matter

3 **Relay neurone** receives nerve impulses from the sensory neurone and passes them to the motor neurone.

neural canal – filled with **cerebrospinal fluid** which circulates food and oxygen

descending fibre carries nerve impulses from the brain

- ventral root
- FROM THE BRAIN

CROSS-SECTION THROUGH THE NERVE CORD

4 **Motor neurone** receives nerve impulses from the relay neurone and passes them to the effector muscle.

Follow the → and track the path of nerve impulses

Neurones, nerves and the nervous system (Checklist on page 73.)

Humans as organisms

The peripheral nervous system is formed by the cranial nerves and spinal nerves that join the central nervous system.

NERVES × 400

Neurones are grouped together into bundles called **nerves** which pass to all parts of the body, forming a nervous system.

CHECK LIST 1

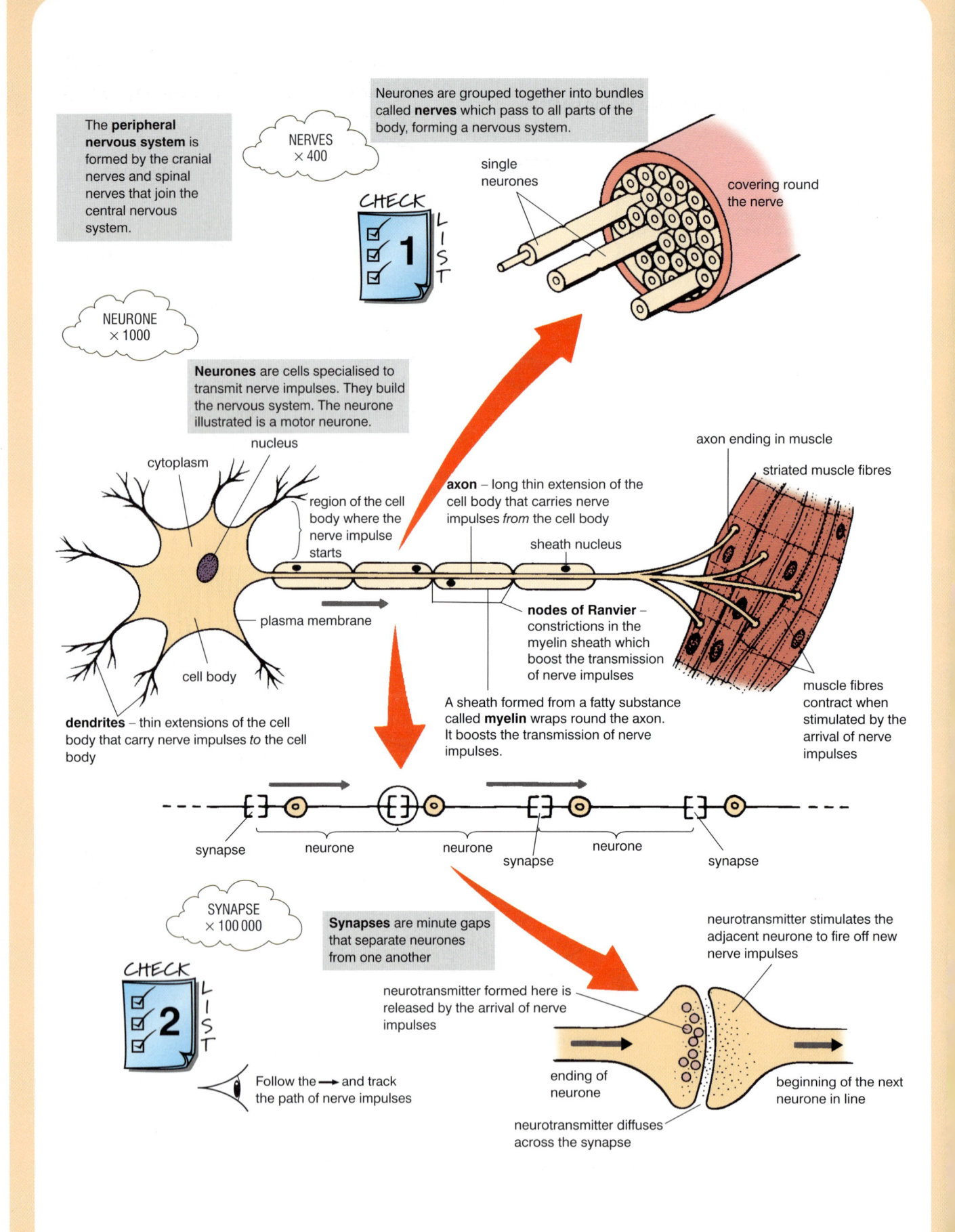

- single neurones
- covering round the nerve

NEURONE × 1000

Neurones are cells specialised to transmit nerve impulses. They build the nervous system. The neurone illustrated is a motor neurone.

- cytoplasm
- nucleus
- region of the cell body where the nerve impulse starts
- **axon** – long thin extension of the cell body that carries nerve impulses *from* the cell body
- sheath nucleus
- axon ending in muscle
- striated muscle fibres
- plasma membrane
- **nodes of Ranvier** – constrictions in the myelin sheath which boost the transmission of nerve impulses
- cell body
- **dendrites** – thin extensions of the cell body that carry nerve impulses *to* the cell body
- A sheath formed from a fatty substance called **myelin** wraps round the axon. It boosts the transmission of nerve impulses.
- muscle fibres contract when stimulated by the arrival of nerve impulses

synapse — neurone — neurone — synapse — neurone — synapse

SYNAPSE × 100 000

Synapses are minute gaps that separate neurones from one another

CHECK LIST 2

Follow the ➝ and track the path of nerve impulses

- neurotransmitter formed here is released by the arrival of nerve impulses
- neurotransmitter stimulates the adjacent neurone to fire off new nerve impulses
- ending of neurone
- beginning of the next neurone in line
- neurotransmitter diffuses across the synapse

Humans as organisms

The nervous system

On pages 71–2 is the concept map for **the nervous system**. The numbers on the concept map refer to the checklist below.

Checklist for the nervous system

1 ★ Each **nerve** of the nervous system consists of a bundle of **neurones**.
   ★ Neurones transmit nerve impulses to an **effector** (muscle or gland).
   ★ Nerve impulses are minute electrical disturbances which carry information about stimuli.
   ★ Nerve impulses stimulate effectors to respond to stimuli in a useful way.
   ★ A nerve impulse takes just milliseconds to travel along a neurone.

2 ★ A **neurotransmitter** is a chemical substance released from the end of a neurone into the **synapse**.
   ★ A neurotransmitter is produced only from the end of the neurone before the synapse.
   As a result, nerve impulses always travel *from* the receptor *to* the effector.
   ★ Once the neurotransmitter has stimulated the neurone after the synapse to fire off new nerve impulses, it is destroyed by an enzyme. If it were not destroyed, it would stimulate the neurone after the synapse to continue to fire off nerve impulses.
   As a result, muscles (the effectors) would be permanently contracted: a condition called **tetanus**. Death quickly follows.

3 ★ **Reflex responses** happen before the brain has had time to process the nerve impulses carrying the information about the stimulus (track the sequence 1–5 in the diagram on page 71).
   ★ When the brain catches up with events, it brings about the next set of reactions – such as a shout of pain.
   ★ **Ascending fibres** form synapses with sensory neurones. The ascending fibres carry nerve impulses to the brain.

As a result, the brain receives information about the stimulus causing the reflex response.
   ★ Nerve impulses from the brain are carried by the **descending fibres**, which synapse with motor neurones.
   As a result, the reflex response is brought under conscious control.

4 ★ The human brain weighs approximately 1.3 kg and occupies a volume of about 1500 cm^3.
   ★ Around 6 million neurones make up 1 cm^3 of brain matter.
   ★ Memory and learning are under the brain's control.
   ★ Different drugs affect the brain. For example, ethanol (the alcohol in beers, wines and spirits) depresses the activity of the cerebral cortex, affecting judgement and the control of movement.

5.6 Sense organs

PREVIEW

At the end of this section you will know that:
- the sense organs consist of sensory cells which are adapted to detect a particular type of stimulus.

Handy hint

The sensory cells of the:
- **T**ongue detect chemicals
- **E**ar detect sound
- **E**ye detect light
- **N**ose detect chemicals
- **S**kin detect heat and cold, touch and pain.

Thinking of the memory aid **TEENS** will help you remember the major sense organs of the body.

Sensing the surroundings

On pages 74–5 is the concept map for **sense organs**. The numbers refer to the checklist on page 76.

Humans as organisms

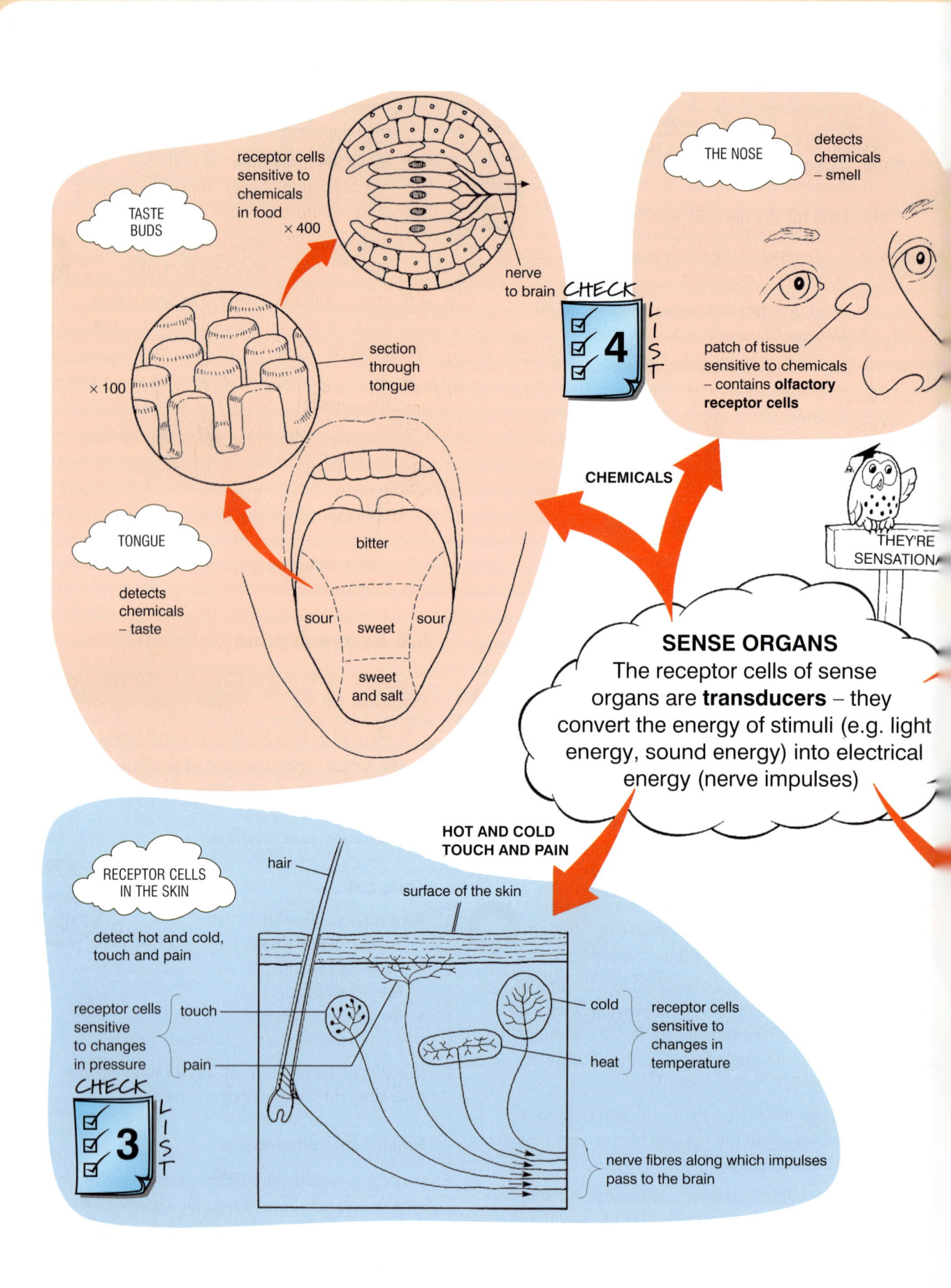

TASTE BUDS
receptor cells sensitive to chemicals in food
× 400
nerve to brain

× 100
section through tongue

TONGUE
detects chemicals – taste

bitter
sour — sweet — sour
sweet and salt

THE NOSE
detects chemicals – smell

patch of tissue sensitive to chemicals – contains **olfactory receptor cells**

CHECK LIST 4

CHEMICALS

THEY'RE SENSATIONAL

SENSE ORGANS
The receptor cells of sense organs are **transducers** – they convert the energy of stimuli (e.g. light energy, sound energy) into electrical energy (nerve impulses)

HOT AND COLD TOUCH AND PAIN

RECEPTOR CELLS IN THE SKIN
detect hot and cold, touch and pain

hair
surface of the skin

receptor cells sensitive to changes in pressure
— touch
— pain

cold
heat
receptor cells sensitive to changes in temperature

nerve fibres along which impulses pass to the brain

CHECK LIST 3

Sense organs (Checklist on page 76.)

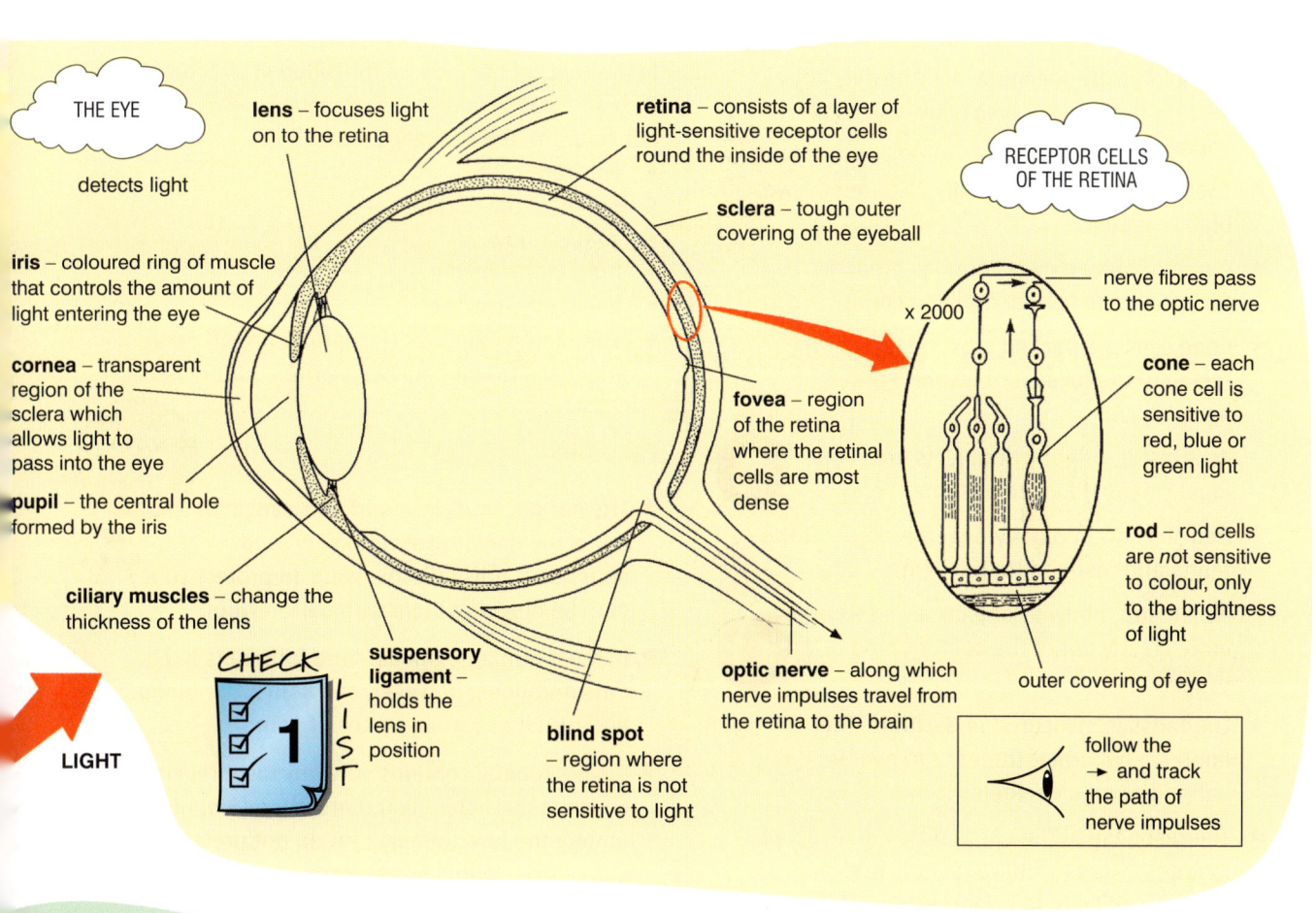

Humans as organisms

THE EYE
detects light

LIGHT →

- **lens** – focuses light on to the retina
- **retina** – consists of a layer of light-sensitive receptor cells round the inside of the eye
- **sclera** – tough outer covering of the eyeball
- **iris** – coloured ring of muscle that controls the amount of light entering the eye
- **cornea** – transparent region of the sclera which allows light to pass into the eye
- **pupil** – the central hole formed by the iris
- **ciliary muscles** – change the thickness of the lens
- **suspensory ligament** – holds the lens in position
- **fovea** – region of the retina where the retinal cells are most dense
- **blind spot** – region where the retina is not sensitive to light
- **optic nerve** – along which nerve impulses travel from the retina to the brain

RECEPTOR CELLS OF THE RETINA

x 2000

- nerve fibres pass to the optic nerve
- **cone** – each cone cell is sensitive to red, blue or green light
- **rod** – rod cells are *not* sensitive to colour, only to the brightness of light
- outer covering of eye

follow the → and track the path of nerve impulses

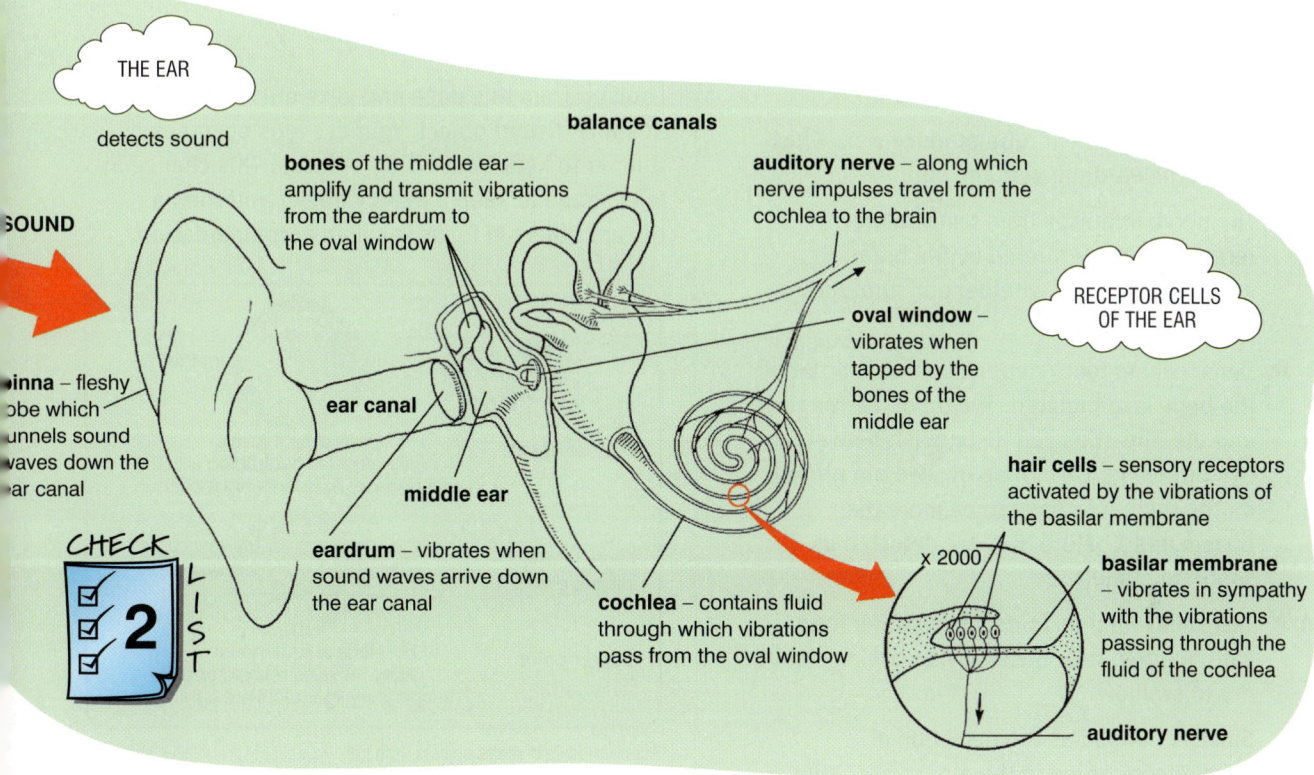

CHECK LIST 1

THE EAR
detects sound

SOUND →

- **pinna** – fleshy lobe which funnels sound waves down the ear canal
- **ear canal**
- **middle ear**
- **eardrum** – vibrates when sound waves arrive down the ear canal
- **bones** of the middle ear – amplify and transmit vibrations from the eardrum to the oval window
- **balance canals**
- **auditory nerve** – along which nerve impulses travel from the cochlea to the brain
- **oval window** – vibrates when tapped by the bones of the middle ear
- **cochlea** – contains fluid through which vibrations pass from the oval window

RECEPTOR CELLS OF THE EAR

x 2000

- **hair cells** – sensory receptors activated by the vibrations of the basilar membrane
- **basilar membrane** – vibrates in sympathy with the vibrations passing through the fluid of the cochlea
- **auditory nerve**

CHECK LIST 2

Humans as organisms

Checklist for sense organs

1. ★ **Tears** lubricate the surface of the eye. They contain the enzyme **lysozyme** which kills bacteria.

   ★ The **iris** of the eye is usually coloured brown, blue or green.

   ★ A pair of human eyes contains around 130 million **rods** and 7 million **cones**.

   ★ **Cone** cells are packed most densely in the region of the **fovea** and respond to bright light.

   As a result, brightly lit objects are seen most clearly if looked at straight on.

   ★ **Rod** cells occur mostly near the edges of the retina and respond to dim light.

   As a result, dimly lit objects are seen more clearly out of the corner of the eye.

2. ★ Loudness is measured in **decibels**. The faintest sound that the ear can hear is defined as zero decibels.

   ★ The response of the ear to different levels of loudness varies with frequency. The ear is most sensitive to frequencies around 3000 Hz, and can detect the softest sounds. It is completely insensitive to sounds over 18 000 Hz and cannot detect them.

   ★ The walls of the ear tube produce wax, which keeps the eardrum soft and supple.

3. ★ The nerve impulses from **temperature receptors** are interpreted by the brain, enabling us to feel whether our surroundings are hot or cold.

   ★ Sensitivity to **touch** depends on which part of the body is stimulated. The tip of the tongue and the fingertips can distinguish between two pin pricks 1.0 mm apart. Two pin pricks on the thigh may have to be more than 60 mm apart before they are detected as separate stimuli.

4. ★ **Taste buds** help us to decide whether food is safe. A bitter taste is usually a warning signal not to swallow.

   ★ **Smell** is defined as the detection of substances carried in the air.

   ★ To be detected, substances which are tasted or smelt must first be dissolved in the watery environment covering the receptor cells.

Check the vibrations

In the concept map, notice the different structures in the ear vibrating in response to sound waves striking the eardrum. The sequence reads:
- eardrum
- bones of the middle ear
- oval window
- fluid in the cochlea
- basilar membrane
- stimulated hair cells (receptors) fire off nerve impulses to the brain along the auditory nerve.

Fact file

★ The ear becomes less and less sensitive if it is regularly exposed to very loud sounds. At noisy discos, you can protect your ears by plugging them with cotton wool.

★ In most humans, the ear lobe (pinna) is fixed. Cats and dogs, however, can adjust the pinna and turn it towards sources of sound.

★ A cat's tongue contains very few taste receptors which respond to sugar. Cats, therefore, are among the few animals that do not prefer substances with a sweet taste.

The eye at work

Look up from this page and gaze out of the window at some distant object. Your eye lens becomes thinner to keep your vision in focus. This change in lens shape to keep a nearby object and then a distant object in focus is called **accommodation**.

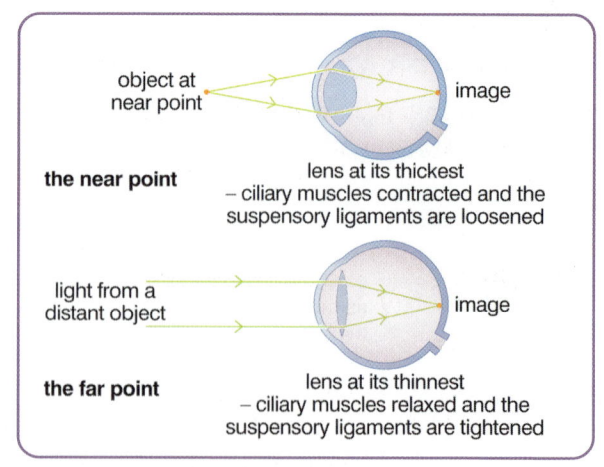

object at near point → image

the near point — lens at its thickest – ciliary muscles contracted and the suspensory ligaments are loosened

light from a distant object → image

the far point — lens at its thinnest – ciliary muscles relaxed and the suspensory ligaments are tightened

Accommodation keeps objects in focus

Humans as organisms

Fact file

★ Human eyes are damaged by ultraviolet light. However, insects' eyes can see in ultraviolet light.

★ A normal eye can see clearly any object from far away (at the **far point**) to 25 cm from the eye (the **near point**).

★ The image of an object on the retina is inverted, but the brain interprets it so you see it the right way up.

Light control

The **iris** controls the amount of light entering the eye. The intensity of light causes a **reflex response**. In bright light:

- the muscle of the iris contracts.

  As a result, the pupil narrows.

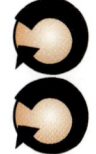

  As a result, the amount of light entering the eye is reduced.

In dim light:

- the muscle of the iris relaxes.

  As a result, the pupil widens.

  As a result, the amount of light entering the eye is increased.

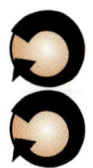

5.7 Hormones

PREVIEW

At the end of this section you will know that:

- chemicals called hormones regulate the activities of the body
- hormones are produced in the tissues of endocrine glands
- endocrine glands are ductless glands – they release their hormones directly into the bloodstream
- hormones circulate in the blood and cause specific effects on the body
- the tissue on which a particular hormone or group of hormones acts is called a target tissue.

The hormonal system

The blood system is the link between a hormone and its **target tissue**. The sequence reads:

$$\text{endocrine gland} \xrightarrow{\text{produces}} \text{hormone} \xrightarrow{\text{circulates}} \text{blood} \xrightarrow{\text{hormone affects}} \text{target tissue}$$

Hormones affect many of the body's activities. For example, the hormones **insulin** and **glucagon** help regulate the level of glucose in the blood and cope with the surge of glucose at mealtimes and when you eat a snack, such as a bar of chocolate.

Fact file

Most hormones produce their effects rather slowly. They bring about long-term changes in the body such as growth and sexual development.

How hormones work

On pages 78–9 is the concept map which revises **hormones**. The numbers on the concept map refer to the checklist below.

Fact file

Hormones called **anabolic steroids** are used illegally by some athletes to improve their performance. The hormones help to develop muscle tissue, giving an unfair advantage over other athletes who do not use them.

Checklist for hormones at work

1 ★ If the pancreas does not produce enough insulin, a condition called **diabetes mellitus** occurs.

  As a result, the glucose level in the blood becomes dangerously high and can cause kidney failure and blindness.

★ People suffering from diabetes (**diabetics**) are taught to inject themselves regularly with insulin to lower their blood glucose level.

★ Glycogen is a polysaccharide whose molecules consist of hundreds of glucose units.

continued on page 80

Humans as organisms

FLIGHT OR FIGHT

Adrenaline at work prepares the body for sudden action.

- brain thinking quickly
- muscles working hard

EFFECTS OF ADRENALINE
- Cells metabolise glucose fast. As a result, more energy is available for sudden action.
- The heart beats more rapidly. As a result, more blood with its load of glucose reaches tissues and organs more rap[idly].
- Blood is diverted to tissues such as the muscles and bra[in].

HORMONE LIST
- adrenaline

CHECK LIST 4

BODY'S WATER CONTENT

Sensory receptors in the brain detect how much water is in the blood.

NOT ENOUGH
Antidiuretic hormone (ADH) is produced from the pituitary gland.
As a result, the walls of the collecting duct of the nephron are more permeable ('leaky') to water.
As a result, water is absorbed back into the body.

LOTS
Reduced production of antidiuretic hormone (ADH) from the pituitary gland.
As a result, most of the surplus water is excreted through the kidneys.

- brain
- pituitary gland
- ADH ✗
- full up!
- iced water
- kidney
- ureter

Excess water is excreted. As a result, large volumes of dilute urine are produced.

- brain
- pituitary gland ADH ✓
- DEAD MAN'S GULCH
- water reabsorbed into the blood

Very little water is excreted. As a result, the urine is scanty and concentrated.

HORMONE LIST
- antidiuretic hormone (ADH)

CHECK LIST 3

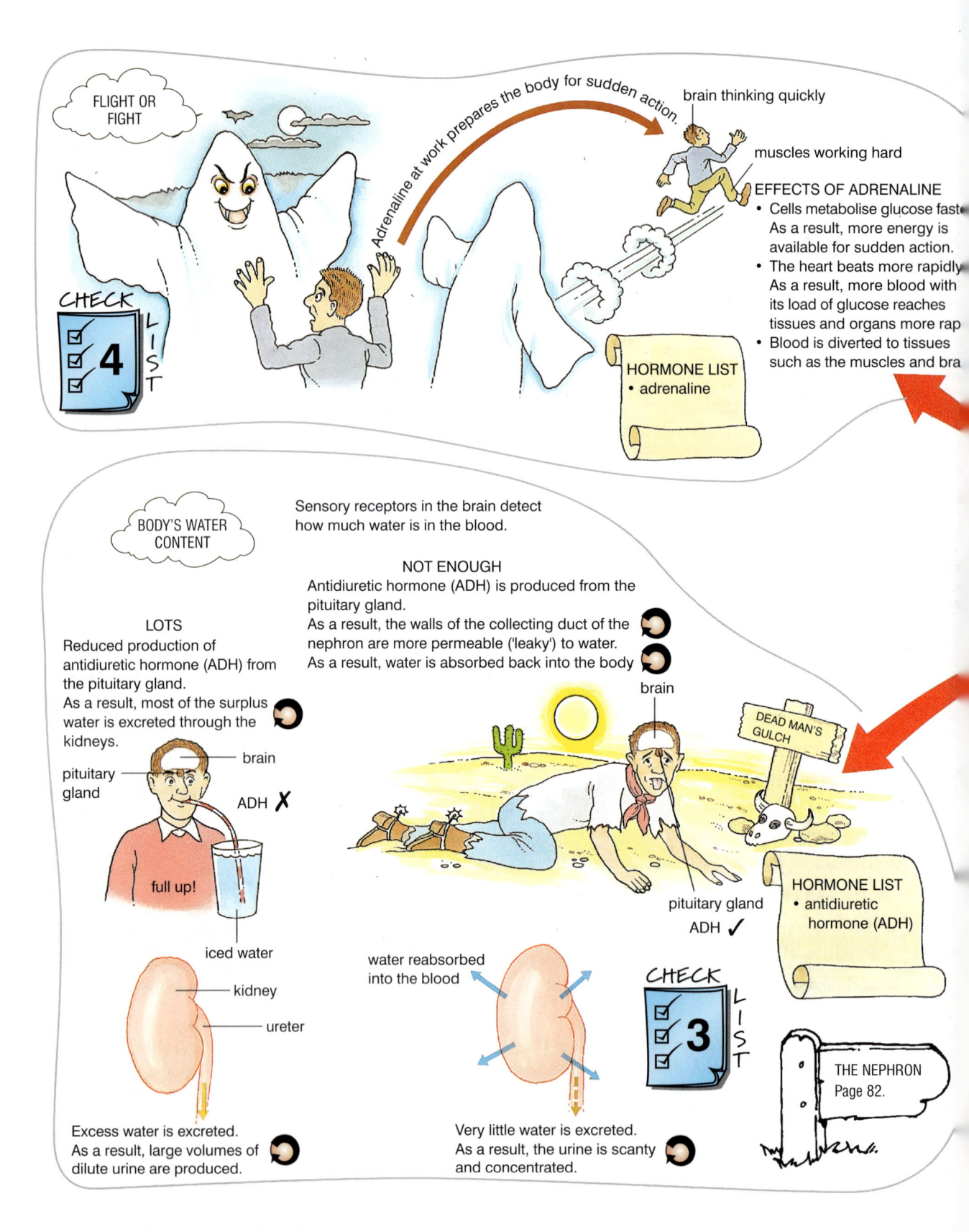

THE NEPHRON Page 82.

Hormones at work (Checklist on pages 77 and 80.)

Humans as organisms

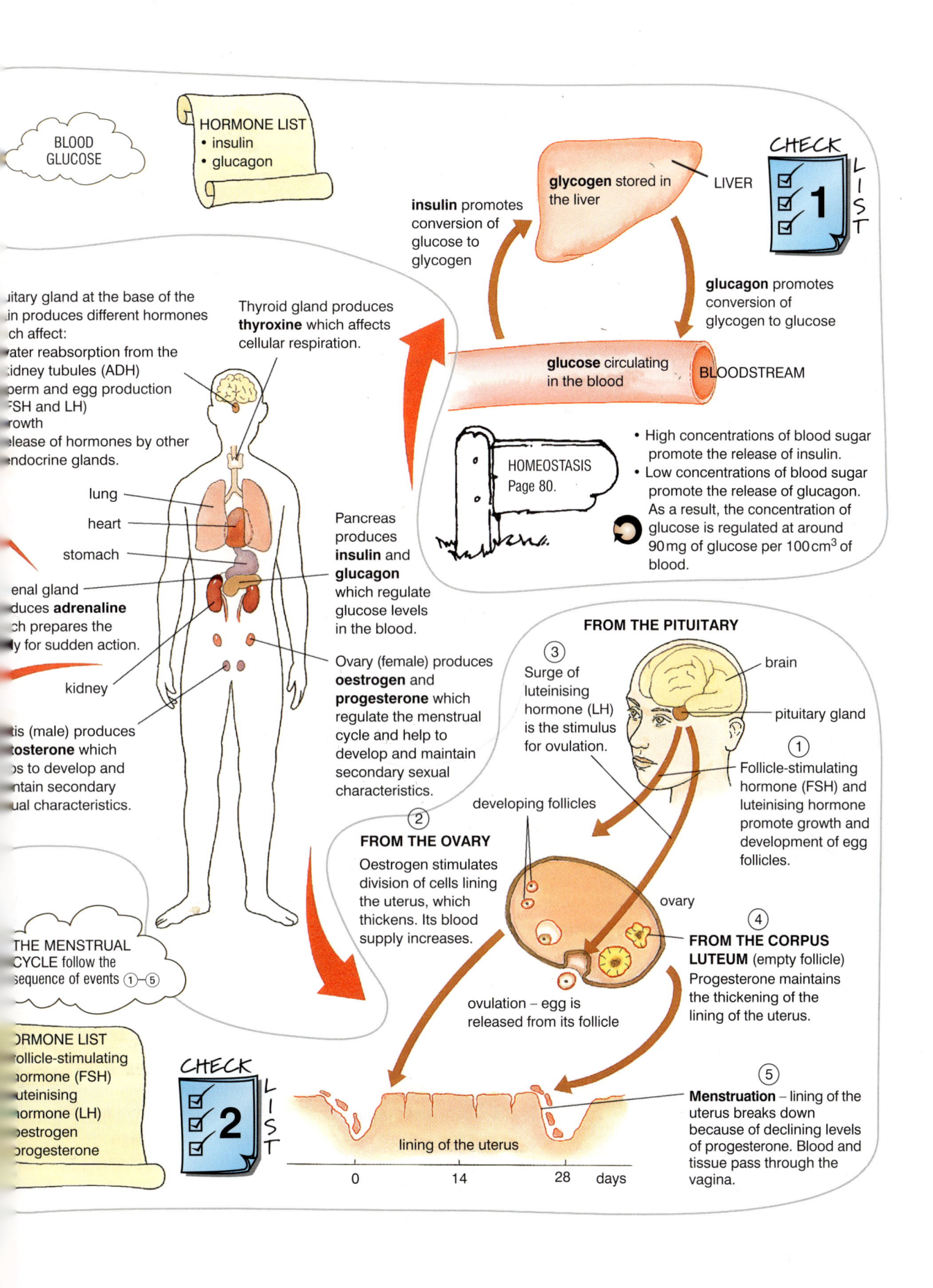

BLOOD GLUCOSE

HORMONE LIST
- insulin
- glucagon

CHECK LIST 1

insulin promotes conversion of glucose to glycogen

glycogen stored in the liver — LIVER

glucagon promotes conversion of glycogen to glucose

glucose circulating in the blood — BLOODSTREAM

HOMEOSTASIS Page 80.

- High concentrations of blood sugar promote the release of insulin.
- Low concentrations of blood sugar promote the release of glucagon. As a result, the concentration of glucose is regulated at around 90 mg of glucose per 100 cm^3 of blood.

...uitary gland at the base of the ...in produces different hormones ...ch affect:
- ...ater reabsorption from the ...idney tubules (ADH)
- ...perm and egg production (FSH and LH)
- ...rowth
- ...elease of hormones by other ...endocrine glands.

lung
heart
stomach

...enal gland ...duces **adrenaline** ...ch prepares the ...y for sudden action.

kidney

...tis (male) produces ...**tosterone** which ...s to develop and ...tain secondary ...ual characteristics.

Thyroid gland produces **thyroxine** which affects cellular respiration.

Pancreas produces **insulin** and **glucagon** which regulate glucose levels in the blood.

Ovary (female) produces **oestrogen** and **progesterone** which regulate the menstrual cycle and help to develop and maintain secondary sexual characteristics.

...THE MENSTRUAL CYCLE follow the ...sequence of events ①–⑤

HORMONE LIST
- ...ollicle-stimulating ...hormone (FSH)
- ...uteinising ...hormone (LH)
- ...estrogen
- ...rogesterone

CHECK LIST 2

FROM THE PITUITARY

③ Surge of luteinising hormone (LH) is the stimulus for ovulation.

brain
pituitary gland

① Follicle-stimulating hormone (FSH) and luteinising hormone promote growth and development of egg follicles.

developing follicles

② **FROM THE OVARY**
Oestrogen stimulates division of cells lining the uterus, which thickens. Its blood supply increases.

ovary

④ **FROM THE CORPUS LUTEUM** (empty follicle)
Progesterone maintains the thickening of the lining of the uterus.

ovulation – egg is released from its follicle

⑤ **Menstruation** – lining of the uterus breaks down because of declining levels of progesterone. Blood and tissue pass through the vagina.

lining of the uterus

0   14   28   days

Humans as organisms

2 ★ The human female usually produces one mature egg each month from the onset of **puberty** (age 11–14 years) to the approach of the menopause (age about 45 years). Egg production becomes more irregular and then stops at the **menopause** (average age around 51 years).

★ The contraceptive pill contains one or both of the hormones oestrogen and progesterone. The hormones stop the ovaries from producing eggs.

★ Treatment with **fertility drugs** aims to stimulate egg development by raising the level of follicle-stimulating hormone (FSH) in the body.

3 ★ **Diuresis** refers to the production of urine. Antidiuretic hormone (ADH) counteracts diuresis.

As a result, less urine leaves the body.

★ Ethanol (the alcohol in beer, wine and spirits) increases diuresis.

4 ★ Unlike most hormones, adrenaline produces its effect very quickly.

As a result, the body is able to respond to sudden shock or danger.

Fact file

Secondary sexual characteristics are the physical features which distinguish boys from girls. Testosterone helps develop and maintain the secondary sexual characteristics of boys. Oestrogen and progesterone help develop and maintain the secondary sexual characteristics of girls.

guys	gals
pubic hair develops	pubic hair develops
penis gets larger	breasts develop and fat is laid down around the thighs
voice breaks	menstruation starts
hair grows on armpits, chest, face and legs	hair grows on armpits

Secondary sexual characteristics

5.8 Maintaining the internal environment

PREVIEW

At the end of this section you will:
- understand that for cells to work efficiently, the composition of the tissue fluid which surrounds them should be kept fairly constant
- know about the important systems which maintain a constant environment in the body: the pancreas and liver (blood glucose), the kidneys (water content) and the skin (temperature).

Conditions in the body

The cells of the body work efficiently when they are:
- at an appropriate temperature
- supplied with an appropriate mixture and concentration of substances
- supplied with sufficient water
- at an appropriate acidity/alkalinity (pH).

These conditions are part of the body's **internal environment**. Different mechanisms help regulate the body, keeping its internal environment fairly constant. Keeping conditions constant is called **homeostasis**.

★ The **skin** regulates the body's temperature.

★ The **kidneys** regulate the concentration of salts in the blood, and the water content of the body.

★ The **liver** and **pancreas** regulate the concentration of sugar in the blood.

Homeostasis

Homeostasis depends on **negative feedback** mechanisms, which enable different processes to correct themselves when they change. In other words, the processes of life are **self-adjusting**. A level of a chemical or a temperature that deviates from a **set point** (a normal value) is returned to that set point. The menstrual cycle pictured on page 79 illustrates the principles. Rising levels of FSH and luteinising hormone stimulate the ovaries to produce the hormone oestrogen. Increasing levels of oestrogen feed back negatively, inhibiting further release of follicle-stimulating hormone. The level of the hormone returns to normal, its role of promoting the growth of egg follicles complete.

On pages 82–3 is the concept map for **homeostasis**. The numbers on the concept map refer to the checklist of points below. Study the concept map and its checklist carefully.

Checklist for homeostasis

1 ★ Each kidney consists of about 1 million tiny tubules called **nephrons**.

   ★ The nephron is the working unit of the kidney. It is the structure that brings about homeostatic control of the:
   - concentration of salts in the blood
   - water content of the body.

   The kidney tubules are also responsible for the excretion of urea and other wastes from the body.

2 ★ Hair is made of the protein keratin.

   ★ **Goose pimples** are bumps on the skin formed when empty hair follicles contract in response to cold.

Fact file

Liver metabolism releases a lot of heat energy, which is distributed all over the body by the blood. Humans (and other mammals and birds) have a high metabolic rate, which releases a large amount of heat. This is why mammals and birds are able to keep body temperature constant, even if the temperature of the environment changes. We say that they are **warm blooded**. Warm bloodedness means that the activity of enzymes (and therefore the activity of cells and the body as a whole) is at the optimum (most efficient) irrespective of the temperature of the surroundings.

5.9 Health and disease

> **PREVIEW**
>
> At the end of this section you will:
> - be able to distinguish between different categories of disease
> - know about the defence mechanisms of the body
> - understand the harmful effects of smoking
> - understand the effects of drug abuse and solvent abuse on the body.

What is disease?

There are several categories of disease.

Infectious diseases are caused by a range of organisms:
- **bacteria**, for example, cause cholera, typhoid fever, tuberculosis, syphilis, gonorrhoea
- **viruses**, for example, cause AIDS, 'flu, poliomyelitis, German measles
- **fungi**, for example, cause thrush, athlete's foot, ringworm
- **protists**, for example, cause malaria, sleeping sickness.

Non-infectious diseases develop because the body is not working properly.

★ **cancer** – the uncontrolled division of cells leads to the development of a cancerous growth (**tumour**)

★ **degenerative diseases** – organs and tissues work less well with wear and tear, for example, joints become arthritic and sight and hearing deteriorate with age

★ **allergies** – reactions to substances which are normally harmless, for example, sensitivity to pollen and dust causes **hay fever**

★ **deficiency** – a poor diet may deprive the body of vitamins and other essential substances, for example scurvy (deficiency of vitamin C), rickets (deficiency of vitamin D), kwashiorkor (deficiency of protein).

Humans as organisms

CONTROLLING WATER CONTENT

Labels on kidney cross-section: cortex, medulla, nephron, ureter

Labels on torso diagram:
- vena cava
- aorta
- diaphragm
- left kidney
- renal artery } the blood supply to the kidneys
- renal vein
- ureter – urine passes through the ureter from each kidney to the bladder
- bladder – stores urine
- sphincter muscle – keeps the bladder closed. When it contracts, the bladder opens and urine passes to the outside.
- urethra – tube through which urine passes to the outside

Section lengthways through a kidney. Two zones of tissue, the cortex and the medulla, can be seen. The horseshoe-shaped Bowman's capsule is in the cortex. The rest of the nephron dips down into the medulla. (The nephron is drawn much larger than life.)

CHECK LIST 1

THE NEPHRON AT WORK

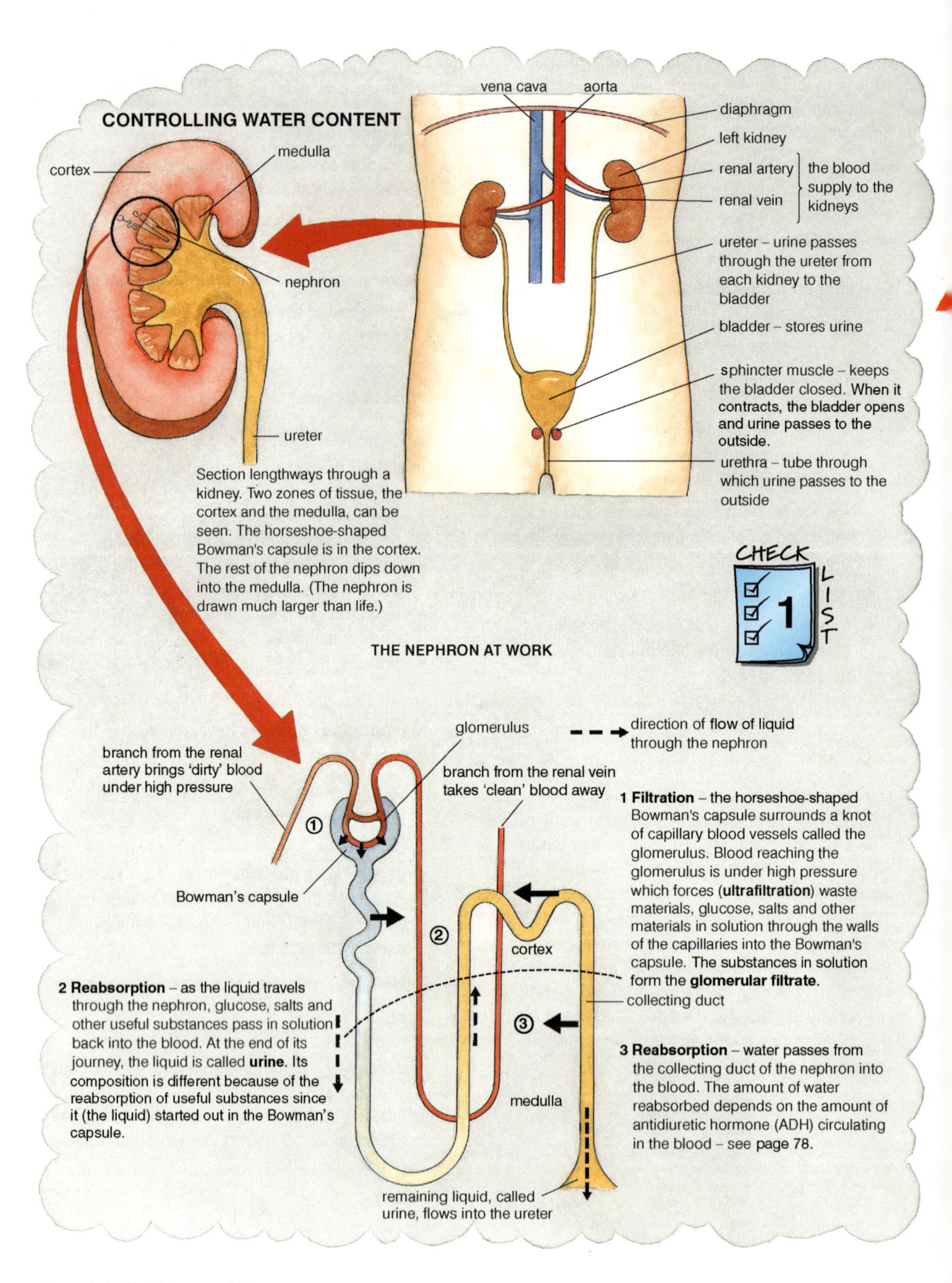

Labels: glomerulus; branch from the renal artery brings 'dirty' blood under high pressure; branch from the renal vein takes 'clean' blood away; Bowman's capsule; cortex; medulla; collecting duct; remaining liquid, called urine, flows into the ureter

- - -> direction of flow of liquid through the nephron

1 Filtration – the horseshoe-shaped Bowman's capsule surrounds a knot of capillary blood vessels called the glomerulus. Blood reaching the glomerulus is under high pressure which forces (**ultrafiltration**) waste materials, glucose, salts and other materials in solution through the walls of the capillaries into the Bowman's capsule. The substances in solution form the **glomerular filtrate**.

2 Reabsorption – as the liquid travels through the nephron, glucose, salts and other useful substances pass in solution back into the blood. At the end of its journey, the liquid is called **urine**. Its composition is different because of the reabsorption of useful substances since it (the liquid) started out in the Bowman's capsule.

3 Reabsorption – water passes from the collecting duct of the nephron into the blood. The amount of water reabsorbed depends on the amount of antidiuretic hormone (ADH) circulating in the blood – see page 78.

Homeostasis (Checklist on page 81.)

Humans as organisms

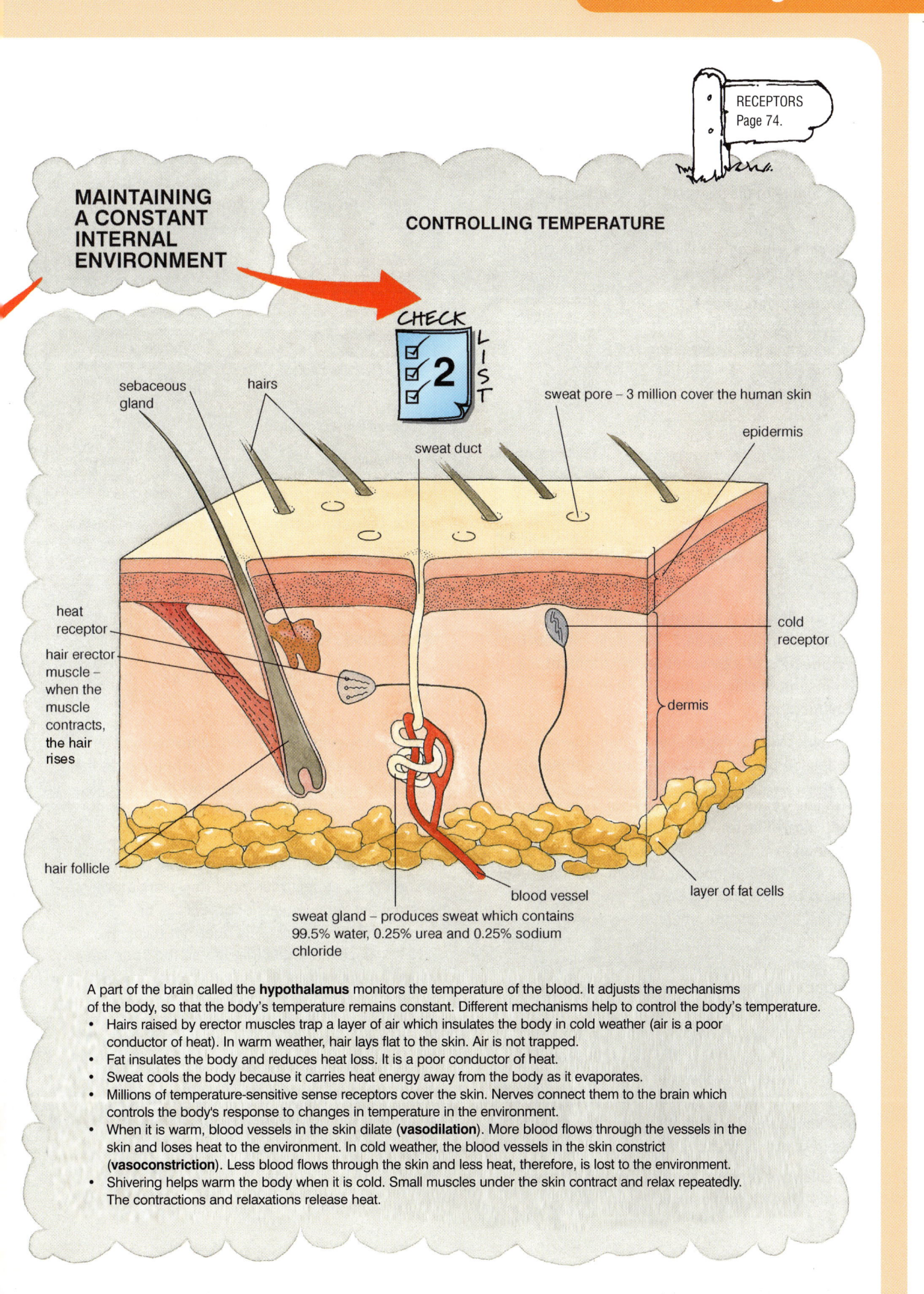

RECEPTORS
Page 74.

MAINTAINING A CONSTANT INTERNAL ENVIRONMENT

CONTROLLING TEMPERATURE

CHECK LIST 2

Labels on diagram:
- sebaceous gland
- hairs
- sweat duct
- sweat pore – 3 million cover the human skin
- epidermis
- heat receptor
- hair erector muscle – when the muscle contracts, the hair rises
- cold receptor
- dermis
- hair follicle
- blood vessel
- sweat gland – produces sweat which contains 99.5% water, 0.25% urea and 0.25% sodium chloride
- layer of fat cells

A part of the brain called the **hypothalamus** monitors the temperature of the blood. It adjusts the mechanisms of the body, so that the body's temperature remains constant. Different mechanisms help to control the body's temperature.
- Hairs raised by erector muscles trap a layer of air which insulates the body in cold weather (air is a poor conductor of heat). In warm weather, hair lays flat to the skin. Air is not trapped.
- Fat insulates the body and reduces heat loss. It is a poor conductor of heat.
- Sweat cools the body because it carries heat energy away from the body as it evaporates.
- Millions of temperature-sensitive sense receptors cover the skin. Nerves connect them to the brain which controls the body's response to changes in temperature in the environment.
- When it is warm, blood vessels in the skin dilate (**vasodilation**). More blood flows through the vessels in the skin and loses heat to the environment. In cold weather, the blood vessels in the skin constrict (**vasoconstriction**). Less blood flows through the skin and less heat, therefore, is lost to the environment.
- Shivering helps warm the body when it is cold. Small muscles under the skin contract and relax repeatedly. The contractions and relaxations release heat.

Humans as organisms

Genetic disorders result from genetic defects and may be inherited. About 4000 genetic disorders affect humans. Genetic make-up also influences our vulnerability to diseases such as diabetes and heart disease.

★ **Down's syndrome** is caused by an extra copy of chromosome 21.

★ **Sickle-cell anaemia** is caused by a mutation of the gene (**allele**) controlling the synthesis of the blood pigment haemoglobin.

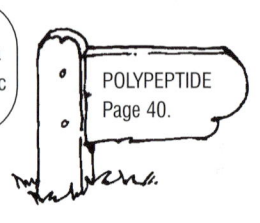

MUTATION Page 43.

Alleles are pairs of genes which control a particular characteristic Page 96.

POLYPEPTIDE Page 40.

★ **Cystic fibrosis** is caused by the mutation of an allele on chromosome 7. The allele controls the production of a polypeptide important for the transport of chloride ions (Cl^-) across the cell membrane.

★ **Haemophilia** is caused by the mutation of an allele on the X chromosome, as described below.

The allele on the X chromosome normally controls production of **factor VIII**, a substance required for the blood to clot. The defective allele is recessive. The Y chromosome does not carry a dominant allele to mask the effect of the defective recessive allele on the X chromosome. Therefore a man with the defective allele produces no factor VIII, and suffers from haemophilia. For a woman to suffer from haemophilia, she would have to receive the recessive allele from both her father and her mother – a rare occurrence. A woman who has the defective allele on *one* of the X chromosomes is called a **carrier**. She does not suffer from haemophilia because the normal allele on the other X chromosome is dominant and therefore masks the effect of the recessive allele.

Muscular dystrophy is another genetic disease linked to the X chromosome.

Fighting disease

The body's natural defences against disease are shown below. **Physical** barriers and **chemical** barriers keep us healthy for most of our lives.

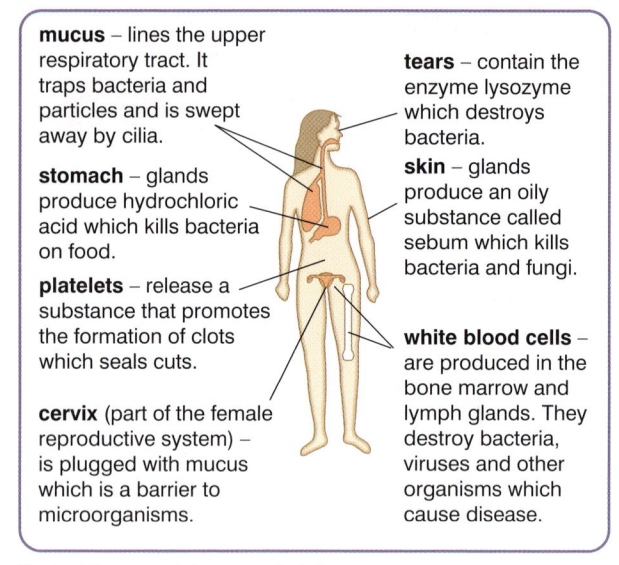

- **mucus** – lines the upper respiratory tract. It traps bacteria and particles and is swept away by cilia.
- **stomach** – glands produce hydrochloric acid which kills bacteria on food.
- **platelets** – release a substance that promotes the formation of clots which seals cuts.
- **cervix** (part of the female reproductive system) – is plugged with mucus which is a barrier to microorganisms.
- **tears** – contain the enzyme lysozyme which destroys bacteria.
- **skin** – glands produce an oily substance called sebum which kills bacteria and fungi.
- **white blood cells** – are produced in the bone marrow and lymph glands. They destroy bacteria, viruses and other organisms which cause disease.

The body's natural defences against disease

White blood cells

Bacteria, viruses and other microorganisms may infect the blood and tissues of the body and cause disease. Microorganisms that cause disease are called **pathogens**. Some release **toxins** (poisons); others damage and destroy cells. Their effects make us feel unwell. Pathogens are more likely to pass from person to person when people are crowded together in unhygienic conditions.

Two types of white blood cell, **lymphocytes** and **phagocytes**, protect the body. They work quickly to destroy bacteria, viruses or other cells or substances which the body does not recognise as its own. Such materials 'foreign' to the body are called **antigens**.

There are two types of lymphocyte.

★ **B-lymphocytes** produce **antibodies** which are proteins that attack antigens.

★ **T-lymphocytes** do not produce antibodies. Instead they bind with an antigen and destroy it.

Humans as organisms

Phagocytes in the blood engulf and destroy antigens. Some phagocytes pass through the walls of blood vessels and migrate through tissues to attack antigens that have entered the body through cuts or scratches. Their action causes an **inflammatory response** – swelling, redness and heat as the phagocytes destroy the invading antigens at the site of the infection. The diagram below shows B-lymphocytes and phagocytes at work in the blood.

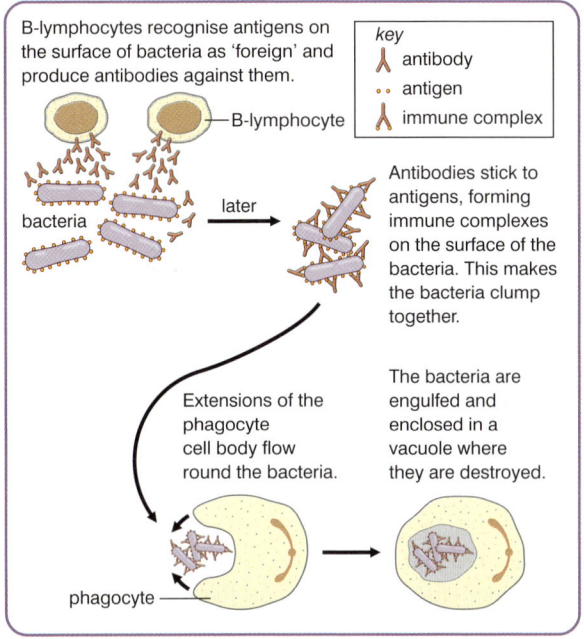

B-lymphocytes produce antibodies which damage bacteria 'foreign' to the body (antigens). Phagocytes engulf the bacteria. (The different cells and antibodies are not drawn to scale.)

Immunisation

Immunisation (or **vaccination**) promotes active immunity against a pathogen (or group of pathogens). It involves you having an injection or swallowing some substance. The substance injected or swallowed is called a **vaccine**.

A vaccine contains antigens from a particular pathogen (or group of pathogens in the case of a multiple vaccine). The antigens stimulate the B-lymphocytes of the person vaccinated to produce antibodies against the particular pathogen (or group of pathogens). So, when the active, harmful pathogen (or pathogens) invade the body, the antibodies made in response to the vaccine destroy it (or them).

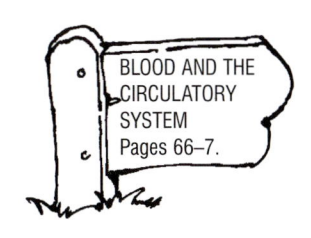

BLOOD AND THE CIRCULATORY SYSTEM Pages 66–7.

Kidney disease

If a person's kidneys are not working (**kidney failure**) then:
- poisonous urea accumulates in the blood
- water accumulates in the tissues of the body.

As a result, the person dies unless treated quickly.

Kidney failure is usually treated by:
- **dialysis** – a **kidney machine** removes urea and other waste substances from the patient's blood. The diagram below shows you how the kidney machine works.

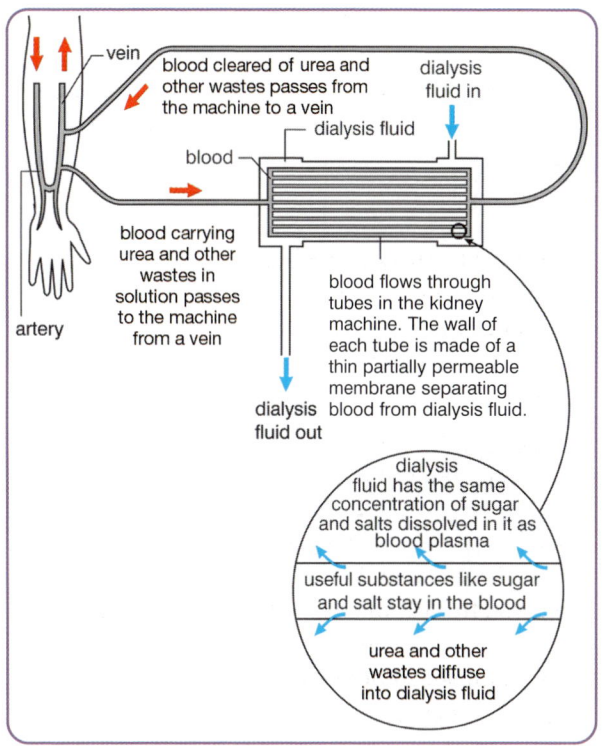

How a kidney machine works

- **transplant surgery** – a healthy kidney taken from a person (the donor) who has just died or from a living person (often a close relative) who wants to help the patient is put inside the patient's body. The transplanted kidney is connected to the blood supply and to the bladder.

Humans as organisms

The table below summarises the benefits and limitations of dialysis and transplant surgery.

dialysis	transplant surgery
Benefits The patient • does not have to take drugs for a lifetime • may be treated more quickly because the availability of kidney machines is restricted only by money	The patient • can enjoy a normal diet • does not depend on a kidney machine • has the freedom of a normal life
Limitations The patient • is restricted to eating a limited diet • must always have easy access to a kidney machine • must be treated two or three times a week. Each treatment takes about 10 hours	The patient • is vulnerable to the body rejecting the new kidney. Transplanting a kidney from a close relative of the patient reduces the risk of rejection • must for their lifetime take drugs which reduce the risk of rejection • is vulnerable to infections because the anti-rejection drugs reduce resistance to disease-causing organisms (e.g. bacteria) • may have to wait for a suitable kidney because donor kidneys are in short supply

Diseases of the upper respiratory tract and lungs

Despite its filtering and cleaning mechanisms, the upper respiratory tract may become infected by disease-causing microorganisms. Infection of the:
- throat (pharynx) is called **pharyngitis**
- voicebox (larynx) is called **laryngitis**
- windpipe (trachea) is called **tracheitis**
- bronchi and bronchioles is called **bronchitis**.

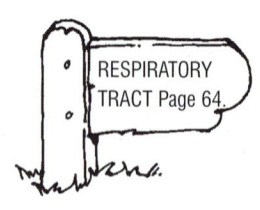

RESPIRATORY TRACT Page 64.

Pneumonia is an infection of the lungs caused by a particular type of bacterium. In pneumonia:
- fluid collects in the lungs.

  As a result, the surface area available for the absorption of oxygen is reduced.

  As a result, the patient becomes breathless.

Pleurisy is an infection of the pleural membranes caused by a particular type of bacterium. In pleurisy:
- infection makes the membranes rough.

  As a result, there is pain when the membranes rub together.

Antibiotic drugs are used to treat pneumonia and pleurisy.

Cystic fibrosis is an inherited condition which affects the pancreas and the bronchioles of the lungs. **Gene therapy** is one approach to treating cystic fibrosis. The healthy gene for normal bronchioles (and pancreas) is taken up into fatty droplets called **liposomes**. The liposomes in a fine aerosol are then sprayed deep into the lungs of the patient. The liposomes may fuse with the patient's alveoli and healthy genes may enter the cells and do their work. 'May', however, is the important word. Treatment is not always successful, and when it is, the benefits are often short lived.

Smoking

Smoking cigarettes is a major cause of lung cancer and heart disease. Cigarette smoke is acidic and contains various substances harmful to health.

★ **Nicotine** is a powerful drug which increases the heart rate and blood pressure.

★ **Carbon monoxide** is a poisonous gas which combines 300 times more readily with haemoglobin than oxygen does.

  As a result, the level of oxygen in the blood is reduced.

★ **Tar** is a mixture of many compounds, some of which cause cancer (are **carcinogens**).

Some substances in cigarette smoke irritate the membrane lining the upper respiratory tract.

As a result, extra mucus (phlegm) forms in the trachea and bronchi.

As a result, the person may develop 'smoker's cough'. Coughing helps remove the excess phlegm.

Other substances in cigarette smoke stop the cilia from beating.

As a result, particles and microorganisms enter the lungs.

As a result, the risk of infection is increased.

Emphysema is caused by cells of the lungs producing protein – digesting enzymes which destroy the walls of the alveoli.

As a result, the surface area available for the absorption of oxygen is reduced.

As a result, the person becomes breathless.

Lung cancer is caused by the carcinogens in tar. Abnormal cell division in lung tissue leads to the development of tumours (growths) which may be difficult to cure. Cancer cells may break away from the tumours and circulate in the blood to start **secondary** growths elsewhere in the body.

The smoking habit

Smoking cigarettes was fashionable in the early 1900s, and many people became smokers. Scientists soon suspected a link between smoking cigarettes and lung cancer.

Today there are fewer smokers than non-smokers in the United Kingdom. However, of the people who do smoke, there are many young people. SMOKING IS A MUG'S GAME – DO NOT START!

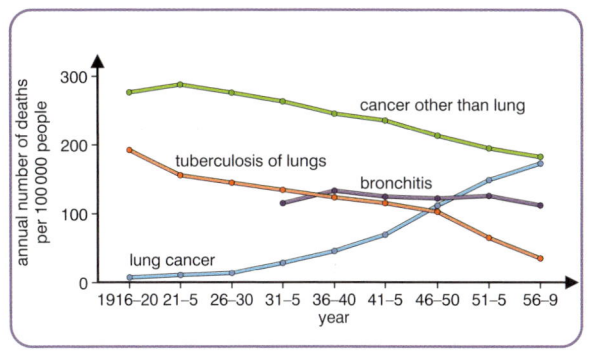

Deaths from lung cancer increased sharply in England and Wales from 1916 to 1960, which was the period when more and more people were smoking cigarettes. Other types of lung disease were declining.

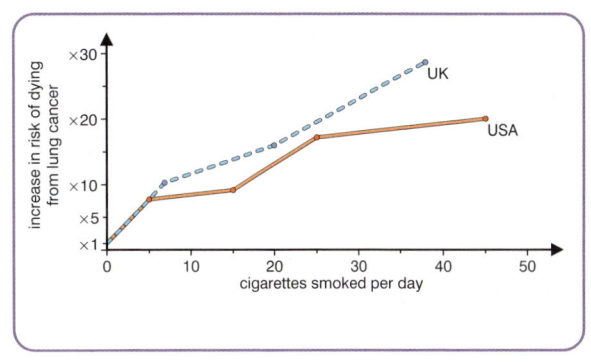

Studies have shown that the more cigarettes smoked, the greater is the risk of dying from lung cancer.

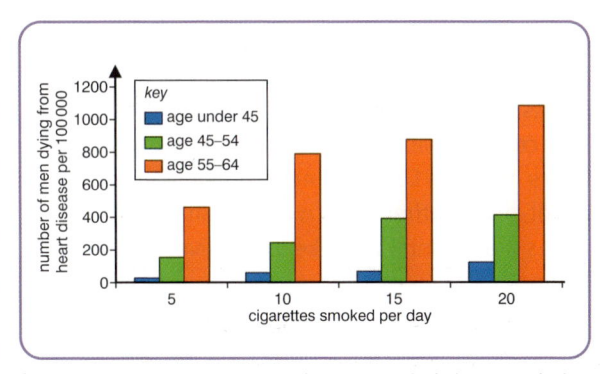

Studies have shown that the more cigarettes smoked, the greater is the risk of dying from heart disease.

REMEMBER – IF YOU DO SMOKE YOU CAN GIVE IT UP. Advice and help are available.

Humans as organisms

Drugs

Drugs are used to help in the fight against disease. For example:
- **antibiotics** are used to attack the different types of bacteria that cause disease
- **analgesics** are drugs that reduce pain (painkillers).

Some drugs may be **abused**. This means they are used for non-medical purposes.

If drugs that affect the nervous system are taken under the wrong circumstances (abused), people can become **addicted** to them, wanting more and more and not caring about the damage caused to the body. **Cocaine** and **heroin** are **addictive** drugs; so too are alcohol and nicotine in tobacco. Cocaine and heroin may be smoked or injected into a vein, causing the 'high' that addicts crave. Injecting the drugs is particularly risky. If addicts share syringes and needles ('**equipment**') when injecting drugs, they risk infection with HIV and hepatitis B virus if the 'equipment' is contaminated with virus-infected blood.

Alcohol

Ethanol (the alcohol in beers, wine and spirits) depresses the activity of the nervous system. Small amounts affect the **cortex** of the brain, which controls judgement. Large quantities affect the **motor cortex**, which controls movement. Even more impairs memory. Drinking increasing amounts of alcohol affects other areas of the brain until it reaches brain centres that keep us alive. Death may follow.

Drinking too much alcohol is one cause of disease of the heart and liver (**cirrhosis**). The liver breaks down (metabolises) alcohol. The link between heavy drinking and cirrhosis is well established.

Solvents

Glues, paints, nail varnish and cleaning fluids (dry cleaners) contain volatile solvents such as esters and ethanol. These are liquids in which other substances dissolve, and which readily produce a vapour at room temperature. Breathing them in gives a warm sense of well-being, but also produces dangerous disorientation. Long-term solvent abuse can damage the brain, kidneys and liver.

BRAIN Page 73.

Humans as organisms

ROUND UP

How much have you improved? Work out your improvement index on page 112.

1. Simple tests identify the nutrients in different foods. Match the nutrient in column **A** with the test result that identifies the nutrient in column **B**.

A nutrients	B test results
starch	forms a milky emulsion when mixed with warm dilute ethanol
glucose	produces a violet/purple colour when mixed with dilute sodium hydroxide and a few drops of copper sulphate solution
fat	produces a blue/black colour when mixed with a few drops of iodine solution
protein	produces an orange/red colour when heated with Benedict's solution [4]

2. Match each enzyme in column **A** with its role in digestion in column **B**.

A enzymes	B roles
amylase	digests maltose to glucose
pepsin	digests fat to fatty acids and glycerol
lipase	digests starch to maltose
maltase	digests protein to polypeptides [4]

3. Complete the following paragraph using the words below. Each word may be used once, more than once or not at all.

   thin   exhalation   fat   oxygen   inhalation   moist   carbon dioxide   exchange   alveoli   surface area

   The uptake of _____ and removal of _____ occur in the _____ of the lungs. These provide a large _____ for efficient gas _____. They are _____-walled, have an excellent blood supply, are _____ and kept well supplied with air by breathing. _____ takes air into the lungs; _____ removes air from the lungs. [9]

4. Distinguish between the following pairs of terms:
   a) oxygenated and deoxygenated blood [4]
   b) antibody and antigen [5]
   c) HIV and AIDS [3]
   d) haemoglobin and haemophilia [5]
   e) thrombus and thrombosis. [3]

5. The different parts of a motor nerve cell are listed in column **A**. Match each part with its description in column **B**.

A parts of a cell	B descriptions
axon	minute electrical disturbance
dendrite	boosts the transmission of nerve impulses
myelin sheath	transmits nerve impulses from the cell body
nerve impulse	carries nerve impulses to the cell body [4]

6. Explain the differences between the following pairs of terms:
   a) blind spot and fovea
   b) pupil and iris
   c) cornea and retina. [6]

7. How do endocrine glands differ from other glands in the body? [2]

8. Briefly explain how antidiuretic hormone (ADH) keeps the water content of the body steady. [2]

9. Briefly explain
   a) why raised body hair helps us keep warm [3]
   b) why sweating helps us keep cool. [2]

10. Identify the cause of each disease in the list by writing either **B** (for bacterium) or **V** (for virus) next to each one.

    cholera   AIDS   syphilis   'flu   pneumonia [5]

11. Identify the substances in cigarette smoke which are harmful to health. Briefly explain why they are harmful. [6]

Well done if you've improved. Don't worry if you haven't. Take a break and try again.

Chapter 6 Inheritance and evolution

How much do you already know? Work out your score on pages 112–13.

Test yourself

1. The diagram shows the reproductive system of a man. Name parts A–E. [5]

2. Match each structure in column **A** with its correct description in column **B**.

A structures	B descriptions
corm	a horizontal stem running above ground
runner	a short, swollen underground stem
tuber	a large underground bud
bulb	a swelling at the end of a rhizome

   [4]

3. In humans, the gene for brown eyes (**B**) is dominant to the gene for blue eyes (**b**).
   a) Using the symbols **B** and **b**, state the genotypes of the children that could be born from a marriage between a heterozygous father and a blue-eyed mother. [2]
   b) State whether the children are brown eyed or blue eyed. [2]

4. Distinguish between the following:
   a) restriction enzyme and ligase (splicing enzyme) [7]
   b) biotechnology and genetic engineering [5]
   c) batch culture and continuous culture. [7]

5. Why are acquired characteristics not inherited? [3]

6. List the different sources of variation in living things. [6]

7. Why does sexual reproduction produce much more genetic variation than asexual reproduction? [5]

8. Distinguish between the following terms:
   a) ancestors and descendants [1]
   b) adaptation and extinction [2]
   c) evolution and natural selection. [3]

9. How are fossils formed? [4]

6.1 Reproduction

PREVIEW

At the end of this section you will:
- know that reproduction gives rise to offspring
- understand that sexual reproduction gives rise to variation in offspring and that asexual reproduction gives rise to identical offspring
- be able to identify the components of the human reproductive system
- know how sexual reproduction occurs in humans and in flowering plants.

Sexual or asexual?

GENES AND ALLELES, GENETICS Pages 43 and 96.

Reproduction passes genetic material from parents to their offspring:

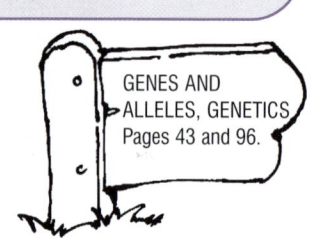

★ In **sexual reproduction**, *two* parents (male and female) produce **gametes** (sex cells). Gametes are formed by **meiosis**. The male gametes are **sperm**. The female gametes are **eggs**. An egg is **fertilised** when a sperm fuses with it. The fertilised egg cell is called a **zygote**. The zygote divides repeatedly by **mitosis**, producing a ball of cells called an **embryo** which develops into the new individual. The offspring formed by sexual reproduction inherit one of each pair of alleles (genes) from each parent, and are genetically *different* from one another (except identical twins) and from their parents. The term **variation** refers to the differences.

IMPORTANT ANNOUNCEMENT
Section 3.3 about meiosis and mitosis is **REALLY** important to your understanding of sexual and asexual reproduction.

Inheritance and evolution

★ In **asexual reproduction**, *one* parent divides by **mitosis**. The daughter cells produced divide by mitosis and develop into new individuals. These offspring are genetically *identical* to one another and to their parent because DNA replicates exact copies of itself during mitosis.

Sexual reproduction in humans and flowering plants

REPLICATION Page 42.

How much do you recall about the structure of the reproductive organs in flowering plants and humans? **Remember** that **flowers** are shoots which are specialised for reproduction. The **genitalia** are the visible parts of the human reproductive system.

Checklist for reproduction

1 ★ The testes hang down between the legs.

   As a result, the testes are protected from injury.

   ★ The position of the testes keeps them about 3 °C lower than body temperature.

   As a result, sperm develop properly in the slightly cooler conditions.

   ★ A woman's genitalia cover and protect the opening to the rest of the reproductive system inside her body.

2 ★ A fertilised egg is called a **zygote**. It develops into a new individual. The sequence reads as follows:

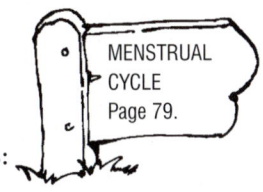

MENSTRUAL CYCLE Page 79.

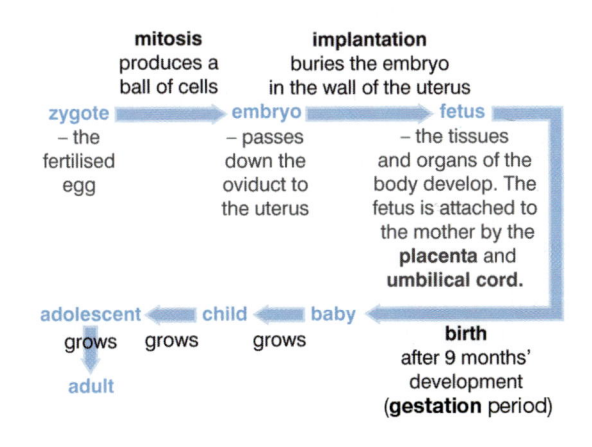

mitosis produces a ball of cells — **implantation** buries the embryo in the wall of the uterus

zygote – the fertilised egg → **embryo** – passes down the oviduct to the uterus → **fetus** – the tissues and organs of the body develop. The fetus is attached to the mother by the **placenta** and **umbilical cord**.

adolescent ← child ← baby ← **birth** after 9 months' development (**gestation** period)
grows grows grows
↓
adult

★ In humans, pregnancy usually results in the birth of only one baby. However, sometimes **twins** are born. The diagram below shows the alternatives.

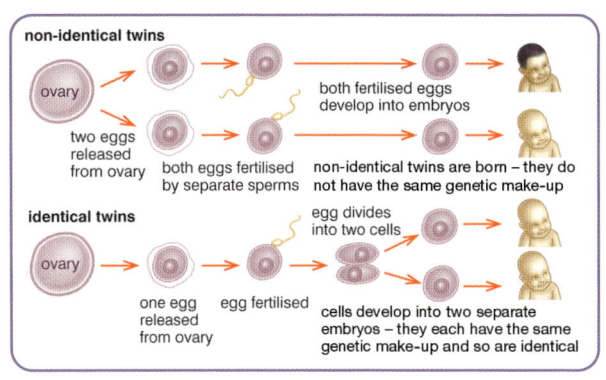

non-identical twins
ovary → two eggs released from ovary → both eggs fertilised by separate sperms → both fertilised eggs develop into embryos → non-identical twins are born – they do not have the same genetic make-up

identical twins
ovary → one egg released from ovary → egg fertilised → egg divides into two cells → cells develop into two separate embryos – they each have the same genetic make-up and so are identical

Producing twins

★ Cells from a developing animal embryo may be split apart before they become specialised. The process, called **embryo cloning**, produces many genetically identical copies (**clones**) of the animal. The identical embryos may then be transplanted into host mothers. The embryos develop normally, resulting in genetically identical offspring. In this way, beneficial characteristics, such as milk-producing abilities, are conserved from generation to generation.

★ Clones of animals can also be produced by inserting the nuclei of the body cells of an animal into its egg cells after the nucleus of each egg cell has been removed. Each egg cell, with the new body nucleus in place, is 'tricked' into developing as if it had been fertilised. Since the nuclei of the animal's body cells are genetically identical, the offspring that result from the treated egg cells are also genetically identical, forming a clone.

3 ★ **Contraception** aims to prevent pregnancy by:
  • preventing sperm from reaching the egg, or
  • preventing eggs from being produced, or
  • preventing the fertilised egg from developing in the uterus.

4 ★ In flowering plants, sexual reproduction involves **pollination**, **fertilisation** and the formation of **fruits** and **seeds**. The diagram at the top of page 92 shows the sequence.

91

Inheritance and evolution

Pollination
is the transfer of pollen from the anther to the stigma.

* **Cross-pollination** is the transfer of pollen between anthers and stigma(s) of different plants.

* **Self-pollination** is the transfer of pollen between the anthers and stigma(s) on the same plant.

Fertilisation
is the fusion of a male sex nucleus with the female egg nucleus. The male sex nucleus passes down the **pollen tube** which grows from a pollen grain.

Seed
is formed from the fertilised egg. It contains the embryo plant with its food store. The **fruit** (usually formed from the wall of the ovary) surrounds and protects the seed.

Remember that asexual reproduction depends on mitosis. It gives rise to **genetically identical** individuals, because DNA replicates during mitosis. This process passes on exact copies of the parent's genetic material to the daughter cells.

replication of DNA → exact copy of parent's genetic material is inherited → develop

parent cells ⇒ mitosis ⇒ daughter cells ⇒ offspring

Remember that genetically identical individuals are called **clones** (see page 91).

Vegetative reproduction

Different parts of flowering plants can reproduce asexually. They are called the **vegetative parts** and are formed from the **root**, **leaf** or **stem**. Asexual reproduction in flowering plants is sometimes called **vegetative reproduction**. Since the new plants come from a single parent, and develop as a result of mitosis, they are genetically the same and are therefore **clones**.

The vegetative parts of plants store food. The stored food is used for the development of the new plant(s). We sometimes eat the organs which store the food, for example, potatoes, carrots.

The concept map for **asexual reproduction in plants** is shown on page 94. It is your revision guide, so study it carefully.

Artificial vegetative reproduction

Gardeners and farmers need to produce fresh stocks of plants that have desirable characteristics such as disease resistance, colour of fruit or shape of flower. The diagram on the following page shows how plants are propagated vegetatively.

Micropropagation is used to grow plants from small pieces, using a technique called **tissue culture**.

★ Small fragments of plant tissue are grown in a liquid or gel that contains all the ingredients the pieces need to grow.

★ Conditions are sterile.

As a result, the new plants are free of disease.

★ The temperature is carefully controlled.

Flowers have features which make pollination more certain.

- **Insect-pollinated** flowers are often brightly coloured and produce nectar and scent to attract insect visitors.
- **Wind-pollinated** flowers are often dull in colour. Clouds of light, smooth pollen grains are easily carried in the wind, scattering them far and wide.

5 ★ Fruits and seeds may be distributed by animals or wind.

- **Spines** and **hooks** attach the fruit to passing animals.
- Animals are attracted to feed on **brightly coloured** fruits. The seeds are protected from the digestive juices in the animal's intestine, and eventually pass out in the animal's faeces.
- **Parachutes** and **wings** increase the surface area of fruits, helping them travel long distances in the wind.

6.2 Asexual reproduction in plants

PREVIEW

At the end of this section you will:
- be able to identify the organs of asexual reproduction in flowering plants
- know that cuttings, graftings and micropropagation are used by farmers and gardeners to produce many identical plants
- understand that asexual reproduction preserves desirable characteristics and so guarantees plant quality.

Inheritance and evolution

Cutting

These leaves are left on to make food by photosynthesis while the cutting establishes itself.

New shoots grow at the points (nodes) where the leaves were stripped off.

A piece of stem is cut from a mature plant. **Adventitious** roots grow from the cut surface.

nodes — growing medium

ARTIFICIAL VEGETATIVE REPRODUCTION

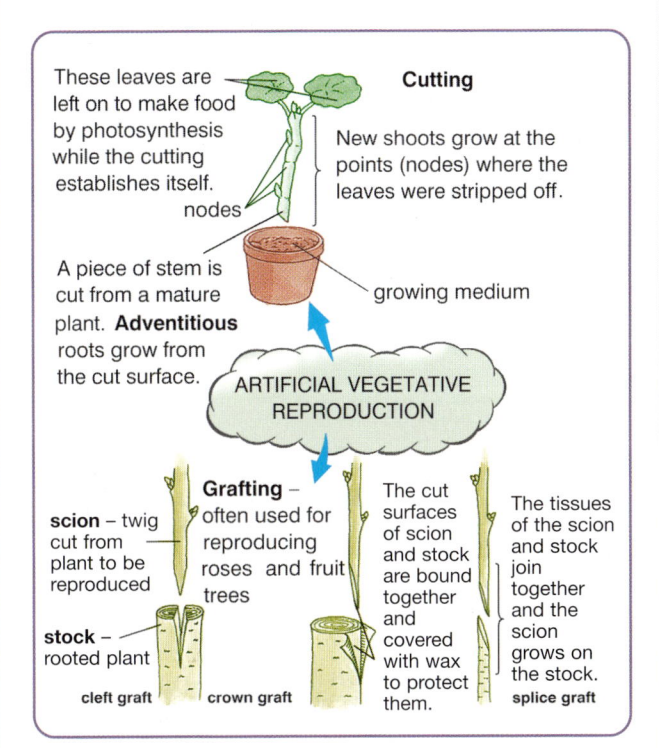

Grafting – often used for reproducing roses and fruit trees

scion – twig cut from plant to be reproduced

stock – rooted plant

The cut surfaces of scion and stock are bound together and covered with wax to protect them.

The tissues of the scion and stock join together and the scion grows on the stock.

cleft graft — crown graft — splice graft

Exploiting vegetative reproduction. Adventitious roots are roots that grow from a part of a stem. A node is the point where a leaf stalk joins the stem.

All the plants grown from pieces of one parent plant will be genetically identical. They are clones. The advantages are that the plants:
- are healthy
- are the same
- retain the desirable characteristics of the parent plant.

Fact file

The widespread use of clones by gardeners and farmers reduces variation. Fewer alleles are available for the selective breeding of new varieties of crops and animals for food.

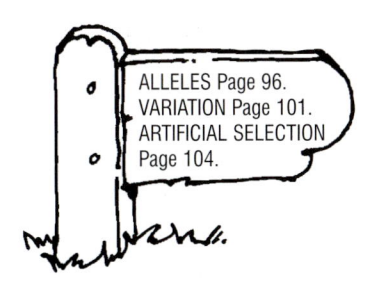

ALLELES Page 96.
VARIATION Page 101.
ARTIFICIAL SELECTION Page 104.

6.3 Monohybrid inheritance

PREVIEW

At the end of this section you will:
- understand genetic terms
- be able to work out the expected outcome of a monohybrid cross
- understand the inheritance of gender
- understand sex-linked inheritance.

Fact file

Gregor Mendel was a monk who lived in the Augustinian monastery at the town of Brünn (now Brno in the Czech Republic). He observed the inheritance of different characteristics in the garden pea, and reported the results of his experiments in 1865. The work established the basis of modern genetics.

However, at the time, nobody realised what Mendel was talking about. The reason probably lay with Mendel's training: he was a mathematician as well as a biologist, which was an unusual combination of skills in the mid-nineteenth century. His report was ignored because then, most scientists were unfamiliar with the mathematical analysis of biological problems.

The vocabulary of genetics

★ **monohybrid inheritance** – the processes by which a single characteristic is passed from parents to offspring, for example flower colour or eye colour

★ **pure breeding** – characteristics that breed true, appearing unchanged generation after generation

★ **parental generation** (symbol **P**) – individuals that are pure breeding for a characteristic

★ **first filial generation** (symbol F_1) – the offspring produced by a parental generation

★ **second filial generation** (symbol F_2) – the offspring produced by crossing members of the first filial generation

continued on page 96

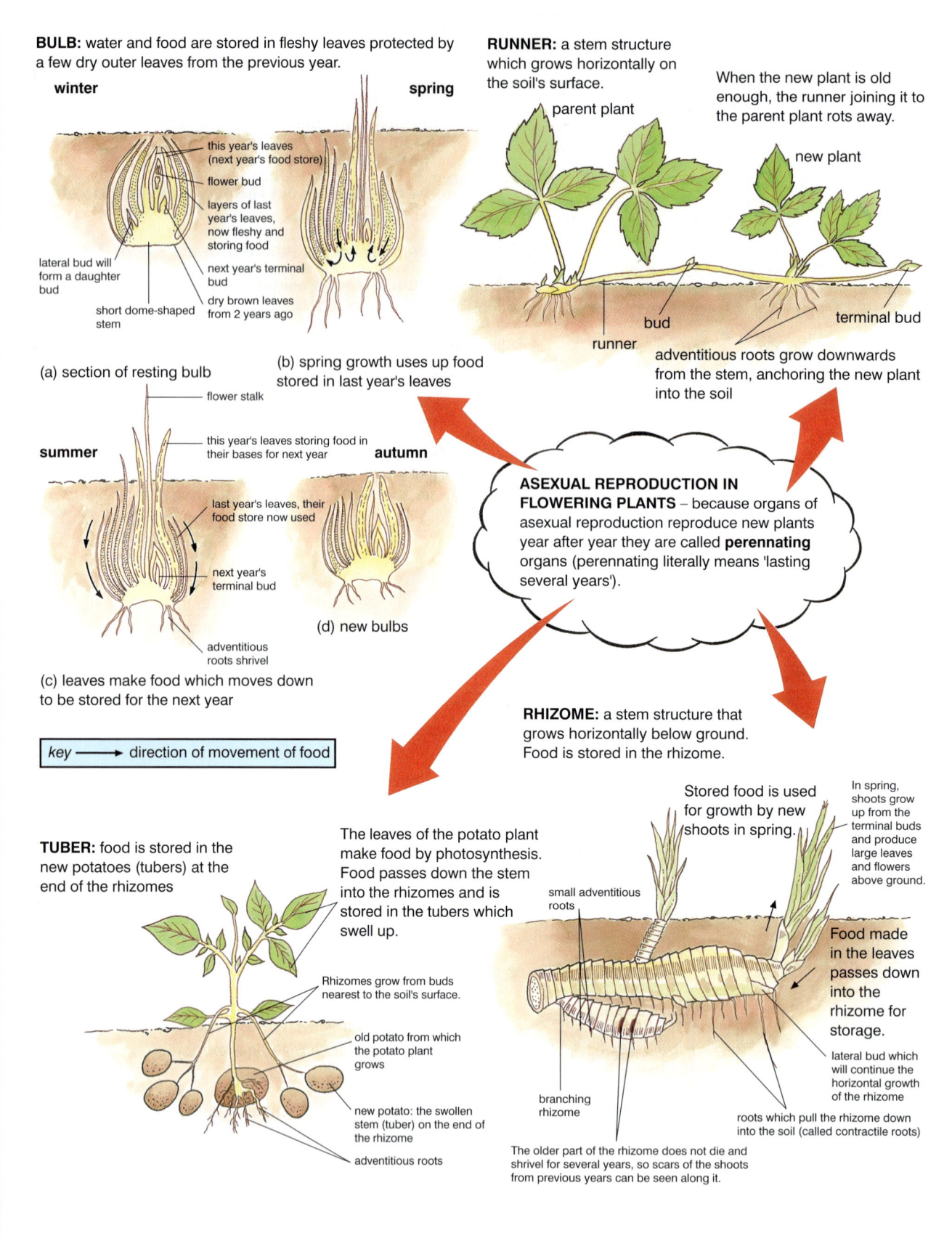

Inheritance and evolution

BULB: water and food are stored in fleshy leaves protected by a few dry outer leaves from the previous year.

winter
- this year's leaves (next year's food store)
- flower bud
- layers of last year's leaves, now fleshy and storing food
- lateral bud will form a daughter bud
- next year's terminal bud
- short dome-shaped stem
- dry brown leaves from 2 years ago

spring

(a) section of resting bulb

(b) spring growth uses up food stored in last year's leaves

summer
- flower stalk
- this year's leaves storing food in their bases for next year
- last year's leaves, their food store now used
- next year's terminal bud
- adventitious roots shrivel

autumn

(c) leaves make food which moves down to be stored for the next year

(d) new bulbs

key ⟶ direction of movement of food

RUNNER: a stem structure which grows horizontally on the soil's surface.

When the new plant is old enough, the runner joining it to the parent plant rots away.

- parent plant
- new plant
- bud
- runner
- terminal bud
- adventitious roots grow downwards from the stem, anchoring the new plant into the soil

ASEXUAL REPRODUCTION IN FLOWERING PLANTS – because organs of asexual reproduction reproduce new plants year after year they are called **perennating** organs (perennating literally means 'lasting several years').

TUBER: food is stored in the new potatoes (tubers) at the end of the rhizomes

The leaves of the potato plant make food by photosynthesis. Food passes down the stem into the rhizomes and is stored in the tubers which swell up.

- Rhizomes grow from buds nearest to the soil's surface.
- old potato from which the potato plant grows
- new potato: the swollen stem (tuber) on the end of the rhizome
- adventitious roots

RHIZOME: a stem structure that grows horizontally below ground. Food is stored in the rhizome.

Stored food is used for growth by new shoots in spring.

In spring, shoots grow up from the terminal buds and produce large leaves and flowers above ground.

- small adventitious roots
- branching rhizome

Food made in the leaves passes down into the rhizome for storage.

- lateral bud which will continue the horizontal growth of the rhizome
- roots which pull the rhizome down into the soil (called contractile roots)

The older part of the rhizome does not die and shrivel for several years, so scars of the shoots from previous years can be seen along it.

Asexual reproduction in flowering plants. **Remember** that adventitious roots are roots that grow from part of a stem.

Inheritance and evolution

Fact file

A **test cross** (or **back cross**) is used to find out if a tall plant is homozygous (TT) or heterozygous (Tt).

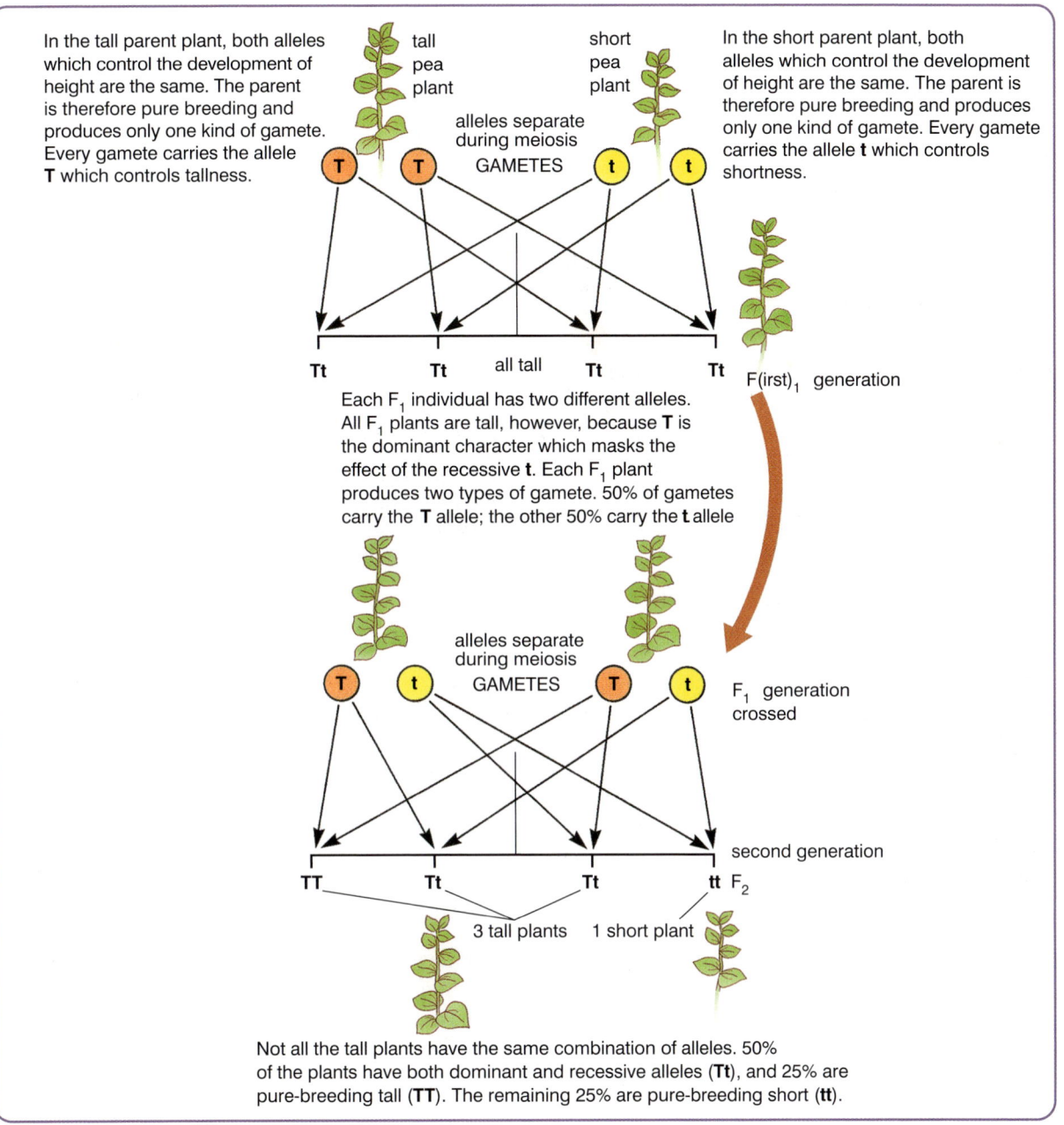

In the tall parent plant, both alleles which control the development of height are the same. The parent is therefore pure breeding and produces only one kind of gamete. Every gamete carries the allele **T** which controls tallness.

tall pea plant

short pea plant

alleles separate during meiosis
GAMETES

In the short parent plant, both alleles which control the development of height are the same. The parent is therefore pure breeding and produces only one kind of gamete. Every gamete carries the allele **t** which controls shortness.

Tt   Tt   all tall   Tt   Tt   F(irst)$_1$ generation

Each F$_1$ individual has two different alleles. All F$_1$ plants are tall, however, because **T** is the dominant character which masks the effect of the recessive **t**. Each F$_1$ plant produces two types of gamete. 50% of gametes carry the **T** allele; the other 50% carry the **t** allele

alleles separate during meiosis
GAMETES

F$_1$ generation crossed

second generation

TT   Tt   Tt   tt   F$_2$

3 tall plants   1 short plant

Not all the tall plants have the same combination of alleles. 50% of the plants have both dominant and recessive alleles (**Tt**), and 25% are pure-breeding tall (**TT**). The remaining 25% are pure-breeding short (**tt**).

How alleles controlling a characteristic (in this case height of plant) pass from one generation to the next

Inheritance and evolution

* **gene** – a length of DNA which codes for the whole of one protein

  GENES Page 43.

* **allele** – one of a pair of genes that control a particular characteristic
* **homozygote** – an individual with identical alleles controlling a particular characteristic. Individuals that are pure breeding for a particular characteristic are **homozygous** for that characteristic
* **heterozygote** – an individual with different alleles controlling a particular characteristic
* **expressed** – a gene is expressed when a protein is produced as a result of the activity of the gene
* **dominant** – any characteristic that appears in the F_1 offspring of a cross between pure-breeding parents with contrasting characteristics, such as tallness and shortness in pea plants, *or* any characteristic expressed by an allele in preference to the form of the characteristic controlled by the allele's partner
* **recessive** – any characteristic present in the parental generation that misses the F_1 generation but reappears in the F_2 generation, *or* any characteristic of an allele that is not expressed because the form of the characteristic of the allele's partner is expressed in preference, *or* any characteristic of an allele that is only expressed in the absence of the allele's dominant partner
* **genotype** – the genetic make-up (all of the genes) of an individual
* **phenotype** – the outward appearance and internal structure and function of an individual which results from the activity of those genes of the genotype actively expressing characteristics.

Some rules of genetics

* Paired genes controlling a particular characteristic are called alleles.
* Letters are used to symbolise alleles.
* A capital letter is used to symbolise the dominant member of a pair of alleles.
* A small letter is used to symbolise the recessive member of a pair of alleles.
* The letter used to symbolise the recessive allele is the same letter as that for the dominant allele.

A monohybrid cross

The diagram on page 95 sets out the results of crosses between tall and short pea plants. Notice that **T** is used to symbolise the allele that results in tallness in pea plants, and **t** is used to symbolise the allele that results in shortness. Other contrasting characteristics of the pea plant such as seed shape (round or wrinkled), flower colour (purple or white) and pod shape (smooth or wrinkled) are inherited in a similar way.

From his results on the inheritance of different characteristics of pea plants, Mendel realised that parents passed 'something' on to their offspring that made them look like their parents. When these offspring became parents, they passed on the 'something' to their offspring, and so on, from generation to generation. Mendel called the 'something' particles; today we call them **genes**.

Fact file

Some scientists have thought that Mendel's ratio of 3:1 in the F_2 generation was statistically too perfect. The doubts do not mean that Mendel's conclusions were wrong; just that 'experimental error' was not properly taken into account.

Inheritance of sex

The photograph opposite shows the chromosomes that determine the sex of a person. The larger chromosome is the **X** chromosome; the smaller chromosome is the **Y** chromosome. The body cells of a woman each carry two **X** chromosomes; those of a man each carry an **X** chromosome and a **Y** chromosome.

Inheritance and evolution

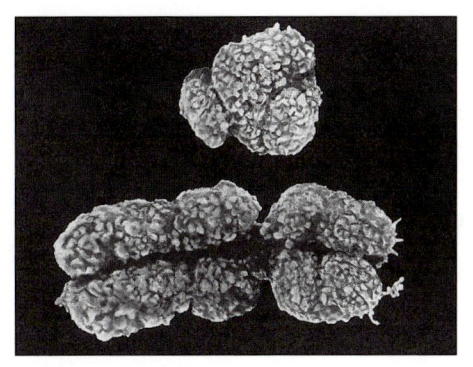

Human sex chromosomes

The diagram below shows how a person's sex is inherited. **Notice** that:
- a baby's sex depends on whether the egg is fertilised by a sperm carrying an X chromosome or one carrying a Y chromosome
- the birth of (almost) equal numbers of girls and boys is governed by the production of equal numbers of X and Y sperm at meiosis.

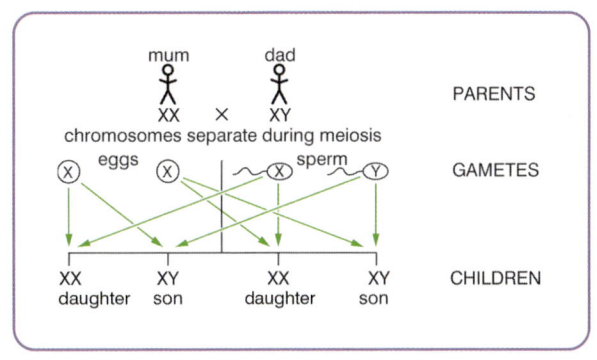

Inheritance of sex in humans

Haemophilia: a sex-linked genetic disease

Characteristics controlled by alleles situated on the sex chromosomes are said to be **sex-linked** characteristics. The genetic disease **haemophilia** is an example.

A haemophiliac (a person suffering from haemophilia) has a mutant version of the allele responsible for the expression of the blood clotting agent factor VIII. The affected person does not produce factor VIII, which means that if s/he is cut, it takes a long time for a clot to form and a lot of blood may be lost. The mutant allele is recessive and located on the X chromosome. The diagrams at the bottom of page 98 show how it passes from one generation to the next in two different circumstances: when the father is haemophiliac and the mother is a carrier.

Fact file

Haemophiliacs are usually male. Although the mutant allele is recessive, the male Y chromosome (remember that men have an X chromosome and a Y chromosome) carries few alleles and does not have a normal dominant partner allele to mask the effects of the mutant allele on the X chromosome. For a female to have haemophilia, she would have to inherit the recessive mutant allele from both of her parents. This happens only very occasionally as the mutant allele is very rare.

Cystic fibrosis: a recessive genetic disease

Cystic fibrosis is a genetic disease that is not sex-linked. It affects the lungs and the pancreas. The bronchioles and the pancreatic duct become blocked with excess mucus and have to be cleared regularly. The mutant allele responsible is recessive. A person suffers from the disease only if s/he has two mutant alleles. A person with a single mutant allele is a **carrier**. The diagram at the top of page 98 shows how it passes from one generation to the next when two parents who are carriers have children.

Huntington's chorea: a dominant genetic disease

Like cystic fibrosis, Huntington's chorea is a genetic disease which is not sex-linked. However, unlike cystic fibrosis, the mutant allele responsible is dominant. Involuntary muscular movement and mental deterioration are characteristics of the disease. A person suffers from the disease even if s/he has only one mutant allele. Unfortunately, the age of onset of symptoms of the disease is about 35 years. Affected people, therefore, can have a family before being aware of their own condition. The diagram in the middle of page 98 shows how the mutant allele passes from one generation to the next when one of the parents is affected.

Inheritance and evolution

Cc x Cc — **PARENTS**
chromosomes separate during meiosis
(C represents the allele which controls the development normal lungs and pancreas; c represents the allele which controls the development of cystic fibrosis)
GAMETES: C c C c

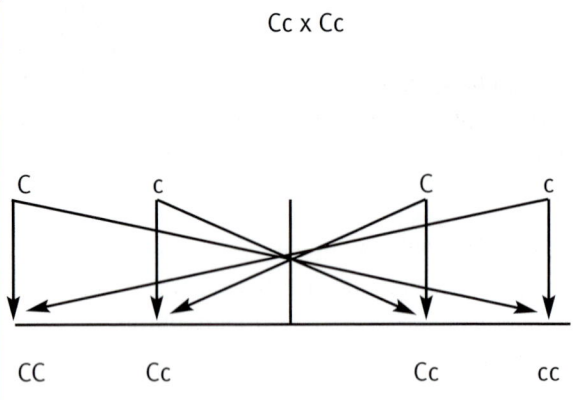

CHILDREN: CC Cc Cc cc

One child is affected by cystic fibrosis; two of the other children are carriers but are not affected by cystic fibrosis. One child does not have the allele for cystic fibrosis.

HChc x hchc — **PARENTS**
chromosomes separate during meiosis
(HC represents the allele which controls the development of Huntington's chorea; hc represents the normal allele)
GAMETES: HC hc hc hc

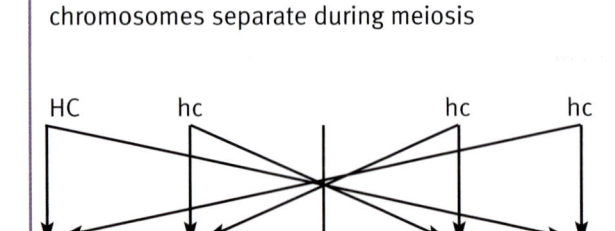

CHILDREN: HChc hchc hchc HChc

Two children are affected by Huntington's chorea; the other two are not. The unaffected children cannot be carriers because the mutant allele is dominant.

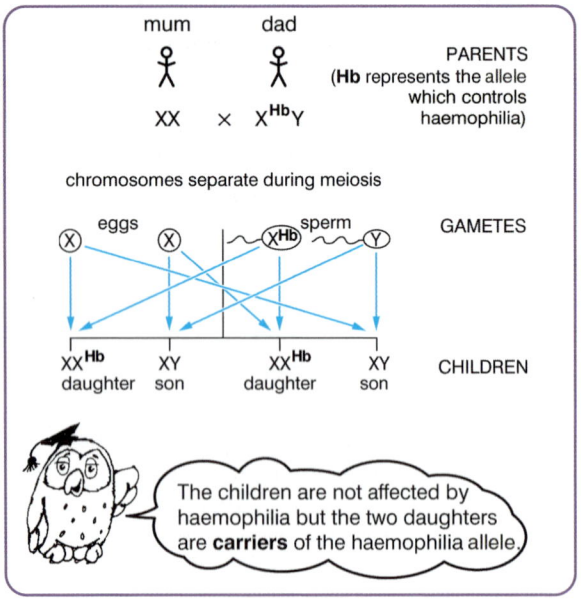

mum XX × dad $X^{Hb}Y$ — **PARENTS**
(Hb represents the allele which controls haemophilia)

chromosomes separate during meiosis

GAMETES: eggs X, X ; sperm X^{Hb}, Y

CHILDREN: XX^{Hb} daughter, XY son, XX^{Hb} daughter, XY son

The children are not affected by haemophilia but the two daughters are **carriers** of the haemophilia allele.

The outcome when a man affected by haemophilia becomes a father

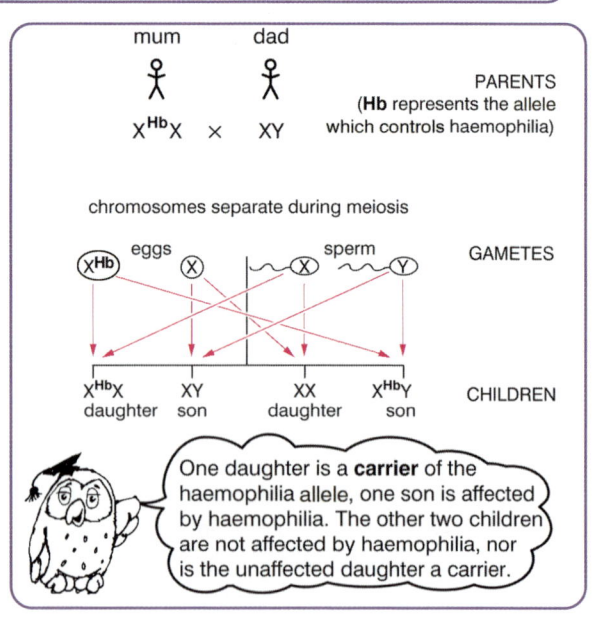

mum $X^{Hb}X$ × dad XY — **PARENTS**
(Hb represents the allele which controls haemophilia)

chromosomes separate during meiosis

GAMETES: eggs X^{Hb}, X ; sperm X, Y

CHILDREN: $X^{Hb}X$ daughter, XY son, XX daughter, $X^{Hb}Y$ son

One daughter is a **carrier** of the haemophilia allele, one son is affected by haemophilia. The other two children are not affected by haemophilia, nor is the unaffected daughter a carrier.

The outcome when a woman who is a carrier of the haemophilia allele becomes a mother

Inheritance and evolution

6.4 Biotechnology

PREVIEW

At the end of this section you will:

- know that the processes of biotechnology have a long history in the production of bread and alcoholic drinks
- understand that the techniques of genetic engineering manipulate genes to human advantage
- realise that genetic engineering has transformed biotechnology into a rapidly expanding industry which provides food, medicines and a range of industrial chemicals.

Fact file

The word **biotechnology** describes the way we use plant cells, animal cells and microorganisms to produce substances that are useful to us.

Using biotechnology

The long history of biotechnology demonstrates the importance of some of the processes of biotechnology.

The traditional: for thousands of years humans have exploited different organisms to make food, using:

- **yeast** to make wine, beer and bread
- **moulds** to make cheese
- **bacteria** to make yogurt and vinegar.

The diagram below sets out the processes in the production of wine and bread.

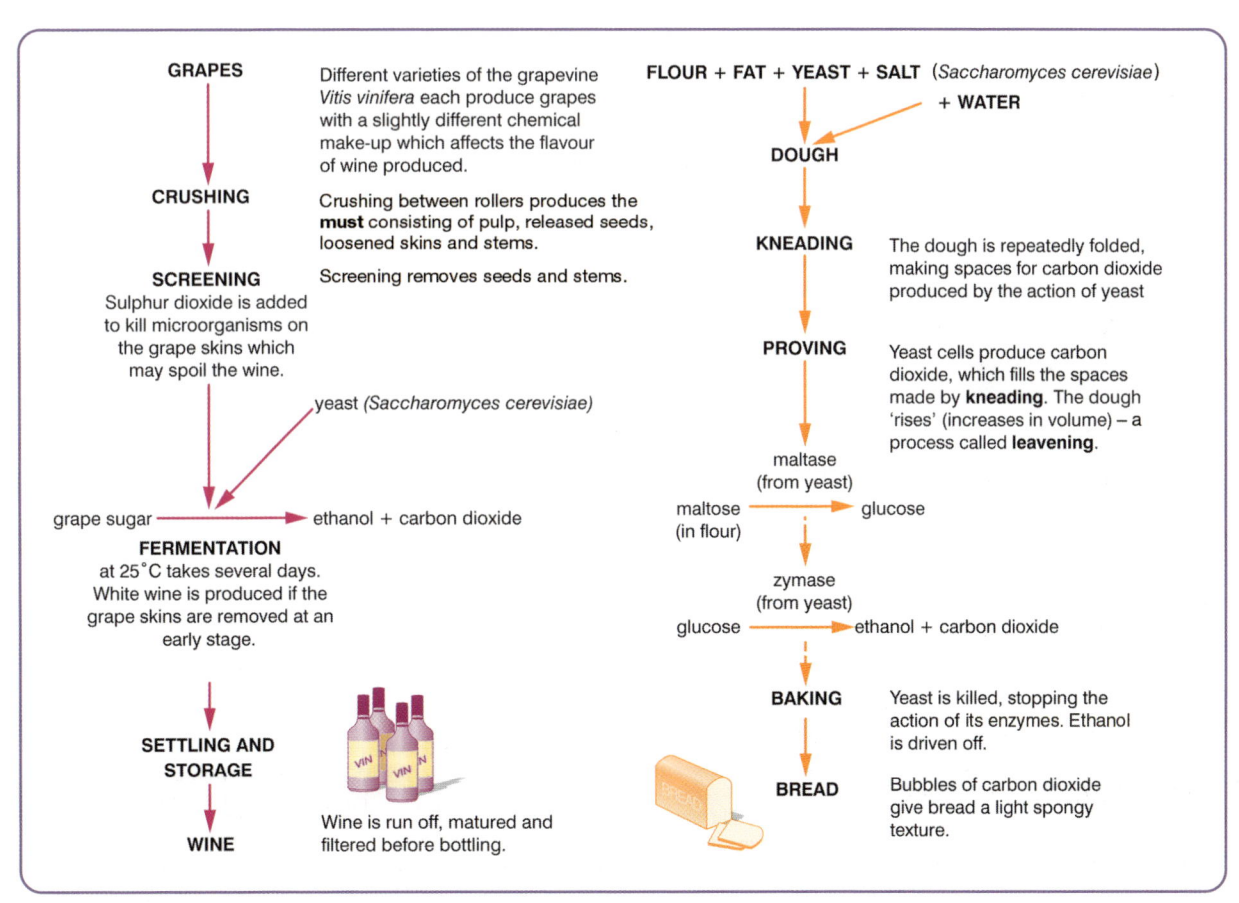

Making wine and bread

Wine production:

GRAPES — Different varieties of the grapevine *Vitis vinifera* each produce grapes with a slightly different chemical make-up which affects the flavour of wine produced.

↓

CRUSHING — Crushing between rollers produces the **must** consisting of pulp, released seeds, loosened skins and stems.

↓

SCREENING — Screening removes seeds and stems. Sulphur dioxide is added to kill microorganisms on the grape skins which may spoil the wine.

↓ yeast (*Saccharomyces cerevisiae*)

grape sugar → ethanol + carbon dioxide

FERMENTATION at 25°C takes several days. White wine is produced if the grape skins are removed at an early stage.

↓

SETTLING AND STORAGE

↓

WINE — Wine is run off, matured and filtered before bottling.

Bread production:

FLOUR + FAT + YEAST + SALT (*Saccharomyces cerevisiae*) + WATER

↓

DOUGH

↓

KNEADING — The dough is repeatedly folded, making spaces for carbon dioxide produced by the action of yeast

↓

PROVING — Yeast cells produce carbon dioxide, which fills the spaces made by **kneading**. The dough 'rises' (increases in volume) – a process called **leavening**.

maltose (in flour) —maltase (from yeast)→ glucose

glucose —zymase (from yeast)→ ethanol + carbon dioxide

↓

BAKING — Yeast is killed, stopping the action of its enzymes. Ethanol is driven off.

↓

BREAD — Bubbles of carbon dioxide give bread a light spongy texture.

Inheritance and evolution

Anaerobic respiration by yeast cells converts glucose into **ethanol** ('alcohol' in wines and beers) and **carbon dioxide** (the gas that makes bread rise). The reaction is an example of **fermentation**. Biotechnology exploits a range of fermentation reactions to produce different substances.

ANAEROBIC RESPIRATION Page 63.

The new: in the 1970s scientists developed the techniques of **genetic engineering**, which introduced the modern era of biotechnology. New methods of manipulating genes became possible because of the discovery of different enzymes in bacteria.

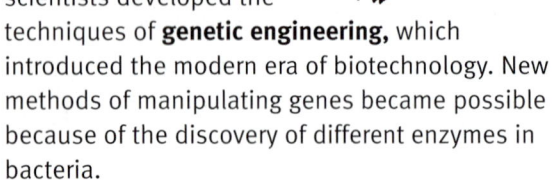

★ **Restriction enzymes** cut DNA into pieces, making it possible to isolate desirable genes (those which are useful to us).

★ **Ligase** (splicing enzyme) allows genes which express substances that are useful to us to be inserted into the genetic material of host cells.

Using genetic engineering we can create **genetically modified** (GM) organisms with specific genetic characteristics, such that they produce substances that we need and want. For example, the microorganisms are cultured in a solution containing all the substances (nutrients) they require for rapid growth and multiplication inside huge containers called **fermenters**. In this way, medicines, foods and industrial chemicals can be made on an industrial scale. The diagram below shows how genetically engineered insulin is made.

INSULIN Page 77.

Remember that the products of biotechnology come from the action of **genes** which results in the production of useful substances.

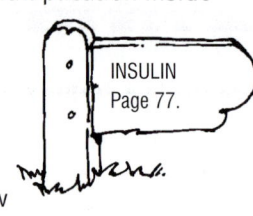

Fact file

★ **Batch culture** produces batches of product in a fermenter. The fermenter is then emptied of the product and the nutrient solution. The fermenter is sterilised with super-heated steam ready for the next batch.

★ **Continuous culture** produces substances as an ongoing process. The product is drawn off the fermenter and nutrients are replaced as they are used.

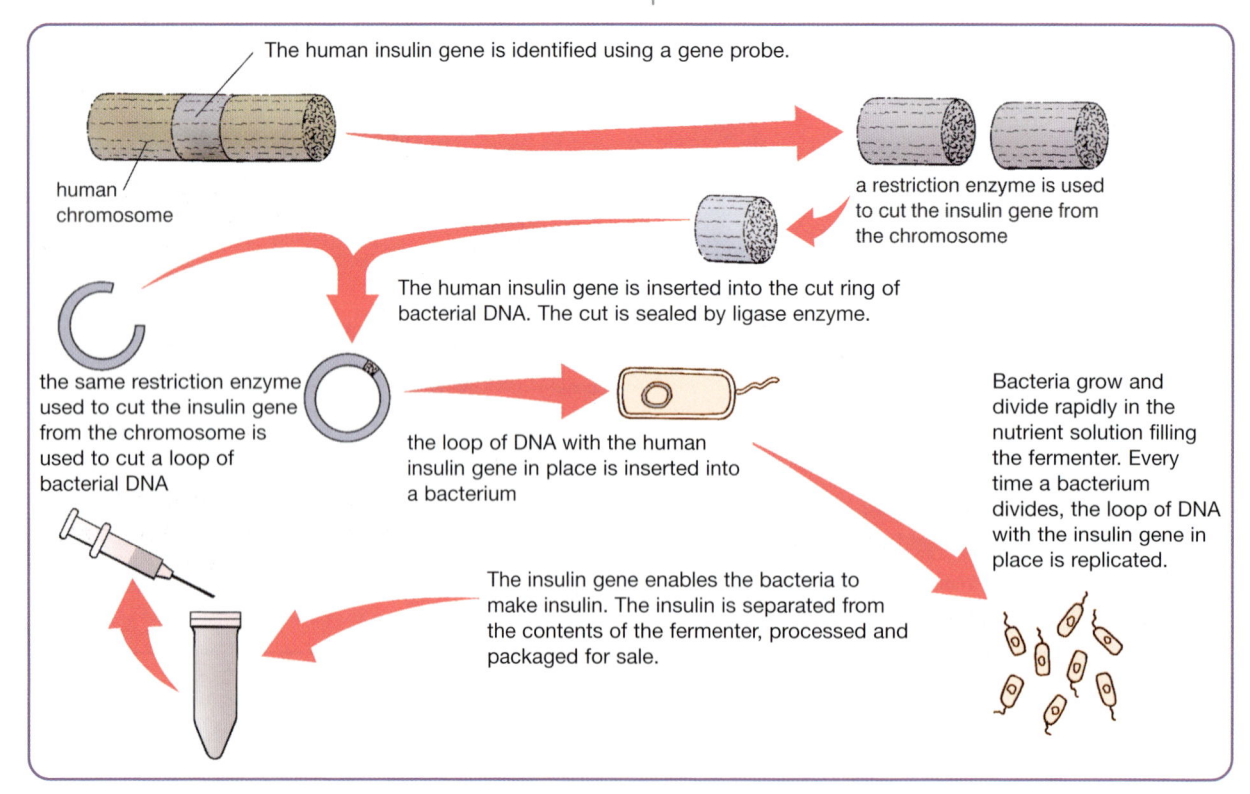

The human insulin gene is identified using a gene probe.

human chromosome

a restriction enzyme is used to cut the insulin gene from the chromosome

the same restriction enzyme used to cut the insulin gene from the chromosome is used to cut a loop of bacterial DNA

The human insulin gene is inserted into the cut ring of bacterial DNA. The cut is sealed by ligase enzyme.

the loop of DNA with the human insulin gene in place is inserted into a bacterium

Bacteria grow and divide rapidly in the nutrient solution filling the fermenter. Every time a bacterium divides, the loop of DNA with the insulin gene in place is replicated.

The insulin gene enables the bacteria to make insulin. The insulin is separated from the contents of the fermenter, processed and packaged for sale.

Making genetically engineered insulin

Inheritance and evolution

6.5 Variation

> **PREVIEW**
>
> At the end of this section you will:
> - understand the difference between continuous variation and discontinuous variation
> - be able to identify the sources of variation
> - know that variation is either inherited or acquired.

Genetic and environmental variation

Look closely at your family, friends and classmates. Notice the differently coloured hair and eyes, and the differently shaped faces. We all show **variations** in the different characteristics that make up our physical appearance (**phenotype**).

GENOTYPE and PHENOTYPE Page 96.

Variation arises from **genetic** causes.

Sexual reproduction (see pages 90–2) involves the fusion of the nucleus of a **sperm** with the nucleus of the **egg**. The process of fusion is called **fertilisation** and recombines the genetic material from each parent in new ways within the **zygote**.

Mutations are either the result of abnormalities in the number of chromosomes (**chromosome mutations**) or of a change (or changes) in the genes themselves (**gene mutations**). Down's syndrome is an example of a chromosome mutation. The affected person has an extra copy of chromosome 21. Gene mutations arise as a result of mistakes in the **replication** of DNA (see page 42). Occasionally the wrong base adds to the growing strand of DNA, making the new DNA slightly different from the original. **Ionising radiation** and some **chemicals** increase the probability of gene mutation.

★ Ionising radiation strips electrons from matter exposed to it (ionises the atoms). Emissions from radioactive substances are ionising radiations. They may cause mutations by damaging DNA directly, or by generating highly active components of molecules called **free radicals** which cause the damage indirectly.

★ Chemicals such as the **carcinogens** (substances that cause cancer) in tobacco may lead to mutations of the genes that normally inhibit cell division.

As a result, cell division runs out of control and a cancer develops.

★ **Crossing over** during **meiosis** exchanges a segment of one chromosome (and the genes it carries) with the corresponding segment of its homologous chromosome (see page 33).

As a result, the sex cells produced by meiosis have a different combination of genes from the parent cell.

Fact file

In rare cases, a mutation may increase an organism's chances of survival. The mutant gene will be favoured by natural selection and therefore inherited by future generations. Some mutations do not affect an organism's chances of survival one way or another. Such mutations are **neutral** in their effects.

Variations that arise from genetic causes are inherited from parents by their offspring, who pass them on to their offspring, and so on from generation to generation. Inherited variation is the raw material on which **natural selection** acts, resulting in **evolution**.

Variation also arises from **environmental** causes. Here, 'environmental' means all the external influences affecting an organism, including the following.

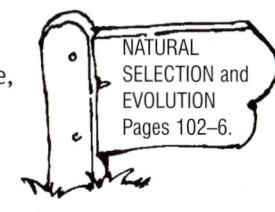

NATURAL SELECTION and EVOLUTION Pages 102–6.

★ **nutrients** in the food we eat and minerals that plants absorb in solution through the roots. In many countries, children are now taller and heavier, age for age, than they were 50 years ago because of improved diet and standards of living.

Inheritance and evolution

- **drugs**, which may have a serious effect on appearance. **Thalidomide** was given to pregnant women in the 1960s to prevent them feeling sick and to help them sleep. The drug can affect the development of the fetus and some women who were prescribed thalidomide gave birth to seriously deformed children.
- **temperature** affects the rate of enzyme-controlled chemical reactions. Warmth increases the rate of photosynthesis, for instance, and therefore improves the rate of growth of plants kept under glass.
- **physical training** uses muscles more than normal, increasing their size and power. Weightlifters, therefore, develop bulging muscles as they train for their sport.

Variations that arise from environmental causes are *not* inherited, because the sex cells are not affected. Instead the characteristics are said to be **acquired**. The fact that the weightlifter has developed bulging muscles does not mean that his or her children will have bulging muscles – unless they take up weightlifting as well! Because variations as a result of acquired characteristics are not inherited, they do not affect evolution.

Continuous and discontinuous variation

The variations shown by some characteristics are spread over a range of measurements. All intermediate forms of a characteristic are possible between one extreme and the other.
We say that the characteristic shows **continuous variation**. The height of a population is an example of continuous variation.

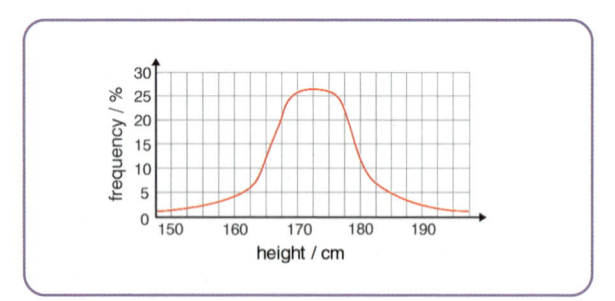

Variation in the height of the adult human population – an example of continuous variation

Other characteristics do not show a continuous trend in variation from one extreme to another. They show categories of the characteristic without any intermediate forms. The ability to roll the tongue is an example – you can either do it or you can't. There are no half-rollers! We say that the characteristic shows **discontinuous variation**.

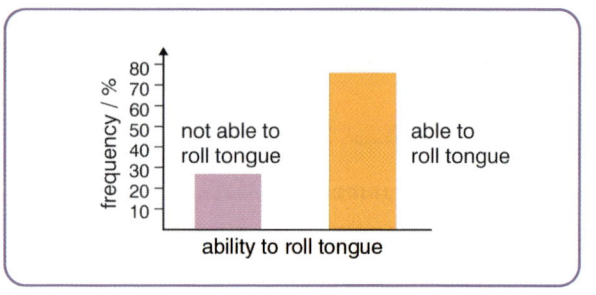

Ability to roll the tongue – an example of discontinuous variation

6.6 Evolution

PREVIEW

At the end of this section you will:
- know that the British naturalist Charles Darwin was the first person to explain *how* species can evolve
- understand Darwin's evidence showing that evolution occurs, and that natural selection is the mechanism of evolution
- be able to interpret examples of evolution in action
- know that fossils are a record of organisms that have become extinct.

Fact file

Charles Darwin (1809–82) was a keen British naturalist who abandoned medicine at Edinburgh and studied theology at Cambridge. His world voyage on HMS *Beagle* (1831–6) provided much of the evidence that:
- organisms **evolve** and that
- **natural selection** is the mechanism of evolution.

It was another 20 years before he published these proposals in his book *Origin of species*.

Inheritance and evolution

Evidence
- The fossils that Darwin collected on expeditions inland showed him that organisms today are not the same as organisms that lived a long time ago. In other words, organisms change through time – they evolve.
- There is an enormous variety of living things.

Darwin travelled around the coast of South America on HMS *Beagle*.

CHECKLIST 1

Evidence
- Lyell's work showed that the geology of the Earth changed through long periods of time.
- Darwin reasoned that if the geology of Earth had changed then so too could organisms.

Charles Lyell
Darwin and Lyell becam friends on Darwin's return to England from the voyage in the *Beagle*. Lyell believed that the Earth was very old.

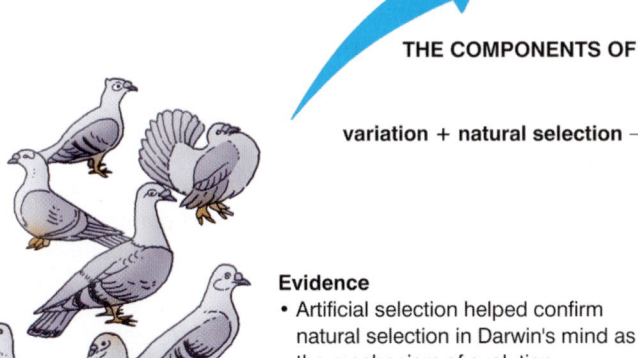

Charles Darwin (1809–82)

CHECKLIST 2

THE COMPONENTS OF EVOLUTION

variation + natural selection $\xrightarrow{\text{time}}$ evolution

Evidence
- Artificial selection helped confirm natural selection in Darwin's mind as the mechanism of evolution.

The variety of pigeons bred by 'fanciers' over hundreds of years originated from a 'wild type' common ancestor.

CHECKLIST 4

Evidence
- Darwin reasoned that since the number of individuals in a population does not increase indefinitely, then limiting factors must check the increase in numbers.

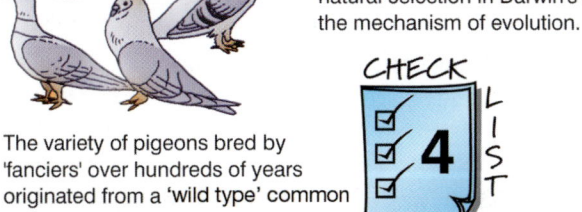

Reverend Thomas Malthus
Malthus suggested that the growth in numbers of a population outstrips resources in limited supply, leading to competition between individuals for the resources, e.g. food, habitats (see page 106), mates.

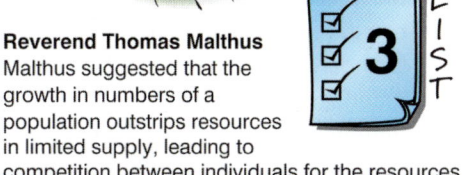

CHECKLIST 3

How Darwin arrived at a theory of evolution through natural selection (Checklist overleaf.)

Inheritance and evolution

The process of evolution

Present-day living things are descended from ancestors that have changed through thousands of generations. The process of change is called **evolution**. The concept map for evolution is shown on page 103. It shows that other people's ideas influenced Darwin's thinking on how species can evolve. The numbers on the concept map refer to the checklist of points below. The concept map and its checklist are your revision guide to evolution.

Fact file

Charles Darwin was not the first person to propose a mechanism by which species evolve. In 1809, the French biologist Jean-Baptiste de Lamarck proposed that organisms evolve because changes in the environment cause changes in the characteristics of organisms. The characteristics are said to be **acquired** and Lamarck believed them to be inherited by offspring.

Checklist for evolution

1. A survey of the South American coast was among the tasks undertaken by the crew of HMS *Beagle* during its world voyage. At that time Darwin took over as the ship's naturalist. He:
   - collected **fossils** and specimens of plants and animals on expeditions inland
   - noticed that one type of organism gave way to another as the *Beagle* sailed around the coast of South America
   - observed that the animals along the Pacific coast of South America were different from those along the Atlantic coast
   - compared the wildlife of the Galapagos Islands with the wildlife of the South American mainland, noting the differences between similar species.

   The variety of species that Darwin discovered on his expeditions in South America and the Galapagos Islands convinced him that species change through time; that is, they **evolve**.

2. The famous geologist Charles Lyell (1797–1875) believed that:
   - Earth's rocks are very old
   - natural forces produce continuous geological change during the course of Earth's history
   - fossils can be used to date rocks
   - the fossil record was laid down over hundreds of millions of years.

   Darwin read Lyell's books.

   As a result, Darwin reasoned that if rocks have changed slowly over long periods of time, living things might have a similar history.

3. In 1798 the Reverend Thomas Malthus wrote *An Essay on the Principle of Population*. He stated that the size of a population would increase indefinitely unless kept in check by shortages of resources such as food and living space. Darwin read the essay in 1838 and reasoned that in nature a 'struggle for existence' must occur. In modern language we say that organisms **compete** for resources in limited supply.

   COMPETITION Page 16.

4. For centuries we have selected animals and plants for their desirable characteristics, and bred from them. This is called **artificial selection**. For example, dogs have been bred for shape, size and coat colour, resulting in a wide variety of breeds. Darwin investigated the work of breeders of animals and plants, and added to his experience by breeding pigeons. He reasoned that if artificial selection produced change in domestic animals and plants, then natural selection should have the same effect on wildlife.

The checklist above sets out the different components which were the key to Darwin's understanding of how species evolve.

Fact file

Francis Galton was a rich Victorian scientist and cousin to Charles Darwin. He believed that the human race could be improved by only allowing couples with 'desirable' characteristics to have children. In other words, he supported the idea of the artificial selection of human beings. This idea is called **eugenics** and is a controversial subject.

Inheritance and evolution

The components of evolution are:

Variation: Darwin's work during the voyage of HMS *Beagle* and his experience of selectively breeding pigeons provided evidence for the large amount of variation in the characteristics of different species (checklist **1** and **4**).

Natural selection: Malthus' work contributed to Darwin's idea of a 'struggle for existence' (competition for resources). The result is the natural selection of those organisms best suited (**adapted**) to survive (checklist **3**).

Time: Lyell's work showed Darwin that the Earth is very old, giving time for the evolution of species to occur (checklist **2**).

Fact file

Evidence suggests that Earth was formed about 4600 million years ago and that very simple forms of life first appeared around 4000 million years ago.

How species evolve – the modern argument summarised

1 Because individuals vary genetically, individuals are slightly different from one another.

2 This variation in a population of individuals is the raw material on which natural selection works, resulting in evolution.

3 All organisms potentially over-reproduce. Individuals, therefore, compete for resources in short supply. Resources include food and space – both required for individuals to survive.

4 Individuals with genes that express characteristics which adapt the individuals to obtain scarce resources are more likely to survive than other less well adapted individuals.

5 The best adapted individuals are more likely to survive and reproduce, and so their offspring will inherit the genes which control those favourable characteristics.

6 In this way, organisms accumulate genes which control favourable characteristics and change through time; that is, they evolve over many generations.

7 If the environment in which individuals are living changes, then genes which control different characteristics might favour survival. Individuals with these characteristics will survive to reproduce and so evolution continues from generation to generation.

It took Darwin nearly 30 years to develop a theory of evolution through natural selection. The ideas were a revolution in scientific thinking.

Evolution in action

Evolution is still happening. Maintaining the balance between the pale (peppered) and the dark (melanic) forms of the peppered moth *Biston betularia* is an example. The diagram on page 106 shows what happens.

The development of resistance of bacteria to antibiotic drugs is another example of evolution in action. Populations of bacteria always contain a few individuals with genes which enable them to resist the effects of an antibiotic. These individuals survive exposure to the antibiotic and reproduce. The new generation of bacteria inherits the genes which control resistance. Resistance quickly develops in bacteria because they reproduce rapidly.

The fossil record

Fossils are the remains of dead organisms, or impressions such as footprints made by them. Fossilisation also occurs when parts of organisms have not decayed because one or more of the conditions (e.g. warmth, oxygen) necessary for decomposition to occur are absent, or when parts of organisms are replaced by other materials (e.g. mineral particles) as they decompose. Fossils are usually preserved in sedimentary rocks which are formed layer on layer by the deposition of mud, sand and silt over millions of years. Provided the layers are undisturbed, then the more recent the layer, the nearer it is to the Earth's surface.

As a result, the fossils in each rock layer are a record of life on Earth at the time when the layer was formed.

As a result, a sequence of layers each with its fossils traces the history of life on Earth.

Inheritance and evolution

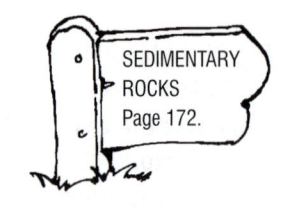

Extinction

Species may die out (become **extinct**) because of the harmful effects of human activities on the environment. Natural extinction also happens over longer periods of time. It makes room for new species to evolve and replace the previous ones. Naturally occurring extinctions are caused by:
- competition between species
- changes in the environment.

SEDIMENTARY ROCKS Page 172.

The mass extinction of whole groups of organisms has occurred at intervals throughout the history of life on Earth. Extinction of the dinosaurs and many other species of reptile about 70 million years ago is a well known example. Their extinction made way for mammals and birds to fill the vacant spaces in the environment.

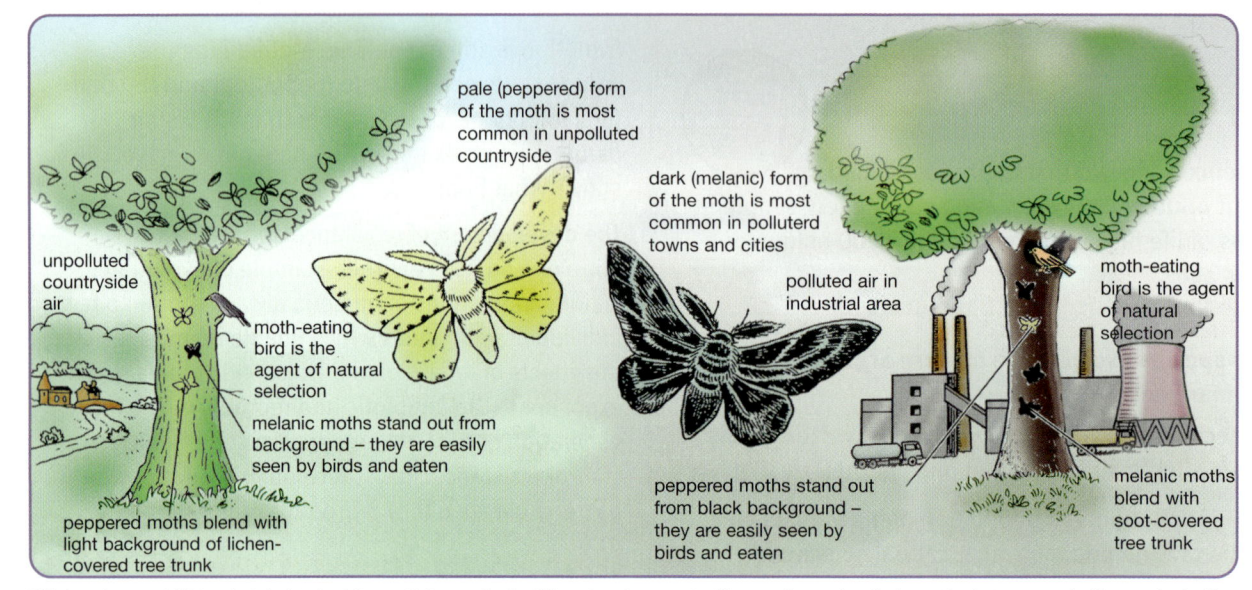

That's why you and I are here!

Different forms of *Biston betularia* adapt the moth to survive in different environments. The numbers of melanic moths in towns and cities are in decline as pollution control makes the urban environment cleaner. At the same time, the numbers of peppered moths are increasing.

Inheritance and evolution

ROUND UP

How much have you improved?
Work out your improvement index on page 113.

1. Match each structure in column **A** with its correct description in column **B**.

A structures	B descriptions
seed	structure to which pollen grains attach
ovule	produces a sugar solution
fruit	contains the egg nucleus
stigma	a fertilised ovule
nectary	develops from the ovary after fertilisation

   [5]

2. What are the advantages to growers of reproducing crops asexually? [3]

3. Name the food stored in the organs of asexual reproduction of plants. [1]

4. Briefly explain why the production of clones depends on the process of mitosis. [5]

5. Match each term in column **A** with its correct description in column **B**.

A terms	B descriptions
allele	the processes by which a single characteristic passes from parents to offspring
pure breeding	offspring of the offspring of the parental generation
second filial generation	characteristics that appear unchanged from generation to generation
monohybrid inheritance	one of a pair of genes that control a particular characteristic

   [4]

6. The diagram shows a glass container called a demijohn, in which wine is produced from the fermentation of grape juice by yeast.

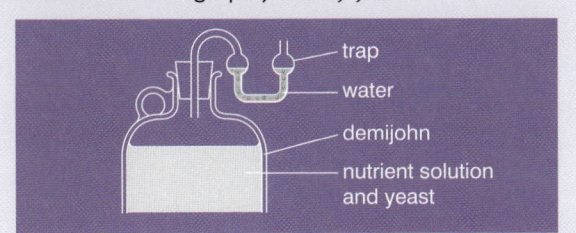

   a) The trap is filled with water. What is the purpose of the trap? [2]

   b) Name the gas bubbling through the water in the trap. [1]

   c) Why is the grape juice called a nutrient solution? [1]

   d) Name the substance in the grape juice fermented by the yeast. [1]

7. In a population of 300 goldfish, variations in two characteristics were measured and the results displayed as charts. Chart A shows variation in the length of the fish; chart B shows variation in their colour.

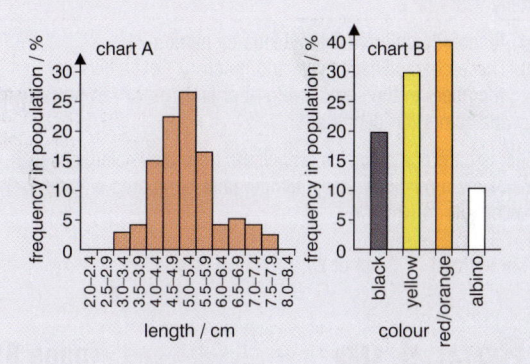

   a) Which chart shows
      (i) continuous variation
      (ii) discontinuous variation?
      (iii) Briefly give reasons for your answers. [6]

   b) Using chart B, calculate the number of yellow goldfish in the population. [1]

   c) Albino goldfish are relatively rare. Give a possible genetic explanation for the occurrence of albino goldfish. [1]

8. a) Look at the diagram on page 106. Briefly explain why the population densities of pale peppered moths and dark peppered moths are different in the countryside from those in industrial areas. [8]

   b) Why is the moth-eating bird called an agent of natural selection? [2]

9. Briefly explain why genes which control characteristics that favour the survival of individuals tend to accumulate from generation to generation. [4]

10. Outline the contributions of the ideas of Charles Lyell and Thomas Malthus to Darwin's development of a theory of evolution through natural selection. [5]

Answers

1 Test yourself (page 2)
Introducing biology

1. **a)** It would increase (✓). **b)** It would decrease (✓).

2. **a)**

	b)	c)
movement	✓	
respiration	✓	✗
sensitivity	✓	✗
growth	✓	✗
reproduction	✓	✗
excretion	✓	✗
nutrition	✓	✗

[✓ × 10]

   d) No – plants do not move from place to place (✓).

3. Annual: a plant that grows from seed to maturity and produces new seeds all within one growing season (✓). It then dies (✓). Perennial: a plant that continues to grow and produce seeds for many years (✓).

4. **a)** To identify different living things by name (✓).
   b) These characteristics vary too much (✓) even between members of the same group of organisms (✓) to be reliable indicators for identification (✓).

5. Soil: is damp (✓); shields organisms from ultraviolet light (✓); maintains a relatively stable temperature compared with air (✓); contains food (✓).

Your score: ☐ out of 24

1 Round up (page 8)
Introducing biology

1. **a)** It would boil away (✓).
   b) It would freeze and form ice (✓).

2. **a)** oxygen (✓)
   b) carbon dioxide (✓)

3. **a)** Respiration releases energy from food (✓). Gaseous exchange takes into the body the oxygen needed for respiration (✓) and removes carbon dioxide produced by respiration from the body (✓).
   b) Excretion removes the waste substances produced by metabolism (✓). Defecation removes the undigested remains of food (✓).

4. The answer should include the idea that although cars move (✓), need fuel (= nutrition) (✓), burn fuel (= respiration) (✓) and produce waste gases (= excretion) (✓) they do not grow (✓) or reproduce (✓) and are not sensitive (✓). Cars therefore do not show all the characteristics associated with living things (✓).

5.
A characteristics		B descriptions
movement	(✓)	changing position
respiration	(✓)	releasing energy from food
sensitivity	(✓)	responding to stimuli
growth	(✓)	increasing in size
reproduction	(✓)	producing new individuals
excretion	(✓)	removing waste substances produced by cells
nutrition	(✓)	making or obtaining food

6.
A animals		B descriptions
insect	(✓)	six legs
worm	(✓)	no legs
spider	(✓)	eight legs
bird	(✓)	two legs

7. The unfamiliar specimen is compared with the descriptions in the key (✓).
The descriptions are followed through (✓) until the description that matches the specimen is found (✓).
The matching description identifies the specimen (✓).

8. The system gives each living organism a name in two parts (✓). The first is the name of the genus (✓); the second is the species name (✓). The genus and species names identify the organism (✓).

9. paired statements (✓)

Your score: ☐ out of 37

Your improvement index: $\dfrac{\boxed{}/37}{\boxed{}/24} \times 100\% = \boxed{}\%$

2 Test yourself (page 9)
Organisms in the environment

1.
A terms		B descriptions
biosphere	(✓)	all the ecosystems of the world
community	(✓)	all the organisms that live in a particular ecosystem
habitat	(✓)	the place where a group of organisms lives
population	(✓)	a group of individuals of the same species

2. **a)** Most animals eat more than one type of plant or other animal (✓). A food web shows the range of different foods eaten (✓).
   b) Plants produce food by photosynthesis (✓). Animals consume this food directly when they eat plants (✓) or indirectly when they eat other animals (✓) which depend on plant food (✓).

Answers

3 a) The pyramid of biomass takes into account differences in size (✓) of producers and consumers (✓).
b) The energy pyramid shows the amount of food being produced (✓) and consumed (✓) in a given time (✓).

4 Improvements in food production (✓); more jobs (✓); new drugs (accept improvement in medicines/medical care) (✓); improvement in public health (✓).

5 Benefits: more food (✓), reliably produced (✓).
Costs: loss of wildlife (✓), loss of habitats (✓), pollution from agrochemicals (✓). (Accept other sensible alternatives.)

Your score: ☐ out of 24

2 Round up (page 26)
Organisms in the environment

1 physical *or* abiotic factors (✓), environment (✓), living *or* biotic factors (✓), community (✓), habitats (✓), niches (✓)

2 a) the non-living part of an ecosystem (✓)
b) The amount of light affects the rate of photosynthesis (✓) and therefore the amount of plant growth under the canopy layer (✓). This in turn affects the animals that depend on plants for food and shelter (✓) and so on along the food chain (✓).

3 a) three (✓)
b) water weed (✓)
c) water weed makes food by photosynthesis (✓)
d) tadpoles (✓)
e) tadpoles eat water weed (accept plants) (✓)
f) minnows (✓) and perch (✓)
g) Minnow and perch eat tadpoles (accept meat) (✓).

4 Light is reflected from the leaf surface (✓). Light passes through the leaf (✓). Only some of the light is absorbed by chlorophyll (✓).

5 When the different organisms in the community show an approximation (are roughly the same) in size (✓).

6 a) saw wrack (✓)
b) dog whelks (✓)
c) The biomass of dog whelks would decrease (✓). The biomass of saw wrack would increase (✓).

7 a) Intraspecific competition – competition between individuals of the same species (✓). Interspecific competition – competition between individuals of different species (✓).
b) Adaptation – an organism is adapted (suited) to survive (✓). Survival – an organism survives (lives) because of its adaptations (✓).
c) Camouflage – coloration that conceals organisms (✓). Warning coloration – colours that deter predators from attacking prey (✓).

8 a) When prey is scarce predator numbers fall (✓). When prey numbers build up predator numbers follow because there is more prey food (✓). Predators breed and reproduce more slowly than prey (✓).
b) The population numbers of each species are stable (✓). (Allow: population numbers of each species fluctuated around a mean (average) number for that species.)
c) Numbers would increase (✓).
d) Numbers would decline (✓) to the former level (✓).
e) Numbers would decline (✓) because of lack of food (✓). (Allow sensible alternative suggestions, e.g. increased mortality due to disease or parasites.)

9
A terms		B descriptions
fertiliser	(✓)	supplies plants with nutrients
herbicide	(✓)	kills plants
irrigation	(✓)	supplies plants with water
monoculture	(✓)	a crop grown over a large area
weed	(✓)	an unwanted plant

Your score: ☐ out of 47

Your improvement index: $\dfrac{\Box/47}{\Box/24} \times 100\% = \Box\%$

3 Test yourself (page 27)
Cell activity

1
A structures		B functions
mitochondrion	(✓)	where energy is released from the oxidation of glucose
plasma membrane	(✓)	partially permeable to substances in solution
chloroplast	(✓)	where light energy is captured
cell wall	(✓)	fully permeable to substances in solution
nucleus	(✓)	contains the chromosomes

2 Because molecules of the substance are moving against their concentration gradient (✓).

3 a) A plasmolysed cell is one from which water has passed out of the vacuole, out of the cytoplasm, and out of the cell through the plasma membrane and cell wall into the solution outside the cell (accept water has passed out of the cell) (✓). As a result the cytoplasm pulls away from the cell wall (accept cell content disrupted) (✓) and the cell becomes limp (✓). A turgid cell is one which contains as much water as it can hold (✓).
b) A fully permeable membrane allows most substances to pass through it (✓). A partially permeable membrane allows some substances to pass through it (✓) and stops other substances (✓).

4 A group of genetically identical cells (or organisms) (✓).

5 During replication each chromosome (and its DNA) (✓) makes an exact copy of itself (✓).

Answers

6 a) Cells die (✓). New cells (✓) which are replicas of the old cells are produced by mitosis (✓).
   b) The daughter cells have the same number of chromosomes as the parent cell (✓). The chromosomes in the daughter cells are identical to those in the parent cells (✓).

7 Haploid cells receive half the diploid number of chromosomes (✓) from their parent cell (✓).
   Diploid cells receive the full number of chromosomes (✓) from their parent cell (✓).

8 cells (✓), cells (✓), tissues (✓), an organ (✓), organs (✓), an organ (✓)

9 cellulose in plant cell walls (✓); chitin in insect exoskeletons (✓)

10 Molecules of unsaturated fats have double bonds between some carbon atoms (✓). Molecules of saturated fats have only single bonds between carbon atoms (✓).

11 A nucleotide consists of the sugar ribose (✓) or deoxyribose (✓), one of five different bases (✓) and a phosphate group (✓).

Your score: ☐ out of 39

3 Round up (page 44)

Cell activity

1 a) nucleus (✓), plasma membrane (✓), mitochondria (✓), cytoplasm (✓)
   b) cell wall (✓), large vacuole (✓), chloroplasts (✓)

2 Water is taken into the cells (✓) by osmosis (✓). The cells become turgid (✓). The wilted plant (✓) will become upright again (✓) as its cells become turgid following watering.

3 down (✓), faster (✓), against (✓), energy (✓), partially (✓), osmosis (✓)

4 Damaged tissues can be replaced by new cells that are identical to the parent cells (✓).

5 Similarities: replication of each chromosome into chromatids (✓); lining up of the chromosomes on the equator of the cell (✓); separation of the chromatids (✓); chromatids form the new chromosomes in daughter cells (✓); breakdown and reformation of the nuclear membrane during the process of cell division (✓).
   Differences: chromosomes form homologous pairs in meiosis but not in mitosis (✓); there are two divisions during meiosis but only one division during mitosis (✓); meiosis results in four haploid daughter cells, mitosis in two diploid daughter cells (✓).

6 cells (✓), tissues (✓), organs (✓), organ systems (✓), organisms (✓)

7
A substances		B functions
fat	(✓)	insulates the body
cellulose	(✓)	a component of the plant cell wall
DNA	(✓)	carries the genetic code
polypeptide	(✓)	made of about 40 amino acids
glycogen	(✓)	a food substance stored in the liver
protein	(✓)	most enzymes are made of this substance

8 a) 4 (✓)   b) 4 (✓)

Your score: ☐ out of 40

Your improvement index: ☐/40 ÷ ☐/39 × 100% = ☐ %

4 Test yourself (page 45)

Green plants as organisms

1 a) carbon dioxide (✓) and water (✓)
   b) oxygen (✓)

2
A substances		B functions
nitrogen	(✓)	used to make protein
phosphorus	(✓)	used to make cell membranes
magnesium	(✓)	used to make chlorophyll

3 increase (✓), xylem (✓), osmosis (✓), active transport (✓), xylem (✓), evaporates (✓), stomata (✓)

4
A tropisms		B descriptions
phototropism	(✓)	growth movement in response to light
geotropism	(✓)	growth movement in response to gravity
hydrotropism	(✓)	growth movement in response to water
thigmotropism	(✓)	growth movement in response to touch

Your score: ☐ out of 18

4 Round up (page 55)

Green plants as organisms

1 palisade cells (✓), spongy mesophyll cells (✓), guard cells (✓)

2 The cells of the upper surface of the leaf do not contain chloroplasts (✓). Most light therefore reaches the palisade cells (✓), which are packed with chloroplasts (✓). Photosynthesis occurs at a maximum rate (✓).

3 temperature (✓), light intensity (✓), supplies of carbon dioxide (✓) and water (✓). A modern greenhouse provides warmth (✓), lighting (✓), a source of carbon dioxide (✓) and water from sprinkler systems (✓)

4 sugar (✓), sugar (✓), phloem (✓), sugar (✓), phloem (✓), active transport (✓), water (✓), phloem (✓), pressure (✓), translocation (✓), sugar (✓), pressure (✓), phloem (✓)

5 warm (✓), windy (✓), low humidity (✓) and bright sunlight (✓)

6 The stomata close (✓). If the plant continues to lose more water than it gains then its cells lose turgor (✓) and it wilts (✓).

7
Xylem		Phloem
dead tissue (cells)	(✓)	living tissue (cells)
tissue (cells) waterproofed with lignin	(✓)	tissue (cells) not waterproofed with lignin
transports water and minerals	(✓)	transports sugar and other substances
transport of materials is one way	(✓)	transport of materials is two ways
xylem tissue does not have companion cells	(✓)	phloem tissue has companion cells

8 growth regulator (✓), tip (✓), weedkiller (✓), unfertilised (✓), seedless (✓), ripens (✓)

9 a) Hypothesis: a substance produced in the shoot tip of a growing seedling (✓) controls the response of the shoot to light (✓).
   b) A: the shoot will remain upright and not bend towards the source of light (✓).
   Explanation: the piece of metal prevents the substance that controls the response of the shoot to light and which is produced in the shoot tip (✓) from diffusing to the region behind the shoot tip where it has its effect (✓).
   B: the shoot will bend towards the source of light (✓).
   Explanation: the substance that controls the response of the shoot to light and which is produced in the shoot tip (✓) is able to diffuse to the region behind the shoot tip where it has its effect (✓).

Your score: ☐ out of 54

Your improvement index: $\frac{\boxed{}/54}{\boxed{}/18} \times 100\% = \boxed{}\%$

5 Test yourself (page 56)

Humans as organisms

1 a) carbohydrates (✓), fats (✓), proteins (✓)
   b) protein (✓)
   c) fat (✓)
   d) minerals (✓) and vitamins (✓)

2
A terms		B descriptions
ingestion	(✓)	food is taken into the mouth
digestion	(✓)	food is broken down
absorption	(✓)	digested food passes into the body
egestion	(✓)	the removal of undigested food through the anus

3 a) There are two bronchi, one branching to each lung (✓). Each bronchus branches many times into small tubes called bronchioles (✓).
   b) A person has two lungs (✓). Within each lung, bronchioles subdivide into even smaller tubes which end in clusters of small sacs called alveoli (✓).

   c) During aerobic respiration, cells use oxygen to oxidise digested food substances (accept glucose) (✓), releasing energy (✓). During anaerobic respiration, cells break down digested food substances (accept glucose) without oxygen (✓). Less energy is released during anaerobic respiration than during aerobic respiration (✓).
   d) Breathing takes in (inhales) (✓) and expels (exhales) (✓) air. Gaseous exchange occurs across the surfaces of the alveoli (✓).

4 The right ventricle pumps blood into the pulmonary artery (✓) on its way to the lungs (✓); the left ventricle pumps blood into the aorta (✓), which takes it around the rest of the body (✓).

5
A components		B descriptions
plasma	(✓)	contains dissolved food substances
red blood cells	(✓)	contain haemoglobin
white blood cells	(✓)	produce antibodies
platelets	(✓)	promote the formation of blood clots

6 receptor (✓), sensory neurone (✓), relay neurone (✓), motor neurone (✓), effector

7 a) The eardrum vibrates (✓) in response to sound waves (✓).
   b) The bones pass vibrations through the middle ear (✓) and also amplify them (✓).
   c) The pinna funnels sound waves down the ear canal (✓) to the eardrum (✓).
   d) The hair cells are stimulated by the vibrations of the basilar membrane (✓). They fire off nerve impulses to the brain along the auditory nerve (✓).

8 Hormones are chemical substances (✓) which circulate in the blood (✓).

9 Insulin decreases the level of glucose in the blood (✓). Glucagon increases the level of glucose in the blood (✓).

10 glomerulus (✓), Bowman's capsule (✓), tubule (✓), collecting duct (✓), ureter (✓), bladder (✓), urethra (✓)

11
A body structures		B roles
tear gland	(✓)	produces the enzyme lysozyme, which destroys bacteria
glands in the stomach wall	(✓)	produce hydrochloric acid, which kills bacteria
skin	(✓)	produces sebum, which kills bacteria and fungi
cilia lining the upper respiratory tract	(✓)	sweep away mucus containing trapped microorganisms and particles
blood	(✓)	white cells produce antibodies, which destroy antigens

Your score: ☐ out of 58

Answers

5 Round up (page 89)

Humans as organisms

1
A nutrients		B test results
starch	(✓)	produces a blue/black colour when mixed with a few drops of iodine solution
glucose	(✓)	produces an orange/red colour when heated with Benedict's solution
fat	(✓)	forms a milky emulsion when mixed with warm dilute ethanol
protein	(✓)	produces a violet/purple colour when mixed with dilute sodium hydroxide and a few drops of copper sulphate solution

2
A enzymes		B roles
amylase	(✓)	digests starch to maltose
pepsin	(✓)	digests protein to polypeptides
lipase	(✓)	digests fat to fatty acids and glycerol
maltase	(✓)	digests maltose to glucose

3 oxygen (✓), carbon dioxide (✓), alveoli (✓), surface area (✓), exchange (✓), thin (✓), moist (✓), inhalation (✓), exhalation (✓)

4
a) Oxygenated blood contains a lot of oxyhaemoglobin (✓). It is bright red (✓). Deoxygenated blood contains little oxyhaemoglobin (✓). It is deep red-purple (✓).
b) Antibodies are proteins (✓) produced by lymphocytes (accept white blood cells) (✓) in response to antigens (✓), which are materials 'foreign' to (accept not recognised by) the body (✓). Antibodies destroy antigens (✓).
c) HIV is the abbreviation for human immunodeficiency virus (✓), which causes the diseases (✓) that characterise AIDS (✓).
d) Haemoglobin is the protein (✓) in red blood cells (✓) that absorbs oxygen (✓). Haemophilia is a genetic disease (✓) characterised by the slow clotting time of blood (✓).
e) A thrombus is a clot (✓) that causes a thrombosis (blockage) (✓) in a blood vessel (✓).

5
A parts of cell		B descriptions
axon	(✓)	transmits nerve impulses from the cell body
dendrite	(✓)	carries nerve impulses to the cell body
myelin sheath	(✓)	boosts the transmission of nerve impulses
nerve impulse	(✓)	minute electrical disturbance

6
a) The blind spot is the region of the retina insensitive to light (✓). The fovea is the most sensitive region of the retina, where cone cells are most dense (✓).
b) The pupil is the central hole formed by the iris (✓). The iris is the coloured ring of muscle that controls the amount of light entering the eye (✓).
c) The cornea bends (refracts) light (✓) and helps to focus light on to the retina (✓).

7 Endocrine glands are ductless glands (✓) which release hormones directly into the blood (✓).

8 Antidiuretic hormone promotes reabsorbtion of water into the body (✓) by making the collecting duct of the nephron more permeable to water (✓).

9
a) Raised hairs trap a layer of air (✓) which insulates the body in cold weather (✓). Air is a poor conductor of heat (✓).
b) Sweat cools the body because heat energy is drawn away from the body (✓) as sweat evaporates (✓).

10 cholera (B) (✓), AIDS (V) (✓), syphilis (B) (✓), 'flu (V) (✓), pneumonia (B) (✓)

11 Nicotine is a poison which increases the heart rate (✓) and blood pressure (✓).
Carbon monoxide combines with haemoglobin (✓) more readily than oxygen (✓).
Tar is a mixture of substances (✓), some of which cause cancer (accept are carcinogens) (✓).

Your score: ☐ out of 67

Your improvement index: $\dfrac{\Box/67}{\Box/58} \times 100\% = \Box\%$

6 Test yourself (page 90)

Inheritance and evolution

1 A = sperm duct (✓), B = urethra (✓), C = scrotal sac (accept scrotum) (✓), D = testis (✓), E = penis (✓)

2
A structures		B descriptions
corm	(✓)	a short, swollen underground stem
runner	(✓)	a horizontal stem running above ground
tuber	(✓)	a swelling at the end of a rhizome
bulb	(✓)	a large underground bud

3
a) **Bb** (✓) or **bb** (✓)
b) 50% of the children would be brown eyed (✓); 50% blue eyed (✓).

4
a) Restriction enzyme cleaves (cuts up) lengths of DNA into different sized fragments (✓) depending on the restriction enzyme used (✓). A particular DNA fragment may correspond to a desired gene (✓). (Accept sensible alternative explanation.)
Ligase splices the desired gene from among the fragments of DNA produced by restriction enzyme (✓) into a plasmid vector (✓), which is a loop of bacterial DNA (✓) into which the desired gene is inserted (✓).
b) Biotechnology uses microorganisms (✓) on a large scale for the production of useful substances (✓).
Genetic engineering manipulates genes (✓) to create organisms (✓) with specific genetic characteristics for producing a range of useful substances (✓).
c) Batch culture produces batches of substances in a fermenter (✓). The fermenter is then emptied of product and nutrient solution (✓) and sterilised (✓) in preparation for the next batch (✓).
Continuous culture produces substances over an extended period (✓). Product is drawn off and nutrients replaced as they are used (✓) during an ongoing process (✓).

5 Acquired characteristics are those produced in the individual as a result of the influence (effects) of the environment (✓). These characteristics are not the result of genetic influence (✓) and are therefore not inherited (✓).

Answers

6 Genetic recombination (✓) as a result of sexual reproduction (✓), mutation (✓), crossing over (✓) during meiosis (✓) and the effects of the environment (✓).

> Well done if you mentioned crossing over!

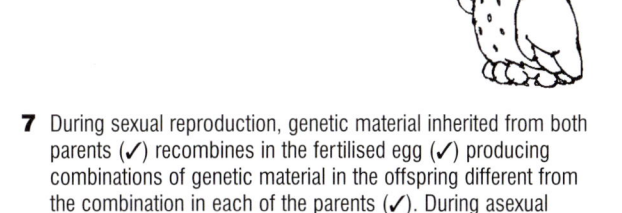

7 During sexual reproduction, genetic material inherited from both parents (✓) recombines in the fertilised egg (✓) producing combinations of genetic material in the offspring different from the combination in each of the parents (✓). During asexual reproduction, offspring inherit identical genetic material from one parent (✓). Mutation is the only source of variation (✓).

8 a) Ancestors are organisms that give rise to offspring, who are their descendants (✓).
b) Adaptation – an organism with a structure and way of life that best suits it to survive is said to be adapted (✓). Extinction occurs when a species dies out (✓).
c) Evolution – the change that occurs through many generations of descendants from different ancestors (✓). Natural selection – the process whereby favourable variations survive (✓) so that descendants evolve from ancestors (✓). (Allow: the mechanism of evolution through the survival of favourable variations.)

9 Fossil formation occurs under the following conditions:
- the replacement of decayed organic material with a permanent alternative (✓)
- the burying of an organism in hardening mud or cooling volcanic ash (✓) followed by the formation of a cast (allow: material that takes on the shape of the original organism) (✓)
- rapid freezing of the organism following its death (✓).

Your score: ☐ out of 56

6 Round up (page 107)

Inheritance and evolution

1 | A structures | | B descriptions |
   |---|---|---|
   | seed | (✓) | a fertilised ovule |
   | ovule | (✓) | contains the egg nucleus |
   | fruit | (✓) | develops from the ovary after fertilisation |
   | stigma | (✓) | structure to which pollen grains attach |
   | nectary | (✓) | produces a sugar solution |

2 Plants are healthy (✓), the same (accept uniform) (✓), and retain desirable characteristics (✓).

3 starch (✓)

4 During mitosis, the DNA of the parent cell replicates (✓) so that daughter cells receive exact copies of the parent cell's genetic material (✓). Daughter cells divide and develop into new individuals which inherit the exact characteristics of the parent (✓). Offspring of the parent are also genetically identical to one another (✓) and are a clone (✓).

5 | A terms | | B descriptions |
  |---|---|---|
  | allele | (✓) | one of a pair of genes that controls a particular characteristic |
  | pure breeding | (✓) | characteristics that appear unchanged from generation to generation |
  | second filial generation | (✓) | offspring of the offspring of the parental generation |
  | monohybrid inheritance | (✓) | the processes by which a single characteristic passes from parents to offspring |

6 a) The trap allows gas to escape (✓) and prevents unwanted airborne microorganisms from contaminating the mixture (✓).
b) carbon dioxide (✓)
c) The grape juice provides the substances yeast cells need to grow and multiply (✓).
d) sugar (accept glucose) (✓)

7 a) (i) A (✓)
    (ii) B (✓)
    (iii) Chart A shows intermediate lengths of fish (✓) over a range of measurements (✓). Chart B shows categories of colour (✓) without any intermediate shades (✓).
b) 90% (✓)
c) Albino fish occur as a result of a mutation of the alleles controlling colour (✓).

8 a) In unpolluted countryside, pale peppered moths blend with the light background of (are camouflaged on) the lichen-covered tree trunk (✓). Fewer are eaten by moth-eating birds (suffer less predation) (✓) than dark peppered moths (✓), which are more conspicuous (✓). In polluted industrial areas, dark peppered moths are less conspicuous against the soot-covered tree trunks (✓). Fewer are eaten by moth-eating birds (suffer less predation) (✓) than pale peppered moths (✓), which are more conspicuous (✓).
b) The bird eats the moths which are conspicuous (✓) and therefore not adapted to blend with their surroundings (✓).

9 Individuals with genes for characteristics that favour survival are more likely to reproduce (✓). Their offspring inherit the favourable genes (✓) and in turn are more likely to survive and reproduce (✓) so handing on the favourable genes to the next generation, and so on (✓).

10 Charles Lyell stated that the Earth was very old (✓). This suggested to Darwin that there was sufficient time for the process of evolution to occur (✓). Malthus suggested that limited resources regulated population numbers (✓) which would otherwise increase indefinitely (✓). Darwin concluded that there must be a struggle for existence (competition for limited resources) (✓).

Your score: ☐ out of 50

Your improvement index: $\dfrac{\Box/50}{\Box/56} \times 100\% = \Box\%$

Materials and their properties

1	**Matter and the kinetic theory**	**116**
	1.1 States of matter	116
	1.2 Change of state	116
	1.3 Some properties of materials	117
	1.4 Composite materials	117
	1.5 The kinetic theory	117
	1.6 What does the kinetic theory explain?	118
2	**Elements, compounds and equations**	**119**
	2.1 Metallic and non-metallic elements	119
	2.2 Structures of elements	119
	2.3 Compounds	119
	2.4 Symbols	120
	2.5 Formulas	120
	2.6 Equations	122
3	**The structure of the atom**	**124**
	3.1 Protons, neutrons and electrons	124
	3.2 Focus on the atom	124
4	**Electrolysis**	**128**
	4.1 Conducting electricity	128
	4.2 Ions	129
	4.3 At the electrodes	129
	4.4 Which ions are discharged?	130
	4.5 Electrodes taking part	130
	4.6 Applications of electrolysis	130
5	**The chemical bond**	**135**
	5.1 Bond formation	135
	5.2 Ionic bonding	135
	5.3 Covalent bonding	136
	5.4 Ionic and covalent substances	137
	5.5 The formula of an ionic compound	137
6	**The periodic table**	**140**
	6.1 Classifying elements	140
	6.2 A repeating pattern	140
7	**Acids, bases and salts**	**145**
	7.1 Acids	145
	7.2 Bases	147
	7.3 Neutralisation	149
	7.4 Indicators	149
	7.5 Salts	149
8	**Air**	**153**
	8.1 How the atmosphere evolved	153
	8.2 Oxygen	154
	8.3 Oxidation and reduction	155
	8.4 Nitrogen	156
	8.5 The nitrogen cycle	156
	8.6 Ammonia and fertilisers	157
	8.7 Carbon dioxide	157
	8.8 The noble gases	159
	8.9 The problem of pollution	159
9	**Water**	**165**
	9.1 The water cycle	165
	9.2 Water underground	166
	9.3 Dissolved oxygen	166
	9.4 Pure water	166
	9.5 Pollution of water	166
10	**Planet Earth**	**169**
	10.1 Structure of the Earth	169
	10.2 Plate tectonics	169
	10.3 Types of rock	172
	10.4 The landscape	173
	10.5 Materials from rocks	173
11	**Metals and alloys**	**177**
	11.1 The metallic bond	177
	11.2 Reactions of metals	177
	11.3 Metals in the periodic table	178
	11.4 Making predictions	179
	11.5 Extracting metals	180
	11.6 Corrosion of metals	181
	11.7 Conservation	181
	11.8 Uses of metals and alloys	182
	11.9 Iron and steel	183
12	**Reaction speeds**	**186**
	12.1 Particle size	186
	12.2 Concentration	187
	12.3 Pressure	187
	12.4 Temperature	187
	12.5 Light	187
	12.6 Catalysts	187
	12.7 Enzymes	188
13	**Tackling chemical calculations**	**190**
	13.1 Some definitions	190
	13.2 Formulas	192
	13.3 Masses of reacting solids	193
14	**Fuels**	**196**
	14.1 Fossil fuels	196
	14.2 Fuels from petroleum	197
	14.3 Alkanes	197
	14.4 Energy and chemical reactions	198
	14.5 Energy change of reaction	198
	14.6 Activation energy	199
	14.7 Using bond energy values	199
15	**Alkenes and plastics**	**202**
	15.1 Alkenes	202
	15.2 Reactions of alkenes	202
	15.3 Uses of plastics	203
	15.4 Some disadvantages of plastics	204
Periodic table		**207**
Answers		**208**
Index		**315**

Chapter 1 Matter and the kinetic theory

PREVIEW

At the end of this topic you will be able to:
- describe the states of matter and changes of state
- apply the kinetic theory of matter to solids, liquids, gases, changes of state, dissolving, diffusion and Brownian motion.

How much do you already know? Work out your score on page 208.

Test yourself

1. Name the three chief states of matter. [3]
2. What can you tell about the purity of a solid from its melting point? [2]
3. What is the difference between evaporation and boiling? [2]
4. How can you tell when a liquid is boiling? [1]
5. Why do vegetables cook faster in a pressure cooker? [2]
6. Why does it take a long time to boil potatoes on a high mountain? [2]
7. What is a) the resemblance b) the difference between a plastic material and an elastic material? [3]
8. Why are crystals shiny? [3]
9. What happens to the heat energy that is supplied to a solid to make it melt? [2]
10. One litre of water forms 1333 litres of steam. Explain the big difference in volume. [2]
11. Explain why a spoonful of salt can flavour a whole pan of soup. [3]

1.1 States of matter

Everything in the Universe is composed of matter. Matter exists in three chief states: the solid, liquid and gaseous states. Their characteristics are shown in the table.

	volume	shape	effect of rise in temperature
solid	fixed	definite	expands slightly
liquid	fixed	flows – changes shape to fit the shape of the container	expands
gas	changes to fit the container	changes to fit the container	expands greatly (gases have much lower densities than solids and liquids)

Characteristics of the solid, liquid and gaseous states

1.2 Change of state

Matter can change from one state into another, as shown in the diagram below.

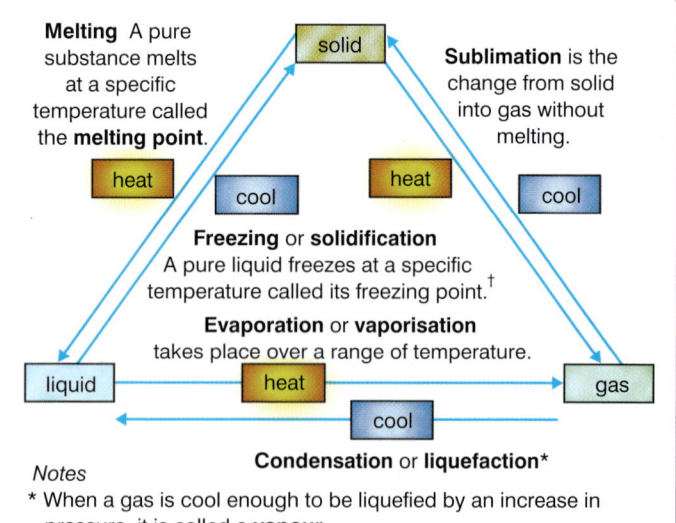

Melting A pure substance melts at a specific temperature called the **melting point**.

Sublimation is the change from solid into gas without melting.

Freezing or **solidification**
A pure liquid freezes at a specific temperature called its freezing point.†

Evaporation or **vaporisation** takes place over a range of temperature.

Condensation or **liquefaction***

Notes
* When a gas is cool enough to be liquefied by an increase in pressure, it is called a **vapour**.
† The melting point of a solid and the freezing point of a liquid are the same temperature.

116

Matter and the kinetic theory

1.3 Some properties of materials

★ **Density:** density = $\dfrac{\text{mass}}{\text{volume}}$

★ **Melting point:** while a pure solid melts, the temperature remains constant at the melting point of the solid.

★ **Boiling point:** while a pure liquid boils, the temperature remains constant at the boiling point of the liquid.

★ **Conductivity** (thermal and electrical): the ability to conduct heat and electricity is a characteristic of metals and alloys.

★ **Solubility:** a solution consists of a **solute** dissolved in a **solvent**. A concentrated solution contains a high proportion of solute; a dilute solution contains a low proportion of solute. A saturated solution contains as much solute as it is possible to dissolve at the stated temperature.

Solubility is the mass of solute that will dissolve in 100 g of solvent at the stated temperature.

Two ways of expressing concentration are:

concentration = $\dfrac{\text{mass of solute}}{\text{volume of solution}}$

concentration = $\dfrac{\text{amount (moles) of solute}}{\text{volume of solution}}$

(For *mole*, see page 191.)

1.4 Composite materials

A **composite material** is a mixture of two or more materials which combines their properties. Here are some examples.

- Reinforced concrete combines the compressive (crushing) strength of concrete with the tensile (stretching) strength of the reinforcing steel rods.
- Glass-fibre-reinforced plastic combines plasticity with the strength of fibres, which prevent cracking.
- Plasterboard combines plaster, a brittle material, with paper fibres that prevent cracking.

1.5 The kinetic theory

According to the **kinetic theory of matter**, all forms of matter are made up of small particles which are in constant motion. The theory explains the states of matter and changes of state.

In a solid, the particles are close together and attract one another strongly. They are arranged in a regular three-dimensional structure. The particles can vibrate, but they cannot move out of their positions in the structure.

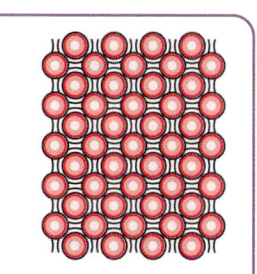

The arrangement of particles in a solid

When the solid is heated, the particles vibrate more energetically. If they gain enough energy, they may break away from the structure and become free to move independently. When this happens, the solid has melted.

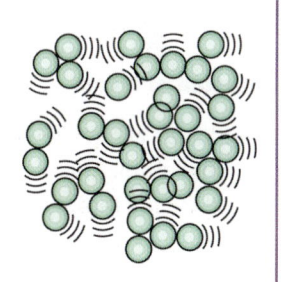

In a liquid, the particles are further apart than in a solid. They are free to move about. This is why a liquid flows easily and has no fixed shape. There are forces of attraction between particles. When a liquid is heated, some particles gain enough energy to break away from the other particles and become a gas.

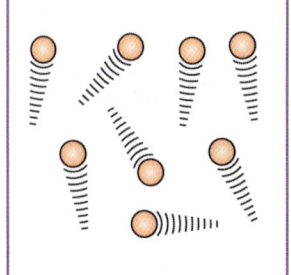

The arrangement of particles in a liquid

Most of a gas is space, through which the particles move at high speed. There are only very small forces of attraction between the particles. When a mass of liquid vaporises, it forms a very much larger volume of gas because the particles are so much further apart in a gas.

The arrangement of particles in a gas

Collisions between the gas particles and the container create pressure on the container.

Matter and the kinetic theory

Crystals

A crystal is a piece of matter with a regular shape and smooth surfaces which reflect light. Viewed through an electron microscope, crystals can be seen to consist of a regular arrangement of particles. The regular arrangement of particles gives the crystal its regular shape.

A beam of X-rays passed through a crystal on to a photographic plate produces a regular pattern of dots called an **X-ray diffraction photograph**. From the pattern of dots, a crystallographer can work out the arrangement of particles in the crystal.

1.6 What does the kinetic theory explain?

Dissolving of a solid

When a solid dissolves, particles of solid separate from the crystal and spread out through the solvent to form a solution.

Diffusion of a gas

When a gas is released into a container, particles of gas move through the container until the gas has spread evenly through all the space available.

Evaporation or vaporisation

Attractive forces exist between the particles in a liquid. Some particles with more energy than the average break away from the attraction of other particles and escape into the vapour phase. The average energy of the particles that remain is lower than before – the liquid has cooled.

Brownian motion

The botanist William Brown used his microscope a century ago to observe grains of pollen suspended in water. He saw that the grains were in constant motion. The explanation is that water molecules collide with a pollen grain and give it a push. The direction of the push changes as different numbers of molecules strike the pollen grain from different sides.

ROUND UP

How much have you improved? Work out your improvement index on page 208.

1. The graph shows temperature against time as a liquid is heated. What is happening at A and B? [3]

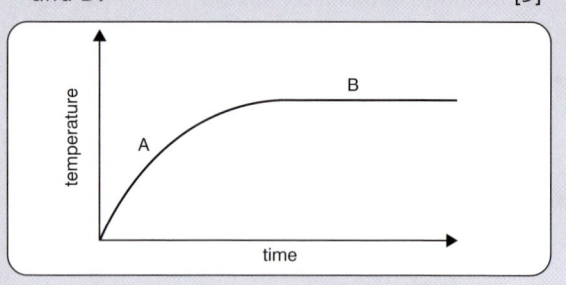

2. The graph below shows temperature of a solid against time as it is heated. What is happening at C, D and E? Is the solid a pure substance? [7]

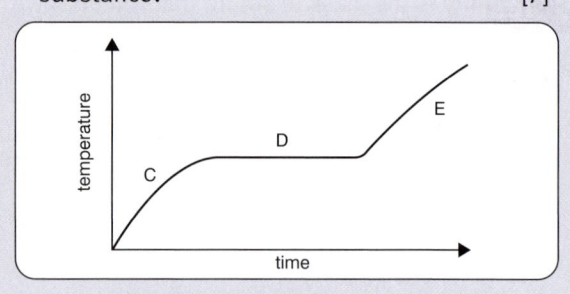

3. Medical instruments are sterilised in an autoclave, which heats them in steam formed from water boiled under pressure. Why is this more effective than heating them in a pan of boiling water? [2]

4. Why do gases have a much lower density than solids and liquids? [1]

5. Why does compression reduce the volume of a gas more than that of a solid or a liquid? [2]

6. Give an example of the expansion of a gas with rising temperature. [1]

7. Give an example of the increase of gas pressure with rising temperature. [1]

8. Angela is wearing 'L'esprit de la chemie'. Explain why her friends can still smell her perfume after she leaves the room. [3]

9. Aftershave lotions contain a liquid which vaporises readily at room temperature. When the lotion is dabbed on the skin, it produces a cooling effect. Explain what causes this cooling effect. [2]

Elements, compounds and equations — Chapter 2

PREVIEW

At the end of this topic you will be able to:
- list the differences between metallic and non-metallic elements
- describe the structures of some elements
- distinguish between an element, a compound and a mixture
- write an equation for a chemical reaction.

CONCEPT MAP Page 123.

How much do you already know? Work out your score on page 208.

Test yourself

1. Explain what is meant by an element. [3]
2. What chemical properties of zinc classify it as a metallic element? [7]
3. Explain why diamond is hard while graphite is soft. [4]
4. Name two methods that can be used to split a compound into elements. [2]
5. How many atoms are there in $2Al(OH)_3$? [1]
6. Balance the equation and insert state symbols. [8]

   $Na + H_2O \rightarrow NaOH + H_2$

2.1 Metallic and non-metallic elements

Elements are pure substances that cannot be split up into simpler substances. Some elements exist as **allotropes** – forms of the same element which have different crystalline structures. Allotropes of carbon are shown on page 121. Elements are classified as metallic and non-metallic, as shown in the table overleaf.

2.2 Structures of elements

Individual molecules

Some elements consist of small individual molecules with negligible forces of attraction between them, e.g. oxygen O_2 and chlorine Cl_2.

Molecular structures

Some elements consist of molecules held in a crystal structure by weak intermolecular forces. Solid iodine is a structure composed of I_2 molecules; iodine vapour consists of individual I_2 molecules.

Giant molecules

Some elements consist of giant molecules or macromolecules, which are composed of millions of atoms bonded together in a three-dimensional structure, e.g. the allotropes of carbon – diamond, graphite and fullerenes – shown on page 121.

2.3 Compounds

A **compound** is a pure substance that consists of two or more elements which are chemically combined in fixed proportions by mass. Some compounds can be **synthesised** from their elements, e.g. calcium burns in oxygen to form calcium oxide; hot copper combines with chlorine to form copper chloride.

It may be possible to split up a compound into its elements:
- by **thermal decomposition**, e.g. silver oxide splits up into silver and oxygen when heated
- by **electrolysis**, e.g. water is electrolysed to hydrogen and oxygen.

A compound differs from a mixture of elements as shown in the table on page 121.

Elements, compounds and equations

metallic elements	non-metallic elements
physical properties	*physical properties*
solids except for mercury	solids and gases, except for bromine (which is a liquid)
dense, hard	Most of the solid elements are softer than metals (diamond is exceptional).
A smooth metallic surface is shiny; many metals tarnish in air.	Most non-metallic elements are dull (diamond is exceptional).
The shape can be changed without breaking by the application of force – either compression, as in hammering, or tension, as in stretching, e.g. drawing out into a wire.	Many non-metallic elements are brittle – they break when a force is applied.
conduct heat (although highly polished surfaces reflect heat)	are poor thermal conductors
are good electrical conductors	are poor electrical conductors, except for graphite; some, e.g. silicon, are semiconductors
are sonorous – make a pleasing sound when struck	are not sonorous
The properties of metals derive from the metallic bond – see pages 177–8.	
chemical properties	*chemical properties*
electropositive – able to donate electrons	electronegative – able to accept electrons
many displace hydrogen from dilute acids to form salts	do not react with acids, except for oxidising acids, e.g. concentrated sulphuric acid
The metal is the cation (positive ion) in the salts, e.g. Na^+, Ca^{2+}; some metals also form oxoanions, e.g. ZnO_2^{2-}, AlO_3^-.	form anions (negative ions), e.g. S^{2-}, and oxoanions, e.g. SO_4^{2-}
form basic oxides and hydroxides, e.g. Na_2O, $NaOH$, CaO, $Ca(OH)_2$	form acidic oxides, e.g. CO_2, SO_2, or neutral oxides, e.g. CO, NO
The chlorides are ionic solids, e.g. $MgCl_2$, $NaCl$.	The chlorides are gases or covalent volatile liquids, e.g. HCl, SCl_2, PCl_3.
Hydrides are formed only by the metals in Groups 1 and 2, and these hydrides are unstable, e.g. NaH.	form stable hydrides, e.g. HBr, H_2S

Characteristics of metallic and non-metallic elements

2.4 Symbols

Every element has its own **symbol**. The symbol is a letter or two letters which stand for one atom of the element, e.g. aluminium Al, iron Fe. See the table on page 126.

2.5 Formulas

Every compound has a **formula**. This is composed of the symbols of the elements present along with numbers which give the ratio in which the atoms are present.

A molecule of sulphuric acid (see below) contains 2 hydrogen atoms, 1 sulphur atom and 4 oxygen atoms, giving the formula H_2SO_4.

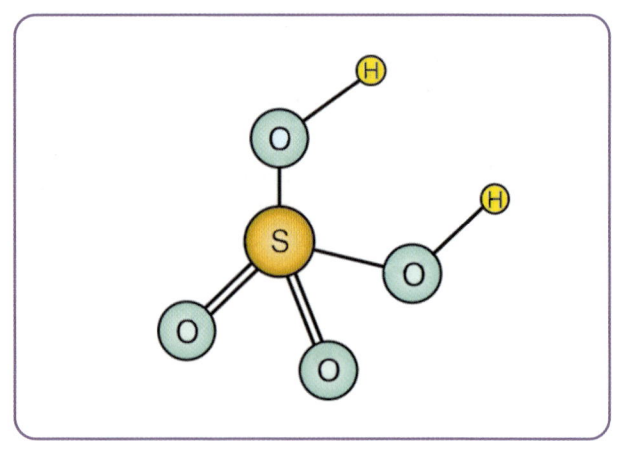

H_2SO_4 – a single molecule

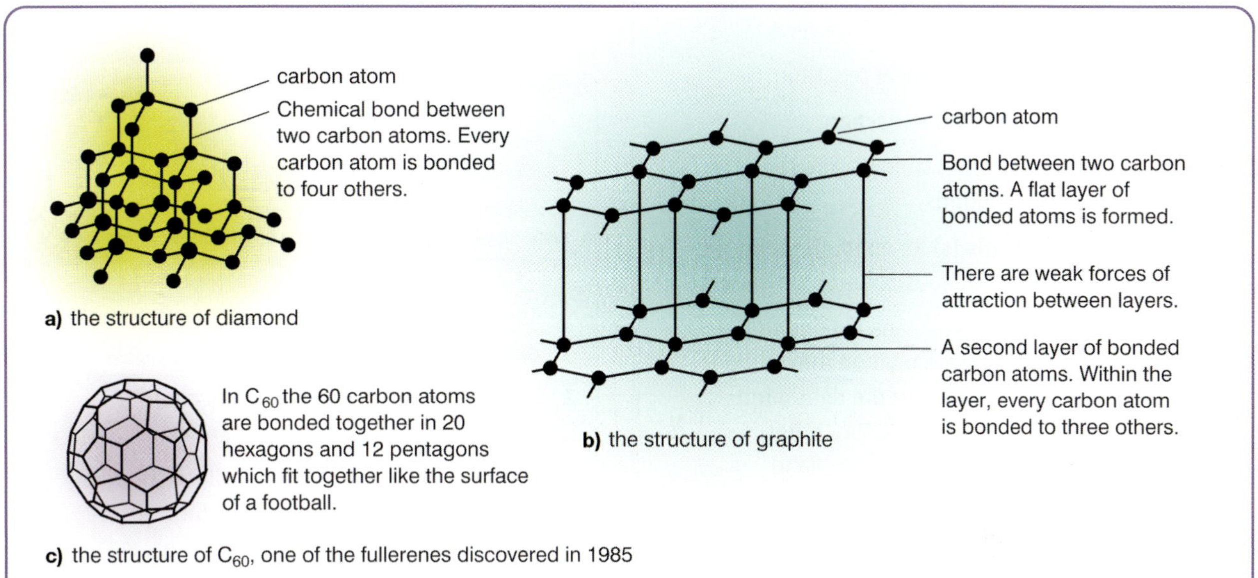

Elements, compounds and equations

a) the structure of diamond
- carbon atom
- Chemical bond between two carbon atoms. Every carbon atom is bonded to four others.

b) the structure of graphite
- carbon atom
- Bond between two carbon atoms. A flat layer of bonded atoms is formed.
- There are weak forces of attraction between layers.
- A second layer of bonded carbon atoms. Within the layer, every carbon atom is bonded to three others.

c) the structure of C_{60}, one of the fullerenes discovered in 1985

In C_{60} the 60 carbon atoms are bonded together in 20 hexagons and 12 pentagons which fit together like the surface of a football.

The allotropes of carbon

mixtures	compounds
No chemical change takes place when a mixture is made.	When a compound is made, a chemical reaction takes place, and heat is often taken in or given out.
A mixture has the same properties as its components.	A compound has a new set of properties; it does not behave in the same way as the components.
A mixture can be separated into its parts by methods such as distillation.	A compound can be split into its elements or into simpler compounds only by a chemical reaction.
A mixture can contain its components in any proportions.	A compound contains its elements in fixed proportions by mass, e.g. magnesium oxide always contains 60% by mass of magnesium.

Differences between mixtures and compounds

Silicon(IV) oxide, shown here, consists of macromolecules which contain twice as many oxygen atoms as silicon atoms, giving the formula SiO_2.

The formula of ammonium sulphate is $(NH_4)_2SO_4$. The '2' multiplies the symbols in brackets: there are 2 nitrogen, 8 hydrogen, 1 sulphur and 4 oxygen atoms.

Writing $2Al_2O_3$ means that the numbers below the line each multiply the symbols in front of them, and the 2 on the line multiplies everything that comes after it, giving a total of 4 aluminium and 6 oxygen atoms.

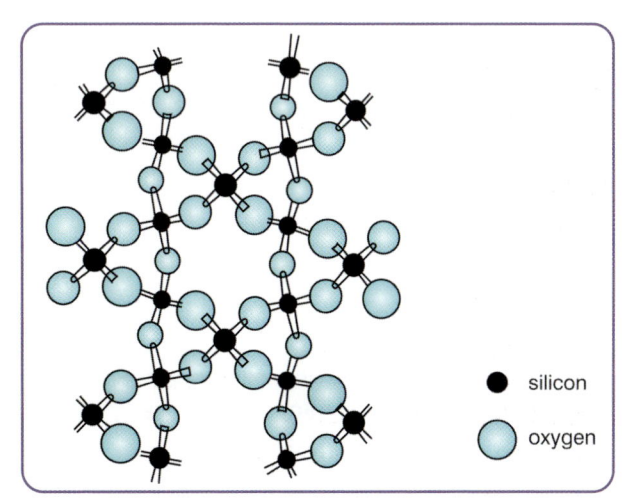

- silicon
- oxygen

SiO_2 – a macromolecule

Elements, compounds and equations

2.6 Equations

To write an equation for a chemical reaction:

1 Write a word equation for the reaction.
2 Put in the symbols for the elements and the formulas for the compounds.
3 Put in the **state symbols** (s) for solid, (l) for liquid, (g) for gas, (aq) for in aqueous solution (in water).
4 **Balance** the equation. This means making the number of atoms of each element on the left-hand side (LHS) equal the number on the right-hand side (RHS). Do this by writing a 2, 3 or other numeral in front of a symbol or a formula to multiply that symbol or formula. **Never try to balance an equation by altering a formula.**

Example

1 calcium + water → hydrogen + calcium hydroxide solution

2 $Ca + H_2O \rightarrow H_2 + Ca(OH)_2$

3 $Ca(s) + H_2O(l) \rightarrow H_2(g) + Ca(OH)_2(aq)$

4 There are 2 hydrogen atoms on the LHS and 4 hydrogen atoms on the RHS. There is 1 oxygen atom on the LHS and 2 oxygen atoms on the RHS. Multiply H_2O by 2:

$Ca(s) + 2H_2O(l) \rightarrow H_2(g) + Ca(OH)_2(aq)$

The equation is now balanced.

Ionic equations

In **ionic equations**, only the ions that take part in the reaction are shown. Here are some examples.

★ **Neutralisation**

acid + alkali → salt + water
$H^+(aq) + OH^-(aq) \rightarrow H_2O(l)$

★ **Displacement**

zinc + copper(II) sulphate solution → zinc sulphate solution + copper
$Zn(s) + Cu^{2+}(aq) \rightarrow Zn^{2+}(aq) + Cu(s)$

★ **Precipitation**

barium chloride solution + sodium sulphate solution → barium sulphate precipitate + sodium chloride solution
$Ba^{2+}(aq) + SO_4^{2-}(aq) \rightarrow BaSO_4(s)$

ROUND UP

How much have you improved? Work out your improvement index on pages 208–9.

1 The element Q forms ions Q^{2+}. Is Q metallic or non-metallic? [1]

2 The element R forms an acidic oxide RO_2. Is R metallic or non-metallic? [1]

3 The element E forms a crystalline chloride ECl_2. Is E metallic or non-metallic? [1]

4 The element G forms a stable hydride HG. Is G metallic or non-metallic? [1]

5 Contrast four physical properties for sulphur and copper (a non-metallic element and a metallic element). [4]

6 How would you distinguish between a mixture of powdered sulphur and iron filings and a compound of iron and sulphur? [4]

7 How many atoms are present in $3(NH_4)_2SO_4$? [1]

8 Balance the equation and insert state symbols. [4]

$CaCO_3 + HCl \rightarrow CaCl_2 + CO_2 + H_2O$

9 Write an ionic equation for the reaction [3]

iron(II) sulphate + sodium hydroxide → iron(II) hydroxide + sodium sulphate

Well done if you've improved. Don't worry if you haven't. Take a break and try again.

Elements, compounds and equations

ELEMENTS

METALS

Physical properties
- solids (except Hg(l)), dense, hard, ductile
- shiny
- good thermal and electrical conductors
- sonorous (2.1, 2.2)

Chemical properties
- form positive ions, e.g. Na^+, Ca^{2+}
- some react with water, e.g. Na, Ca, to give hydrogen and the metal hydroxide
- many react with dilute acids to give hydrogen + the salt of the acid, e.g. Mg, Zn, Fe (2.1, 2.2)

Compounds
- oxides and hydroxides are bases, e.g. $MgO(s)$, $Fe(OH)_2(s)$
- soluble oxides and hydroxides are alkalis, e.g. $Na_2O(s)$, $Ca(OH)_2(s)$
- chlorides are ionic solids, e.g. $Na^+Cl^-(s)$ (2.3)

NON-METALS

Physical properties
- solids or gases (except $Br_2(l)$)
- dull
- poor conductors of heat and electricity
- not sonorous (2.1)

Chemical properties
- form negative ions, e.g. Cl^-, O^{2-}, and oxoanions, e.g. SO_4^{2-}
- some react with water
- do not react with dilute acids (2.1)

Compounds
- oxides are acidic, e.g. $SO_2(g)$, or neutral, e.g. $NO(g)$
- chlorides are covalent and are volatile liquids, e.g. $SCl_2(l)$ (2.3)

Chapter 3: The structure of the atom

PREVIEW

At the end of this topic you will:

- know the names of the particles of which atoms are composed
- know how particles are arranged in the atom
- understand the terms atomic number, mass number, relative atomic mass, relative molecular mass and isotope.

CONCEPT MAP Page 125.

How much do you already know? Work out your score on page 209.

Test yourself

1. An atom is made of charged particles called protons and electrons. Why is an atom uncharged? [2]

2. An atom of potassium has mass number 39 and atomic number 19. What is
   a) the number of electrons and
   b) the number of neutrons? [2]

3. Why do the isotopes of an element have the same chemical reactions? [2]

4. What is meant by a) the atomic number and b) the mass number of an element? [3]

5. Write the symbol, with mass number and atomic number, for each of the following isotopes:
   a) phosphorus with atomic number 15 and mass number 31 [2]
   b) potassium with atomic number 19 and mass number 39. [2]

6. An atom of carbon has 6 electrons. Say how the electrons are divided between shells. [2]

3.1 Protons, neutrons and electrons

The concept map opposite gives a summary of the nature of the subatomic particles, their masses and charges and some ways of expressing the masses of atoms.

3.2 Focus on the atom

The diagram below shows how protons, neutrons and electrons are arranged in the atom.

The nucleus occupies a tiny volume in the centre of the atom. It consists of protons and neutrons.

The electrons occupy the space surrounding the nucleus. They repel the electrons of neighbouring atoms. The electrons are in constant motion, moving round the nucleus in circular paths called orbitals.

The arrangement of particles in the atom

The electrons moving in orbitals further away from the nucleus have more energy than those close to the nucleus. A group of orbitals of similar energy is called a shell (see diagram on page 126). In the outermost shell of any atom, the maximum number of electrons is eight.

The structure of the atom

Mass
Mass of proton
= mass of neutron
= 1 atomic mass unit, a.m.u.
Mass of electron
= 0.0005 a.m.u.

Charge
Negative charge on electron = −1 elementary charge unit.
Positive charge on proton = +1.
Neutrons are uncharged.

The protons and neutrons are located in the **nucleus** of the atom. The electrons are present in the space outside the nucleus (see diagram opposite).

THE ATOM consists of subatomic particles: **protons**, **neutrons** and **electrons**.

Atomic number Z of element
= number of protons in the nucleus of an atom of the element
= number of electrons in the atom.
Mass number A of atom = sum of number of protons + number of neutrons.
Number of neutrons = $A - Z$.

Relative atomic mass A_r = mass of one atom of element ÷ $\frac{1}{12}$ mass of one atom of carbon-12.
Relative molecular mass M_r = mass of one molecule or one formula unit of a compound ÷ $\frac{1}{12}$ mass of one atom of carbon-12.

Electrons occupy orbitals. They are arranged in shells of orbitals, with orbitals of lowest energy filled first (see page 12). The **electron arrangement** of an atom can be predicted from its atomic number, e.g. Ca with $Z = 20$ has the arrangement 2.8.8.2.

Some elements consist of **isotopes** – forms of the element which have the same number of protons but different numbers of neutrons (the same atomic number but different mass numbers.)

Chlorine consists of two kinds of atoms, one with 17 protons and 18 neutrons, called chlorine-35, and one with 17 protons and 20 neutrons, called chlorine-37. The **isotopes** can be written as:
mass number → $^{35}_{17}$Cl ← symbol
atomic number → 17
and $^{37}_{17}$Cl.

The relative atomic mass of the element is the **weighted average** of the relative atomic masses of its isotopes. There are three chlorine-35 atoms for every chlorine-37 atom. Therefore
$$A_r(Cl) = \frac{(3 \times 35) + (1 \times 37)}{4} = 35.5$$

The isotopes of carbon are $^{12}_{6}$C and $^{14}_{6}$C.

The isotopes of hydrogen are $^{1}_{1}$H, $^{2}_{1}$H and $^{3}_{1}$H.

Concept map: the nature of the atom

The structure of the atom

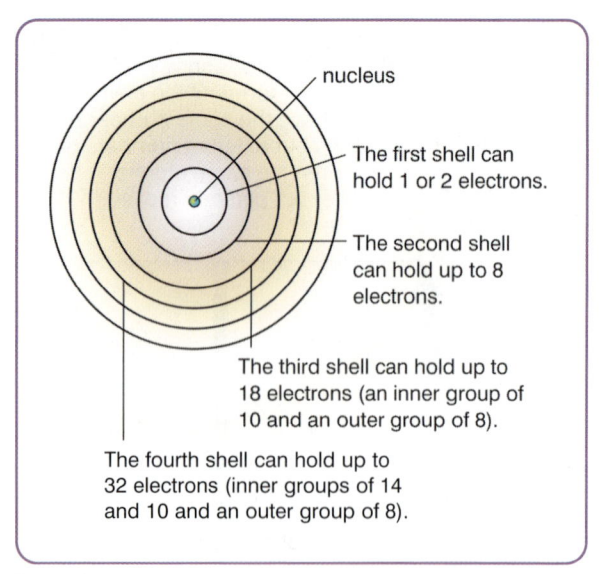

- nucleus
- The first shell can hold 1 or 2 electrons.
- The second shell can hold up to 8 electrons.
- The third shell can hold up to 18 electrons (an inner group of 10 and an outer group of 8).
- The fourth shell can hold up to 32 electrons (inner groups of 14 and 10 and an outer group of 8).

Shells of electrons

If you know the atomic number of an element, you can work out the arrangement of electrons. The lower energy levels are filled before the higher energy levels. The arrangements of electrons in an atom of carbon (atomic number 6) and an atom of magnesium (atomic number 12) are shown here.

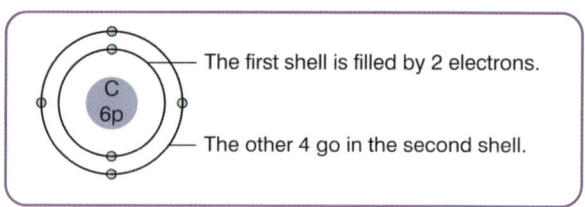

- The first shell is filled by 2 electrons.
- The other 4 go in the second shell.

The arrangement of electrons in the carbon atom (2.4)

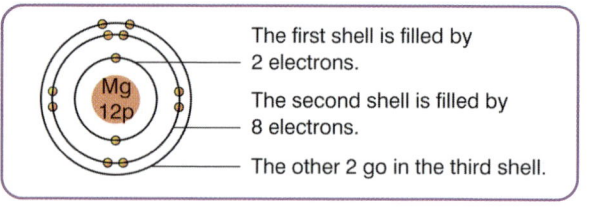

- The first shell is filled by 2 electrons.
- The second shell is filled by 8 electrons.
- The other 2 go in the third shell.

The arrangement of electrons in the magnesium atom (2.8.2)

The table below gives the electron arrangements of the first 20 elements.

element	symbol	atomic number	number of electrons in				electron arrangement
			1st level	2nd level	3rd level	4th level	
hydrogen	H	1	1				1
helium	He	2	2				2
lithium	Li	3	2	1			2.1
beryllium	Be	4	2	2			2.2
boron	B	5	2	3			2.3
carbon	C	6	2	4			2.4
nitrogen	N	7	2	5			2.5
oxygen	O	8	2	6			2.6
fluorine	F	9	2	7			2.7
neon	Ne	10	2	8			2.8
sodium	Na	11	2	8	1		2.8.1
magnesium	Mg	12	2	8	2		2.8.2
aluminium	Al	13	2	8	3		2.8.3
silicon	Si	14	2	8	4		2.8.4
phosphorus	P	15	2	8	5		2.8.5
sulphur	S	16	2	8	6		2.8.6
chlorine	Cl	17	2	8	7		2.8.7
argon	Ar	18	2	8	8		2.8.8
potassium	K	19	2	8	8	1	2.8.8.1
calcium	Ca	20	2	8	8	2	2.8.8.2

Electron arrangements of the first 20 elements

The structure of the atom

ROUND UP

RELATIVE ATOMIC MASSES Page 190.

How much have you improved? Work out your improvement index on page 209.

1. **a)** How many times heavier is one atom of aluminium than one atom of hydrogen? [1]
   b) How many times heavier is one atom of mercury than one atom of calcium? [1]
   c) What is the ratio
   $$\frac{\text{mass of one Fe atom}}{\text{mass of one Br atom}}$$ [1]
   d) How many atoms of nitrogen equal the mass of one atom of iron? [1]

2. Write the symbol, with mass number and atomic number, for each of the following isotopes:
   a) arsenic (atomic number 33 and mass number 75) [1]
   b) uranium-235, uranium-238 and uranium-239 (atomic number 92). [3]

3. Calculate the relative atomic masses of the following elements:
   a) copper, which consists of 69% of copper-63 and 31% of copper-65 [1]
   b) gallium, which consists of 60% of gallium-69 and 40% of gallium-71. [1]

4. The electron arrangement of phosphorus is (2.8.5). Sketch the arrangement of electrons in the atom, as in the diagrams on page 126. [1]

5. Sketch the arrangements of electrons in the atoms of
   a) B (atomic number 5)
   b) N (atomic number 7)
   c) F (atomic number 9)
   d) Al (atomic number 13). [4]

Well done if you've improved. Don't worry if you haven't. Take a break and try again.

Chapter 4 Electrolysis

PREVIEW

At the end of this topic you will be able to:

- explain what happens when compounds are electrolysed
- predict which ions will be discharged in electrolysis
- give examples of the use of electrolysis in industry.

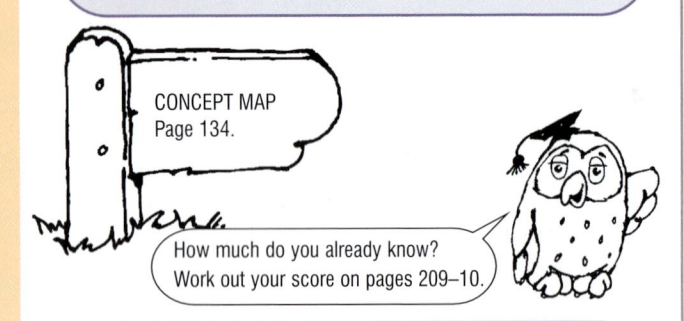

CONCEPT MAP Page 134.

How much do you already know? Work out your score on pages 209–10.

Test yourself

1. Which of the following solids conduct electricity?
   A zinc   B sulphur   C bronze
   D crystalline copper(II) sulphate   [2]

2. Which of the following liquids conduct electricity?
   A a solution of dilute sulphuric acid
   B a solution of sodium sulphate
   C ethanol
   D a solution of ethanoic acid   [3]

3. What do the following terms mean?
   a) an electrolyte   b) an electrode   [4, 1]

4. a) Explain the terms cation and anion, and give two examples of each.   [6]
   b) Explain why ions move towards electrodes.   [2]
   c) Explain why solid copper(II) chloride does not conduct electricity, but an aqueous solution of copper(II) chloride does.   [2]

5. Sodium is obtained by the electrolysis of molten sodium chloride. Why is it important that the sodium chloride electrolysed to give sodium is anhydrous?   [1]

6. Some parts of a car body are painted to protect against rusting, and others are chromium-plated. What advantage does chromium-plating have over painting?   [1]

7. What is the advantage of gold-plated jewellery over   a) gold jewellery   b) brass jewellery?   [2]

8. Aluminium is obtained by the electrolysis of aluminium oxide.
   a) Why is aluminium oxide dissolved in molten cryolite before electrolysis?   [1]
   b) Write the equations for the electrode processes.   [5]
   c) Suggest why this method of extracting aluminium is expensive.   [1]

4.1 Conducting electricity

When substances conduct electricity, changes happen at the electrodes. For example, a solution of copper(II) chloride gives a deposit of copper at the negative electrode and a stream of chlorine at the positive electrode. The explanation is that copper(II) chloride consists of positively charged particles of copper, called copper(II) ions, and negatively charged particles of chlorine, called chloride ions. Experiments show that the copper(II) ion carries two units of positive charge, Cu^{2+}, whereas the chloride ion carries one unit of negative charge, Cl^-. Copper(II) chloride contains two chloride ions for every copper(II) ion so that the charges balance, and the formula is $CuCl_2$.

In solid copper(II) chloride, the ions are not free to move because they are held in a three-dimensional crystal structure, and the solid does not conduct electricity. When the salt is dissolved in water, the ions become free to move, the solution conducts electricity and electrolysis occurs.

There is another way of giving the ions freedom to move – to melt the solid. The electrolysis of molten sodium chloride is used for the extraction of sodium.

Electrolysis

4.2 Ions

How is an ion formed from an atom? Atoms are uncharged. The number of protons in an atom is the same as the number of electrons. If an atom either gains or loses electrons, it will become electrically charged. Metal atoms and hydrogen atoms form positive ions (**cations**) by losing one or more electrons. Atoms of non-metallic elements form negative ions (**anions**) by gaining one or more electrons.

sodium atom Na → electron e⁻ + sodium ion Na⁺

(11 protons, 11 electrons, charge = 0)   (11 protons, 10 electrons, charge = +1)

chlorine atom Cl + electron e⁻ → chloride ion Cl⁻

(17 protons, 17 electrons, charge = 0)   (17 protons, 18 electrons, charge = −1)

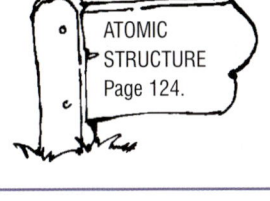

ATOMIC STRUCTURE Page 124.

The table below gives the symbols and formulas of some ions.

cations	anions
hydrogen ion H^+	bromide ion Br^-
sodium ion Na^+	chloride ion Cl^-
copper(II) ion Cu^{2+}	iodide ion I^-
lead(II) ion Pb^{2+}	hydroxide ion OH^-
aluminium ion Al^{3+}	nitrate ion NO_3^-
	sulphate ion SO_4^{2-}

4.3 At the electrodes

Copper(II) chloride solution

The diagram below shows what happens at the electrodes when copper(II) chloride is electrolysed.

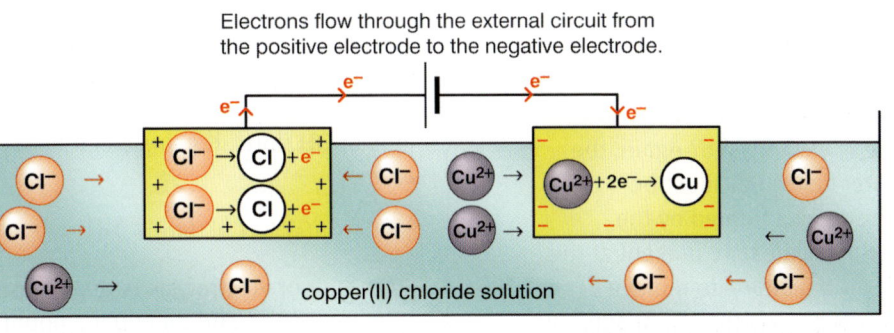

Electrons flow through the external circuit from the positive electrode to the negative electrode.

Chloride ions are attracted to the positive electrode. The positive charge enables the electrode to take electrons from chloride ions, discharging them to form chlorine atoms. Chlorine atoms then combine to form molecules. The electrode process is

chloride ion → chlorine atom + electron

$Cl^-(aq) \rightarrow Cl(g) + e^-$

followed by

$2Cl(g) \rightarrow Cl_2(g)$

Copper ions are attracted to the negative electrode. The negative charge on the electrode is due to the presence of electrons, and copper ions take electrons and are discharged to become copper atoms. The electrode process is

copper(II) ion + 2 electrons → copper atom

$Cu^{2+}(aq) + 2e^- \rightarrow Cu(s)$

The electrolysis of copper(II) chloride with carbon electrodes

Electrolysis

Sodium chloride solution

The products of electrolysis are hydrogen and chlorine. Why is sodium not formed when sodium chloride solution is electrolysed? The water present in the solution is ionised to a very small extent:

water $\rightleftharpoons$ hydrogen ions + hydroxide ions

$H_2O(l) \rightleftharpoons H^+(aq) + OH^-(aq)$

The hydrogen ions are attracted to the cathode (negative electrode). It is easier for the cathode to discharge a hydrogen ion than a sodium ion, and hydrogen is formed:

electrode process $\quad H^+(aq) + e^- \rightarrow H(g)$

followed by $\quad 2H(g) \rightarrow H_2(g)$

Although the concentration of hydrogen ions in water is small, when these hydrogen ions are discharged more water molecules ionise to replace them, and the discharge of hydrogen ions continues. As more water molecules ionise, the concentration of hydroxide ions increases and the solution of sodium chloride gradually turns into a solution of sodium hydroxide.

The electrolysis of sodium chloride solution is used commercially to obtain the important products sodium hydroxide, hydrogen and chlorine.

Copper(II) sulphate solution

The products of electrolysis are copper and oxygen. How is oxygen formed when an aqueous solution of copper(II) sulphate is electrolysed? Again, the dissociation of water molecules must be considered. Hydroxide ions formed by the ionisation of water molecules are present at the anode. It is easier for the anode to remove electrons from hydroxide ions than from sulphate ions. Consequently hydroxide ions are discharged, and the OH groups which are formed rearrange to give oxygen and water:

electrode process $\quad OH^-(aq) \rightarrow OH(aq) + e^-$

followed by $\quad 4OH(aq) \rightarrow O_2(g) + 2H_2O(l)$

The hydroxide ions that are discharged are replaced by the ionisation of more water molecules. Hydrogen ions are also formed by the dissociation of water, and the solution gradually turns into a solution of sulphuric acid.

4.4 Which ions are discharged?

Anions

★ Sulphate ions and nitrate ions are very difficult to discharge. In solutions of these ions, hydroxide ions are discharged to form oxygen.

Cations

★ The ions of very reactive metals, e.g. sodium and potassium, are difficult to discharge. In solutions of these ions, hydrogen ions are discharged instead.

★ The ions of less reactive metals, e.g. copper and lead, are easier to discharge. In a solution that contains a mixture of metal ions, the ions are discharged in order of the reactivity of the metals. Ions of the least reactive metals are discharged first. For example, in a solution containing Cu^{2+} ions and Zn^{2+} ions, Cu^{2+} ions are discharged while Zn^{2+} ions remain in solution.

4.5 Electrodes taking part

Sometimes electrodes are changed by the cell reaction. For example, when copper(II) sulphate is electrolysed with copper electrodes, the products differ from those just described. At the cathode, copper is deposited as before. The copper anode, the positive electrode, needs to gain electrons. Instead of gaining electrons by discharging SO_4^{2-} ions or OH^- ions, it gains electrons by ionising Cu atoms:

$$Cu(s) \rightarrow Cu^{2+}(aq) + 2e^-$$

The result of electrolysis is that copper is dissolved from the anode and an equal amount of copper is deposited on the cathode.

The table opposite shows the products of electrolysis of some electrolytes.

4.6 Applications of electrolysis

Extraction of metals from their ores

★ **Sodium** is obtained from sodium chloride in the mineral rock salt. When molten anhydrous sodium chloride is electrolysed, the products are sodium and chlorine.

Electrolysis

electrolyte	products of electrolysis and electrode processes	
	cathode (negative electrode)	**anode (positive electrode)**
molten sodium chloride	sodium $Na^+(l) + e^- \rightarrow Na(l)$	chlorine $Cl^-(l) \rightarrow Cl(g) + e^-$ $2Cl(g) \rightarrow Cl_2(g)$
sodium chloride solution	hydrogen $H^+(aq) + e^- \rightarrow H(g)$ $2H(g) \rightarrow H_2(g)$	chlorine $Cl^-(aq) \rightarrow Cl(g) + e^-$ $2Cl(g) \rightarrow Cl_2(g)$
copper(II) sulphate solution	copper $Cu^{2+}(aq) + 2e^- \rightarrow Cu(s)$	oxygen $OH^-(aq) \rightarrow OH(aq) + e^-$ $4OH(aq) \rightarrow O_2(g) + 2H_2O(l)$
copper(II) sulphate solution, with copper electrodes	copper is discharged $Cu^{2+}(aq) + 2e^- \rightarrow Cu(s)$	copper dissolves $Cu(s) \rightarrow Cu^{2+}(aq) + 2e^-$
dilute sulphuric acid	hydrogen $H^+(aq) + e^- \rightarrow H(g)$ $2H(g) \rightarrow H_2(g)$	oxygen $OH^-(aq) \rightarrow OH(aq) + e^-$ $4OH(aq) \rightarrow O_2(g) + 2H_2O(l)$

The products of electrolysis of some electrolytes

★ **Potassium, calcium** and **magnesium** are also obtained by electrolysis of molten anhydrous chlorides. The cost of electricity makes this method of extracting metals expensive.

★ **Aluminium** is mined as the ore bauxite, $Al_2O_3.2H_2O$. Purified anhydrous aluminium oxide is obtained from the ore. Before the oxide can be electrolysed, it must be melted. The high melting point of aluminium oxide, 2050 °C, makes this difficult so it is dissolved in molten cryolite, Na_3AlF_6, at 1000 °C before electrolysis. See diagram below.

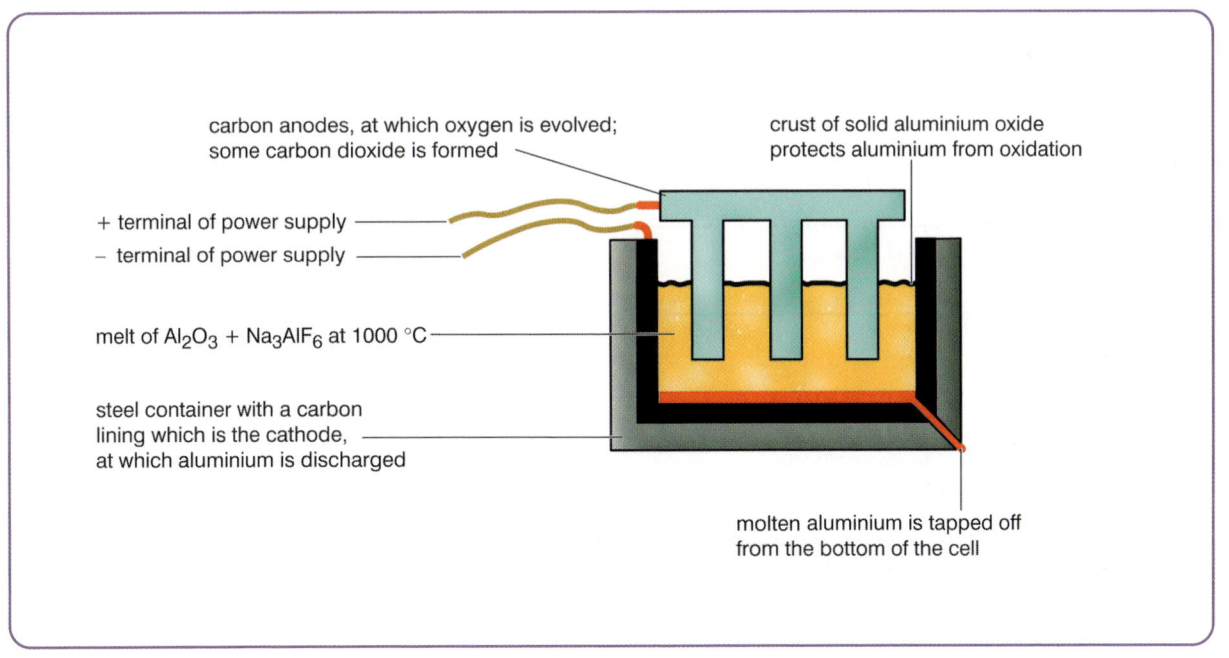

- carbon anodes, at which oxygen is evolved; some carbon dioxide is formed
- crust of solid aluminium oxide protects aluminium from oxidation
- + terminal of power supply
- − terminal of power supply
- melt of Al_2O_3 + Na_3AlF_6 at 1000 °C
- steel container with a carbon lining which is the cathode, at which aluminium is discharged
- molten aluminium is tapped off from the bottom of the cell

Electrolysis of molten aluminium oxide

Electrolysis

Purification of copper

The electrolysis of copper(II) sulphate with copper electrodes is used in the purification of copper. The top diagram below shows the setup.

Electroplating

Electrolysis is used to coat a metal with a thin even film of another metal, as shown in the second diagram below.

1. A cheaper metal may be coated with a more beautiful and more expensive metal, e.g. silver or gold.
2. To prevent steel from rusting, it is electroplated with nickel and chromium which give the steel a bright surface that is not corroded in air.
3. Food cans are made of iron plated with a layer of tin. Tin is not corroded by food juices.
4. A layer of zinc is applied to iron in the manufacture of galvanised iron. Electroplating is one of the methods employed.

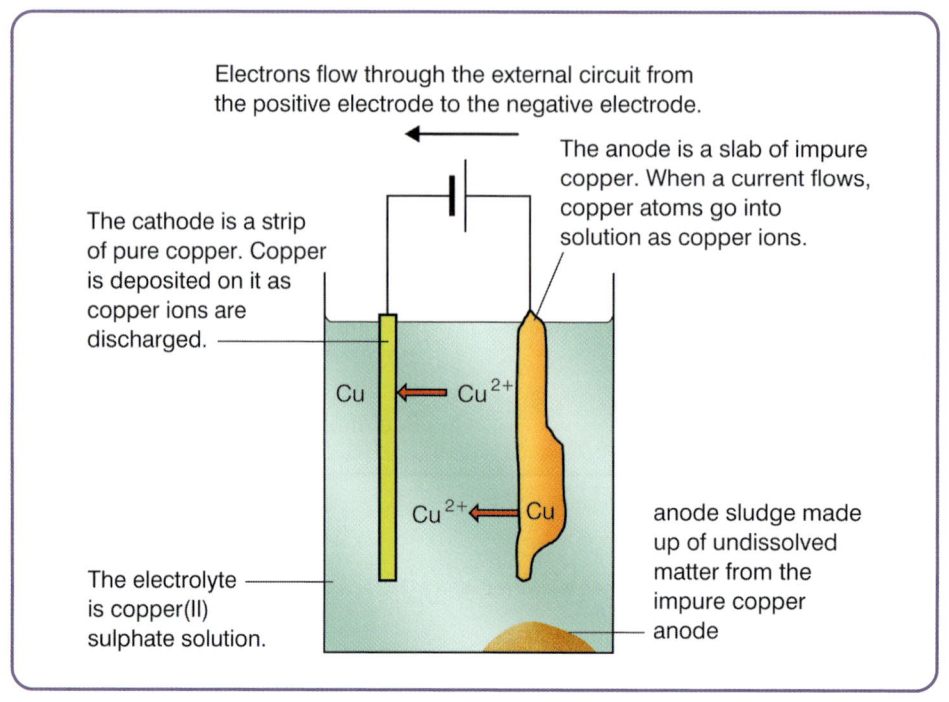

Electrons flow through the external circuit from the positive electrode to the negative electrode.

The cathode is a strip of pure copper. Copper is deposited on it as copper ions are discharged.

The anode is a slab of impure copper. When a current flows, copper atoms go into solution as copper ions.

Cu ← Cu^{2+}

Cu^{2+} ← Cu

The electrolyte is copper(II) sulphate solution.

anode sludge made up of undissolved matter from the impure copper anode

Electrolytic purification of copper

The object to be plated is made the negative electrode (the cathode).

The electrolyte is a solution of one of the salts of the metal.

The positive electrode (the anode) is made of the plating metal. Metal atoms dissolve to form metal ions, keeping the concentration of metal ions in the solution constant.

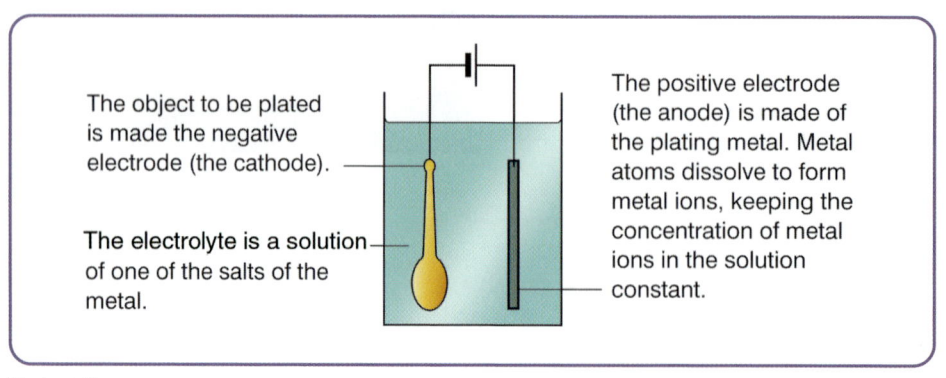

Electroplating

Electrolysis

ROUND UP

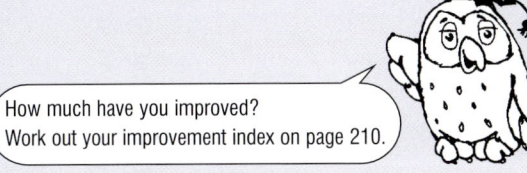

How much have you improved? Work out your improvement index on page 210.

1. Copper is purified by an electrolytic method.
   a) Why do impurities in the copper such as zinc and iron not interfere? [1]
   b) What happens to impurities in the copper such as silver? [2]

2. Iron nails are electroplated with nickel to make them rust-resistant.
   a) Why is electroplating a good method of applying the nickel coating? [2]
   b) Sketch an apparatus which you could use to do this in the laboratory. [2]

3. When an aqueous solution of potassium bromide is electrolysed, a brown colour appears at one electrode.
   a) What is the brown substance? [1]
   b) At which electrode is it formed? [1]
   c) What is formed at the other electrode? [1]
   d) Name an ion which increases in concentration during the electrolysis. [1]
   e) Write equations for the electrode processes. [6]

4. Copper(II) sulphate solution can be electrolysed between platinum electrodes.
   a) State what products are formed at the electrodes. [2]
   b) Write equations for the electrode reactions. [7]
   c) What difference in the products of electrolysis is observed when copper electrodes are used? [2]
   d) Write the equations for the electrode reactions when copper electrodes are used. [4]

Well done if you've improved. Don't worry if you haven't. Take a break and try again.

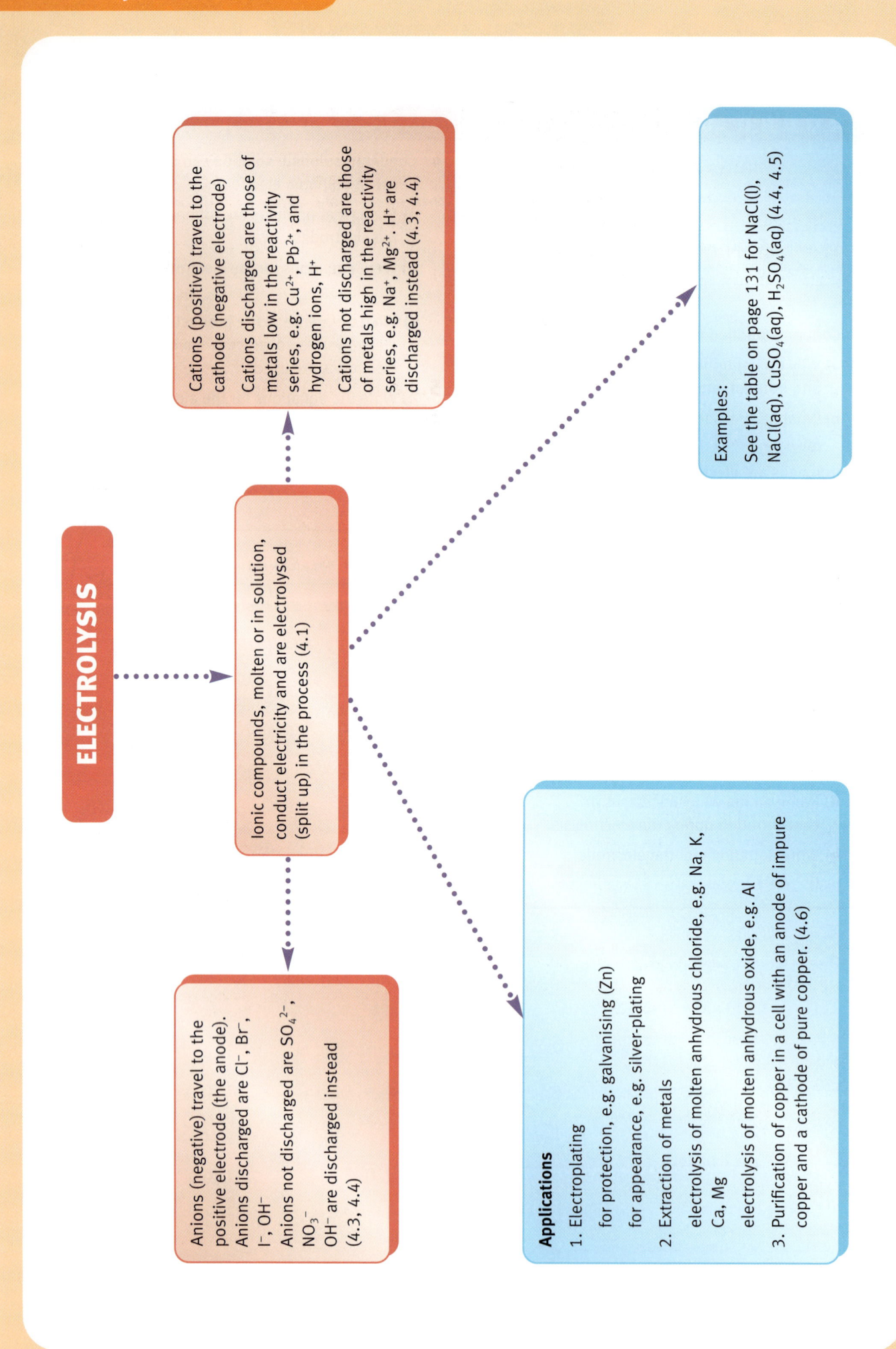

Electrolysis

ELECTROLYSIS

Ionic compounds, molten or in solution, conduct electricity and are electrolysed (split up) in the process (4.1)

Cations (positive) travel to the cathode (negative electrode).

Cations discharged are those of metals low in the reactivity series, e.g. Cu^{2+}, Pb^{2+}, and hydrogen ions, H^+

Cations not discharged are those of metals high in the reactivity series, e.g. Na^+, Mg^{2+}. H^+ are discharged instead (4.3, 4.4)

Anions (negative) travel to the positive electrode (the anode).

Anions discharged are Cl^-, Br^-, I^-, OH^-

Anions not discharged are SO_4^{2-}, NO_3^-

OH^- are discharged instead (4.3, 4.4)

Examples:
See the table on page 131 for $NaCl(l)$, $NaCl(aq)$, $CuSO_4(aq)$, $H_2SO_4(aq)$ (4.4, 4.5)

Applications

1. Electroplating
   - for protection, e.g. galvanising (Zn)
   - for appearance, e.g. silver-plating
2. Extraction of metals
   - electrolysis of molten anhydrous chloride, e.g. Na, K, Ca, Mg
   - electrolysis of molten anhydrous oxide, e.g. Al
3. Purification of copper in a cell with an anode of impure copper and a cathode of pure copper. (4.6)

The chemical bond — Chapter 5

PREVIEW

At the end of this topic you will be able to:
- understand how atoms combine by forming ionic bonds and covalent bonds
- understand how ionic compounds and covalent compounds differ in properties and structure.

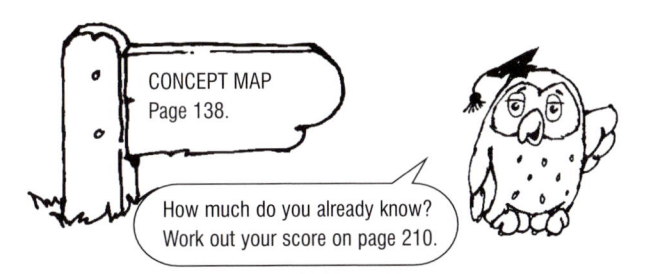

CONCEPT MAP Page 138.

How much do you already know? Work out your score on page 210.

Test yourself

1. Write words in the spaces to complete the sentences.

   When an ionic compound is formed, some atoms lose electrons to become _____ ions while other atoms gain electrons to become _____ ions. Ions are held together by _____ attraction in a three-dimensional structure called a _____. [4]

2. The element E has the electron arrangement E(2.8.2). The element Q has the electron arrangement Q(2.8.7). Explain what happens to atoms of E and Q when they combine to form an ionic compound, and give the formula of the compound. [3]

3. The element T has the electron arrangement T(2.7). Sketch the arrangement of electrons in an atom of T and in the molecule T_2. [2]

4. Name the following compounds:
   a) $MgBr_2$ b) $FeCl_2$ c) $FeCl_3$ d) Na_2O
   e) $BaSO_4$. [5]

5. State the formulas of the following compounds:
   a) potassium bromide b) calcium carbonate
   c) lead(II) oxide d) lead(II) sulphate
   e) silver chloride. [5]

5.1 Bond formation

When chemical reactions take place, it is the electrons in the outer shell that are involved in the formation of bonds. The resistance of the noble gases to chemical change is believed to be due to the stability of the full outer shell of eight electrons (two for helium). When atoms react, they gain, lose or share electrons to attain an outer shell of eight electrons. Metallic elements frequently combine with non-metallic elements to form compounds.

5.2 Ionic bonding

Example 1

Sodium burns in chlorine to form sodium chloride. The diagram below shows what happens to the electrons.

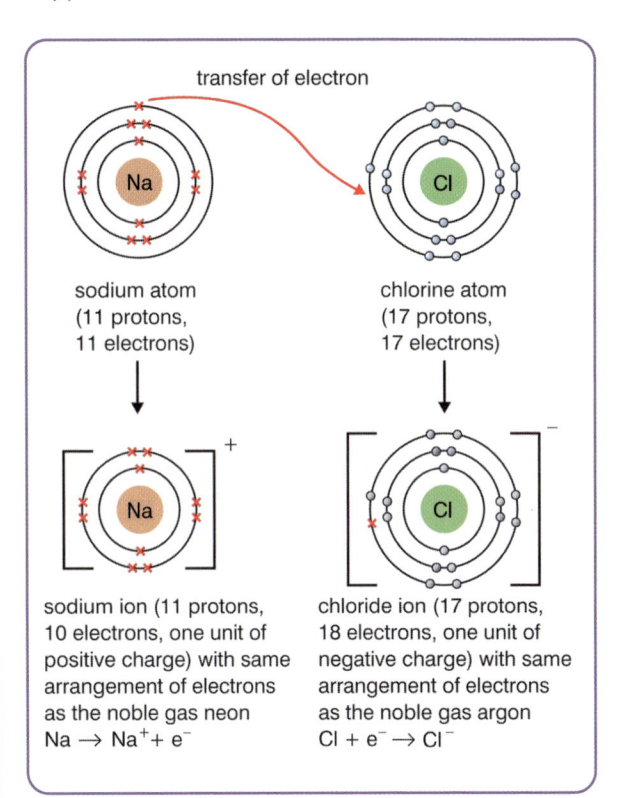

transfer of electron

sodium atom (11 protons, 11 electrons)

chlorine atom (17 protons, 17 electrons)

sodium ion (11 protons, 10 electrons, one unit of positive charge) with same arrangement of electrons as the noble gas neon
$Na \rightarrow Na^+ + e^-$

chloride ion (17 protons, 18 electrons, one unit of negative charge) with same arrangement of electrons as the noble gas argon
$Cl + e^- \rightarrow Cl^-$

The formation of sodium chloride

The chemical bond

There is an electrostatic force of attraction between oppositely charged ions. This force is called an **ionic bond** or **electrovalent bond**. The ions Na$^+$ and Cl$^-$ are part of a **giant ionic structure** (a crystal). The ions cannot move out of their positions in the structure, and the crystal cannot conduct electricity. When the solid is melted or dissolved, the ions become free to move and conduct electricity (see page 128).

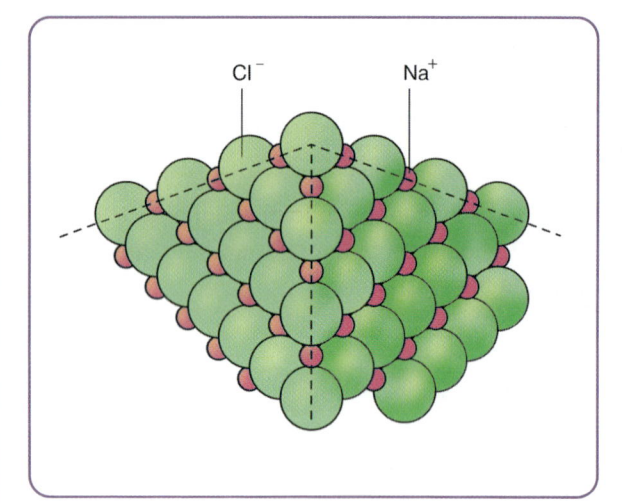

The structure of sodium chloride

Example 2

magnesium + fluorine → magnesium fluoride

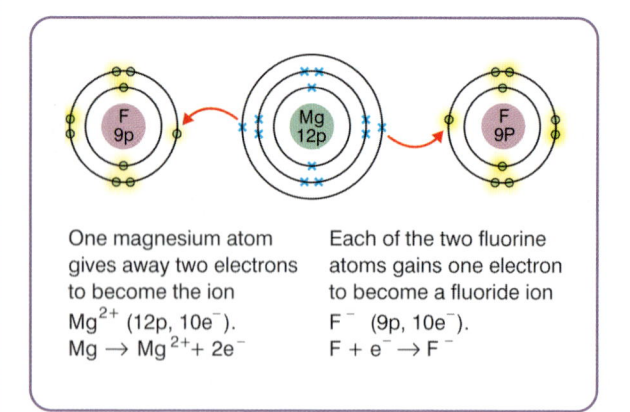

One magnesium atom gives away two electrons to become the ion Mg^{2+} (12p, 10e$^-$).
Mg → Mg^{2+} + 2e$^-$

Each of the two fluorine atoms gains one electron to become a fluoride ion F$^-$ (9p, 10e$^-$).
F + e$^-$ → F$^-$

The formation of magnesium fluoride

The formula of magnesium fluoride is Mg^{2+}2F$^-$ or MgF$_2$.

Example 3

magnesium + oxygen → magnesium oxide

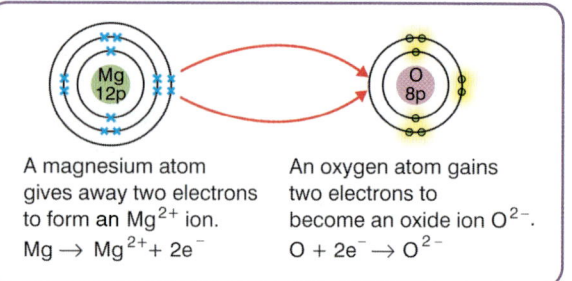

A magnesium atom gives away two electrons to form an Mg^{2+} ion.
Mg → Mg^{2+} + 2e$^-$

An oxygen atom gains two electrons to become an oxide ion O^{2-}.
O + 2e$^-$ → O^{2-}

The formation of magnesium oxide

The formula of magnesium oxide is Mg^{2+}O^{2-} or MgO.

5.3 Covalent bonding

When two non-metallic elements combine, both want to gain electrons; neither wants to form positive ions. They combine by sharing electrons. A shared pair of electrons is a **covalent bond**. If two pairs of electrons are shared, the bond is a **double bond**.

Example 1

hydrogen + fluorine → hydrogen fluoride, HF

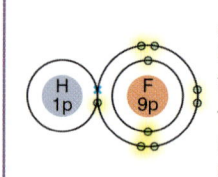

The hydrogen atom shares its electron with the fluorine atom. H has a full shell of two electrons, the same arrangement as helium.

The fluorine atom shares one of its electrons with the hydrogen atom. F has a full shell of eight electrons, the same arrangement as neon.

The formation of hydrogen fluoride

The shared pair of electrons is attracted to the hydrogen nucleus and to the fluorine nucleus, and bonds the two nuclei together.

The chemical bond

Example 2

hydrogen + oxygen → water, H_2O

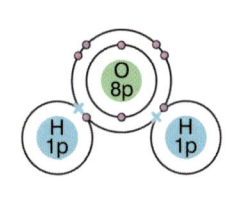

Two hydrogen atoms each share an electron with an oxygen atom. Each hydrogen atom has an outer shell of two electrons, and the oxygen atom has an outer shell of eight electrons.

The formation of water

Example 3

nitrogen + hydrogen → ammonia, NH_3

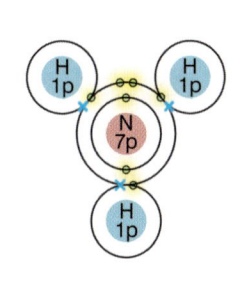

One nitrogen atom shares three electrons, one with each of three hydrogen atoms. The nitrogen atom has eight electrons in its outer shell (like neon), and each hydrogen has two electrons in its outer shell (like helium).

The formation of ammonia

Example 4

carbon + hydrogen → methane, CH_4

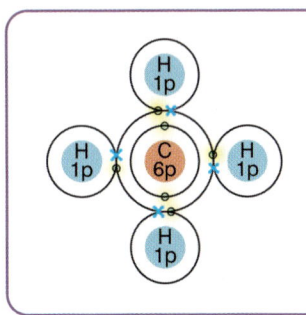

The carbon atom shares four electrons, one with each of four hydrogen atoms.

The formation of methane

Example 5

carbon + oxygen → carbon dioxide, CO_2

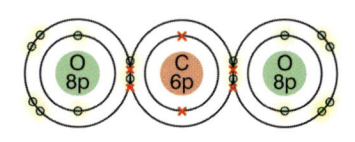

The carbon atom shares four electrons, two with each of two oxygen atoms. Each oxygen atom shares two electrons with the carbon atom. Two pairs of electrons are shared between the carbon atom and each oxygen atom. Each C═O bond is called a double bond.

The formation of carbon dioxide

5.4 Ionic and covalent substances

The concept map overleaf summarises the types of bonds formed by different substances.

5.5 The formula of an ionic compound

Ionic compounds consist of positive and negative ions. A sample of the compound is uncharged because the positive and negative charges balance exactly. In a sample of calcium chloride, $CaCl_2$, the number of chloride ions, Cl^-, is exactly twice the number of calcium ions, Ca^{2+}, so the formula is $Ca^{2+}2Cl^-$ or $CaCl_2$.

Worked example

Compound: sodium sulphate

Ions present are: Na^+ and SO_4^{2-}

To balance the charges: two Na^+ are needed to balance one SO_4^{2-}

The ions needed are: $2Na^+$ and SO_4^{2-}

The formula is: Na_2SO_4

The chemical bond

IONIC AND COVALENT SUBSTANCES

Ionic bonding
Ionic compounds are formed when a metallic element combines with a non-metallic element. An **ionic bond** is formed by **transfer of electrons** from one atom to another to form ions.

Covalent bonding
Atoms of non-metallic elements combine with other non-metallic elements by **sharing pairs of electrons** in their outer shells. A shared pair of electrons is a **covalent bond**.

There are three **types of covalent substances**.

1 Many covalent substances are composed of small individual molecules with only very small forces of attraction between molecules, e.g. the gases HCl, SO_2, CO_2, CH_4.

2 Some covalent substances consist of small molecules with weak forces of attraction between molecules, e.g. the volatile liquid ethanol, C_2H_5OH, and solid carbon dioxide.

3 Some covalent substances consist of giant molecules, e.g. quartz (silicon(IV) oxide). These substances have high melting and boiling points.

Atoms of **metallic elements** form positive ions (cations). Elements in Groups 1, 2 and 3 of the periodic table form ions with charges +1, +2 and +3, e.g. Na^+, Mg^{2+}, Al^{3+}. Atoms of **non-metallic elements** form negative ions (anions). Elements in Groups 6 and 7 of the periodic table form ions with charges −2 and −1, e.g. O^{2-} and Cl^-.

The maximum number of covalent bonds that an atom can form is equal to the number of electrons in the outer shell. An atom may not use all its outer electrons in bond formation.

Ionic compounds are **electrolytes** – they conduct electricity when molten or in solution and are split up (**electrolysed**) in the process. Covalent compounds are **non-electrolytes**.

The strong electrostatic attraction between ions of opposite charge is an **ionic bond**. An ionic compound is composed of a giant regular structure of ions (see diagram of sodium chloride structure on page 135). This regular structure makes ionic compounds **crystalline**. The strong forces of attraction between ions make it difficult to separate the ions, and ionic compounds therefore have **high melting and boiling points**.

Organic solvents, e.g. ethanol and propanone, have covalent bonds. They dissolve covalent compounds but not ionic compounds.

Concept map: ionic and covalent substances

Compound: *iron(II) sulphate*

Ions present are: Fe^{2+} and SO_4^{2-}

To balance the charges: one Fe^{2+} balances one SO_4^{2-}

The ions needed are: Fe^{2+} and SO_4^{2-}

The formula is: $FeSO_4$

Compound: *iron(III) sulphate*

Ions present are: Fe^{3+} and SO_4^{2-}

To balance the charges: two Fe^{3+} balance three SO_4^{2-}

The ions needed are: $2Fe^{3+}$ and $3SO_4^{2-}$

The formula is: $Fe_2(SO_4)_3$

Note

The sulphates of iron are named iron(II) sulphate and iron(III) sulphate. The Roman numerals II and III show which type of ion, Fe^{2+} or Fe^{3+}, is present.

Handy hint

If you know the symbols and charges of these ions, you can work out the formulas of their compounds.

H^+ Na^+ K^+ Ag^+ NH_4^+	OH^- NO_3^- HCO_3^- Cl^- Br^- I^-
Ca^{2+} Cu^{2+} Zn^{2+} Pb^{2+} Mg^{2+} Fe^{2+} Ba^{2+}	SO_4^{2-} SO_3^{2-} CO_3^{2-} O^{2-} S^{2-}
Al^{3+} Fe^{3+}	

The chemical bond

ROUND UP

How much have you improved? Work out your improvement index on page 210.

1. a) What are the particles in a crystal of sodium chloride? [2]
   b) What holds the particles together? [1]
   c) Describe the arrangement of particles in the crystal. [2]

2. Draw the arrangement of electrons in a molecule of hydrogen chloride. [2]

3. Give an example of a covalent substance which
   a) has individual molecules
   b) is a molecular solid
   c) has giant molecules. [3]

4. Name the following compounds:
   a) $Ca(OH)_2$ b) Na_2SO_3 c) $CuCO_3$
   d) $Mg(HCO_3)_2$ e) KNO_3. [5]

5. State the formulas of the following compounds:
   a) ammonium nitrate   b) sodium sulphate
   c) ammonium sulphate   d) aluminium oxide
   e) zinc hydroxide. [5]

Well done if you've improved. Don't worry if you haven't. Take a break and try again.

Chapter 6 The periodic table

PREVIEW

At the end of this topic you will:
- understand the structure of the periodic table
- know the nature of the elements in Groups 0, 1, 2, 7 and the transition elements.

CONCEPT MAP Page 144.

How much do you already know? Work out your score on page 211.

Test yourself

1. a) What are the noble gases? [2]
   b) In which group of the periodic table are they? [1]
   c) What do the noble gases have in common regarding
      (i) their electron arrangements and
      (ii) their chemical reactions? [2]
2. X is a metallic element. It reacts slowly with water to give a strongly alkaline solution. In which group of the periodic table would you place X? [1]
3. Y is a non-metallic element. It reacts vigorously with sodium to give a salt of formula NaY. In which group of the periodic table would you place Y? [1]
4. Z is a metallic element which reacts rapidly with water to give a flammable gas and an alkaline solution. In which group of the periodic table would you place Z? [1]
5. a) Name the halogens. [4]
   b) In which group of the periodic table are they? [1]
   c) Does the chemical reactivity of the halogens increase or decrease with atomic number? [1]
   d) Give the formulas of the products of the reactions of
      (i) sodium (ii) iron with each of the halogens. [8]
6. a) What is a transition metal? [1]
   b) Name two transition metals. [1]

6.1 Classifying elements

Chapter 2 dealt with the classification of elements as metallic and non-metallic elements. A major advance was made by John Newlands in 1866 and Dmitri Mendeleev in 1871 when they originated the periodic table. The modern periodic table is based on arranging the elements in order of increasing atomic number. A vertical row of elements is called a **group** and a horizontal row is called a **period**.

The following patterns can be seen in the arrangement of the elements in the periodic table.

1. The reactive metals are at the left-hand side of the table, less reactive metallic elements in the middle block and non-metallic elements at the right-hand side.
2. The differences between the metals in Group 1, those in Group 2 and the transition metals are summarised in the table at the top of page 142.
3. Silicon and germanium are on the borderline between metals and non-metals. These elements are semiconductors, intermediate between metals, which are electrical conductors, and non-metals, which are non-conductors of electricity. Semiconductors are vital to the computer industry.
4. Group 7 is a set of very reactive non-metallic elements called the **halogens**. They react with metals to form salts; see the table at the foot of page 142.
5. When Mendeleev drew up his periodic table in 1871, only 55 elements were known. He left gaps in the table and predicted that new elements would be discovered which would fit the gaps. When the noble gases were discovered, one by one, their atomic numbers placed them in between Groups 1 and 7, and a new Group 0 had to be created for them.

6.2 A repeating pattern

You can see that the arrangement on page 143 has the following features:

★ The elements are listed in order of increasing atomic number.
★ Elements which have the same number of electrons in the outermost shell fall into the same **group** (vertical column) of the periodic table.

continued on page 143

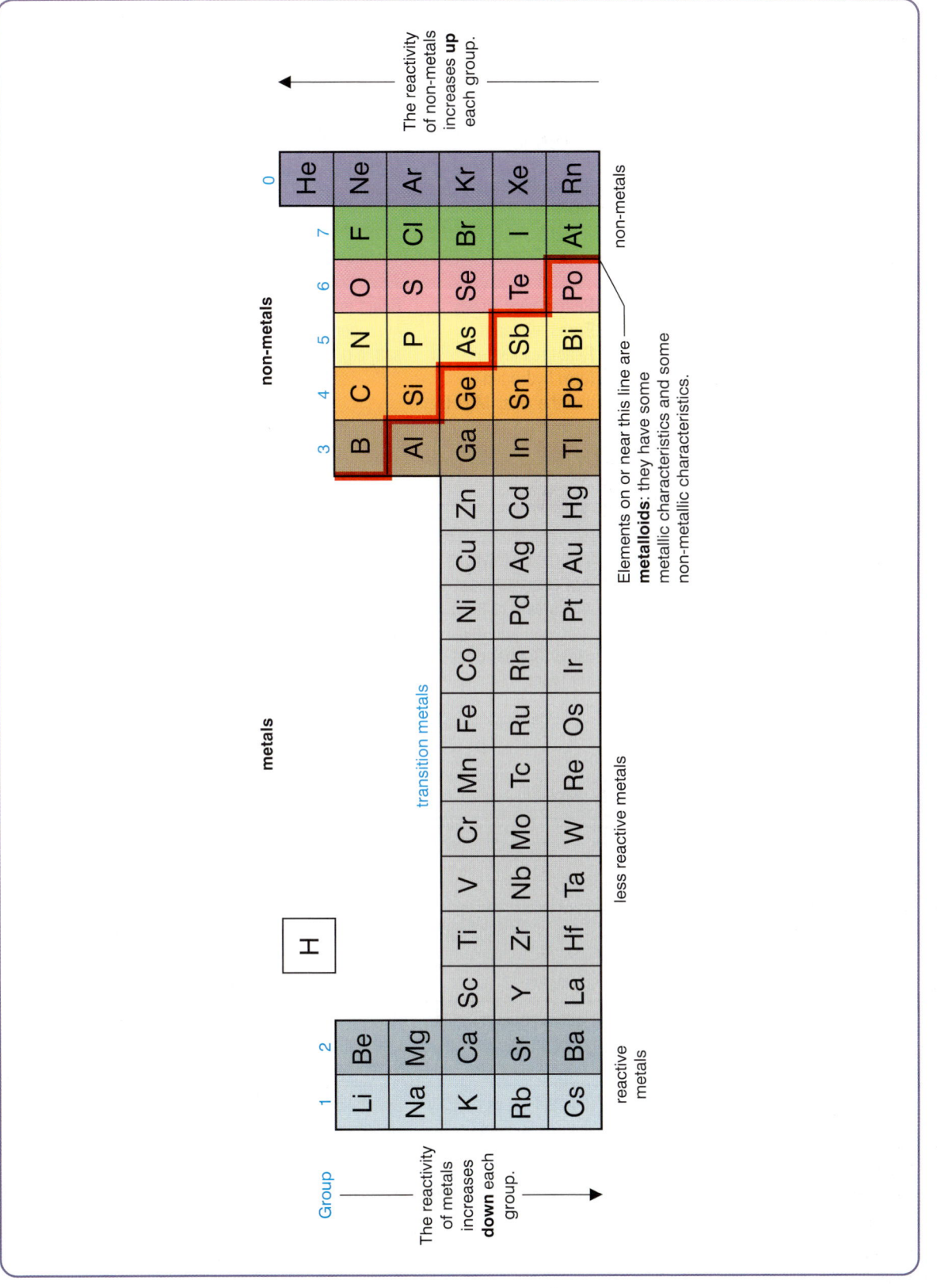

The periodic table

Group	1	2												3	4	5	6	7	0
	H																		He
	Li	Be												B	C	N	O	F	Ne
	Na	Mg				transition metals								Al	Si	P	S	Cl	Ar
	K	Ca	Sc	Ti	V	Cr	Mn	Fe	Co	Ni	Cu	Zn		Ga	Ge	As	Se	Br	Kr
	Rb	Sr	Y	Zr	Nb	Mo	Tc	Ru	Rh	Pd	Ag	Cd		In	Sn	Sb	Te	I	Xe
	Cs	Ba	La	Hf	Ta	W	Re	Os	Ir	Pt	Au	Hg		Tl	Pb	Bi	Po	At	Rn

reactive metals

less reactive metals

metals

non-metals

The reactivity of metals increases **down** each group. →

The reactivity of non-metals increases **up** each group. ←

Elements on or near this line are **metalloids**: they have some metallic characteristics and some non-metallic characteristics.

The periodic table

The periodic table

metal	reaction with air	reaction with water	reaction with dilute hydrochloric acid	trend
Group 1 the alkali metals				
lithium sodium potassium rubidium caesium	Burn vigorously to form the strongly basic oxide M_2O which dissolves in water to give the strong alkali MOH.	React vigorously to form hydrogen and a solution of the strong alkali MOH.	The reaction is dangerously violent.	The vigour of all these reactions increases down the group. ↓
Group 2 the alkaline earths				
beryllium magnesium calcium strontium barium	Burn to form the strongly basic oxides MO, which are sparingly soluble or insoluble.	Reacts very slowly. Burns in steam. React readily to form hydrogen and the alkali $M(OH)_2$.	React readily to give hydrogen and a salt, e.g. MCl_2.	The vigour of all these reactions increases down the group. Group 2 elements are less reactive than Group 1. ↓
Transition metals				
iron zinc copper	When heated, form oxides without burning. The oxides and hydroxides are weaker bases than those of Groups 1 and 2 and are insoluble.	Iron rusts slowly. Iron and zinc react with steam to form hydrogen and the oxide. Copper does not react.	Iron and zinc react to give hydrogen and a salt. Copper does not react.	Transition metals are less reactive than Groups 1 and 2. In general, their compounds are coloured; they are used as catalysts.

Some reactions of metals

Note
M stands for the symbol of a metallic element. Dilute sulphuric acid reacts with metals in the same way as dilute hydrochloric acid. Dilute nitric acid is an oxidising agent and attacks metals, e.g. copper, which are not sufficiently reactive to react with other dilute acids.

OXIDISING AGENT
Page 155.

halogen	state at room temperature	reaction with sodium	reaction with iron	trend
fluorine	gas	explosive	explosive	
chlorine	gas	Heated sodium burns in chlorine to form sodium chloride.	Reacts vigorously with hot iron to form iron(III) chloride.	The vigour of these reactions decreases down the group. ↓
bromine	liquid	Reacts less vigorously to form sodium bromide.	Reacts less vigorously to form iron(III) bromide.	
iodine	solid	Reacts less vigorously than bromine to form sodium iodide.	Reacts less vigorously than bromine to form iron(II) iodide.	

Some reactions of the halogens

The periodic table

★ The noble gases are in Group 0. For the rest of the elements, the group number is the number of electrons in the outermost shell.

★ The first **period** (horizontal row) contains only hydrogen and helium. The second period contains the elements lithium to neon. The third period contains the elements sodium to argon.

								Group 0
Period 1	H (1)							He (2)
	Group 1	Group 2	Group 3	Group 4	Group 5	Group 6	Group 7	
Period 2	Li (2.1)	Be (2.2)	B (2.3)	C (2.4)	N (2.5)	O (2.6)	F (2.7)	Ne (2.8)
Period 3	Na (2.8.1)	Mg (2.8.2)	Al (2.8.3)	Si (2.8.4)	P (2.8.5)	S (2.8.6)	Cl (2.8.7)	Ar (2.8.8)
Period 4	K (2.8.8.1)	Ca (2.8.8.2)						

A section of the periodic table

ROUND UP

How much have you improved? Work out your improvement index on page 211.

1 Magnesium chloride, $MgCl_2$, is a solid of high melting point, and tetrachloromethane, CCl_4, is a volatile liquid. Explain how differences in chemical bonding account for these differences. [4]

2 Choose from the elements: Na, Mg, Al, Si, P, S, Cl, Ar.
   a) List the elements that react readily with cold water to form alkaline solutions. [2]
   b) List the elements that form sulphates. [3]
   c) Name the elements which exist as molecules containing (i) one atom (ii) two atoms. [2]
   d) Which element has both metallic and non-metallic properties? [1]

3 Write the symbol for the reducing agent in each of the following reactions:
   a) $2Na(s) + 2H_2O(l) \rightarrow H_2(g) + 2NaOH(aq)$ [1]
   b) $O_2(g) + S(s) \rightarrow SO_2(g)$ [1]
   c) $2Al(s) + 3Cl_2(g) \rightarrow 2AlCl_3(s)$ [1]
   d) $Cu(s) + S(s) \rightarrow CuS(s)$ [1]

REDUCING AGENTS Page 155.

4 Give the formulas of the oxides of sodium, magnesium, aluminium and silicon. [4]

5 What do the sulphate of chlorine, the carbonate of silicon and the hydride of argon have in common? [1]

6 The elements sodium and potassium have the electron arrangements Na(2.8.1) and K(2.8.8.1). How does this explain the similarity in their reactions? [2]

7 Radium, Ra, is a radioactive element of atomic number 88 which falls below barium in Group 2. What can you predict about
   a) the nature of radium oxide [3]
   b) the reaction of radium with water [3]
   c) the reaction of radium with dilute hydrochloric acid? [4]

   Give the physical state and type of bonding in any compounds you mention. Include the names and formulas of any compounds formed.

8 Astatine, At, is a radioactive element of atomic number 85 which follows iodine in Group 7. What can you predict about
   a) the nature of its compound with hydrogen [3]
   b) the reaction of astatine with sodium? [4]

   Give the physical state and type of bonding in any compounds you mention. Include the names and formulas of any compounds formed.

The periodic table

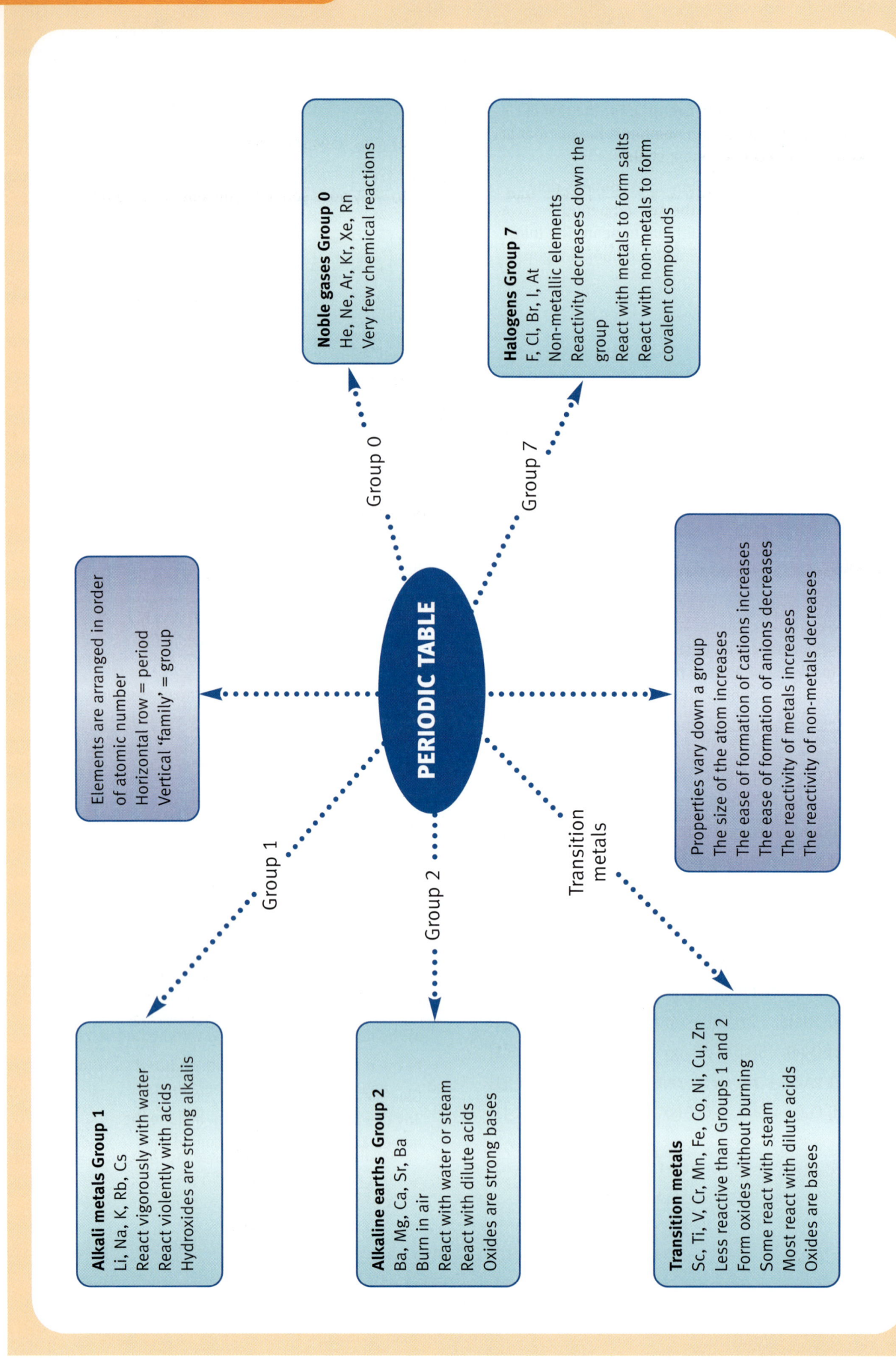

PERIODIC TABLE

- Elements are arranged in order of atomic number
- Horizontal row = period
- Vertical 'family' = group

Noble gases Group 0
- He, Ne, Ar, Kr, Xe, Rn
- Very few chemical reactions

Halogens Group 7
- F, Cl, Br, I, At
- Non-metallic elements
- Reactivity decreases down the group
- React with metals to form salts
- React with non-metals to form covalent compounds

Properties vary down a group
- The size of the atom increases
- The ease of formation of cations increases
- The ease of formation of anions decreases
- The reactivity of metals increases
- The reactivity of non-metals decreases

Alkali metals Group 1
- Li, Na, K, Rb, Cs
- React vigorously with water
- React violently with acids
- Hydroxides are strong alkalis

Alkaline earths Group 2
- Ba, Mg, Ca, Sr, Ba
- Burn in air
- React with water or steam
- React with dilute acids
- Oxides are strong bases

Transition metals
- Sc, Ti, V, Cr, Mn, Fe, Co, Ni, Cu, Zn
- Less reactive than Groups 1 and 2
- Form oxides without burning
- Some react with steam
- Most react with dilute acids
- Oxides are bases

Acids, bases and salts — Chapter 7

PREVIEW

At the end of this topic you will:

- be able to define the terms 'acid', 'base' and 'alkali'
- know the typical reactions of acids and bases
- know how to prepare salts and know the uses of some important salts.

CONCEPT MAPS
Pages 146, 148, 150.

How much do you already know? Work out your score on page 211.

Test yourself

1. Say whether the substances listed are strongly acidic (SA), weakly acidic (WA), strongly basic (SB), weakly basic (WB) or neutral (N).
   - a) battery acid, pH 0 [1]
   - b) rainwater, pH 6.5 [1]
   - c) blood, pH 7.4 [1]
   - d) sea water, pH 8.5 [1]
   - e) cabbage juice, pH 5.0 [1]
   - f) saliva, pH 7.0 [1]
   - g) washing soda, pH 11.5 [1]

2. You are given two bottles labelled 'acid 1' and 'acid 2'. One is a weak acid and the other is a strong acid. Describe two tests you could do to find out which is which. [3]

3. Name
   - a) a strong acid present in your stomach [1]
   - b) a base present in indigestion tablets [1]
   - c) a weak acid present in fruits [1]
   - d) a weak base used as a domestic cleaning fluid. [1]

4. Kleenit is an oven spray for cleaning greasy ovens. It contains a concentrated solution of sodium hydroxide.

   - a) Why does sodium hydroxide remove grease? [1]
   - b) Why does sodium hydroxide work better than ammonia? [1]
   - c) What two safety precautions should you take when using Kleenit? [2]
   - d) Why does Moppit, a fluid used for cleaning floors, contain ammonia rather than sodium hydroxide? [1]
   - e) Why do soap manufacturers use sodium hydroxide, not ammonia? [1]

7.1 Acids

Where are acids found?

The following are strong acids:

★ Hydrochloric acid occurs in the stomach, where it aids digestion.

★ Nitric acid is used in the production of fertilisers and explosives.

★ Sulphuric acid is used in car batteries and in the production of fertilisers.

The following are weak acids:

★ Carbonic acid is used in fizzy drinks.

★ Citric acid occurs in lemons and other citrus fruits.

★ Ethanoic acid occurs in vinegar.

★ Lactic acid is present in sour milk.

What do acids do?

Acids are compounds that release hydrogen ions when dissolved in water. The hydrogen ions are responsible for the typical reactions of acids. Strong acids are completely ionised; for example, hydrochloric acid solution consists of the ions H^+ and Cl^- and water molecules. There are no molecules of HCl in the solution. Weak acids consist chiefly of molecules, but a small fraction of the molecules are ionised. Weak acids therefore have a low concentration of hydrogen ions in solution and react less readily than strong acids.

The concept map overleaf gives a summary of the properties of acids.

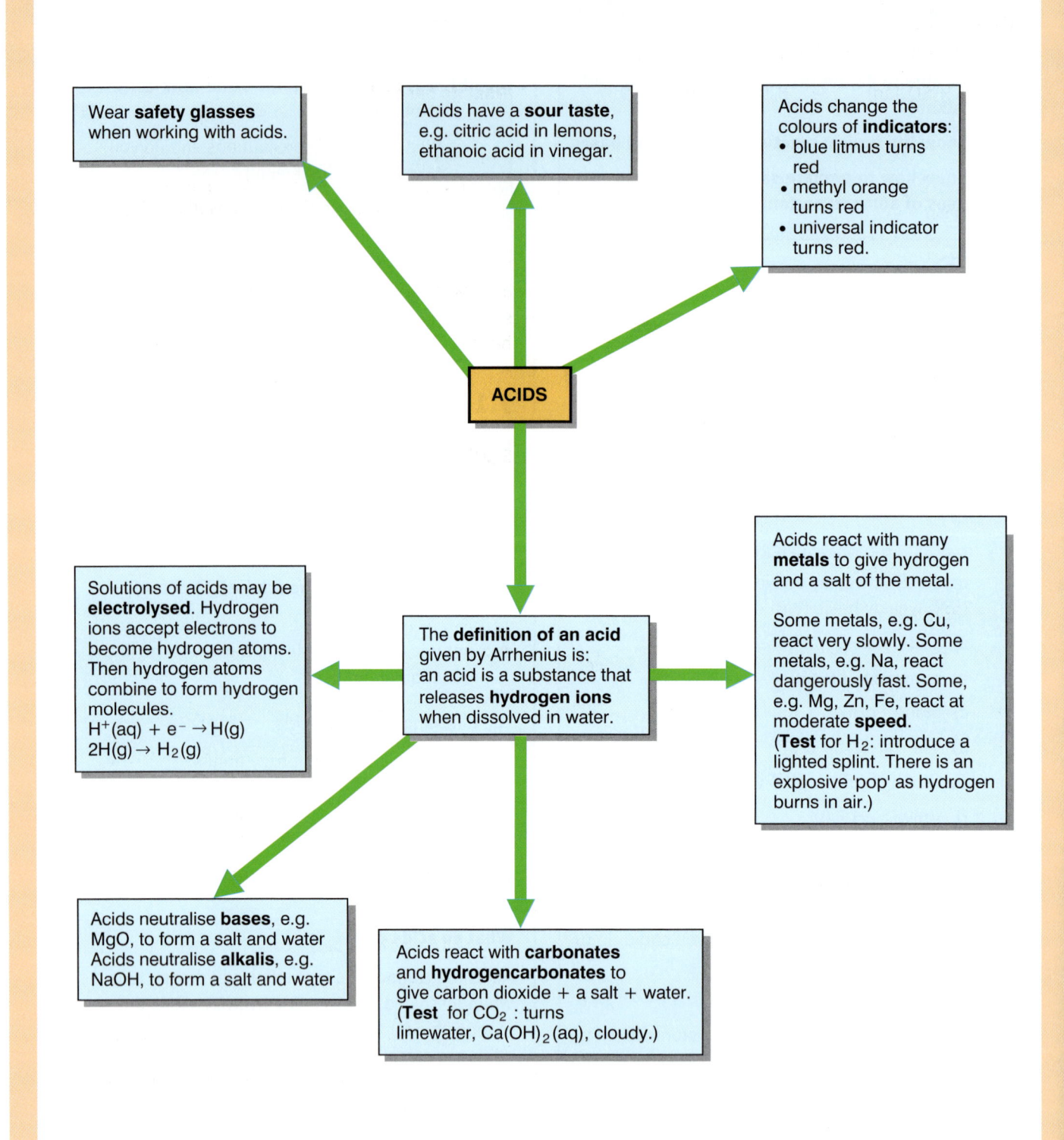

Acids, bases and salts

ACIDS

- Wear **safety glasses** when working with acids.

- Acids have a **sour taste**, e.g. citric acid in lemons, ethanoic acid in vinegar.

- Acids change the colours of **indicators**:
  - blue litmus turns red
  - methyl orange turns red
  - universal indicator turns red.

The **definition of an acid** given by Arrhenius is: an acid is a substance that releases **hydrogen ions** when dissolved in water.

- Solutions of acids may be **electrolysed**. Hydrogen ions accept electrons to become hydrogen atoms. Then hydrogen atoms combine to form hydrogen molecules.
  $H^+(aq) + e^- \rightarrow H(g)$
  $2H(g) \rightarrow H_2(g)$

- Acids react with many **metals** to give hydrogen and a salt of the metal.

  Some metals, e.g. Cu, react very slowly. Some metals, e.g. Na, react dangerously fast. Some, e.g. Mg, Zn, Fe, react at moderate **speed**.
  (**Test** for H_2: introduce a lighted splint. There is an explosive 'pop' as hydrogen burns in air.)

- Acids neutralise **bases**, e.g. MgO, to form a salt and water
  Acids neutralise **alkalis**, e.g. NaOH, to form a salt and water

- Acids react with **carbonates** and **hydrogencarbonates** to give carbon dioxide + a salt + water.
  (**Test** for CO_2: turns limewater, $Ca(OH)_2(aq)$, cloudy.)

Concept map: The properties of acids

Acids, bases and salts

Equations for some reactions in the concept map

With metals

zinc + sulphuric acid → hydrogen + zinc sulphate

$Zn(s) + H_2SO_4(aq) \rightarrow H_2(g) + ZnSO_4(aq)$

or the ionic equation:

$Zn(s) + 2H^+(aq) \rightarrow Zn^{2+}(aq) + H_2(g)$

With bases

magnesium oxide + sulphuric acid → magnesium sulphate + water

$MgO(s) + H_2SO_4(aq) \rightarrow MgSO_4(aq) + H_2O(l)$

or the ionic equation:

$O^{2-}(s) + 2H^+(aq) \rightarrow H_2O(l)$

calcium hydroxide + hydrochloric acid → calcium chloride + water

$Ca(OH)_2(s) + 2HCl(aq) \rightarrow CaCl_2(aq) + 2H_2O(l)$

or the ionic equation:

$OH^-(aq) + H^+(aq) \rightarrow H_2O(l)$

With carbonates

calcium carbonate + hydrochloric acid → carbon dioxide + calcium chloride + water

$CaCO_3(s) + 2HCl(aq) \rightarrow CO_2(g) + CaCl_2(aq) + H_2O(l)$

or the ionic equation:

$CO_3^{2-}(s) + 2H^+(aq) \rightarrow CO_2(g) + H_2O(l)$

With alkalis

ammonia + sulphuric acid → ammonium sulphate

$2NH_3(aq) + H_2SO_4(aq) \rightarrow (NH_4)_2SO_4(aq)$

7.2 Bases

Where do you find bases?

The following are strong bases:

★ Calcium hydroxide is used to treat soil which is too acidic.
★ Calcium oxide is used in the manufacture of cement and concrete.
★ Magnesium hydroxide is used in anti-acid indigestion tablets.
★ Sodium hydroxide is used in soap manufacture and as a degreasing agent.

★ The weak base ammonia is used in cleaning fluids, as a degreasing agent and in the manufacture of fertilisers.

What do bases do?

A **base** is a substance that reacts with an acid to form a salt and water as the only products. A soluble base is called an **alkali**. Sodium hydroxide, NaOH, is a strong base and a strong alkali. It is completely ionised in solution as Na^+ and OH^- ions. Ammonia is only slightly ionised and the concentration of hydroxide ions in the solution is small. Ammonia is therefore a weak base.

The concept map overleaf gives a summary of the properties of bases.

Equations for some reactions in the concept map

With acids

magnesium oxide + hydrochloric acid → magnesium chloride + water

$MgO(s) + 2HCl(aq) \rightarrow MgCl_2(aq) + H_2O(l)$

or the ionic equation:

$O^{2-}(s) + 2H^+(aq) \rightarrow H_2O(l)$

sodium hydroxide + hydrochloric acid → sodium chloride + water

$NaOH(aq) + HCl(aq) \rightarrow NaCl(aq) + H_2O(l)$

sodium hydroxide + sulphuric acid → sodium sulphate + water

$2NaOH(aq) + H_2SO_4(aq) \rightarrow Na_2SO_4(aq) + 2H_2O(l)$

or the ionic equation:

$OH^-(aq) + H^+(aq) \rightarrow H_2O(l)$

With metal salts

sodium hydroxide + iron(II) sulphate → iron(II) hydroxide + sodium sulphate

$2NaOH(aq) + FeSO_4(aq) \rightarrow Fe(OH)_2(s) + Na_2SO_4(aq)$

or the ionic equation:

$Fe^{2+}(aq) + 2OH^-(aq) \rightarrow Fe(OH)_2(s)$

Acids, bases and salts

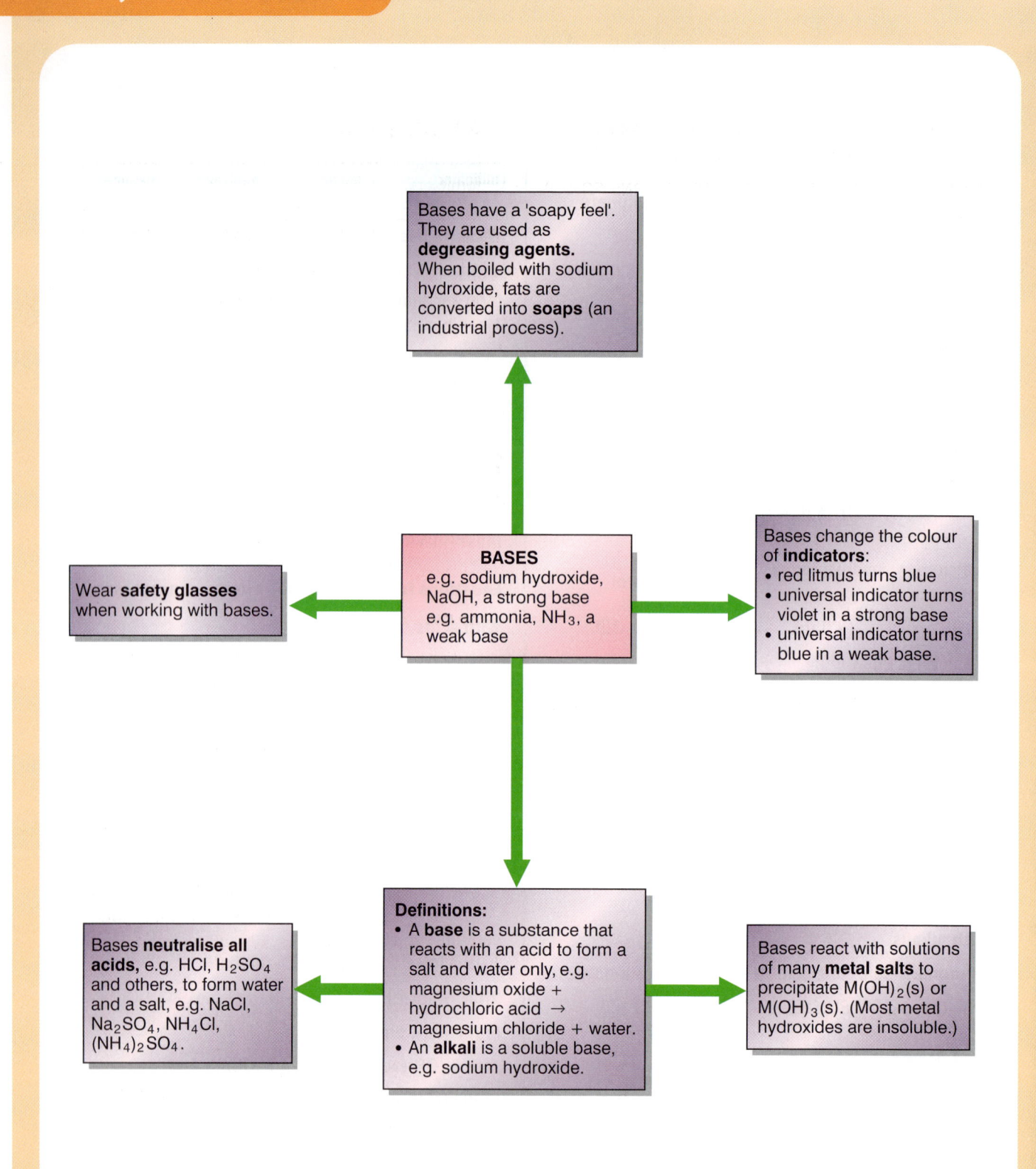

BASES
e.g. sodium hydroxide, NaOH, a strong base
e.g. ammonia, NH_3, a weak base

Bases have a 'soapy feel'. They are used as **degreasing agents**. When boiled with sodium hydroxide, fats are converted into **soaps** (an industrial process).

Wear **safety glasses** when working with bases.

Bases change the colour of **indicators**:
- red litmus turns blue
- universal indicator turns violet in a strong base
- universal indicator turns blue in a weak base.

Definitions:
- A **base** is a substance that reacts with an acid to form a salt and water only, e.g. magnesium oxide + hydrochloric acid → magnesium chloride + water.
- An **alkali** is a soluble base, e.g. sodium hydroxide.

Bases **neutralise all acids**, e.g. HCl, H_2SO_4 and others, to form water and a salt, e.g. NaCl, Na_2SO_4, NH_4Cl, $(NH_4)_2SO_4$.

Bases react with solutions of many **metal salts** to precipitate $M(OH)_2(s)$ or $M(OH)_3(s)$. (Most metal hydroxides are insoluble.)

Concept map: the properties of bases

Acids, bases and salts

sodium hydroxide + iron(III) sulphate → iron(III) hydroxide + sodium sulphate

6NaOH(aq) + Fe$_2$(SO$_4$)$_3$(aq) → 2Fe(OH)$_3$(s) + 3Na$_2$SO$_4$(aq)

or the ionic equation:

Fe^{3+}(aq) + 3OH$^-$(aq) → Fe(OH)$_3$(s)

7.3 Neutralisation

Neutralisation is the combination of hydrogen ions (from an acid) and hydroxide ions (from an alkali) or oxide ions (from an insoluble base) to form water. In the process a salt is formed. For example, with an alkali:

hydrochloric acid + sodium hydroxide → sodium chloride + water

HCl(aq) + NaOH(aq) → NaCl(aq) + H$_2$O(l)

acid + alkali → salt + water

The hydrogen ions and hydroxide ions combine to form water molecules.

H$^+$(aq) + OH$^-$(aq) → H$_2$O(l)

Sodium ions and chloride ions remain in the solution, which becomes a solution of sodium chloride.

With a base:

sulphuric acid + copper(II) oxide → copper(II) sulphate + water

H$_2$SO$_4$(aq) + CuO(s) → CuSO$_4$(aq) + H$_2$O(l)

acid + base → salt + water

Hydrogen ions and oxide ions combine to form water:

2H$^+$(aq) + O^{2-}(s) → H$_2$O(l)

Copper(II) ions and sulphate ions remain in the solution, which becomes a solution of copper(II) sulphate.

7.4 Indicators

indicator	acidic colour	neutral colour	alkaline colour
litmus	red	purple	blue
phenolphthalein	colourless	colourless	red
methyl orange	red	yellow	yellow

The colours of some indicators

Universal indicator can distinguish between strong and weak bases, as shown in the diagram below.

7.5 Salts

Common salt

The importance of common salt, sodium chloride, NaCl, is outlined in the concept map overleaf.

Some useful salts

★ **Sodium carbonate-10-water**, Na$_2$CO$_3$.10H$_2$O, 'washing soda', is used as a water softener, an ingredient of washing powders and bath salts.

★ **Sodium hydrogencarbonate**, NaHCO$_3$, 'baking soda', is added to self-raising flour. It decomposes at oven temperature to give carbon dioxide and steam, which make bread and cakes rise.

★ **Calcium sulphate-$\frac{1}{2}$-water**, CaSO$_4$.$\frac{1}{2}$H$_2$O, is plaster of Paris. When mixed with water it combines and sets to form a strong 'plaster cast'. It is also used for plastering walls.

★ **Silver bromide**, AgBr, is used in black-and-white photographic film.

★ **Iron(II) sulphate-7-water**, FeSO$_4$.7H$_2$O, is used in some kinds of 'iron tablets' which people take for anaemia.

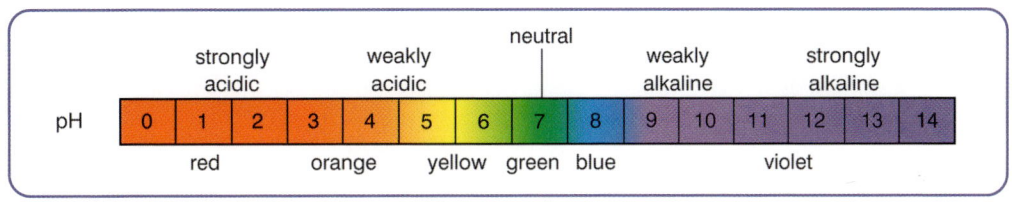

The colour of universal indicator in solutions of different pH

Acids, bases and salts

Table salt is pure sodium chloride. The food industry uses salt for
- seasoning foods
- preserving foods e.g. curing meats and canning vegetables
- making margarine, butter and cheese.

Rock salt is impure salt. It is spread on icy roads in winter and used as a fertiliser for crops such as sugar beet.

SALT sodium chloride, NaCl

Salt is used in the manufacture of sodium carbonate and sodium hydrogencarbonate in the **Solvay process**.

Electrolysis of a solution of sodium chloride (brine) gives sodium hydroxide + hydrogen + chlorine.

- **Sodium carbonate-10-water**, washing soda, $Na_2CO_3.10H_2O$, is used in washing powders.
- **Sodium hydrogencarbonate**, $NaHCO_3$, is an ingredient of baking powders.
- **Sodium carbonate**, Na_2CO_3, is used in making glass.

Sodium hydroxide is used in
- the extraction of aluminium
- the manufacture of drugs, textiles, paper, soap, antiseptics and other products.

Chlorine is used
- to disinfect drinking water and swimming pools
- as a bleach
- in the manufacture of plastics, rubber, herbicides, refrigerants, paints and dyes.

Hydrogen is used
- in the hydrogenation of oils to give solid fats
- for the reduction of some metal oxides
- as a fuel
- in the manufacture of ammonia, which is used to make fertilisers.

Concept map: common salt

Acids, bases and salts

★ **Barium sulphate**, $BaSO_4$, is used in 'barium meals' because barium ions show up well on X-rays and reveal the position of a stomach ulcer (see page 263).

★ **Copper(II) sulphate**, $CuSO_4$, is used as a fungicide for spraying grapes, potatoes and other crops.

★ **Calcium fluoride**, CaF_2, is added to toothpastes. Tooth enamel reacts with fluorides to form a harder enamel which is better at resisting attack by mouth acids. Many water companies add a small amount of calcium fluoride to drinking water.

★ **NPK fertilisers** contain ammonium nitrate, NH_4NO_3, and ammonium sulphate, $(NH_4)_2SO_4$, as sources of nitrogen; calcium phosphate, $Ca_3(PO_4)_2$, as a source of phosphorus; and potassium chloride, KCl, as a source of potassium.

Making soluble salts

To make a soluble salt, an acid is neutralised by adding a metal, a solid base, a solid metal carbonate or a solution of an alkali.

★ **Method 1:** acid + metal → salt + hydrogen

★ **Method 2:** acid + metal oxide → salt + water

★ **Method 3:**
acid + metal carbonate → salt + water + carbon dioxide

★ **Method 4:** acid + alkali → salt + water

Here are the practical details for methods 1, 2 and 3.

a) Carry out the neutralisation as shown in the table and diagram below.

b) Filter to remove the excess of solid, using a filter funnel and filter paper.

c) Evaporate the filtrate, preferably on a water bath.

d) As the solution cools, crystals of the salt form. Separate the crystals by filtration. Using a little distilled water, wash the crystals in the filter funnel. Leave the crystals to dry.

method 1 (acid + metal)	method 2 (acid + metal oxide)	method 3 (acid + metal carbonate)
Warm the acid, then switch off the Bunsen burner.	Warm the acid.	
Add an excess of the metal to the acid. When no more hydrogen is evolved, the reaction is complete.	Add an excess of the metal oxide to the acid. When the solution no longer turns blue litmus paper red, the reaction is complete.	Add an excess of the metal carbonate to the acid. When no more carbon dioxide is evolved, the reaction is complete.

Neutralisation details for methods **1** to **3**

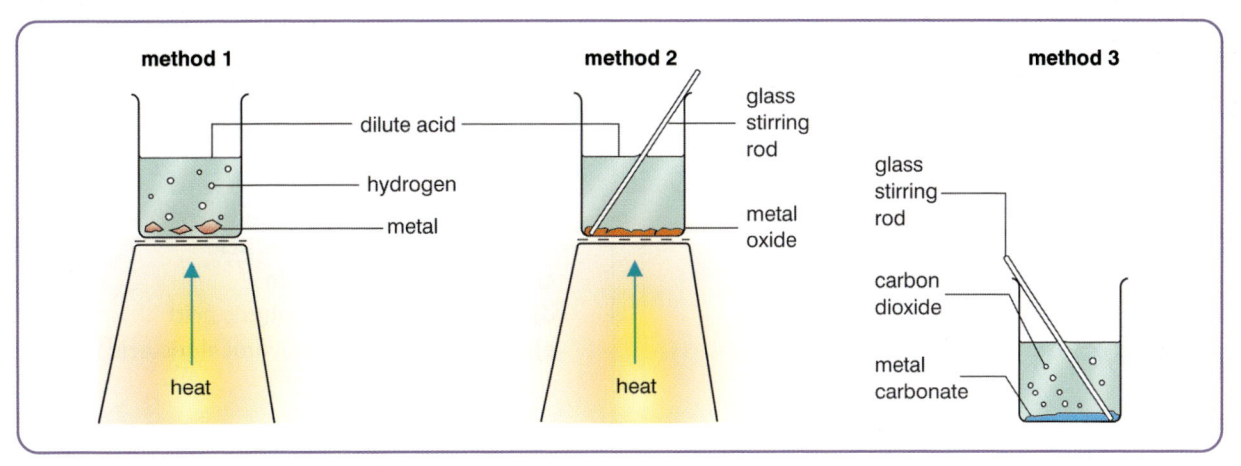

Adding an excess of a solid reactant to an acid

Acids, bases and salts

1 Add ammonia solution to dilute sulphuric acid, stirring constantly.

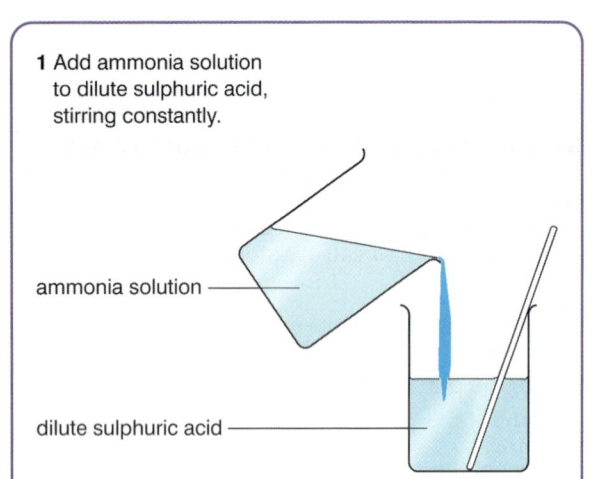

2 From time to time, use the glass rod to remove a drop of acid. Spot it onto a strip of indicator paper. When the indicator shows that the solution has become alkaline, stop adding ammonia.

3 Evaporate the solution until it begins to crystallise. Leave it to stand. Filter to obtain crystals of ammonium sulphate.

Laboratory preparation of ammonium sulphate

Here are the practical details for method **4** (acid + alkali). For example, the neutralisation of an acid by ammonia solution can be used to make ammonium salts. The diagram above shows the steps in the preparation of ammonium sulphate.

Making insoluble salts: precipitation

Insoluble salts are made by mixing two solutions. For example, barium sulphate is insoluble. A soluble barium salt and a soluble sulphate must be chosen to make barium sulphate. The precipitate is separated by filtering or centrifuging.

The equation for the reaction is:

barium chloride + sodium sulphate → barium sulphate + sodium chloride

$BaCl_2(aq) + Na_2SO_4(aq) \rightarrow BaSO_4(s) + 2NaCl(aq)$

or the ionic equation:

$Ba^{2+}(aq) + SO_4^{2-}(aq) \rightarrow BaSO_4(s)$

ROUND UP

How much have you improved? Work out your improvement index on page 211.

1. Refer to the methods of making soluble salts.
   a) Explain why it is easier to remove an excess of solid base than an excess of acid. [1]
   b) Explain why it is important that all the acid is used up. [1]
   c) Say how you find out when all the acid has been used up in the reaction **(i)** with a metal **(ii)** with a metal oxide **(iii)** with a metal carbonate. [3]

2. Complete the following word equations:
   a) zinc + sulphuric acid → ___ sulphate + ___ [2]
   b) cobalt oxide + sulphuric acid → ___ sulphate + ___ [2]
   c) nickel carbonate + hydrochloric acid → nickel ___ + ___ + ___ [3]
   d) potassium hydroxide + nitric acid → ___ nitrate + ___ [2]
   e) ammonia + nitric acid → ___ ___ [2]

3. Lead(II) sulphate is insoluble. Lead(II) nitrate and all sodium salts are soluble.
   a) Suggest two solutions that could be mixed to make lead(II) sulphate. [2]
   b) Write a word equation, a chemical equation and an ionic equation for the reaction. [11]
   c) Lead salts are poisonous. What precaution should you take if you do this preparation? [1]

4. The following pairs of substances react to form a salt. Name the salt formed and say what else is formed.
   a) sodium hydroxide + sulphuric acid [2]
   b) ammonia + hydrochloric acid [1]
   c) zinc + hydrochloric acid [2]
   d) copper(II) oxide + sulphuric acid [2]
   e) calcium carbonate + hydrochloric acid [3]

Well done if you've improved. Don't worry if you haven't. Take a break and try again.

Chapter 8 — Air

PREVIEW

At the end of this topic you will:

- know how Earth's atmosphere originated
- know the reactions and importance of oxygen
- understand oxidation–reduction reactions
- know the importance of the nitrogen cycle and the carbon cycle
- appreciate the effects of pollutants in the atmosphere.

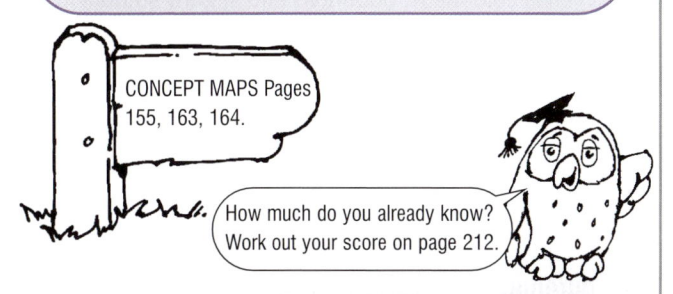

CONCEPT MAPS Pages 155, 163, 164.

How much do you already know? Work out your score on page 212.

Test yourself

1. How did Earth's original atmosphere, formed billions of years ago, differ from today's atmosphere in its content of water vapour, carbon dioxide, oxygen and nitrogen? [4]
2. Give the percentage by volume in pure dry air of oxygen and nitrogen. [2]
3. Give two industrial uses for oxygen. [2]
4. What is the name for an oxidation reaction in which energy is released? [1]
5. Describe a test for oxygen. [1]
6. Suggest identities for the following elements: [4]
   - A burns with a blue flame to give an acidic gas.
   - B burns with a yellow flame to give a basic solid.
   - C burns with a bright white flame to give a basic solid.
   - D burns with a red glow to give an invisible gas.
7. Complete the sentence.
   Oxidation is the _____ of oxygen or the _____ of hydrogen or the _____ of electrons. [3]
8. Name two processes which turn atmospheric nitrogen into compounds. [2]
9. Name two processes which take carbon dioxide out of the atmosphere. [2]
10. How would you test an invisible gas to find out if it is carbon dioxide? [2]
11. Name four atmospheric pollutants and state one source of each. [8]

8.1 How the atmosphere evolved

A mixture of gases was released from the interior of Earth about 4.6 billion years ago. The mixture was probably similar to the gases released from volcanoes today: water vapour 64% by mass, carbon dioxide 24%, sulphur dioxide 10%, nitrogen 1.5%. Water vapour condensed to make oceans. Carbon dioxide dissolved in the oceans, where it was used by the first living things in a process which developed into photosynthesis:

$$\text{carbon dioxide} + \text{water} + \text{sunlight} \rightarrow \text{organic matter} + \text{oxygen}$$

$$CO_2 + H_2O \rightarrow (CH_2O) + O_2$$

The oxygen formed in photosynthesis would have poisoned primitive plants. It was not released into the air, but was converted into iron oxides.

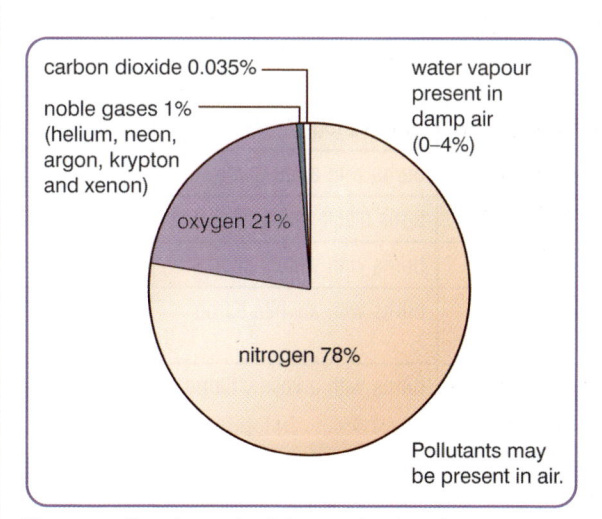

- carbon dioxide 0.035%
- noble gases 1% (helium, neon, argon, krypton and xenon)
- oxygen 21%
- nitrogen 78%
- water vapour present in damp air (0–4%)
- Pollutants may be present in air.

The composition of pure, dry air in percentage by volume

Air

Eventually bacteria living in the ocean developed the ability to use oxygen in respiration. Oxygen began to accumulate in the atmosphere, and the ozone layer formed. This shields Earth from receiving too much radiation from the Sun, and makes Earth an environment in which things can live. About 450 million years ago land plants emerged, followed by land animals 400 million years ago. The composition of the atmosphere has remained the same for about 300 million years.

Separating gases from air

Oxygen, nitrogen and argon are obtained by fractional distillation of liquid air. Liquid air at −190 °C is fed into an insulated fractionation column. Nitrogen (boiling point −196 °C) vaporises at the top of the column, argon (boiling point −186 °C) vaporises from the middle of the column, and oxygen (boiling point −183 °C) is left at the bottom of the column.

8.2 Oxygen

Plants and animals need oxygen for respiration. Aquatic plants and animals depend on the oxygen dissolved in water. Pollutants such as excess decaying organic matter use up dissolved oxygen and put aquatic animals and plants at risk.

Uses of pure oxygen

★ Aeroplanes which fly at high altitude, and all space flights, carry oxygen.

★ Deep-sea divers carry cylinders which contain a mixture of oxygen and helium.

★ An oxyacetylene torch (which burns ethyne, C_2H_2, in oxygen) has a very hot flame, about 4000 °C, and is used for welding and cutting metals.

★ Cast iron contains carbon, which is burnt off in a stream of oxygen to make steel.

★ Oxygen is pumped into polluted rivers and lakes.

Reactions of oxygen

Oxygen is colourless, odourless and slightly soluble in water. Many elements react with oxygen to form oxides as shown in the table below.

★ Combination with oxygen is called **oxidation**.

★ Oxidation in which energy is given out is called **combustion**.

★ Combustion accompanied by a flame is called **burning**.

★ Substances which undergo combustion to give out a lot of energy are called **fuels**.

★ Many substances burn in oxygen, and all substances burn more rapidly in oxygen than in air.

★ **Test for oxygen:** a glowing wooden splint lowered into oxygen starts to burn brightly.

The concept map opposite shows the properties of oxides.

element	observation	product	action of product on water
calcium (metal)	burns with a red flame	calcium oxide (white solid)	dissolves to give a strongly alkaline solution
copper (metal)	turns black without burning	copper(II) oxide (black solid)	insoluble
iron (metal)	burns with yellow sparks	iron oxide, Fe_3O_4	insoluble
magnesium (metal)	burns with a white flame	magnesium oxide (white solid)	dissolves slightly to give an alkaline solution
sodium (metal)	burns with a yellow flame	sodium oxide	dissolves readily to give a strongly alkaline solution
carbon (non-metal)	glows red	carbon dioxide (invisible gas)	dissolves slightly to give a weakly acidic solution
sulphur (non-metal)	burns with a blue flame	sulphur dioxide (fuming gas)	dissolves readily to give a strongly acidic solution

Reactions of oxygen with some elements

Air

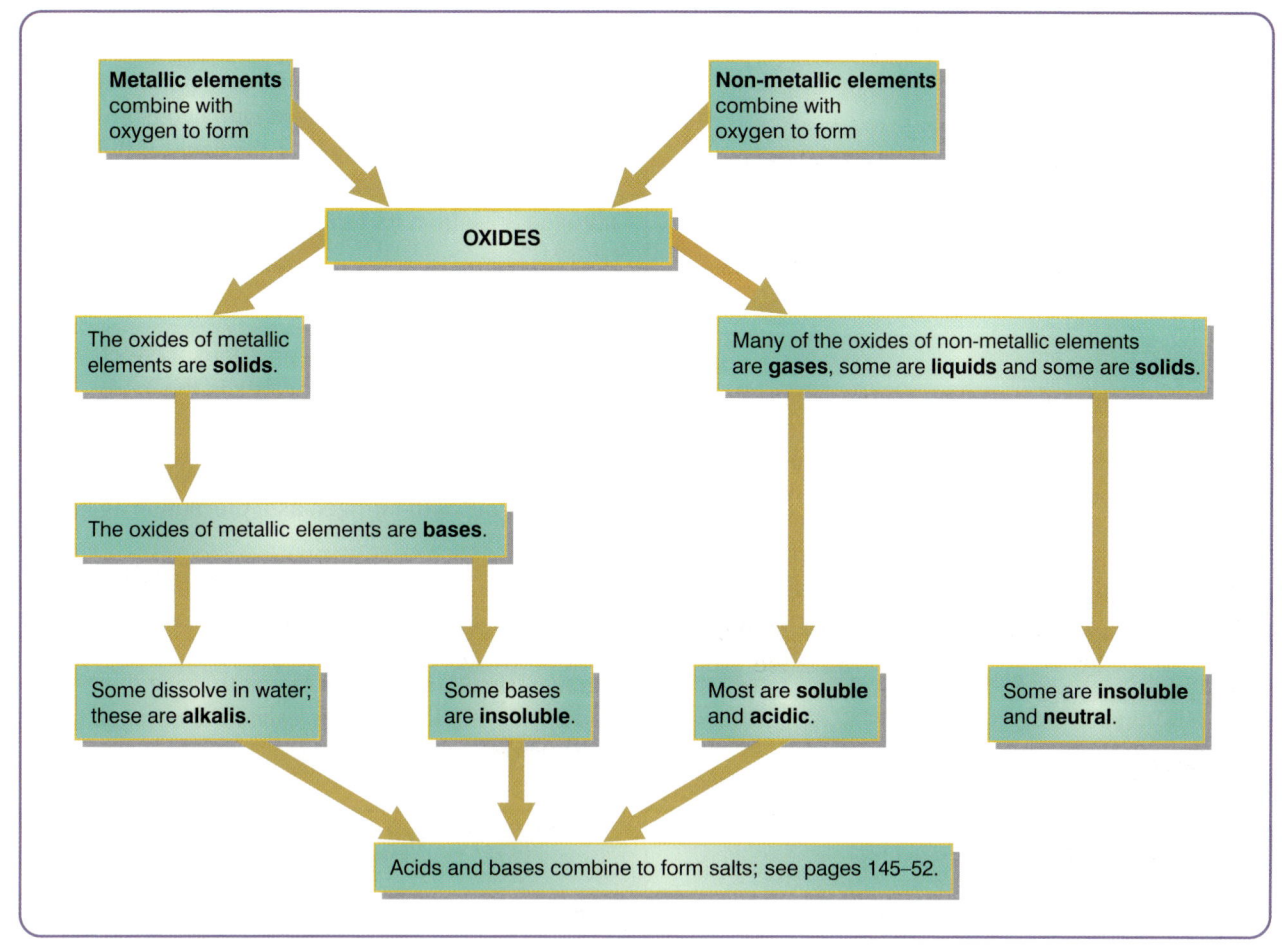

```
Metallic elements          Non-metallic elements
combine with               combine with
oxygen to form             oxygen to form
                ↓       ↓
              OXIDES
         ↙              ↘
The oxides of metallic    Many of the oxides of non-metallic elements
elements are solids.      are gases, some are liquids and some are solids.
    ↓                          ↓                        ↓
The oxides of metallic elements are bases.
    ↓              ↓           ↓                        ↓
Some dissolve    Some bases    Most are soluble    Some are insoluble
in water;        are           and acidic.         and neutral.
these are        insoluble.
alkalis.
         ↘       ↓       ↙          ↙
    Acids and bases combine to form salts; see pages 145–52.
```

Concept map: properties of oxides

8.3 Oxidation and reduction

Fact file

★ **Oxidation** = gain of oxygen or loss of hydrogen

★ **Reduction** = loss of oxygen or gain of hydrogen

★ An **oxidising agent** gives oxygen or takes hydrogen.

★ A **reducing agent** takes oxygen or gives hydrogen.

★ Oxidation and reduction occur together in **oxidation–reduction reactions** or **redox reactions**.

Here is an example of a redox reaction:

lead(II) oxide + hydrogen → lead + water

$PbO(s) + H_2(g) \rightarrow Pb(s) + H_2O(l)$

In this reaction:
- hydrogen has gained oxygen: hydrogen has been oxidised
- lead(II) oxide has lost oxygen: lead(II) oxide has been reduced
- hydrogen has taken oxygen from another substance: hydrogen is a reducing agent
- lead(II) oxide has given oxygen to another substance: lead(II) oxide is an oxidising agent
- oxidation and reduction are occurring together.

Air

$$PbO(s) + H_2(g) \longrightarrow Pb(s) + H_2O(l)$$

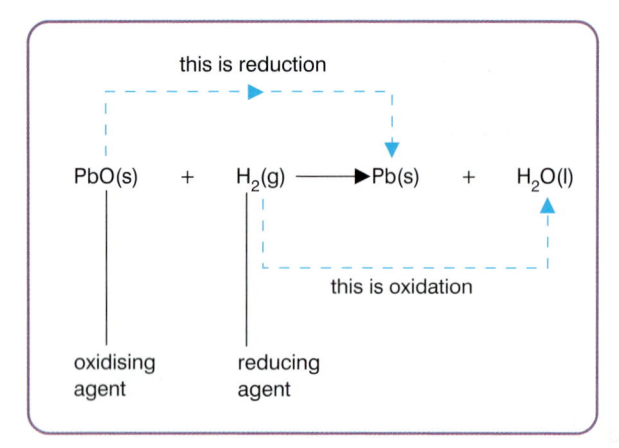

- this is reduction (PbO → Pb)
- this is oxidation (H$_2$ → H$_2$O)
- PbO: oxidising agent
- H$_2$: reducing agent

You can also think of oxidation and reduction in terms of electron transfer:

Oxidation	**R**eduction
Is	**I**s
Loss	**G**ain
of electrons	of electrons

8.4 Nitrogen

Nitrogen is a gas which does not take part in many chemical reactions. It combines with hydrogen to form ammonia. This reaction is the basis of the fertiliser industry; see opposite. Many uses of nitrogen arise from its lack of reactivity.

★ Liquid nitrogen is used in the fast-freezing of foods.

★ Many foods are packed in an atmosphere of nitrogen to prevent oils and fats in the foods from being oxidised to rancid products.

★ Oil tankers, road tankers and grain silos are flushed out with nitrogen as a precaution against fire.

8.5 The nitrogen cycle

Nitrogen circulates from air to soil to living things and back again in a process called the **nitrogen cycle**, shown below.

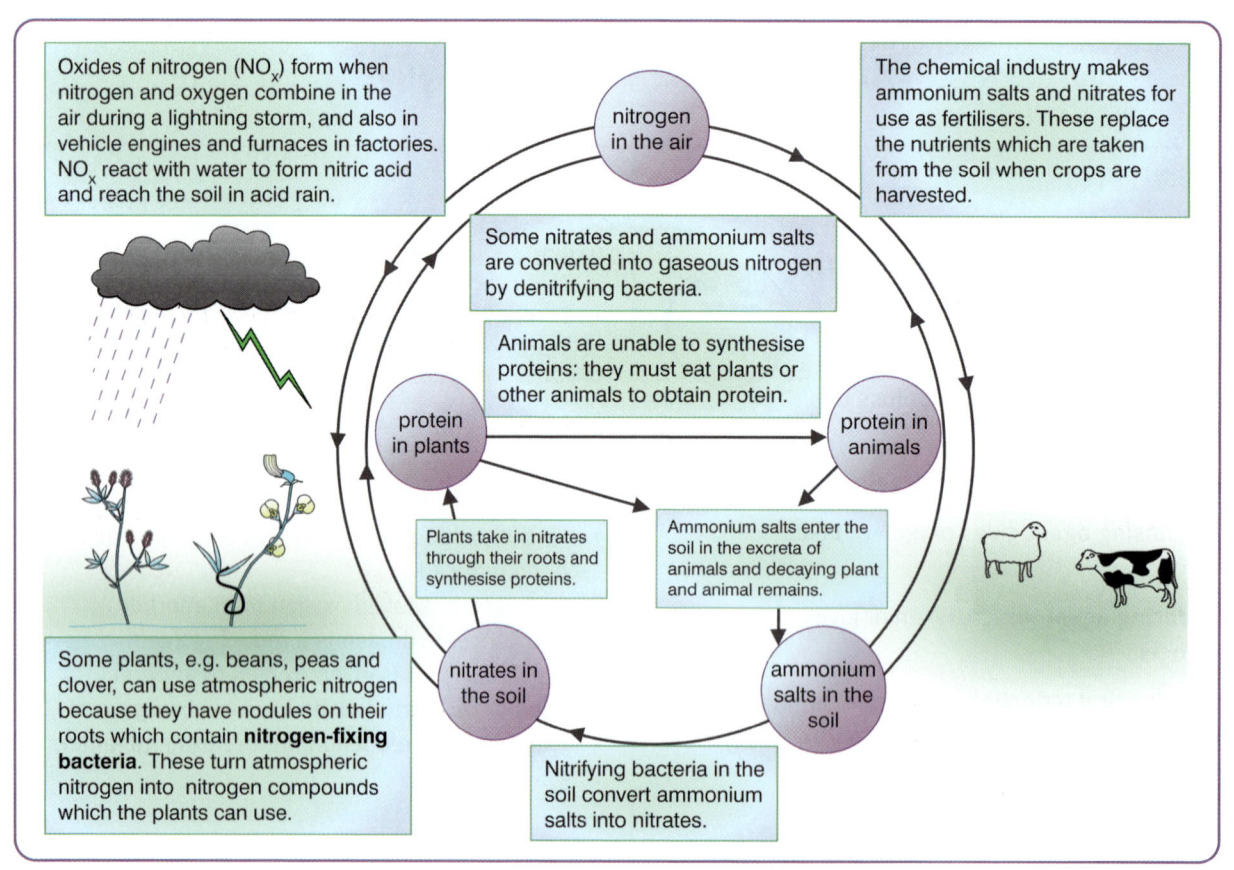

Oxides of nitrogen (NO$_x$) form when nitrogen and oxygen combine in the air during a lightning storm, and also in vehicle engines and furnaces in factories. NO$_x$ react with water to form nitric acid and reach the soil in acid rain.

The chemical industry makes ammonium salts and nitrates for use as fertilisers. These replace the nutrients which are taken from the soil when crops are harvested.

Some nitrates and ammonium salts are converted into gaseous nitrogen by denitrifying bacteria.

Animals are unable to synthesise proteins: they must eat plants or other animals to obtain protein.

Plants take in nitrates through their roots and synthesise proteins.

Ammonium salts enter the soil in the excreta of animals and decaying plant and animal remains.

Some plants, e.g. beans, peas and clover, can use atmospheric nitrogen because they have nodules on their roots which contain **nitrogen-fixing bacteria**. These turn atmospheric nitrogen into nitrogen compounds which the plants can use.

Nitrifying bacteria in the soil convert ammonium salts into nitrates.

Cycle nodes: nitrogen in the air → protein in plants → protein in animals → ammonium salts in the soil → nitrates in the soil →

The nitrogen cycle

8.6 Ammonia and fertilisers

Ammonia

The nitrogen in the air is used to make nitrogenous fertilisers. Under the conditions of the **Haber process** (named after the chemist Fritz Haber) nitrogen will combine with hydrogen.

nitrogen + hydrogen $\rightleftharpoons$ ammonia

$$N_2(g) + 3H_2(g) \rightleftharpoons 2NH_3(g)$$

The reaction is reversible: some of the ammonia formed dissociates into nitrogen and hydrogen. The product is a mixture of nitrogen, hydrogen and ammonia. Two factors increase the percentage of ammonia in the mixture: a **high pressure** and a **low temperature**. However, the reaction is very slow to reach equilibrium at a low temperature, and industrial plants use a compromise temperature and a catalyst to speed up the reaction, as shown in the flow diagram. The ammonia made by the Haber process can be oxidised to nitric acid.

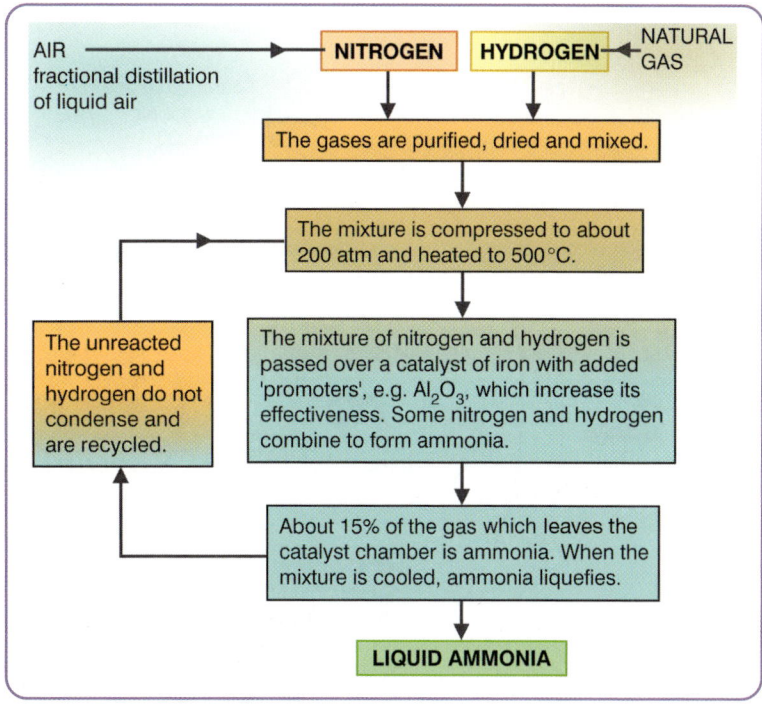

NPK fertilisers

Ammonia solution can be used as a fertiliser. However, it is more common to use the solid fertilisers ammonium nitrate, ammonium sulphate and ammonium phosphate.

Mixtures of ammonium nitrate, ammonium phosphate and potassium chloride contain the elements nitrogen, phosphorus and potassium, which are essential for plant growth and are sold as **NPK fertilisers**.

8.7 Carbon dioxide

The carbon cycle

Plants are able to make sugars by the process of **photosynthesis**:

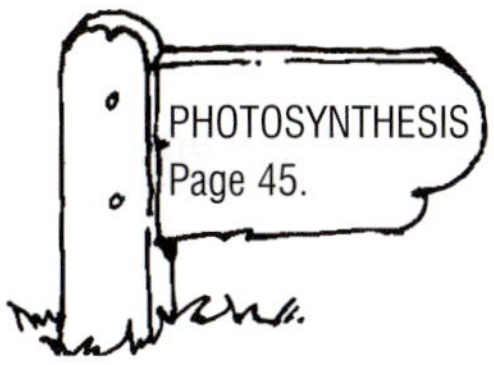

carbon dioxide + water + sunlight $\xrightarrow{\text{catalysed by chlorophyll}}$ glucose + oxygen

Flow diagram of the Haber process

The energy of sunlight is converted into the energy of the chemical bonds in the sugar glucose.

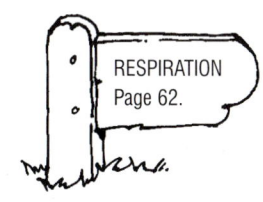

Animals obtain energy by **cellular respiration**:

glucose + oxygen → carbon dioxide + water + energy

The balance between the processes which take carbon dioxide from the air and those which put carbon dioxide into the air is called the **carbon cycle**. The cycle is shown on the next page.

Uses of carbon dioxide

★ Soft drinks are made by dissolving carbon dioxide in water under pressure and adding sugar and flavourings.

★ Solid carbon dioxide sublimes (turns into a vapour on warming). It is used as the refrigerant 'dry ice'.

★ Carbon dioxide is used in fire extinguishers because it does not support combustion and is denser than air.

Air

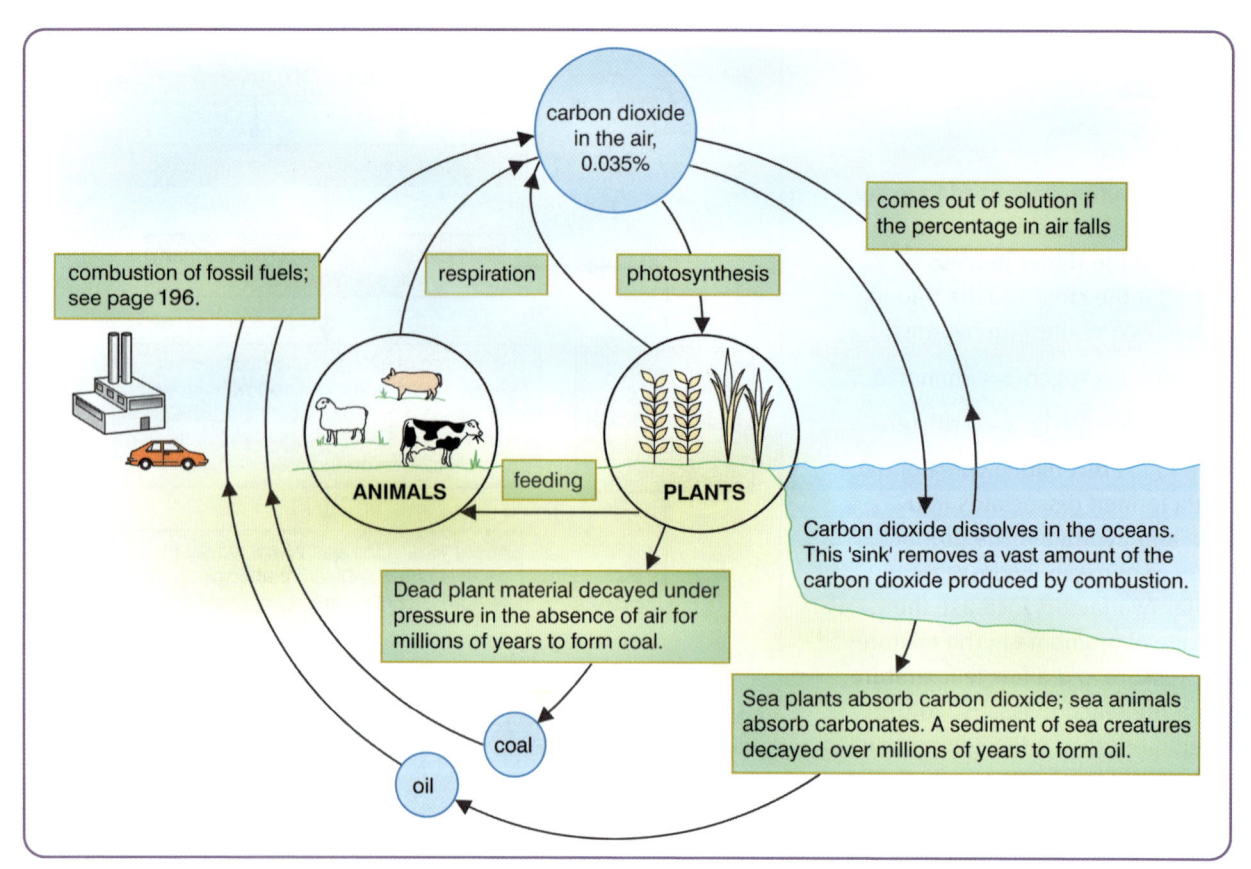

The carbon cycle

Test for carbon dioxide

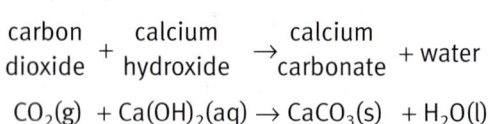

Carbon dioxide reacts with a solution of calcium hydroxide (limewater) to form a white precipitate of calcium carbonate.

carbon dioxide + calcium hydroxide → calcium carbonate + water

$$CO_2(g) + Ca(OH)_2(aq) \rightarrow CaCO_3(s) + H_2O(l)$$

The greenhouse effect

The Earth receives radiation from the Sun, and also radiates heat into space. Carbon dioxide and water vapour reduce the escape of heat energy from the Earth by means of the **greenhouse effect** (see diagram on opposite page). Without these 'blankets' of water vapour and carbon dioxide, the temperature of the Earth's surface would be at −18 °C, and life on Earth would be impossible.

The combustion of fossil fuels is causing an increase in the level of carbon dioxide at a rate which could raise the average temperature of the Earth. One result would be that the massive icecaps of the Arctic and Antarctic regions would slowly begin to melt. The levels of oceans would rise, and coastal areas would be flooded. A rise in temperature could decrease food production over vast areas, e.g. the mid-west USA and Russia. Secondary effects would make matters worse. The increase in temperature would make more water vaporise from the oceans and drive out some of the carbon dioxide dissolved in the oceans to add to a still thicker greenhouse blanket. Other 'greenhouse gases' are methane, chlorofluorocarbons (CFCs), nitrogen oxides and ozone.

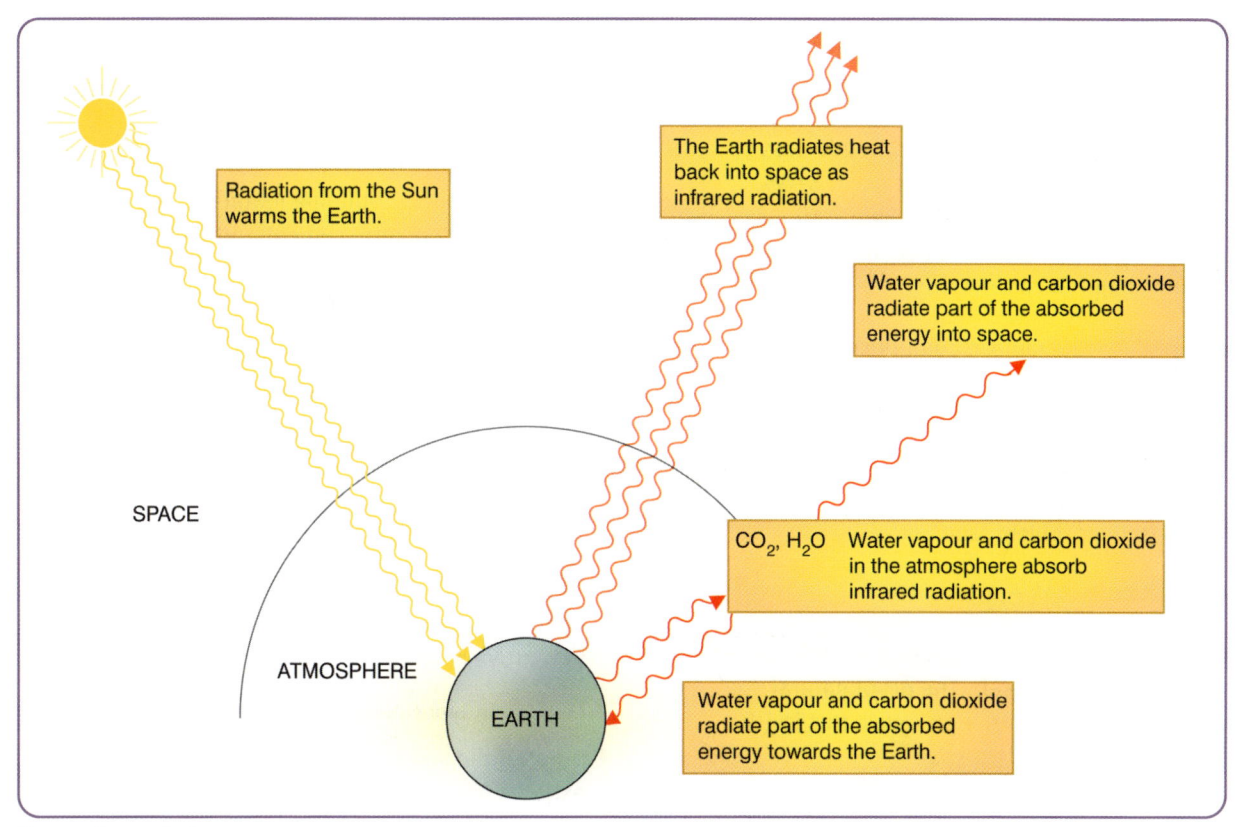

The greenhouse effect

8.8 The noble gases

Helium, neon, argon, krypton and xenon are the noble gases.

★ Helium is used in airships because of its low density.
★ Neon and other noble gases are used in illuminated signs.
★ Argon is used to fill light bulbs.

GROUPS OF THE PERIODIC TABLE Page 141.

8.9 The problem of pollution

Carbon monoxide

Source: most of the carbon monoxide in the air comes from vehicle engines, where it is formed by the incomplete combustion of petrol.

Soil organisms remove carbon monoxide from the air. However, in cities, where the concentration of carbon monoxide is high, there is little soil to remove it.

Effects: carbon monoxide combines with haemoglobin, the red pigment in the blood, and prevents haemoglobin from combining with oxygen. At a level of 1%, carbon monoxide will kill quickly; at lower levels, it causes headaches and dizziness and affects reaction times. Being colourless and odourless, carbon monoxide gives no warning of its presence.

Solutions to the problem may come from:
- tuning vehicle engines to use more air and produce only carbon dioxide and water. However, this increases the emission of oxides of nitrogen.
- fitting vehicles with catalytic converters
- using fuels which burn more cleanly than hydrocarbons, e.g. ethanol.

Air

Sulphur dioxide

Sources: major sources of the sulphur dioxide in the air are:
- the extraction of metals from sulphide ores
- the burning of coal, which contains 0.5–5% sulphur, mostly in electricity power stations
- oil-burning power stations, because fuel oil contains sulphur compounds.

Effects: sulphur dioxide is a colourless gas with a very penetrating and irritating smell. Atmospheric sulphur dioxide is thought to contribute to bronchitis and lung diseases. It is a cause of acid rain.

Solutions to the problem: see below.

Acid rain

Rain is naturally weakly acidic because it dissolves carbon dioxide from the air. The pH of natural rainwater is 5.2. Rain with a pH below this is described as **acid rain**.

The many effects of acid rain include:
- damage to lakes and the fish and plants in them; see diagram below
- washing of nutrients out of topsoil, resulting in poor crops and damage to trees
- costly damage to building materials, e.g. limestone, concrete, cement and metal.

What can be done?

Sweden has tackled the problem by spraying tonnes of calcium hydroxide into acid lakes.

Members of the European Community (EC) agreed to make a 60–70% cut in their emissions of sulphur dioxide. Power stations must make a big contribution to solving the problem. Some lines of attack are given below.

★ Coal can be crushed and washed with a solvent to remove much of the sulphur content.

★ Fuel oil can be purified at the refinery – at a cost.

★ Sulphur dioxide can be removed from the exhaust gases of power stations. In **flue gas desulphurisation** (**FGD**), jets of wet powdered limestone neutralise acidic gases as they pass up the chimney of the power station.

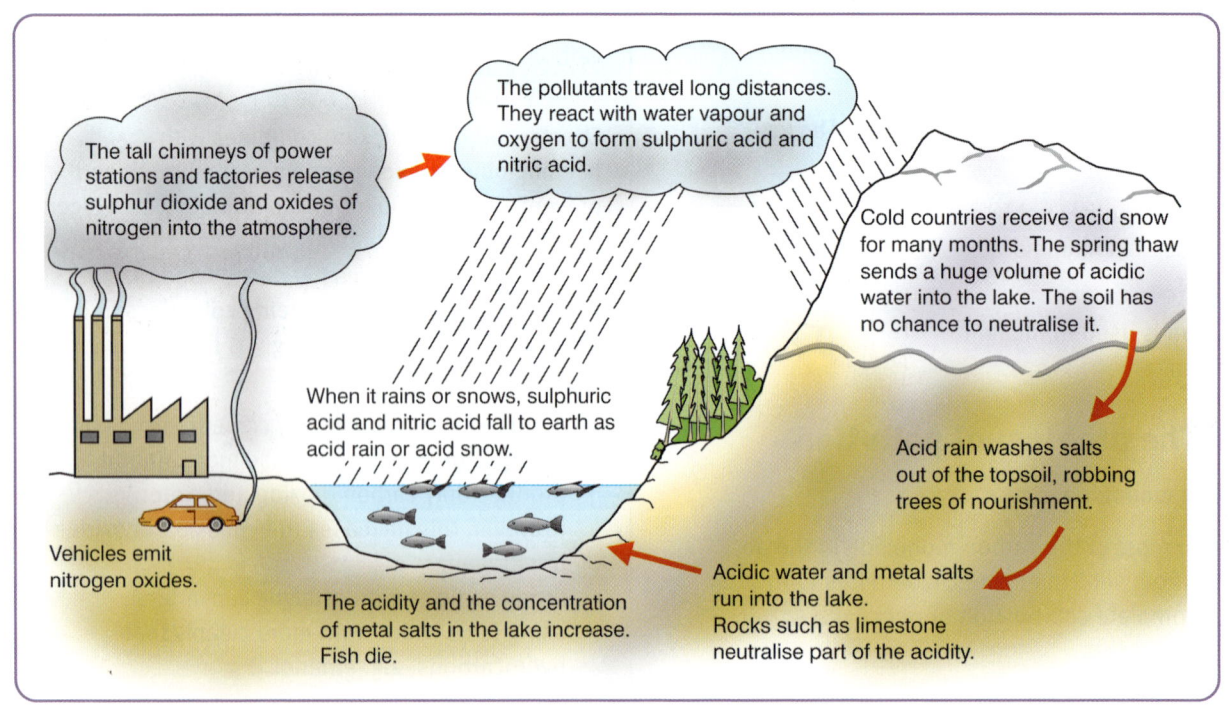

Acid rain; its source and its effect on lake water

★ In a **pulverised fluidised bed combustion** (**PFBC**) furnace, the coal is pulverised (broken into small pieces) and burnt on a bed of powdered limestone, which is 'fluidised' (kept in motion by an upward flow of air). As the coal burns, sulphur dioxide reacts with the limestone.

★ Nuclear power stations do not send pollutants into the air. However, they create the problem of storing radioactive waste.

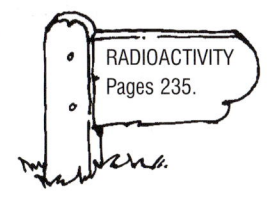

RADIOACTIVITY Pages 235.

Smoke, dust and grit

Particles enter the air from natural sources such as dust storms, forest fires and volcanic eruptions. Coal-burning power stations, incinerators, industries and vehicles add to the pollution. When smoke particles mix with fog, **smog** is formed. Smog contains sulphuric acid, which has been formed from sulphur dioxide in the smoke. Breathing smog makes the lungs produce mucus, making it more difficult to breathe.

Methods of removing particles include:
- using sprays of water to wash out particles from waste gases
- passing exhaust gases through filters
- using electrostatic precipitators which attract particles to charged plates.

The exhaust gases of vehicles are not treated by any of these methods.

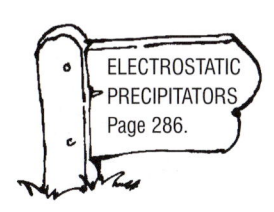

ELECTROSTATIC PRECIPITATORS Page 286.

Oxides of nitrogen

Source: when fuels are burned in air, the temperature rises. Some of the nitrogen and oxygen in the air combine to form nitrogen monoxide, NO, and nitrogen dioxide, NO_2. This mixture (shown as NO_x) is emitted by power stations, factories and vehicles.

Effects: nitrogen monoxide is soon converted into nitrogen dioxide which is highly toxic, and which contributes to the formation of acid rain (see previous page).

Solution to the problem: the presence of a catalyst (platinum) brings about the reaction:

nitrogen monoxide + carbon monoxide → nitrogen + carbon dioxide

$$2NO(g) + 2CO(g) \rightarrow N_2(g) + 2CO_2(g)$$

The **catalytic converters** which are now fitted in the exhausts of cars reduce the emission of oxides of nitrogen in this way. Unleaded petrol must be used because lead compounds in the exhaust gases would stop the catalyst working.

Hydrocarbons

Sources: the hydrocarbons in the air come from natural sources, such as the decay of plant material (85%), and from vehicles (15%).

Effects: in sunlight, hydrocarbons react with oxygen and oxides of nitrogen to form **photochemical smog**. This contains irritating and toxic compounds.

Solutions to the problem: if the air supply in a vehicle engine is increased, the petrol burns completely. However, at the same time, the formation of NO_X increases. A solution may be found by running the engine at a lower temperature and employing a catalyst to promote combustion.

Lead

Sources: lead compounds enter the air from the combustion of coal, the roasting of metal ores and from vehicle engines. Since the introduction of unleaded petrol, the level of lead in the atmosphere has fallen.

Effects: lead causes depression, tiredness, irritability and headaches. Higher levels of lead cause damage to the brain, liver and kidneys.

Air

ROUND UP

How much have you improved? Work out your improvement index on page 212.

1 zinc oxide + carbon → zinc + carbon monoxide

$$ZnO(s) + C(s) \rightarrow Zn(s) + CO(g)$$

   a) In this reaction, name **(i)** the oxidising agent and **(ii)** the reducing agent. [2]

   b) Say which substance is **(i)** oxidised **(ii)** reduced. [2]

2 State which is **(i)** the oxidising agent and **(ii)** the reducing agent in each of these reactions:

   a) aluminium + iron oxide → iron + aluminium oxide [2]

   b) tin sulphide + oxygen → tin oxide + sulphur dioxide [2]

   c) tin oxide + carbon → tin + carbon monoxide [2]

3 a) Why is air not used for 'airships'? [1]

   b) Helium has a density twice that of hydrogen. Why is helium used in preference to hydrogen for filling airships? [2]

4 Explain the danger to health from the presence in the air of

   a) carbon monoxide

   b) sulphur dioxide and

   c) particles of smoke and dust.

   Say how nature removes each of these pollutants from the air. [6]

5 a) How do oxides of nitrogen get into the air?

   b) What damage do they cause?

   c) What is the solution to this problem? [3]

6 a) Explain how the 'greenhouse effect' makes life on Earth possible. [2]

   b) Explain why people are worried about an 'enhanced greenhouse effect'. [2]

   c) If Earth warms up, what do people predict will happen
   (i) at the North Pole **(ii)** in Thailand
   (iii) in the mid-west of the USA? [3]

7 Explain why power stations have tall chimneys. Would the problem of pollution from power stations be solved by still taller chimneys? [2]

8 a) Why do cold countries, e.g. Sweden, suffer badly from acid rain? [1]

   b) In Sweden, the base calcium hydroxide is added to acid lakes. Write a word equation and a chemical equation for the reaction between calcium hydroxide and sulphuric acid in the lake water. [4]

   c) What name is given to this type of reaction? [1]

9 What chemical reactions take place between acid rain and

   a) iron railings

   b) marble statues

   c) fresh mortar? [2, 3, 2]

10 a) In petrol engines and diesel engines, hydrocarbons burn to form a number of products. What are these products? [4]

   b) What other substances are present in vehicle exhaust gases? [3]

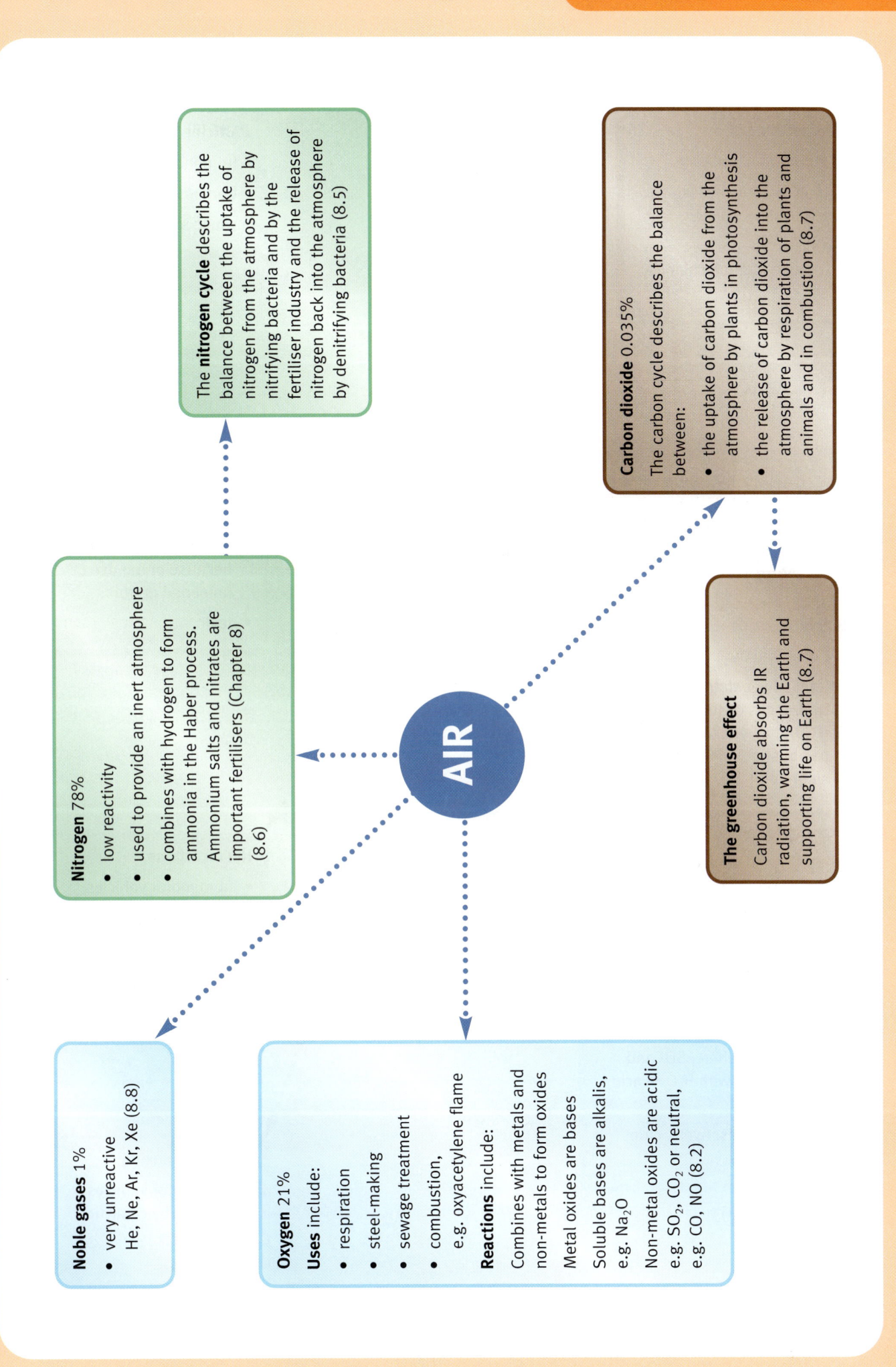

Air

AIR

Nitrogen 78%
- low reactivity
- used to provide an inert atmosphere
- combines with hydrogen to form ammonia in the Haber process. Ammonium salts and nitrates are important fertilisers (Chapter 8) (8.6)

The **nitrogen cycle** describes the balance between the uptake of nitrogen from the atmosphere by nitrifying bacteria and by the fertiliser industry and the release of nitrogen back into the atmosphere by denitrifying bacteria (8.5)

Carbon dioxide 0.035%

The carbon cycle describes the balance between:
- the uptake of carbon dioxide from the atmosphere by plants in photosynthesis
- the release of carbon dioxide into the atmosphere by respiration of plants and animals and in combustion (8.7)

The greenhouse effect

Carbon dioxide absorbs IR radiation, warming the Earth and supporting life on Earth (8.7)

Noble gases 1%
- very unreactive
He, Ne, Ar, Kr, Xe (8.8)

Oxygen 21%

Uses include:
- respiration
- steel-making
- sewage treatment
- combustion, e.g. oxyacetylene flame

Reactions include:

Combines with metals and non-metals to form oxides

Metal oxides are bases

Soluble bases are alkalis, e.g. Na_2O

Non-metal oxides are acidic e.g. SO_2, CO_2 or neutral, e.g. CO, NO (8.2)

Air

AIR POLLUTION

Nitrogen oxides
- from power stations
- from motor vehicles; reduced by catalytic converters
- a cause of photochemical smog

Particles
- from industry
- from motor vehicles
- cause smog

Lead compounds
- from the combustion of leaded petrol in motor vehicles; now a decreasing problem because of the use of unleaded petrol
- toxic

Sulphur dioxide
- from industry
- from power stations; reduced by flue-gas desulphurisation (FGD), pulverised fluidised bed combustion (PFBC) and low-sulphur fuels
- poisonous, causes bronchitis and acid rain

Hydrocarbons
- from motor vehicles; reduced by catalytic converters
- a cause of photochemical smog

Acid rain
- in the atmosphere, SO_2 and NO_x combine with H_2O ➡ acid rain (8.9)
- damages lakes, rivers, crops and buildings

Carbon monoxide
- from motor vehicles; reduced by catalytic converters
- poisonous

Water — Chapter 9

PREVIEW

At the end of this topic you will:

- appreciate the importance of the water cycle
- know how to purify water and how to test for water
- appreciate the dangers of water pollution.

CONCEPT MAP Page 168.

How much do you already know? Work out your score on page 212.

Test yourself

1. Name three processes which send water vapour into the atmosphere. [3]
2. Explain why rainwater is weakly acidic. [1]
3. Explain how weakly acidic rainwater leads to the formation of underground caves in limestone regions. Write a word equation and a chemical equation for the process. [5]
4. State **a)** a test to find out whether a liquid contains water **b)** a test to show whether a liquid is pure water. [3]
5. Name three types of living things for which dissolved oxygen is important. [3]

9.1 The water cycle

The water cycle is shown in the diagram below.

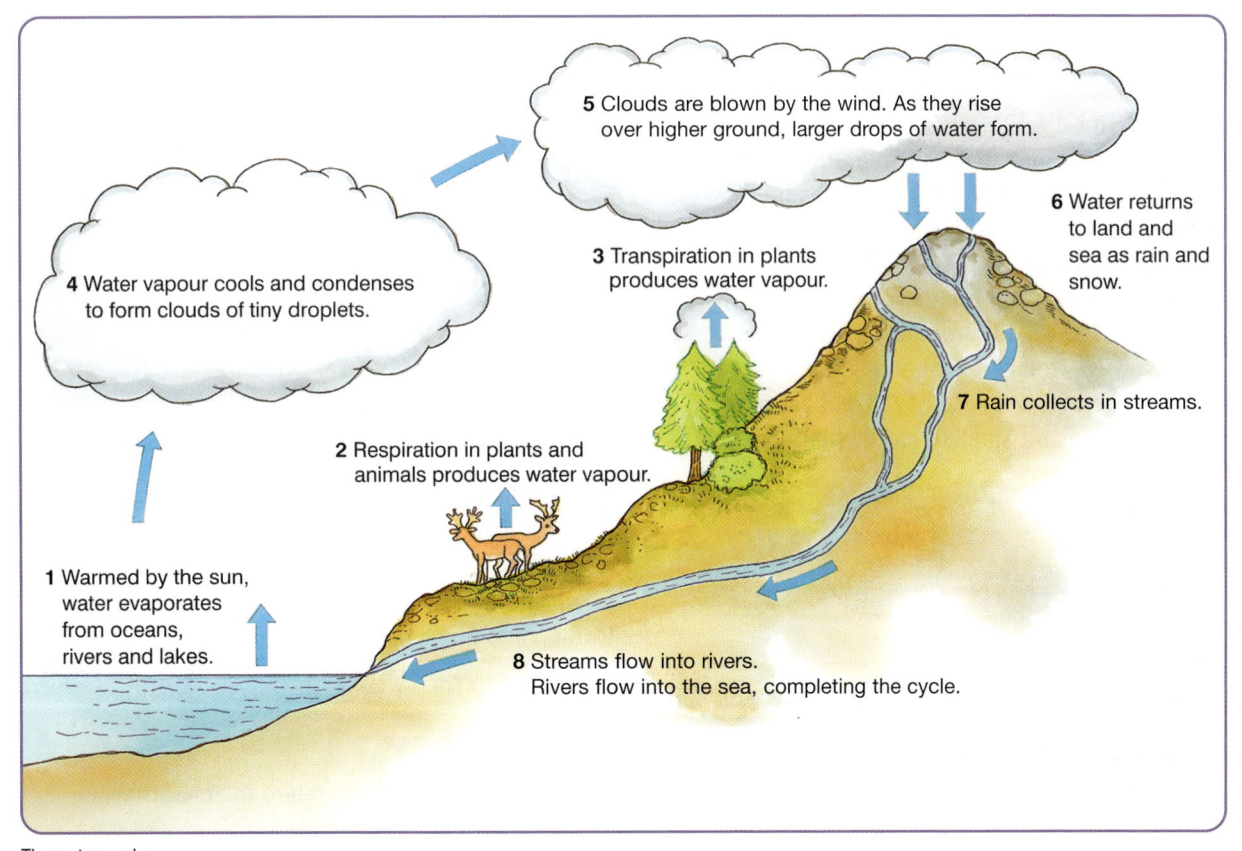

1. Warmed by the sun, water evaporates from oceans, rivers and lakes.
2. Respiration in plants and animals produces water vapour.
3. Transpiration in plants produces water vapour.
4. Water vapour cools and condenses to form clouds of tiny droplets.
5. Clouds are blown by the wind. As they rise over higher ground, larger drops of water form.
6. Water returns to land and sea as rain and snow.
7. Rain collects in streams.
8. Streams flow into rivers. Rivers flow into the sea, completing the cycle.

The water cycle

9.2 Water underground

Rainwater dissolves carbon dioxide as it falls through the air, and natural rainwater is therefore weakly acidic. In limestone regions, rain trickles over rocks containing calcium carbonate and magnesium carbonate. The acidic rainwater reacts with the rocks:

calcium carbonate + water + carbon dioxide → calcium hydrogencarbonate

$CaCO_3(s) + H_2O(l) + CO_2(aq) \rightarrow Ca(HCO_3)_2(aq)$

Over a period of thousands of years, calcium carbonate and magnesium carbonate have been dissolved out of the rocks to form the underground caves and potholes that occur in limestone regions.

The reverse reaction can take place. In an underground cavern, dissolved calcium hydrogencarbonate can turn into a grain of solid calcium carbonate. Over thousands of years, tiny grains of calcium carbonate can build up into **stalactites** and **stalagmites**.

9.3 Dissolved oxygen

The solubility of oxygen in water is 10 p.p.m. (parts per million), only about 10 g oxygen per tonne of water. Fish and other water-living animals and plants depend on this dissolved oxygen. **Aerobic** bacteria which feed on plant and animal debris in the water also depend on the dissolved oxygen. If the oxygen is used up, for example to oxidise untreated sewage, the aerobic bacteria die and **anaerobic** bacteria take over. They digest biomass to produce unpleasant-smelling decay products.

9.4 Pure water

Tests for water

or for any liquid that contains water:

1 Water turns white anhydrous copper(II) sulphate blue:

copper(II) sulphate + water → copper(II) sulphate-5-water

$CuSO_4(s) + 5H_2O(l) \rightarrow CuSO_4.5H_2O$

2 Water turns blue anhydrous cobalt(II) chloride pink:

cobalt(II) chloride + water → cobalt(II) chloride-6-water

$CoCl_2(s) + 6H_2O(l) \rightarrow CoCl_2.6H_2O$

The water in copper(II) sulphate-5-water and cobalt(II) chloride-6-water is combined as **water of crystallisation**. It gives these hydrates their crystalline form and their colour.

Tests for pure water

1 The boiling point is 100 °C at 1 atm.
2 The freezing point is 0 °C at 1 atm.

Methods of obtaining pure water

1 **Distillation**
2 **Deionisation**: water can be passed through an **ion-exchange column**, which contains a resin. An exchange takes place between cations (M^+) and anions (A^-) in the water and H^+ and OH^- ions bonded to the resin.

$M^+(aq) + H^+(resin) \rightarrow M^+(resin) + H^+(aq)$

$A^-(aq) + OH^-(resin) \rightarrow A^-(resin) + OH^-(aq)$

Then hydrogen ions and hydroxide ions combine to form water:

$H^+(aq) + OH^-(aq) \rightarrow H_2O(l)$

9.5 Pollution of water

Pollution by industry

Many industrial firms have their factories on the banks of rivers and estuaries and discharge waste into the water. The National Rivers Authority was set up in 1989 to watch over the quality of rivers and prosecute polluters. It does not watch over tidal waters, and much sewage and industrial waste is poured into coastal waters and estuaries.

Pollution by sewage

Much sewage is discharged into rivers and estuaries without being treated. This gives swimmers at some of Britain's bathing beaches some nasty surprises. Some British beaches fail to meet European Community standards because they have too high a level of coliform bacteria and faecal bacteria in the water.

Pollution by agriculture

Fertilisers: when an excess of fertiliser is used, some of it is not absorbed by the crop. Rain washes it out of the soil, and it accumulates in groundwater. The water industry uses groundwater as a source of drinking water. There is concern that nitrates in drinking water can lead to the formation of nitrosoamines, compounds which cause cancer.

Fertiliser which plants fail to absorb may be carried into the water of a lake, where it nourishes the growth of algae and water plants. This accidental enrichment of the water causes algae to form a thick mat of **algal bloom**, and weeds flourish. When algae die and decay, they use up dissolved oxygen. The fish in the lake are deprived of oxygen and die. The lake becomes a 'dead lake'. This process is called **eutrophication**.

Pesticides: these may enter lakes and become part of a food chain.

FOOD CHAINS AND EUTROPHICATION Page 11.

Thermal pollution

Industries take water from rivers to use as a coolant and return it at a higher temperature. At the higher temperature, the solubility of oxygen in the water is decreased. At the same time, fish and aerobic bacteria become more active and need more oxygen. The **biochemical oxygen demand** has increased.

Pollution by oil

Modern oil tankers are huge, each carrying up to 500 000 tonnes of crude oil.

If a tanker has an accident at sea, oil is spilt, and a huge oil slick floats on the surface of the ocean. It is very slowly oxidised by air and decomposed by bacteria. While the oil slick remains, it poisons fish and glues the feathers of sea birds together so that they cannot fly. When the oil slick washes ashore, it fouls beaches. The following methods can be used to deal with oil slicks:

1 **dispersants** – powerful detergents
2 **sinking** the oil by spreading it with e.g. powdered chalk
3 **absorption** in e.g. straw and polystyrene
4 **booms** placed in the water to prevent oil from spreading
5 **natural processes** if the oil spill occurs far out to sea.

ROUND UP

How much have you improved? Work out your improvement index on page 213.

1 a) What is a food chain? [2]
   b) Explain how the existence of a food chain can lead to poisoning even when the concentration of a pollutant in a body of water is low. [3]
2 What are the effects of thermal pollution? [4]
3 When they change the oil in their car engine, some people pour the waste oil down the drain. Why is this wrong? [2]
4 Why has the incidence of pollution by oil increased? [2]
5 Accidental oil spills from tankers cause oil slicks at sea. List four methods of treating oil slicks. [4]
6 a) Why do some lakes develop an algal bloom? [1]
   b) Why is algal bloom less common in rivers? [1]
   c) What harm does algal bloom do to a lake that is used as (i) a reservoir (ii) a boating lake (iii) a fishing lake? [3]
7 The concentration of nitrates in drinking water is rising. Explain a) why this is happening and b) why some people are worried about the increase. [3]

Well done if you've improved. Don't worry if you haven't. Take a break and try again.

Water

WATER

Water cycle
Water enters the atmosphere by evaporation, respiration, transpiration

It returns to Earth as rain and snow (see diagram in 9.1)

Underground water
Rainwater is weakly acidic. It can slowly dissolve limestone rocks to leave underground caves. Stalactites and stalagmites may form in them (see 9.2)

Tests for water
- Anhydrous $CuSO_4$ turns blue
- Anhydrous $CoCl_2$ turns pink

Pure water has m.p. 0 °C, b.p. 100 °C

It is obtained by distillation or by deionisation (see 9.4)

Aquatic life
Oxygen dissolves in water, making it possible for plants and animals to live in water (see 9.3)

Pollution of water
- Industrial waste discharged into rivers and estuaries
- Sewage discharged without treatment
- Agriculture: excess fertilisers and pesticides enter lakes and rivers
- Thermal pollution from e.g. power stations
- Oil from tankers discharged at sea (see 9.5)

Planet Earth — Chapter 10

> **PREVIEW**
>
> At the end of this chapter you will:
> - know how Earth and its atmosphere evolved
> - understand the theory of plate tectonics
> - know about the different types of rock
> - know how useful materials are obtained from rocks.

CONCEPT MAPS Pages 173, 174, 176.

How much do you already know? Work out your score on page 213.

Test yourself

1. Name the outermost layer of the Earth. [1]
2. Name the thick layer of solid rock, parts of which move slowly. [1]
3. What theory says that the Earth's outermost layer is made of separate pieces? [2]
4. What happens where these pieces collide? [4]
5. What happens when the pieces move apart? [3]
6. Name
   a) the type of rock which is formed when lava solidifies
   b) the type of rock which is formed by compressing deposits of solid particles
   c) the type of rock formed by the action of heat and pressure on types **a** and **b**. [3]
7. Of which type of rock was the original crust of Earth made? [1]
8. The original atmosphere of Earth contained about 25% carbon dioxide by volume. Why is the percentage of carbon dioxide in today's atmosphere so much lower? [2]
9. Name three weathering agents which act on rocks and shape the landscape. [3]
10. Give one method for dating rocks. [2]
11. State three uses for limestone. [3]
12. Name two materials that can be made from silica (sand). [2]

10.1 Structure of the Earth

The planet called Earth was formed as a molten mass of material cooled over a period of millions of years (see diagram overleaf).

As Earth cooled, water vapour condensed and rivers, lakes and oceans formed on its surface.

Earth's crust is of two kinds: **continental crust** and **oceanic crust**.

continental crust	oceanic crust
forms continents and their shelves	beneath deep sea floors
50–70 km thick	6 km thick on average
density 2.7 g/cm^3	density 3.0 g/cm^3
aged up to 3700 million years	aged up to 210 million years
has the same composition as granite	has the same composition as basalt

Earth's crust

10.2 Plate tectonics

Earthquakes and volcanoes occur in belts of activity, which run:

- along chains of high mountains, e.g. the Alps and the Andes
- along chains of high mountains beneath the sea called **oceanic ridges**
- through chains of volcanic islands, e.g. the Philippines.

ATMOSPHERE Page 153.

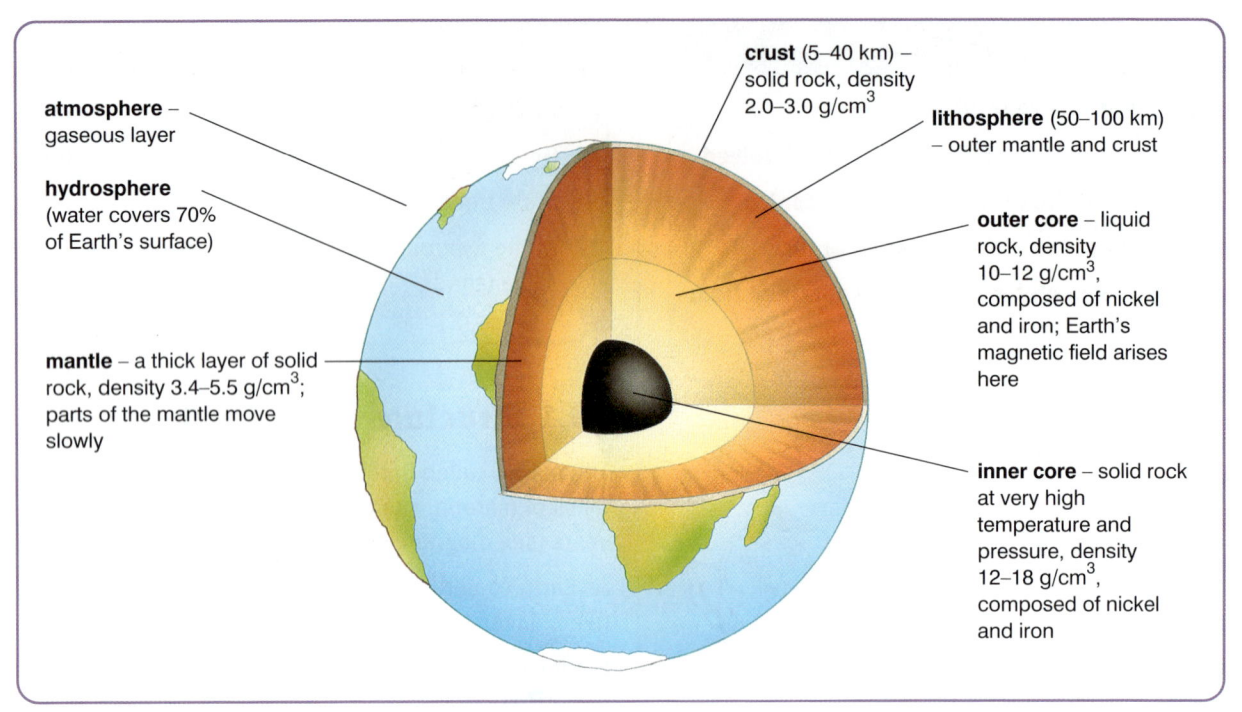

Planet Earth

atmosphere – gaseous layer

hydrosphere (water covers 70% of Earth's surface)

mantle – a thick layer of solid rock, density 3.4–5.5 g/cm^3; parts of the mantle move slowly

crust (5–40 km) – solid rock, density 2.0–3.0 g/cm^3

lithosphere (50–100 km) – outer mantle and crust

outer core – liquid rock, density 10–12 g/cm^3, composed of nickel and iron; Earth's magnetic field arises here

inner core – solid rock at very high temperature and pressure, density 12–18 g/cm^3, composed of nickel and iron

The layered structure of the Earth

Why do earthquakes and volcanoes occur in some parts of Earth's crust and not others? The theory of **plate tectonics** holds that the lithosphere (crust + outer mantle) is made up of a number of separate **plates** (see diagram on opposite page). Movements in the mantle make the plates move very slowly, at a rate of about 5 cm a year. As a result, plates may push against each other, creating stress. As the stress builds up, the plates may bend more and more until suddenly and violently they spring back into shape. Then the shock is felt as an earthquake. The energy required for the movements of the mantle comes from the decay of radioactive elements in the lithosphere.

Plate boundaries

There are three types of boundaries between tectonic plates:
- constructive boundaries, where rock is added to the plates (see figure opposite)
- destructive boundaries, where crust is lost from the edges of the plates (see figure on page 171)
- conservative boundaries, where the plates slide past one another with no loss or gain of crust.

A constructive boundary

Two tectonic plates are moving apart, creating a gap between them. **Magma** (molten mantle) rises to fill the gap. It erupts as a volcano. **Lava** (magma that has reached the surface) solidifies along the edges of the plates. Over millions of years, the process is repeated and mountain ranges form.

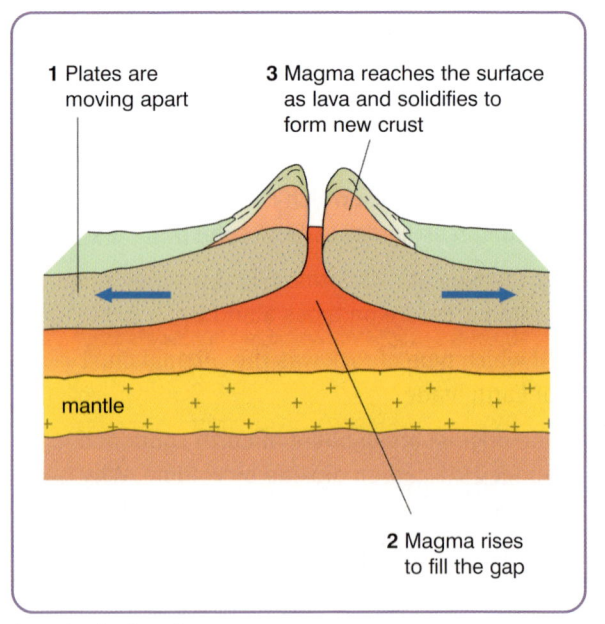

1 Plates are moving apart

3 Magma reaches the surface as lava and solidifies to form new crust

mantle

2 Magma rises to fill the gap

A constructive boundary

Planet Earth

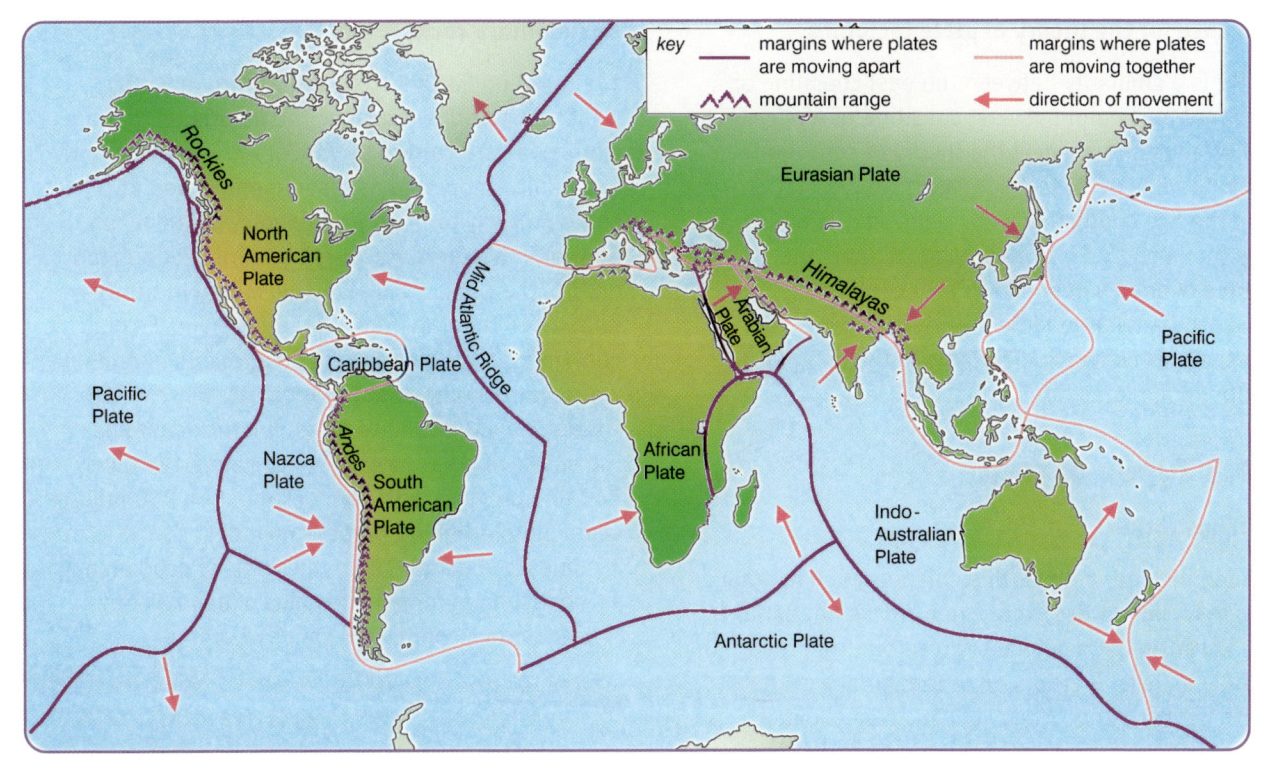

The plates that make up Earth's crust

A destructive boundary

The diagram below shows what happens when two plates collide. In this case, one is oceanic and the other is continental. The edge of the denser oceanic plate is forced to slide beneath the less dense continental plate. As the oceanic plate moves downwards it melts to become part of the mantle. Crust is lost at the boundary by **subduction**.

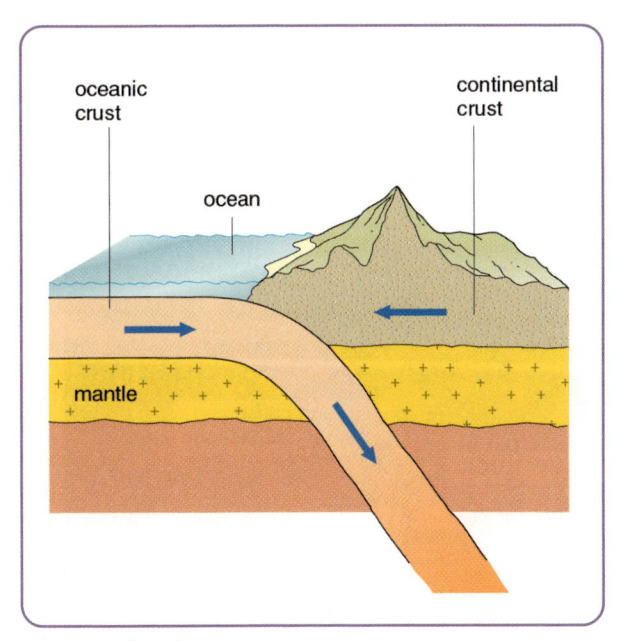

A destructive boundary

The movement of plates

If material is removed (by subduction) from one edge of a tectonic plate and added (by magma from a volcano solidifying) at another edge, the plate moves. As plates move across the fluid mantle beneath them, the continents on them move. This has been happening for thousands of millions of years. Continents move only a few centimetres a year, but they have already travelled thousands of kilometres. The figure above shows the direction in which the tectonic plates are moving.

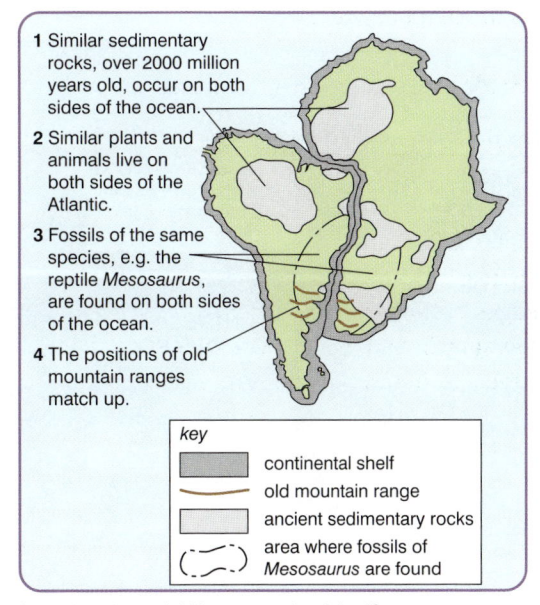

1 Similar sedimentary rocks, over 2000 million years old, occur on both sides of the ocean.
2 Similar plants and animals live on both sides of the Atlantic.
3 Fossils of the same species, e.g. the reptile *Mesosaurus*, are found on both sides of the ocean.
4 The positions of old mountain ranges match up.

South America and Africa – were they joined?

Planet Earth

Evidence for the theory of plate tectonics

There is a similarity between the east coastline of South America and the west coastline of Africa. This led scientists to suggest the theory of **continental drift**. There is evidence (see figure on page 171) that the two continents were, ages ago, joined together and slowly drifted apart. What is the source of energy needed to move continents? The heat produced from radioactive decay inside the Earth drives convection currents in the magma. The continental plates ride on these currents.

10.3 Types of rock

Igneous rocks

Molten rock beneath Earth's crust is called **magma**. Magma tends to rise, and, when cracks appear in the Earth's crust, magma is forced out from the mantle as lava. It erupts on to the surface of the Earth as a volcano. When volcanic lava cools, it crystallises to form **extrusive igneous rocks**. The faster the rate of cooling, the smaller the crystals that are formed. When magma crystallises below Earth's surface, **intrusive igneous rocks** are formed. Igneous rocks include:
- basalt, an extrusive igneous rock formed by free-flowing mobile lava
- granite, an intrusive igneous rock
- pumice, formed from a foam of lava and volcanic gases.

Sedimentary rocks

The rocks on Earth's surface are worn down by weathering and by erosion. The fragments that are worn away are carried by winds, ice and rivers and eventually deposited as a **sediment**. A bed of sediment may form on a sea shore, on an ocean floor or in a desert. As more material is deposited on top, the pressure makes the sediment **lithify** – form a sedimentary rock. Sedimentary rocks may contain fossils – imprints of dead plants or animals which were included in the rocks as they formed. Fossils are used to date rocks. If a rock contains the marks of creatures known to have been alive 250 million years ago, the rock must be 250 million years old. Sedimentary rocks include:
- limestone, formed from the shells of dead animals
- coal, formed from the remains of dead plants
- sandstone, compacted grains of sand.

Metamorphic rocks

Metamorphic rocks are formed from igneous and sedimentary rocks at high temperature or high pressure. Included among metamorphic rocks are:
- marble, formed from limestone at high temperature
- slate, formed from clay, mud and shale at high pressure.

Earth's crust is composed of 8% sedimentary rocks, 65% igneous rocks and 27% metamorphic rocks.

The rock cycle

The interconversion between igneous rocks, sedimentary rocks and metamorphic rocks is called the **rock cycle** (see diagram below).

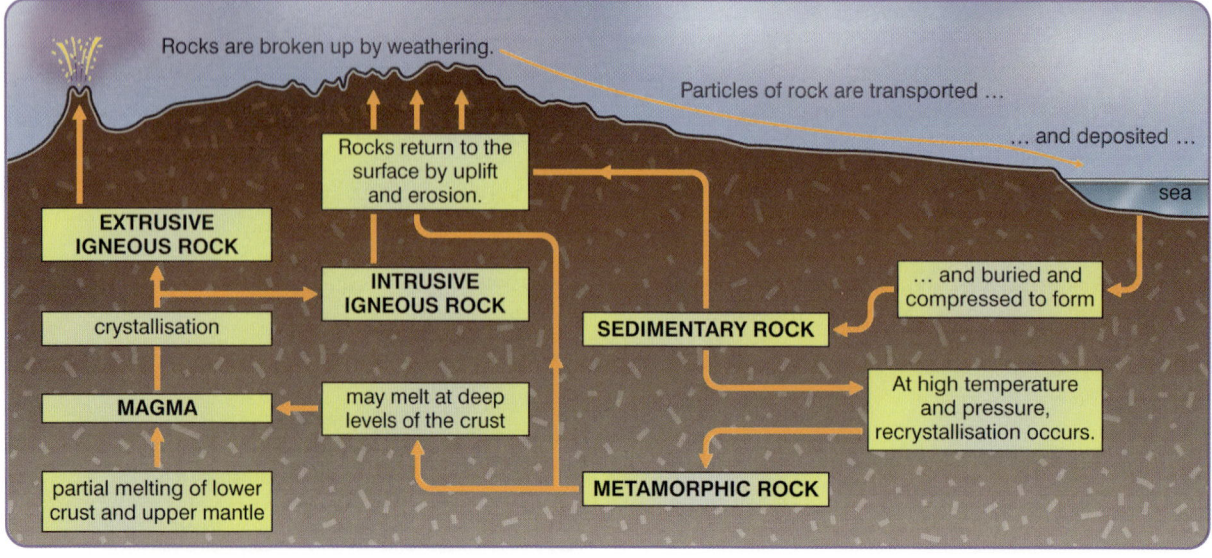

The rock cycle

10.4 The landscape

Rocks are constantly being slowly broken down into smaller particles by **physical forces**, such as the wind, and **chemical reactions** which attack rocks. These processes are called **weathering**. When rocks are broken down and the particles are carried away by an agent such as water or wind, the process is called **erosion**. Weathering and erosion shape the landscape.

The following agents shape the landscape:
- rainwater enters cracks in a rock, freezes, expands and opens the cracks wider
- rivers and streams carry material in solution and in suspension
- erosion happens when minerals dissolve slightly in water
- chemical reactions occur, e.g. between acidic water and limestone rocks
- glaciers move slowly over a landscape, wearing down rocks
- wind has a landscaping effect which is strongest in desert areas.

10.5 Materials from rocks

Many useful materials are obtained from rocks. Metals are extracted from compounds which occur in rocks; see page 180. Limestone and silica are important rocks.

Limestone

The concept map on page 174 shows the uses of limestone.

A lime kiln

The reaction that takes place in a lime kiln is:

calcium carbonate (limestone) $\rightarrow$ calcium oxide (quicklime) + carbon dioxide

$$CaCO_3(s) \rightarrow CaO(s) + CO_2(g)$$

This reaction is **reversible**; it can take place in the reverse direction as well as in the forward direction:

calcium oxide (a base) + carbon dioxide (an acid) $\rightarrow$ calcium carbonate (a salt)

In the lime kiln, a draught of air blowing through the kiln carries away carbon dioxide so that it cannot recombine with calcium oxide.

Silica

The concept map below shows the uses of silicon(IV) oxide (silica).

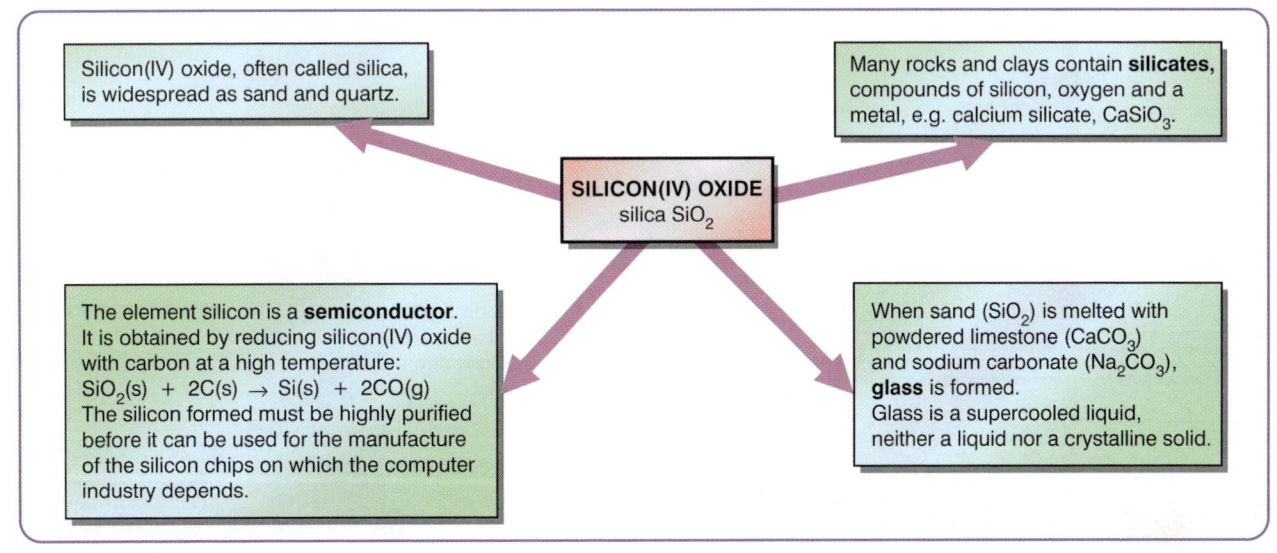

- Silicon(IV) oxide, often called silica, is widespread as sand and quartz.
- Many rocks and clays contain **silicates**, compounds of silicon, oxygen and a metal, e.g. calcium silicate, $CaSiO_3$.
- **SILICON(IV) OXIDE** silica SiO_2
- The element silicon is a **semiconductor**. It is obtained by reducing silicon(IV) oxide with carbon at a high temperature: $SiO_2(s) + 2C(s) \rightarrow Si(s) + 2CO(g)$ The silicon formed must be highly purified before it can be used for the manufacture of the silicon chips on which the computer industry depends.
- When sand (SiO_2) is melted with powdered limestone ($CaCO_3$) and sodium carbonate (Na_2CO_3), **glass** is formed. Glass is a supercooled liquid, neither a liquid nor a crystalline solid.

Concept map: silica

Planet Earth

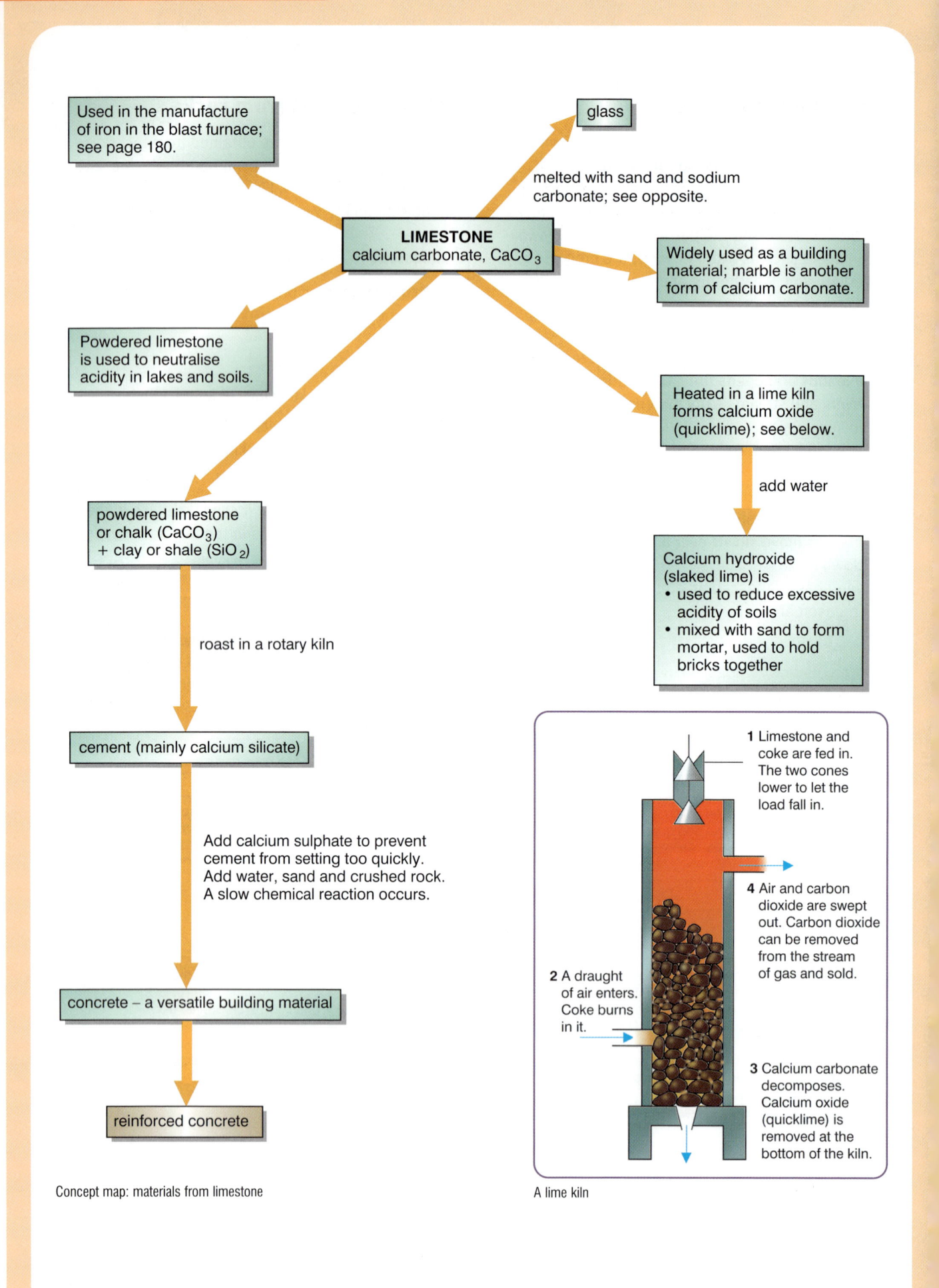

LIMESTONE — calcium carbonate, $CaCO_3$

- Used in the manufacture of iron in the blast furnace; see page 180.
- glass — melted with sand and sodium carbonate; see opposite.
- Widely used as a building material; marble is another form of calcium carbonate.
- Powdered limestone is used to neutralise acidity in lakes and soils.
- Heated in a lime kiln forms calcium oxide (quicklime); see below.
  - add water → **Calcium hydroxide (slaked lime)** is
    - used to reduce excessive acidity of soils
    - mixed with sand to form mortar, used to hold bricks together
- powdered limestone or chalk ($CaCO_3$) + clay or shale (SiO_2)
  - roast in a rotary kiln →
- cement (mainly calcium silicate)
  - Add calcium sulphate to prevent cement from setting too quickly. Add water, sand and crushed rock. A slow chemical reaction occurs.
- concrete – a versatile building material
- reinforced concrete

Concept map: materials from limestone

A lime kiln

1. Limestone and coke are fed in. The two cones lower to let the load fall in.
2. A draught of air enters. Coke burns in it.
3. Calcium carbonate decomposes. Calcium oxide (quicklime) is removed at the bottom of the kiln.
4. Air and carbon dioxide are swept out. Carbon dioxide can be removed from the stream of gas and sold.

Planet Earth

ROUND UP

How much have you improved?
Work out your improvement index on page 213.

1. What is **a)** magma [2]
   b) a tectonic plate? [2]
2. What happens when
   a) magma reaches a crack in the Earth's crust [1]
   b) tectonic plates collide and stress is created? [1]
3. **a)** Suggest a method by which a geologist might find the age of a sedimentary rock. [2]
   b) Suggest two conditions necessary for the conversion of sedimentary rocks into metamorphic rocks. [2]
4. Classify the following rocks as
   a) sedimentary **b)** igneous **c)** metamorphic:

   granite, basalt, marble, limestone, slate, sandstone, pumice [7]
5. Give three examples of erosion changing the landscape. [3]
6. **a)** Briefly describe how cement is made from limestone. [2]
   b) Name three substances added to cement to make concrete. [3]
7. **a)** What is a reversible reaction? [1]
   b) How does the lime kiln ensure that the reaction $CO_2(g) + CaO(s) \rightarrow CaCO_3(s)$ does not take place? [1]
   c) Give two commercial uses for
   (i) CaO **(ii)** CO_2. [4]
8. Name three substances used for making glass. [3]
9. What importance does silica, SiO_2, have in the computer industry? [2]

Well done if you've improved. Don't worry if you haven't. Take a break and try again.

Planet Earth

EARTH
Atmosphere
Hydrosphere
Crust
Lithosphere (crust + outer mantle)
Mantle
Core, inner and outer (see 10.1)

Lithosphere = crust + outer mantle
Consists of tectonic plates
Boundaries between tectonic plates:
- constructive – crust added
- destructive – crust lost
- conservative – no loss or gain of crust (10.2)

Lead to **continental drift** (see illustration in 10.2)

Rocks
Igneous – from molten magma by volcanic eruption (extrusive) or solidification below Earth's surface (intrusive)
Sedimentary – formed from plant and animal remains by settling and compacting of particles; contain fossils
Metamorphic – formed from igneous and metamorphic rocks at high temperature or under high pressure
Rock cycle – see diagram in 10.3

Limestone $CaCO_3$
Uses:
- building material
- in lime kiln gives calcium oxide (quicklime) and carbon dioxide
- manufacture of cement and concrete
- treatment of acidic lakes and soil (see 10.5)

Silica, SiO_2
Reduce → silicon, used in manufacture of silicon chips for the computer industry
Reacts with sodium carbonate and limestone to form glass (see 10.5)

Weathering and **erosion** of rocks:
- rain water, rivers, wind, glaciers
- chemical reactions (see 10.4)

Metals and alloys — Chapter 11

PREVIEW

At the end of this topic you will:

- understand the nature of the metallic bond
- be familiar with the chemical reactions of metals
- use the reactivity series to make predictions about metals and their compounds and methods used for extracting metals
- know methods of preventing the rusting of iron.

CONCEPT MAP Page 185.

How much do you already know? Work out your score on page 214.

Test yourself

1. List three characteristics of metals that are explained by the metallic bond. [3]
2. Name three metals that burn in air to form oxides. [3]
3. Name two metals that do not react when heated in air. [2]
4. Name three metals that react with cold water and say what products are formed. [5]
5. What is formed when a metal reacts with hydrochloric acid? [2]
6. In which groups of the periodic table do you find
   a) sodium   b) magnesium   c) transition metals? [3]
7. What method is used to extract very reactive metals from their ores? [2]
8. How is iron extracted from its ore? [3]
9. Name two metals which become coated with a film of oxide on exposure to the air. [2]

11.1 The metallic bond

A block of metal consists of positive metal ions and free electrons, as shown in the diagram.

The presence of free electrons explains how metals can conduct electricity. Electrons can be supplied at one end of a piece of metal and removed at the other end. The nature of the metallic bond also explains how metals can change their shape without breaking.

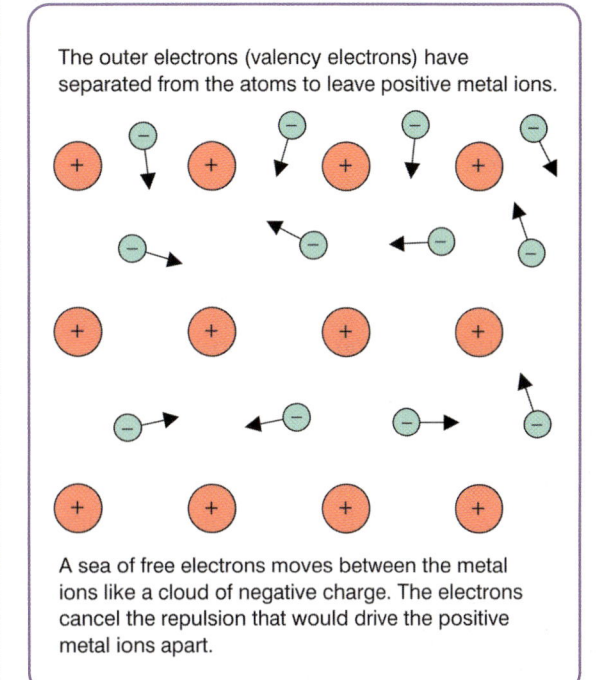

The outer electrons (valency electrons) have separated from the atoms to leave positive metal ions.

A sea of free electrons moves between the metal ions like a cloud of negative charge. The electrons cancel the repulsion that would drive the positive metal ions apart.

The metallic bond

11.2 Reactions of metals

Most metals react slowly with air to form a surface film of metal oxide. This reaction is called **tarnishing**. Gold and platinum do not tarnish in air. Aluminium rapidly forms a surface layer of aluminium oxide and only shows its true reactivity if this layer is removed. The table on the next page shows some of the reactions of metals.

Metals and alloys

metal	reaction when heated in oxygen	reaction with cold water	reaction with dilute hydrochloric acid
potassium sodium lithium calcium	burn to form the oxides	displace hydrogen; form alkaline hydroxides	react dangerously fast to form hydrogen and the metal chloride
magnesium aluminium zinc iron		reacts slowly do not react, except for slow rusting of iron; all react with steam	displace hydrogen; form metal chlorides
tin lead copper	slowly form oxides without burning	do not react even with steam	react very slowly to form hydrogen and the metal chloride
silver gold platinum	do not react		do not react

Reactions of metals

Here are equations for some of the reactions mentioned in the table:

sodium + water → hydrogen + sodium hydroxide

$2Na(s) + 2H_2O(l) \rightarrow H_2(g) + 2NaOH(aq)$

(Sodium must be kept under oil to prevent it being attacked by water in the air.)

calcium + water → hydrogen + calcium hydroxide

$Ca(s) + 2H_2O(l) \rightarrow H_2(g) + Ca(OH)_2(aq)$

magnesium + water → hydrogen + magnesium hydroxide

$Mg(s) + 2H_2O(l) \rightarrow H_2(g) + Mg(OH)_2(aq)$

magnesium + steam → hydrogen + magnesium oxide

$Mg(s) + H_2O(g) \rightarrow H_2(g) + MgO(s)$

zinc + steam → hydrogen + zinc oxide

$Zn(s) + H_2O(g) \rightarrow H_2(g) + ZnO(s)$

iron + steam → hydrogen + tri-iron tetraoxide

$3Fe(s) + 4H_2O(g) \rightarrow 4H_2(g) + Fe_3O_4(s)$

zinc + hydrochloric acid → hydrogen + zinc chloride

$Zn(s) + 2HCl(aq) \rightarrow H_2(g) + ZnCl_2(aq)$

Fact file

The metals can be placed in an order of reactivity which is called the **reactivity series**:

potassium	K	↑	
sodium	Na		
lithium	Li	increase in	
calcium	Ca	reactivity	
magnesium	Mg		
aluminium	Al	increase in	increase in
zinc	Zn	the ease	the ease of
iron	Fe	with which	discharge
tin	Sn	metals	of metal ions
lead	Pb	react to	in electrolysis
copper	Cu	form ions	
silver	Ag		
gold	Au		
platinum	Pt		↓

Part of the reactivity series of metals

11.3 Metals in the periodic table

PERIODIC TABLE Page 141.

In Group 1 of the periodic table are the **alkali metals**, and in Group 2 are the **alkaline earths**. Aluminium is in Group 3. The less reactive metals tin and lead are in Group 4. The metals in the block between Group 2 and Group 3 are called the **transition metals**, e.g. iron, nickel, copper and zinc. For the differences between the physical and chemical properties of metallic and non-metallic elements, see page 120.

Metals and alloys

11.4 Making predictions

Competition between metals for oxygen

When aluminium is heated with iron(III) oxide, the two metals are in competition for oxygen. Aluminium wins because it is above iron in the reactivity series.

aluminium + iron(III) oxide → iron + aluminium oxide

$$2Al(s) + Fe_2O_3(s) \rightarrow 2Fe(s) + Al_2O_3(s)$$

The reaction that occurs is highly exothermic. It is called the **thermit reaction**. Since the iron forms in a molten state, it can be used to weld pieces of metal together.

Competition between metals to form ions

Metals high in the reactivity series form ions with ease. A metal which is higher in the reactivity series will displace a metal which is lower in the reactivity series from a salt. Examples are:

copper + silver nitrate solution → silver + copper(II) nitrate solution

(colourless solution) (silver crystals, turn black in light) (blue solution)

$$Cu(s) + 2AgNO_3(aq) \rightarrow 2Ag(s) + Cu(NO_3)_2(aq)$$

or $\quad Cu(s) + 2Ag^+(aq) \rightarrow Cu^{2+}(aq) + 2Ag(s)$

zinc + copper(II) sulphate → copper + zinc sulphate

(blue solution) (reddish brown solid) (colourless solution)

$$Zn(s) + CuSO_4(aq) \rightarrow Cu(s) + ZnSO_4(aq)$$

or $\quad Zn(s) + Cu^{2+}(aq) \rightarrow Zn^{2+}(aq) + Cu(s)$

Discharge of ions in electrolysis

When metal ions are discharged in electrolysis, the ions of metals high in the reactivity series are difficult to discharge, and the ions of metals low in the reactivity series are easy to discharge. For example:

- when a solution containing copper ions and iron ions is electrolysed, copper is formed at the cathode, while iron ions remain in solution
- when a solution containing copper ions and silver ions is electrolysed, silver is discharged at the cathode, while copper ions remain in solution.

Handy hint

Compounds and the reactivity series

The higher a metal is in the reactivity series,
- the more readily it forms compounds
- the more difficult it is to split up its compounds.

Oxides

★ Hydrogen will reduce the oxides of metals which are low in the reactivity series, e.g:

copper(II) oxide + hydrogen $\xrightarrow{\text{heat}}$ copper + water

$$CuO(s) + H_2(g) \rightarrow Cu(s) + H_2O(l)$$

★ Carbon, when heated, will reduce the oxides of metals which are low in the reactivity series, e.g:

lead(II) oxide + carbon $\xrightarrow{\text{heat}}$ lead + carbon monoxide

$$PbO(s) + C(s) \rightarrow Pb(s) + CO(g)$$

★ Carbon monoxide is used to reduce hot iron oxide to iron.

iron(III) oxide + carbon monoxide $\xrightarrow{\text{heat}}$ iron + carbon dioxide

$$Fe_2O_3(s) + 3CO(g) \rightarrow 2Fe(s) + 3CO_2(g)$$

★ The oxides of metals which are high in the reactivity series, e.g. aluminium, are not reduced by hydrogen or carbon or carbon monoxide.

★ Silver and mercury are very low in the reactivity series. Their oxides decompose when heated.

Other compounds

The position of the metal in the reactivity series ties in with the stability of its compounds to heat, as shown in the table on the next page.

Metals and alloys

cation	anion				
	oxide	chloride	sulphate	carbonate	hydroxide
potassium sodium	no decomposition	no decomposition	no decomposition		
calcium magnesium aluminium zinc iron lead copper			oxide + sulphur trioxide, $MO + SO_3$ some also give SO_2	oxide + carbon dioxide, $MO + CO_2$	oxide + water, $MO + H_2O$
silver	metal + oxygen		metal + O_2 + SO_3	metal + O_2 + CO_2	do not form hydroxides
gold	not formed				

Action of heat on compounds

11.5 Extracting metals

The method chosen for extracting a metal from its ore depends on the position of the metal in the reactivity series; see the table on the right.

Iron

The chief ores of iron are haematite, Fe_2O_3, magnetite, Fe_3O_4, and iron pyrites, FeS_2. The sulphide ore is roasted in air to convert it into an oxide. The oxide ores are reduced to iron in a blast furnace (see diagram below). The blast furnace is run continuously. The low cost of extraction and the plentiful raw materials make iron cheaper than other metals.

Fact file

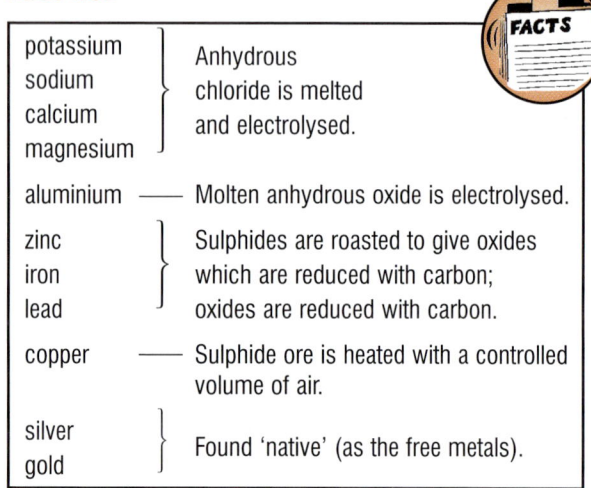

potassium sodium calcium magnesium	Anhydrous chloride is melted and electrolysed.
aluminium	Molten anhydrous oxide is electrolysed.
zinc iron lead	Sulphides are roasted to give oxides which are reduced with carbon; oxides are reduced with carbon.
copper	Sulphide ore is heated with a controlled volume of air.
silver gold	Found 'native' (as the free metals).

Methods used for the extraction of metals from their ores

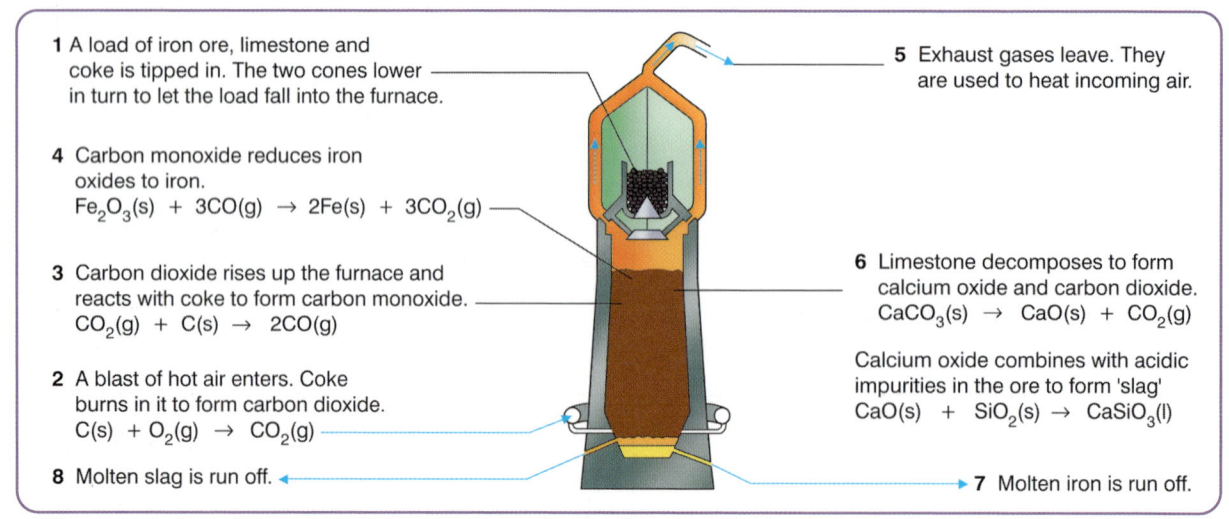

1 A load of iron ore, limestone and coke is tipped in. The two cones lower in turn to let the load fall into the furnace.

4 Carbon monoxide reduces iron oxides to iron.
$Fe_2O_3(s) + 3CO(g) \rightarrow 2Fe(s) + 3CO_2(g)$

3 Carbon dioxide rises up the furnace and reacts with coke to form carbon monoxide.
$CO_2(g) + C(s) \rightarrow 2CO(g)$

2 A blast of hot air enters. Coke burns in it to form carbon dioxide.
$C(s) + O_2(g) \rightarrow CO_2(g)$

8 Molten slag is run off.

5 Exhaust gases leave. They are used to heat incoming air.

6 Limestone decomposes to form calcium oxide and carbon dioxide.
$CaCO_3(s) \rightarrow CaO(s) + CO_2(g)$

Calcium oxide combines with acidic impurities in the ore to form 'slag'
$CaO(s) + SiO_2(s) \rightarrow CaSiO_3(l)$

7 Molten iron is run off.

A blast furnace

11.6 Corrosion of metals

★ **Copper**: the green roofs you see on some buildings are of copper, which has corroded in the air to copper carbonate hydroxide, $Cu(OH)_2.CuCO_3$.

★ **Aluminium**: as soon as a fresh surface of aluminium meets the air, it is corroded to form a thin film of the oxide, which prevents air from reaching the metal below.

★ **Chromium** forms a protective oxide layer in the same way as aluminium. Stainless steel cutlery is made of a chromium–steel alloy (mixture).

★ **Nickel** forms a protective oxide layer as soon as a fresh surface of nickel meets the air. Nickel-plated steels are very useful.

★ **Lead** water pipes were used for centuries. However, water attacks lead slowly to form soluble lead compounds.

★ **Zinc** corrodes quickly in air to form a film of zinc carbonate. This protects the zinc beneath from further attack. Iron can be coated with zinc (**galvanised**) to protect it from rusting.

Rusting of iron and steel

The corrosion of iron and steel is called rusting. Rust has the formula $Fe_2O_3.nH_2O$, where n, the number of water molecules in the formula, varies.

The combination of reagents that attacks iron is water, air and acid. The carbon dioxide in the air provides the acidity. If the water contains salts, the speed of rusting is increased. In a warm climate, rusting is more rapid than at lower temperatures.

The rusting of iron is an expensive problem. The table below lists some of the methods used to protect iron and steel against rusting.

11.7 Conservation

The Earth's resources of metals are limited. It makes sense to collect scrap metals and recycle them. In addition, there is a saving in fuel resources because less energy is needed for recycling than for extracting metals from their ores. There is another reason for conserving metals: the impact which mining has on the environment. Before recycling, scrap metals must be collected, sorted and stored until there is enough to process.

method	where used	comment
1 a coat of paint	large objects, e.g. ships and bridges	If the paint is scratched, the iron beneath it starts to rust.
2 a film of oil or grease	moving parts of machinery	The protective film must be renewed.
3 a coat of metal a) chromium plating	trim on cars, cycle handlebars, taps	Applied by electroplating, decorative as well as protective.
b) galvanising (zinc plating)	galvanised steel girders are used in buildings	Even if the layer of zinc is scratched, the iron underneath does not rust. Zinc cannot be used for food cans because zinc and its compounds are poisonous.
c) tin plating	food cans	If the layer of tin is scratched, the iron beneath it rusts.
4 stainless steel	cutlery, car accessories	Steels containing chromium (10–25%) or nickel (10–20%) do not rust.
5 sacrificial protection	ships	Bars of zinc attached to the hull of a ship corrode and protect the ship from rusting.
	underground pipes	Bags of magnesium scrap attached to underground iron pipes corrode in preference to the pipes. The scrap must be replaced from time to time.

Rust prevention

TAKE A BREAK

Metals and alloys

11.8 Uses of metals and alloys

The strengths of metals and **alloys** (mixtures of metals) find them thousands of uses; the table below lists just some of these.

metal/alloy	characteristics	uses
aluminium	low density good electrical conductor good thermal conductor reflector of light non-toxic resistant to corrosion	aircraft manufacture (Duralumin) overhead electrical cable saucepans, etc. car headlamps food packaging door frames, window frames, etc.
brass, an alloy of copper and zinc	golden colour, harder than copper, resists corrosion	ships' propellers, taps, screws, electrical fittings
bronze, an alloy of copper and tin	golden colour, hard, sonorous, resistant to corrosion	coins, medals, statues, springs, church bells
copper	good electrical conductor not corroded readily	electrical circuits water pipes and tanks
Duralumin, an alloy of aluminium	low density, stronger than aluminium	aircraft and spacecraft
gold	beautiful colour never tarnishes	jewellery, dentistry, electrical contacts
iron	hard, strong, inexpensive, rusts	construction, transport
lead	dense, unreactive, soft, not very strong	car batteries, divers' weights, roofing
magnesium	bright flame	flares and flash bulbs
mercury	liquid at room temperature	thermometers, dental amalgam for filling teeth
nickel	resists corrosion, strong, tough, hard	stainless steel
silver	beautiful colour and shine good electrical conductor good reflector of light	jewellery, silverware contacts in computers, etc. mirrors, dental amalgam
solder, alloy of tin and lead	low melting point	joining metals in an electrical circuit
steel, an iron alloy	strong	buildings, machinery, transport
tin	low in reactivity series	coating 'tin cans'
titanium	low in density, strong, very resistant to corrosion	high-altitude planes, nose-cones of spacecraft
zinc	high in reactivity series	protection of iron and steel by galvanising

The uses of some metals and alloys

Metals and alloys

11.9 Iron and steel

Cast iron

The iron that comes out of the blast furnace is called cast iron. It contains 3–4% carbon which lowers the melting point, making cast iron easier to melt and mould than pure iron. By casting, objects with complicated shapes can be made, such as the engine blocks of motor vehicles. The carbon content makes cast iron brittle.

Steel

Steel is made from iron by burning off carbon and other impurities in a stream of oxygen. A number of elements may be added to give different types of steel:
- chromium in stainless steels for cutlery, car accessories and tools
- cobalt steel in permanent magnets
- manganese in all steels to increase strength
- molybdenum steel for rifle barrels and propeller shafts
- nickel in stainless steel cutlery and industrial plants
- tungsten steel in high-speed cutting tools
- vanadium steel in springs.

ROUND UP

(continues on page 184)

PERIODIC TABLE Page 141.

How much have you improved? Work out your improvement index on page 214.

1. Write equations for the reactions with oxygen of
   a) sodium (to form Na_2O) [3]
   b) magnesium [3]
   c) zinc [3]
   d) iron (to form Fe_3O_4) [3]
   e) tin (to form SnO) [3]
   f) lead (to form PbO) [3]
   g) copper (to form CuO). [3]

2. a) Write equations for the reactions of
      (i) magnesium and hydrochloric acid [4]
      (ii) iron and hydrochloric acid (to form $FeCl_2$) [4]
      (iii) tin and hydrochloric acid (to form $SnCl_2$). [4]
   b) Write equations for the reactions between
      (i) magnesium and sulphuric acid [4]
      (ii) iron and sulphuric acid (to give $FeSO_4$). [4]

3. Copy and complete these word equations. If there is no reaction, write 'no reaction'. [8]
   a) magnesium + sulphuric acid →
   b) platinum + sulphuric acid →
   c) silver + hydrochloric acid →
   d) gold + hydrochloric acid →
   e) zinc + sulphuric acid →
   f) tin + water →

4. Why are copper and its alloys used as coinage metals in preference to iron? [3]

5. The following metals are listed in order of reactivity:

   calcium > magnesium > iron > copper

   Describe how the metals follow this order in their reactions with
   a) water [4]
   b) dilute hydrochloric acid. [4]

6. What would you see if you dropped a piece of zinc into a test tube of
   a) copper(II) sulphate solution
   b) lead(II) nitrate solution?

   Write word equations and chemical equations for the reactions. [11]

7. A metal X displaces another metal Y from a solution of a salt of Y. X is displaced by a metal Z from a solution of a salt of X. List the metals in order of reactivity with the most reactive first. [2]

8. The following metals are listed in order of reactivity, with the most reactive first:

   Na Mg Al Zn Fe Pb Cu Hg Au

   List the metals which
   a) occur as the free elements in the Earth's crust [1]
   b) react at an observable speed with cold water [2]
   c) react with steam but not with cold water [2]
   d) react at an observable speed with dilute acids [4]
   e) react dangerously fast with dilute acids [1]
   f) displace lead from lead(II) nitrate solution. [4]

183

ROUND UP
continued

9 Suggest what method could be used to extract each of the metals A, B, C and D from a chloride ore or an oxide ore.
- Metal A reacts with cold water. [3]
- Metal B reacts only very, very slowly with water. [2]
- Metal C does not react with steam or with dilute hydrochloric acid. [2]
- Metal D when exposed to air immediately becomes coated with a layer of oxide. [3]

10 Predict the reaction of
 a) rubidium and cold water
 b) palladium and dilute hydrochloric acid. [5]

11 Copy and complete the following word equations. If no reaction occurs, write 'no reaction'.
 a) copper + oxygen → [1]
 b) aluminium + iron(III) oxide → [1]
 c) iron + aluminium oxide → [1]
 d) carbon monoxide + iron(III) oxide → [1]
 e) carbon monoxide + aluminium oxide → [1]
 f) zinc + copper(II) sulphate solution → [1]

12 List four different uses for aluminium. Say what property of aluminium makes it suitable for each use. [8]

13 What method of rust prevention is used on
 a) a bicycle chain   b) bicycle handlebars
 c) steel girders   d) cutlery   e) parts of a ship above the waterline   f) parts of a ship below the waterline   g) food cans? [7]

14 List three savings which are made when metal objects are recycled. [3]

Well done if you've improved. Don't worry if you haven't. Take a break and try again.

Metals and alloys

Physical properties
See Chapter 2

Alloys
Steel, Fe + C + many other metals
Bronze, Cu + Sn,
Brass, Cu + Zn
Duralumin, Al + Cu
Solder, Sn + Pb (11.9)

Methods of extraction
1. Some are native, e.g. Cu, Ag
2. Reduction of oxides by carbon or carbon monoxide, e.g. Fe
3. Electrolysis of molten anhydrous chloride, e.g. Na or oxide, e.g. Al
4. Reduction of chloride by Mg, e.g. Ti (11.5)

Corrosion
Many metals corrode in air to form oxides, e.g. rusting of iron. For methods of prevention, see 11.6

Metallic bond
A metal consists of cations and a cloud of free electrons (11.1)

METALLIC ELEMENTS

Reactivity series
Metals are ranked in order of the vigour of reaction with
- air
- water
- dilute acids.

Predictions can be made from the reactivity series about
- the ease of reduction of metal oxides
- the ease of displacement of a metal from its compounds
- the ease of decomposition of oxides, hydroxides, carbonates and sulphates
- whether electrolysis of an aqueous salt will give the metal or hydrogen (11.4)

Periodic table
Group 1 Alkali metals, Li, Na, K, Rb, Cs
Group 2 Alkaline earths, Mg, Ca, Sr, Ba
Group 3 Aluminium
Group 4 Tin and lead
Transition metals, e.g. Fe, Co, Ni (11.3)

Reactions
1. Some react with water to give hydrogen and the metal hydroxide: Group 1 metals and Ca and (slowly) Mg
2. Some react with steam but not with water: Mg, Zn, Fe
3. Many react with dilute acids to give hydrogen and a salt:
   - Dangerously fast: Group 1
   - Moderate speed: Ca, Mg, Zn, Fe
   - Very slowly: Sn, Pb
   - No reaction: Cu, Ag, Au, Pt (11.2)

Chapter 12 Reaction speeds

PREVIEW

At the end of this topic you will:
- **understand the factors which can change the speed of a chemical reaction.**

CONCEPT MAP Page 189.

How much do you already know? Work out your score on page 215.

Test yourself

1. Which act faster to cure acid indigestion, indigestion tablets or indigestion powders? Explain your answer. [2]

2. a) Suggest three ways in which you could speed up the reaction between zinc and dilute sulphuric acid.
   $$Zn(s) + H_2SO_4(aq) \rightarrow H_2(g) + ZnSO_4(aq)$$ [3]

   b) Explain why each of these methods increases the speed of the reaction. [4]

3. Sketch an apparatus in which you could collect a gaseous product of a reaction and measure the rate at which it was formed. [5]

4. What is a catalyst? [2]

5. Why are catalysts important in industry? [2]

6. Name two reactions which depend on the absorption of light energy. [2]

12.1 Particle size

The reaction between a solid and a liquid is speeded up by using smaller particles of the solid reactant. The reason is that it is the atoms or ions at the surface of the solid that react, and the ratio of surface area:mass is greater for small particles than for large particles.

The diagram below shows an apparatus which you may have used to investigate the effect of particle size on the reaction:

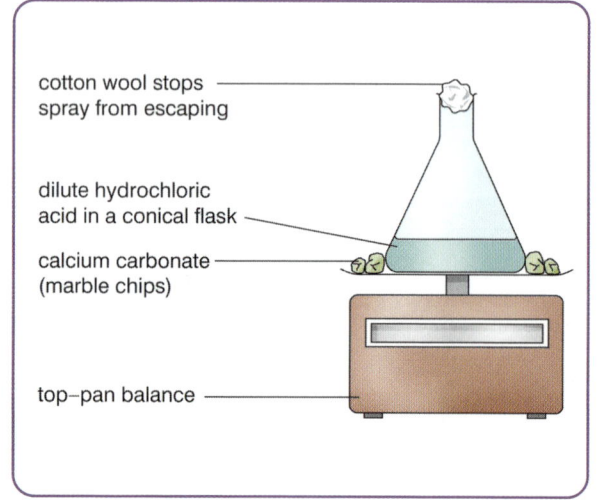

calcium carbonate + hydrochloric acid → carbon dioxide + calcium chloride + water

$$CaCO_3(s) + 2HCl(aq) \rightarrow CO_2(g) + CaCl_2(aq) + H_2O(l)$$

- cotton wool stops spray from escaping
- dilute hydrochloric acid in a conical flask
- calcium carbonate (marble chips)
- top–pan balance

The effect of particle size on the speed of a reaction

As the reaction happens, carbon dioxide is given off and the mass of the reacting mixture decreases.

1. Note the mass of flask + acid + marble chips.

2. Add the marble chips to the acid, and start a stopwatch.

3. Note the mass after 10 seconds and then every 30 seconds for 5–10 minutes.

4. Plot the mass against time since the start of the reaction.

5. Repeat with the same mass of smaller chips.

Reaction speeds

12.2 Concentration

A precipitate of sulphur is formed in the reaction:

sodium thiosulphate + hydrochloric acid → sulphur + sulphur dioxide + sodium chloride + water

$Na_2S_2O_3(aq) + 2HCl(aq) \rightarrow S(s) + SO_2(g) + 2NaCl(aq) + H_2O(l)$

1. Watch the precipitate of sulphur appear.
2. Note the time when the precipitate is thick enough to block your view of a cross on a piece of paper.
3. Repeat for various concentrations of acid and for various concentrations of thiosulphate.

The experiment shows that, for this reaction:
- the rate of reaction is proportional to concentration of thiosulphate
- the rate of reaction is proportional to concentration of acid.

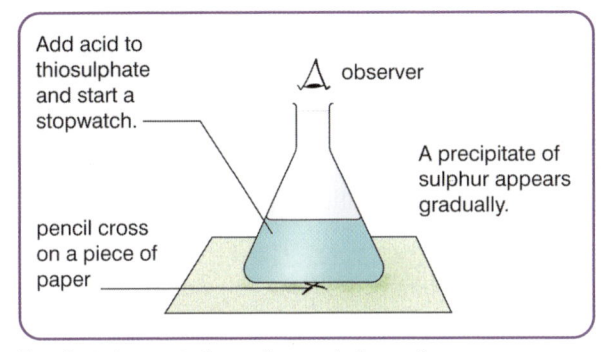

The effect of concentration on the speed of a reaction

12.3 Pressure

An increase in pressure increases the rates of reactions between gases. As the molecules are pushed more closely together, they react more rapidly.

12.4 Temperature

The reaction between thiosulphate and acid can be used to study the effect of temperature on the rate of a reaction, as shown in the following graphs. This reaction goes twice as fast at 30 °C as it does at 20 °C. At higher temperatures, ions have more kinetic energy and collide more often and more vigorously, giving them a greater chance of reacting.

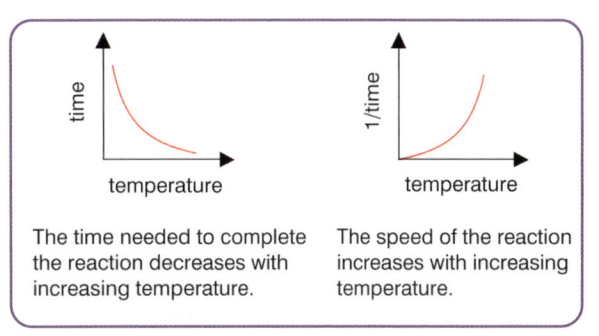

The time needed to complete the reaction decreases with increasing temperature.

The speed of the reaction increases with increasing temperature.

The effect of temperature on the speed of a reaction

12.5 Light

Heat is not the only form of energy that speeds up chemical reactions. Light energy enables many reactions to take place, e.g. photosynthesis and photography.

12.6 Catalysts

Hydrogen peroxide decomposes to form oxygen and water:

hydrogen peroxide → oxygen + water

$2H_2O_2(aq) \rightarrow O_2(g) + 2H_2O(l)$

The decomposition takes place very slowly unless a **catalyst**, e.g. manganese(IV) oxide, is present. The rate at which the reaction takes place can be found by collecting the oxygen formed and measuring its volume at certain times after the start of the reaction, as shown in the diagram.

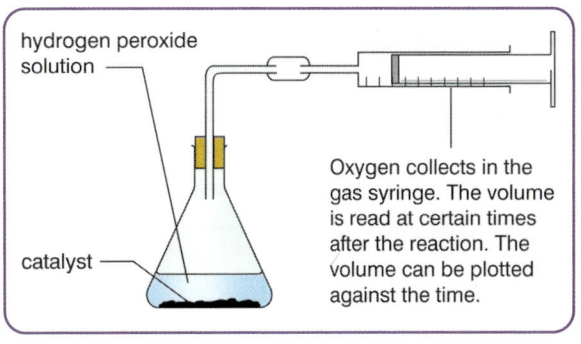

Oxygen collects in the gas syringe. The volume is read at certain times after the reaction. The volume can be plotted against the time.

Collecting and measuring a gas

Reaction speeds

Fact file

★ A catalyst is a substance which increases the rate of a chemical reaction without being used up in the reaction.

★ A catalyst will catalyse a certain reaction or group of reactions. Platinum catalyses certain oxidation reactions, and nickel catalyses some hydrogenation reactions.

★ Catalysts are very important in industry. They enable a manufacturer to make a product more rapidly or at a lower temperature.

12.7 Enzymes

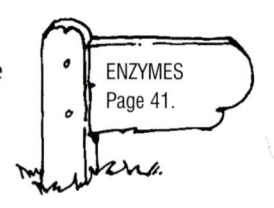

Chemical reactions take place in the cells of living things. These reactions happen at reasonably fast rates at the temperatures which exist in plants and animals. They can do this because the cells contain powerful catalysts called **enzymes**.

ENZYMES Page 41.

Enzymes are proteins. They have large molecules which are twisted into complicated three-dimensional structures. The structures are damaged by temperatures above about 45 °C. Here are some examples of enzyme-catalysed reactions:

★ Enzymes in yeast catalyse the conversion of sugar into ethanol and carbon dioxide. The process is called **fermentation**. It is used to make ethanol (alcohol) by the fermentation of carbohydrates. It also produces bubbles of carbon dioxide which make bread rise.

★ Enzymes in bacteria produce yoghurt from milk. They catalyse the conversion of lactose, the sugar in milk, into lactic acid.

ROUND UP

How much have you improved? Work out your improvement index on page 215.

1 The three graphs were obtained in experiments as described on page 186.

   a) Why is there a decrease in mass? [1]

   b) Which of the graphs relates to (i) small chips (ii) large chips (iii) medium-sized chips? [2]

   c) Explain why there is a difference. [1]

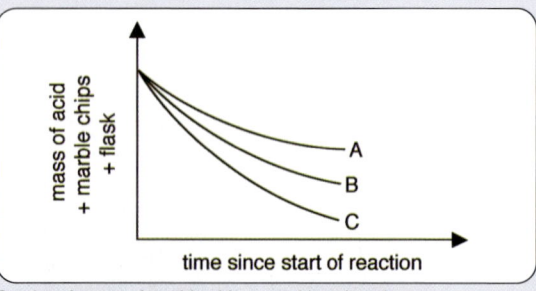

Graphs of mass of marble chips + acid against time

2 Suggest two ways of cooking potatoes faster. [2]

3 Someone tells you that there is an enzyme in potatoes that is better than manganese(IV) oxide as a catalyst for the decomposition of hydrogen peroxide. Describe the experiments you would do to find out whether this is true. [4]

4 You are asked to study the effect of temperature on the reaction:

magnesium + sulphuric acid → magnesium sulphate + hydrogen

Describe the measurements you would make and what you would do with your results. [6]

5 Catalysts A and B catalyse the decomposition of hydrogen peroxide.

time / minutes	0	3	6	9	12	15	18	21
volume of oxygen with A / cm^3	0	4	8	12	16	17	18	18
volume of oxygen with B / cm^3	0	5	10	15	16.5	18	18	18

   a) Plot a graph to show both sets of results. [4]

   b) Say which is the better catalyst, A or B. [1]

   c) Add a line to your graph to show the uncatalysed reaction. [1]

Well done if you've improved. Don't worry if you haven't. Take a break and try again.

Reaction speeds

SPEEDS OF REACTIONS

Temperature
The speed of a reaction increases as the temperature is raised ...
... because particles of reactants collide more frequently ... and with more energy
e.g. sodium thiosulphate + acid reaction (12.4)

Catalysts
Catalysts are substances that increase the speeds of chemical reactions
e.g. MnO_2 catalyses the decomposition of H_2O_2
e.g. enzymes in biochemical reactions
e.g. transition metals in industrial processes such as the Haber process and the Contact process (12.6)

Light
Light increases the speeds of many reactions
e.g. photosynthesis, photography (12.5)

Pressures of gases
Gases react faster under pressure ...
... because molecules collide more frequently (12.3)

Particle size
Small particles react more rapidly than large particles ...
... because the ratio of surface area to mass is greater
e.g. marble chips + acid reaction (12.1)

Concentrations of solutions
A concentrated solution reacts faster than a dilute solution ...
... because molecules and ions collide more frequently
e.g. sodium thiosulphate + acid reaction, e.g. magnesium + acid reaction (12.2)

Chapter 13 Tackling chemical calculations

PREVIEW

At the end of this topic you will be able to:

- calculate the relative molecular mass and molar mass of a compound
- understand 'the mole'
- calculate the empirical formula and molecular formula of a compound
- use the equation for a reaction to calculate the masses of solids that react.

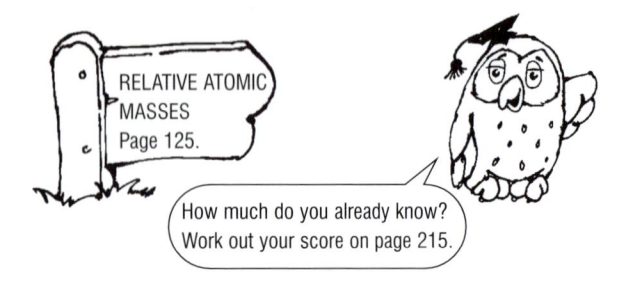

RELATIVE ATOMIC MASSES Page 125.

How much do you already know? Work out your score on page 215.

Test yourself

1. State the relative molecular masses of
   a) SO_2 b) SO_3 c) H_2SO_4 d) CH_3CO_2H
   e) $CuSO_4.5H_2O$. [5]

2. State the amount in moles of a) sodium in 46 g of sodium b) sulphur atoms in 64 g of sulphur c) S_8 molecules in 64 g of sulphur. [3]

3. State the mass of a) mercury in 0.100 mol of mercury b) sulphuric acid in 0.25 mol of H_2SO_4 c) magnesium oxide in 3.0 mol of MgO. [3]

4. Calculate the empirical formulas of
   a) the compound containing 55.5% mercury and 44.5% bromine by mass [1]
   b) the compound formed from 14.9 g of copper and 17.7 g of chlorine [1]
   c) the compound formed when 0.69 g of sodium forms 0.93 g of an oxide. [1]

5. Calculate the percentage by mass of sulphur in
   a) SO_2 b) SO_3 c) H_2SO_4. [3]

6. When a mixture of 8 g of iron and 4 g of sulphur is heated, the elements react to form iron(II) sulphide, FeS. How much iron will be left over at the end of the reaction? [1]

7. a) Calculate the mass of carbon dioxide formed by the action of acid on 15 g of calcium carbonate in the reaction [1]

   $CaCO_3(s) + 2HCl(aq) \rightarrow CO_2(g) + CaCl_2(aq) + H_2O(l)$

   b) State the volume at room temperature and pressure (rtp) of the carbon dioxide formed. [1]

8. A sulphuric acid plant uses 2500 tonnes of sulphur dioxide each day.
   a) What mass of sulphur must be burned to produce this quantity of sulphur dioxide? [1]
   b) What is the volume at rtp of this mass of sulphur dioxide? [1]

9. A company buys 100 kg of $Na_2CO_3.10H_2O$ at 30p/kg with the intention of selling it as bath salts. While standing in the warehouse, the bag punctures, and the crystals lose some of their water of crystallisation to form $Na_2CO_3.H_2O$. The company sells this powder at 50p/kg. Does the company make a profit or a loss? [2]

13.1 Some definitions

Relative atomic mass

Relative atomic mass A_r of element =

$$\frac{\text{mass of one atom of compound}}{\frac{1}{12} \text{ mass of one atom of carbon-12}}$$

Relative molecular mass

Relative molecular mass M_r of compound =

$$\frac{\text{mass of one molecule or formula unit}}{\frac{1}{12} \text{ mass of one atom of carbon-12}}$$

The relative molecular mass M_r of a compound is the sum of the relative atomic masses of all the atoms in a molecule of the compound. For sulphuric acid, H_2SO_4,

$M_r = 2(A_r \text{ H}) + 1(A_r \text{ S}) + 4(A_r \text{ O}) = 2 + 32 + 64 = 98$

Tackling chemical calculations

Relative formula mass

The term relative formula mass (symbol M_r) is used for compounds that do not consist of molecules. An ionic compound consists of formula units, e.g. the formula unit of sodium chloride is NaCl. Then,

Relative formula mass of compound =

$$\frac{\text{mass of one formula unit of compound}}{\frac{1}{12}\text{ mass of one atom of carbon-12}}$$

The relative formula mass of a compound is the sum of the relative atomic masses of all the atoms in the formula unit of the compound.

The mole

The amount of an element that contains 6.022×10^{23} atoms (the same number of atoms as 12 g of carbon-12) is called **one mole** (symbol mol) of that element.

Take the relative atomic mass expressed in grams of any element:

12 g of carbon	24 g of magnesium	56 g of iron
40 g of calcium	108 g of silver	238 g of uranium

All these masses contain the same number of atoms: 6.022×10^{23} atoms.

The ratio 6.022×10^{23}/mol is called the **Avogadro constant**. Each of these masses represents one mole (1 mol) of the element. One mole of sulphuric acid contains 6.022×10^{23} molecules of H_2SO_4, that is, 98 g of H_2SO_4 (the molar mass in grams). To write 'a mole of nitrogen' is imprecise: one mole of nitrogen atoms, N, has a mass of 14 g; one mole of nitrogen molecules, N_2, has a mass of 28 g.

Fact file

Molar mass

The molar mass of a substance, symbol M, is defined by the equation:

$$\frac{\text{amount (in moles) of substance}}{} = \frac{\text{mass of substance}}{\text{molar mass of substance}}$$

The molar mass of carbon is 12 g/mol; that is the relative atomic mass expressed in grams per mole. The molar mass of sulphuric acid, H_2SO_4, is 98 g/mol. Notice the units: relative molecular mass has no unit; molar mass has the unit g/mol.

Example 1

What is the amount of calcium present in 120 g of calcium?

A_r of calcium = 40; molar mass of calcium = 40 g/mol

$$\text{amount of calcium} = \frac{\text{mass of calcium}}{\text{molar mass of calcium}}$$

$$= \frac{120 \text{ g}}{40 \text{ g/mol}}$$

$$= 3.0 \text{ mol}$$

The amount of calcium is 3.0 mol.

Example 2

If you need 2.25 mol of magnesium carbonate, what mass of the substance do you have to weigh out?

relative molecular mass of $MgCO_3$ = $24 + 12 + (3 \times 16)$

$$= 84$$

molar mass of $MgCO_3$ = 84 g/mol

$$\text{amount of substance} = \frac{\text{mass of substance}}{\text{molar mass of substance}}$$

$$2.25 \text{ mol} = \frac{\text{mass}}{84 \text{ g/mol}}$$

$$\text{mass} = 84 \text{ g/mol} \times 2.25 \text{ mol} = 189 \text{ g}$$

You need to weigh out 189 g of magnesium carbonate.

Tackling chemical calculations

ROUND UP

On the mole

RELATIVE ATOMIC MASSES Page 194.

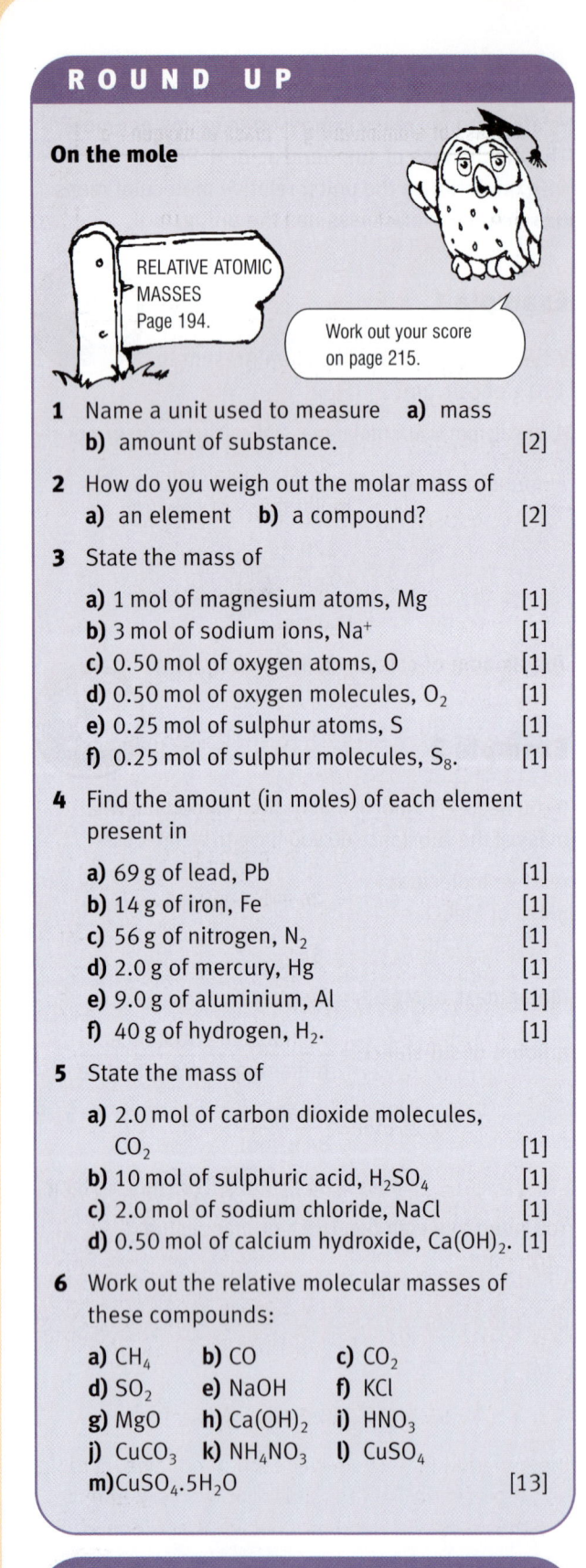

Work out your score on page 215.

1. Name a unit used to measure a) mass b) amount of substance. [2]

2. How do you weigh out the molar mass of a) an element b) a compound? [2]

3. State the mass of
   a) 1 mol of magnesium atoms, Mg [1]
   b) 3 mol of sodium ions, Na^+ [1]
   c) 0.50 mol of oxygen atoms, O [1]
   d) 0.50 mol of oxygen molecules, O_2 [1]
   e) 0.25 mol of sulphur atoms, S [1]
   f) 0.25 mol of sulphur molecules, S_8. [1]

4. Find the amount (in moles) of each element present in
   a) 69 g of lead, Pb [1]
   b) 14 g of iron, Fe [1]
   c) 56 g of nitrogen, N_2 [1]
   d) 2.0 g of mercury, Hg [1]
   e) 9.0 g of aluminium, Al [1]
   f) 40 g of hydrogen, H_2. [1]

5. State the mass of
   a) 2.0 mol of carbon dioxide molecules, CO_2 [1]
   b) 10 mol of sulphuric acid, H_2SO_4 [1]
   c) 2.0 mol of sodium chloride, NaCl [1]
   d) 0.50 mol of calcium hydroxide, $Ca(OH)_2$. [1]

6. Work out the relative molecular masses of these compounds:
   a) CH_4 b) CO c) CO_2
   d) SO_2 e) NaOH f) KCl
   g) MgO h) $Ca(OH)_2$ i) HNO_3
   j) $CuCO_3$ k) NH_4NO_3 l) $CuSO_4$
   m) $CuSO_4.5H_2O$ [13]

TAKE A BREAK

13.2 Formulas

Molecular formula

The molecular formula of a compound shows the elements present and how many atoms of each element are present in a molecule or formula unit of the compound. For example, the molecular formula of ethanoic acid is $C_2H_4O_2$.

Empirical formula

The empirical formula of a compound shows the elements present and the **ratio** of the numbers of atoms of each element present in a molecule or formula unit of the compound. For example, the empirical formula of ethanoic acid is CH_2O. The empirical formula is calculated from the composition by mass of the compound. It is also possible to find the percentage composition by mass of the compound if its empirical formula is known.

Calculation of empirical formula

3.72 g of phosphorus react with 4.80 g of oxygen to form an oxide. What is the empirical formula of the oxide?

	phosphorus	oxygen
mass	3.72 g	4.80 g
A_r	31	16
amount (moles)	$\frac{3.72}{31}$	$\frac{4.80}{16}$
	= 0.12	0.30
ratio of amounts	= 1 to	2.5
ratio of numbers of atoms	= 2 to	5

Empirical formula is P_2O_5.

Calculation of percentage composition

Find the percentages by mass of carbon, hydrogen and oxygen in propanol, C_3H_7OH.

The empirical formula is C_3H_8O.

$M_r = (3 \times 12) + 8 + 16 = 60$

$$\text{percentage of carbon} = \frac{A_r(C) \times \text{no. of C atoms}}{M_r(C_3H_8O)} \times 100\%$$

$$= \frac{(12 \times 3)}{60} \times 100\% = 60.0\%$$

percentage of hydrogen $= \dfrac{A_r(H) \times \text{no. of H atoms}}{M_r(C_3H_8O)} \times 100\%$

$= \dfrac{(1 \times 8)}{60} \times 100\% = 13.3\%$

percentage of oxygen $= \dfrac{A_r(O) \times \text{no. of O atoms}}{M_r(C_3H_8O)} \times 100\%$

$= \dfrac{(16 \times 1)}{60} \times 100\% = 26.7\%$

You can check on your calculation by adding up the percentages:

carbon 60.0% + hydrogen 13.3% + oxygen 26.7% = 100%

Calculation of molecular formula

The molecular formula is a multiple of the empirical formula:

molecular formula = (empirical formula)$_n$

Therefore

relative molecular mass = $n \times$ relative empirical formula mass

For ethanoic acid:

empirical formula = CH_2O

relative empirical formula mass = (12 + 2 + 16) = 30

The relative molecular mass of ethanoic acid is found by experiment to be 60, therefore

molecular formula = 2 × empirical formula
= $C_2H_4O_2$

ROUND UP

On formulas

RELATIVE ATOMIC MASSES
Page 194.

Work out your score on page 215.

1 Which of the following shows the mass of each element present in one mole of aluminium oxide, Al_2O_3? [1]

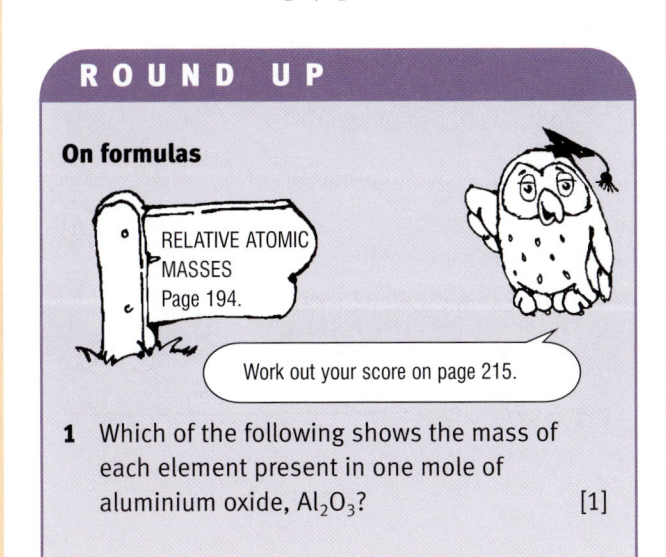

mass of aluminium / g	mass of oxygen / g
A 2	3
B 27	16
C 54	32
D 54	48

2 Calculate the empirical formulas of the following compounds: [5]

   A contains 0.72 g of magnesium and 0.28 g of nitrogen

   B contains 1.68 g of iron and 0.64 g of oxygen

   C contains 3.5 g of silicon and 4.0 g of oxygen

   D contains 20.0% magnesium, 26.6% sulphur and 53.3% oxygen

   E contains 40.0% carbon, 6.7% hydrogen and 53.3% oxygen.

3 Find the percentage by mass of
   a) carbon and hydrogen in ethane, C_2H_6 [2]
   b) sulphur and oxygen in sulphur trioxide, SO_3 [2]
   c) nitrogen, hydrogen and oxygen in ammonium nitrate, NH_4NO_3 [3]
   d) calcium and bromine in calcium bromide, $CaBr_2$. [2]

TAKE A BREAK

13.3 Masses of reacting solids

The equation for a chemical reaction enables us to calculate the masses of solids that react together, and the masses of solid products that are formed.

Example 1

What mass of copper(II) oxide is formed by the complete oxidation of 3.175 g of copper?

Tackling chemical calculations

Equation: $2Cu(s) + O_2(g) \rightarrow 2CuO(s)$

The equation shows that 2 mol of copper form 2 mol of copper(II) oxide; that is, 1 mol of copper forms 1 mol of copper(II) oxide.

Putting in the values $A_r(Cu) = 63.5$, $A_r(O) = 16$, $M_r(CuO) = 79.5$:

63.5 g of copper form 79.5 g of copper(II) oxide

3.175 g of copper gives $\left(\frac{3.175}{63.5}\right) \times 79.5 = 3.98$ g of copper(II) oxide

Example 2

What mass of calcium carbonate must be decomposed to give 50 tonnes of calcium oxide? (1 tonne = 1×10^3 kg = 1×10^6 g)

Equation: $CaCO_3(s) \rightarrow CaO(s) + CO_2(g)$

Putting in the values $A_r(Ca) = 40$, $A_r(C) = 12$, $A_r(O) = 16$:

M_r of $CaCO_3 = 40 + 12 + (3 \times 16) = 100$

M_r of $CaO = 40 + 16 = 56$

Therefore, 56 g of CaO are formed from 100 g of $CaCO_3$.

50 tonnes of CaO are formed from $(50 \times 10^6 / 56) \times 100$ g of $CaCO_3$ = 89 tonnes of $CaCO_3$.

element	symbol	relative atomic mass
aluminium	Al	27
bromine	Br	80
calcium	Ca	40
carbon	C	12
chlorine	Cl	35.5
copper	Cu	63.5
hydrogen	H	1
iron	Fe	56
lead	Pb	207
magnesium	Mg	24
mercury	Hg	200
nitrogen	N	14
oxygen	O	16
phosphorus	P	31
potassium	K	39
silicon	Si	28
sodium	Na	23
sulphur	S	64

Table of selected relative atomic masses

ROUND UP

On reacting masses

How much have you improved? Work out your improvement index on page 216.

1. Find the mass of sodium hydroxide needed to neutralise a solution containing 7.3 g of hydrogen chloride in the reaction

   $NaOH(aq) + HCl(aq) \rightarrow NaCl(aq) + H_2O(l)$ [1]

2. Find the mass of sodium sulphate formed when a solution containing 49 g of sulphuric acid is neutralised by the reaction

   $H_2SO_4(aq) + 2NaOH(aq) \rightarrow Na_2SO_4(aq) + 2H_2O(l)$ [1]

3. An anti-acid tablet contains 0.10 g of magnesium hydrogencarbonate, $Mg(HCO_3)_2$. What mass of stomach acid, HCl, will it neutralise? [1]

4. Wine is made by fermenting the sugar in grapes.

   $C_6H_{12}O_6(aq) \rightarrow 2C_2H_6O(aq) + 2CO_2(g)$
   sucrose   ethanol   carbon dioxide

   What mass of ethanol is obtained from 6.00 kg of sucrose? [1]

5. Aspirin, $C_9H_8O_4$, is made by the reaction

   salicylic acid + ethanoic anhydride → aspirin + ethanoic acid

   $C_7H_6O_3 + C_4H_6O_3 \rightarrow C_9H_8O_4 + C_2H_4O_2$

   What mass of salicylic acid, $C_7H_6O_3$, is needed to make one aspirin tablet, which contains 0.33 g of aspirin? [1]

Well done if you've improved. Don't worry if you haven't. Take a break and try again.

Tackling chemical calculations

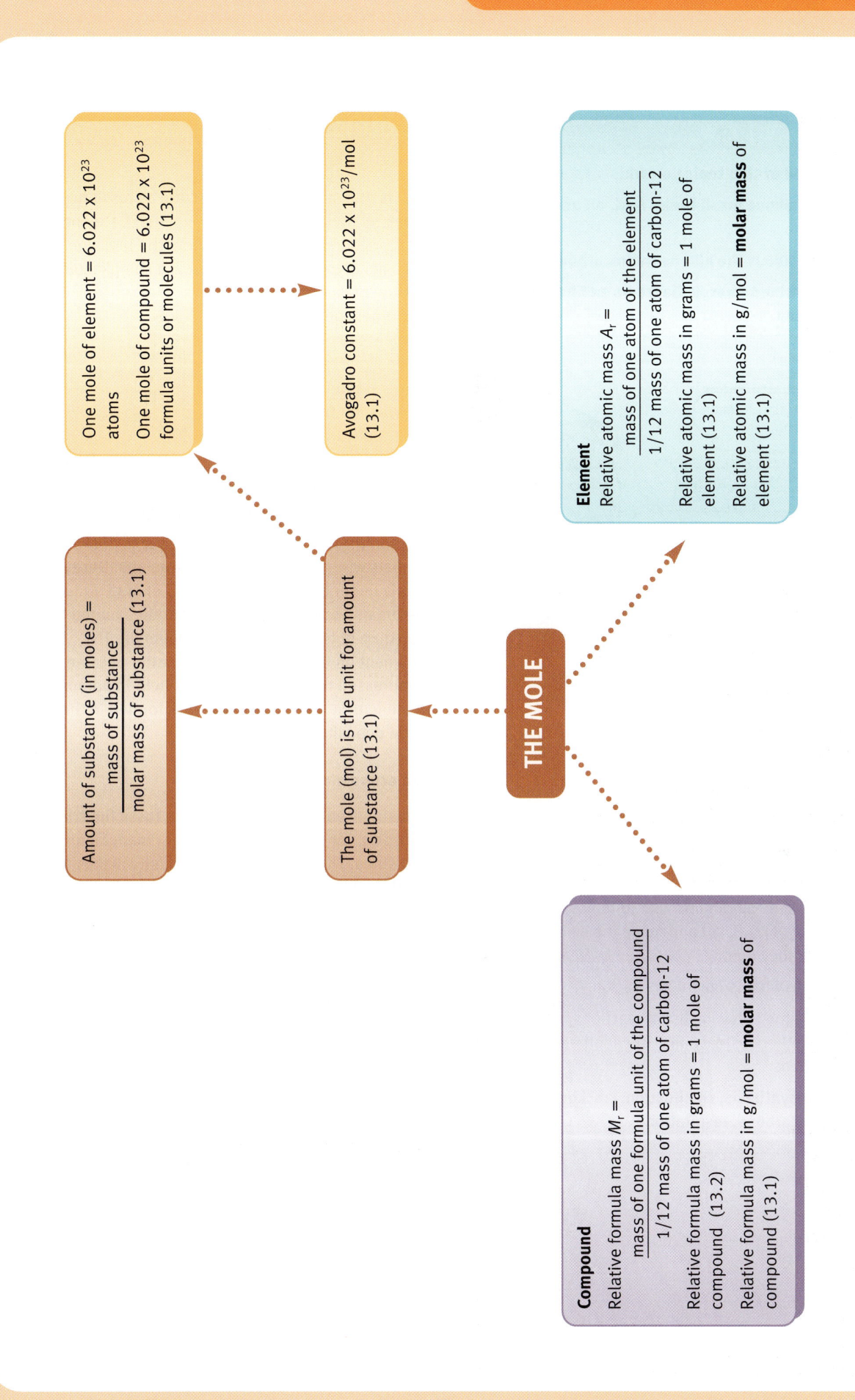

- One mole of element = 6.022×10^{23} atoms
- One mole of compound = 6.022×10^{23} formula units or molecules (13.1)

- Avogadro constant = 6.022×10^{23}/mol (13.1)

- Amount of substance (in moles) = $\dfrac{\text{mass of substance}}{\text{molar mass of substance}}$ (13.1)

- The mole (mol) is the unit for amount of substance (13.1)

THE MOLE

Element
- Relative atomic mass A_r = $\dfrac{\text{mass of one atom of the element}}{1/12 \text{ mass of one atom of carbon-12}}$
- Relative atomic mass in grams = 1 mole of element (13.1)
- Relative atomic mass in g/mol = **molar mass** of element (13.1)

Compound
- Relative formula mass M_r = $\dfrac{\text{mass of one formula unit of the compound}}{1/12 \text{ mass of one atom of carbon-12}}$
- Relative formula mass in grams = 1 mole of compound (13.2)
- Relative formula mass in g/mol = **molar mass** of compound (13.1)

Chapter 14 Fuels

PREVIEW

At the end of this topic you will:
- know about fossil fuels: coal, oil and natural gas
- know about the alkane hydrocarbons
- understand energy diagrams and heat of reaction.

CONCEPT MAP Page 201.

How much do you already know? Work out your score on page 216.

Test yourself

1. Why are coal and oil called 'fossil fuels'? [3]
2. What is most of the world's coal used for? [1]
3. Crude oil can be separated into useful fuels and other substances.
   a) Name the process which is used. [1]
   b) Name four fuels obtained from crude oil. [4]
   c) Name two other useful substances separated from crude oil. [2]
4. Name the compounds with formulas a) CH_4 b) C_2H_6 c) C_3H_8 d) and name the series to which they belong. [4]
5. Explain what is meant by 'cracking'. [4]
6. Divide the following list of reactions into:
   a) exothermic reactions b) endothermic reactions [4]

   photosynthesis, combustion, cracking of hydrocarbons, respiration

14.1 Fossil fuels

Coal

Coal is one of the fuels we describe as **fossil fuels**. It was formed from dead plant material decaying slowly over millions of years under the pressure of deposits of mud and sand. Coal is a complicated mixture of carbon, hydrocarbons and other compounds. Much of the coal used in the world is burned in power stations. The main combustion products are carbon dioxide and water.

COMBUSTION Page 198.

Petroleum oil and natural gas

Petroleum oil (usually called simply oil) and natural gas are fossil fuels: they are the remains of sea animals which lived millions of years ago. Decaying slowly under the pressure of layers of mud and silt, the organic part of the creatures' bodies turned into a mixture of hydrocarbons: petroleum oil. The sediment on top of the decaying matter became compressed to form rock, so oil is held in porous oil-bearing rock. Natural gas is always formed in the same deposits as oil.

The economic importance of oil

Industrialised countries depend on fossil fuels for transport, for power stations and for manufacturing industries. The petrochemicals industry makes a vast number of important chemicals from oil, including fertilisers, herbicides, insecticides and the raw materials needed by the pharmaceutical industry. When we have used the Earth's deposits of coal, oil and gas, there will be no more forthcoming. The economies of all industrial countries will depend on alternative energy sources.

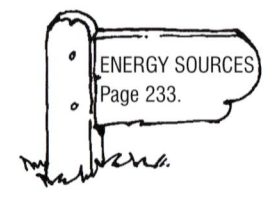

ENERGY SOURCES Page 233.

14.2 Fuels from petroleum

Fractional distillation

Crude oil is separated by fractional distillation into a number of important fuels. Each fraction is collected over a certain boiling point range. Each fraction is a mixture of hydrocarbons (compounds which consist of hydrogen and carbon only). The use that is made of each fraction depends on the following factors, all of which increase with the size of the molecules.

★ Its boiling point range: the higher the boiling point range, the more difficult it is to vaporise in a vehicle engine.

★ Its viscosity: the more viscous a fraction is, the less easily it flows.

★ Its ignition temperature: the less easily a fraction ignites, the less flammable it is.

Cracking

We use more naphtha, petrol and kerosene than heavy fuel oil. The technique called **cracking** is used to convert the high boiling point range fractions into the lower boiling point range fractions petrol and kerosene.

vapour of hydrocarbon with large molecules and high boiling point $\xrightarrow[\text{e.g. } Al_2O_3 \text{ or } SiO_2]{\text{cracking passed over a heated catalyst}}$ mixture of hydrocarbons with smaller molecules and low boiling point, and hydrogen. The mixture is separated by fractional distillation.

14.3 Alkanes

Most of the hydrocarbons in crude oil belong to the **homologous series** called **alkanes**; they are shown in the table. A homologous series is a set of compounds with similar chemical properties in which one member of the series differs from the next by a $-CH_2-$ group. Physical properties such as boiling point vary gradually as the size of the molecules increases.

Fact file

The alkanes	
name	formula
methane	CH_4
ethane	C_2H_6
propane	C_3H_8
butane	C_4H_{10}
pentane	C_5H_{12}
hexane	C_6H_{14}
general formula	C_nH_{2n+2}

Petroleum fractions and their uses (fractional distillation column):

- **below 25 °C** — **Petroleum gases** are liquefied under pressure, and sold in cylinders as 'bottled gas' for use in gas cookers.
- **40–75 °C** — **Petrol** (gasoline) vaporises easily at the temperature of vehicle engines.
- **75–150 °C** — **Naphtha** is used in the manufacture of plastics, fabrics, medicines, agricultural chemicals, etc.
- **150–260 °C** — **Kerosene** needs a higher temperature for combustion. It is used as aviation fuel.
- **260–340 °C** — **Diesel oil** is used in the diesel engine which has a special fuel injection system to allow this fuel to burn. It is used in buses, lorries, etc.
- **340–500 °C** — **Lubricating oil** is used as a lubricant to reduce engine wear.
- **>500 °C** — **Fuel oil** is a viscous liquid with a high ignition temperature. It is used in ships, heating plants and power stations. To help it to ignite, fuel oil must be sprayed into the combustion chambers as a fine mist.
- **Bitumen** is left as a residue at the bottom of the distillation column. It is used to waterproof roofs and pipes and to tar roads.

(vapour of crude oil enters at the base of the column)

Fuels

Here are the structural formulas for the first three alkanes:

methane, ethane, propane

Alkanes do not take part in many chemical reactions. Their important reaction is combustion.

Alkanes contain only single bonds between carbon atoms. Such hydrocarbons are called **saturated hydrocarbons**. This is in contrast to the alkenes, which contain double bonds and are **unsaturated hydrocarbons**.

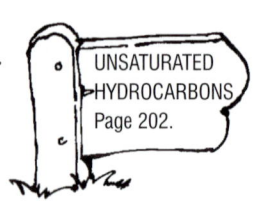

UNSATURATED HYDROCARBONS Page 202.

14.4 Energy and chemical reactions

Exothermic reactions

1. **Combustion**: the combustion of hydrocarbons is an exothermic reaction – heat is given out.

   methane + oxygen → carbon dioxide + water; heat is given out

   $CH_4(g) + 2O_2(g) \rightarrow CO_2(g) + 2H_2O(l)$

   octane + oxygen → carbon dioxide + water; heat is given out

   ★ An oxidation reaction in which heat is given out is **combustion**.

   ★ Combustion accompanied by a flame is **burning**.

   ★ A substance which is oxidised with the release of energy is a **fuel**.

2. **Respiration**: our bodies obtain energy from the oxidation of foods, e.g. glucose, in cells. This process is called **cellular respiration**.

   RESPIRATION Page 62.

   glucose + oxygen → carbon dioxide + water; energy is given out

   $C_6H_{12}O_6(aq) + 6O_2(g) \rightarrow 6CO_2(g) + 6H_2O(l)$

3. **Neutralisation**

   hydrogen ion + hydroxide ion → water; heat is given out

   $H^+(aq) + OH^-(aq) \rightarrow H_2O(l)$

Endothermic reactions

1. **Photosynthesis**: plants convert carbon dioxide and water into sugars in the process of photosynthesis.

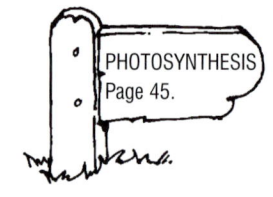

   PHOTOSYNTHESIS Page 45.

   catalysed by chlorophyll

   carbon dioxide + water → glucose + oxygen; energy of sunlight is taken in

   $6CO_2(g) + 6H_2O(l) \rightarrow C_6H_{12}O_6(aq) + 6O_2(g)$

2. **Thermal decomposition**; for example the cracking of hydrocarbons and the decomposition of calcium carbonate:

   calcium carbonate $\xrightarrow{heat}$ calcium oxide + carbon dioxide; heat is taken in

   $CaCO_3(s) \rightarrow CaO(s) + CO_2(g)$

14.5 Energy change of reaction

The atoms, ions or molecules in a substance are held together by chemical bonds. Energy must be supplied if these chemical bonds are to be broken. When bonds are created, energy is given out. The reactants and the products possess different amounts of energy because they have different chemical bonds; see diagram below.

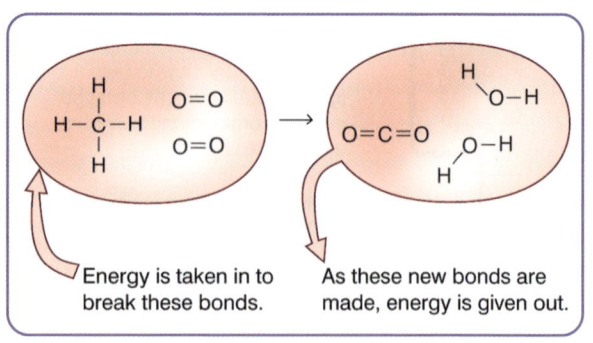

Energy is taken in to break these bonds. As these new bonds are made, energy is given out.

Bonds broken and made when methane burns

In the reaction shown, the energy taken in is less than the energy given out: this reaction is exothermic.

The graphs below are energy diagrams, in which
energy change of reaction = energy of products − energy of reactants

★ In an **exothermic reaction**, the products of the reaction contain less energy than the reactants. When the reactants change into the products, they get rid of their extra energy by giving out heat to the surroundings.

★ In an **endothermic reaction**, the reactants have to climb to a higher energy level to change into the products. To do this, they take energy from the surroundings: they cool the surroundings.

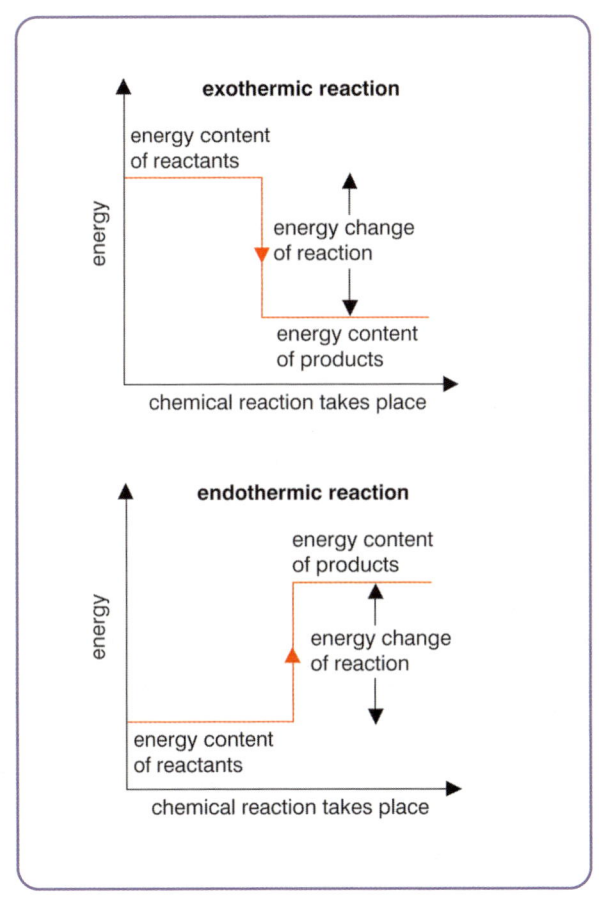

Energy diagrams for an exothermic reaction and an endothermic reaction

14.6 Activation energy

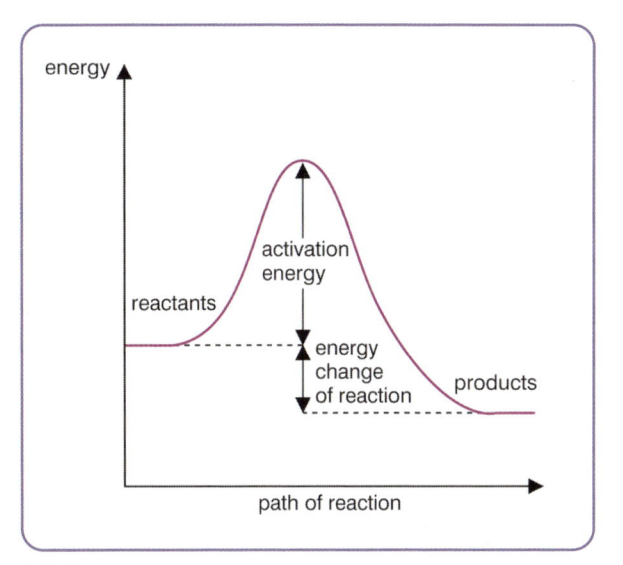

Activation energy

The graph shows how the energy of the reactants changes during an exothermic reaction. The products possess less energy than the reactants, but the reactants cannot just slide down an energy hill to form the products. There is an energy barrier which the reactants must climb before they can be converted into the products. The energy barrier is called the **activation energy** or the **energy of activation**. Reactant molecules which collide with energy equal to the activation energy are converted into the products. A catalyst alters the speed of a reaction by altering the activation energy.

CATALYSTS Page 187.

14.7 Using bond energy values

It is possible to measure exactly how much energy it takes to break different chemical bonds. To break 1 mol of C—C bonds requires 348 kJ; the **bond energy** of the C—C bond is 348 kJ/mol. To break a chemical bond, energy must be supplied, so all bond energies are positive. Energy is given out when new bonds are made. This energy change has a negative value. Some bond energies are shown in the following table (overleaf).

Fuels

We can use bond energy values to calculate a value for the energy change of reaction.

bond	bond energy / kJ/mol
H—H	436
O=O	496
C—C	348
C=C	612
C—H	412
C—O	360
C=O	743
H—O	463

Bond energy values

Example

Use bond energies to calculate the energy change for the reaction:

$CH_4(g) + 2O_2(g) \rightarrow CO_2(g) + 2H_2O(l)$

First, show the bonds that are broken and the bonds that are made.

Next, list the bonds that are broken and the bonds that are made along with their bond energies.

Bonds broken:

4(C—H) bonds; energy = 4 × 412 = 1648 kJ/mol

2(O=O) bonds; energy = 2 × 496 = 992 kJ/mol

total energy required = 2640 kJ/mol

Bonds made:

2(C=O) bonds; energy = 2 × 743 = 1486 kJ/mol

2(H—O) bonds; energy = 4 × 463 = 1852 kJ/mol

total energy change = 3338 kJ/mol

energy change of reaction = energy given out when new bonds are made – energy required to break old bonds

= 3338 – 2640

= **698 kJ/mol**

ROUND UP

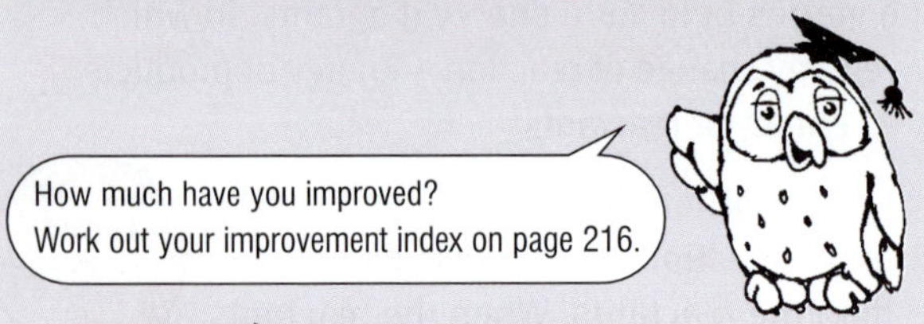

How much have you improved?
Work out your improvement index on page 216.

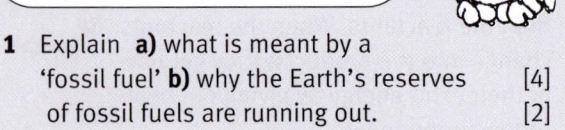

1. Explain a) what is meant by a 'fossil fuel' b) why the Earth's reserves [4] of fossil fuels are running out. [2]

2. Suggest three methods of dealing with oil slicks. [3]

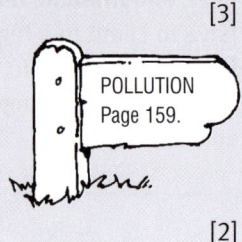

3. a) Briefly explain how crude oil is separated into natural gas, gasoline, naphtha, kerosene, diesel oil and fuel oil. [2]
   POLLUTION Page 159.
   b) State one use for each of the fractions. [6]
   c) Give three differences in properties between gasoline and fuel oil. [3]
   d) A barrel of oil yields less gasoline than fuel oil. The demand for gasoline is, however, greater than the demand for fuel oil. Explain why fuel oil cannot be used in car engines. [2]
   e) Briefly explain why an increase in the price of oil has a great impact worldwide. [4]

4. Draw an energy diagram for the combustion of petrol to form carbon dioxide and water. Mark the energy change of reaction on your diagram, and state whether the reaction is exothermic or endothermic. [3]

5. Draw an energy diagram for the cracking of heavy fuel oil to form kerosene. Mark the energy change of reaction on your diagram, and state whether the reaction is exothermic or endothermic. [3]

6. Find the energy change of reaction for the following reactions:

   a)
   $$H_2C=CH_2 + H_2 \rightarrow H_3C-CH_3$$
   (drawn with full structural formulae: H—C=C—H with H's on each carbon + H₂ → H—C—C—H with H's on each carbon)

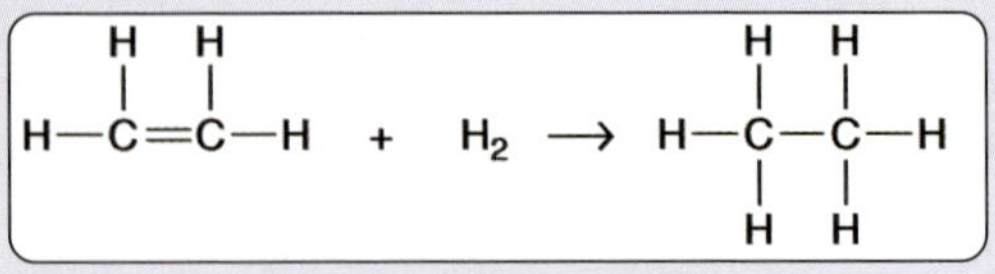

   Hint: add the energies of the bonds that are broken and the energies of the bonds that are created.

   b) $2H_2(g) + O_2(g) \rightarrow 2H_2O(l)$

   c)
   $$CH_3-\overset{O}{\underset{\|}{C}}-CH_3(g) + H_2(g) \rightarrow CH_3-\underset{H}{\overset{O-H}{\underset{|}{C}}}-CH_3(g)$$

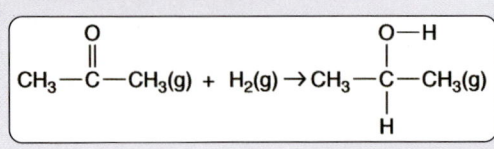

   [3]

Fuels

Alkanes
Petroleum oil consists of hydrocarbons, chiefly alkanes, formula C_nH_{2n+2}. They are a homologous series. (see 14.3)

Cracking
Converts high boiling point fractions into lower boiling point fractions, e.g. petrol. (14.2)

Bond energies*
Energy change of reaction = energy given out when new bonds are made − energy required to break old bonds (see 14.7)

* = Check your specification

Fuels from petroleum
'Bottled gas', petrol, naphtha, kerosene, diesel oil, lubricating oil, fuel oil, bitumen. (see diagram in 14.2)

FUELS

Energy change of reaction
The combustion of fuels is exothermic.
Chemical reactions may be exothermic – heat given out
or
endothermic – heat taken in
Energy change of reaction = energy of products − energy of reactants (see 14.5)

Fossil fuels
Coal was formed from dead plant material decaying over millions of years under pressure

Petroleum oil and natural gas were formed from sea animals decaying over millions of years under pressure

Importance of fossil fuels:
- transport
- power stations
- manufacturing industries
- petrochemicals industry (14.1)

Activation energy*
Reactants have to overcome an energy barrier (the activation energy) before they can form the products (see 14.6)

Chapter 15   Alkenes and plastics

PREVIEW

At the end of this topic you will:

- know the general formula and reactions of alkenes
- understand the differences between thermoplastic and thermosetting plastics
- know the names and uses of some poly(alkenes)
- appreciate the difficulties of disposing of plastic waste.

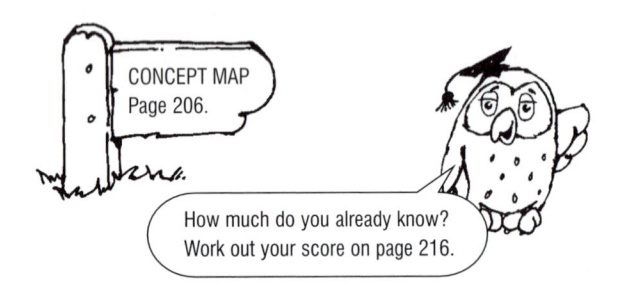

CONCEPT MAP Page 206.

How much do you already know? Work out your score on page 216.

Test yourself

1. Draw the functional group of an alkene. Say in what type of reactions this functional group takes part. [2]

2. Unlike alkanes, alkenes are not used as fuels. Why is this? [2]

3. Why does ethene decolourise a solution of bromine? Give the formula of the product. [1]

4. a) What is hydration? [1]
   b) What important compound is formed by the hydration of ethene? Give its name and formula. [1]

5. a) What is hydrogenation? [1]
   b) What is the industrial importance of hydrogenation? [1]

6. Explain what is meant by addition polymerisation. [2]

7. Name two sets of plastics which differ in their reaction to heat. Describe the difference in behaviour. [4]

8. By what types of process are the two different kinds of plastics moulded? [2]

15.1 Alkenes

The alkenes are a **homologous series** of hydrocarbons, as shown in the table.

Fact file

The alkenes	
name	formula
ethene	C_2H_4
propene	C_3H_6
butene	C_4H_8
general formula	C_nH_{2n}

The double bond (see page 135) between the carbon atoms is the **functional group** of alkenes, and is responsible for their reactions. Alkenes are described as **unsaturated hydrocarbons**. They will react with hydrogen in an **addition reaction** to form saturated hydrocarbons (alkanes).

ethene + hydrogen → ethane

15.2 Reactions of alkenes

Alkenes are not used as fuels because they are an important source of other compounds. The double bond makes them chemically reactive, and they are starting materials in the manufacture of plastics, fibres, solvents and other chemicals.

Addition reactions

1. **Halogens add** to alkenes. A solution of bromine in an organic solvent is brown. If an alkene is bubbled through such a bromine solution, the solution loses its colour. Bromine has added to the alkene to form a colourless compound, for example:

    ethene + bromine → 1, 2-dibromoethane

Alkenes and plastics

$$\text{CH}_2=\text{CH}_2 + \text{Br}_2 \rightarrow \text{CH}_2\text{Br}-\text{CH}_2\text{Br}$$

The decolourisation of a bromine solution is used to distinguish between an alkene and an alkane. Chlorine adds to alkenes in a similar way.

2 **Hydration**: a molecule of water will add across the double bond. Addition of water is called **hydration**.

ethene + water → ethanol

$$\text{CH}_2=\text{CH}_2 + \text{H}-\text{O}-\text{H} \rightarrow \text{CH}_3-\text{CH}_2-\text{O}-\text{H}$$

Ethene and steam are passed over a heated catalyst under pressure. The product is ethanol, an important industrial solvent.

3 **Hydrogenation**: animal fats, such as butter, are saturated compounds and are solid. Vegetable oils, such as sunflower seed oil, are unsaturated compounds and are liquid. An unsaturated vegetable oil can be converted into a saturated fat by hydrogenation (the addition of hydrogen):

vegetable oil + hydrogen $\xrightarrow{\text{pass over heated nickel catalyst}}$ solid fat
(unsaturated) (saturated)

The solid fat produced is sold as margarine.

4 **Addition polymerisation**: in this reaction, many molecules of the **monomer**, e.g. ethene, join together (**polymerise**) to form the **polymer**, e.g. poly(ethene).

The conditions needed are:

ethene $\xrightarrow{\text{pass at high pressure over a heated catalyst}}$ poly(ethene)

$$n\text{CH}_2=\text{CH}_2 \rightarrow (-\text{CH}_2-\text{CH}_2-)_n$$

In poly(ethene), n is between 30 000 and 40 000. Poly(ethene) is used for making plastic bags, for kitchenware (buckets, bowls, etc.), for laboratory tubing and for toys. It is flexible and difficult to break. Polymers of alkenes are called poly(alkenes).

15.3 Uses of plastics

Plastics are:
- strong
- low in density
- good insulators of heat and electricity
- resistant to attack by chemicals
- smooth
- able to be moulded into different shapes.

There are two kinds of plastics, **thermoplastics** and **thermosetting plastics**. The difference is shown in the diagram below.

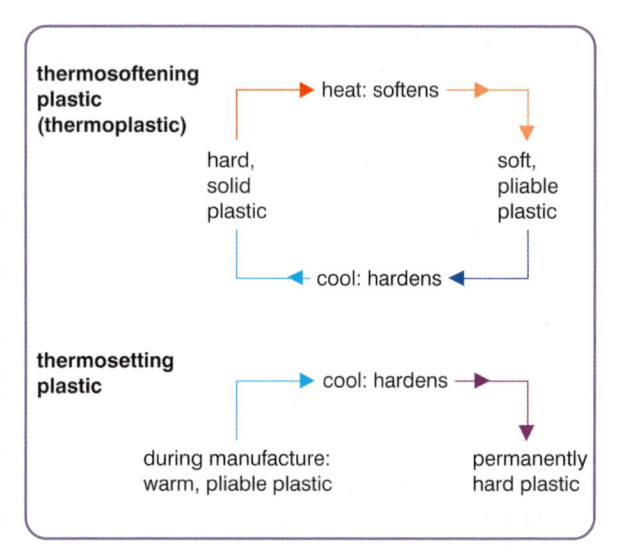

Thermosetting and thermosoftening plastics

Alkenes and plastics

The reason for the difference in behaviour is a difference in structure, as shown below.

> (a) **Thermoplastics** consist of long polymer chains. The forces of attraction between chains are weak.
>
> (b) When a **thermosetting plastic** sets, the chains react with one another. Cross-links are formed, and a huge three-dimensional structure is built up. This is why thermosetting plastics can be formed only once.

The structure of (a) a thermosoftening plastic (b) a thermosetting plastic

Moulding of thermoplastics can be a **continuous process**: solid granules of the plastic are fed into one end of the moulding machine, softened by heat and then moulded to come out of the other end in the shape of tubes, sheets or rods. It is easy to manufacture coloured articles by adding a pigment to the plastic.

The moulding of thermosetting plastics is a **batch process**. The monomer is poured into the mould and heated. As it polymerises, the plastic solidifies and a press forms it into the required shape while it is setting.

Both types of plastic have their advantages. A material used for electrical fittings and counter tops must be able to withstand high temperatures without softening. For these purposes, 'thermosets' are used.

Sometimes gases are mixed with softened plastics to make low density plastic foam for use in car seats, thermal insulation, sound insulation and packaging. Plastics can be strengthened by the addition of other materials; for example the composite material **glass fibre-reinforced plastic** is used for the manufacture of boat hulls and car bodies.

15.4 Some disadvantages of plastics

There is a danger in the use of plastics as building materials. Plastics catch fire at lower temperatures than wood, metals, brick and glass. Some burning plastics give off poisonous gases, e.g. hydrogen chloride and hydrogen cyanide.

Plastics are non-biodegradable. They are not decomposed by natural processes in the soil. This makes waste plastics difficult to dispose of. When they are tipped into landfill sites, plastics remain there for many years without decomposing. Chemists have invented some biodegradable plastics that are attacked by microorganisms in the soil. At present these plastics are costly.

An alternative to dumping is burning waste plastics to provide energy. This cannot be done with plastics that burn to form poisonous gases.

Plastics can be recycled, but different types of plastic need different treatments. They must therefore be collected and sorted into different types of plastic before recycling.

Alkenes and plastics

ROUND UP

How much have you improved? Work out your improvement index on page 217.

1. **a)** Write (i) the molecular formulas
      (ii) the structural formulas of ethane and ethene. [4]
   b) State the difference between the chemical bonding in the two compounds. [4]

2. **a)** Give two examples of substances which react with ethene but not with ethane. [2]
   b) What name is given to the type of reactions in **a**? [1]
   c) How can ethene be converted into ethane? [2]

3. Alkanes and alkenes burn in a similar way. Alkanes are important fuels.
   a) What are the main products of combustion of alkanes and alkenes? [2]
   b) Why are alkenes not used as fuels? [1]

4. **a)** Sketch the structural formulas of propane and propene. [2]
   b) Which of the two compounds will decolourise bromine water? [1]
   c) Sketch the structural formula of the product formed in the reaction between bromine and the compound in **b**. [1]

5. State the advantage that plastic has
   a) over china for making cups and saucers and dolls [1]
   b) over lead for making toy farmyard animals and soldiers [1]
   c) over glass for making motorbike windscreens. [1]

6. The formula of propenamide is

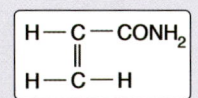

   $$\begin{array}{c} H-C-CONH_2 \\ \parallel \\ H-C-H \end{array}$$

   Draw the formula of the polymer poly(propenamide). [1]

7. **a)** What does the word 'plastic' mean? [2]
   b) There are two big classes of plastics, which behave differently when heated. Name the two classes. Describe the difference in behaviour. Say how this difference is related to the molecular nature of the plastics. [5]

8. Name two addition polymers, and give uses for them. [4]

9. **a)** What is meant by the statement that plastics are non-biodegradable? [1]
   b) Why is this a disadvantage? [1]
   c) What is wrong with burning plastic waste? [2]
   d) Suggest an alternative to burning plastic waste. [1]

Alkenes and plastics

Alkenes
hydrocarbons with the formula C_nH_{2n}
e.g. ethene $CH_2=CH_2$, propene $CH_3CH=CH_2$ (15.1)

Reactions
The C=C double bond makes alkenes take part in addition reactions,
- with bromine:
  $CH_2=CH_2 + Br_2 \rightarrow BrCH_2CH_2Br$
- with water:
  ethene + $H_2O \rightarrow$ ethanol C_2H_5OH
- with hydrogen (Ni catalyst):
  unsaturated oils + $H_2 \rightarrow$ solid fats
- polymerisation: many molecules of monomer combine to form a large molecule of polymer, e.g.
  ethene $\rightarrow$ poly(ethene)
  propene $\rightarrow$ poly(propene) (15.2)

Plastics
Poly(alkenes) are plastics. (15.3)

Thermosoftening plastics
can be softened by heat, moulded, and set by cooling many times. They consist of long polymer chains.

Thermosetting plastics
can be moulded while they are warm, during manufacture, and once set cannot be re-softened by heat. There are cross-links between the long polymer chains. (15.3)

Drawbacks of plastics
The low ignition temperatures are a hazard in building materials.

Non-biodegradable, therefore pose a problem for disposal in landfill sites.

Can be burnt to provide useful energy unless they form toxic combustion products.

Can be sorted and recycled.

Research into biodegradable plastics continues. (15.4)

Properties
Plastics are strong, low in density, thermal and electrical insulators, resistant to chemicals, easy to colour. (15.3)

Periodic table

THE PERIODIC TABLE OF THE ELEMENTS

Group 1	2											3	4	5	6	7	0
				H hydrogen 1													He helium 2
Li lithium 3	Be beryllium 4											B boron 5	C carbon 6	N nitrogen 7	O oxygen 8	F fluorine 9	Ne neon 10
Na sodium 11	Mg magnesium 12											Al aluminium 13	Si silicon 14	P phosphorus 15	S sulphur 16	Cl chlorine 17	Ar argon 18
K potassium 19	Ca calcium 20	Sc scandium 21	Ti titanium 22	V vanadium 23	Cr chromium 24	Mn manganese 25	Fe iron 26	Co cobalt 27	Ni nickel 28	Cu copper 29	Zn zinc 30	Ga gallium 31	Ge germanium 32	As arsenic 33	Se selenium 34	Br bromine 35	Kr krypton 36
Rb rubidium 37	Sr strontium 38	Y yttrium 39	Zr zirconium 40	Nb niobium 41	Mo molybdenum 42	Tc technetium 43	Ru ruthenium 44	Rh rhodium 45	Pd palladium 46	Ag silver 47	Cd cadmium 48	In indium 49	Sn tin 50	Sb antimony 51	Te tellurium 52	I iodine 53	Xe xenon 54
Cs caesium 55	Ba barium 56	La lanthanum 57	Hf hafnium 72	Ta tantalum 73	W tungsten 74	Re rhenium 75	Os osmium 76	Ir iridium 77	Pt platinum 78	Au gold 79	Hg mercury 80	Tl thallium 81	Pb lead 82	Bi bismuth 83	Po polonium 84	At astatine 85	Rn radon 86
Fr francium 87	Ra radium 88	Ac actinium 89															

lanthanum series: elements 58–71
actinium series: elements 90–103

Answers

1 Test yourself (page 116)
Matter and the kinetic theory

1. solid (✓), liquid (✓), gas (✓)
2. A pure solid melts at a fixed temperature (✓); an impure solid melts over a range of temperature (✓).
3. Evaporation takes place over a range of temperatures (✓). Boiling takes place at a certain temperature (✓).
4. Bubbles of vapour appear in the body of the liquid (✓).
5. In a pressure cooker, water boils at a temperature above 100 °C (✓) and foods cook faster at higher temperature (✓).
6. On a high mountain, air pressure is lower than at sea level (✓), and water boils below 100 °C (✓).
7. a) Both change shape when a force is applied (✓).
   b) When the force ceases, a plastic material retains its new shape (✓), but an elastic material returns to its previous shape (✓).
8. Crystals consist of a regular arrangement of particles (✓). As a result the surfaces are smooth (✓) and reflect light (✓).
9. The particles that make up the solid gain enough energy to break free from the attractive forces (✓) between particles which maintain the solid structure, and the particles move independently (✓).
10. In a gas, e.g. steam, the molecules are very much further apart (✓) than in a liquid (✓).
11. Particles (✓) of salt dissolve (✓) and spread out (✓) through the soup.

Your score: ☐ out of 25

1 Round up (page 118)
Matter and the kinetic theory

1. At A, the temperature of the liquid is rising (✓). At B, the temperature stays constant because the liquid is boiling (✓) and all the heat is being used to convert liquid into gas (✓).
2. At C, the temperature of the solid is rising as it is heated (✓). At D the solid starts to melt (✓), and the temperature stays constant at the melting point (✓) while heat is used in the conversion of solid into liquid (✓). At E all the solid has melted (✓), and the temperature of the liquid rises as it is heated (✓). The sharp melting point shows that the solid is a pure substance (✓).
3. Under pressure, water boils at a temperature above 100 °C (✓) and the hotter steam kills more bacteria than steam at 100 °C (✓).
4. Most of a gas is space; the molecules are far apart (✓).
5. There is so much space between the molecules of a gas (✓) that it is easy for them to move closer together (✓) when the pressure is increased.
6. One example, e.g. heating a lump of bread dough, e.g. air in a hot air balloon expands and is less dense than the air outside the balloon (✓).
7. One example, e.g. increase in the pressure of air in car tyres, e.g. removing a dent from a table tennis ball by warming, e.g. a balloon filled with gas bursts if it is heated (✓).
8. The liquid vaporises (✓). A gas diffuses (✓) to occupy the whole of its container, i.e. the whole of the room (✓).
9. Liquids need energy to vaporise (see page 116) (✓). Aftershave lotion takes this energy from the skin (✓).

Your score: ☐ out of 22

Your improvement index: $\dfrac{\boxed{}/22}{\boxed{}/25} \times 100\% = \boxed{}\%$

2 Test yourself (page 119)
Elements, compounds and equations

1. An element is a pure substance (✓) that cannot be split up (✓) into simpler substances (✓).
2. Zinc reacts with dilute acids (✓) to form hydrogen (✓) and a salt (✓). It forms the cation Zn^{2+} (✓). The oxide and hydroxide are basic (✓) (and amphoteric). The chloride is a solid salt (✓). It forms no hydride (✓).
3. In diamond every carbon atom is covalently bonded to four other carbon atoms (✓). In graphite carbon atoms are covalently bonded together in layers (✓). The layers are joined by weak forces (✓), so one layer can slide over another (✓).
4. thermal decomposition (✓), electrolysis (✓)
5. 14 (✓)
6. $2Na(s) + 2H_2O(l) \rightarrow 2NaOH(aq) + H_2(g)$
   (✓✓✓✓ for state symbols, ✓✓✓✓ for balancing)

Your score: ☐ out of 25

2 Round up (page 122)
Elements, compounds and equations

1. metallic (✓)
2. non-metallic (✓)
3. metallic (✓)
4. non-metallic (✓)

Answers

5 For example:
   a) Appearance: sulphur is dull, whereas copper is shiny (✓).
   b) Sulphur is shattered by hammering, whereas copper can be hammered into shape (✓).
   c) Sulphur does not conduct heat or electricity, whereas copper is a good thermal and electrical conductor (✓).
   d) Sulphur is not sonorous; copper is sonorous (✓).

6 The appearance of the mixture (speckled yellow and grey) is different from that of the compound (dark grey throughout) (✓). The iron in the mixture reacts with dilute acids to give hydrogen (✓). The compound, iron(II) sulphide, reacts with acids to give hydrogen sulphide (✓), with a characteristic smell. The iron in the mixture is attracted to a magnet (✓).

7 45 (✓)

8 $CaCO_3(s) + 2HCl(aq) \rightarrow CaCl_2(aq) + CO_2(g) + H_2O(l)$
   (✓✓✓ for state symbols, ✓ for factor 2)

9 $Fe^{2+}(aq) + 2OH^-(aq) \rightarrow Fe(OH)_2(s)$ (✓✓✓)

Your score: ☐ out of 20

Your improvement index: $\frac{\Box/20}{\Box/25} \times 100\% = \Box\%$

3 Test yourself (page 124)

The structure of the atom

1 The number of protons = number of electrons (✓) and the positive charge on a proton has the same value as the negative charge on an electron (✓).

2 a) 19 (✓)   b) 20 (✓)

3 Their chemical reactions are identical because it is the electrons that determine the chemical behaviour (✓), and isotopes have the same electron arrangement (✓).

4 a) The number of protons (= number of electrons) in an atom of the element (✓).
  b) The number of protons + neutrons in an atom of the element (✓✓).

5 a) $^{31}_{15}P$ (✓✓)   b) $^{39}_{19}K$ (✓✓)

6 Two in the first shell (✓), four in the second shell (✓).

Your score: ☐ out of 15

3 Round up (page 127)

The structure of the atom

1 a) 27 (✓)   b) 5 (✓)   c) 0.7 (✓)   d) 4 (✓)

2 a) $^{75}_{33}As$ (✓)   b) $^{235}_{92}U$ (✓), $^{238}_{92}U$ (✓), $^{239}_{92}U$ (✓)

3 a) 63.6 (✓)   b) 69.8 (✓)

4 [Diagram of P atom, 15p] (✓)

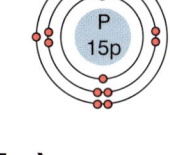

5 a) [B, 5p]   b) [N, 7p]   c) [F, 9p]

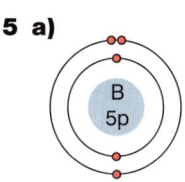

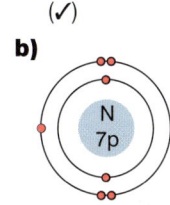

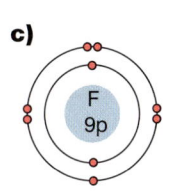

d) [Al, 13p]

(✓✓✓✓)

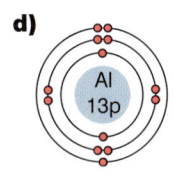

Your score: ☐ out of 15

Your improvement index: $\frac{\Box/15}{\Box/15} \times 100\% = \Box\%$

4 Test yourself (page 128)

Electrolysis

1 A (✓)   C (✓)

2 A (✓)   B (✓)   D (✓)

3 a) A compound which conducts electricity (✓) when molten (✓) or in solution (✓) and is split up in the process (✓).
  b) An object which conducts electricity into or out of a cell (✓).

4 a) cation – a positively charged atom or group of atoms (✓)
     anion – a negatively charged atom or group of atoms (✓)
     For examples see table on page 133 (✓✓✓✓).
  b) Ions are charged (✓) and move towards the electrode of opposite charge (✓).
  c) In the solid the ions are held in place in a crystal structure (✓). In solution, they are free to move (✓).

209

Answers

5 If water is present, hydrogen ions are discharged in preference to sodium (see page 130) (✓).
6 Chromium plate is not easily chipped off, as paint would be on door handles, etc. (✓).
7 a) Gold plate is cheaper than gold (✓).
   b) Gold does not tarnish as brass does (✓).
8 a) The melting point of the mixture is much lower than that of aluminium oxide (✓).
   b) Cathode: $Al^{3+}(l) + 3e^- \rightarrow Al(l)$ (✓✓)
      Anode: $O^{2-}(l) \rightarrow O(g) + 2e^-$ (✓✓)
      followed by: $2O(g) \rightarrow O_2(g)$ (✓)
   c) It requires a lot of energy (✓).

Your score: ☐ out of 31

4 Round up (page 133)
Electrolysis

1 a) Copper(II) ions are discharged in preference to the ions of more reactive metals (see page 124) (✓).
   b) Metals which are less reactive than copper, e.g. silver and gold, do not go into solution (✓); they are part of the anode sludge (✓).
2 a) The coating is even (✓) and it can be as thin as required (✓).
   b) Your diagram should similar to be the one on page 132, using an iron nail as cathode and a solution of e.g. nickel(II) sulphate as electrolyte (✓✓).
3 a) bromine (✓)   b) positive electrode/anode (✓)
   c) hydrogen (✓)   d) hydroxide ion (✓)
   e) cathode: $H^+(aq) + e^- \rightarrow H(g)$ (✓✓)
      followed by: $2H(g) \rightarrow H_2(g)$ (✓)
      anode: $Br^-(aq) \rightarrow Br(aq) + e^-$ (✓✓)
      followed by: $2Br(aq) \rightarrow Br_2(aq)$ (✓)
4 a) Cathode: copper (✓), anode: oxygen (✓).
   b) Cathode: $Cu^{2+}(aq) + 2e^- \rightarrow Cu(s)$ (✓✓)
      Anode: $OH^-(aq) \rightarrow OH(aq) + e^-$ (✓✓)
      followed by: $4OH(aq) \rightarrow O_2(g) + 2H_2O(l)$ (✓✓✓)
   c) Oxygen is not evolved at the anode (✓). Copper dissolves from the anode (✓).
   d) Cathode: $Cu^{2+}(aq) + 2e^- \rightarrow Cu(s)$ (✓✓)
      Anode: $Cu(s) \rightarrow Cu^{2+}(aq) + 2e^-$ (✓✓)

Your score: ☐ out of 32

Your improvement index: $\dfrac{☐/32}{☐/31} \times 100\% = $ ☐ %

5 Test yourself (page 135)
The chemical bond

1 positive (✓), negative (✓), electrostatic (✓), crystal (✓)
2 Each atom of E loses two electrons to become E^{2+} (2.8) (✓).
   Each atom of Q gains one electron to become Q^- (2.8.8) (✓).
   The compound EQ_2 is formed (✓).
3

T (✓) T_2 (✓)

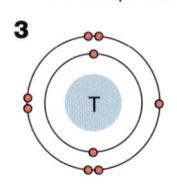

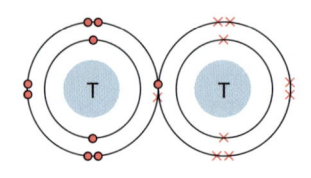

4 a) magnesium bromide (✓)   b) iron(II) chloride (✓)
   c) iron(III) chloride (✓)   d) sodium oxide (✓)
   e) barium sulphate (✓)
5 a) KBr (✓) b) $CaCO_3$ (✓) c) PbO (✓) d) $PbSO_4$ (✓)
   e) AgCl (✓)

Your score: ☐ out of 19

5 Round up (page 139)
The chemical bond

1 a) sodium ions, Na^+ (✓) and chloride ions, Cl^- (✓)
   b) electrostatic attraction (✓)
   c) A three-dimensional arrangement (✓) of alternate Na^+ ions and Cl^- ions (✓).
2

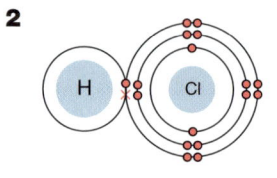

(✓✓)

3 For example, one of a) O_2, CH_4 (✓) b) $I_2(s)$, $CO_2(s)$ (✓)
   c) Diamond, graphite, silcon(IV) oxide (✓).
4 a) calcium hydroxide (✓)   b) sodium sulphite (✓)
   c) copper(II) carbonate (✓)   d) magnesium hydrogencarbonate (✓)
                                  e) potassium nitrate (✓)
5 a) NH_4NO_3 (✓) b) Na_2SO_4 (✓) c) $(NH_4)_2SO_4$ (✓)
   d) Al_2O_3 (✓)   e) $Zn(OH)_2$ (✓)

Your score: ☐ out of 20

Your improvement index: $\dfrac{☐/20}{☐/19} \times 100\% = $ ☐ %

Answers

6 Test yourself (page 140)
The periodic table
1. a) He, Ne, Ar, Kr, Xe (✓), a set of very unreactive gases present in air (✓).
   b) Group 0 (✓)
   c) (i) They have a full outer shell of electrons (✓).
      (ii) They are very unreactive (✓). (Some take part in no chemical reactions. Krypton and xenon react with fluorine.)
2. Group 2 (✓)
3. Group 7 (✓)
4. Group 1 (✓)
5. a) fluorine (✓), chlorine (✓), bromine (✓), iodine (✓)
   b) Group 7 (✓) c) decreases (✓)
   d) (i) NaF (✓), NaCl (✓), NaBr (✓), NaI (✓)
      (ii) FeF_3 (✓), $FeCl_3$ (✓), $FeBr_3$ (✓), FeI_2 (✓)
6. a) An element in the block of the periodic table between Groups 2 and 3 (✓).
   b) See page 145 (✓).

Your score: ☐ out of 24

6 Round up (page 143)
The periodic table
1. Magnesium chloride is a three-dimensional structure of ions (✓) with strong forces of attraction between them (✓). Tetrachloromethane consists of individual covalent molecules (✓) with only weak forces of attraction between them (✓).
2. a) Na (✓), Mg (✓) b) Na (✓), Mg (✓), Al (✓)
   c) (i) Argon (✓) (ii) Chlorine (✓) d) Silicon (✓)
3. a) Na (✓) b) S (✓) c) Al (✓) d) S (✓)
4. Na_2O (✓), MgO (✓), Al_2O_3 (✓), SiO_2 (✓)
5. They do not exist (✓).
6. They both have one electron in the outermost shell (✓). It is the electrons in the outermost shell that decide chemical reactions (✓).
7. a) basic (✓), ionic solid (✓), formula RaO (✓)
   b) Reacts readily to form hydrogen (✓) and the alkali radium hydroxide (✓), $Ra(OH)_2$ (✓).
   c) Reacts readily to form hydrogen (✓) and a solution of the ionic compound (✓) radium chloride (✓), $RaCl_2$ (✓).
8. a) Hydrogen astatide is a gas (✓), a covalent compound (✓) which forms an acidic solution in water (✓).
   b) Astatine reacts slowly with sodium (✓) to form the ionic solid (✓) sodium astatide (✓), NaAt (✓).

Your score: ☐ out of 40

Your improvement index: $\dfrac{☐/40}{☐/24} \times 100\% = ☐\%$

7 Test yourself (page 145)
Acids, bases and salts
1. a) SA (✓) b) WA (✓) c) WB (✓) d) WB (✓)
   e) WA (✓) f) N (✓) g) SB (✓)
2. You could compare the rates (✓) at which hydrogen is given off (✓) in the reactions of the two acids with magnesium or another metal (✓),
   or the rates (✓) at which carbon dioxide is given off (✓) in the reactions of the acids with a carbonate or hydrogencarbonate (✓).
3. a) hydrochloric acid (✓) b) for example, magnesium hydroxide (✓) c) citric acid (✓) d) ammonia (✓)
4. a) Sodium hydroxide converts grease into soap (✓).
   b) Sodium hydroxide is a stronger base than ammonia (✓).
   c) Wear glasses (✓) and rubber gloves (✓).
   d) Sodium hydroxide would be too dangerous or corrosive (✓).
   e) The saponification of fats by a weak base, e.g. ammonia, is very slow (✓).

Your score: ☐ out of 20

7 Round up (page 152)
Acids, bases and salts
1. a) A solid base can be separated by filtration (✓).
   b) If any acid remains it will be concentrated in the evaporation step (✓).
   c) (i) Note when the evolution of hydrogen stops (✓).
      (ii) Test with indicator paper to find out when the solution is no longer acidic (✓).
      (iii) Note when the evolution of carbon dioxide stops (✓).
2. a) zinc + sulphuric acid → zinc sulphate + hydrogen (✓✓)
   b) cobalt oxide + sulphuric acid → cobalt sulphate + water (✓✓)
   c) nickel carbonate + hydrochloric acid → nickel chloride + carbon dioxide + water (✓✓✓)
   d) potassium hydroxide + nitric acid → potassium nitrate + water (✓✓)
   e) ammonia + nitric acid → ammonium nitrate (✓✓)
3. a) mix e.g. lead(II) nitrate solution and sodium sulphate solution (✓✓)
   b) lead(II) nitrate + sodium sulphate → lead(II) sulphate + sodium nitrate (✓✓✓✓)
   $Pb(NO_3)_2(aq) + Na_2SO_4(aq) \rightarrow PbSO_4(s) + 2NaNO_3(aq)$ (✓✓✓✓)
   $Pb^{2+}(aq) + SO_4^{2-}(aq) \rightarrow PbSO_4(s)$ (✓✓✓)
   c) Do not touch the lead salts with your hands. Wash your hands after the experiment (✓).
4. a) sodium sulphate + water (✓✓)
   b) ammonium chloride, no other product (✓)
   c) zinc chloride + hydrogen (✓✓)
   d) copper(II) sulphate + water (✓✓)
   e) calcium chloride + carbon dioxide + water (✓✓✓)

Your score: ☐ out of 40

Your improvement index: $\dfrac{☐/40}{☐/20} \times 100\% = ☐\%$

Answers

8 Test yourself (page 153)

Air

1. More water vapour (✓), more carbon dioxide (✓), no oxygen (✓), same amount of nitrogen (✓).
2. 21% O_2 (✓), 78% N_2 (✓)
3. Two from, for example, oxyacetylene flame, steel-making, sewage treatment, combating pollution (✓✓).
4. combustion (✓)
5. It makes a glowing splint burn more brightly (✓).
6. A = S (✓), B = Na (✓), C = Mg (✓), D = C (✓)
7. gain (✓), loss (✓), loss (✓)
8. Two from, for example, lightning, vehicle engines, Haber process, fixation by bacteria (✓✓).
9. For example, dissolving in oceans, photosynthesis (✓✓).
10. Pass through limewater, $Ca(OH)_2(aq)$ (✓). A white precipitate shows that the gas is carbon dioxide (✓).
11. Four from, for example, carbon monoxide – vehicle engines; sulphur dioxide – combustion of fuels; hydrocarbons – combustion of fuels; NO_x – vehicle engines; dust – combustion of fuels, mining, factories; lead compounds – vehicle engines (✓✓✓✓✓✓).

Your score: ☐ out of 31

8 Round up (page 162)

Air

1. a) (i) zinc oxide (✓)   (ii) carbon (✓)
   b) (i) carbon (✓)   (ii) zinc oxide (✓)
2. a) (i) iron oxide (✓)   (ii) aluminium (✓)
   b) (i) oxygen (✓)   (ii) tin sulphide (✓)
   c) (i) tin oxide (✓)   (ii) carbon (✓)
3. a) Airships need to be lighter than air (✓).
   b) Helium is a noble gas (✓); hydrogen forms an explosive mixture with air (✓).
4. a) poisonous (✓); removed by soil bacteria (✓)
   b) causes respiratory difficulties (✓); acid rain (✓)
   c) causes respiratory difficulties (✓); washed out in rain (✓)
5. a) From vehicle exhausts, power stations, factories (✓).
   b) One of the causes of acid rain (✓).
   c) catalytic converters (✓)
6. a) See pages 158–9 (✓✓).
   b) See pages 158–9 (✓✓).
   c) (i) Icecaps will melt (✓)   (ii) Flooding (✓)
      (iii) Decrease in wheat crop (✓).
7. Tall chimneys carry pollutants away from the area of the power station (✓). Taller chimneys do not prevent acid rain (✓).
8. a) Acidic water is released suddenly in the spring thaw (✓).
   b) calcium hydroxide + sulphuric acid → calcium sulphate + water (✓✓)
      $Ca(OH)_2(s) + H_2SO_4(aq) \rightarrow CaSO_4(aq) + 2H_2O(l)$ (✓✓)
   c) neutralisation (✓)
9. a) iron + sulphuric acid → iron(II) sulphate + water (✓✓)
   b) calcium carbonate + sulphuric acid → calcium sulphate + carbon dioxide + water (✓✓✓)
   c) calcium hydroxide + sulphuric acid → calcium sulphate + water (✓✓)
      (Nitric acid can be stated instead of sulphuric acid.)
10. a) carbon dioxide (✓), carbon monoxide (✓), carbon (✓), water (✓)
    b) oxides of nitrogen (✓), hydrocarbons (✓), sulphur dioxide (✓)

Your score: ☐ out of 51

Your improvement index: $\dfrac{☐/51}{☐/31} \times 100\% = $ ☐%

9 Test yourself (page 165)

Water

1. evaporation (✓), respiration (✓), transpiration (✓)
2. Carbon dioxide dissolves in rainwater (✓).
3. Limestone reacts with acidic rainwater to form the soluble salt calcium hydrogencarbonate (✓).
   calcium carbonate + carbon dioxide + water → calcium hydrogencarbonate (✓✓)
   $CaCO_3(s) + CO_2(aq) + H_2O(l) \rightarrow Ca(HCO_3)_2(aq)$ (✓✓)
4. a) Water turns anhydrous copper(II) sulphate (✓) from white to blue (✓) (or anhydrous cobalt(II) chloride from blue to pink).
   b) Pure water boils at 100 °C (or freezes at 0 °C) (✓).
5. For example, aquatic plants (✓), fish (✓), aerobic bacteria (✓).

Your score: ☐ out of 15

Answers

9 Round up (page 167)

Water

1. a) Small animals are eaten by predators (✓); larger predators eat the smaller predators (✓), and so on.
   b) A pollutant in the water becomes incorporated into the bodies of small animals (✓). A predator which eats many small animals has a higher concentration of the pollutant in its body (✓). A larger predator eats many smaller predators and builds up a still higher concentration of the pollutant in its body, and so on up the food chain (✓).
2. A rise in temperature decreases the solubility of oxygen in water (✓). It makes fish (✓) and aerobic bacteria more active (✓) thus increasing the biochemical oxygen demand (✓).
3. Oil is discharged from sewers into waterways (✓). The oxidation of hydrocarbons in the oil uses up dissolved oxygen in the water (✓).
4. Modern tankers are very large (✓). Any accident that happens involves a large loss of oil (✓).
5. Disperse oil with detergents (✓), sink it with e.g. chalk (✓), absorb the oil in straw etc. (✓), contain the oil in booms and suck it up (✓).
6. a) Eutrophication leads to an increase in the growth of algae (✓).
   b) Fertilisers do not accumulate as much in running water (✓).
   c) (i) You cannot drink water full of algae (✓).
      (ii) Propellers get entangled in algae (✓).
      (iii) Fish die because decaying algae use up all the dissolved oxygen (✓).
7. a) Excess fertiliser washes off fields in the rain and passes into groundwater (✓).
   b) Nitrates can be converted into nitrites which can cause 'blue baby syndrome' and stomach cancer (✓✓).

Your score: ☐ out of 25

Your improvement index: $\dfrac{\boxed{}/25}{\boxed{}/15} \times 100\% = \boxed{}\%$

10 Test yourself (page 169)

Planet Earth

1. crust (✓)
2. mantle (✓)
3. theory of plate (✓) tectonics (✓)
4. subduction (✓): crust moves downwards (✓) and melts (✓) to become part of the mantle (✓)
5. addition of new crust (✓) as lava (✓) from a volcano (✓) cools (✓)
6. a) igneous (✓) b) sedimentary (✓)
   c) metamorphic (✓)
7. igneous (✓)
8. Carbon dioxide is removed from the atmosphere by photosynthesis (✓) and by dissolution in oceans (✓).
9. Three from, for example, rain, rivers, glaciers, wind (✓✓✓).
10. For example, identify fossils in the rock and date them (✓).
11. Three from, for example, to neutralise acidity in lakes and soils; used as a building material; in the manufacture of cement, quicklime, glass and iron (✓✓✓).
12. For example, silicon, glass (✓✓).

Your score: ☐ out of 26

10 Round up (page 175)

Planet Earth

1. a) molten mantle (rock) (✓) below the surface of the Earth (✓)
   b) a separate piece (✓) of Earth's crust (✓)
2. a) a volcanic eruption (✓)
   b) an earthquake (✓)
3. a) Look for fossils and date the fossils (✓✓).
   b) high pressure and temperature (✓✓)
4. a) limestone (✓), sandstone (✓)
   b) basalt (✓), granite (✓), pumice (✓)
   c) marble (✓), slate (✓)
5. Three from, for example, dissolution of minerals in water, acidic rain reacting with rocks, glaciers wearing down rocks, wind blowing away rock particles (✓✓✓).
6. a) Powdered limestone is mixed with clay or shale (✓) in a rotary kiln (✓).
   b) Three from water, sand, crushed rock, calcium sulphate (✓✓✓).
7. a) The reaction can take place in the reverse direction as well as the forward direction (✓).
   b) Carbon dioxide is removed by air blowing through the kiln (✓).
   c) For example, (i) CaO is used to make Ca(OH)$_2$ which is used to reduce excess acidity in soil (✓) and mixed with sand to form mortar (✓). (ii) CO$_2$ is used to make fizzy drinks (✓) and as a fire extinguisher (✓).
8. silicon(IV) oxide (silica), calcium carbonate, sodium carbonate (✓✓✓)
9. Silicon is made from it (✓) and it is used in silicon chips (✓).

Your score: ☐ out of 36

Your improvement index: $\dfrac{\boxed{}/36}{\boxed{}/26} \times 100\% = \boxed{}\%$

Answers

11 Test yourself (page 177)

Metals and alloys

1. Metals can change shape without breaking (✓), conduct heat (✓), conduct electricity (✓).
2. Three from, for example, potassium, sodium, lithium, calcium, magnesium, aluminium, zinc, iron (✓✓✓).
3. Two from, for example, silver, gold, platinum (✓✓).
4. Three from, for example, lithium, sodium, potassium, calcium, magnesium (slowly) (✓✓✓). Products are hydrogen (✓) and the metal hydroxide (✓).
5. hydrogen (✓) and the metal chloride (✓)
6. a) Group 1 (✓) b) Group 2 (✓)
   c) Between Group 2 and Group 3 (✓).
7. Electrolysis (✓) of the molten anhydrous chloride or oxide (✓).
8. The ore is heated with limestone and coke in a blast furnace (✓✓✓).
9. Two from, for example, aluminium, chromium, nickel (✓✓).

Your score: ☐ out of 25

11 Round up (pages 183–4)

Metals and alloys

1. a) $4Na(s) + O_2(g) \rightarrow 2Na_2O(s)$ (✓✓✓, one for each symbol or formula)
   b) $2Mg(s) + O_2(g) \rightarrow 2MgO(s)$ (✓✓✓)
   c) $2Zn(s) + O_2(g) \rightarrow 2ZnO(s)$ (✓✓✓)
   d) $3Fe(s) + 2O_2(g) \rightarrow Fe_3O_4(s)$ (✓✓✓)
   e) Similar to **b** (✓✓✓)
   f) Similar to **b** (✓✓✓)
   g) Similar to **b** (✓✓✓)
2. a) (i) $Mg(s) + 2HCl(aq) \rightarrow MgCl_2(aq) + H_2(g)$ (✓✓✓✓, one for each)
      (ii) $Fe(s) + 2HCl(aq) \rightarrow FeCl_2(aq) + H_2(g)$ (✓✓✓✓)
      (iii) $Sn(s) + 2HCl(aq) \rightarrow SnCl_2(s) + H_2(g)$ (✓✓✓✓)
   b) (i) $Mg(s) + H_2SO_4(aq) \rightarrow MgSO_4(aq) + H_2(g)$ (✓✓✓✓)
      (ii) $Fe(s) + H_2SO_4(aq) \rightarrow FeSO_4(aq) + H_2(g)$ (✓✓✓✓)
3. a) magnesium sulphate and hydrogen (✓✓)
   e) zinc sulphate and hydrogen (✓✓)
   b), c), d) and f) no reaction (✓✓✓✓)
4. Copper alloys do not rust (✓). They are softer than iron (✓) and easier to mint (✓).
5. a) With water, calcium reacts steadily (✓), magnesium over several days (✓), iron rusts over a period of weeks (✓), and copper does not react (✓).
   b) With dilute hydrochloric acid, calcium reacts extremely vigorously (✓), magnesium reacts in minutes (✓), iron reacts at moderate speed with warm acid (✓), and copper does not react (✓).
6. a) The blue colour of the solution fades (✓) and a reddish brown solid is precipitated (✓).
   zinc + copper(II) sulphate → copper + zinc sulphate (✓✓)
   $Zn(s) + CuSO_4(aq) \rightarrow Cu(s) + ZnSO_4(aq)$ (✓✓)
   b) Grey crystals appear (✓).
   zinc + lead(II) nitrate → lead + zinc nitrate (✓✓)
   $Zn(s) + Pb(NO_3)_2(aq) \rightarrow Pb(s) + Zn(NO_3)_2(aq)$ (✓✓)
7. Z > X > Y (✓✓)
8. a) Au (✓) b) Na (✓), Mg (✓) c) Zn (✓), Fe (✓)
   d) Na (✓), Mg (✓), Zn (✓), Fe (✓) e) Na (✓)
   f) Mg (✓), Al (✓), Zn (✓), Fe (✓) (Na reacts with water instead of with Pb^{2+}.)
9. A: electrolysis (✓) of the molten anhydrous (✓) chloride or oxide (✓)
   B: reduction of the oxide (✓) with carbon or carbon monoxide (✓)
   C: electrolysis of a solution of the chloride (✓) or reduction of the oxide (✓)
   D: electrolysis (✓) of the molten anhydrous (✓) chloride or oxide (✓)
10. a) Rubidium (Group 1) reacts vigorously with cold water (✓), bursting into flame because of the hydrogen formed (✓) and forming a solution of the alkali rubidium hydroxide (✓).
    b) Palladium (transition metal, resembling iron) reacts with warm dilute hydrochloric acid to form hydrogen and palladium chloride (✓✓).
11. a) copper(II) oxide (✓) b) aluminium oxide + iron (✓)
    d) carbon dioxide + iron (✓) f) copper + zinc sulphate solution (✓) c) and e) no reaction (✓✓).
12. For uses of aluminium related to properties, see table on page 182. (✓✓✓✓ for four uses, ✓✓✓✓ for four properties).
13. a) oiling (✓) b) chromium-plating (✓)
    c) galvanising (coating with zinc) (✓)
    d) stainless steel (✓) e) painting (✓)
    f) sacrificial protection by e.g. zinc (✓)
    g) tin-plating (✓)
14. Saving of Earth's resources (✓), saving of energy used in extracting the metal, (✓) limiting damage to the environment through mining (✓).

Your score: ☐ out of 126

Your improvement index: $\dfrac{\Box/126}{\Box/25} \times 100\% = \Box \%$

Answers

12 Test yourself (page 186)
Reaction speeds
1. Indigestion powders (✓) because the ratio surface area : mass is greater (✓).
2. a) Use smaller pieces of zinc (✓), use a more concentrated solution of acid (✓), raise the temperature (✓).
   b) In smaller particles, the ratio surface area : mass is larger (✓). At a higher concentration, collisions take place more frequently between hydrogen ions and zinc (✓). At a higher temperature, the hydrogen ions have higher energy (✓), and collide more frequently with the particles of zinc (✓).
3. An apparatus with a gas syringe, see page 187, and a clock (✓✓✓✓).
4. A catalyst is a substance which increases the rate of a chemical reaction without being used up in the reaction (✓✓).
5. Industrial manufacturers can make their product more rapidly or at a lower temperature with the use of a catalyst (✓✓).
6. photosynthesis, photography (✓✓)

Your score: ☐ out of 20

12 Round up (page 188)
Reaction speeds
1. a) Carbon dioxide is given off (✓).
   b) (i) C   (ii) A   (iii) B (✓✓).
   c) The ratio of surface area : volume differs (✓).
2. Cut them into smaller pieces (✓). Use a higher temperature by using a pressure cooker (✓).
3. Use an apparatus such as that shown on page 187 (bottom) (✓). Using potato, measure the volume of oxygen formed at certain times after the start of the reaction (✓). Plot volume against time (✓). Repeat the measurement using manganese(IV) oxide. Compare the two graphs (✓).
4. You could take pieces of magnesium ribbon of the same length and therefore approximately the same mass (✓). You could find out how long it took (✓) for a piece of magnesium ribbon to react completely with a certain volume of acid (✓) of a certain concentration (✓) at different temperatures (✓). You could plot time against temperature or 1/time (rate) against temperature (✓).
5. a) Axes labelled correctly and units shown (✓), points plotted correctly (✓), points covering at least half of each scale (✓), smooth lines drawn through the points (✓).
   b) B (✓)
   c) Your line should show very slow evolution of oxygen (✓).

Your score: ☐ out of 22

Your improvement index: $\dfrac{\boxed{}/22}{\boxed{}/20} \times 100\% = \boxed{}\%$

13 Test yourself (page 190)
Tackling chemical calculations
1. a) 64 (✓)   b) 80 (✓)   c) 98 (✓)   d) 60 (✓)
   e) 249.5 (✓)
2. a) 2.0 mol (✓)   b) 2 mol (✓)   c) 0.25 mol (✓)
3. a) 20.1 g (✓)   b) 24.5 g (✓)   c) 120 g (✓)
4. a) $HgBr_2$ (✓)   b) $CuCl_2$ (✓)   c) Na_2O (✓)
5. a) 50% (✓)   b) 40% (✓)   c) 33% (✓)
6. 1 g (✓)
7. a) 6.6 g (✓)   b) 3.6 dm^3 at rtp (✓)
8. a) 1250 tonnes (✓)   b) 9.4×10^8 dm^3 (✓)
9. Loss (✓) of £8.30 (✓)

Your score: ☐ out of 24

13 Round up
The mole (page 192)
1. a) gram, kilogram (✓)   b) mole (✓)
2. Weigh out a) the relative atomic mass in grams (✓)
   b) the relative molecular mass in grams (✓).
3. a) 24 g (✓)   b) 69 g (✓)   c) 8 g (✓)   d) 16 g (✓)
   e) 8 g (✓)   f) 16 g (✓)
4. a) 0.33 mol (✓)   b) 0.25 mol (✓)   c) 2.0 mol (✓)
   d) 0.010 mol (✓)   e) 0.33 mol (✓)   f) 20 mol (✓)
5. a) 88 g (✓)   b) 980 g (✓)   c) 117 g (✓)   d) 37 g (✓)
6. a) 16 (✓)   b) 28 (✓)   c) 44 (✓)   d) 64 (✓)   e) 40 (✓)
   f) 74.5 (✓)   g) 40 (✓)   h) 74 (✓)   i) 63 (✓)
   j) 123.5 (✓)   k) 80 (✓)   l) 159.5 (✓)   m) 249.5 (✓)

Your score: ☐ out of 33

Formulas (page 193)
1. D (✓)
2. A = Mg_3N_2 (✓),   B = Fe_3O_4 (✓),   C = SiO_2 (✓),
   D = $MgSO_4$ (✓),   E = C_3H_8 (✓)
3. a) C = 80%, H = 20% (✓✓)
   b) S = 40%, O = 60% (✓✓)
   c) N = 35%, H = 5%, O = 60% (✓✓✓)
   d) Ca = 20%, Br = 80% (✓✓)

Your score: ☐ out of 15

Answers

Reacting masses (page 194)
1. 8.0 g (✓)
2. 71 g (✓)
3. 0.05 g (✓)
4. 3.06 kg (✓)
5. 0.26 g (✓)

Your score: ☐ out of 5

Total round-up score: ☐ + ☐ + ☐ = ☐ out of 53

Your improvement index: $\dfrac{\square/53}{\square/24} \times 100\% = \square\%$

14 Test yourself (page 196)
Fuels
1. Coal and oil were formed from the remains of plants and trees (coal) (✓) and sea animals and plants (oil) (✓) which lived millions of years ago (✓).
2. It is burnt in power stations (✓).
3. a) fractional distillation (✓)
   b) Four from: petroleum gas, gasoline, kerosene, diesel oil, fuel oil (✓✓✓✓).
   c) Two from lubricating oil, bitumen, naphtha (✓✓)
4. a) methane (✓) b) ethane (✓) c) propane (✓)
   d) the alkane series (✓)
5. Converting hydrocarbons with large molecules (✓) and high boiling points (✓) into hydrocarbons with smaller molecules (✓) and lower boiling points (✓).
6. a) combustion (✓), respiration (✓)
   b) photosynthesis (✓), cracking of hydrocarbons (✓)

Your score: ☐ out of 23

14 Round up (page 200)
Fuels
1. a) Fossil fuels are formed by the decay (✓) of the remains of plants (✓) and animals (✓) over long periods of time (✓).
   b) Fossil fuels took millions of years to form (✓) and we are using them up much more quickly (✓).
2. Three of the five methods mentioned on page 167 (✓✓✓).
3. a) Fractional distillation (✓) separates the fractions on the basis of their different boiling point ranges (✓).
   b) For uses see the diagram on page 197 (✓✓✓✓✓).
   c) Gasoline has a lower boiling point (✓), lower ignition temperature (✓) and lower viscosity than fuel oil (✓).
   d) It does not vaporise (✓) and does not ignite (✓).
   e) Fuels from petroleum oil are important in transport (✓), industry (✓) and power generation (✓). Oil is a source of valuable petrochemicals (✓).

4. As for exothermic energy diagram on page 199 (✓✓), exothermic (✓).
5. As for endothermic energy diagram on page 199 (✓✓), endothermic (✓).
6. a) 124 kJ/mol (✓)
   b) 484 kJ/mol (✓)
   c) 56 kJ/mol (✓)

Your score: ☐ out of 35

Your improvement index: $\dfrac{\square/35}{\square/23} \times 100\% = \square\%$

15 Test yourself (page 202)
Alkenes and plastics
1. $\mathrm{>C=C<}$ (✓), addition reactions (✓)
2. Alkenes are reactive (✓) and are therefore the starting materials for the manufacture of many other compounds (✓).
3. Bromine adds across the double bond to form $BrCH_2CH_2Br$ (✓).
4. a) Addition of water across the double bond (✓).
   b) ethanol, C_2H_5OH (✓)
5. a) Addition of hydrogen across a double bond (✓).
   b) Catalytic hydrogenation is used to convert unsaturated oils (vegetable oils) into saturated fats, which are solid, in the manufacture of margarine (✓).
6. The addition of many identical small molecules to form a large molecule (✓). The substance with small molecules is the monomer; the substance with large molecules is the polymer (✓).
7. Thermosetting plastics can be softened by heat and hardened by cooling (✓) many times (✓). Thermosetting plastics are softened by heat (✓) only during manufacture (✓).
8. For thermosoftening plastics a continuous process is used (✓). For thermosetting plastics, a batch process is used (✓).

Your score: ☐ out of 17

15 Round up (page 205)

Alkenes and plastics

1 a) (i) ethane C_2H_6 (✓), ethene C_2H_4 (✓)

(ii) ethane: H—C(H)(H)—C(H)(H)—H ; ethene: H—C(H)=C(H)—H (✓✓)

b) Ethane has only single bonds (✓); it is a saturated compound (✓). Ethene has a carbon–carbon double bond (✓); it is an unsaturated compound (✓).

2 a) Two from hydrogen, bromine, water, sulphuric acid (✓✓).
b) addition reactions (✓)
c) hydrogen with a nickel catalyst (✓✓)

3 a) carbon dioxide (✓) and water (✓)
b) Alkenes are a source of valuable chemicals (✓).

4 a) propane: H—C(H)(H)—C(H)(H)—C(H)(H)—H ; propene: H—C(H)(H)—C(H)=C(H)—H (✓✓)
b) propene (✓)
c) H—C(H)(H)—C(H)(Br)—C(H)(Br)—H (✓)

5 a) less breakable (✓)
b) cheaper, less breakable, non-toxic (✓)
c) much less breakable (✓)

6 $-(-C(H)(H)-C(H)(CONH_2)-)_n-$ (✓)

7 a) When deformed, a plastic changes shape (✓) and retains the new shape when the deforming force is removed (✓).
b) Thermoplastic – can be softened by heat (✓) many times (✓).
Thermosetting – can be moulded only once (✓).
Thermoplastic – individual chains can move with respect to one another (✓).
Thermosetting – chains are cross-linked (✓).

8 Two from, for example, poly(ethene), poly(chloroethene), poly(propene) (✓✓). Uses: poly(ethene) for plastic bags, kitchenware, laboratory tubing, toys; poly(chloroethene) for plastic bottles, wellington boots, raincoats, electrical insulation, gutters; poly(propene) for hospital equipment that must be sterilised, as fibres for ropes and fishing nets (✓✓).

9 a) Most plastics cannot be decomposed by natural biological processes (✓).
b) Plastic rubbish accumulates in landfill sites and never decomposes (✓).
c) Some plastics form toxic combustion products (✓). Also, burning them is a waste of Earth's resources (✓).
d) recycling (✓)

Your score: ☐ out of 40

Your improvement index: $\dfrac{\Box/40}{\Box/17} \times 100\% = \Box\%$

Physical processes

1	**Beyond the Earth**	**219**
1.1	Gravity	220
1.2	The Solar System	221
1.3	Life as a star	223
1.4	The expansion of the Universe	225
2	**Energy resources and energy transfer**	**227**
2.1	Work and energy	228
2.2	More about kinetic and potential energy	229
2.3	Power and efficiency	230
2.4	Heat transfer	231
2.5	Controlling heat transfer	232
2.6	Energy resources	233
3	**Radioactivity**	**235**
3.1	Inside the atom	235
3.2	Radioactive isotopes	237
3.3	Radioactive emissions	238
3.4	Half-life	239
3.5	Using radioactivity	240
3.6	Nuclear reactors	241
4	**Waves**	**244**
4.1	What is a wave?	244
4.2	Transverse and longitudinal waves	245
4.3	Measuring waves	246
4.4	Wave properties	247
5	**Sound waves and seismic waves**	**249**
5.1	Properties of sound	249
5.2	Ultrasound	251
5.3	Seismic waves	252
6	**Light**	**254**
6.1	Reflection	255
6.2	Refraction	256
6.3	Fibre optics	257
6.4	Light and colour	258
7	**The electromagnetic spectrum**	**261**
7.1	Using electromagnetic waves	261
7.2	Electromagnetic waves in medicine	263
7.3	Communications	264
8	**Force and motion**	**267**
8.1	Speed and distance	268
8.2	Acceleration	269
8.3	On the road	270
8.4	Force and acceleration	271
8.5	Work and energy	272
9	**Forces in balance**	**275**
9.1	Equilibrium	276
9.2	Strength of solids	278
9.3	Pressure and its measurement	279
9.4	Hydraulics	280
9.5	Gases	281
10	**Electric charge**	**283**
10.1	Electrostatics	284
10.2	Electrostatics at work	286
10.3	Current and charge	287
10.4	Electrolysis	288
11	**Electric circuits**	**290**
11.1	Current and potential difference	291
11.2	Resistance	292
11.3	Components	293
11.4	Mains electricity	294
11.5	Electrical safety	295
12	**Electromagnetism**	**297**
12.1	Magnetism	298
12.2	The electric motor	299
12.3	Electromagnetic induction	300
12.4	Transformers	302

Equations and symbols you should know	**304**
Answers	**305**
Index	**315**

Beyond the Earth — Chapter 1

PREVIEW

At the end of this topic you will be able to:

- recall the main features of the planets
- interpret data about the planets
- use the theory of gravity to explain the motion of the planets, the Moon, satellites and comets
- describe the life cycle of a star
- describe evidence for the expansion of the Universe.
- describe how the future of the Universe depends on the amount of mass present.

How much do you already know? Work out your score on page 305.

Test yourself

1. List the planets Mars (M), Jupiter (J), Neptune (N), Uranus (U) and Venus (V) in order of *increasing* distance from the Sun. [5]

2. State two factors that determine the force of gravity due to the Sun on a planet. [2]

3. Why does the brightness of a planet vary? [2]

4. Why can you see different constellations in the night sky during the year? [2]

5. a) Of the planets Mercury, Venus, Mars and Jupiter, which one is rocky and further from the Sun than Earth is? [1]

    b) Which of the above four planets does not have a solid surface? [1]

6. A comet X orbits the Sun once every 76 years. It was last seen from Earth in 1985 when it was visible for about a year. By the year 2050, is it likely to be

    a) slowing down or speeding up [1]

    b) moving towards or away from the Sun? [1]

7. What is the name of the process that releases energy in the core of a star? [1]

8. What is a supernova? [2]

9. What is meant by 'red shift'? [2]

10. What did the astronomer Edwin Hubble discover? [2]

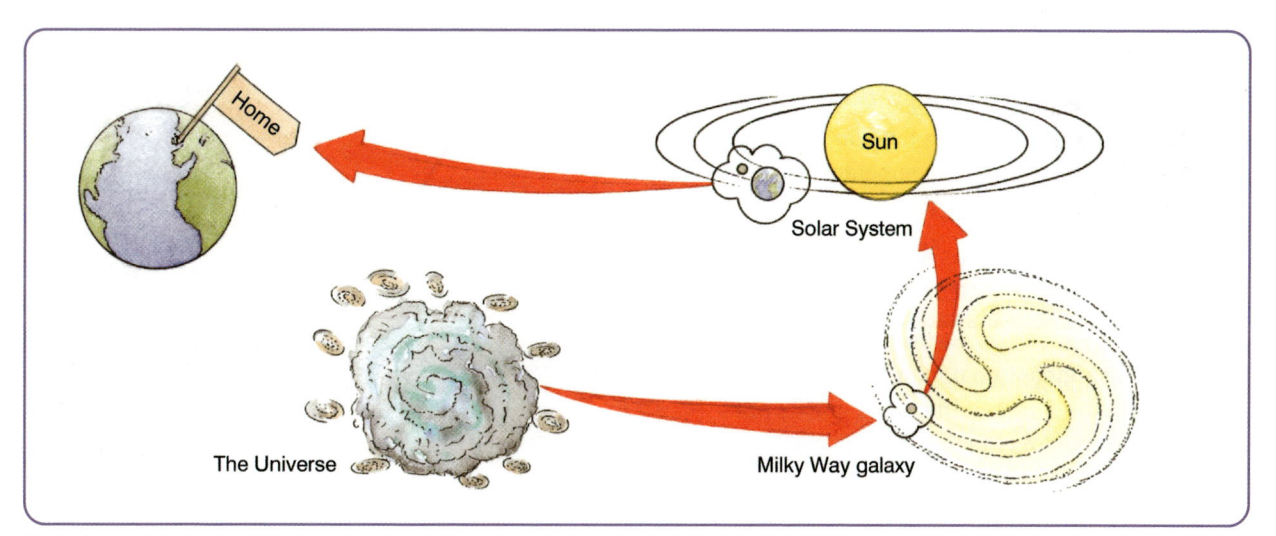

Where do you fit in?

Beyond the Earth

1.1 Gravity

A mysterious force

Any two objects attract each other. This force of attraction is called **gravity**. The greater the masses of the two objects or the closer they are, the stronger the force of gravity between them. The planets, the Moon, satellites and comets all stay in their orbits because of the force of gravity. You stay on the Earth because of the force of gravity between you and the Earth.

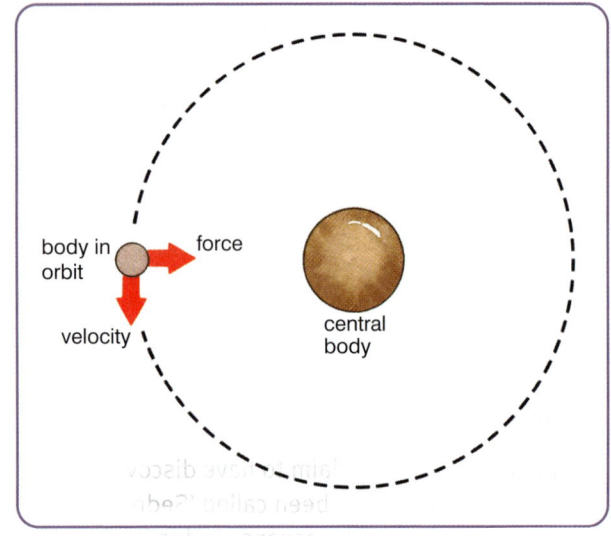

In orbit

Comets

★ Comets move round the Sun in elliptical orbits, usually in a different plane from the Earth's orbit.

★ As a comet approaches the Sun, it moves faster because the Sun's gravity is stronger closer in.

★ It also becomes visible near the Sun because solar heating raises the comet's temperature until it glows.

★ A comet usually develops a tail when it is near the Sun, as particles streaming from the Sun 'blow' glowing matter away from the comet.

★ Comets disappear into darkness as they move away from the Sun, but the Sun's gravity pulls them back towards the Sun again.

Scaling down

If the Sun was represented by a football, the Earth would be a pea 50 metres away from it. Pluto would be a small seed over 2 km away, still held in the Solar System by the force of gravity between it and the Sun.

Satellites

★ **Artificial satellites** are kept in their orbits because of the Earth's gravity. The greater the radius of orbit, the longer its **time period** (the time it takes to go round Earth once).

★ **Communication satellites** orbit the Earth at a certain height above the equator, with a time period of 24 hours. This means that they are always in the same place as seen from the Earth.

★ **Polar satellites** are in low orbits which take them over both poles once every few hours. They have a wide range of uses, including weather forecasting, surveying and spying.

★ **The Moon** is a natural satellite of the Earth. Its radius of orbit is so great that it takes over 27 days to orbit the Earth once.

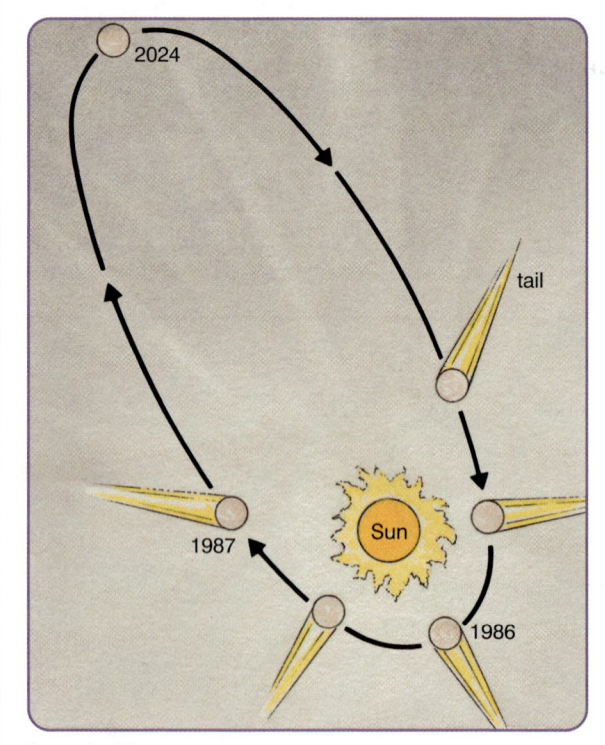

A comet orbit

Beyond the Earth

1.2 The Solar System

Planets in perspective

★ The planets all move round the Sun in the same direction.

★ Their orbits are almost circular, except for Pluto, and in the same plane as the Earth's orbit.

★ The planets reflect sunlight, which is why we can see them.

★ The further a planet is from the Sun, the longer it takes to go round its orbit.

★ When we observe the planets from Earth, they appear to move through the constellations as they go round the Sun.

★ The brightness of a planet varies as its distance from Earth changes and the amount of its sunlit surface we can see changes.

On another planet

Mercury and **Venus** are called the 'inner planets' because they are closer to the Sun than Earth is. They are rocky, without moons. **Mars** is a rocky planet like the Earth and the inner planets. **Jupiter**, **Saturn**, **Uranus** and **Neptune** are giant spinning balls of fluid. **Pluto** is a small rocky planet.

Handy hint

To remember the order of the planets from the Sun, use the mnemonic '**M**ake **V**ery **E**asy **M**ash, **J**ust **S**tart **U**sing **N**ew **P**otatoes'!

Wandering stars

Ancient astronomers called the planets 'wandering stars' because they move through the constellations gradually. This is because the time each planet takes to move round its orbit is different for each planet. Seen from the Earth, the position of a planet against the constellations therefore changes because it moves round its orbit at a different speed from the speed of the Earth.

Questions

1. Use the chart of the planets on the next page to answer each of the following questions:
   a) Which planets do not have any moons?
   b) Which planets have just one moon each?
   c) Which planet has a ring system that can be seen from Earth?

2. Use the table of data on the next page to answer each of the following questions:
   a) What is the closest distance, in astronomical units, that the Earth and Venus come to each other?
   b) How much bigger in diameter is the Sun than Jupiter?
   c) How much greater in mass is the Sun than Jupiter?

3. Use the information in the chart to explain why Saturn's rings can be seen from Earth whereas Jupiter's rings cannot.

Welcome to Sedna!

Astronomers in 2004 claim to have discovered a tenth planet which has been called 'Sedna' after the Inuit goddess of the oceans. Sedna is thought to be about the same size as Pluto but three times further from the Sun than Pluto.

Answers

1 a) Mercury and Venus b) Earth and Pluto c) Saturn
2 a) 0.3 A.U. b) 10 times c) 1050 times
3 Saturn's rings reflect sunlight much better than Jupiter's ring system.

Beyond the Earth

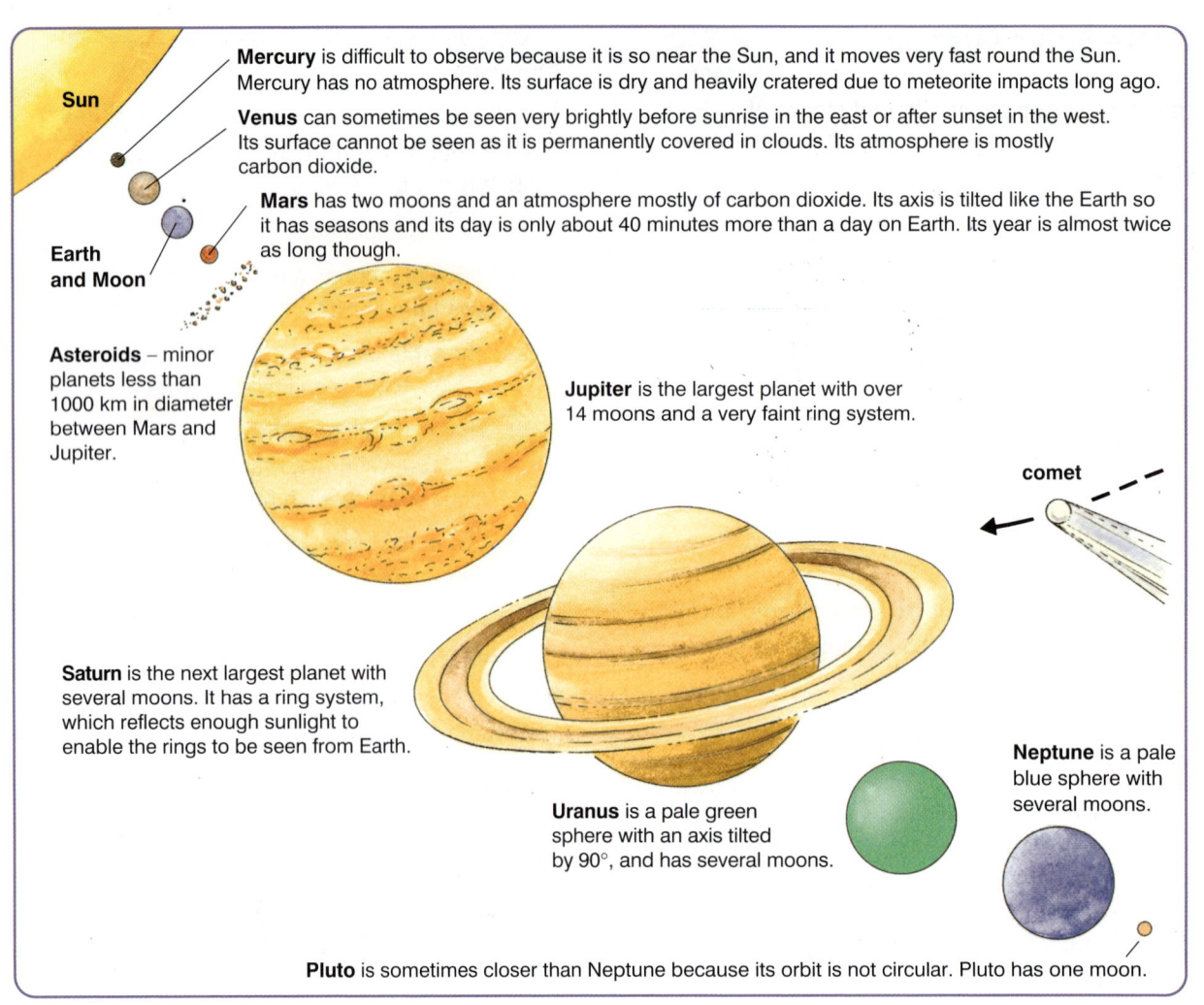

Mercury is difficult to observe because it is so near the Sun, and it moves very fast round the Sun. Mercury has no atmosphere. Its surface is dry and heavily cratered due to meteorite impacts long ago.

Venus can sometimes be seen very brightly before sunrise in the east or after sunset in the west. Its surface cannot be seen as it is permanently covered in clouds. Its atmosphere is mostly carbon dioxide.

Mars has two moons and an atmosphere mostly of carbon dioxide. Its axis is tilted like the Earth so it has seasons and its day is only about 40 minutes more than a day on Earth. Its year is almost twice as long though.

Asteroids – minor planets less than 1000 km in diameter between Mars and Jupiter.

Jupiter is the largest planet with over 14 moons and a very faint ring system.

Saturn is the next largest planet with several moons. It has a ring system, which reflects enough sunlight to enable the rings to be seen from Earth.

Uranus is a pale green sphere with an axis tilted by 90°, and has several moons.

Neptune is a pale blue sphere with several moons.

Pluto is sometimes closer than Neptune because its orbit is not circular. Pluto has one moon.

The planets

planet	distance from the sun in AU	time to orbit the sun in years	Mass of planet / Mass of Earth	Diameter of planet / Diameter of Earth
Mercury	0.4	0.24	0.06	0.4
Venus	0.7	0.61	0.8	1.0
Earth	1	1	1	1
Mars	1.5	1.9	0.11	0.5
Jupiter	5.2	11.9	318	11.2
Saturn	9.5	29.5	95	9.5
Uranus	19.2	84	15	3.7
Neptune	30	165	17	3.5
Pluto	39	250	0.002	0.4

1 astronomical unit (AU) = 150 million km
mass of Sun = 330 000 × mass of Earth
diameter of Sun = 110 × diameter of Earth

Beyond the Earth

1.3 Life as a star

★ The stars we see are at different stages of evolution and they vary in size, brightness and lifetime.

★ Massive bright stars last no more than a few million years.

★ Small dim stars shine for thousands of millions of years.

★ The Sun is thought to be a typical middle-aged star about half way through its life cycle of about 10 000 million years.

Formation
- A star forms from dust and gas in space pulled in by its own gravity.
- As its density rises, it becomes hotter and hotter due to the release of gravitational energy.
- The planets are thought to have formed from the dust clouds left over at this stage.

Birth
- At a temperature of about 10 million degrees, the nuclei of hydrogen atoms fuse together, releasing nuclear energy.
- This energy keeps the star temperature high enough for nuclear fusion to continue. A star is born!

Equilibrium
- For most of its life, the star gradually fuses the hydrogen nuclei in its core into heavier nuclei such as helium.
- The nuclear reactions in the core release vast amounts of electromagnetic and particle radiation.
- The inward gravitational attraction on the core is balanced by outward pressure due to this radiation.

Expansion
- Eventually, the hydrogen in the core is used up and the star expands to become a **red giant**.
- This is thought to occur because the helium nuclei and other light nuclei formed from the hydrogen nuclei fuse to form heavier nuclei, releasing more radiation, which forces the star to swell out.

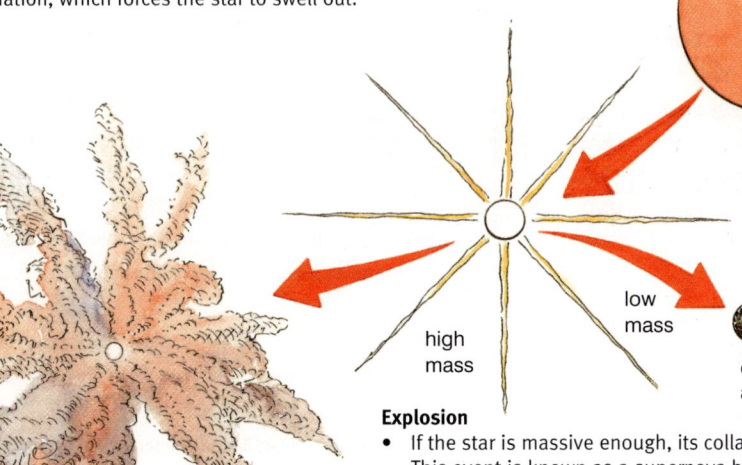

Collapse
- Once there are no more light nuclei to fuse together, the star collapses due to its own gravity.
- It becomes very hot, very dense and very small. It is now referred to as a **white dwarf**.

Explosion
- If the star is massive enough, its collapse is followed by a massive explosion. This event is known as a supernova because the star suddenly outshines entire galaxies.
- The supernova event is thought to leave behind an extremely dense object known as a **neutron star**, which is composed only of neutrons.
- If the star was very massive, a **black hole** is left behind. Nothing can escape from a black hole, not even light, because its gravity is so strong.

The life cycle of a star

Beyond the Earth

Sandaluk II

Supernovae are rare events. The Crab Nebula in the constellation Taurus is thought to be the remnants of an eleventh century supernova. In 1987, a supernova was observed in the Andromeda galaxy. It was thought to be the death throes of a star called Sandaluk II.

In a supernova explosion, large heavy nuclei are formed from the fusion of lighter nuclei. Dense elements like uranium found in the Earth mean that the Earth and the Sun probably formed from the debris of a supernova explosion.

SETI, the search for extra-terrestrial intelligence

★ Astronomers now know that planets orbit other stars. Large telescopes enable astronomers to see planets in orbit round nearby stars. Some stars 'wobble' because of the gravitational pull of a planet too small to see.

★ Other solar systems exist, probably containing small planets like Earth. They are too far away for space travel.

★ Radio telescopes are being used to find out if intelligent life exists beyond Earth, capable of transmitting radio signals. This search for extra-terrestrial intelligence (SETI) has not discovered any such signals yet.

★ Life in the form of microbes might exist or have existed on the other planets of our own solar system. Evidence of microbes has been found in a meteorite discovered in Antarctica, and thought to be from Mars. Space probes sent to one or two areas of Mars have not yet found evidence of life.

Are we alone?

About one in ten stars might have planets. About one in ten planets could be Earth-like. Intelligent life perhaps exists on a planet for about ten thousand years, a period of time less than a millionth of its existence. Even though our galaxy contains about a billion stars, intelligent life may not exist elsewhere in our galaxy at the present time.

Questions

1 When a star forms from dust clouds, it becomes so hot that its nuclei fuse together and release more energy. Why does it become hot when it forms from dust?

2 List the main stages in the life cycle of a massive star.

3 What evidence is there that the Sun and its solar system formed from the remnants of a supernova?

4 List the main points in support of the view that
   a) life probably exists elsewhere in our galaxy,
   b) life in our galaxy beyond Earth, if it exists at all, may not be intelligent.

Answers

1 The dust clouds attract each other due to their own gravity and become more and more dense. Gravitational potential energy is converted into kinetic energy of the dust particles, which become very hot when they collide with each other.

2 Formation from dust and cloud; heating up until fusion starts; steady emission of light as a star; sudden expansion as a red giant; collapse to a white dwarf; sudden explosion as a supernova.

3 Atoms heavier than iron atoms are present in our solar system. These atoms can only be formed in a supernova explosion. Therefore, our solar system must have formed from the remnants of a supernova explosion.

4 (a) Evidence of microbes in a meteorite thought to have come from Mars; about 1 in 100 stars probably have Earth-like planets, (b) SETI radio telescopes have not detected any extra-terrestrial radio signals yet.

Beyond the Earth

1.4 The expansion of the Universe

Galaxies

★ The Sun is just one of billions of stars in the Milky Way galaxy.

★ There are many other galaxies.

★ The nearest galaxy is about 10 million light years away.

★ The furthest is about 12 000 million light years away.

The red shift

The spectrum of light from a star is crossed by dark vertical lines. These are caused by substances in the star's outer layers absorbing light of certain wavelengths. **Edwin Hubble** discovered that the absorption lines due to the same substances in the light spectra of distant galaxies are red-shifted towards longer wavelengths in the spectrum. This is because these galaxies are moving away from us very quickly so their light waves are lengthened.

Hubble made precise measurements and discovered that the speed of a galaxy is greater the more distant the galaxy is. This important discovery is known as **Hubble's law**.

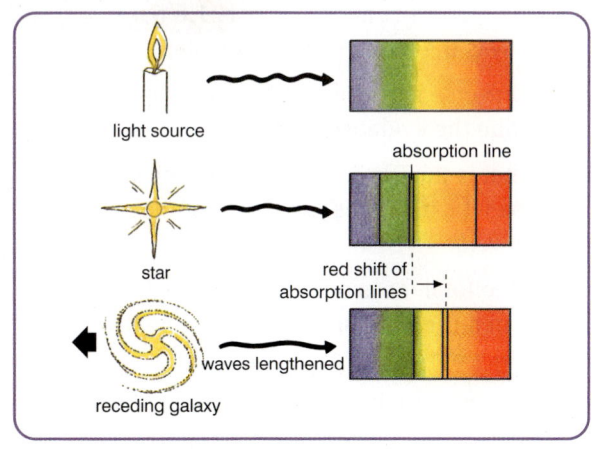

Starlight spectra

Question

If the age of the Universe at 15 000 million years was scaled down to start 24 hours ago, when would life on Earth (one million years ago) have started?

The Big Bang

All the distant galaxies are rushing away from us. Scientists think the Universe is expanding. This would explain why distant galaxies are moving away faster and faster the further they are from us. The expansion started about 15 billion years ago in a huge explosion called the **Big Bang**. At present, it is not known whether the expansion will continue indefinitely or reverse – ending perhaps in the Big Crunch!

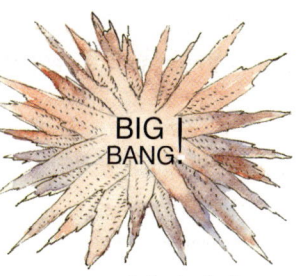

In the beginning

The Big Bang theory was only accepted after astronomers detected background microwave radiation from **all** directions in space. Before this discovery, many scientists doubted the Big Bang theory and they favoured the **Steady State** theory. This theory is based on the idea that the Universe has always existed and is the same now as it always was. Matter was thought to be entering the Universe at so-called 'white holes' in space, pushing the galaxies away from each other. The Steady State theory could not explain the presence of background microwave radiation whereas the Big Bang theory predicts its presence as radiation released in the Big Bang.

The future of the Universe

★ No object can travel faster than light. Light from the Big Bang defines the edge of the Universe, which is expanding at present. Hubble estimated that the edge of the Universe is about 12 000 million light years away!

★ The expansion of the Universe could continue forever or slow down and reverse, depending on the total mass of the Universe, which is not known at present. If the mass of the Universe is sufficiently large, the expansion will slow down and reverse leading to the Big Crunch! If it is too small, the expansion will continue forever at a decreasing rate of expansion.

Recent measurements suggest an increasing rate of expansion, indicating the existence of a cosmic repulsion force.

Answer 7 seconds ago

Beyond the Earth

ROUND UP

How much have you improved? Work out your improvement index on page 305.

1. **a)** Explain why the planets of the Solar System do not leave the Solar System. [2]

   b) Why does the Earth orbit the Sun whereas the Moon orbits the Earth? [1]

2. During the night, the constellations move across the sky. Explain why this happens. [2]

3. **a)** Stars produce their own light but planets do not. Explain why we can see the planets. [1]

   b) The diagram shows the planet Venus in two different positions on its orbit relative to the Earth. A sketch was made of Venus in each of these positions, viewed through a large telescope. Decide which sketch is for which position, and explain your reasons. [2]

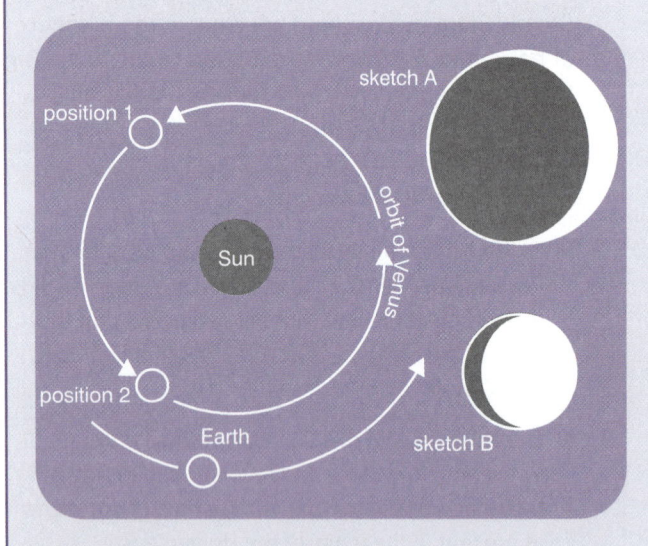

4. List the following astronomical objects in order of increasing distance from Earth:

   Andromeda galaxy, Moon, Pole star, Sun [4]

5. **a)** Draw a sketch to show the relative positions of the Sun, the Earth and Jupiter when Jupiter is easily visible in the night sky. [1]

   b) State four differences between the Earth and **(i)** Mars **(ii)** Jupiter **(iii)** Saturn. [12]

6. **a)** Mercury is very difficult to observe. Why? [3]

   b) Pluto is the most distant planet, yet it can be closer than Neptune to the Sun. Why? [2]

   c) Uranus is closer to the Sun than Neptune is. Which takes longer to go round the Sun? [1]

   d) Why do comets disappear and then return? [3]

7. **a)** Betelgeuse is a red giant star. Why is it described as a red giant? [2]

   b) Describe what will happen to the Sun when it uses up all the hydrogen nuclei in its core. [4]

   c) What is a supernova? [2]

8. **a)** Why is it difficult to launch satellites into orbit? [3]

   b) The Earth's surface gravity is 10 N/kg. The Moon's surface gravity is 1.6 N/kg. Why is the Moon's gravity smaller? [2]

9. The Universe is thought to be expanding. Describe the evidence for this. [4]

10. **a)** What is the Big Bang theory and how does it explain the expansion of the Universe? [2]

    b) If the total mass of the Universe is less than a certain amount, what will be the future of the Universe? [2]

    c) Write a short account of the possibilities of life in the Universe beyond Earth. [5]

Well done if you've improved. Don't worry if you haven't. Take a break and try again.

Energy resources and energy transfer — Chapter 2

PREVIEW

At the end of this topic you will be able to:

- describe different forms of energy
- explain what is meant by work, energy and power
- describe the energy changes when work is done or when heat transfer takes place
- explain what is meant by conservation of energy, efficiency and energy waste
- carry out calculations using the formulae for kinetic energy, potential energy, power and efficiency.

How much do you already know? Work out your score on pages 305–6.

Test yourself

Assume $g = 10$ N/kg where necessary.

1. A cyclist freewheels down a road and eventually comes to rest. Which one of the following sequences **A** to **D** best describes the energy changes in this process?

    A chemical ⟶ potential ⟶ kinetic
    B potential ⟶ kinetic ⟶ thermal
    C potential ⟶ chemical ⟶ kinetic
    D chemical ⟶ kinetic ⟶ thermal [1]

2. State the correct units for weight and power, respectively. [2]

3. A weightlifter raises an object of mass 60 kg from the floor to a height of 2.0 m. Calculate the gain of potential energy of the object. [1]

4. An object of weight 2.0 N is held 4.0 m above a floor and then released. Calculate its kinetic energy and its potential energy in joules
    a) when it is 1.0 m above the floor [2]
    b) just before it hits the floor. [2]

5. A person uses a 1.0 kW electric heater for 4 hours and a 3.0 kW electric oven for 2 hours. Calculate the total number of kilowatt hours used. [2]

6. A trolley of mass 20 kg is released at the top of a slope of height 10 m and allowed to run down the slope. Its speed at the bottom of the slope is 5.0 m/s. Calculate the ratio of the trolley's loss of potential energy to its gain of kinetic energy. [3]

7. Why are metals good conductors of heat? [3]

8. Home heating bills may be reduced by installing
    a) double glazed windows instead of ordinary windows
    b) felt insulation in the loft
    c) draught excluders round the door frames.

    Which of the above measures reduces heat loss due to thermal conduction or thermal radiation? [2]

9. Which of the above measures reduces heat loss due to thermal convection? [1]

10. A falling weight is used to turn an electricity generator which is used to light a bulb, as shown in the diagram. Complete the energy flow diagram below. [5]

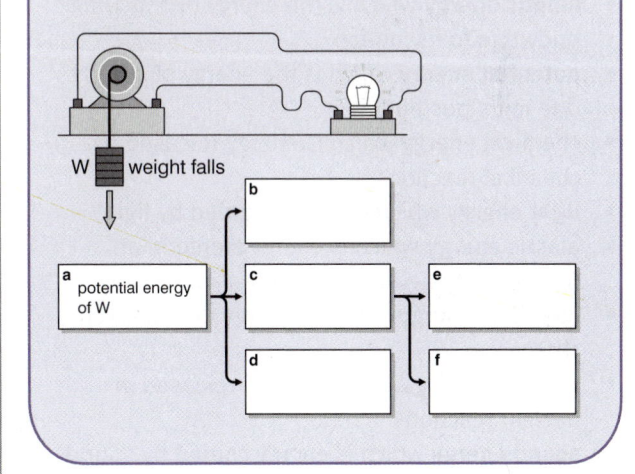

227

Energy resources and energy transfer

2.1 Work and energy

Time for work

Work is done when a force makes an object move. The greater the force or the further the movement, the greater the amount of work done. For example, the work done to lift a box to a height of 2 m is twice the work done to lift the same box to a height of 1 m.

Energy is the capacity to do work. A battery-operated electric motor used to raise a weight does work on the weight. The battery therefore contains energy because it has the capacity to make the motor do work.

Heat is energy transferred due to a difference of temperature. Heat and work are two methods by which energy can be transferred to or from a body. Work is energy transferred due to force and heat is energy transferred due to temperature difference. Heat as a method of transferring energy is discussed in more detail on page 231.

Energy can be changed from one form into other forms.

Forms of energy

Energy exists in different forms, including:
- **kinetic energy** which is the energy of a moving body due to its motion
- **potential energy** which is the energy of a body due to its position
- **chemical energy** which is energy released by chemical reactions
- **light energy** which is energy carried by light
- **elastic energy** which is energy stored in an object by changing its shape
- **electrical energy** which is energy due to electric charge
- **nuclear energy** which is energy released in nuclear reactions
- **sound energy** which is energy carried by sound waves
- **thermal energy** which is the energy of an object due to its temperature.

Temperature is the hotness of an object and is measured in degrees Celsius (°C).

The Celsius scale of temperature is defined in terms of **ice point**, 0°C, which is the temperature of pure melting ice, and **steam point**, 100 °C, which is the temperature of steam at atmospheric pressure.

Measuring energy

Work and energy are measured in joules (J), where one joule is defined as the work done when a force of one newton acts over a distance of one metre in the direction of the force.

The following equation is used to calculate the work done (or energy transferred) by a force:

work done (or energy transferred) = force × distance moved in the direction of the force

$$W = F \times s$$
(in joules)   (in newtons)   (in metres)

Questions

a) A student applies a force of 600 N to a wardrobe and pushes it a distance of 2.0 m across a floor. Calculate the work done by the student.

b) If the wardrobe had been emptied, it could have been pushed across the floor using a force of 200 N. How far could it have been moved for the same amount of work?

c) Describe the energy changes in the picture below.

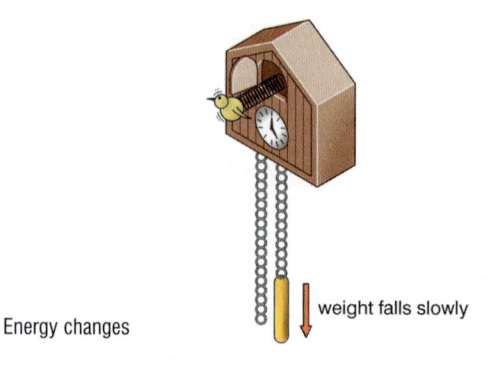

Energy changes — weight falls slowly

Answers

a) 1200 J b) 6.0 m
c) Potential energy of the weight → kinetic energy of the moving parts of the clock + sound

Energy resources and energy transfer

2.2 More about kinetic and potential energy

Gravitational potential energy (GPE)

For an object of mass m raised through a height h,

$$\text{its gain of potential energy} = mgh$$

where g is the gravitational field strength.

Note that for an object of mass m, its **weight** = mg because g is the force of gravity per unit mass on an object. Also, the mass must be in kilograms and the height gain in metres to give the gain of potential energy in joules. The value of g on the Earth is 10 N/kg.

Kinetic energy (KE)

For an object of mass m moving at speed v,

$$\text{its kinetic energy} = \tfrac{1}{2}mv^2$$

Proof of this formula is not required at GCSE. Note that the mass must be in kilograms and the speed in metres per second to give the kinetic energy in joules.

Questions

1. How much gravitational potential energy does a 60 kg swimmer gain as a result of climbing a height of 15 m?

2. a) If the swimmer in question 1 dives from a diving board 15 m above the water, how much kinetic energy does the swimmer have just before impact?

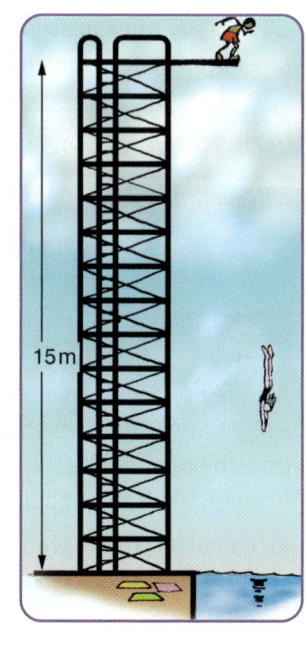

   b) Calculate the swimmer's speed just before impact.

A very important principle

The principle of conservation of energy states that in any change, the total energy before the change is equal to the total energy after the change. In other words, the total amount of energy is conserved, even though it may change from its initial form into other forms as a result of the change.

Consider the energy changes if a 100 N weight is released at a height of 1.0 m above the floor.

★ Its initial potential energy (relative to the floor) is $mgh = 100\,\text{N} \times 1.0\,\text{m} = 100\,\text{J}$.

★ Its potential energy (relative to the floor) just before impact = 0, since its height is effectively zero just before impact.

It loses 100 J of potential energy as a result of falling to the floor. Just before impact, its kinetic energy is therefore 100 J since it had no kinetic energy at the start and all its potential energy is transformed into kinetic energy – assuming no air resistance!

But

The trouble with energy is that it tends to spread out when it changes from one form into other forms. For example, in a bicycle freewheeling down a slope, friction at the wheel bearings causes the bearings to become warm. Some of the initial potential energy is therefore converted into thermal energy. Such thermal energy is lost to the surroundings and can never be recovered and used to do work. The thermal energy is therefore wasted.

Even where energy is concentrated, such as when a car battery is charged, energy is wasted in the process. For example, the electric current passing through a car battery when it is being charged would warm the circuit wires a little.

Answers 1 9000 J 2 a) 9000 J b) 17 m/s

TAKE A BREAK

Energy resources and energy transfer

2.3 Power and efficiency

Power is defined as the work done or energy transferred per second.

$$\frac{\text{power}}{\text{(in watts)}} = \frac{\text{energy transferred (in joules)}}{\text{time taken (in seconds)}}$$

The unit of power is the **watt** (W), equal to one joule per second. Note that one kilowatt (kW) equals 1000 W and one megawatt (MW) equals 1 000 000 W.

Question

1. Calculate the muscle power of a student of mass 50 kg who climbs a height of 5.0 m up a rope in 10 s. (Hint: remember that weight = mass × g where g = 10 N/kg. Also, the student uses both arms to climb the rope.)

Electrical power

The electrical power supplied to an electrical appliance is the electrical energy transferred per second to the appliance. For example, a 1000 W electrical heater is supplied with 1000 J of electrical energy each second. This is changed into thermal energy by the heater.

The electrical power of an appliance depends on the current and potential difference (i.e. voltage), in accordance with this equation:

electrical power = current × potential difference

$$P = I \times V$$
(in watts) (in amperes) (in volts)

The unit of electrical energy used to cost mains electricity is the **kilowatt hour**, sometimes written as kWh. One kilowatt hour is the electrical energy supplied to a 1000 W appliance in one hour and is equal to 3.6 million joules (1000 W × 3600 s).

The electrical energy supplied to a mains appliance in a certain number of hours is calculated by multiplying the power of the appliance in kilowatts by the number of hours. For example, the electrical energy used by:
- a 3.0 kW heater in 2 hours is 6.0 kWh
- a 100 W light bulb in 24 hours is 2.4 kWh (= 0.1 kW × 24 hours).

Electrical energy supplied in kWh = power in kilowatts × the number of hours.

Notes

1. *The kilowatt hour (kWh) is the unit which is used to cost electricity.*
2. *The cost of the electrical energy supplied = the number of 'units' used × the cost per 'unit'.*

Machines at work

A machine is a device designed to do work. Energy is supplied to a machine enabling it to do **useful work**. The useful work done by a machine is always less than the energy supplied to it because of friction between its moving parts. This causes heating and therefore wastes energy. Energy may be wasted in other ways in a machine as well as through friction.

Efficiency

The efficiency of a machine is the proportion of the energy supplied to the machine which is transferred to useful work. This may be expressed as an equation:

$$\text{efficiency} = \frac{\text{useful work done by the machine}}{\text{energy supplied to the machine}}$$

Notes

1. *Efficiency is sometimes expressed as a percentage (the fraction above multiplied by 100).*
2. *The efficiency of any machine is always less than 100% because of friction.*
3. *Efficiency may be expressed in terms of power as*

$$\frac{\text{output power}}{\text{input power}}$$

Questions

2. A pulley system is used to raise a crate of weight 500 N through a height of 2.4 m. To do this, the operator must pull on the rope with a force of 300 N through a distance of 4.8 m.

   a) Calculate (i) the work done by the operator (ii) the potential energy gain of the crate.

   b) Hence calculate the efficiency of the pulley system and give two reasons why it is not 100%.

Answers

1. 125 W
2. a) (i) 1440 J (ii) 1200 J b) 83%
   Heat and sound energy losses due to friction.

2.4 Heat transfer

Heat transfer occurs by means of thermal **conduction**, **convection** and **radiation**. Cooling also takes place during **evaporation** from a hot liquid, and matter as well as heat is transferred in this process, which is not the case with conduction, convection or radiation.

Thermal conduction – five facts

1 Thermal conduction is heat transfer through a substance without the substance moving.

2 Solids, liquids and gases all conduct heat.

3 Good thermal conductors are also good electrical conductors. They contain free electrons which can transport both energy and charge through the substance.

4 Metals and alloys are the best conductors of heat.

5 Insulating materials such as wood, fibreglass and air are very poor conductors of heat. The presence of air pockets in an insulating material improves its insulating properties.

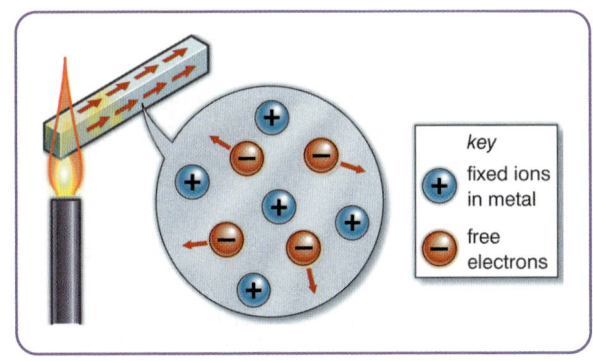

Thermal conduction in a metal

Thermal convection – five facts

1 Thermal convection is heat transfer in a liquid or a gas due to internal circulation of particles.

2 Thermal convection occurs only in fluids (liquids or gases).

3 Natural convection occurs because hot fluids, being less dense than cold fluids, rise, whereas cold fluids sink. When a fluid is heated, circulation is caused by hot fluid rising and cold fluid sinking.

4 Forced convection happens when a cold fluid is pumped over a hot surface and takes away energy from the surface.

5 Cooling fins on an engine increase the surface area of the engine and therefore enable more thermal convection to occur.

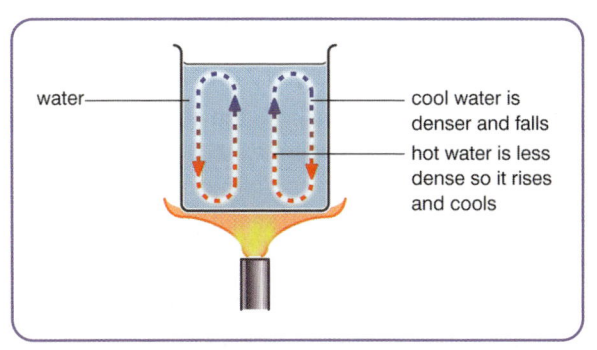

Thermal convection in water

Thermal radiation – five facts

1 Thermal radiation is electromagnetic radiation emitted by any surface at a temperature greater than absolute zero.

2 The hotter a surface is, the more thermal radiation it emits.

3 Thermal radiation can pass through a vacuum and does not need a substance to carry it.

4 A black surface is a better emitter and absorber of thermal radiation than a silvered surface.

5 A matt (rough) surface is a better emitter and absorber of thermal radiation than a shiny surface.

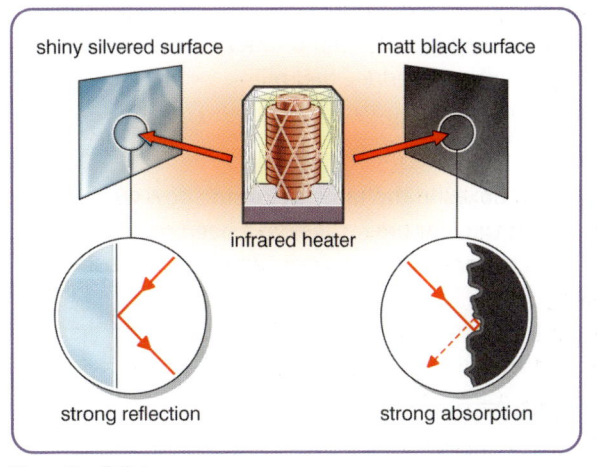

Thermal radiation

Energy resources and energy transfer

2.5 Controlling heat transfer

Designers need to take account of the thermal properties of materials when considering what materials to use in any given device or situation.

★ A car radiator transfers heat from the engine to the surroundings. Forced convection occurs as water pumped round the engine block carries away heat to the radiator. Heat is conducted through the radiator walls so the outside of the radiator becomes hot. Air circulates round the outside of the radiator, carrying away heat, and the radiator surface is blackened so it emits thermal radiation.

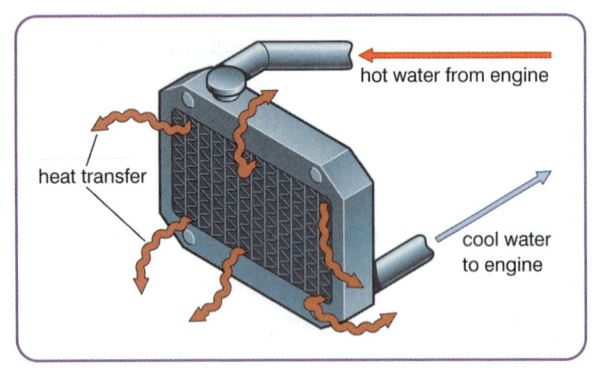

A car radiator

★ A domestic hot water tank is fitted with an insulating jacket to reduce heat losses. The outer surface of the jacket is shiny to reduce heat losses due to thermal radiation.

Keeping warm in winter

Home heating bills can be greatly reduced by fitting loft insulation and double glazing. The picture of the house shows these and other measures that can be taken to reduce fuel bills.

Question

1 Tick boxes in the table below to show which heat transfer processes have been reduced by each measure.

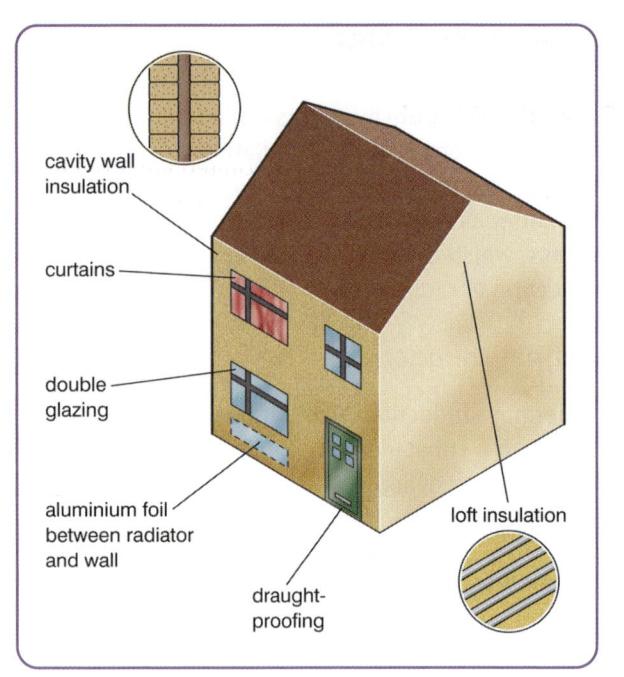

Reducing home heating bills

Maintaining body temperature

If you are outdoors in winter, you need warm, dry clothing made of fibres which trap layers of air. Since air is a very poor conductor of heat, it reduces heat transfer from the body to the surroundings. A white outer surface reduces thermal radiation. A smooth shiny surface would be even better but might be expensive! In addition, the outer surface needs to be waterproof and the inner layers need to prevent water vapour caused by sweat penetrating the fibres.

Question

2 List the materials you would use to make a winter coat, giving a reason for each material chosen.

Answers

1 conduction ✓✓✓XXX
  convection X✓XXX✓ radiation ✓✓XXX✓X
2 wool or polyester fibres to trap layers of air, silk lining for smooth fit

	loft insulation	double glazing	cavity wall insulation	radiator foil	heavy curtains	draught excluder
conduction						
convection						
radiation						

Energy resources and energy transfer

2.6 Energy resources

Demand and supply

The total energy demand for the United Kingdom in one year is about 10 million million million joules. This works out at about 5000 joules per second for every person in the country.

Fuels are substances which release energy as a result of changing into another substance. Fuels cannot be reused.

- Fossil fuels – coal, oil, gas
- Nuclear fuels – uranium, plutonium

Renewable energy resources are sources of useful energy which do not change the substances involved, allowing them to be reused. The energy usually comes from the Sun:

- solar-driven resources – solar panels for water heating, solar cells
- weather-driven resources (indirectly powered by the Sun's heating effect on the atmosphere) – hydroelectricity, wind turbines, wave-powered generators
- tidal generators (powered by the gravitational potential energy between the Earth and the Moon)
- geothermal power (powered by thermal energy in the Earth's interior).

Electricity supplies need to be matched to demand which is usually lowest at night and greatest at meal times:

★ Mains electricity in Britain is mostly supplied from fossil fuel and nuclear power stations.

★ Electricity power stations need to be started and stopped quickly to match sudden changes of demand during each day.

★ The start-up time of each type of power station is, from shortest to longest:

hydroelectric   gas   oil   coal   nuclear.

Energy efficiency

Reasons why energy should not be wasted:

1. Fuel supplies are finite and cannot be renewed once used.
2. Fossil fuels release carbon dioxide gas, which is thought to be causing global warming, resulting in melting icecaps and rising sea levels. Sulphur dioxide from power stations is a cause of acid rain.
3. Nuclear fuel creates radioactive waste which must be stored safely for hundreds of years to prevent it harming us.
4. Small-scale renewable resources may damage the environment, for example turbine noise from wind turbines, and plant and animal life are affected when tidal power stations are built.
5. It costs money to make energy useful and to distribute it.

How to use energy resources more efficiently

★ Use machines and vehicles more efficiently.

★ Replace inefficient machines and vehicles with more efficient ones.

★ Improve thermal insulation in buildings.

★ Fit automatic lighting and temperature sensors to reduce unnecessary lighting and heating.

★ Supply waste heat from power stations for district heating (combined heat and power stations).

★ Use more pumped storage schemes.

★ Make energy-efficient lifestyle choices, for example teleworking, car sharing, better public transport.

A pumped storage station. Electricity is used to pump water uphill when the demand for electricity is low. Electricity is generated by allowing water to flow downhill when demand is high.

Energy resources and energy transfer

ROUND UP

How much have you improved? Work out your improvement index on page 306.

1. Describe the energy changes that take place when

   a) the alarm sounds on a battery-operated clock [1]

   b) a parachutist jumps from a plane and descends safely to the ground. [2]

2. An elevator is used in a factory to lift packages each weighing 200 N through a height of 4.0 m from the production line to a loading platform. The elevator is designed to deliver three packages per minute to the loading bay.

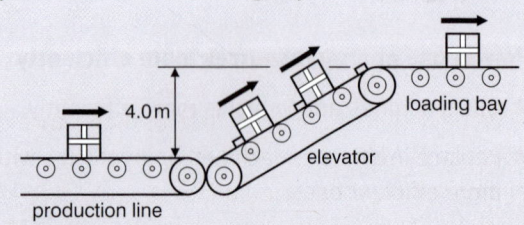

   a) Calculate
      (i) the potential energy gain of each package [1]
      (ii) the work done per second by the elevator to lift the packages. [1]

   b) A 200 W electric motor is used to drive the elevator. Calculate the efficiency of the elevator and motor system. [1]

3. a) An athlete of mass 55 kg is capable of running at a top speed of 10 m/s. Calculate the athlete's kinetic energy at this speed. [1]

   b) If the athlete could convert all the kinetic energy in a) into potential energy, how much would the athlete's centre of gravity rise? [1]

4. A passenger aeroplane of mass 25 000 kg accelerates on a level run from rest to reach its take-off speed of 80 m/s in a time of 50 s. Calculate

   a) its kinetic energy at take-off [1]

   b) the power developed by its engines to achieve this speed in 50 s. [1]

5. A student records the usage of electrical appliances in her household over a period of 24 hours.

   > 2.0 kW electric heater for 2.5 hours
   > 100 W electric light for 3 hours
   > 40 W electric light for 5 hours
   > 750 W microwave oven for 20 minutes
   > 3.0 kW electric kettle used 4 times for 5 minutes each time

   a) Calculate the total number of units of electricity (kWh) used by the appliances. [1]

   b) Calculate the total cost of using all these appliances if each unit of electricity costs 6.0p. [1]

6. A 12 V electric heater, rated at 25 W, is designed for use in a car and is capable of heating a flask of tea from 20 °C to 50 °C in 15 minutes.

   a) Calculate the energy supplied by a 25 W electric heater in 15 minutes. [1]

   b) A student decides to test the heater by filling the flask with 0.2 kg of water. She has discovered in a separate test that 4200 J of energy is needed to raise the temperature of 1.0 kg of water by 1 °C. She finds that the heater takes 650 seconds to heat the water from 20 °C to 40 °C.
      (i) Calculate the energy needed to heat 0.2 kg of water from 20 °C to 40 °C. [1]
      (ii) Calculate the actual power of the heater. [1]

7. a) Explain whether hot tea in a china teapot would cool faster than hot tea in a shiny metal teapot. [2]

   b) Explain why hot tea cools faster in a wide-brimmed cup than in a narrow cup. [3]

   c) Explain why heat loss through a single-glazed window can be reduced by fitting double glazing. [2]

   d) (i) Condensation often forms on single-glazed classroom windows in winter. Explain how this happens. [2]
      (ii) Double glazing reduces condensation. Why? [2]

Well done if you've improved. Don't worry if you haven't. Take a break and try again.

Radioactivity — Chapter 3

PREVIEW

At the end of this topic you will be able to:

- explain the structure of the atomic nucleus and the term isotope
- explain radioactivity in simple terms
- describe the characteristics of the three main types of emission from radioactive substances
- explain what is meant by background radioactivity
- explain the term half-life and interpret half-life graphs and related data
- know that emissions from radioactive substances have harmful effects
- describe uses of radioactivity.

How much do you already know? Work out your score on page 306.

Test yourself

1. State whether each of the following particles carries positive charge, negative charge or is uncharged:
   a) the electron b) the proton c) the neutron d) the alpha particle e) the beta minus particle. [5]

2. State how many protons and how many neutrons are present in each nucleus of the following isotopes:
   a) $^{4}_{2}He$ b) $^{235}_{92}U$. [4]

3. What type of charge does the nucleus of the atom carry? [1]

4. State the three types of emissions from naturally occurring radioactive substances, and state which type of radioactive emission is most easily absorbed. [4]

5. What is background radioactivity? [1]

6. Name a scientific instrument used to measure radioactivity. [1]

7. The *half-life* of the *isotope* of carbon $^{14}_{6}C$ is 5500 years. Explain what is meant by the terms in italics. [2]

8. What is meant by nuclear fission? [2]

9. Why is it important to store radioactive waste from a nuclear reactor for thousands of years? [2]

10. State two uses of radioactive isotopes. [2]

3.1 Inside the atom

A scientific puzzle

Radioactivity was discovered in 1896 by **Henri Becquerel**. When he developed an unused photographic plate, he found an image of a key on it. He realised this was caused by radiation from a packet containing uranium salts, which had been on top of a key with the photographic plate underneath. The puzzle of explaining the radiation was passed by Becquerel to a young research worker, **Marie Curie**. She painstakingly analysed the uranium salts and discovered the radiations were emitted from the uranium atoms, which formed other types of atoms in the process. She and her husband Pierre discovered and named two new radioactive elements, polonium and radium. It was shown that the emissions contained two types of radiation: alpha radiation which is positively charged and easily absorbed, and beta radiation which is negatively charged and much less easily absorbed. Later gamma radiation was discovered which is uncharged and much more penetrating.

Symbol for radioactive sources

Radioactivity

The structure of the atom

Ernest Rutherford used alpha radiation to probe the atom. He knew that alpha radiation consisted of positively charged particles. He found that when a beam of alpha particles was directed at a thin metal foil, some of the particles bounced back off the foil. He deduced that:
- the atom contains a tiny positively charged nucleus, where most of its mass is located
- the rest of the atom consists of empty space through which negatively charged electrons move as they orbit the nucleus.

Further investigations showed that the nucleus contains two types of particles, **protons** and **neutrons**.

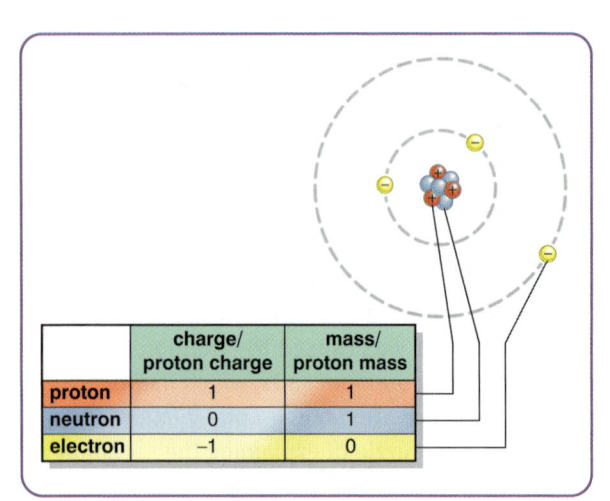

	charge/proton charge	mass/proton mass
proton	1	1
neutron	0	1
electron	−1	0

A lithium atom

Atoms and molecules

★ An **element** is a substance which cannot be split into simpler substances. A **compound** is a substance containing two or more elements combined in fixed proportions.

★ An **atom** is the smallest particle of an element which is characteristic of that element.

★ A **molecule** is formed when two or more atoms join together.

★ The lightest atom is hydrogen. The heaviest naturally occurring atom is uranium.

★ The **periodic table of the elements** places the elements in order of increasing **atomic number** (symbol Z). The atomic number of an element is the number of protons in its nucleus.

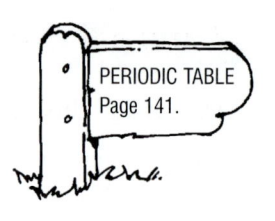

PERIODIC TABLE Page 141.

Isotopes

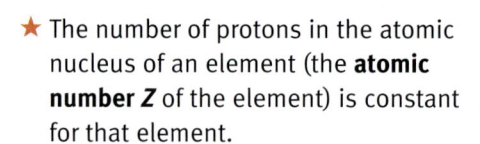

★ The number of protons in the atomic nucleus of an element (the **atomic number Z** of the element) is constant for that element.

★ The number of neutrons in the atomic nuclei of a given element can vary from one atom to another.

★ The term **isotope** describes a particular type of atom of a given element. For example, chlorine has two isotopes, one with 17 protons and 18 neutrons, and the other with 17 protons and 20 neutrons.

★ Since protons and neutrons each have a mass of one atomic mass unit, the total number of protons and neutrons in a nucleus gives the mass of the nucleus in atomic mass units. This is called the **mass number A** of the nucleus. Because electrons have very little mass in comparison, the mass of an atom in atomic mass units is equal to A.

★ An isotope is defined by the symbol

$$^{A}_{Z}X$$

where X is the chemical symbol of the element, Z is the number of protons in the nucleus (the atomic number) and A is the number of protons and neutrons in the nucleus (the mass number).

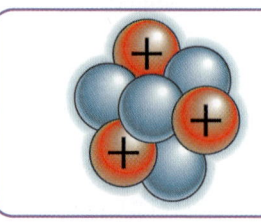

Why doesn't the nucleus fly apart due to repulsion of the positive protons? The nucleus is held together by the **strong nuclear force**.

Questions

Work out the number of protons and neutrons in each of the following isotopes: **a)** $^{238}_{92}U$ **b)** $^{14}_{6}C$ **c)** $^{22}_{10}Ne$.

Answers a) 92p + 146n b) 6p + 8n c) 10p + 12n

Radioactivity

3.2 Radioactive isotopes

Stable and unstable nuclei

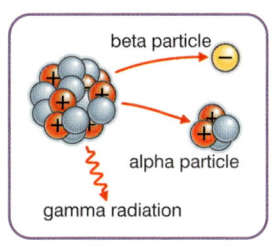

A nucleus is **stable** if the strong nuclear force between its neutrons and protons is much greater than the electrostatic force of repulsion between the protons. Some nuclei are **unstable** because the electrostatic forces of repulsion are larger than the strong attractive forces.

An unstable nucleus

★ A large nucleus with **too many protons and neutrons** is unstable. It becomes stable by emitting an **alpha particle**. This is a particle consisting of two protons and two neutrons.

★ A smaller nucleus with **too many neutrons** is unstable. It becomes stable by emitting a **beta particle**. This is an electron created in the nucleus and instantly emitted.

★ A nucleus may still possess **excess energy** after an alpha or beta particle has been emitted. It may then release the excess energy as **gamma radiation**. This is electromagnetic radiation of very short wavelength.

★ The daughter nucleus might itself be radioactive, and may emit a further alpha or beta particle.

★ An unstable nucleus is said to **disintegrate** when it emits an alpha particle or beta particle. When it emits gamma radiation, it is said to **de-excite**.

★ The **activity** of a radioactive source is the number of nuclei per second that disintegrate.

The Geiger counter

This consists of a Geiger tube connected to an electronic counter. Each particle from a radioactive source that enters the tube is registered on the electronic counter as one count. If the Geiger tube is pointed at a radioactive source, the activity of the source can be monitored by counting the number of particles entering the tube in a measured time interval and calculating the **count rate** (the number of counts per second), which is proportional to the activity.

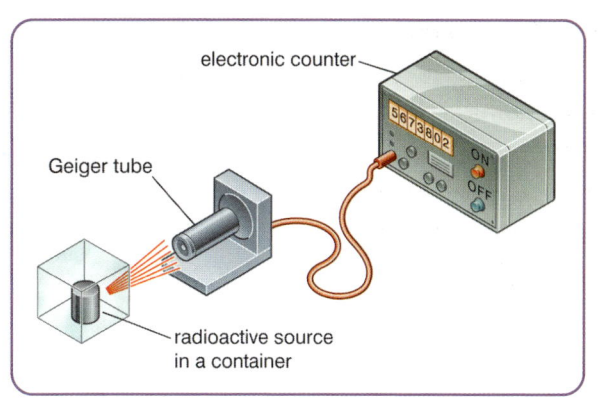

Using a Geiger counter

Background radioactivity

A Geiger counter will detect a low level of radioactivity even with no source present. This is called **background radioactivity** and is due to cosmic radiation and naturally occurring radioactive isotopes in rocks such as granite.

Questions

A Geiger counter records 1980 counts in 300 seconds when it is held at a fixed distance from a radioactive source. Without the source present, it records 120 counts in 300 seconds.

a) Why does the Geiger tube count when no source is present?

b) Calculate the count rate due to the source.

c) Give two reasons why the count rate is less than the activity of the source.

$E = mc^2$

This famous equation was first derived by **Albert Einstein**. He showed that if energy E is given to (or taken away from) an object, the mass of the object increases (or decreases) by a mass m in accordance with the equation $E = mc^2$, where c is the speed of light. The energy given out when a nucleus disintegrates can be calculated from the difference in mass of the parent nucleus and its products.

Answers

a) Background radioactivity
b) 6.2 counts per second
c) The radiation spreads out from the source in all directions so most of it misses the tube; absorption by the air between the tube and the source.

Radioactivity

3.3 Radioactive emissions

Ionisation

Ions are atoms that have become charged, either by removing electrons or by adding them.

When the particles produced from radioactive substances pass through a gas, they cause the gas molecules to ionise. In a **cloud chamber**, tiny droplets form along the path of an alpha particle due to the trail of ions created by the particle. The path of each alpha particle is visible in the cloud chamber.

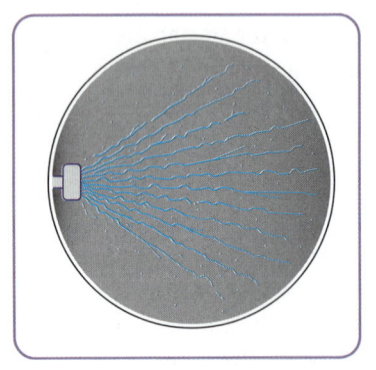

Alpha-particle tracks in a cloud chamber

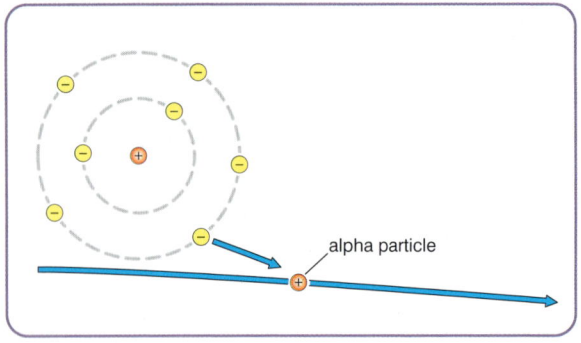

Ionisation

The properties of alpha, beta and gamma radiation

	alpha	beta	gamma
charge	+2	−1	0
absorption	thin paper	few mm of aluminium	several cm of lead
range in air	fixed*, up to 10 cm	variable*, up to 1 m	spreads without limit
ionising effect	strong	weak	very weak

(* = for a given source)

Equations for radioactive change

★ Alpha emission

An alpha particle (symbol $^4_2\alpha$) consists of two protons and two neutrons. An unstable nucleus that emits an alpha particle therefore loses two units of charge and four units of mass. (Remember each proton has a mass of 1 atomic mass unit and a charge of +1 and a neutron has the same mass as a proton and is not charged.)

An unstable nucleus $^A_Z X$ has Z protons and $(A-Z)$ neutrons in its nucleus. If it emits an alpha particle, it becomes a nucleus with two fewer protons and two fewer neutrons.

$$^A_Z X \longrightarrow {}^{A-4}_{Z-2} Y + {}^4_2 \alpha$$

★ Beta minus emission

A beta particle (symbol β) is an electron created in an unstable nucleus, then instantly emitted. A neutron in the nucleus suddenly becomes a proton, creating the beta particle at the same time. The total number of neutrons and protons in the nucleus is therefore unchanged, but there is one more proton.

$$^A_Z X \longrightarrow {}^A_{Z+1} Y + {}^0_{-1} \beta$$

The mass number of the beta particle is 0 because it is an electron. Its charge is opposite to that of a proton, so its proton number is written as −1.

Note
In both equations, the numbers balance along the top and along the bottom.

Questions

a) Write down the equation representing
   (i) alpha emission from the unstable nucleus $^{238}_{92}U$ to form a nucleus of thorium (Th).
   (ii) beta emission from the unstable nucleus $^{27}_{12}Mg$ to form a nucleus of aluminium (Al).

b) State how many protons and how many neutrons are present in each nucleus in your equations.

Answers

a) (i) $^{238}_{92}U \rightarrow {}^{234}_{90}Th + {}^4_2\alpha$
(ii) $^{27}_{12}Mg \rightarrow {}^{27}_{13}Al + {}^0_{-1}\beta$
b) U-238 = 92 p + 146 n; Th-234 = 90 p + 144 n; Mg-27 = 12 p + 15 n; Al-27 = 13 p + 14 n

Radioactivity

3.4 Half-life

The **half-life** of a radioactive isotope is the time taken for half its atoms to disintegrate. This time is a characteristic of the isotope. Long-lived radioactive isotopes have nuclei that are less unstable than short-lived isotopes. For example, uranium-238 has a half-life of more than 4500 million years.

The **number of atoms** of a radioactive isotope decreases with time. Radioactive disintegration is a **random** process, and the number of atoms that disintegrate per second is proportional to the number of radioactive atoms present at that time. For example, suppose 10% of the atoms of a certain radioactive isotope X disintegrate every 10 seconds. The table below shows how the number of atoms of X changes, starting with 10 000.

A graph showing how the number of atoms of X decreases with time is shown below. This type of curve is called a **decay curve**.

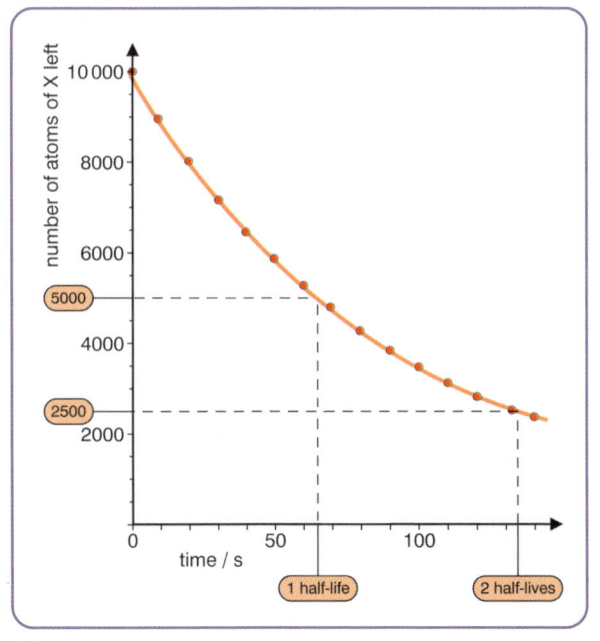

A decay curve

> **Questions**
>
> a) Use the graph to estimate the half-life of X.
>
> b) Estimate the time taken for the number of atoms to fall to 25% of 10 000.

The **activity** of a radioactive isotope decreases with time. This is because the activity is proportional to the number of atoms of the isotope left. The shape of the activity–time curve is the same as the decay curve, provided the 'daughter' isotope is stable.

Radioactive dating

Rocks formed millions of years ago can be dated using radioactivity. Ancient materials can also be dated using radioactivity.

★ Some igneous rocks contain the uranium isotope U-238, formed by volcanic activity long ago. These can be dated by measuring the proportion of an isotope of lead, Pb-206, relative to U-238. The uranium isotope has a half-life of 4500 million years, emitting alpha particles and forming the stable isotope Pb-206 via a series of relatively short-lived radioactive isotopes. A decay curve like the one on the left may be used to work out the age of a rock from the proportion of U-238 remaining.

★ Rocks containing trapped argon gas can be dated by measuring the proportion of the gas to the radioactive potassium isotope, K-40, which produces the gas as a result of radioactive change. K-40 is an unstable isotope with a half-life of 1250 million years, producing the argon isotope Ar-40. This gas is trapped when the molten rock solidifies. Hence the age of the rock can be determined by measuring the relative proportions of the two isotopes and then using a decay curve.

> **Answers**   a) 66 s   b) 134 s

Time/s	0	10	20	30	40	50	60	70
Number of atoms left	10 000	9000	8100	7290	6561	5905	5314	4783
Decrease in number of atoms of X	1000	900	810	729	656	591	531	478

Radioactivity

3.5 Using radioactivity

In each of the uses of radioactivity described below, think about the choice of the radioactive isotope in terms of:
- the half-life of the isotope
- absorption of radioactive emissions
- whether or not the daughter isotope is stable.

Medical uses

Tracers for diagnosis: the cause of certain illnesses can be pinpointed using **radioactive tracers**. For example, an underactive thyroid gland can be detected by giving the patient food containing the radioactive isotope iodine-131. This is a beta emitter with a half-life of 8 days.

A correctly functioning thyroid gland will absorb iodine and store it. A Geiger tube pointed at the neck will therefore show an increased reading if the patient's thyroid gland is functioning correctly. The amount of radioactivity is too small to harm the gland, and the isotope decays after a few weeks.

Questions

1 a) Why is a beta emitter chosen?
   b) Why is an isotope with a half-life of a few minutes not chosen?

Gamma therapy: gamma radiation from the radioactive isotope cobalt-60 is used to destroy cancerous tissues. The gamma radiation penetrates the body and passes into the diseased tissue. A lead collimator (filter) is used to direct the gamma radiation onto the cancer cells. The half-life of cobalt-60 is 5 years.

Questions

2 a) Why is a gamma emitter chosen?
   b) Why is an isotope with a half-life of a few years chosen?

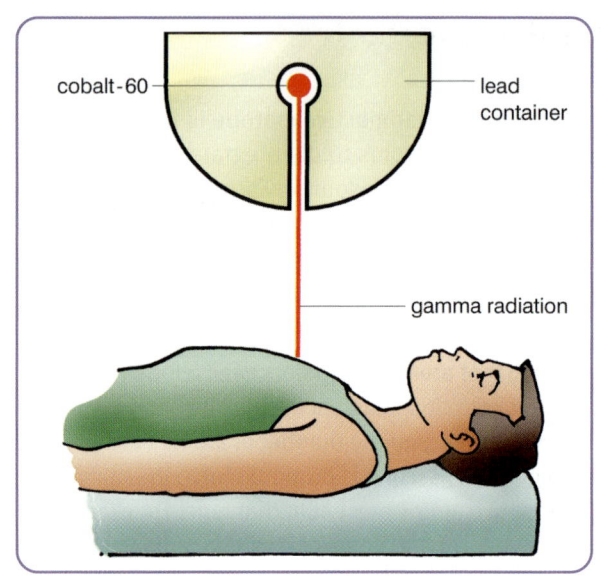

Treating cancer

Industrial uses

Thickness of metal foil: a detector measures the amount of beta radiation passing through the metal foil feeding out of a production line. If the foil becomes too thick, the detector reading falls and feeds a signal back to increase the pressure on the foil and make it thinner.

Pipeline cracks: the crack in a leaking underground pipe can be located by putting a radioactive tracer into the flow. A Geiger counter is then moved on the ground along the pipeline. Its reading is higher where the fluid in the pipe leaks into the ground. A beta-emitting isotope with a half-life of a few hours is suitable for this purpose.

Some other uses

Irradiation of food: gamma radiation is used to kill the bacteria responsible for food poisoning in certain foods. This makes the food safer to eat, and prolongs its shelf-life.

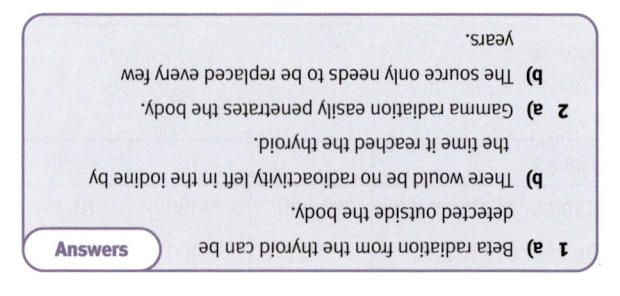

Answers

1 a) Beta radiation from the thyroid can be detected outside the body.
  b) There would be no radioactivity left in the iodine by the time it reached the thyroid.
2 a) Gamma radiation easily penetrates the body.
  b) The source only needs to be replaced every few years.

Radioactivity

3.6 Nuclear reactors

Releasing energy from the nucleus

★ The uranium-235 nucleus is unstable and splits into two approximately equal 'daughter' nuclei, and two or three neutrons. This splitting process is called **fission**.

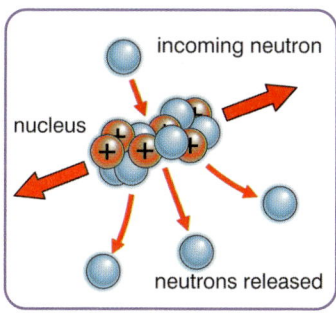

Fission

★ Energy is released when a U-235 nucleus splits, which is carried away as kinetic energy by the daughter nuclei and neutrons.

★ Fission can be induced by bombarding U-235 nuclei with neutrons.

★ A controlled **chain reaction** is created if there are sufficient U-235 nuclei. One neutron from each fission event goes on to cause the fission of another nucleus.

Radioactive waste

Radioactive waste from a nuclear reactor is classified as:
- **low level waste** such as clothing worn by personnel – the clothing fibres may contain radioactive dust particles
- **intermediate level waste** such as metal cladding from spent fuel rods – the cladding becomes radioactive inside the reactor
- **high level waste** such as fission products, unused uranium and plutonium.

Treatment and storage of radioactive waste

★ Low level radioactive waste from Britain's nuclear reactors is stored in sealed containers in a shallow trench at Sellafield.

★ Intermediate level waste is stored in sealed drums at several sites in Britain. An underground storage site at Sellafield is being developed to store all Britain's intermediate level and low level waste.

★ High level waste includes spent fuel rods, which are highly radioactive because the nuclei produced by fission of uranium-235 are unstable. The spent fuel rods therefore generate heat due to radioactive decay. The rods are placed initially in cooling ponds until they are cool enough to be transported safely to Sellafield. There they are reprocessed to recover unused uranium and plutonium. The rest of the high level waste is stored in sealed containers at Sellafield.

Why radioactivity is harmful

Radiation from radioactive substances produces ions. Ionising radiation damages living cells in two ways:
1. by penetrating the cell membranes which causes the cell to die
2. by breaking the strands of DNA molecules in the cell nucleus, which may cause cell mutation.

★ **Alpha radiation** is easily absorbed, highly ionising and therefore very harmful.

★ **Beta radiation** is less easily absorbed and less ionising. However, it can penetrate deep into the body from outside so it too is very harmful.

★ **Gamma radiation** easily penetrates soft tissue and is absorbed by bones, where its ionising effect can produce immense damage.

There is no lower limit below which ionising radiation is harmless. Therefore, extreme care is essential when radioactive substances are used and legal regulations for using radioactive substances must be observed. In a school laboratory, students under the age of 16 are not allowed to carry out experiments with radioactive materials.

Questions

a) Why is a storage box for radioactive substances made of lead?

b) Why is it essential for tongs used for handling radioactive substances to have long handles?

Answers
a) Lead is the best absorber of radioactivity.
b) The tongs keep the source as far away from the user as possible.

Radioactivity

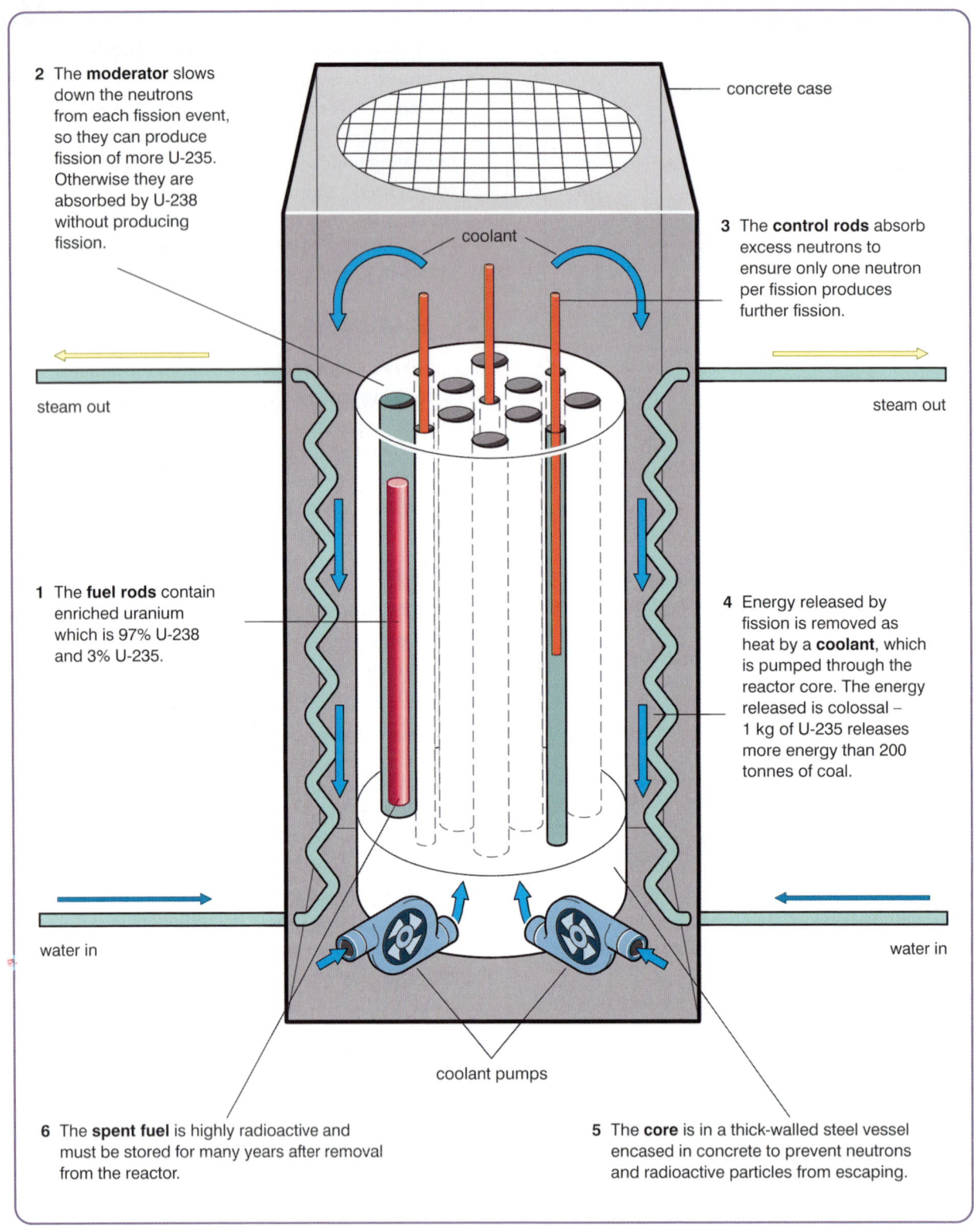

2 The **moderator** slows down the neutrons from each fission event, so they can produce fission of more U-235. Otherwise they are absorbed by U-238 without producing fission.

concrete case

coolant

3 The **control rods** absorb excess neutrons to ensure only one neutron per fission produces further fission.

steam out

steam out

1 The **fuel rods** contain enriched uranium which is 97% U-238 and 3% U-235.

4 Energy released by fission is removed as heat by a **coolant**, which is pumped through the reactor core. The energy released is colossal – 1 kg of U-235 releases more energy than 200 tonnes of coal.

water in

water in

coolant pumps

6 The **spent fuel** is highly radioactive and must be stored for many years after removal from the reactor.

5 The **core** is in a thick-walled steel vessel encased in concrete to prevent neutrons and radioactive particles from escaping.

Inside a nuclear reactor

Radioactivity

ROUND UP

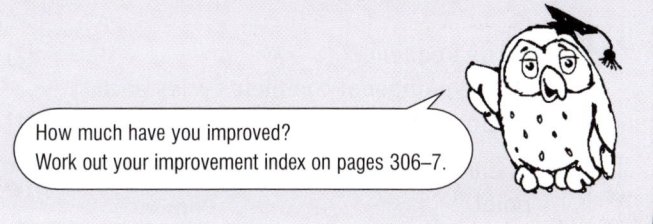

How much have you improved?
Work out your improvement index on pages 306–7.

1. Natural uranium consists of about 99% $^{238}_{92}$U and about 1% $^{235}_{92}$U.

   a) How many protons and how many neutrons are present in each type of atom? [4]

   b) What is the name for different types of atoms of the same element? [1]

   c) $^{238}_{92}$U has a half-life of about 4500 million years. Explain what is meant by *half-life*. [1]

2. One type of smoke detector uses an alpha particle source, as shown.

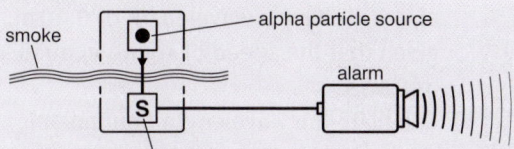

   a) Why is an alpha source used rather than a beta or a gamma source? [2]

   b) Why is it important for the alpha source to have a half-life of more than 5 years? [1]

3. a) $^{220}_{82}$Rn emits alpha particles to form an isotope of the element polonium (Po). Write down the equation for this process. [2]

   b) Radon-220 has a half-life of 52 s. A pure sample of this isotope had an initial activity of 400 disintegrations per second. What was its activity after (i) 104 s (ii) 208 s? [2]

4. The thickness of hot rolled steel plate produced in a factory was monitored using a gamma source and detector, as shown below.

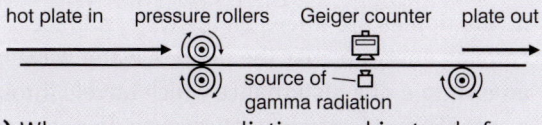

   a) Why was gamma radiation used instead of alpha or beta radiation? [3]

   b) The counter reading increased every second as shown in the table below.

Time / s	0	1	2	3	4	5	6	7	8	9	10
Counter reading	0	204	395	602	792	1004	1180	1340	1505	1660	1825

   (i) What was the average count rate over the first 5 seconds? [1]

   (ii) What was the average count rate over the last 2 seconds? [1]

   (iii) What happened to the thickness of the plate? [1]

5. a) Background radioactivity accounts for 87% of the exposure to ionising radiations of the average person in Britain. Explain what is meant by

   (i) background radioactivity [1]
   (ii) ionising radiation. [1]

   b) State two further sources of ionising radiation. [2]

   c) Explain how you would use a Geiger counter and a stopwatch to measure background radioactivity. [2]

6. In a test to identify the type of radioactivity produced by a radioactive source, the following results were obtained with different sheets of materials placed between the source and the Geiger tube.

material	count rate / counts per second
none	450
tin foil	235
1 mm aluminium	230
10 mm aluminium	228
10 mm lead	160

Use these results to decide what types of radiation are emitted by the source. Explain your answer. [4]

7. a) Why is it essential to use long-handled tongs to move a radioactive source? [1]

   b) Cobalt-60 is a radioactive isotope that emits gamma radiation. It is used in hospitals to treat cancer.

   (i) What is gamma radiation and why is it necessary to use gamma radiation for this purpose? [2]

   (ii) With the aid of a diagram, explain how the gamma radiation is concentrated on the tumour. [3]

Chapter 4 Waves

PREVIEW

At the end of this topic you will be able to:

- describe different types of waves
- explain what is meant by a transverse wave and a longitudinal wave
- explain what is meant by the amplitude, wavelength and frequency of a wave
- relate the speed of a wave to its wavelength and its frequency
- describe reflection, refraction and diffraction as wave properties.

How much do you already know? Work out your score on page 307.

Test yourself

1. State four different types of waves. [4]

2. a) What is the difference between a longitudinal wave and a transverse wave? [2]
   b) Is the primary component of a seismic wave longitudinal or transverse? [1]

3. State one type of wave that can travel through a vacuum, and one type that cannot. [2]

4. The diagram shows a snapshot of a wave travelling from left to right.

   Use a millimetre rule to measure its wavelength and its amplitude. [2]

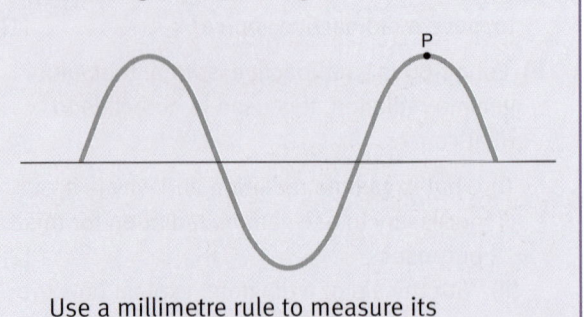

5. If the wave in **4** is travelling at 20 mm/s, what is
   a) its frequency? [1]
   b) the number of complete cycles each point goes through in 1 minute? [1]

6. In the diagram in **4**, what is the position of point P
   a) exactly 1.0 s after the snapshot shown?
   b) exactly 4.0 s after the snapshot shown? [2]

7. Why are waves on the seashore not reflected when they run up the beach? [2]

8. What is meant by refraction of waves? [2]

9. When waves pass through a gap they spread out. Is the spreading increased or decreased when
   a) the gap is made narrower?
   b) the wavelength is decreased? [2]

10. a) Calculate the frequency of sound waves in air which have a wavelength of 0.40 m, given that the speed of sound in air is 340 m/s. [1]
    b) Calculate the wavelength of ultrasonic waves of frequency 1.5 MHz in water, given that the speed of the waves is 1500 m/s. [1]

4.1 What is a wave?

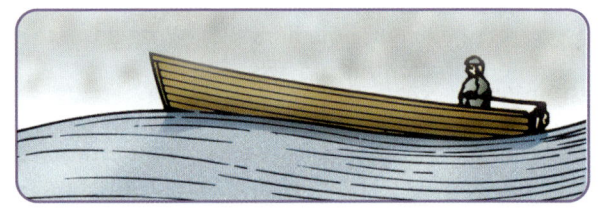

Waves can carry energy without carrying matter. Drop a stone in a pond and observe the ripples as they spread out. A small object floating on the water would bob up and down as the ripples pass it. The ripples are waves on the water surface carrying energy across the pond. A water wave is an example of a disturbance which travels through a substance. Electromagnetic waves do not need a substance to travel through; all other types of waves do.

Waves

4.2 Transverse and longitudinal waves

Different types of waves

Some types of waves are listed below. You need to know how they are produced, what they have in common and how they differ from each other. They include:
- water waves
- waves on a string or a rope
- seismic waves
- sound waves
- electromagnetic waves (radio waves, microwaves, infrared radiation, visible light, ultraviolet light, X-rays, gamma rays).

Making waves

All waves except electromagnetic waves need a substance to travel through. Waves are sent through the medium when one part of the substance is made to vibrate. For example, waves can be sent along a long stretched coil by making one end vibrate. The vibrations can be in any direction, but there are two particular ways of sending waves down the coil.

★ **Longitudinal waves** can be created by making one end vibrate to and fro along the coil. At any point, the vibrations are parallel to the direction in which the waves travel. The coil windings are squeezed and stretched as the waves pass down the coil.

★ **Transverse waves** can be created by making one end vibrate at right angles to the coil. At any point along the coil, the vibrations are at 90° to the direction in which the waves travel.

More about transverse waves

'Transverse' means 'across', so transverse waves vibrate in a direction that is across (perpendicular to) the direction in which the wave travels. Examples of transverse waves include:
- waves on a rope or a string
- electromagnetic waves
- secondary (S) seismic waves.

Transverse waves are **polarised** if their vibrations are in one plane only. However, if the plane of vibration continually changes, the waves on the rope are **unpolarised**.

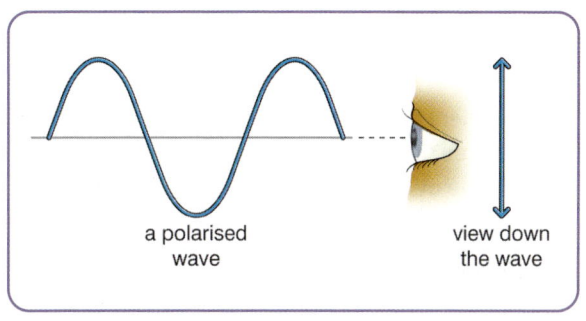

Polarisation

More about longitudinal waves

'Longitudinal' means 'along', so longitudinal waves vibrate along (parallel to) the direction in which the wave travels. They squeeze and stretch the medium. Examples of longitudinal waves include:
- sound waves
- primary (P) seismic waves.

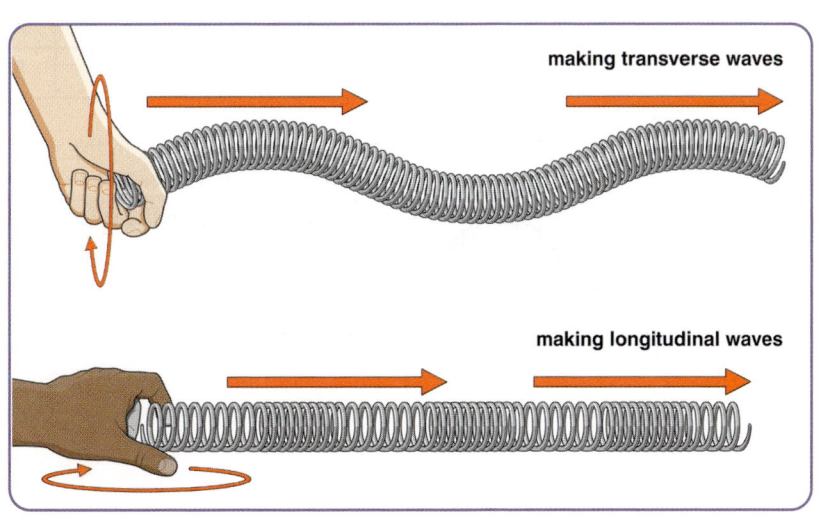

Transverse and longitudinal waves

Waves

4.3 Measuring waves

Look at the snapshot of a transverse wave in the diagram below. The wave is travelling from left to right, but you can't tell this from the snapshot. Each point on the wave vibrates at 90° to the wave direction.

★ **One complete cycle** of vibration of any point returns the point to the same position and direction it had at the start of the cycle. In this time, a wave crest at the point is replaced by the next wave crest.

★ **The amplitude of a wave** is the height of the wave crest above the centre. This is the same as the depth of a wave trough below the centre.

★ **The wavelength of a wave** (symbol λ, pronounced 'lambda') is the distance from one crest to the next crest. This is the same as the distance from a trough to the next trough.

★ **The frequency of a wave** (symbol f) is the number of crests passing a given position each second. This is the same as the number of complete cycles of vibration per second of any point. The unit of frequency is the hertz (symbol Hz), equal to 1 cycle per second.

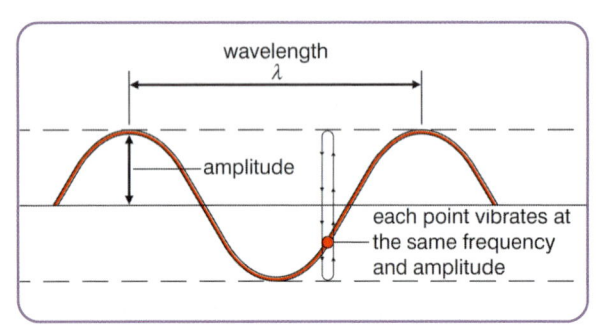

Wave measurements

Question

1. What are the wavelength and the amplitude of the wave shown above?

Speed

★ The speed v of a wave is the distance travelled by a crest in one second. The unit of speed is the metre per second (m/s).

★ The speed of a wave can be calculated from its frequency and wavelength using the following equation:

speed = frequency × wavelength
(in m/s)   (in Hz)   (in m)

Maths workshop

- The equation for speed can be written in symbols as $v = f\lambda$, where v is the speed, f is the frequency and λ is the wavelength.

- To find the frequency f from $v = f\lambda$, the equation needs to be rearranged to make f its subject.

  Start with $\quad f\lambda = v$

  then divide both sides by λ to give

  $$\frac{f\lambda}{\lambda} = \frac{v}{\lambda}$$

  then cancel λ top and bottom on the left-hand side of the equation to give

  $$f = \frac{v}{\lambda}$$

- To find the wavelength λ from $v = f\lambda$, transfer f from the top on one side to the bottom on the other side to give

  $$\lambda = \frac{v}{f}$$

Questions

2. Complete the table below by calculating the missing value of speed, frequency or wavelength.

wavelength/m	2.5	0.1			5×10^{-7}
frequency/Hz		3400	500	3750	
speed/m/s	340		80	1500	3×10^8

3. Suppose the wave in the diagram is travelling at a speed of 60 mm/s to the left. Calculate its frequency using the wavelength measurement from question **1**.

Answers
1. Amplitude = 10 mm, wavelength = 40 mm
2. 136 Hz, 340 m/s, 0.160 m, 0.40 m, 6×10^{14} Hz
3. 1.5 Hz

Waves

4.4 Wave properties

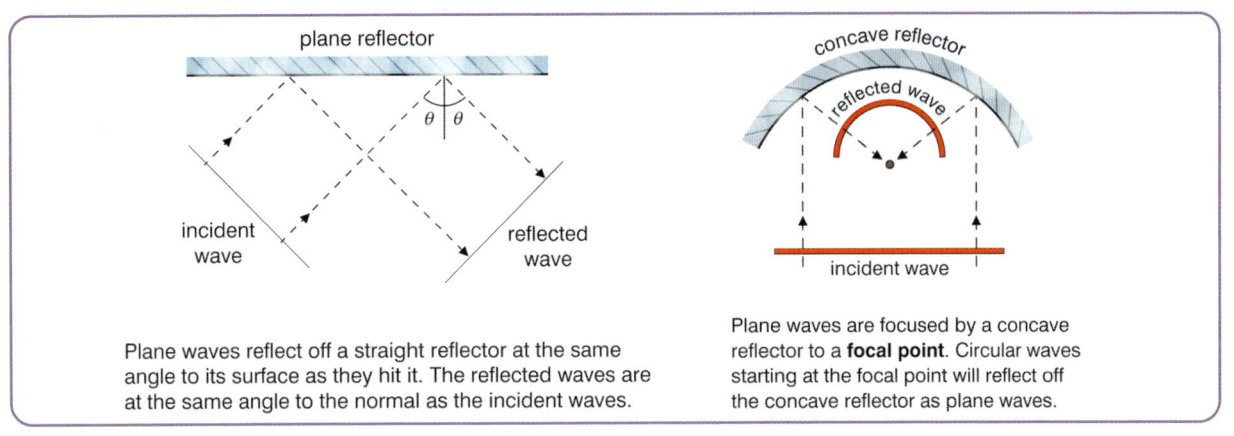

Plane waves reflect off a straight reflector at the same angle to its surface as they hit it. The reflected waves are at the same angle to the normal as the incident waves.

Plane waves are focused by a concave reflector to a **focal point**. Circular waves starting at the focal point will reflect off the concave reflector as plane waves.

Reflections on reflection

Reflection

The shape and the direction of a reflected wave depend on the shape of the incident wave and on the shape of the reflecting surface.

Note
*Straight waves are sometimes called **plane waves**. A line perpendicular to a wall or boundary is called a **normal**.*

Refraction

When a plane wave passes across a straight boundary:
- its wavelength changes if the wave speed changes at the boundary; the frequency does not change
- its direction of motion changes if its direction is not perpendicular to the boundary.

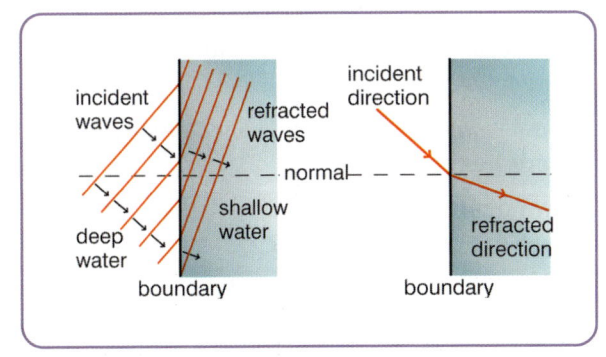

Refraction

Diffraction

★ Waves spread out when they pass through a gap or behind an obstacle. This process is called **diffraction**.

★ The spreading is greater the longer the wavelength or the narrower the gap.

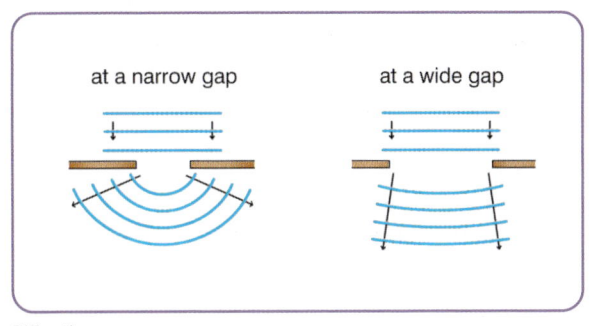

Diffraction

Questions

A satellite TV dish needs to be pointed in the correct direction to obtain a picture.

a) Using a diagram, explain how a satellite dish works.

b) Why are larger dishes needed in northern Europe than in southern Europe?

Answers

a) The dish is a concave reflector which focuses radio waves from the satellite onto an aerial at the focal point.

b) The satellite is over the equator so the radio waves travel further through the atmosphere to reach northern Europe, so they become weaker. Hence a larger dish is needed to collect more radio waves.

Waves

ROUND UP

How much have you improved?
Work out your improvement index on page 307.

1. **a)** Which of the following can be classified as (i) longitudinal waves (ii) transverse waves?

   water waves, radio waves, sound waves, waves on a rope [3]

   b) State three differences between sound waves and light waves. [3]

2. Copy and complete each of these sketches, showing the wave after reflection. [4]

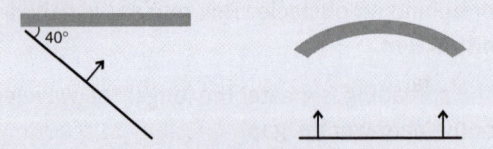

3. **a)** What is the name for the process that takes place when waves spread out after passing through a gap? [1]

   b) Does the spreading increase or decrease if
   - (i) the gap is made narrower and the wavelength of the waves is not changed
   - (ii) the wavelength is made shorter and the gap width is not changed
   - (iii) the gap is made narrower and the wavelength is made longer? [3]

4. **a)** When light passes from air into glass, it slows down. What happens to its wavelength and its frequency? [2]

   b) The diagram shows plane waves about to cross a boundary between shallow and deep water. Copy and complete the diagram by showing the waves in the deep water as well as the shallow water. [2]

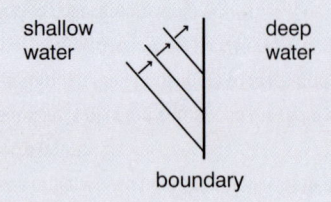

5. **a)** Sound travels at a speed of 1500 m/s in water. Calculate the wavelength in water of sound waves of frequency 3000 Hz. [1]

   b) Plane water waves of wavelength 0.2 m travel past five ducks spaced 0.3 m apart in a straight line. Each crest takes 3.0 s to pass from the mother duck at one end to the last duck at the other end. Calculate (i) the speed (ii) the frequency of the waves. [2]

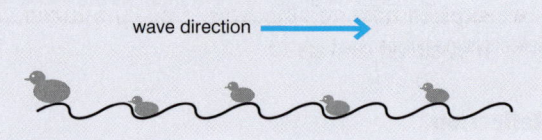

6. **a)** When sound waves pass through an open door, they spread out. What is the name for this process? [1]

   b) If the frequency of the sound waves is increased, what happens to the amount of spreading? [1]

7. **a)** A local radio station broadcasts at a frequency of 100 MHz. Calculate the wavelength of these radio waves, given that radio waves travel through air at a speed of 300 000 km/s. [1]

   b) The aerial of a portable radio is turned through 90°, causing the reception to become weaker. Explain why this happens. [3]

   c) A radio telescope consists of a large concave dish made from wire mesh with an aerial at its focal point. What is the purpose of the wire mesh? [1]

8. A boat travelling at constant speed produces bow waves as shown.

   How would the bow waves differ if the boat travelled **a)** faster **b)** slower? [2]

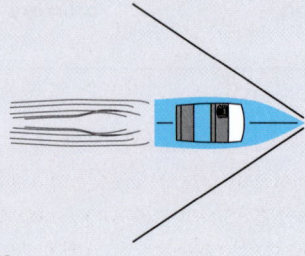

   Bow waves

Sound waves and seismic waves — Chapter 5

PREVIEW

At the end of this topic you will be able to:
- describe how sound is produced and transmitted
- explain how pitch and loudness are related to frequency and amplitude
- describe reflection, refraction, diffraction and absorption of sound
- explain what ultrasound is and describe some uses of ultrasound
- explain how seismic waves are produced, measured and used.

How much do you already know? Work out your score on page 308.

Test yourself

1. a) Are sound waves longitudinal or transverse? [1]
   b) Are seismic waves longitudinal or transverse? [2]
2. What is special about the sound produced by a vibrating tuning fork? [1]
3. a) The pitch of a note produced by plucking a guitar string can be altered by changing the tension or changing the length of the vibrating section of the string. How does the pitch of the note change when the string is **(i)** tightened **(ii)** lengthened? [2]
   b) Two guitar strings of the same material have equal lengths but different thicknesses. They are tuned to produce notes of the same pitch when plucked. Which string is under the greater tension? [2]
4. What is an echo? [1]
5. How do the amplitude and the wavelength of the sound waves from a loudspeaker change if the sound is made **a)** louder at the same pitch **b)** quieter at higher pitch? [4]
6. A teacher is talking in a classroom with the door to the corridor open. The teacher's voice can be heard down the corridor even though the teacher cannot be seen from there. What property of sound is responsible for this? [1]
7. a) Which frequency **A** to **D** is nearest to the highest sound frequency that can be heard by the human ear? [1]

   A 200 Hz   **B** 2000 Hz   **C** 20 000 Hz
   D 200 000 Hz

   b) Which frequency **A** to **D** is nearest to the frequency at which the human ear is most sensitive? [1]
   c) A telephone circuit does not transmit frequencies above 4000 Hz. Explain how this affects voice signals. [1]
8. a) Outline how an ultrasonic depth gauge on a ship works. [5]
   b) State two other uses of ultrasonics. [2]
9. a) Ultrasonic waves of frequency 2 MHz in air travel at a speed of 340 m/s. Calculate the wavelength of these waves. [1]
   b) These waves travel faster in water than in air. On entering water from air, what change occurs in **(i)** the frequency **(ii)** the wavelength of the waves? [2]
10. a) What causes earthquakes? [2]
    b) Why are secondary (S) waves from an earthquake unable to travel through the Earth's centre to the opposite side of the Earth? [3]

5.1 Properties of sound

Sound waves are longitudinal. They are created by an object vibrating in a medium. The object pushes and pulls on the medium. The particles of the medium vibrate to and fro along the direction in which the sound travels.

249

Sound waves and seismic waves

Sound waves can be displayed using a microphone and an oscilloscope, as shown below.

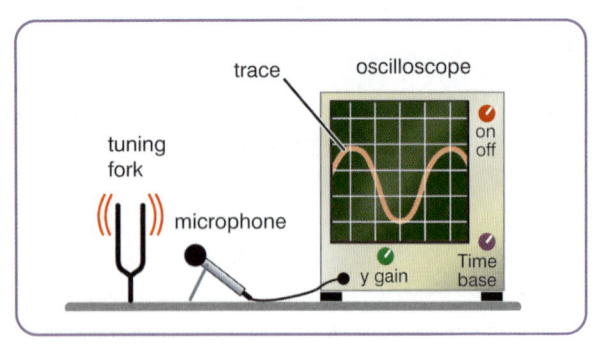

Displaying sound

The oscilloscope trace shows how the amplitude of the sound wave varies with time. The trace is usually referred to as the **waveform**. The trace on the screen is a transverse wave; the sound wave that creates the trace is a longitudinal wave.

★ If the sound is made louder, the trace becomes taller. The amplitude of a sound wave represents the volume.

★ If the sound is lowered in pitch, the trace is stretched out on the screen. The frequency of a sound wave represents the pitch.

★ Most sounds have more complicated waveforms than the pure waveform shown in the diagram.

Echoes

Sound is reflected by a hard surface such as a brick wall. **Echoes** are caused by sound reflections. First the original sound is heard, then an echo may be heard a little later due to reflection off the wall. The echo is delayed because the echo sound waves travel further than the direct sound waves.

Absorption of sound

Soft surfaces such as curtains absorb sound instead of reflecting it or transmitting it. This is why a curtained room sounds different from a bare room.

Refraction of sound

Like all waves, sound waves can be refracted. The speed of sound in air will change if the air temperature changes with height. Sound created on the ground may then be refracted, and may be heard a long way away from where it was produced.

Diffraction of sound

Sound waves spread through gaps and round obstacles. The sound from a car engine may be heard on the other side of a large building because of diffraction. The sound waves from the car engine pass round the edge of the building and spread round it on the other side.

Sound cannot travel through a vacuum

This fact is demonstrated by removing the air surrounding a ringing bell in a bell jar. The ringing bell can be heard before the air is pumped out. The sound of the bell fades away as the air is removed. If the air is allowed back into the bell jar, the sound returns.

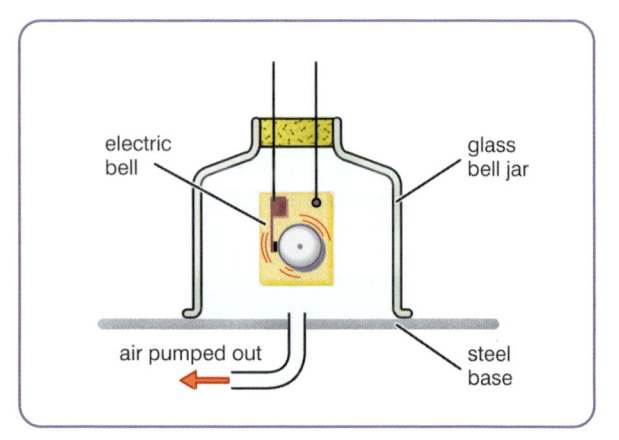

A soundless bell

Measuring the speed of sound

Two people stand a measured distance apart, at least 500 m. The starter makes a loud short sound, for example with a large gong, in view of the other person (the timer). The timer times the interval between observing the sound being created and hearing it. The speed of sound is calculated from the distance divided by the time taken.

To account for wind speed, the two people change roles and the experiment is repeated to give an average value.

Sound waves and seismic waves

5.2 Ultrasound

Hearing

The human ear is a remarkable organ. The loudest sounds your ears can withstand without damage are about one million million times more powerful than the faintest sound you can hear. Loudness levels are expressed in **decibels** (dB) where 0 dB is at the lower threshold of hearing and every 10 dB extra corresponds to ten times more power. The graph shows how the lower threshold of hearing varies with frequency.

★ The human ear is most sensitive at a frequency of about 3000 Hz.

★ The upper frequency limit for the human ear is about 20 000 Hz.

★ Hearing usually deteriorates with age – your upper frequency limit will decrease as you become older.

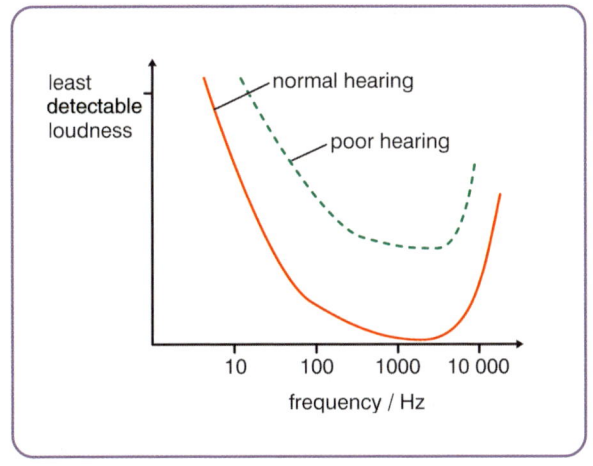

Hearing response

Ultrasound

Ultrasound is defined as sound at frequencies above the upper limit of the human ear. In other words, any sound waves of frequency above 20 kHz will be ultrasound.

Ultrasonic cleaning: dirt particles are removed from street lamps by immersing the lamp in an ultrasonic cleaning tank operating at 40 kHz. The ultrasonic waves in the water agitate the dirt particles which are then dispersed by the water.

Depth finding: the depth of the sea bed can be determined by sending ultrasonic pulses from a ship towards the sea bed, and timing how long the reflected pulses take to return to the ship. If the speed of sound c in water is known, the depth of the sea bed can be calculated from $\frac{1}{2}ct$, where t is the time taken for each pulse to travel to the sea bed and back.

Metal fatigue tests: cracks inside a metal weaken the metal, but cannot be seen from the outside. Such cracks can be detected using an ultrasonic probe. This sends ultrasonic waves into the metal and picks up reflections from internal boundaries within the metal.

Ultrasonic medical scanner: this is used to obtain images of organs within the body. It is also widely used to form images of unborn babies to monitor the health of the baby and the mother. An ultrasonic probe moved across the body surface directs ultrasonic waves into the human body. Internal boundaries partially reflect the ultrasonic waves, and the reflected waves are detected by the same probe, which is connected to a computer. The probe builds up an image of the reflecting boundaries inside the body. Unlike X-rays, ultrasonic waves do not cause ionisation, and are therefore thought to be harmless at low power.

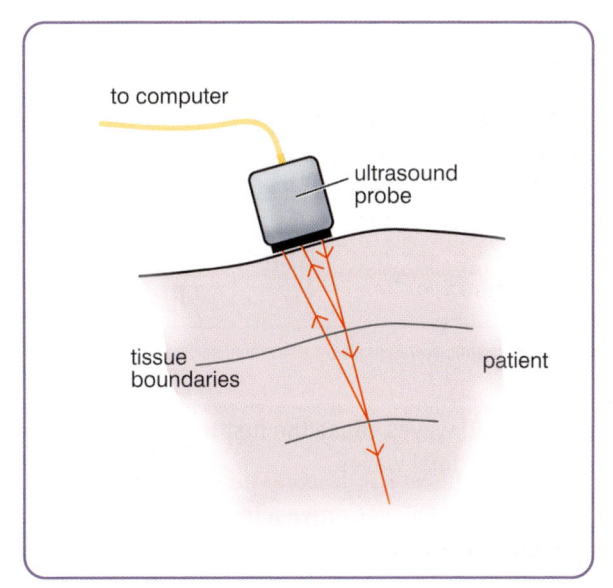

Ultrasonic scanner

Sound waves and seismic waves

5.3 Seismic waves

Inside the Earth

The Earth is thought to have formed about 4600 million years ago, originally in a molten state which gradually cooled and solidified. More dense materials such as iron sank to the centre when it was molten. The least dense material formed the Earth's crust.

Earthquakes

★ Earthquake belts occur where two plates press against each other or slide past each other. Stress builds up which is suddenly released when one plate gives way to the other. The crust shakes violently and seismic waves spread out through the Earth.

★ The point where the seismic waves originate from is called the **focus** of the earthquake. The nearest point on the surface directly above the focus is called the **epicentre**.

★ The energy released by an earthquake is measured on the **Richter scale** which is a 'times ten' scale. An earthquake that registers at a certain point on the Richter scale releases ten times as much energy as an earthquake that registers on the next point below.

Analysing seismic waves

An instrument called a **seismometer** is used to detect seismic waves.

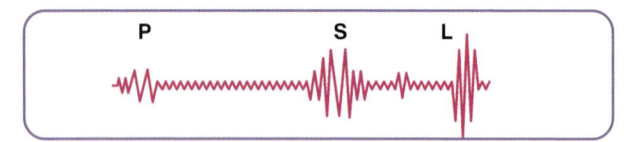

Recording of seismic waves made by a seismometer

★ **Primary (P)** waves cause the first tremors. These are longitudinal waves.

★ **Secondary (S)** waves arrive a few minutes later, causing more tremors. They travel more slowly than P waves. These are transverse waves.

★ **Long (L)** waves arrive last to cause the main shock. These travel along the crust only, making the surface move violently up and down as well as to and fro.

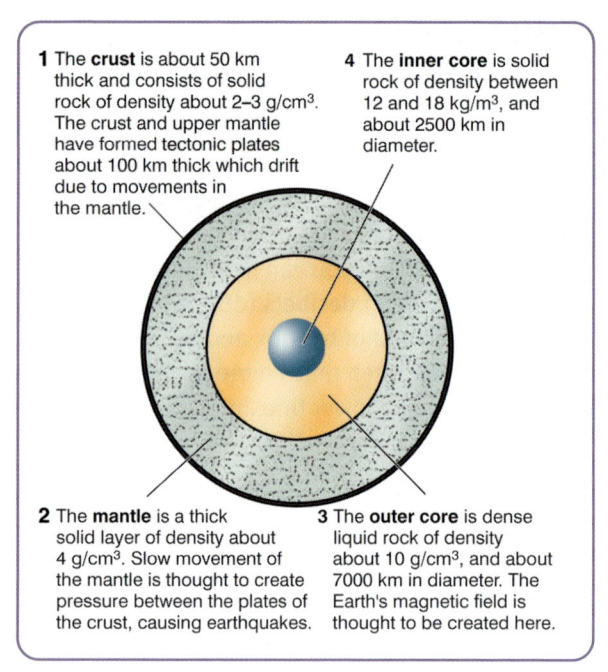

1 The **crust** is about 50 km thick and consists of solid rock of density about 2–3 g/cm³. The crust and upper mantle have formed tectonic plates about 100 km thick which drift due to movements in the mantle.

2 The **mantle** is a thick solid layer of density about 4 g/cm³. Slow movement of the mantle is thought to create pressure between the plates of the crust, causing earthquakes.

3 The **outer core** is dense liquid rock of density about 10 g/cm³, and about 7000 km in diameter. The Earth's magnetic field is thought to be created here.

4 The **inner core** is solid rock of density between 12 and 18 kg/m³, and about 2500 km in diameter.

The structure of the Earth

Continental drift is due to the gradual movement of tectonic plates. (See page 169 for plate tectonics.)

Handy hint

P waves **P**ush and **P**ull.
S waves **S**hake **S**ide to **S**ide.
L waves go the **L**ong way round.

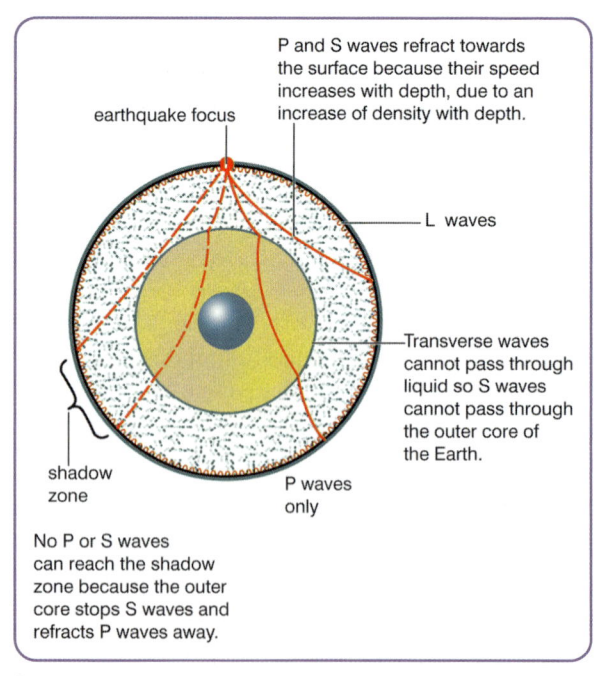

P and S waves refract towards the surface because their speed increases with depth, due to an increase of density with depth.

earthquake focus

L waves

Transverse waves cannot pass through liquid so S waves cannot pass through the outer core of the Earth.

shadow zone

P waves only

No P or S waves can reach the shadow zone because the outer core stops S waves and refracts P waves away.

Seismic waves inside the Earth

Sound waves and seismic waves

ROUND UP

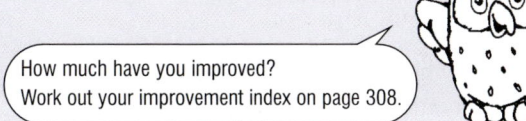

How much have you improved? Work out your improvement index on page 308.

1. The diagram shows a ship at sea near a cliff.

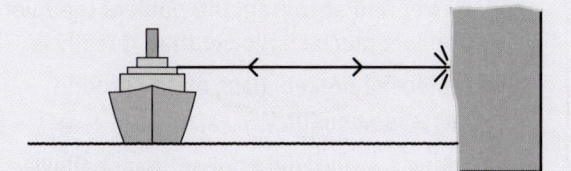

   An echo from the ship's siren is heard 5.0 s after the siren is sounded.

   a) Calculate the distance from the ship to the cliff. The speed of sound in air is 340 m/s. [1]

   b) If the ship was fog-bound, explain how the ship's captain could find out if the ship was moving towards or away from the cliffs. [2]

2. A loudspeaker connected to a signal generator is used to produce a continuous sound of constant pitch and loudness.

   a) Explain how the vibrating surface of the loudspeaker creates sound waves. [2]

   b) Why is a small loudspeaker likely to be able to produce sound waves of high frequency better than a large loudspeaker? [2]

3. The waveform of a note from a musical instrument is shown in the diagram below. Copy and draw on the diagram the waveform you would expect if the same instrument is

   a) played more quietly [2]

   b) played at a lower pitch. [1]

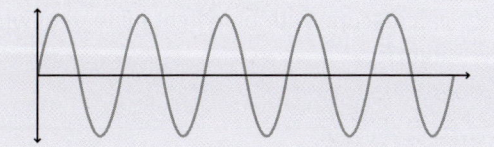

4. The speed of sound in air is 340 m/s.

   a) Calculate the frequency of sound waves of wavelength 0.10 m in air. [1]

   b) Calculate the wavelength of sound waves of frequency 5000 Hz in air. [1]

5. When indoors, noise from outside may be reduced by closing any open windows. How does this reduce the noise from outside? [2]

6. a) An ultrasonic cleaning tank operates at a frequency of 40 kHz. Calculate the wavelength of ultrasonic waves in water. The speed of sound waves in water is 1500 m/s. [1]

   b) When using an ultrasonic hospital scanner, a paste is applied to the body surface where the probe is used.

   (i) Explain why this is necessary. [2]

   (ii) Give two reasons why each reflected pulse is weaker than the pulse emitted by the probe. [2]

7. a) The diagram shows a cross-section of the Earth. The inner core is labelled A.

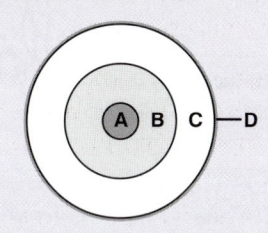

   (i) What are the parts labelled B, C and D? [3]

   (ii) State which of the parts A to D are molten and which are solid. [4]

   b) Why are earthquakes more common in certain parts of the world than in other parts? [1]

8. a) Are primary seismic waves longitudinal or transverse? [1]

   b) (i) Sketch and describe a typical seismic wave trace, labelling the P waves, the S waves and the L waves. [3]

   (ii) Why are S waves unable to travel through the Earth's core? [2]

   (iii) Why do P waves and S waves in the mantle curve towards the surface? [2]

   (iv) Copy the diagram above and use it to explain why shock waves from an earthquake can arrive without being preceded by tremors. [3]

Well done if you've improved. Don't worry if you haven't. Take a break and try again.

Chapter 6 Light

PREVIEW

At the end of this topic you will be able to:
- state the law of reflection and explain what is meant by refraction of light
- describe image formation by a plane mirror and describe some uses of a plane mirror
- explain how total internal reflection can occur
- describe some applications of fibre optics
- explain how diffraction affects image detail
- describe how to split white light into a spectrum using a prism.

How much do you already know? Work out your score on pages 308–9.

Test yourself

1. a) State the law of reflection at a plane mirror. [1]
   b) A person stands 0.6 m in front of a plane mirror and observes his own image. How far away is the image from the person? [1]

2. a) When a light ray passes from air into glass at a non-zero angle to the normal, does it bend towards or away from the normal? [1]
   b) A light ray passes from a pool of water into air, emerging at an angle of 30° to the vertical, as in the following diagram. Is the angle between the light ray in the water and the vertical more than, less than or equal to 30°? [1]

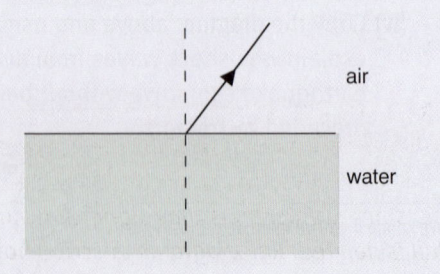

   c) In b), the angle between the light ray in the water and the vertical is increased until the refracted ray emerges along the water surface. What happens if this angle is made larger? [1]

3. State whether each of the following observations is due to reflection or refraction of light.
   (i) You look at yourself in a mirror.
   (ii) A river bed seen from the bank of the river appears much shallower than it really is.
   (iii) A piece of broken glass on the ground glints in sunlight. [3]

4. Why does a swimming pool appear shallower than it really is? [3]

5. When light travels from air into glass,
   a) does its speed increase or decrease?
   b) does its wavelength increase or decrease? [2]

6. State the colours of the visible spectrum. [1]

7. a) A beam of white light is split into a spectrum by passing it through a glass prism. Which colour of the spectrum is refracted least? [1]
   b) A surface that appears blue in white light will appear black in red light. Why? [3]

8. a) Explain what is meant by total internal reflection of light. [1]
   b) State one application of total internal reflection of light. [1]
   c) How does total internal reflection of light differ from reflection of light by a flat mirror? [2]

9. State two uses of fibre optics. [2]

10. a) Is the wavelength of red light less or more than the wavelength of blue light? [1]
    b) Why can you see more detail using a microscope with blue light instead of white light? [3]

Light

6.1 Reflection

The **law of reflection** states that the angle between the reflected ray and the normal is equal to the angle between the incident ray and the normal.

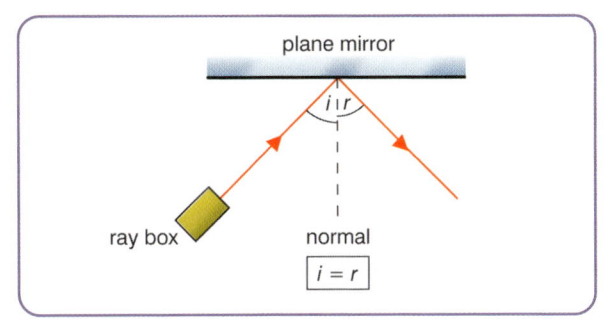

The law of reflection

The diagram above shows how this can be tested using a ray box and a plane mirror. Note that the normal is the line which is perpendicular to the mirror at the point where the light ray meets the mirror.

Mirror images

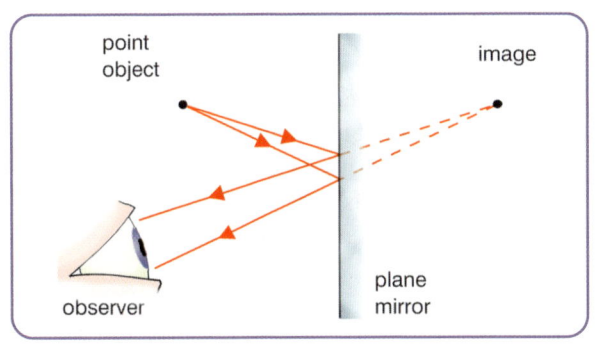

Image formation

The diagram above shows how a plane mirror forms an image. Note that the image of an object viewed by reflection using a plane mirror is:
- the same distance behind the mirror as the object is in front
- upright and the same size as the object
- virtual, which means it is formed where the reflected rays *appear* to come from
- laterally inverted, which means the image of a left-handed person is right-handed and vice versa. Try it if you don't believe it!

Uses of a plane mirror

1. A **wall mirror** needs to be at least half the height of the tallest person who uses it. It also needs to be mounted with its top edge level with the top of the head.

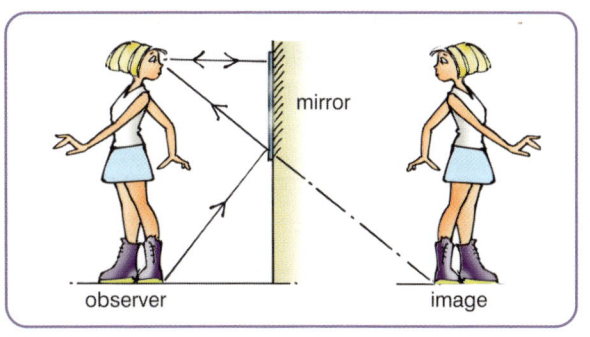

   Using a wall mirror

2. A **periscope** is useful for seeing over a crowd. It is also used in submarines to see above the surface when the submarine is under water.

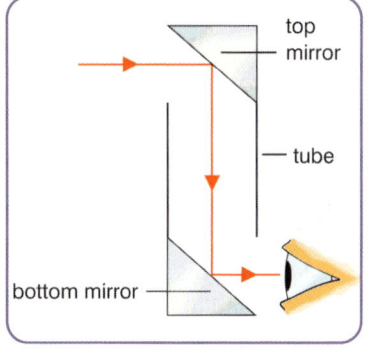

   Using a periscope

3. **Parallax errors** caused by incorrectly reading the position of a pointer on a scale can be eliminated using a plane mirror. The image of the pointer must be directly under the pointer when reading the scale.

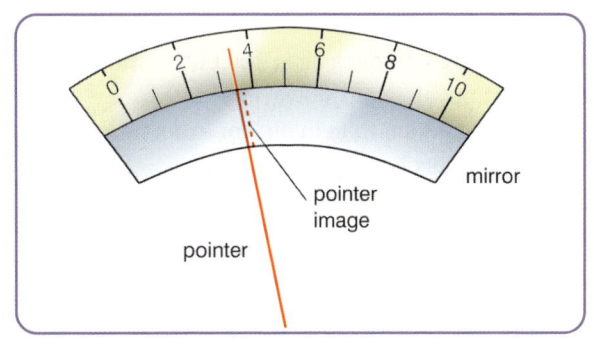

   Parallax errors

Note on rays and waves

A light ray shows the direction in which light travels. Light rays are usually drawn as straight lines, since diffraction is only significant where fine detail is needed. Ray diagrams describe how light is affected by mirrors and lenses.

255

Light

6.2 Refraction

Investigating refraction

★ If a light ray is directed at a glass block as shown, the light ray changes its direction when it enters the glass. It is closer to the normal in glass than in air. This is an example of the **refraction** of light. It occurs because light waves travel more slowly in glass than in air.

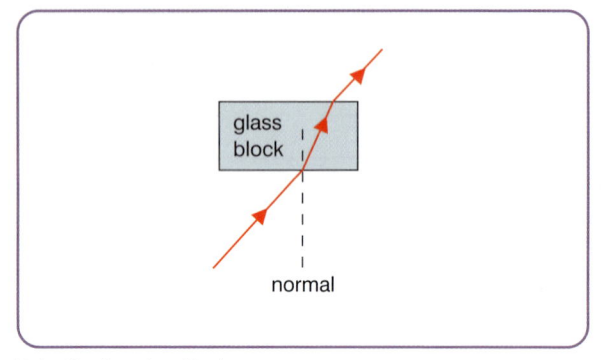

Refraction in a glass block

★ When a light ray passes from glass into air at a non-zero angle to the normal, it bends away from the normal. This happens because the light waves speed up when they pass from glass into air.

★ Refraction happens when light passes from one transparent medium into another. The light ray is always closer to the normal in the 'slower' medium.

Fact file

The speed of light through air is 300 000 km/s. Light travels more slowly in a transparent medium than in air. For example, its speed in glass is 200 000 km/s.

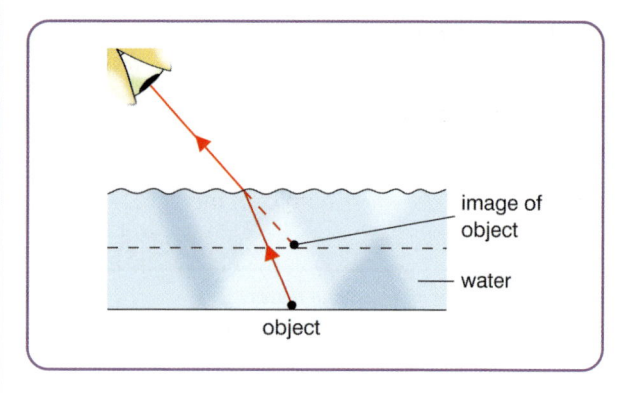

In deep water

A swimming pool appears shallower than it really is because light from the bottom of the pool is refracted away from the normal when it passes into air at the surface. Someone looking into the water from above sees an image of the bottom of the pool nearer the surface.

Questions

1. A light ray passes into and out of a glass block in air, as shown in the diagram opposite. Describe how its speed changes along this path.

2. Light travels more slowly in glass than in water and it travels more slowly in water than in air. In each of the following situations, a light ray travels across a boundary at non-normal incidence. State whether the light ray bends towards or away from the normal if it passes from

   a) glass to air
   b) air to water
   c) water to glass
   d) glass to water.

Answers

1. When it passes from air into glass, its speed becomes less. When it passes from glass to air, its speed increases.
2. a) away b) towards c) towards d) away

Light

6.3 Fibre optics

Total internal reflection

This occurs when light in a transparent medium strikes the boundary at an angle of incidence greater than a **critical angle**. The light ray reflects internally just as if the boundary is a mirror.

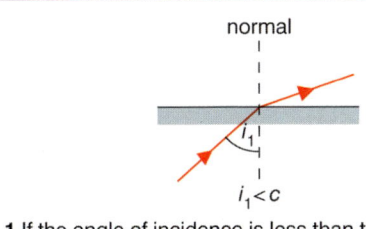

1 If the angle of incidence is less than the critical angle, the light ray bends away from the normal on leaving the glass. ($i_1 < c$)

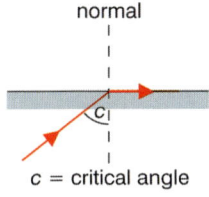

2 If the angle of incidence is equal to the critical angle, the light refracts along the boundary. (c = critical angle)

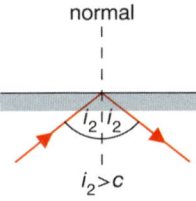

3 If the angle of incidence exceeds the critical angle, the light ray is totally internally reflected. ($i_2 > c$)

Total internal reflection

Optical fibres

An optical fibre is a thin fibre of transparent flexible material. A light ray that enters the fibre at one end emerges at the other end, even if the fibre is curved round. This happens because the light ray is totally internally reflected at the fibre surface wherever it hits the boundary. Each light ray in the fibre travels along a straight line through the fibre between successive reflections. Provided the bends in the fibre are not too tight, light rays in the fibre do not emerge from its sides.

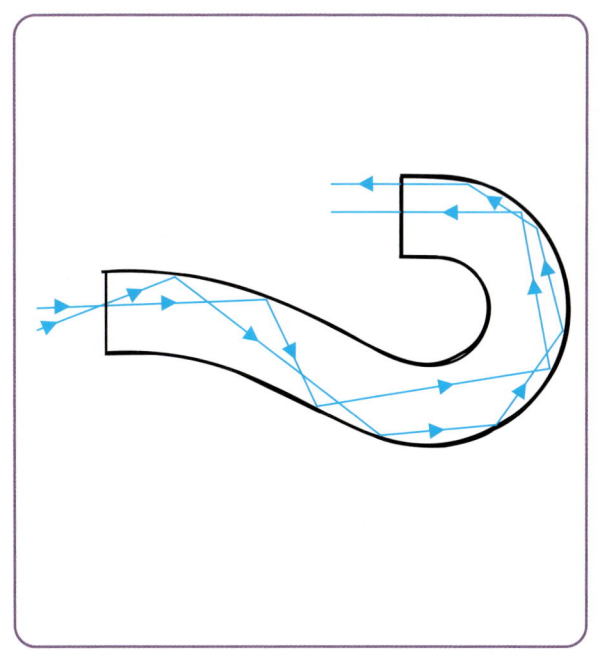

An optical fibre

Questions

1. The critical angle of glass in air is 47°. A light ray travelling in a glass block in air is incident on the boundary of the glass block. State whether the light ray is refracted or totally internally reflected if the angle of incidence in the glass is **a)** 40° **b)** 50°.

2. White light consists of all the colours of the spectrum. In glass, the speed of light decreases from red to blue. A ray of white light is directed into an optical fibre at one end. If the fibre is curved more and more, blue light is seen emerging from its sides where it bends.

   a) Why does this happen?

   b) What colour emerges at the other end? Explain your answer.

Answers

1 a) Refracted **b)** Totally internally reflected
2 a) The critical angle is bigger for red light than for blue light. Therefore blue light emerges first when the fibre is bent.
b) Yellow (white light minus blue light).

Light

Using optical fibres

1. The **endoscope** consists of two bundles of optical fibres.
2. One bundle delivers light to the organ to be inspected.
3. A small lens near the end of the other bundle forms a real image of the organ on the end of the bundle. Each fibre in the bundle transmits a 'dot' of light from this image so it can be seen at the other end. The fibres in this bundle must be positioned the same way at each end otherwise the image is 'scrambled'.
4. Special surgical tools can be pushed down the endoscope and used to remove tumours. Powerful pulses of laser light can also be sent down one of the bundles to destroy unwanted tissues.

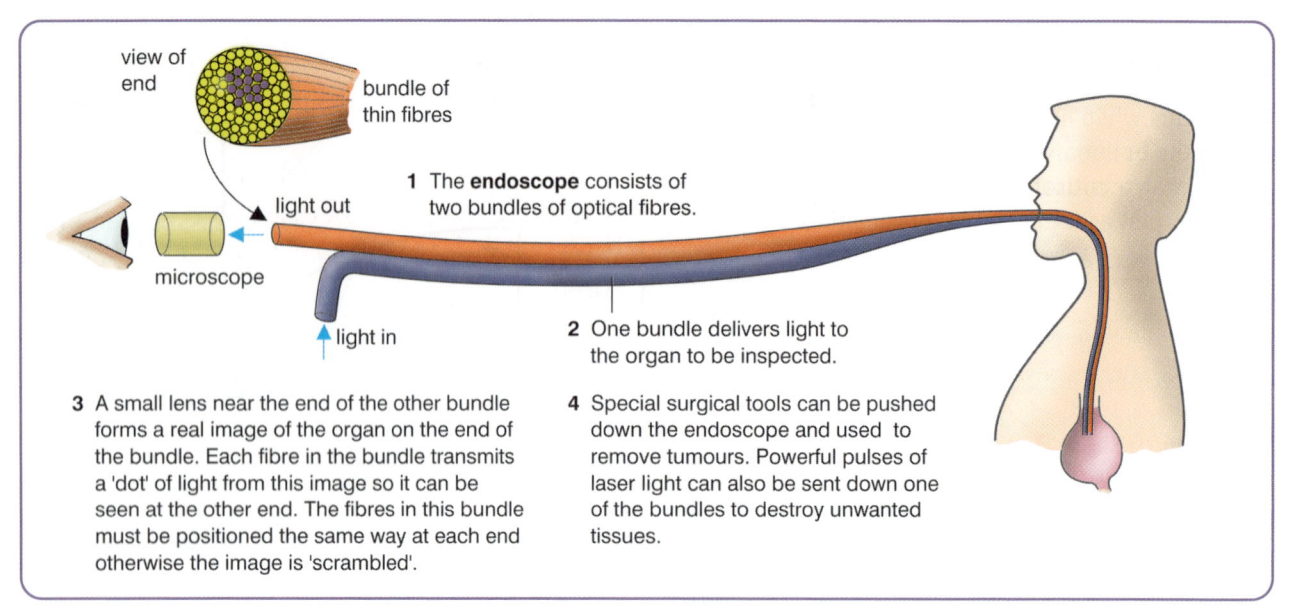

The endoscope

In communications, optical fibres are used to guide pulses of infrared light. Because the frequency of light is much higher than that of radio waves or microwaves, an infrared light beam can carry many more pulses per second than radio waves or microwaves. This means much more information can be carried using optical fibres than by other means.

In medicine, optical fibres are used in an **endoscope** to see inside the body, and to treat internal tumours. Use of an endoscope avoids the need to cut open the body and therefore shortens the post-operation recovery period.

Reflectors for road safety

The back surface of a cycle reflector consists of lots of triangles. Light rays falling directly on the reflector are totally internally reflected twice at this surface, so they are reflected back.

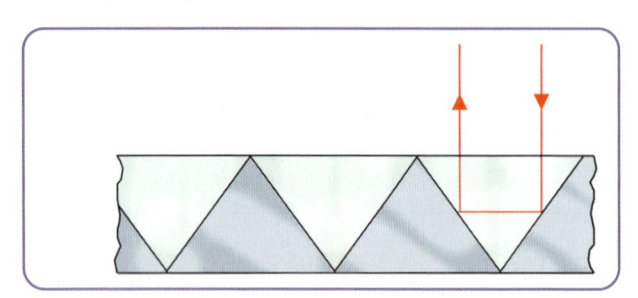

A reflector

6.4 Light and colour

The visible spectrum

This is produced by passing a beam of white light through a prism. Because the speed of light in glass decreases from red to blue, blue light is bent more than red light.

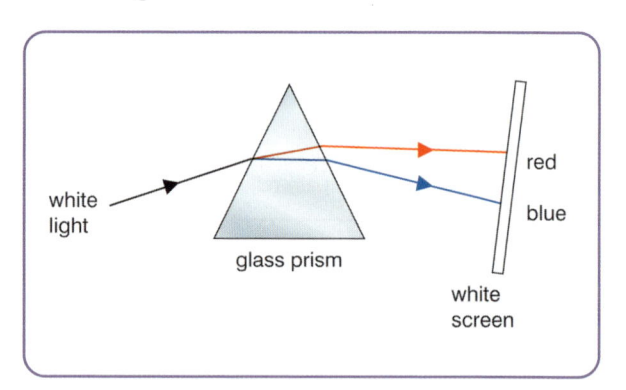

Producing a spectrum

★ **Remember** that blue bends better than red!

★ Also remember the colours of the spectrum (**R**ed **O**range **Y**ellow **G**reen **B**lue **I**ndigo **V**iolet) from a mnemonic, such as **R**ichard **O**f **Y**ork **G**ave **B**attle **I**n **V**ain, or remember Roy G Biv.

Light

Colour and wavelength

★ Light is diffracted when it passes through a gap, because it consists of waves. The narrower the gap or the longer the wavelength, the greater the amount of diffraction (spreading).

★ For a gap of constant width, the spreading depends on the colour of the light. The closer the light is to the red part of the spectrum, the more it spreads.

★ It therefore follows that the wavelength of light increases across the spectrum from blue to red. The amount of spreading can be used to work out the wavelength of the light.

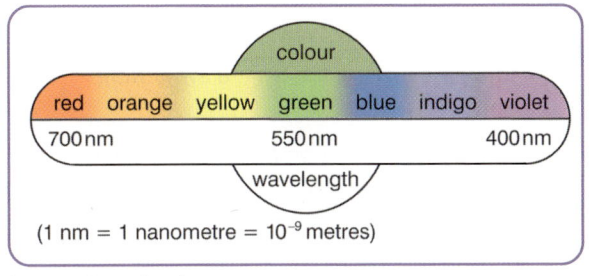

colour: red, orange, yellow, green, blue, indigo, violet
wavelength: 700 nm — 550 nm — 400 nm
(1 nm = 1 nanometre = 10^{-9} metres)

Colour and wavelength

Diffraction at work

A **telescope** is used to magnify distant objects. It does not necessarily produce a detailed image.

★ Light from a point object entering the telescope is diffracted at the entrance and so an image 'spot' is formed.

★ If two point objects are too close, their image spots will merge and be seen as one spot.

★ The wider the objective lens of a telescope, the less diffraction it produces, so the greater the image detail that can be seen.

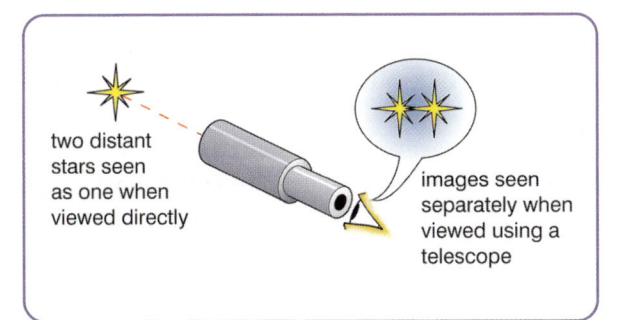

two distant stars seen as one when viewed directly — images seen separately when viewed using a telescope

Using a telescope

A **microscope** is used to observe details of small objects.

★ Light from each point of an object under view spreads when it enters the microscope and forms an image spot.

★ The spreading is less for blue light than for any other colour. This is because blue light has a shorter wavelength than other colours of light.

★ Therefore, two points that are very close together can be better distinguished in blue light than in any other colour. This is why more detail can be seen in an image if blue light is used instead of white light.

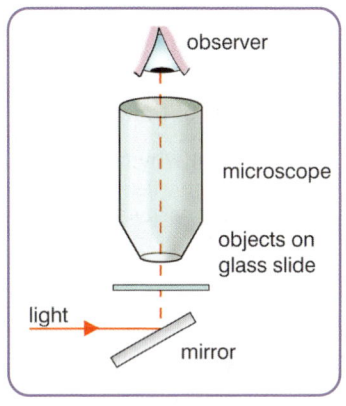

Using a microscope

Questions

Cheap cameras often produce images which are tinged in colours. The sketch below shows two rays of white light entering a convex lens at opposite edges. Each ray is split into coloured rays by the lens. The sketch shows the blue rays forming a point image on a colour film.

a) Describe what you would expect to see when the film is developed.

b) Which direction would you move the object to form a point image in red light?

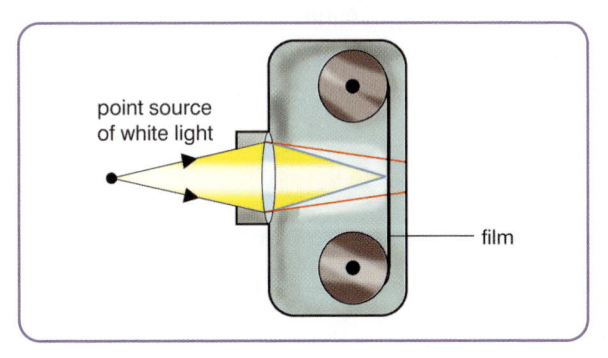

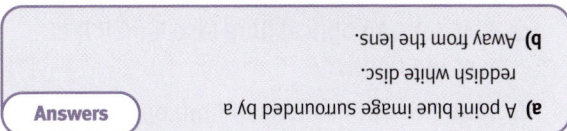

Answers

a) A point blue image surrounded by a reddish white disc.
b) Away from the lens.

Light

ROUND UP

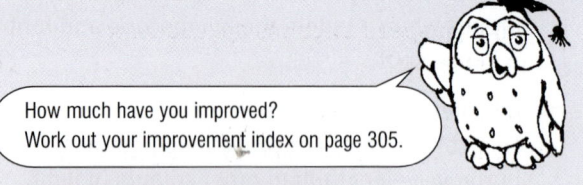

How much have you improved? Work out your improvement index on page 305.

1 a) Complete the ray diagram to show where the image of point object O_1 is formed. [2]

b) Without drawing further rays on your diagram, mark the position where the image of point object O_2 is formed. [1]

c) Explain why the image of the arrow between O_1 and O_2 is the same length as the object. [2]

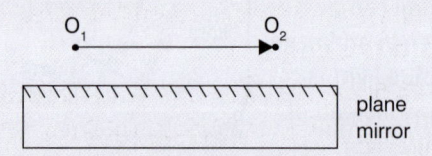

plane mirror

2 a) A student stands 1.0 m in front of a wall-mounted plane mirror. What is the distance from the student to her image? [1]

b) The student is 1.80 m tall. With the aid of a diagram, explain why the mirror needs to be at least 0.9 m in length if she is to be able to see a full-length image. [4]

c) State two further uses of a plane mirror. [2]

3 a) Explain with the aid of a diagram what is meant by total internal reflection of light. [2]

b) The diagram shows a light ray entering an optical fibre. Complete the diagram showing the path of the light ray after it enters the optical fibre. [2]

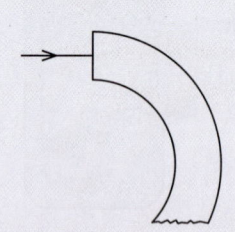

c) Why does an optical fibre lose light if it is bent too tightly? [1]

d) State two applications of fibre optics. [2]

4 Light travels more slowly in glass than in water and more slowly in water than in air. State whether or not a light ray incident on a boundary at a non-zero angle of incidence bends towards or away from the normal if it travels across the boundary from

(i) air to glass (ii) glass to air

(iii) glass to water. [3]

5 State whether reflection, refraction or diffraction takes place in each of the following situations.

(i) Light spreads out when it passes through a narrow gap.

(ii) Sunlight causes glare from a swimming pool.

(iii) Light passes along an optical fibre coiled round a tube.

(iv) An object viewed through a magnifying glass appears larger. [4]

6 Sketch a diagram to show how a glass prism can be used to split a ray of white light into a spectrum of colours.

Mark the order of the colours in the spectrum from red to blue. [3]

7 a) Blue light rays are refracted more by glass than red light rays. What does this statement tell you about the speed of blue light in glass compared with the speed of red light in glass? [1]

b) Explain why a microscope image is more detailed if it is observed using blue light than using white light. [3]

8 A military satellite is used to observe hostile troop movements. Explain why the satellite's camera must be fitted with a wide lens. [2]

Well done if you've improved. Don't worry if you haven't. Take a break and try again.

The electromagnetic spectrum — Chapter 7

PREVIEW

At the end of this topic you will be able to:
- state the six main bands of the electromagnetic spectrum in order of increasing wavelength
- outline the similarities and the main differences between the different bands
- describe some uses of electromagnetic waves in the home, in medicine and in communications
- relate uses of electromagnetic waves to their properties.

How much do you already know? Work out your score on page 309.

Test yourself

1. Name the six main bands of the electromagnetic spectrum in order of increasing frequency. [6]
2. State one use for each of the main bands of the electromagnetic spectrum. [6]
3. Which two bands of the electromagnetic spectrum are not absorbed by the atmosphere? [2]
4. a) Which type(s) of electromagnetic radiation can cause ionisation? [2]
   b) Which type of electromagnetic radiation are you emitting at this very moment? [1]
   c) Which type of electromagnetic radiation causes sunburn? [1]
5. Name one type of electromagnetic radiation that can pass through a metal plate and one type that cannot. [2]
6. Which type of electromagnetic radiation is emitted when
   a) high-speed electrons are suddenly stopped? [1]
   b) a sunbed is used? [1]
7. a) A satellite broadcasts at a frequency of 10 GHz. What type of electromagnetic radiation is at this frequency? [1]
   b) Why is a satellite dish (i) concave (ii) made from metal? [2]
8. How does an invisible marker pen work? [3]
9. a) What type of electromagnetic radiation is detected by (i) a blackened thermometer (ii) a Geiger counter? [2]
   b) Which type(s) of electromagnetic radiation cannot be detected using photographic film? [1]
10. a) A fibre optic link uses electromagnetic radiation of wavelength 1000 nm. What part of the electromagnetic spectrum is this? [1]
    b) Which two types of electromagnetic radiation are emitted by a filament lamp? [1]

7.1 Using electromagnetic waves

All electromagnetic waves:
- do not need to be carried by a medium
- travel at the same speed of 300 000 km/s in a vacuum
- can be diffracted, refracted and reflected (although X-rays and gamma rays need special techniques)
- make charged particles vibrate
- are transverse waves and can be polarised.

The electromagnetic spectrum

INCREASING WAVELENGTH

10^{-15} m 10^{-12} m 10^{-9} m 10^{-6} m 10^{-3} m 1 m 10^{3} m

X-rays and gamma rays | ultraviolet radiation | infrared radiation | microwaves | radio waves

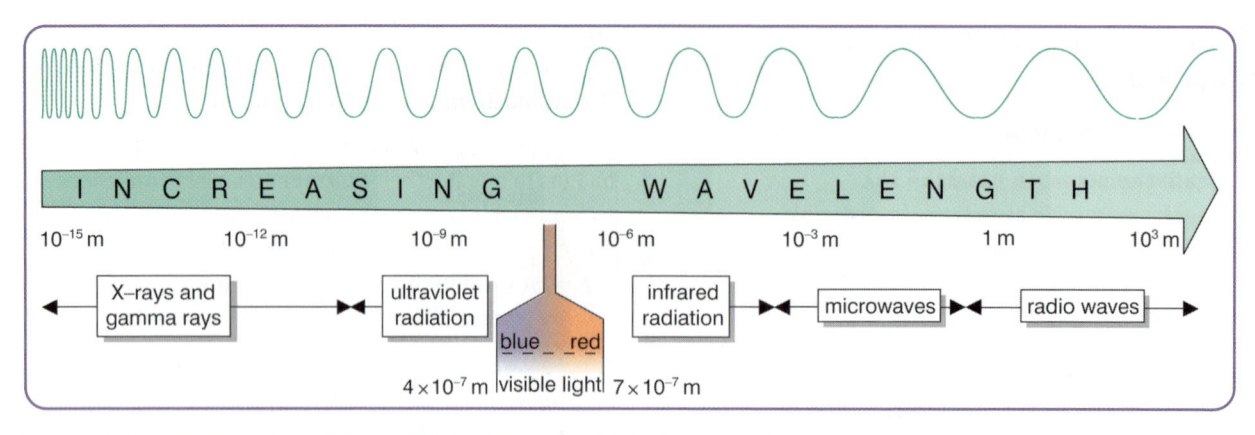

blue — red
4×10^{-7} m visible light 7×10^{-7} m

	production	detection	absorption or reflection	uses
radio waves	transmitter aerial, Sun	receiver aerial	reflected by metal	communications
microwaves	microwave transmitter	microwave detector	reflected by metal	communications, heating
infrared light	any object	blackened thermometer	reflected by shiny silvered surfaces, absorbed best by matt black surfaces	communications, heating, TV remote control handsets
visible light	glowing objects	eye, photographic film, electronic pixels	reflected by metal, absorbed by pigments	sight, communications
ultraviolet light	UV lamps, Sun	photocell, photographic film	absorbed by skin	security coding, sunbeds
X-rays and gamma rays	X-ray tube, radioactive isotopes	Geiger tube, photographic film	penetrates matter	medical

Electromagnetic waves at home

Microwave cookers: microwaves penetrate food and agitate water molecules within the food. This happens if the frequency is 2.5 GHz, so microwave cookers operate at this frequency. The oven case is metal, which reflects microwaves, so the oven does not heat up. All the electrical power supplied is used to heat the food.

Microwaves are also used for industrial heating, for example to dry wet fabrics after dyeing.

Infrared sensors: these are used for security purposes. **Passive** sensors detect infrared radiation emitted by intruders. **Active** sensors emit infrared rays and detect reflections from intruders. Infrared sensors fitted to TV cameras allow surveillance in the dark.

Halogen hobs: cookers fitted with transparent ceramic cooker rings use halogen lamp bulbs that emit mostly infrared radiation. Little energy is used to heat the ceramic plate, and when the cooker ring is switched off it cools much more rapidly than an ordinary cooker ring.

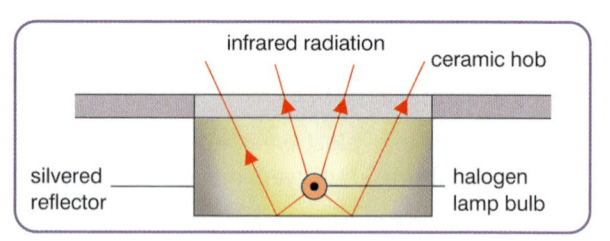

A halogen hob

UV-sensitive inks: these inks can only be seen using ultraviolet light. They are used for security marking.

Fluorescent lights: when one is switched on, ultraviolet light is produced in the tube. This radiation is absorbed by a fluorescent coating on the inside surface of the tube. As a result, this coating emits visible light, which illuminates the room.

The electromagnetic spectrum

7.2 Electromagnetic waves in medicine

A health warning

X-rays and gamma rays penetrate living tissues and so can be used in medicine to diagnose disorders and for treatment. These electromagnetic radiations are ionising, so excessive amounts will damage living cells. Great care is taken to ensure radiation doses given to patients are as low as possible and to ensure personnel are not exposed.

X-rays

These are produced in an **X-ray tube**. The X-ray beam consists of a continuous spread of wavelengths. The longer wavelengths are easily absorbed by tissues, unlike the shorter wavelengths which easily pass through tissues. A metal plate is placed in the path of the beam before the patient to remove longer wavelengths. This reduces absorption of X-rays by the patient.

X-ray photographs of internal organs are made with the aid of a suitable contrast medium. For example, a patient about to undergo a stomach X-ray may be given a barium meal in advance. Barium absorbs X-rays so the X-ray photograph shows a light image of the stomach on a darker background.

Personnel in a hospital X-ray department wear **film badges** to monitor their exposure to ionising radiations. If a film badge is over-exposed when it is developed, the wearer has been over-exposed too!

Gamma radiation

This is produced by radioactive isotopes. Gamma radiation is used at high doses to destroy unwanted tissue inside the body, and at low doses to 'image' internal organs.

★ **Treatment** – the use of gamma radiation from the radioactive isotope cobalt-60 is described on page 250. Re-read this section.

★ **Diagnosis** – the **gamma camera** is used with a suitable radioactive tracer to form an image of an internal organ. The tracer must emit gamma radiation and its half-life must be a suitable length. The tracer is given to the patient in advance, either by mouth or by injection.

Gamma radiation is also used to sterilise surgical instruments and to kill harmful bacteria in food.

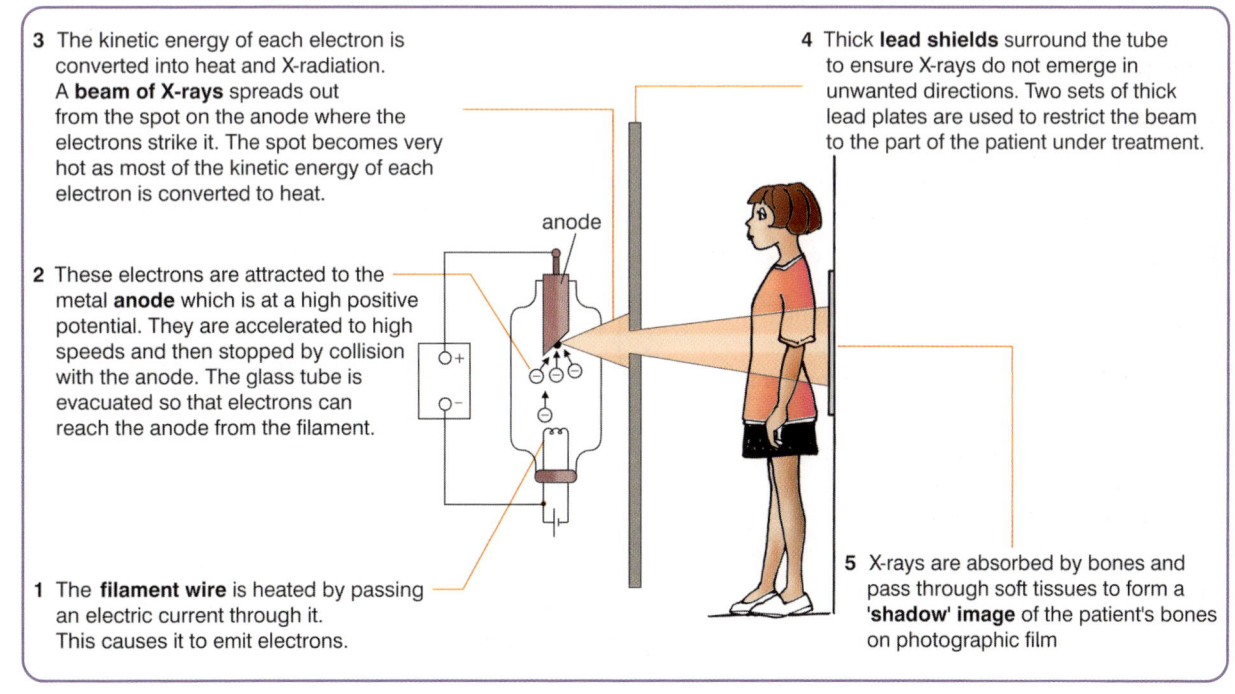

---

3 The kinetic energy of each electron is converted into heat and X-radiation. A **beam of X-rays** spreads out from the spot on the anode where the electrons strike it. The spot becomes very hot as most of the kinetic energy of each electron is converted to heat.

2 These electrons are attracted to the metal **anode** which is at a high positive potential. They are accelerated to high speeds and then stopped by collision with the anode. The glass tube is evacuated so that electrons can reach the anode from the filament.

1 The **filament wire** is heated by passing an electric current through it. This causes it to emit electrons.

4 Thick **lead shields** surround the tube to ensure X-rays do not emerge in unwanted directions. Two sets of thick lead plates are used to restrict the beam to the part of the patient under treatment.

5 X-rays are absorbed by bones and pass through soft tissues to form a **'shadow' image** of the patient's bones on photographic film

An X-ray tube in use

The electromagnetic spectrum

7.3 Communications

Radio waves, microwaves, infrared light and visible light are all used to carry information. The higher the frequency of the **carrier waves**, the more information can be carried. The information is carried by **modulating** the carrier wave:
- in **analogue form**, by modulating the amplitude (AM) or the frequency (FM) of the carrier wave
- in **digital form** as a stream of pulses.

The spread of frequencies in the signal determines the **bandwidth** of the carrier wave. Each carrier wave is allocated a frequency channel wide enough to transmit the bandwidth of the signal. For example, a channel width of 4000 Hz in telephone channels covers most of the audio range. A TV channel needs to be 8 MHz wide to carry all the information for TV pictures.

Electrical **noise** is created in amplifiers used to boost weak signals, causing loss of information. Digital pulses can be 'cleaned up' to eliminate noise. This is one of the main reasons why digital communication is much more effective than analogue communication. Noise cannot be removed from an analogue signal as easily as it can be from a digital signal.

In addition, analogue signals can be distorted by amplifiers, which amplify different frequencies by different amounts, whereas digital regenerators always recreate a strong pulse from a weak pulse. One further advantage of digital transmission over analogue transmission is that more information can be carried.

Optical fibre communications

Optical fibres can carry pulses of infrared light hundreds of kilometres without interruption. The frequency of light is about 1 million times higher than the frequency of microwave radiation, so an optical fibre can carry much more information than a microwave beam or an electrical cable.

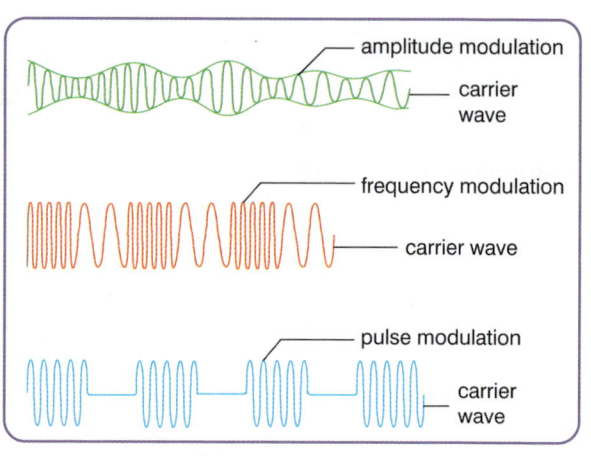

Amplitude modulation, frequency modulation and pulse modulation

Radio communications

★ Radio waves and microwaves create alternating voltages of the same frequency as the radiation itself when they are absorbed. This is why a receiver aerial picks up a signal from a transmitter.

★ Microwaves are used for satellite links because they pass straight through the atmosphere. They are also used for 'line of sight' links between communications towers because they do not spread out as much as radio waves do.

★ Radio waves of frequencies below 30 MHz reflect from the 'ionosphere', a layer of ionised gas in the upper atmosphere. Local radio and TV signals and mobile phone signals use frequencies well above 30 MHz.

Frequency bands

	frequency range	uses
long wave (LW)	up to 300 kHz	international AM radio
medium wave (MW)	300 kHz–3 MHz	AM radio
high frequency (HF)	3–30 MHz	AM radio
very high frequency (VHF)	30–300 MHz	FM radio
ultra high frequency (UHF)	300–3000 MHz	TV broadcasting, mobile phones
microwave	above 3000 MHz	satellite TV, global phone links
light	500 THz approx.	fibre optic communication links

Note: 1 MHz = 1 million Hz
       1 THz = 1 million MHz

The electromagnetic spectrum

Mobile phone links are only possible if the receiver is near a transmitter. A mobile phone signal is allocated a channel of bandwidth 25 kHz in the UHF band at a frequency of about 900 MHz. The transmitter is linked to the international phone network which uses undersea cable links, local microwave links and satellite links.

Satellite TV signals are carried by microwaves from a geostationary satellite. This orbits the Earth once every 24 hours round the equator, so stays in the same place above the Earth. A reflecting dish pointed towards the satellite focuses the microwaves on an aerial, which detects the signal and passes it on to a decoder.

Radio broadcasts at frequencies below 30 MHz travel long distances due to reflection from a layer of ionised gases in the upper atmosphere. Long wave broadcasts spread round the Earth because long wavelength radio waves follow the Earth's curvature.

Terrestrial TV signals are carried by radio waves in the UHF band range. Receiving aerials need to be in the line of sight of the transmitter. TV pictures from the other side of the world reach us via satellite links and ground stations.

Questions

1. a) Draw a diagram to show a wave that is modulated in **(i)** analogue form **(ii)** digital form.
   b) State two advantages of digital transmission in comparison with analogue transmission.
   c) What is meant by the bandwidth of a carrier wave?

2. a) What type of electromagnetic radiation is used for **(i)** optical fibre communications **(ii)** mobile phone communications **(iii)** satellite communications?
   b) State two advantages of optical fibre communications in comparison with radio communications.

3. a) What is a geostationary orbit?
   b) State one advantage and one disadvantage of putting a communications satellite in a geostationary orbit in comparison with putting it in a lower orbit.

Fact file

It is possible sometimes to pick up foreign radio stations on a radio receiver. If the atmospheric conditions are suitable, medium wave broadcasts from abroad can be picked up if they bounce between the ionosphere and the ground repeatedly. This happens best in summer at night when the ionosphere is most effective as a reflector. Long wave broadcasts from abroad can also be picked up sometimes but this is because they follow the Earth's curvature.

Answers

1. a) See the diagram on page 264 b) Noise and distortion are eliminated; more information can be carried c) It is the range of frequencies that can be carried.
2. a) (i) visible light or infrared radiation (ii) UHF radio waves (iii) microwaves b) It can carry more information, it is easier to maintain privacy.
3. a) An orbit in the same plane as the equator and in which a satellite remains at a fixed position relative to the ground.
   b) Advantage: transmitters and receivers point in one direction only all the time; disadvantage: more energy is needed to put a satellite into a higher orbit so the launch rocket needs to be more powerful.

The electromagnetic spectrum

ROUND UP

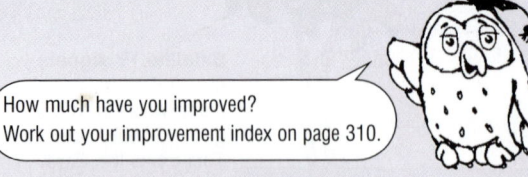

How much have you improved? Work out your improvement index on page 310.

1. **a)** List the six main bands of the electromagnetic spectrum in order of increasing wavelength. [6]
   b) (i) State two common properties of all electromagnetic waves. [2]
   (ii) List the types of electromagnetic waves that blacken photographic film. [3]
   (iii) List the types of electromagnetic waves that are used in communications. [4]

2. **a)** Microwave cookers operate at 2500 MHz and microwave satellites operate at about 10 000 MHz. Calculate the wavelength in air in each case. The speed of light in air is 300 000 km/s. [2]
   b) Food can be heated using a microwave oven or an ordinary oven. What are the advantages of using a microwave oven? [1]

3. **a)** Why is it possible to detect radio broadcasts from distant countries? [2]
   b) (i) What is meant by the carrier frequency of a radio or TV broadcast? [1]
   (ii) Why is it necessary for TV transmitter stations in adjacent regions to broadcast at different carrier frequencies? [1]
   c) Why is it necessary to use a concave metal dish to detect electromagnetic waves from a satellite but not from a TV transmitter mast? [2]

4. **a)** A soap powder manufacturer decides to mix a substance into the powder which absorbs ultraviolet light and emits visible light as a result. Why would this make clothes washed in this powder seem very white in bright sunlight? [2]
   b) (i) Why is ultraviolet light harmful? [2]
   (ii) Why is it important to use protective skin cream if you are outdoors for a long time in summer? [2]

5. **a)** Why can an infrared TV camera see people and animals in darkness? [1]
   b) (i) What main type of electromagnetic radiation is emitted by a halogen lamp in a ceramic cooker hob? [1]
   (ii) Why does a ceramic hob heat food up more quickly than a conventional cooker ring? [2]

6. **a)** In an X-ray tube, why is it essential to
   (i) make the anode positive relative to the filament?
   (ii) focus the electron beam onto a small spot of the anode? [3]
   b) (i) A photograph of a broken limb can be obtained using X-rays. What properties of X-rays are made use of in this process? [2]
   (ii) Before a stomach X-ray is taken, the patient is given a barium meal. Why? [2]

7. **a)** The diagram shows the waveform of two carrier waves with different frequencies. Identify the high frequency carrier wave and explain why it can carry more pulses than the low frequency carrier wave. [3]

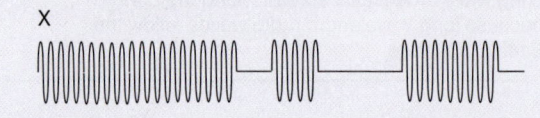

   X

   Y

   b) Mobile phones operate at a frequency of about 900 MHz, each channel occupying a bandwidth of 25 kHz.
   (i) How many mobile phone channels can be carried in the frequency band from 890 to 915 MHz? [1]
   (ii) Terrestrial TV programmes are carried at lower frequencies and satellite TV is carried at higher frequencies. Why are no TV channels allocated to the frequency band from 890 to 915 MHz? [1]

8. A communications satellite must be in a geostationary orbit.
   a) What is meant by a geostationary orbit? [2]
   b) Why is it necessary for a communications satellite to be in such an orbit? [1]

Well done if you've improved. Don't worry if you haven't. Take a break and try again.

Force and motion — Chapter 8

PREVIEW

At the end of this topic you will be able to:

- define speed, velocity, acceleration, force, weight and work and state the unit of each quantity
- carry out calculations relating the above quantities to each other and to measurements of distance and time
- carry out calculations using the formulae for kinetic energy and potential energy
- sketch and interpret graphs of distance against time and speed against time
- describe the motion of a falling object with and without drag forces, including its energy changes.

How much do you already know? Work out your score on page 310.

Test yourself

The acceleration of a freely falling object, $g = 10$ m/s^2.

1. A walker travelled a distance of 10 km in 2 hours. Calculate the walker's average speed in **a)** km/h **b)** m/s. [2]

2. **a)** What feature of a graph of speed against time gives the distance travelled? [1]
   b) What does the gradient of a distance against time graph represent? [1]

3. A 1000 kg car accelerates from rest to a speed of 10 m/s in 20 s. Calculate the acceleration of the car and the force needed to produce this acceleration. [2]

4. A car is travelling at a speed of 15 m/s when the driver sees a tree lying across the road ahead and is forced to brake. The graph shows how its speed changed with time.

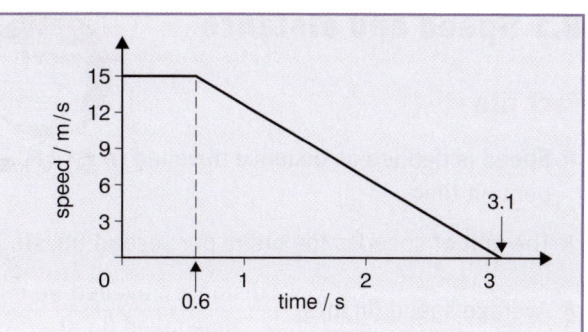

   a) If the driver's reaction time is 0.6 s, how far does the car travel before the driver applies the brakes? [1]

   b) The car takes 2.5 s to stop after the brakes are first applied. Calculate its deceleration. [1]

   c) (i) Use the graph to calculate the braking distance. [1]

   (ii) Hence calculate the total stopping distance. [1]

5. A lift of total mass 400 kg descends at a constant speed of 2 m/s.

   a) Calculate **(i)** its weight and its kinetic energy **(ii)** its loss of potential energy per second. [3]

   b) What happens to the potential energy lost by the lift? [3]

6. Explain why the shape of a vehicle affects its top speed. [3]

7. Why does a parachutist fall at constant speed? [3]

8. An aeroplane of total mass 8000 kg is in level flight at a constant speed of 60 m/s.

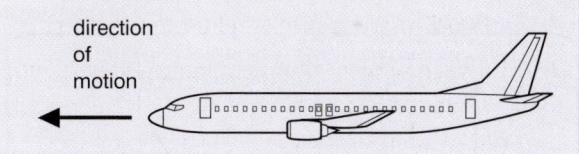

   a) Calculate its weight and the lift force acting on the aeroplane. [2]

   b) The output power of its engines is 200 kW. Calculate **(i)** the distance it moves in 100 s **(ii)** the energy output from the engine in this time. [2]

   c) What happens to the energy supplied by the engine when the aeroplane is moving at constant speed in level flight? [1]

Force and motion

8.1 Speed and distance

Fact file

- **Speed** is defined as distance travelled per unit time.
- The **unit** of speed is the metre per second (m/s).
- Average speed (in m/s) = $\dfrac{\text{distance travelled (in m)}}{\text{time taken (in s)}}$
- **Velocity** is speed in a given direction.

Distance–time graphs for a moving object

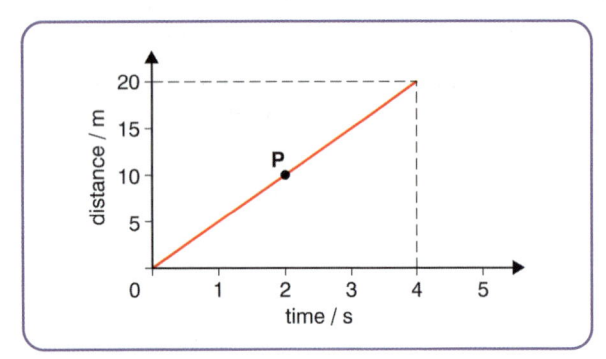

Constant speed

At **constant speed**, the distance travelled increases steadily with time as shown on the graph above.

1. The graph is a straight line with a constant gradient.
2. The steeper the line, the greater the speed.
3. The gradient of the graph is equal to the speed of the object.

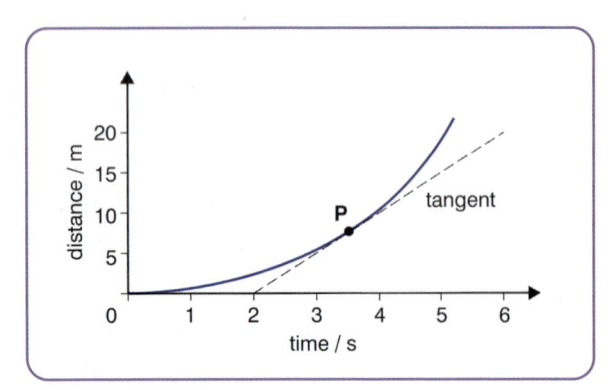

Distance–time graph for an object that accelerates from rest

At **changing speed**, the gradient of the line changes, as in the distance–time graph for an object that accelerates from rest.

1. The gradient changes with time.
2. The speed at any point is equal to the gradient of the tangent to the curve.
3. The speed is zero where the gradient is zero. This is at the origin 0 on the graph.

Questions

a) Determine the speed at point P on each graph.

b) On the second graph, how can you tell if the object is moving faster or slower after point P?

Speed and velocity

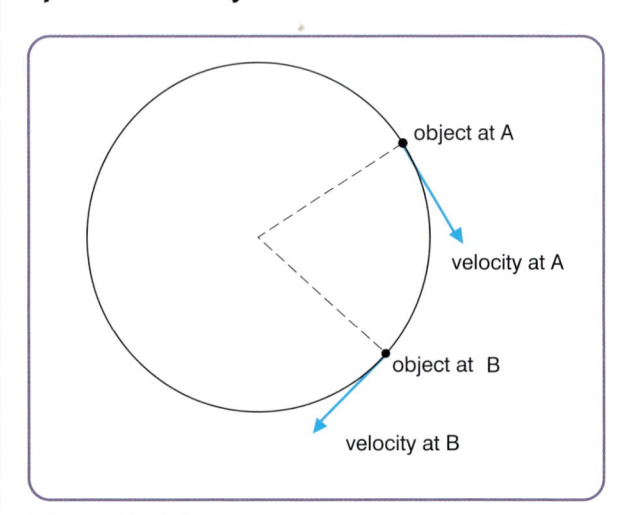

Going round in circles

Velocity is defined as speed in a given direction. An object moving round a circular path at a steady rate has a constant speed. However, it is continuously changing its direction so its velocity continually changes. Velocity is an example of a **vector** quantity, which is any quantity that has magnitude *and* direction. Other examples of vectors include acceleration, force and weight. Non-directional quantities such as speed, mass and energy are called **scalar** quantities.

Answers

a) 5 m/s, 5 m/s b) The gradient becomes steeper so the speed is increasing.

Force and motion

8.2 Acceleration

Fact file

★ **Acceleration** is defined as change of velocity per unit time.

★ The **unit** of acceleration is the metre per second per second (m/s²).

★ Acceleration is a vector quantity.

Constant acceleration

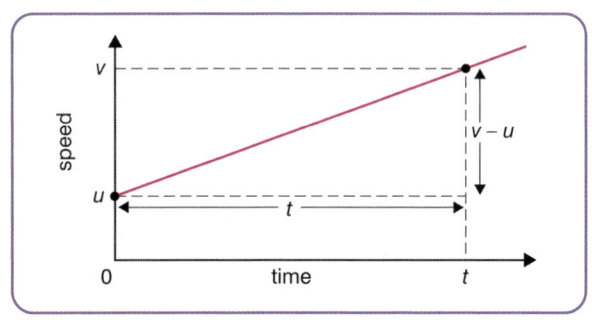

Velocity-time graph for constant acceleration

The graph shows how the speed changes with time for an object moving along a straight line at constant acceleration.

1. The gradient of the line is equal to the acceleration of the object.

2. The acceleration can be calculated using the equation

   $$\text{acceleration} = \frac{\text{change of velocity}}{\text{time taken}}$$

   If u represents the initial velocity and v represents the velocity at time t, the equation can be written as

   $$\text{acceleration } a = \frac{(v-u)}{t}$$

3. The distance moved s in time t can be calculated using the equation

   $$\text{distance moved} = \text{average speed} \times \text{time}$$

   Since the average speed $= \frac{(u+v)}{2}$,

   this equation can written as $s = \frac{(u+v)t}{2}$

4. The area under the line gives the distance travelled.

Note: *deceleration* means decrease of velocity per unit time and has a negative value in a calculation.

Maths workshop

The equation

$$a = \frac{(v-u)}{t}$$

can be rearranged to find v.

Step 1: multiply both sides of the equation by t to give $at = (v - u)$.

Step 2: Take u across to the other side to give $u + at = v$ or $v = u + at$.

Questions

The graph below shows how the speed of a train changed as it travelled between two stations.

a) Determine the acceleration and the distance moved in each of the three parts of the journey.

b) Hence calculate the average speed of the train.

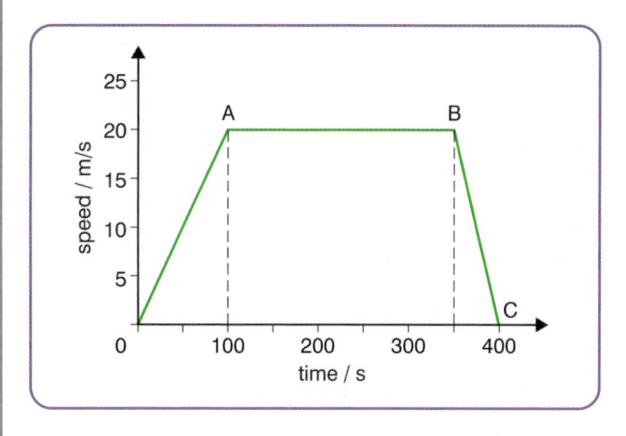

Acceleration due to gravity, g

The acceleration of an object falling freely is constant, equal to 10 m/s². This means that an object falling freely increases its speed by 10 m/s every second – it accelerates at a constant rate.

Non-uniform acceleration

The acceleration can be determined at any point by drawing the tangent to the curve at that point and measuring the gradient of this line.

Answers

a) Acceleration = 0.2 m/s²; 0; −0.4 m/s²
Distance = 1000 m; 5000 m; 500 m
b) 16 m/s

269

Force and motion

8.3 On the road

Stopping distances

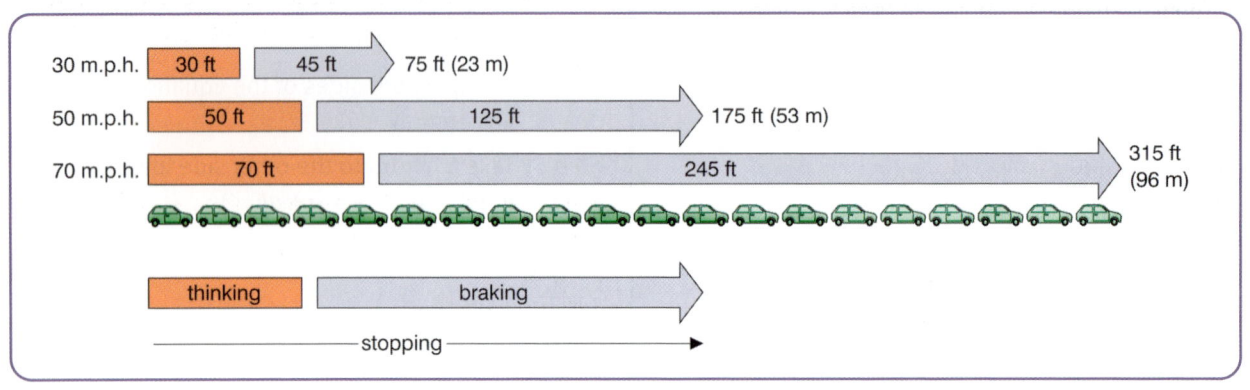

Shortest stopping distances of a car in good condition on a dry road for different speeds

- ★ **The thinking distance** is the distance travelled by the car in the time it takes the driver to react.
- ★ **The braking distance** is the distance travelled by the car from the point where the brakes are applied to where it comes to rest.
- ★ **The stopping distance** is the thinking distance added to the braking distance.

The graphs below show how each of these distances (in m) increases with speed (in m/s).

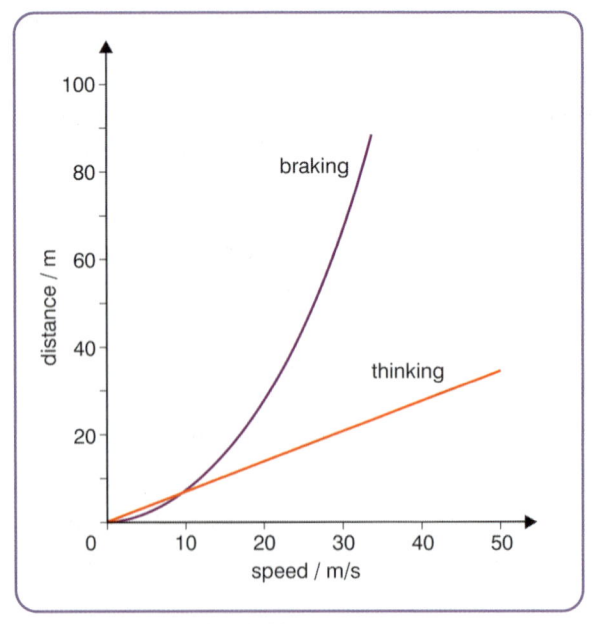

Distance–speed graphs for a braking car

1 **The thinking distance is proportional to the speed**. This is because the vehicle travels at constant speed during the reaction period before the brakes are applied. For constant speed, distance moved = speed × time. Prove for yourself from the graph that the reaction time for the data is 0.7 s. This is the average reaction time for a driver in an alert state of mind.

2 **The braking distance is proportional to the square of the speed**. This assumes the vehicle's deceleration is constant during braking.

Question

Determine the thinking distance and the stopping distance at a speed of 27 m/s (= 60 m.p.h.).

What affects the stopping distance?

1 **Reaction time:** the driver's reaction time depends on alertness.

2 **Road conditions:** when the brakes are applied, friction between the brakes and the wheels reduces the vehicle's speed, provided the tyres don't skid on the road. Skidding occurs if the braking force exceeds the grip (the maximum amount of friction possible) between the tyres and the road. Grip depends on the road conditions as well as the tyre conditions.

Answer

thinking distance = 18 m, stopping distance = 55 m

Force and motion

8.4 Force and acceleration

Balanced forces

★ A **force** is anything that can change the velocity of an object.

★ If there is no force acting on an object, the object moves at constant velocity (constant speed without changing direction) or remains stationary.

★ If an object is acted on by two or more forces which balance each other out, the object either remains at rest or continues to move at constant velocity.

Changing velocity

The velocity of an object changes if the object is acted on by a force or by several forces which do not balance out. The combined effect of different forces acting on an object is called the **resultant force** on the object.

If an object is at rest or moving at constant velocity, the resultant force on it must be zero. This is known as **Newton's first law of motion**.

If an object's velocity is changing, the resultant force on it is not zero. Experiments show that the acceleration of an object is proportional to the resultant force on the object. This is known as **Newton's second law of motion** and it can be written as an equation:

force = mass × acceleration
(in newtons, N) (in kg) (in m/s^2)

The unit of force is the **newton** (abbreviated N), equal to the force needed to give a 1 kg mass an acceleration of 1 m/s^2.

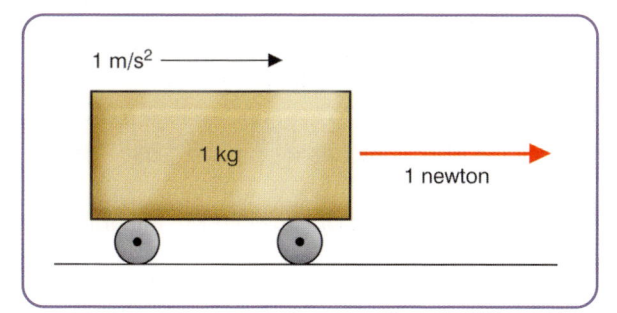

The newton

Weight

The **weight** of an object is the force of gravity on it. An object falling freely is acted on by gravity only. Since the acceleration due to gravity g is constant, then the force of gravity on an object (its weight) must be equal to its mass × g:

weight = mass × g
(in N) (in kg) (in m/s^2)

Note that the unit of g may be written as N/kg or m/s^2 since 1 N = 1 kg m/s^2.

Terminal speed

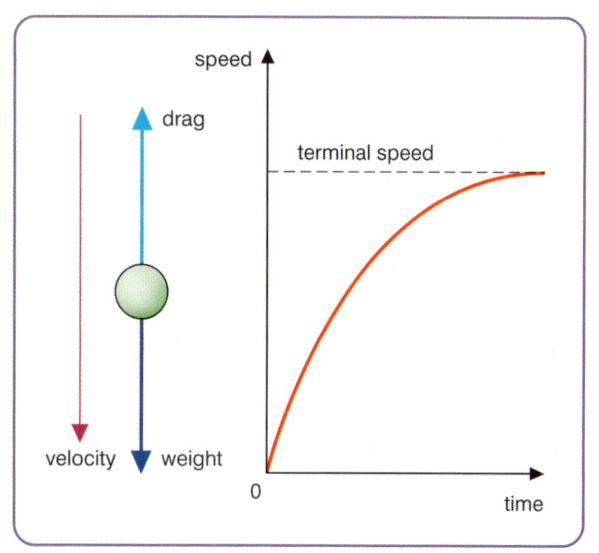

Terminal speed

When an object moves through a liquid or a gas, it experiences friction due to the liquid or gas, which opposes its motion. This resistance to its motion is called **drag**. The drag force increases with speed, and depends on the shape of the object and the substance the object is moving through.

★ An object released in air accelerates gradually until its speed is such that the drag force is equal and opposite to its weight. This speed is called the **terminal speed** (or terminal velocity).

★ A vehicle reaches its top speed when the drag force is equal and opposite to the engine force. The top speed can be increased by reshaping a vehicle to reduce the drag force on it.

Force and motion

> **Questions**
>
> A car of total mass 800 kg can accelerate from rest to a speed of 20 m/s in 20 s. Calculate
> a) the acceleration of the car
> b) the force producing this acceleration, assuming the drag force is negligible
> c) the ratio of this force to the total weight of the car. Assume $g = 10$ m/s^2.

8.5 Work and energy

At work

Fact file

★ A force does **work** on an object when it moves the object in the direction of the force.

★ **Work done** = force × distance moved in the direction of the force.

★ **Energy** is the capacity to do work.

★ The unit of work and of energy is the **joule** (J), which is equal to the work done when a force of 1 N moves its point of application through a distance of 1 m.

★ **Power** is defined as rate of transfer of energy. The unit of power is the **watt** (W), which is equal to 1 J/s.

Gaining height

Gravitational potential energy

If a mass m is moved through a height h, its

change of gravitational potential energy = mgh,

where g is the acceleration due to gravity. This is because the force of gravity on the object (its weight) is mg.

1 Any object at rest is acted on by a support force which is equal and opposite to its weight.

2 If the object is raised, the work done by the support force is mgh (equal to force × distance). This is therefore the gain of potential energy of the object.

3 If the object is lowered, the work done by gravity is mgh (equal to force × distance). This is therefore the decrease of potential energy of the object.

Kinetic energy

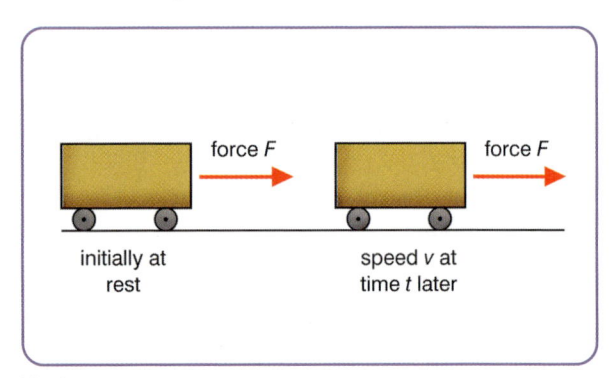

Kinetic energy

For a mass m moving at speed v, its

kinetic energy = $\tfrac{1}{2}mv^2$.

This can be proved by considering a constant force F acting on an object of mass m, initially at rest, for time t. From pages 269, 271 and above,

1 its distance moved $s = \dfrac{vt}{2}$ where v is its speed at time t

2 its acceleration $a = \dfrac{v}{t}$ hence $F = ma = \dfrac{mv}{t}$

3 Hence the work done $= Fs = \dfrac{mv}{t} \times \dfrac{vt}{2} = \tfrac{1}{2}mv^2$

which is therefore the kinetic energy of the object.

> **Answers**
>
> a) 1 m/s^2 b) 800 N c) 0.1

Force and motion

Questions

Set out your answers clearly. In an examination, if you slip up on a calculation, you will only lose one mark if you have shown clearly that you understand the principles involved. Where necessary, assume $g = 10\,\text{m/s}^2$.

1. A tennis ball of mass 0.20 kg is released from rest at a height of 2.0 m above a concrete floor. It rebounds to a height of 1.5 m.

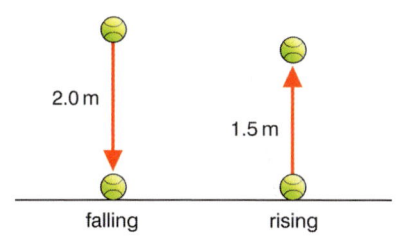

   a) Calculate its kinetic energy and speed just before impact.
   b) Calculate its kinetic energy and speed just after impact.
   c) Calculate its loss of energy between release and its maximum height after rebounding.

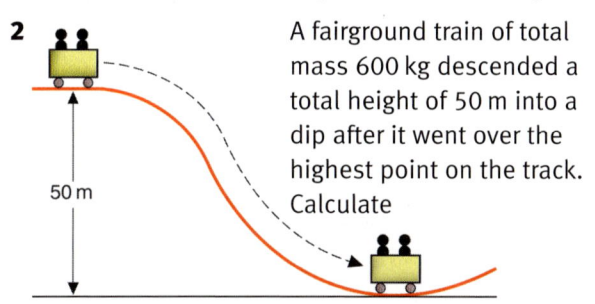

2. A fairground train of total mass 600 kg descended a total height of 50 m into a dip after it went over the highest point on the track. Calculate

   a) its loss of potential energy in this descent
   b) its kinetic energy and speed at the bottom of the dip, assuming air resistance was negligible and its kinetic energy at the highest point was zero.

3. An aeroplane of mass 600 kg takes off from rest in 50 s over a distance of 1500 m.

   a) Calculate (i) its speed when it lifts off
   (ii) its acceleration during take-off
   (iii) the force needed to produce this acceleration.
   b) Why is the engine force greater than the force calculated in a) (iii)?

4. A hot air balloon and its occupants have a total weight of 5000 N. It is descending at a constant speed of 0.5 m/s.

   a) What is the total upward force on it during this descent?
   b) Calculate its kinetic energy.
   c) Calculate its loss of height and loss of potential energy in 1 minute.
   d) Explain why it does not gain kinetic energy.

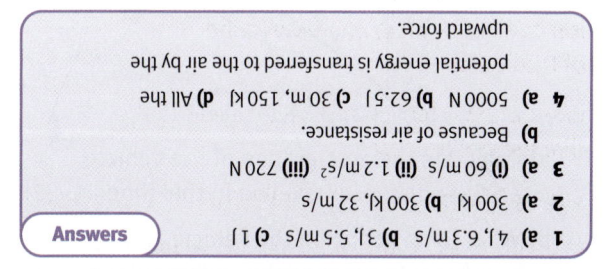

Answers

1 a) 4 J, 6.3 m/s b) 3 J, 5.5 m/s c) 1 J
2 a) 300 kJ b) 300 kJ, 32 m/s
3 a) (i) 60 m/s (ii) 1.2 m/s² (iii) 720 N
   b) Because of air resistance.
4 a) 5000 N b) 62.5 J c) 30 m, 150 kJ d) All the potential energy is transferred to the air by the upward force.

ROUND UP

continues on page 274

How much have you improved?
Work out your improvement index on pages 310–11.

The acceleration of a freely falling object, $g = 10\,\text{m/s}^2$.

1. a) A walker leaves a car park and walks at a steady speed of 1.2 m/s for 1 hour. How far did the walker travel in this time in
   (i) metres (ii) kilometres? [2]
   b) A runner leaves the same car park 40 minutes after the walker and catches up with the walker at a distance of 4 km from the car park. What was the runner's speed? [1]

2. The graph shows the progress of two cyclists in a 10 km road race.

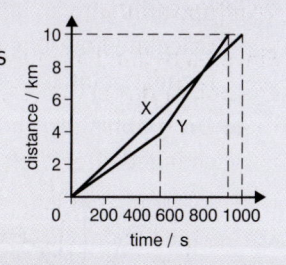

   a) One cyclist X maintained a constant speed throughout. What can you deduce from the graph about the speed of the other cyclist Y? [4]
   b) (i) From the graph, calculate the speed of X. [1]
   (ii) From the graph, calculate the speed of Y when Y overtook X. [1]

273

Force and motion

ROUND UP continued

3 a) Explain the difference between speed and velocity. [2]

b) A police car joins a motorway and travels north at a constant speed of 30 m/s for 5 minutes. It then leaves the motorway at a motorway junction, rejoins it immediately and travels south in the opposite direction for 20 minutes at a steady speed of 20 m/s to the scene of an accident.

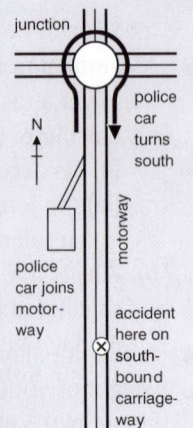

  (i) How far did the police car travel in each direction? [2]
  (ii) How far from the point where the police car first joined the motorway was the scene of the accident? [1]

4 A vehicle of mass 700 kg accelerates steadily from rest to a speed of 8 m/s in a time of 5 s. The graph shows how the speed of the vehicle increased with time.

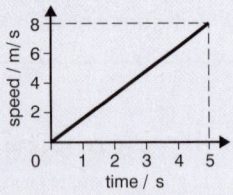

a) Calculate the acceleration of the vehicle and the distance travelled in this time. [2]

b) What force acting on the vehicle is necessary to produce this acceleration? [1]

5 a) A ball of mass 0.2 kg is thrown directly upwards with an initial speed of 25 m/s. Calculate how long it took to reach its highest point. [1]

b) The graph shows how its vertical position changed after it left the thrower's hand.

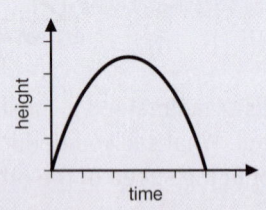

  (i) What was its initial kinetic energy? [1]
  (ii) Calculate its maximum gain of potential energy. [1]
  (iii) Calculate its maximum gain of height. [1]

6 a) An athlete runs a distance of 100 m in a time of 10.5 s. Calculate the athlete's average speed over this distance. [1]

b) The athlete's mass is 60 kg. Calculate the athlete's kinetic energy at the speed calculated in **a)**. [1]

c) If all the kinetic energy calculated in **b)** could be converted into potential energy by the athlete, what height gain would be possible? [1]

d) A pole vaulter is capable of jumping considerably higher. Discuss how this is achieved. [1]

7 A train of total mass 30 000 kg is travelling at a constant speed of 10 m/s when its brakes are applied, bringing it to rest with a constant deceleration in 50 s.

a) Sketch a graph to show how the speed of the train changed with time. [2]

b) Calculate (i) the distance moved by the train in this time (ii) its deceleration. [2]

c) Hence calculate the force of the brakes on the train. [1]

d) Calculate the ratio of the braking force to the train's weight. [1]

8 a) Explain why a moving car skids if the brakes are applied too hard. [1]

b) Explain why the stopping distance of a car travelling at a certain speed is greater if the road surface is wet. [4]

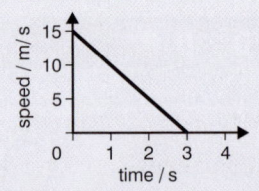

c) The graph shows how the speed of a car of mass 1200 kg on a dry road decreases with time when it stops safely in the shortest possible distance. The car is initially moving at a speed of 15 m/s. Calculate (i) the braking distance (ii) the deceleration of the car and the braking force. [3]

d) On a wet road, the braking force is reduced by half. Calculate the time it would take to brake safely from a speed of 15 m/s on a wet road and determine the braking distance in this condition. [2]

Forces in balance — Chapter 9

PREVIEW

At the end of this topic you will be able to:

- identify the forces acting on a body in equilibrium
- explain what is meant by centre of gravity
- describe the use of levers as force multipliers*
- state and use Hooke's law and describe elastic and plastic behaviour*
- carry out simple pressure and density calculations*
- describe pressure applications, including hydrostatic pressure and hydraulics*
- explain gas pressure and relate it to volume*

*Not needed for AQA, EDEXCEL and OCR specifications.

How much do you already know? Work out your score on page 311.

Test yourself

1. What forces are acting on your body at the moment? [2]

2. State whether each of the following is in stable, unstable or neutral equilibrium
   a) a ball at rest on the floor
   b) a child sitting on a fence
   c) a coat hanger hanging from a rail. [3]

3. The diagram shows a person pushing a wheelbarrow containing sand. The total weight of the wheelbarrow and its contents is 800 N.

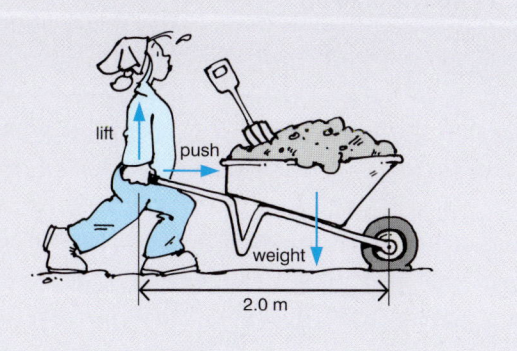

   a) Estimate how far the centre of gravity of the wheelbarrow is from the handle. [1]
   b) Explain why the force needed to lift the wheelbarrow is much less than 800 N. [2]
   c) The wheelbarrow contains 0.020 m^3 of sand. The density of the sand is 2500 kg/m^3. Calculate the mass of sand in the wheelbarrow. [1]

4. a) (i) Explain why a sharp knife cuts more easily than a blunt knife. [1]
      (ii) Explain why a suction cap pushed onto a smooth vertical tile doesn't fall off. [2]
   b) A spade has a rectangular blade which measures 25 cm × 20 cm. It is used to flatten a mound of earth. Each impact of the blade's flat surface on the mound creates a force of 300 N. Calculate the pressure due to this force. [2]

5. a) What is meant by elastic behaviour? [1]
   b) What is meant by plastic behaviour? [1]

6. A steel spring stretches by 4 cm when it is stretched by a 1 N force applied at either end.
   a) What is the extension of the spring when it is stretched by a force of 5 N? [1]
   b) How much force is needed to extend the spring by 10 cm? [1]

7. A spanner is used to unscrew a wheel nut on a bicycle. Why is it easier to do this using a long spanner rather than a short spanner? [2]

8. A metre rule is pivoted on a knife edge at its centre with a 1.0 N weight on a thread suspended from the 10 cm mark of the rule. The rule is then balanced by suspending an object of unknown weight W at its 65 cm mark. The arrangement is shown in the diagram below. Calculate
   a) the moment of the 1.0 N weight about the pivot [1]
   b) the weight W of the unknown object. [2]

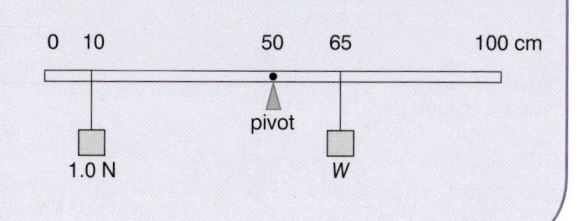

Forces in balance

9.1 Equilibrium

Fact file

★ Different types of force include **weight** (the force of gravity), **tension** (forces that stretch), **compression** (forces that squeeze), **twisting forces**, **electrical forces** and **magnetic forces**.

★ The unit of force is the newton (N). Note that 10 N is the weight of a mass of 1 kg at the Earth's surface.

★ The centre of gravity of an object is the point where its weight may be considered to act.

Balanced forces

An object at rest is said to be in **equilibrium**. The forces acting on an object at rest balance each other out. If an object is acted on by two forces only, the object will be in equilibrium if the two forces are:
1. equal to each other, and
2. acting on the object along the same line in opposite directions.

Some examples of objects in equilibrium are shown in the diagram below.

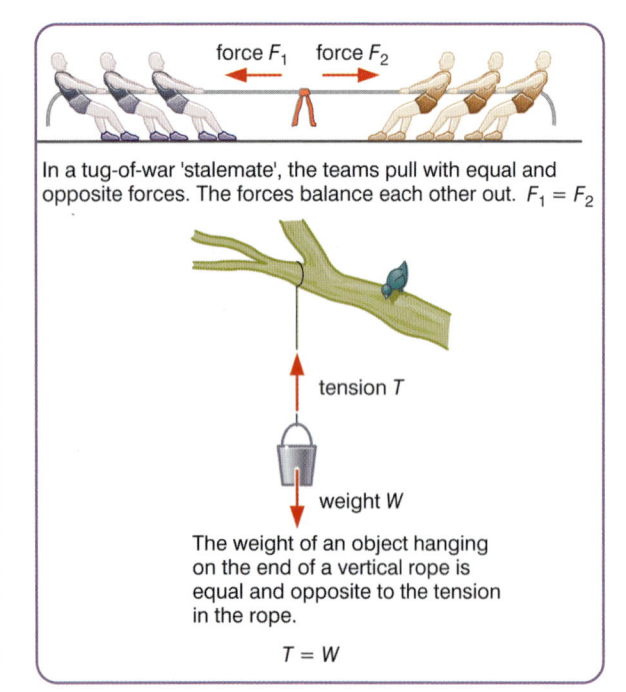

In a tug-of-war 'stalemate', the teams pull with equal and opposite forces. The forces balance each other out. $F_1 = F_2$

The weight of an object hanging on the end of a vertical rope is equal and opposite to the tension in the rope.
$T = W$

Equal and opposite forces

Stability

If an object at equilibrium is displaced slightly then released, it is said to be:
- **in stable equilibrium** if it returns to equilibrium
- **in neutral equilibrium** if it stays at its new position
- **in unstable equilibrium** if it moves away from the point where it was in equilibrium.

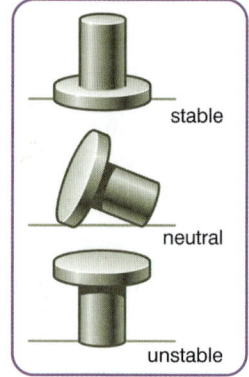

Turning effects

A force acting on an object can have a turning effect on the object. For example, the diagram below shows a force acting on a spanner that is used to turn a nut. The turning effect of such a force depends on the size of the force and its perpendicular distance from the line of action of the force to the nut.

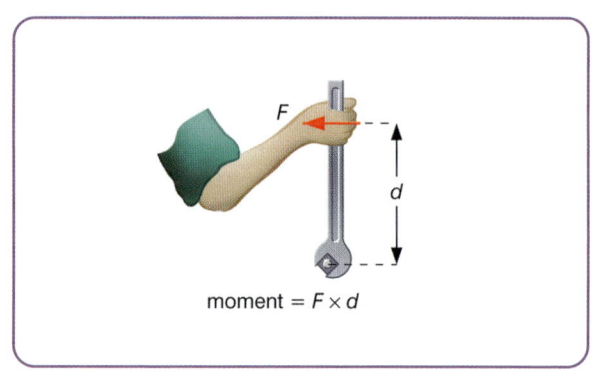

moment = $F \times d$

Turning a nut

★ The **moment** of a force about a point is defined as the force × the perpendicular distance from the line of action of the force to the pivot.

For example, in the diagram, if $F = 40$ N and $d = 0.20$ m, then the moment of the force is 8 Nm (= 40 N × 0.20 m).

Forces in balance

★ For any object in equilibrium, the moments of the forces about the same point balance each other out. This is known as the **principle of moments**. Two examples are shown in the diagram below.

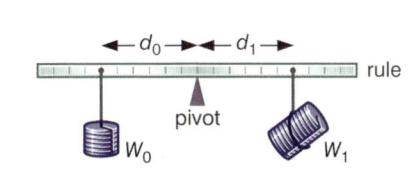

The unknown weight W_1 can be measured by adjusting its distance from the pivot until the rule is balanced. The moment of W_1 = the moment of the known weight W_0.

$$W_0 d_0 = W_1 d_1$$

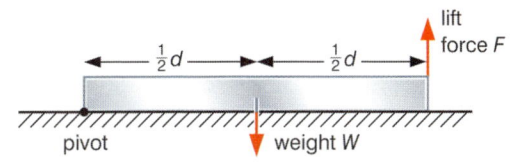

The force F required to lift the concrete post at one end is half the weight W. This is because the moment of this force about the pivot must be at least equal to the moment of the weight about the pivot.

$$Fd = \tfrac{1}{2}dW$$

Equal and opposite moments

Tilting and toppling

The diagram shows a tall cupboard tilted on one side. It will topple if released because the perpendicular from its centre of gravity to the ground falls outside its base. This means its weight tries to turn it anticlockwise about the edge which acts as the pivot. A force F as shown is necessary to provide an equal and opposite moment.

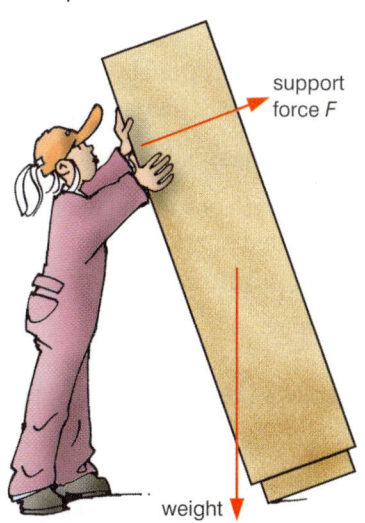

Action and reaction

Whenever two objects interact, they exert equal and opposite forces on each other. For example, if you lean on a wall with a certain force, you experience an equal and opposite force from the wall. The same rule applies when two objects collide; they push on each other with an equal and opposite force.

Questions

1 A spanner of length 0.3 m is used to turn a nut by applying a force of 50 N to the free end of the spanner. Calculate the moment of this force.

2 In the top diagram above, a ruler pivoted at its centre supports two weights W_0 and W_1. The rule is horizontal. If W_0 = 1.5 N, d_0 = 0.20 m and d_1 = 0.30 m, calculate

   a) the moment of W_0 about the pivot
   b) the unknown weight W_1.

3 A plank of weight 200 N rests horizontally on two bricks, one at either end as shown.

   a) What force does the plank exert on each brick?
   b) What force is necessary to lift the plank at one end?

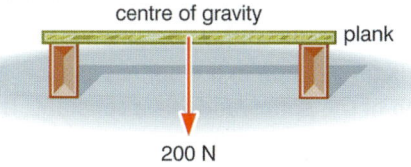

Answers
1 15 N m
2 a) 0.30 N m b) 1.0 N
3 a) 100 N b) 100 N

Forces in balance

9.2 Strength of solids

Solids and strength

★ **Stiffness** is the ability to withstand being stretched or bent.

★ **Toughness** is the ability to withstand fracture.

★ **Strength** is a measure of how much force is needed to break an object.

★ **Brittleness** is a measure of how easily an object snaps.

Hooke's law

This law states that **the extension of a spiral spring is proportional to the force used to stretch it**. The diagram shows how Hooke's law may be tested, and a graph of some typical results for a steel spring. Note that the extension is the change of length from its unstretched length.

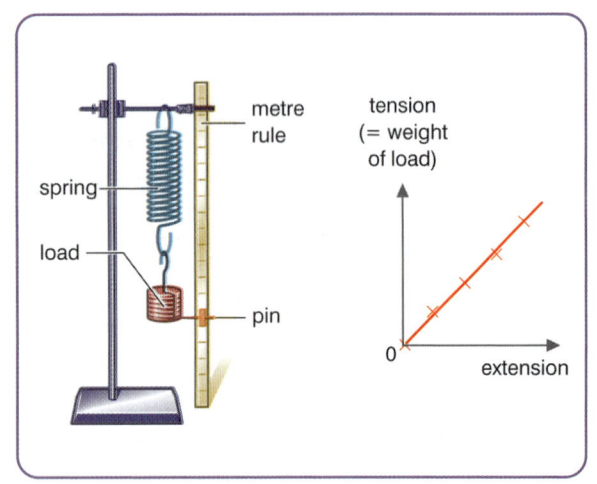

Hooke's law

Hooke's law may be written in the form $T = ke$, where T is the tension in the spring, e is the extension of the spring and k is a constant. This is the equation for the line in the graph. The line is straight and it passes through the origin because the tension is proportional to the extension. Its gradient is equal to the spring constant k. Note that the equation $T = ke$ may be rearranged to give

$$e = \frac{T}{k} \quad \text{or} \quad k = \frac{T}{e}$$

Elastic and plastic behaviour

★ **Elastic behaviour** is the ability of a solid to regain its shape when the external forces are removed. The atoms return to their original positions when the external forces are removed.

★ The **elastic limit** of a solid is the limit of its ability to regain its shape. Beyond its elastic limit, it deforms permanently.

★ **Plastic behaviour** occurs when the shape of a solid is permanently changed by external forces. The atoms are pulled out of position permanently.

The graphs below show how the extension of different objects under tension increases with the external force.

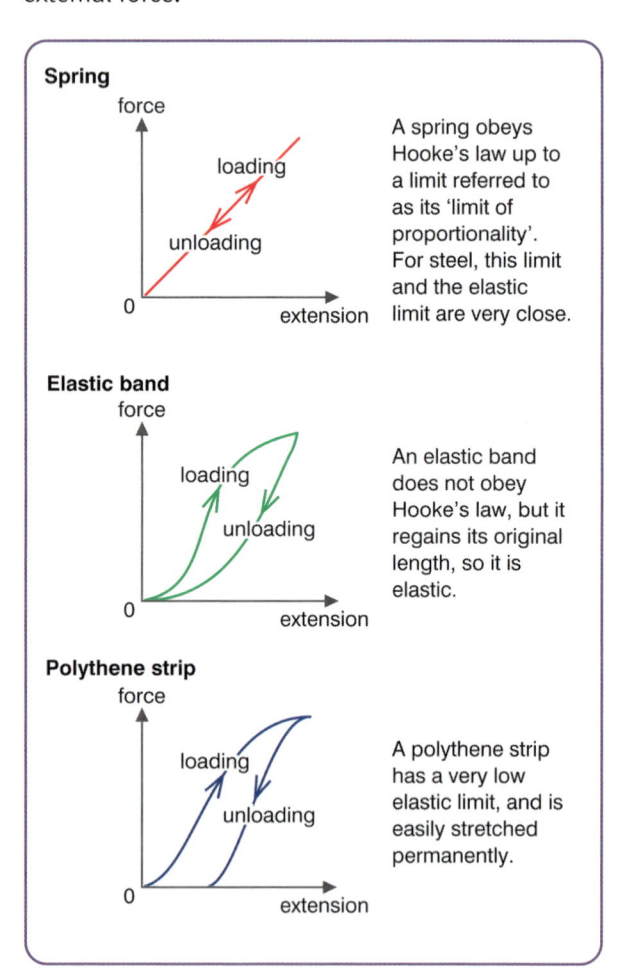

Spring: A spring obeys Hooke's law up to a limit referred to as its 'limit of proportionality'. For steel, this limit and the elastic limit are very close.

Elastic band: An elastic band does not obey Hooke's law, but it regains its original length, so it is elastic.

Polythene strip: A polythene strip has a very low elastic limit, and is easily stretched permanently.

Stretching materials

Forces in balance

9.3 Pressure and its measurement

Fact file

★ **Pressure** is defined as force per unit area acting normally on a surface.

★ The unit of pressure is the **pascal** (Pa), equal to 1 N/m².

★ Density = $\dfrac{\text{mass}}{\text{volume}}$

★ The unit of density is the kilogram per cubic metre (kg/m³).

★ The pressure p due to a force F acting normally on an area A may be calculated from the equation

$$p = \dfrac{F}{A}$$

★ Note that an area of 1 m² is equal to 10 000 cm² (= 100 cm × 100 cm).

Therefore, a force of 1 N acting on an area of 1cm² gives a pressure of 10 kPa (= 10 000 Pa).

Pressure points

The larger the area of surface over which a force acts, the smaller the pressure. The smaller the area, the greater the pressure.

Question

Calculate the pressure in kPa exerted by a 60 kg person standing on the floor if the total area of contact between the person's feet and the floor is 100 cm². Assume g = 10 N/kg.

Pressure in a liquid

The pressure in a liquid:
- acts equally in all directions
- increases with depth
- is the same at all points at the same depth
- depends on the density of the liquid.

Floating and sinking

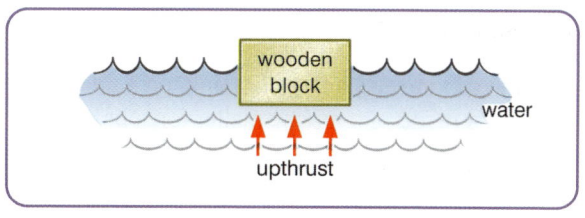

A floating object

An **upthrust** acts on any object in a fluid. This is because the pressure of the fluid is greater on the bottom of the object than on the top. If an object is slowly lowered into a liquid, the upthrust on it increases gradually. The object will:
- **float** if the upthrust becomes large enough to support its weight
- **sink** if the upthrust at maximum depth is not enough to support its weight.

The U-tube manometer

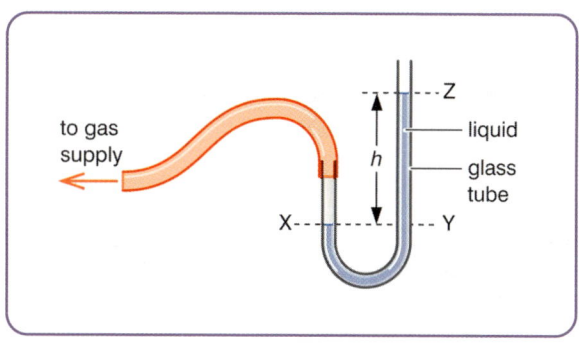

The U-tube manometer

This device is used to measure gas pressure.

★ The pressure at X is due to the gas supply.

★ The pressure at Y is caused by atmospheric pressure at Z + the pressure of the liquid column YZ.

★ The pressure at Y = the pressure at X since they are on the same level.

★ Therefore, the gas supply pressure = the pressure due to YZ + atmospheric pressure.

★ Hence the height of column YZ is a measure of how much the gas supply pressure exceeds atmospheric pressure (the 'excess' gas pressure).

Answer 60 kPa

Forces in balance

9.4 Hydraulics

Vehicle brakes

A brake system exerts a large braking force on the wheels as a result of a much smaller force being applied to the foot pedal.

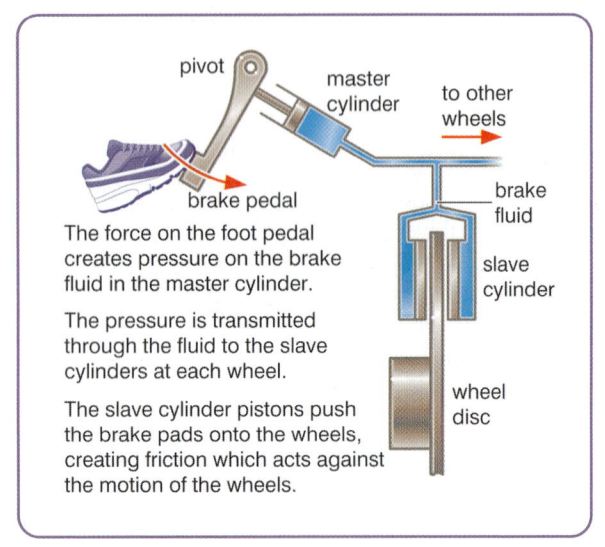

The force on the foot pedal creates pressure on the brake fluid in the master cylinder.

The pressure is transmitted through the fluid to the slave cylinders at each wheel.

The slave cylinder pistons push the brake pads onto the wheels, creating friction which acts against the motion of the wheels.

Disc brakes

Using the pressure equation

1. The pressure exerted on the fluid is given by the equation $p = \dfrac{F_1}{A_1}$ where F_1 is the force on the master cylinder and A_1 is the area of the master cylinder.

2. This pressure is transmitted to the slave cylinders without loss. This assumes no air in the brake system.

3. The force exerted by each slave cylinder $F_2 = pA_2$, where A_2 is the area of each slave cylinder.

4. Hence $F_2 = \dfrac{F_1 A_2}{A_1}$.

Since A_2 is much larger than A_1, then it follows that F_2 is much larger than F_1.

Questions

A brake system has a master cylinder of area 5 cm² and each slave cylinder has an area of 100 cm². A force of 20 N is applied to the master cylinder.

a) Calculate (i) the pressure in the system in pascals (ii) the force exerted by each slave piston.

b) Why is it important not to allow any air into the brake system?

More hydraulic machines

A hydraulic car jack is used to raise a car wheel off the ground. The car jack handle is a lever which multiplies the effort applied to it. The lever force is then magnified further by the hydraulic cylinders which contain oil. The force of the slave cylinder on the vehicle is enough to raise the vehicle at that point.

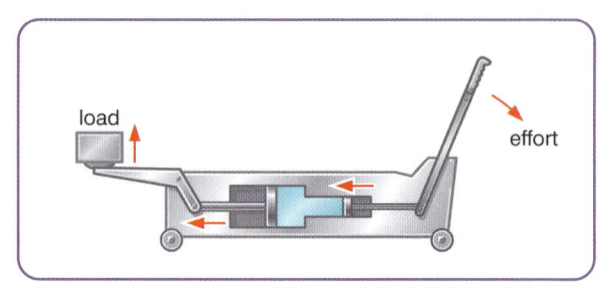

A hydraulic car jack

A hydraulic press is capable of exerting enough force to stamp metals into shape. The effort is applied to a lever which acts on the master piston. The pressure in the oil is then transmitted to the much wider slave cylinders which then exert a much greater force on the object to be stamped.

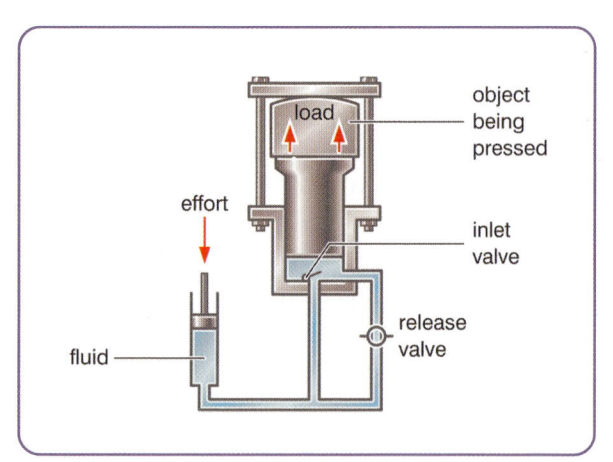

A hydraulic press

Answers

a) (i) 40 000 Pa (ii) 400 N
b) Unlike a liquid, air can be compressed. Therefore the pressure would not be transmitted to the slave cylinders.

Forces in balance

9.5 Gases

Fact file

★ A gas does not have its own surface, unlike a liquid or a solid. It fills any container it is released into. Its volume is therefore the volume of the space it fills.

★ A gas can easily be compressed. This means its density can easily be changed, unlike a solid or a liquid.

★ A gas exerts pressure on any surface it is in contact with.

★ The pressure of a gas can be increased by increasing its temperature or by reducing its volume.

Gas pressure

A gas consists of molecules which move about very fast in random motion, colliding repeatedly with each other and with solid surfaces present. Each impact on a surface exerts a force on the surface. These impacts are what causes the pressure exerted by the gas on the surface. The pressure is constant because there is an enormous number of impacts per second, so the surface is under continuous bombardment. Heating a gas makes the molecules move faster, causing harder and more frequent impacts – hence the pressure goes up.

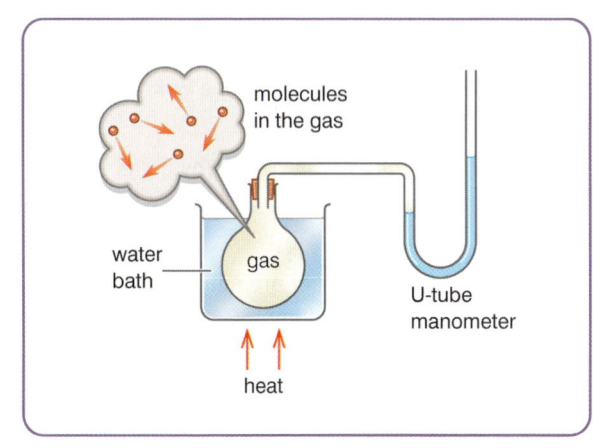

Gas pressure

Boyle's law

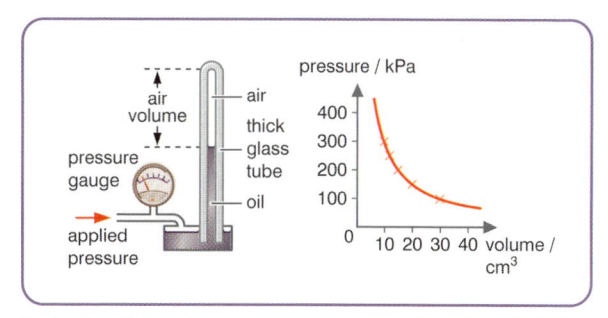

Testing Boyle's law

For a fixed mass of gas at constant temperature, its pressure × its volume is constant. The diagram above shows how this law can be tested. The table below shows some typical results, which are also plotted on the graph of pressure against volume above.

pressure / kPa	100	150	200	250	300
volume / cm³	30	20	15	12	10
pressure × volume	3000	3000	3000	3000	3000

Questions

For the gas at the same temperature which gave the results in the table, calculate

a) the pressure necessary to reduce the volume to 5 cm³

b) the volume at which the pressure would be 50 kPa.

Atmospheric pressure

Some applications of atmospheric pressure are shown below. Each application works because of the force due to atmospheric pressure.

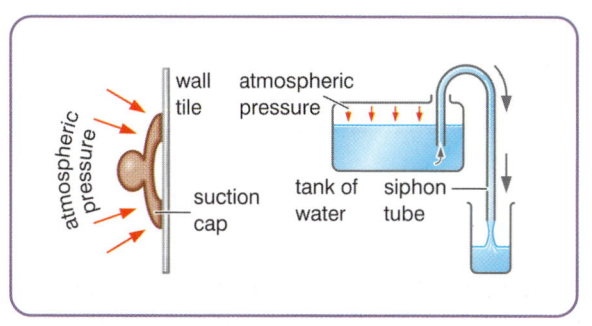

Using atmospheric pressure

Answers a) 600 kPa b) 60 cm³

Forces in balance

ROUND UP

How much have you improved? Work out your improvement index on page 311.

1   a) Why do the rear wheels of a tractor need to be much larger than the wheels of a van of equal weight? [2]

    b) With the aid of a diagram, explain why the shape of a bowling alley pin makes it easy to knock over. [2]

2   a) Calculate the pressure exerted by a person of weight 600 N when she is

    (i) standing on both feet, with an area of contact between each foot and the floor of 0.0015 m² [1]

    (ii) sitting on a chair, with a total area of contact on the chair of 0.10 m². [1]

    b) Calculate the total area of contact between the tyres of a bicycle and the ground if the air pressure in each tyre is 150 kPa and the total weight of the bicycle and cyclist is 600 N. [1]

3   A student proposes to replace a steel spring in a spring balance with an elastic band. She tests the stiffness of the elastic band and the spring in separate experiments. The graphs show her results.

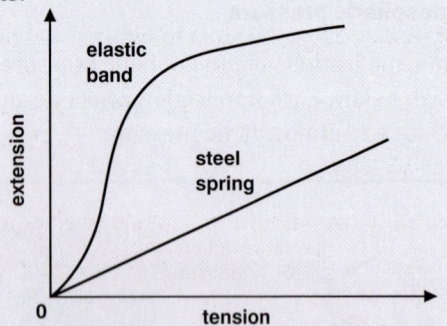

    a) Use these results to compare the stiffness of the elastic band and the steel spring. [2]

    b) Would the elastic band be satisfactory in place of the steel spring? Give a reason for your answer. [2]

4   The diagram shows a metre rule in equilibrium in a horizontal position. The rule is pivoted at its midpoint and it supports two weights W_1 and W_2 at distances d_1 and d_2 from the pivot.

The following table shows four incomplete sets of measurements taken with different weights. Calculate each missing measurement. [4]

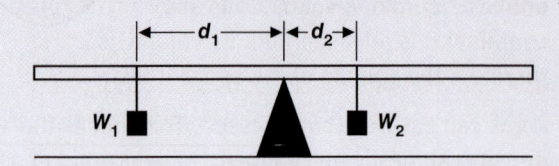

	W_1 / N	W_2 / N	d_1 / m	d_2 / m
set 1	3.2	1.6	0.2	?
set 2	?	1.5	0.4	0.3
set 3	2.5	?	0.4	0.1
set 4	4.5	3.2	?	0.27

5   A steel spring of length 300 mm was used to measure the weight of an object. With the spring hanging vertically from a fixed point, its length was measured when it supported different known weights. Then its length was measured when it supported the unknown weight W. The measurements are given below.

weight / N	0	1	2	3	4
spring length / mm	300	340	382	419	461

Spring length for the unknown weight = 376 mm

    a) Plot a graph of weight (vertical axis) against the extension of the spring. [4]

    b) Use your graph to determine the unknown weight W. [1]

6   a) Explain in terms of molecules why a gas exerts pressure on any surface it is in contact with. [3]

    b) A gas and some powder are sealed in a hollow cylinder of internal volume 50 cm³ at a pressure of 100 kPa. The volume is reduced to 20 cm³ at constant temperature, causing the pressure to rise to 400 kPa. Use these results to calculate the volume of the powder. [2]

Well done if you've improved. Don't worry if you haven't. Take a break and try again.

Electric charge — Chapter 10

PREVIEW

At the end of this topic you will be able to:
- explain how objects become charged
- describe the law of force between charged objects
- describe some of the uses and some of the dangers associated with charged objects
- explain how earthing works and why it is necessary
- recall that an electric current is a flow of charge, and recall the units of current and charge
- describe examples of electrolysis
- explain how electricity is conducted by a metal and by an electrolyte.

How much do you already know? Work out your score on pages 311–12.

Test yourself

1. Two charged objects X and Y repel each other. Which of the following statements could be true?

   A X is positive and Y is negative.
   B X is positive and Y is positive.
   C X is negative and Y is negative. [2]

2. a) When a polythene rod is charged by rubbing it with a dry cloth, it becomes negatively charged. This happens because

   A electrons transfer from the rod to the cloth
   B protons transfer from the rod to the cloth
   C electrons transfer from the cloth to the rod
   D protons transfer from the cloth to the rod. [1]

   b) A negatively charged rod is touched on a metal sphere which is insulated. As a result, electrons transfer

   A to earth   B to the sphere
   C to the rod   D from the sphere. [1]

3. a) Why does a metal conduct electric charge? [2]
   b) Why is an electrical insulator unable to conduct electric charge? [2]

4. The diagram shows a gold leaf electroscope. When a charged rod is held above the cap of the electroscope, the electroscope leaf rises. Explain why this happens. [4]

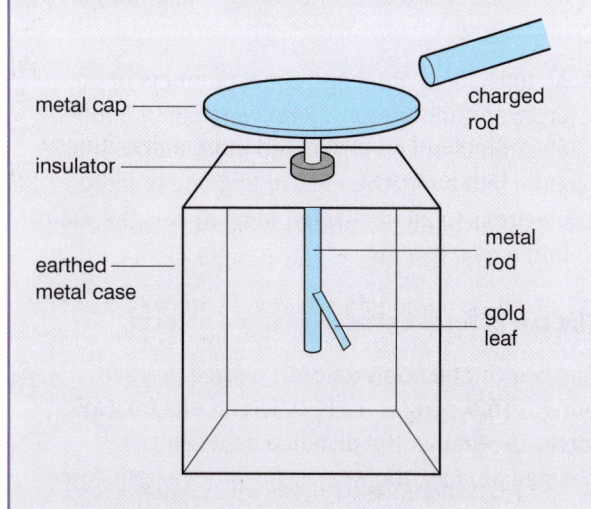

The gold leaf electroscope

5. In a photocopier, an image is formed on the surface of an electrically charged plate or drum.
   (i) What happens to the charge where the image is bright?
   (ii) Why do particles of the toner powder stick to the plate where the image is dark? [2]

6. A road tanker is used to deliver heating oil from a refinery to homes and offices. When oil is being pumped from the road tanker, the outlet pipe must be earthed. Why is this necessary? [2]

7. State two applications of static electricity. [2]

8. In a copper-plating experiment, a current of 0.2 A is passed through the electrolytic cell for 30 minutes exactly. How much charge passes through the cell in this time? [2]

9. When current is passed through an electrolytic cell, chlorine gas bubbles off at the anode and hydrogen gas at the cathode. Explain why this happens. [3]

10. State two applications of electrolysis. [2]

Electric charge

10.1 Electrostatics

Atomic structure

★ An atom consists of a nucleus surrounded by electrons. The nucleus is made up of neutrons and protons. Most of the mass of an atom is carried by the nucleus. A proton and an electron carry equal and opposite charge. A neutron is uncharged.

★ An uncharged atom has equal numbers of electrons and protons. Removing one or more electrons from an uncharged atom makes the atom into a positive ion. Adding one or more electrons to an uncharged atom makes the atom into a negative ion.

The law of force between charged objects

Any two charged objects exert a force on each other. This type of force is called an **electrostatic force**. The greater the distance between two charged objects, the weaker the electrostatic force between them.
- **Like charges repel; unlike charges attract.**

Conductors and insulators

1. In an **insulator**, all the electrons are firmly attached to atoms.
2. In a **conductor**, such as a metal, some electrons have broken away from the atoms. These electrons move about freely inside the conductor.

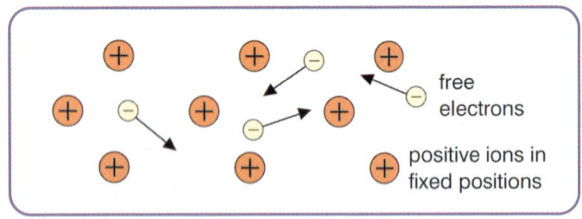

Inside a metal

Charging by friction

★ Certain insulators can be charged by rubbing with a dry cloth.

★ This happens as a result of the transfer of electrons to or from the surface atoms of the insulator.

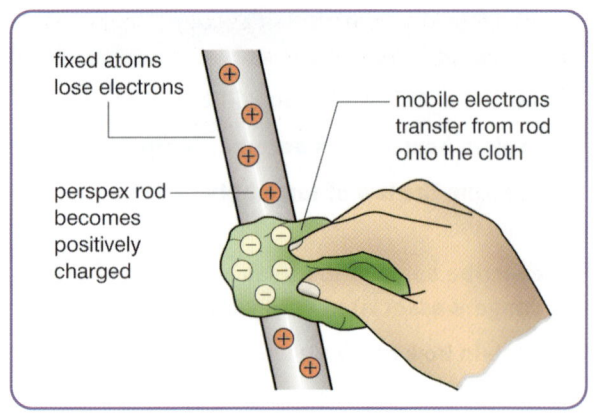

Charging by friction

★ Insulators that lose electrons to the cloth become positively charged (e.g. pers**P**ex; **P** for positive!).

★ Insulators that gain electrons from the cloth become negatively charged (e.g. polythe**N**e; **N** for negative!).

Charging an insulated metal object by direct contact

An uncharged insulated metal object can be charged by direct contact with a charged insulator.

1. **To make the metal object positive**, a positively charged rod is touched on the object. Free electrons in the metal transfer onto the positive rod, where they become trapped by the surface atoms. As a result, the metal object becomes positively charged and the rod becomes less positive.

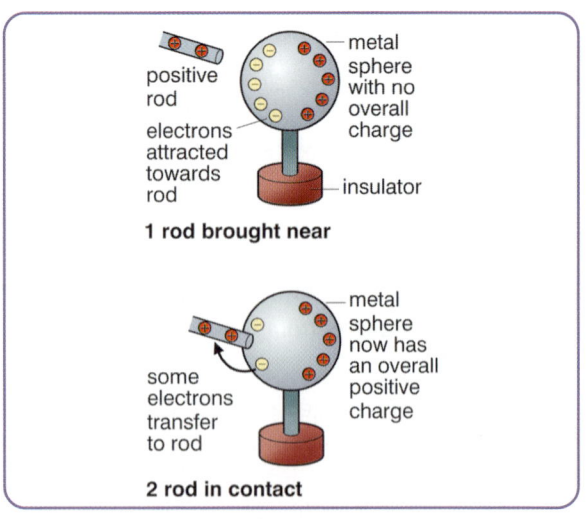

1 rod brought near

2 rod in contact

Charging a metal object positively

Electric charge

2 To make the metal object negative, a negatively charged rod is touched on the object. Electrons from the rod's surface atoms transfer to the metal. As a result, the metal object becomes negatively charged and the rod becomes less negative.

Earthing

A charged metal object can be discharged by connecting it to the earth with a wire. Electrons transfer between the object and the earth so the object loses its charge. This process is called **earthing**.

The gold leaf electroscope

This device is used to detect charge, and to determine whether the charge is positive or negative. If a charged object is touched on the cap of the electroscope, electron transfer makes the electroscope charged.

★ **If the charge on the object is negative**, the electroscope gains electrons. The leaf and the stem of the electroscope both become negative so the leaf rises as it is repelled from the stem.

★ **If the charge on the object is positive**, the electroscope loses electrons. The leaf and the stem of the electroscope both become positive so the leaf rises as it is repelled from the stem.

The diagram below shows the use of an electroscope to detect whether an object is positively or negatively charged.

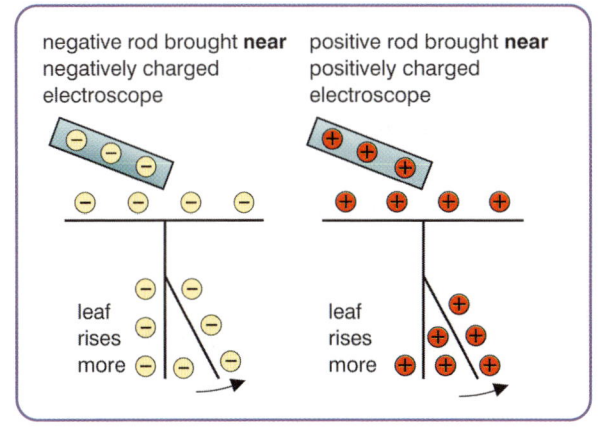

Detecting negative charge   Detecting positive charge

Electrostatic hazards

In an operating theatre, a tiny spark could make an anaesthetic gas leak explode. Such a spark could be generated if charge builds up on an insulated metal object. All metal objects, and the theatre floor itself, must therefore be earthed.

Pipe flow: powders and non-conducting fluids being pumped out of a metal pipe charge the pipe up, unless it is earthed. This occurs because of friction between the metal and the powder or fluid. If the pipe is not earthed, charge builds up on it until a spark jumps from the pipe to earth. If the powder or the fluid is flammable, a disaster could follow! Earthing the pipe prevents the pipe becoming charged.

Computer damage: expensive computer chips need to be handled with care since they are damaged by static electricity. Anyone handling a computer chip should not touch the pins of the chip, otherwise the pins will become charged if a charged object is nearby. This process, known as **charging by induction**, is explained in the diagram below.

Charging without direct contact

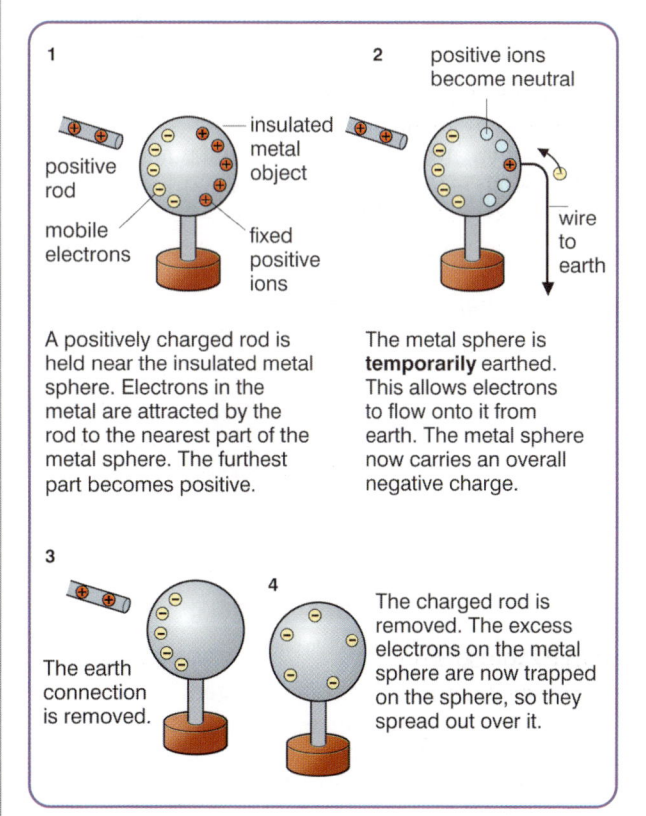

A positively charged rod is held near the insulated metal sphere. Electrons in the metal are attracted by the rod to the nearest part of the metal sphere. The furthest part becomes positive.

The metal sphere is **temporarily** earthed. This allows electrons to flow onto it from earth. The metal sphere now carries an overall negative charge.

The earth connection is removed.

The charged rod is removed. The excess electrons on the metal sphere are now trapped on the sphere, so they spread out over it.

Charging by induction

Electric charge

10.2 Electrostatics at work

Electrostatics is used in a wide range of devices. In addition, safety measures are necessary to eliminate static electricity as a hazard in a wide range of situations.

The electrostatic paint spray

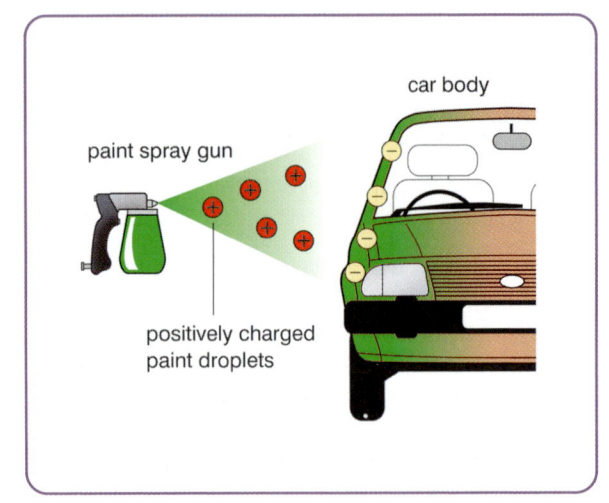

Electrostatic paint spray

A fixed potential difference is maintained between the paint spray nozzle and the metal panel to be painted. The paint droplets in the spray become charged when they are forced out of the spray gun. They are then attracted onto the metal panel to form an even layer of paint on the panel.

The electrostatic precipitator

The ash and dust from coal burned at a power station is prevented from entering the atmosphere by an electrostatic precipitator in the chimney. The dust particles touch the charged wire grid of the precipitator and become charged. The particles are then attracted onto the earthed metal tube surrounding the grid.

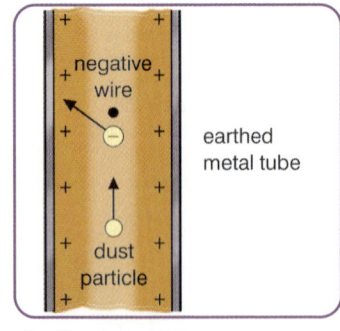

Attracting dust particles

The photocopier

When a photocopier is used:
- a copying plate or drum is charged electrostatically with a uniform layer of charge across its surface
- an image of the page to be copied is projected on to the copying plate
- charge leaks away from the areas of the plate where the image is bright. This is because the plate surface is made of material that conducts electricity when it is illuminated
- black 'toner' powder applied to the surface sticks to the charged areas of the surface because the powder particles are electrostatically attracted to the surface
- the powder is transferred onto a sheet of white paper pressed against the surface
- heating the paper makes the black powder melt, stick to the paper and dry to form a copy of the original page.

Handy hint

The process can be summarised as:

charge plate, project image, leak charge, apply powder, press paper and heat

The inkjet printer

This is used to print characters on paper. Each character is formed from closely spaced tiny ink dots. Each character is represented by a digital signal from a computer linked to the printer. The signal is a string of 1s and 0s which control the direction of tiny droplets of ink forced out of a fine nozzle onto a sheet of paper.

★ The droplets are charged electrically when they are forced out of the nozzle.

★ Each droplet then passes between two metal plates. A voltage can be applied to these plates to make one plate positive and the other one negative. This causes each droplet to be deflected because it experiences an electrostatic force towards the plate with the opposite charge as it passes between the plates.

★ The deflection of each droplet depends on the size and the direction of the voltage applied to the plates. This voltage therefore determines where the ink dot produced by each droplet appears on the paper.

Electric charge

10.3 Current and charge

Fact file

★ An **electric current** is a flow of electric charge.

★ The unit of electric current is the **ampere** (A); the unit of electric charge is the **coulomb** (C).

★ **Electrons** are responsible for the flow of charge through a **metal** when it conducts electricity.

★ **Positive and negative ions** are responsible for the flow of charge through an **electrolyte** when it conducts electricity.

Steady currents

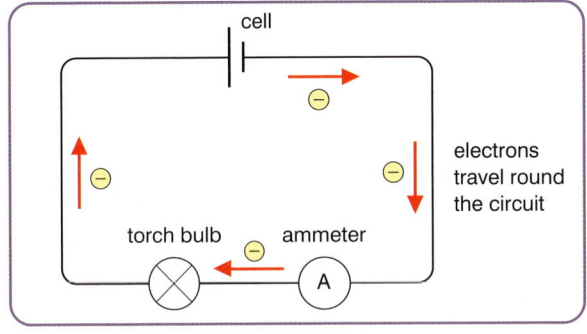

A steady current

The diagram shows a simple electric circuit in which a cell is connected in series with an ammeter and a torch bulb.

★ **The current in this circuit is constant.** This means that charge passes through each component at a steady rate. Electrons pass through each component at a steady rate.

★ **The current through each component is the same.** Equal amounts of charge pass through each component in a set period of time. The number of electrons per second passing through each component is the same.

Equation for charge flow

★ **One coulomb of charge** is defined as the amount of charge passing a point in a circuit in one second when the current is one ampere.

★ **The charge passing a point in a circuit** that is carrying a steady current is calculated as follows:

charge passed = current × time taken
    (in C)   (in A)   (in s)

At a junction

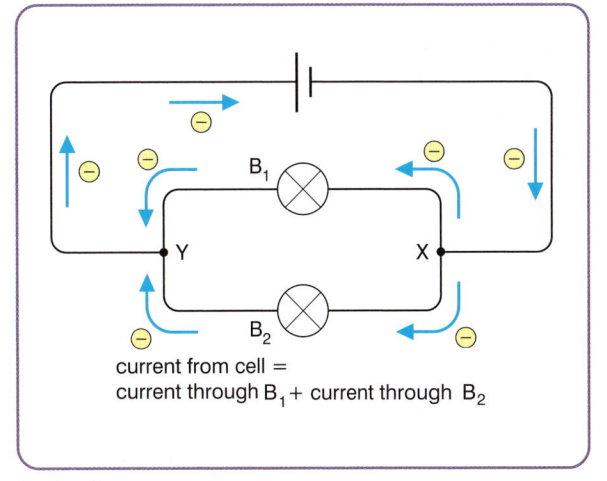

current from cell =
current through B_1 + current through B_2

At a junction

In this circuit, two torch bulbs B_1 and B_2 are in parallel with each other. Each electron from the cell passes through one of the torch bulbs and then returns to the positive terminal of the cell. The flow of electrons from the cell divides at junction X and recombines at junction Y.

The charge flow per second from the cell = charge flow per second through B_1 + charge flow per second through B_2. Since charge flow per second is current, it follows that cell current = current through B_1 + current through B_2.

In other words, at a junction in a circuit,

the total current entering the junction is equal to the total current leaving the junction.

Questions

a) Calculate the charge that flows through a torch bulb carrying a steady current of 0.25 A in

  (i) 1 minute

  (ii) 5 minutes.

b) Calculate how long it takes for a charge of 100 C to pass through a torch bulb that is carrying a steady current of 0.2 A.

Answers

a) (i) 15 C (ii) 75 C
b) 500 s

Electric charge

10.4 Electrolysis

Electrolytic conduction

This occurs when a substance is decomposed by an electric current passing through it. Decomposition does not happen when an electric current passes through a wire – the chemical composition of the wire is unaffected by the electric current. In comparison, the passage of an electric current through sodium chloride solution causes a gas to bubble off at each electrode. In an electrolytic cell:
- the **electrolyte** is the conducting liquid
- the **anode** is the positive electrode
- the **cathode** is the negative electrode.

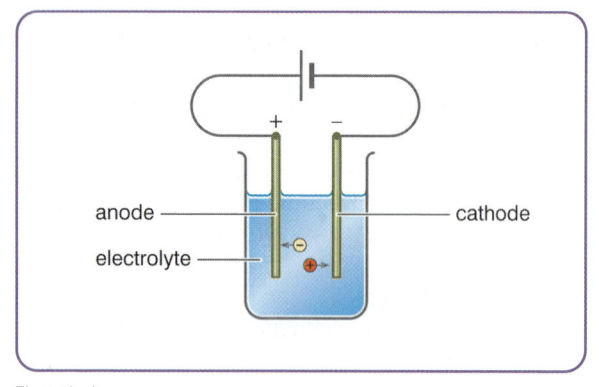

Electrolysis

In an electrolyte

An electrolyte is a liquid which contains positive and negative ions. For example, in sodium chloride solution, the positive ions are hydrogen ions (H^+) and sodium ions (Na^+). The negative ions are chloride ions (Cl^-) and hydroxide ions (OH^-).

The positive ions are attracted to the cathode because they carry the opposite charge. Where there is more than one type of positive ion, the ion that attracts an electron most easily off the cathode is discharged. In sodium chloride solution, hydrogen gas bubbles off the cathode because the hydrogen ions are more easily discharged than the sodium ions.

The negative ions are attracted to the anode. The ion that gives up an electron most easily is discharged at the anode. In sodium chloride solution, chlorine gas bubbles off at the anode.

Copper-plating

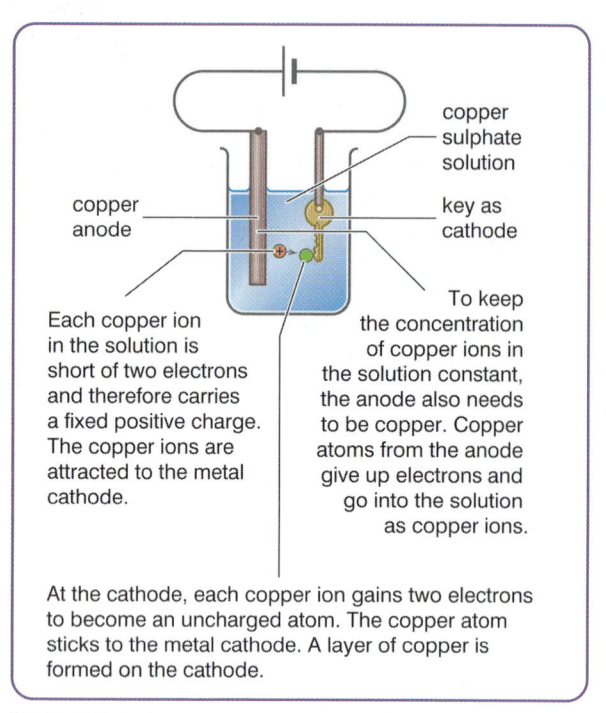

Each copper ion in the solution is short of two electrons and therefore carries a fixed positive charge. The copper ions are attracted to the metal cathode.

To keep the concentration of copper ions in the solution constant, the anode also needs to be copper. Copper atoms from the anode give up electrons and go into the solution as copper ions.

At the cathode, each copper ion gains two electrons to become an uncharged atom. The copper atom sticks to the metal cathode. A layer of copper is formed on the cathode.

Copper-plating a key

A metal object can be copper-plated by making the object the cathode in an electrolytic cell containing copper sulphate solution.

Each copper atom deposited on the cathode adds the same mass and gains the same amount of charge (2 electrons). The mass of copper deposited is therefore proportional to the charge flow through the cell. Hence the mass deposited is proportional to the **current** and the **time taken**.

Questions

In a copper-plating experiment, a metal key was used as the cathode. Its initial mass was 25.25 g. After being used for 30 minutes as the cathode with a steady current of 0.25 A, its mass had increased to 25.40 g. Calculate

a) the amount of charge needed to deposit 1 g of copper

b) the mass of copper that would be deposited by a current of 0.1 A for exactly 3 hours.

Answers: a) 3000 C b) 0.36 g

Electric charge

ROUND UP

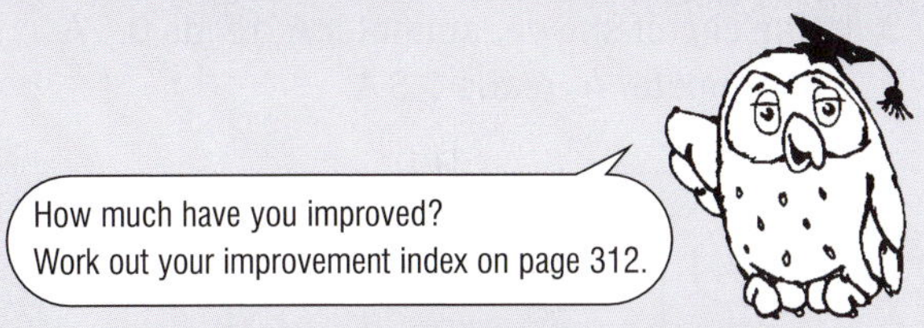

How much have you improved? Work out your improvement index on page 312.

1. An insulated metal object M can become charged without making direct contact with a charged object O. The diagram shows how one stage in this process could happen. The complete sequence of actions including the stage shown in the diagram are listed below in the wrong order.

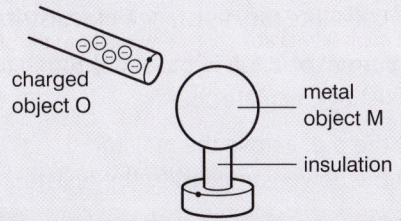

    (i) The earth connection to the metal object M is removed.
    (ii) The charged body O is brought near the metal object M.
    (iii) The charged body O is removed.
    (iv) The metal object M is earthed.

    a) Rewrite the list in the correct order. [4]
    b) What type of charge is left on the metal object M if the charged body O carries a negative charge? [1]
    c) Does the total charge on the charged object O alter as a result of M being charged in this way? [1]

2. A gold leaf electroscope is charged by direct contact with a positively charged rod, as shown.

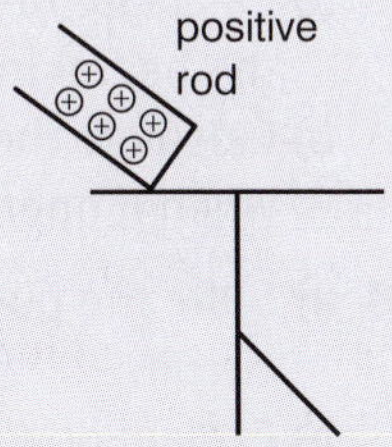

    a) Explain in terms of electrons why the leaf rises when the electroscope is charged in this way. [3]
    b) Explain why the leaf remains in the position shown when the charged rod is removed. [1]
    c) Explain how the electroscope could be charged negatively using a positively charged rod. [4]
    d) Describe how the electroscope could be used to determine the type of charge on a charged object. [3]

3. a) In dry weather, the metal body of a car becomes charged when the car is in motion on a dry road. If the car is not fitted with a trailing conductor,
    (i) explain why someone who touches the car when it stops would receive a shock [2]
    (ii) explain why the car driver would receive a shock on getting out of the car after it stops. [2]
    b) Why does the metal body of a car not become charged
    (i) if a trailing conductor is fitted to the car? [1]
    (ii) in wet weather? [2]

4. In an electroplating experiment, a layer of copper was being deposited on a metal plate. The initial mass of the plate was measured at 64.50 g. The current was maintained at 0.1 A for 30 minutes, then the plate was carefully dried and reweighed at 64.56 g. It was then reconnected and the current was increased to 0.30 A for a further 60 minutes.
    a) Calculate the charge passed through the cell in each of the two parts of the experiment. [2]
    b) Calculate the increase in mass of the plate in the first part of the experiment. [1]
    c) Hence calculate the increase in mass in the second part of the experiment. [1]
    d) What steady current would have given the same total increase in mass in a total time of 1 hour? [1]

5. a) (i) A photocopier sometimes produces copies on which the print is too light. State and explain one reason why this can happen.
    (ii) Explain why a photocopy is sometimes smudged when it emerges from the photocopier. [4]
    b) In an ink jet printer, an ink droplet is deflected to a certain point on the paper when a certain voltage is applied. How would the deflection change if the voltage is
    (i) changed to zero? (ii) reversed? [2]

6. a) Describe the principle of operation of an electrostatic precipitator used to remove ash and dust particles from the flue gases of a power station. [3] 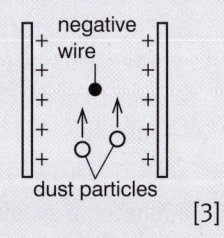
    b) An electronic chip may be damaged if its metal pins become charged. With the aid of a diagram, explain how it is possible to charge an insulated metal pin simply by touching the pin in the presence of a nearby charged object. [2]

Chapter 11 — Electric circuits

PREVIEW

At the end of this topic you will be able to:

- explain what is meant by potential difference
- describe series and parallel circuits in terms of current and voltage
- describe how to use an ammeter to measure current and a voltmeter to measure voltage
- recognise the circuit symbols for common electrical components and know their characteristics
- define resistance and carry out calculations involving current, voltage, resistance and power
- describe how mains electricity is supplied and costed
- identify dangers of mains electricity and explain safety features and devices to minimise dangers.

How much do you already know? Work out your score on pages 312–13.

Test yourself

1. Two identical torch bulbs, a switch, an ammeter and a 1.5 V cell are connected in series with each other.
   a) Draw the circuit diagram. [2]
   b) The ammeter reading was 0.20 A when the switch was closed. How much energy was delivered to each torch bulb in one minute? [2]

2. A 1.5 V cell was connected in series with an ammeter, a switch and a torch bulb X. A second torch bulb Y was connected in parallel with X. The switch was then closed to light both torch bulbs.
   a) Draw the circuit diagram. [2]
   b) The ammeter reading was 0.30 A. Calculate the energy supplied by the cell in
      (i) one second (ii) one minute. [2]

3. In the circuit shown, ammeter A_1 reads 0.5 A and ammeter A_2 reads 0.3 A.

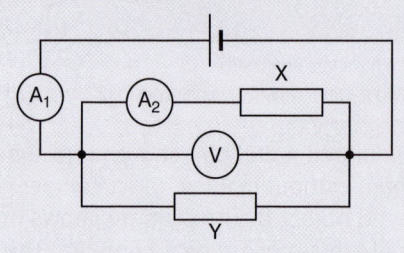

   a) Calculate the current through resistor Y. [1]
   b) The voltmeter in parallel with resistor Y reads 1.0 V when ammeter A_1 reads 0.5 A. Calculate the resistance of resistor Y. [2]

4. A current of 2.5 A is passed through a 6.0 Ω resistor. Calculate
   a) the p.d. across the resistor
   b) the power supplied to the resistor. [2]

5. a) Draw a circuit diagram to show a diode connected in series with a 1.5 V cell and a torch bulb lit up. [2]
   b) If the 1.5 V cell is connected in the circuit in the reverse direction, the torch bulb would not light. Why? [2]

6. Give the symbol and state the main characteristic of each of the following components:
   a) a light-dependent resistor
   b) a thermistor. [4]

7. An electric heater is rated at 240 V, 1000 W.
   a) Calculate the electrical energy delivered to the heater in 300 s.
   b) Calculate the current through the heater when it operates at its rated power. [3]

8. a) State the purpose of a fuse in an electric circuit.
   b) Explain how a fuse achieves its purpose. [3]

9. A set of Christmas tree lights contains 20 light bulbs rated at 6 W. The light bulbs are connected in series to be operated from 240 V mains. When in normal use, calculate
   a) the current through each bulb
   b) the voltage across each bulb. [4]

10. A microwave oven rated at 800 W is used for 15 minutes to heat some food. Calculate
    a) the number of units of electricity used
    b) the cost of the electricity used, if each unit of electricity is priced at 6.0p. [3]

Electric circuits

11.1 Current and potential difference

Note
The symbols used in the current diagrams in this chapter are explained on page 304.

Fact file

★ An **electric current** is a **flow of charge**. The unit of electric current is the **ampere** (A).

★ The **potential difference** (p.d.) between any two points in a circuit is the **work done per unit charge** when charge moves from one point to the other point. Voltage is an alternative word for potential difference.

★ The unit of charge is the **coulomb** (C). One coulomb is equal to the charge passing a point in a circuit in one second when the current is one ampere.

★ The unit of potential difference is the **volt** (V), equal to one joule per coulomb.

Four rules about current

1. The current entering a component is the same as the current leaving it. A component does not use up current; it uses the electrical energy supplied to it by the charge that passes through it.

2. At a junction, the total current leaving the junction is equal to the total current entering the junction.

3. Components in series pass the same current.

4. An ammeter is a meter designed to measure current. It is always connected in series with a component. An ideal ammeter has zero resistance.

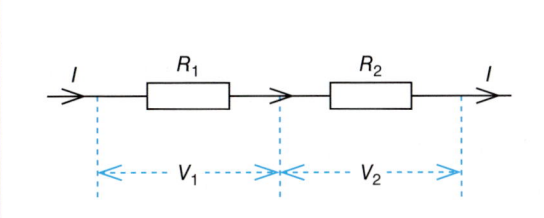

The combined resistance of two or more resistors in series = the sum of the individual resistances

Series resistors

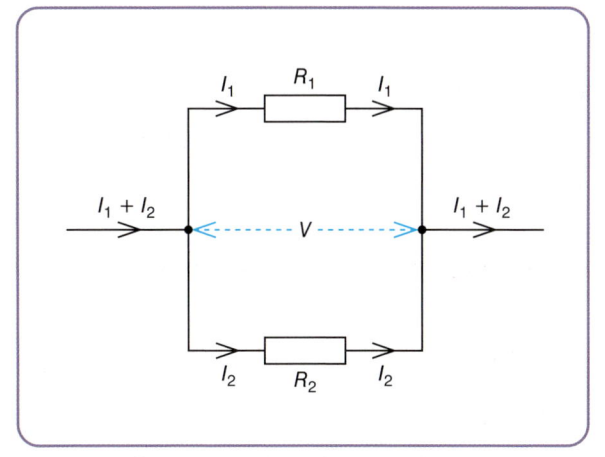

Parallel resistors

Four rules about voltage

1. The voltage across a component is the number of joules delivered to the component by each coulomb of charge that passes through it.

2. Components in parallel have the same voltage across them.

3. For two or more components in series, the total voltage is equal to the sum of the individual voltages.

4. A voltmeter is a meter designed to measure voltage (potential difference). It is always connected in parallel with a component. An ideal voltmeter has infinite resistance.

Four rules about power

Consider a component in a circuit which has voltage V across its terminals and which passes a steady current I.

1. In a time interval t, charge Q flows through the component where $Q = It$.

2. The electrical energy E delivered by charge Q is QV, since V is defined as the electrical energy delivered per unit charge.

3. Hence the electrical energy E delivered in time t is ItV.

4. The electrical power = $\dfrac{\text{electrical energy delivered}}{\text{time taken}} = IV$

Electric circuits

11.2 Resistance

Fact file

★ The **resistance** R of an electrical component in a circuit is given by

$$R = \frac{\text{the voltage across the component}}{\text{the current through the component}}$$

★ The unit of resistance is the **ohm** (Ω), defined as one volt per ampere.

★ **To calculate resistance**, use the equation

$$\text{resistance} = \frac{\text{voltage}}{\text{current}}$$

★ **Ohm's law** states that for a wire under constant physical conditions, the current is proportional to the voltage. This is equivalent to stating that its resistance is constant.

★ A **resistor** is a component designed to have a particular value of resistance. This resistance is caused by opposition to the motion of electrons round the circuit.

Note

The following prefixes are used for large or small values of current, voltage or resistance:

mega (M)	kilo (k)	milli (m)	micro (μ)
1 000 000	1000	0.001	0.000 001
10^6	10^3	10^{-3}	10^{-6}

What does current depend on?

Current depends on:
- the voltage of the cell, battery or power supply unit
- the resistance of the components in the circuit.

Resistors can be used to control the current in a circuit.

Measuring resistance

The diagram at the top of the next column shows how the resistance of a resistor may be determined using an ammeter and a voltmeter. Note that the voltmeter is in parallel with the resistor, and the ammeter is in series.

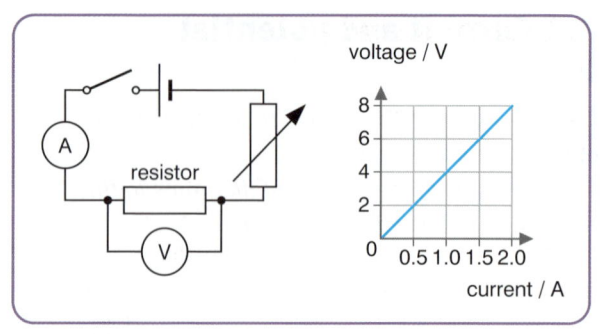

Measuring resistance

Voltage against current

1. With the switch closed, the variable resistor is adjusted to change the current in steps. At each step, the current and voltage are measured from the ammeter and the voltmeter, respectively.

2. The measurements are plotted as a graph of voltage (on the vertical axis) against current, as shown. The plotted points define a straight line passing through the origin.

3. The gradient of the line is measured. This is equal to the resistance of the resistor.

Questions

a) Determine the resistance of the resistor that gave the results plotted on the graph.

b) Calculate the current through this resistor when the voltage across it is **(i)** 5.0 V **(ii)** 0.1 V.

Resistance heating

All the electrical energy supplied to a resistor is transformed to thermal energy, heating the surroundings as a result.

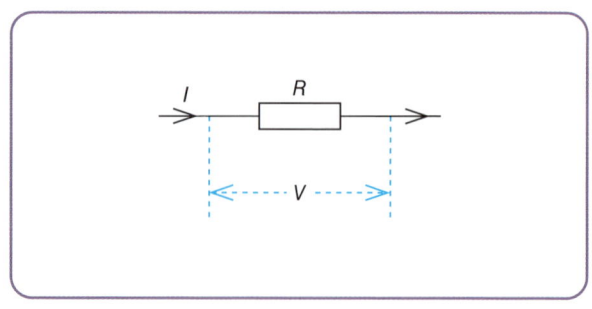

Heating effect

1. The voltage V across the resistor = IR, where I is the current through the component.

2. The power supplied to the resistor $P = IV = I^2R$. This is the rate of heat produced in the resistor.

Answers

a) 4.0 Ω b) (i) 1.25 A (ii) 25 mA

Electric circuits

11.3 Components

The circuit shown on the previous page (top right) for measuring resistance may be used to investigate the variation of current with voltage for any device. The graphs below show the results of such investigations for different components, plotted with current on the *y*-axis and voltage on the *x*-axis.

★ For a wire-wound resistor at constant temperature, the graph is a straight line – the resistance is constant.

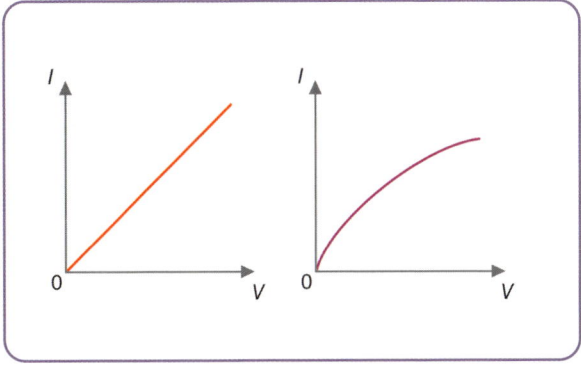

Fixed resistor   Filament bulb

★ For a filament bulb such as a torch bulb, the graph is a curve – the resistance increases as the filament becomes hotter.

★ For a diode in its forward direction, the graph shows that the resistance decreases as the current increases. In the reverse direction, the graph shows that the diode has an extremely high resistance.

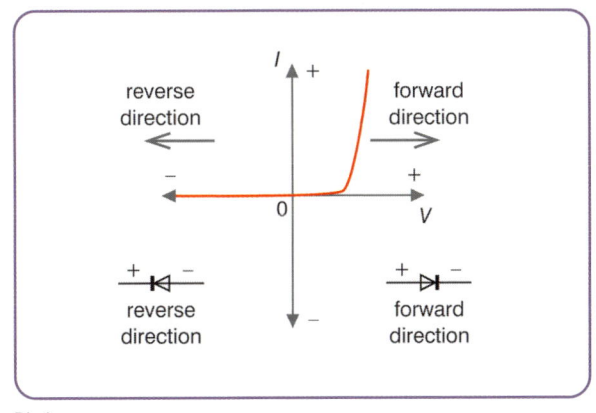

Diode

★ For a light-dependent resistor (LDR), its resistance depends on the intensity of light falling on it. Increasing the intensity makes the resistance lower; conversely, decreasing the intensity makes the resistance higher. More electrons are freed from the atoms if the light intensity is increased, causing the resistance to fall.

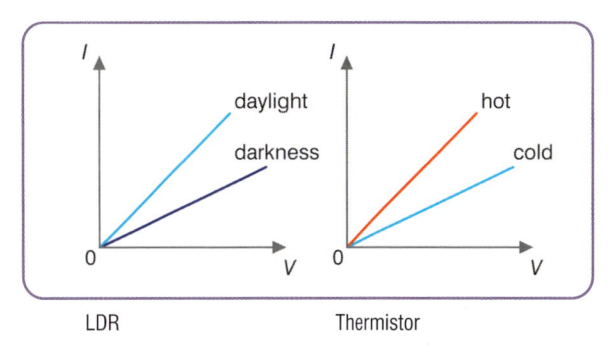

LDR   Thermistor

★ For a thermistor, the resistance decreases with increasing temperature and vice versa. More electrons are freed from the atoms if the temperature is increased, causing the resistance to fall.

Questions

A $1000\,\Omega$ resistor was connected in series with a thermistor, a milliammeter and a 2.0 V cell. The reading on the milliammeter was 1.0 mA. Calculate

a) the voltage across the $1000\,\Omega$ resistor when its current was 1.0 mA

b) the voltage across the thermistor when its current was 1.0 mA.

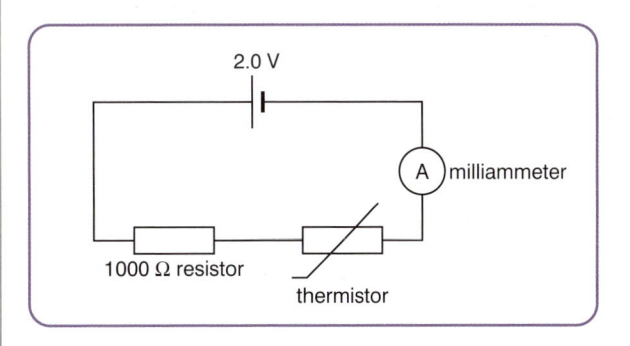

Answers

a) 1.0 V   b) 1.0 V

Electric circuits

11.4 Mains electricity

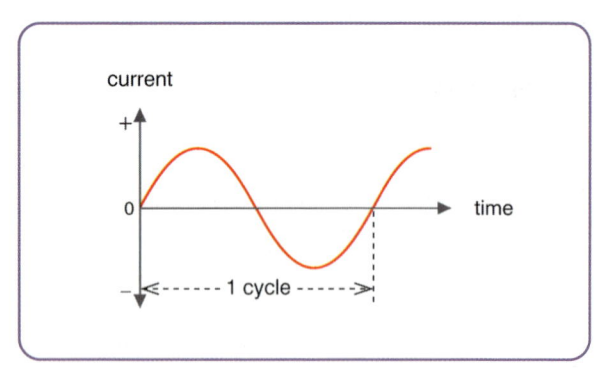

Alternating current

Alternating current

★ The electric current through a mains appliance alternates in direction. The current reverses direction then reverses back each cycle.

★ The **frequency** of an alternating current is the number of cycles per second. In the UK, the mains frequency is 50 Hz.

The three-pin plug

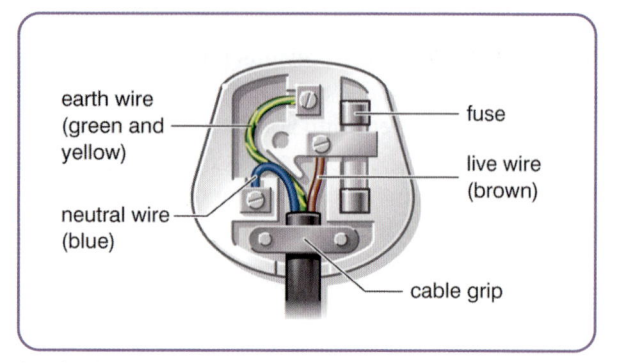

A mains plug

Electricity costs

★ One kilowatt hour (kWh) is the electrical energy supplied to a one kilowatt appliance in exactly one hour.

★ The kilowatt hour is the unit of electricity for costing purposes.

★ A domestic electricity meter records the total number of units used.

Each circuit from the fuse board is protected with its own fuse. If the fuse 'blows', the live wire is therefore cut off from appliances supplied by that circuit.

The mains cable from the substation to a building is connected via the electricity meter to the circuits in the building at the distribution fuse board. The live wire from the substation is connected via a main fuse to the electricity meter.

The two wires used to supply an electric current to an appliance are referred to as the **live** and the **neutral** wires. The neutral wire is earthed at the nearest mains substation.

Mains wires need to have as low a resistance as possible, otherwise heat is produced in them by the current. This is why mains wires are made from copper. All mains wires and fittings are insulated.

The fuse in a lighting circuit is in the fuse box. Each light bulb is turned on or off by its own switch. When the switch is in the off position, the appliance is not connected to the live wire of the mains supply.

A **ring main** is used to supply electricity to appliances via wall sockets. A ring main circuit consists of a live wire, a neutral wire and the **earth wire** which is earthed at the fuse board. The wires of a ring main are thicker than the wires of a lighting circuit because appliances connected to a ring main require more current than light bulbs.

Each appliance is connected to the ring main by means of a three-pin plug which carries a fuse. An appliance with a metal chassis is earthed via the three-pin plug and the earth wire. This prevents the metal chassis from becoming live if a fault develops in the appliance. Appliances connected to the ring main can be switched on or off independently since they are in parallel with each other.

Mains circuits

Electric circuits

11.5 Electrical safety

Faults and fuses

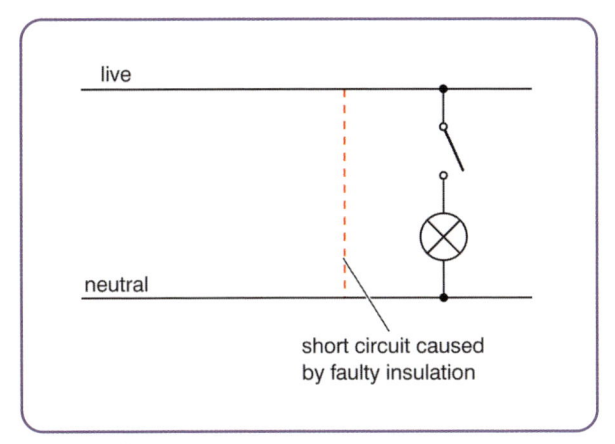

A short circuit

A **short circuit** occurs where a fault creates a low resistance path between two points at different voltages. The current through the short circuit is much greater than the current along the correct path between the two points; enough to create a fire through overheating.

Fuses are intended to prevent excessive currents flowing. A fuse is a thin piece of resistance wire which overheats and melts if too much current passes through it. The fuse wire breaks when it melts, thus cutting the current off and protecting the appliance or the wires leading to it from overheating due to excessive current.

Faults in mains circuits can arise due to:
- **poor maintenance**, e.g. frayed cables or damaged plugs or fittings such as sockets and switches
- **carelessness**, e.g. coiling cables that are too long which prevents heat escaping from them
- **overloading a circuit**, e.g. too many appliances connected to the same circuit or connecting a powerful appliance to a low current circuit.

Earthing

Any appliance with a metal case must be earthed through the ring main to protect the user. If such an appliance is not earthed and a fault develops in which a live wire touches the case, anyone who subsequently touches the case will be electrocuted. The victim effectively provides a short circuit path to earth from the live case.

Circuit breakers

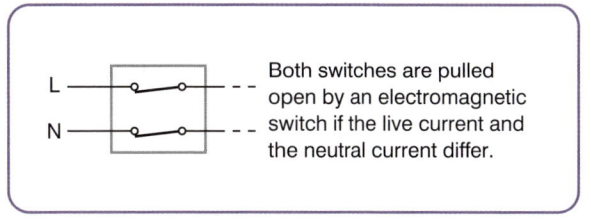

A residual current circuit breaker

Both switches are pulled open by an electromagnetic switch if the live current and the neutral current differ.

A lethal electric shock is possible with currents as small as 50 mA passing through the body. The **residual current circuit breaker** is designed to cut an appliance off from the mains if the current in the live wire differs from the current in the neutral wire by more than 30 mA. This difference would arise if current leaks to earth from a poorly insulated live wire.

A **simple circuit breaker** is a switch operated by an electromagnet in series with the switch. When the switch is closed, if the current reaches a certain value, the electromagnet pulls the switch open and cuts the current off. The circuit breaker switch then needs to be reset once the fault causing the current rise has been remedied. A circuit breaker does not need to be replaced like a fuse each time it cuts the current off.

Double insulation

This is a safety feature of mains appliances like hand-held hair dryers and electric shavers which have insulated cases.

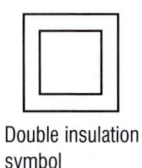

Double insulation symbol

Questions

State the purpose of **a)** a fuse **b)** a residual current circuit breaker.

Answers
a) To protect the appliance or the wiring from overheating due to excessive current.
b) To protect the user from shocks.

Electric circuits

ROUND UP

How much have you improved?
Work out your improvement index on page 313.

1. In this circuit, the ammeter reading was 0.25 A and the voltmeter reading was 3.0 V.

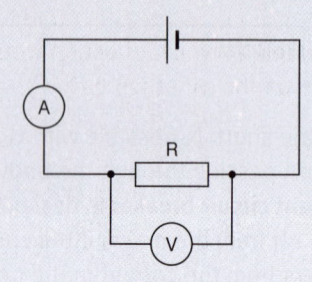

   a) Calculate the resistance of resistor R. [1]
   b) If a second resistor identical to R was connected in parallel with R how would the ammeter and voltmeter readings alter? [2]

2. a) A 1500 W, 240 V electric heater is connected to the ring main in a house and then switched on.
      (i) Calculate the current through the heater. [1]
      (ii) How many units of electricity would be used by this heater in 2 hours? [1]
   b) (i) What is the function of the earth wire in a ring main circuit? [2]
      (ii) Given mains fuses rated at 3 A, 5 A and 13 A, which one would you choose for a microwave oven rated at 650 W, 240 V? [1]
      (iii) In (ii), if the wrong fuse is chosen, what problems might occur? [2]

3. The circuit diagram shows two 5 Ω resistors P and Q in series with each other, an ammeter and a 3.0 V cell.

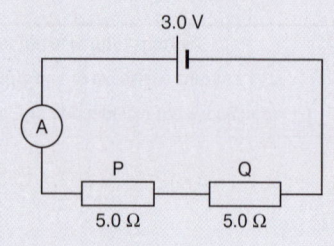

   a) (i) What is the voltage across each resistor? [1]
      (ii) What is the current through each resistor? [1]
   b) Hence calculate the power supplied to each resistor. [1]
   c) A third 5 Ω resistor R is then connected in parallel with resistor P. How does this affect the current passing through each of the other two resistors? [2]

4. A 24 W heating element for a 12 V heater is to be made using a suitable length of resistance wire.
   a) Calculate the expected current and the required resistance. [2]
   b) The resistance wire has a resistance of 5 Ω per metre. Calculate the length of wire required to make this heating element. [2]
   c) With the aid of a circuit diagram, describe how you could check the resistance per metre of a reel of this resistance wire. [5]

5. The following mains appliances were used in a household over a period of 24 hours:
   (i) two 100 W light bulbs, each for 6 hours
   (ii) a 5000 W electric oven for 2 hours
   (iii) a 3000 W electric kettle used four times for 5 minutes each time.
   a) Calculate the number of units of electricity used in each case. [3]
   b) Calculate the total cost of the electricity used if the unit price of electricity was 5p. [1]
   c) How long would it take a 5000 W electric oven to use the same number of electricity units as a 100 W electric light bulb in 24 hours? [2]

6. a) Why is it dangerous to touch a mains appliance when you have wet hands? [3]
   b) A mains electric mower should never be connected to the mains unless a residual current circuit breaker is used. Why? [3]
   c) Why is it dangerous to use a mains electric mower with its mains cable coiled up? [2]

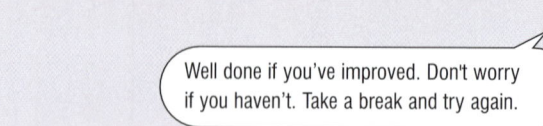

Well done if you've improved. Don't worry if you haven't. Take a break and try again.

Electromagnetism — Chapter 12

> **PREVIEW**
>
> At the end of this topic you will be able to:
>
> - describe the operation of devices that contain an electromagnet
> - explain the principle and operation of a moving-coil loudspeaker and an electric motor
> - explain the principle and operation of an alternating current generator and a transformer
> - explain how electric power is transmitted via the grid system.

How much do you already know? Work out your score on page 313–14.

Test yourself

1. State a suitable material from which to make
   a) the core of an electromagnet
   b) a permanent magnet. [2]

2. a) One end of a bar magnet is held near a plotting compass, as shown. What is the polarity of this end of the bar magnet? [1]

   b) The north pole of a bar magnet repels pole P of another bar magnet. What is the polarity of P? [1]

3. Describe the lines of the magnetic field produced by
   a) a long, straight, vertical wire carrying a direct current [2]
   b) a solenoid carrying a direct current. [2]

4. State whether each of the following devices contains a permanent magnet or an electromagnet:
   a) a loudspeaker b) a relay c) an electric motor. [3]

5. a) The diagram shows a vertical wire between the poles of a U-shaped magnet, arranged so the magnetic field of the magnet is horizontal. When a current passes up the wire, the wire is forced outwards. If the magnetic field is reversed and the current is reversed, in which direction would the force on the wire then be? [1]

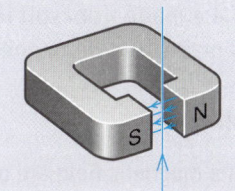

   b) Explain why a direct current electric motor cannot work on alternating current. [2]

6. a) State two ways in which the voltage from an alternating current generator would change if its rate of rotation was reduced. [2]

   b) Why is alternating current used to transmit electric power through the grid system? [3]

7. An aluminium plate placed between the poles of an electromagnet supplied with alternating current, as shown, becomes warm. Explain how this happens. [2]

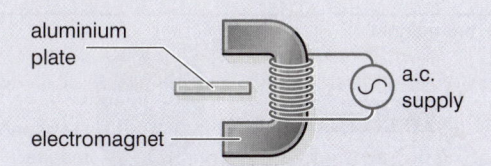

8. A transformer has 60 turns in its primary coil and 1200 turns in its secondary coil. A 240 V, 100 W lamp is connected to the terminals of its secondary coil. The primary coil is connected to an alternating voltage supply.

   a) Calculate the voltage of this supply if the lamp lights normally. [1]

   b) Calculate the maximum possible current through the primary coil when the 100 W lamp is on. [1]

297

Electromagnetism

12.1 Magnetism

Fact file

★ Two magnets act on each other at a distance.

★ The law of force for magnetic poles is that **like poles repel and unlike poles attract**.

★ Iron and steel can be magnetised and demagnetised.

★ Permanent magnets are made from steel because it is hard to demagnetise once magnetised.

★ Electromagnets are made from soft iron because it is easy to magnetise and demagnetise.

Magnetic field patterns

The lines of force of a magnetic field are defined by the direction of a plotting compass in the magnetic field. A bar magnet suspended on a thread aligns itself with the Earth's magnetic field. The end that points north is the north-seeking pole; the other end is the south-seeking pole.

Permanent magnets

A bar magnet produces lines of force which loop round from one end to the other end. The lines emerge from the north-seeking pole and end at the south-seeking pole. A U-shaped magnet has straight lines of force between its poles.

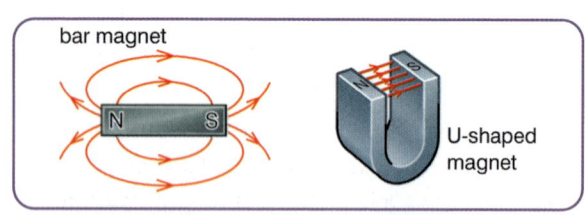

Magnetic fields

The magnetic effect of a steady electric current

Near a long straight wire, the magnetic field lines are concentric circles centred on the wire in a plane perpendicular to it.

Near a long solenoid, the magnetic field lines are concentrated at the ends, similar to the field of a bar magnet. The lines pass through the solenoid along its axis. In both examples, reversing the current reverses the field lines.

Electromagnets

An electromagnet consists of a solenoid with an iron core. When a current is passed through the coil of wire, the iron bar is magnetised. The magnetic field is much stronger than the field created by the empty coil. It can be switched off by switching the current off, and its strength can be altered by changing the current.

Using electromagnets

To lift scrap iron: a powerful electromagnet suspended from a crane cable is used to lift scrap iron in scrapyards. Switching the electromagnet off causes the scrap iron to fall off the electromagnet.

The relay: when current is passed through the coil of a relay, the electromagnet attracts a soft iron armature. The movement of this armature closes a switch which is part of a different circuit. When the current is switched off, the armature springs back to its normal position and the switch reverts to its original state.

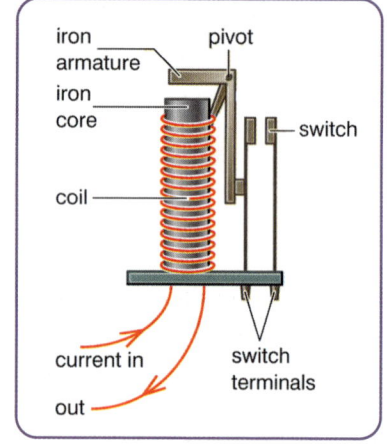

A normally open relay

The electric bell: the electromagnet coil is part of a 'make-and-break' switch. When current passes through the coil, the electromagnet attracts the soft iron armature which makes the hammer hit the bell. The movement of the armature opens the 'make-and-break' switch which switches the electromagnet off, allowing the armature to spring back to its initial position and close the switch. Current then passes through the electromagnet again, causing the sequence to be repeated.

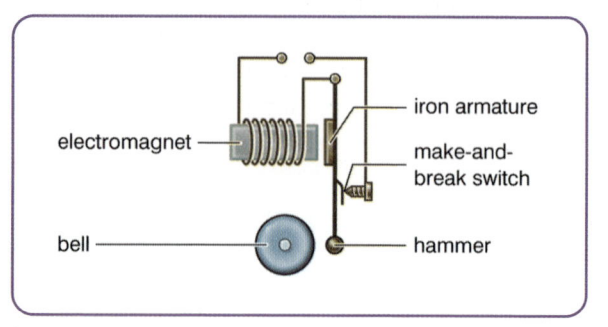

An electric bell

Electromagnetism

12.2 The electric motor

The motor effect

A force is exerted on a current-carrying wire placed at right angles to the lines of force of a magnetic field. The diagram shows a current-carrying wire between the poles of a U-shaped magnet. The force is perpendicular to the wire and to the lines of force of the magnet.

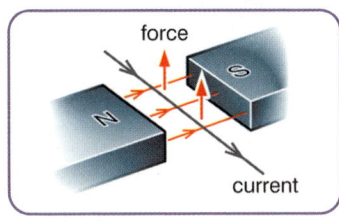

The motor effect

The force occurs because the magnetic field created by the wire interacts with the applied magnetic field (the magnetic field in which the wire is placed). The combined field is very weak on one side where the two fields are in opposite directions to each other. The force acts towards the side where the combined field is very weak.

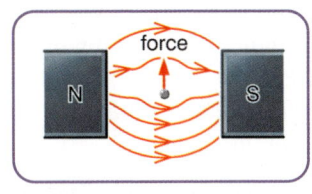

Combined fields

Fleming's left-hand rule is a convenient way to remember the force direction if you know the current direction and the direction of the applied magnetic field.

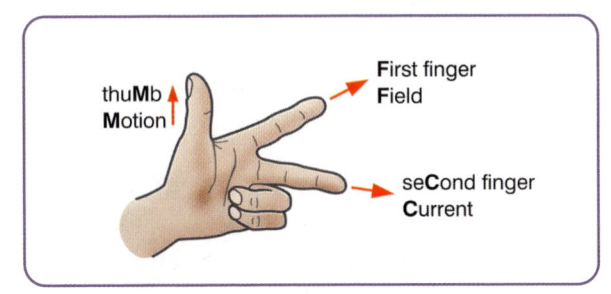

Fleming's left-hand rule

The electric motor

A model electric motor is shown in the next diagram. The rectangular coil is on a spindle between the poles of a U-shaped magnet. Current enters and leaves the coil via a split-ring commutator.

Current passes along each side of the coil in opposite directions. Each side is therefore acted on by a force due to the magnetic field. The force on one side is in the opposite direction to the force on the other side.

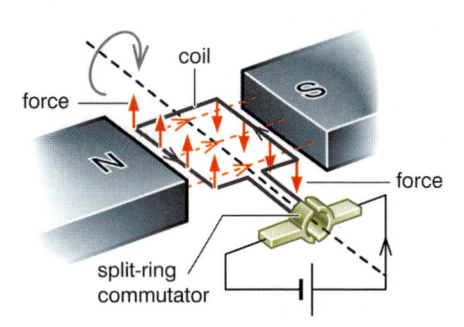

When the coil is parallel to the field, the forces on the sides rotate the coil. As the coil turns through the position at 90° to the field, the split-ring commutator reverses its connections to the battery, reversing the current direction round the coil. Therefore, the forces acting on each side continue to turn the coil in the same direction as before, so the coil rotates continuously in one direction.

The electric motor

Questions

For the electric motor above, what would be the effect of **a)** reversing the current direction **b)** reversing the current direction *and* reversing the direction of the magnetic field?

Practical electric motors

★ A mains electric motor works with alternating current because it has an electromagnet, not a permanent magnet. Each time the current reverses, the magnetic field does too, so the rotation direction is unchanged.

★ The armature may comprise 20 different coils, each at a fixed angle to the next. Each coil has its own pair of segments of a split-ring commutator. This produces a much steadier speed of rotation than a single coil.

★ The power supply is connected to the split-ring commutator using two spring-loaded graphite brushes which press on the commutator. Graphite conducts electricity and allows the commutator to turn with very little friction.

Answers The rotation direction would **a)** reverse **b)** be unchanged

Electromagnetism

The loudspeaker

This contains a coil of insulated wire on a plastic tube in a magnetic field, as shown. The coil is at the centre of a diaphragm. When current is passed through the coil, it is forced to move by the magnetic field. With alternating current, the coil is forced to move to and fro. This vibrating motion makes the diaphragm vibrate, creating sound waves in the surrounding air with the same frequency as the alternating current.

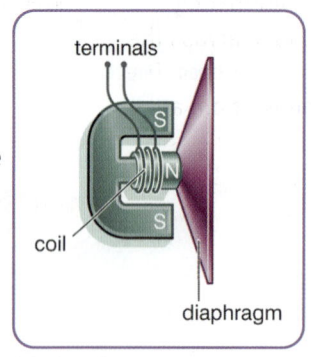

A loudspeaker

12.3 Electromagnetic induction

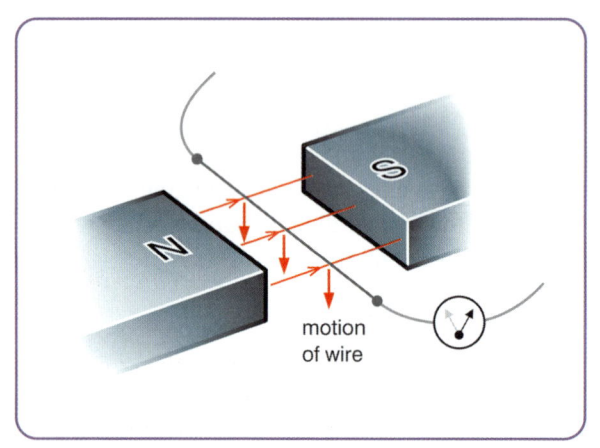

Electromagnetic induction

Fact file

★ When a wire cuts across the lines of force of a magnetic field, a voltage is induced in the wire.

★ If the wire is part of a complete circuit in which there is no other voltage source, the induced voltage drives a current round the circuit.

★ The faster the wire moves across the field lines, the greater the induced voltage.

★ The stronger the magnetic field, the greater the induced voltage.

Laws of electromagnetic induction

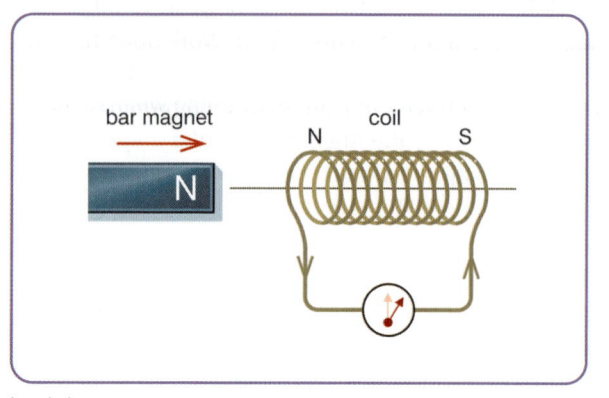

Lenz's law

Lenz's law: the induced current in a circuit is always in such a direction as to oppose the change which causes it. This can be tested by inserting a bar magnet into a coil connected to a centre-reading milliammeter. The direction of the induced current is given by the deflection of the pointer of the meter. Inserting the magnet generates a current which creates a magnetic pole to oppose the incoming pole.

Faraday's law of electromagnetic induction: the induced voltage is proportional to the speed at which the wire cuts the magnetic field lines. The induced current is small if the magnet is inserted slowly. If the magnet is inserted rapidly, the induced current is much larger.

The alternating current generator

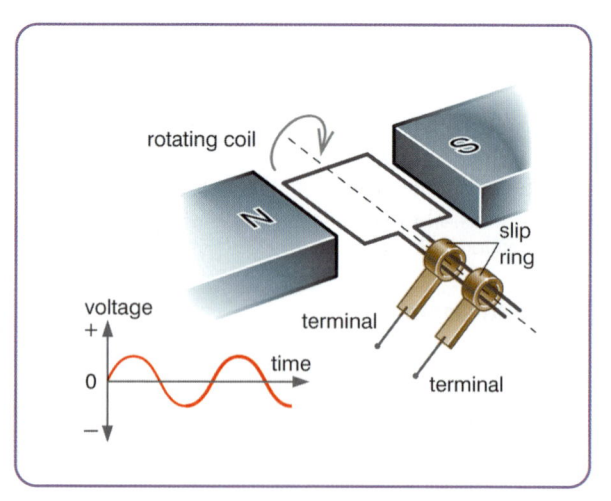

An a.c. generator

The a.c. generator consists of a rectangular coil of insulated wire which is made to rotate at steady speed in a uniform magnetic field. Work done to turn the coil is converted into electrical energy. The alternating voltage induced across the terminals of the coil can be displayed on an oscilloscope.

★ The frequency of the alternating voltage is equal to the frequency of rotation of the coil.

★ The peak voltage is proportional to the speed of rotation of the coil (Faraday's law). Rotating the coil faster would show more waves on an oscilloscope screen (because the frequency is greater) and make them higher (because the peak voltage is larger).

★ The peak voltage occurs when the sides of the coil cut across the field lines at 90°. The voltage is zero when the coil sides move parallel to the field lines.

★ A direct voltage can be generated if the two slip rings are replaced by a split-ring commutator, as shown. An oscilloscope display of this voltage would show each cycle as two positive half-cycles instead of a positive half-cycle followed by a negative half-cycle. Note that a battery connected to an oscilloscope would display a flat line above or below the zero level.

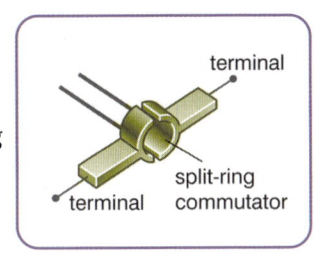

Producing direct current

The dynamo

In a dynamo, the magnet rotates and the coil remains stationary. The magnet and coil move relative to each other such that the coil windings cut across the magnetic field lines. Hence a voltage is induced.

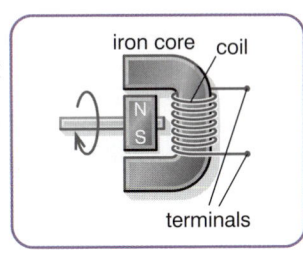

A dynamo

The microphone

Sound waves make the microphone diaphragm vibrate. A coil attached to the diaphragm moves in and out of the magnetic field of a permanent magnet, generating an alternating voltage across the coil terminals. The voltage from a microphone is usually referred to as an audio signal.

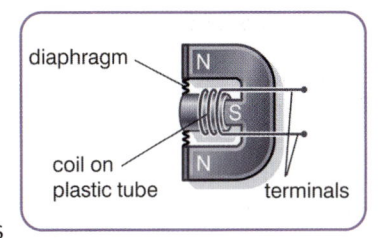

A microphone

Question

A bicycle is fitted with a dynamo lamp. Explain why the cyclist must pedal harder after switching the lamp on.

Magnetic recording

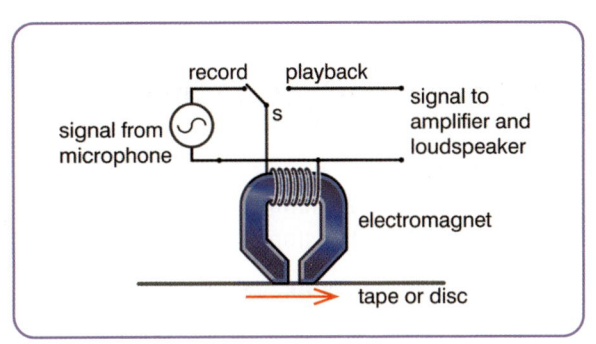

Magnetic recording

The tape or disc is coated on one side with a thin film of magnetic material.

Recording: the tape or disc is made to run at a steady speed past a recording head. This is a small electromagnet to which the audio signal is supplied. The changes of magnetism due to the audio signal are recorded by the magnetic film.

Playback: the tape or disc is made to run at a steady speed past the same recording head. This time, the recording head is connected to an amplifier and a loudspeaker. The changes in magnetism on the film induce an alternating voltage in the coil of the electromagnet. This is the audio signal recreated.

Answer

Electrical energy for the lamp is provided from work done by the cyclist. Hence the cyclist must do more work by exerting more force to keep the speed the same.

Electromagnetism

12.4 Transformers

How a transformer works

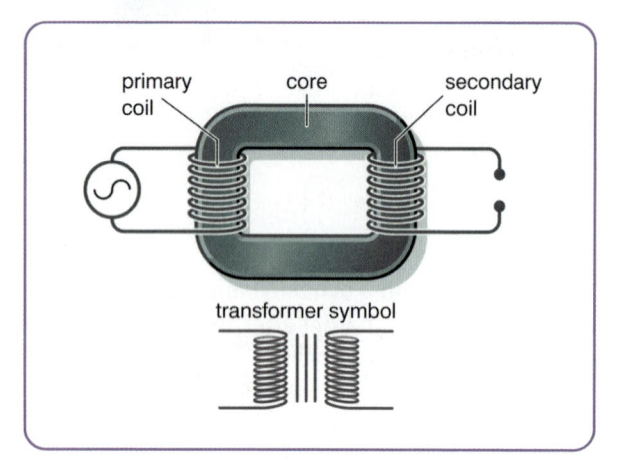

A model transformer

A transformer steps an alternating voltage up or down. It consists of two coils wound on an iron core.

1. The voltage to be transformed is applied to the **primary coil** of the transformer.

2. The alternating current through the windings of the primary coil creates an alternating magnetic field in the transformer's iron core.

3. The continuously changing magnetic field through the core induces an alternating voltage in the **secondary coil**.

The transformer rule

$$\frac{\text{voltage induced in the secondary coil } V_s}{\text{voltage applied to the primary coil } V_p} = \frac{\text{number of turns on the secondary coil } N_s}{\text{number of turns on the primary coil } N_p}$$

For a **step-up transformer**, the number of secondary turns is greater than the number of primary turns. Hence the secondary voltage is greater than the primary voltage.

For a **step-down transformer**, the number of secondary turns is less than the number of primary turns. Hence the secondary voltage is less than the primary voltage.

Transformer efficiency

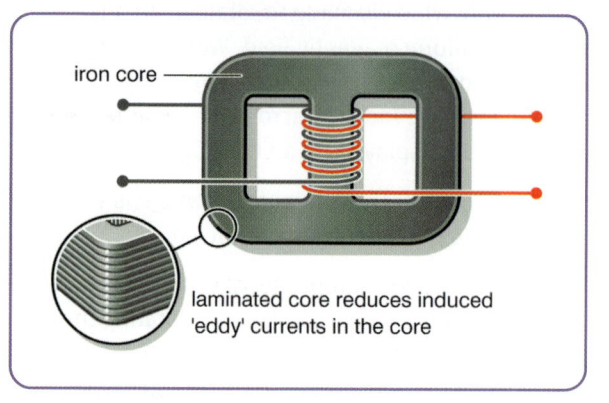

A practical transformer

The percentage efficiency of a transformer is defined as $\frac{\text{output power}}{\text{input power}} \times 100\%$.

For a transformer that is 100% efficient, the output power equals the input power. In other words, primary current × primary voltage = secondary current × secondary voltage. Thus if the voltage is stepped up, the current is stepped down and vice versa.

Questions

A transformer has a 100-turn primary coil and a 2000-turn secondary coil. A 240 V, 60 W lamp is connected to the secondary coil. Calculate **a)** the primary voltage needed to make the lamp light normally **b)** the primary current when the lamp lights normally, assuming the transformer is 100% efficient.

High-voltage transmission of electrical power

The grid system operates at high voltage because the higher the voltage, the less the current needed for the same power. Less power is therefore wasted due to resistance heating in the cables used to carry the current. Alternating voltages can easily be stepped up or down using transformers. Hence power is transmitted on the grid system using alternating voltage.

Answers

a) 12 V b) 5 A

Electromagnetism

ROUND UP

How much have you improved?
Work out your improvement index on page 314.

1 a) With the aid of a diagram, explain the operation of a make-and-break switch in an electric bell or a buzzer. [8]

b) The diagram shows the construction of a different type of electric bell. When the switch is closed, the iron bar is pulled into the electromagnet, causing the wooden striker X to hit the metal plate with a 'ding'. When the switch is released, the iron bar springs back and the other wooden striker Y hits the other plate with a 'dong'.

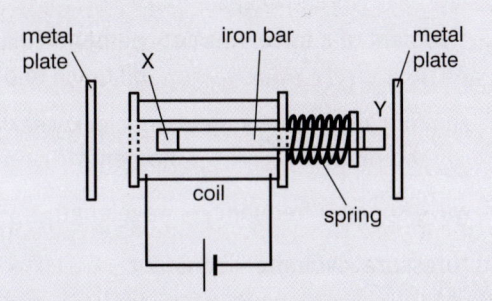

  (i) Why is it essential that the bar is made of iron? [1]
  (ii) When the switch is open, why is it necessary for the iron bar to be partly in and partly out of the solenoid? [1]
  (iii) Explain whether or not the device would work with an alternating current supply instead of a direct current supply. [2]

2 a) With the aid of a labelled diagram, explain the operation of a relay that is normally open. [6]

b) A metal-detector consists of an electromagnet connected to a low voltage alternating current supply. When a piece of metal is held near the electromagnet, the current through the coil increases. Explain why this increase of current occurs. [2]

3 a) With the aid of a labelled diagram, explain the operation of an alternating current generator. [6]

b) (i) Sketch the waveform produced by an alternating current generator. [2]

  (ii) Show on the waveform you have drawn a point where the coil is parallel to the magnetic field. [1]

c) How does the voltage waveform of an alternating current generator change if the generator turns more quickly? [2]

4 a) The diagram shows the construction of a step-down transformer.

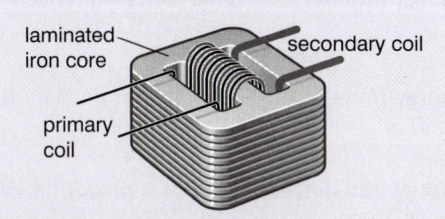

  (i) Explain the operation of this transformer. [2]
  (ii) Why are the windings of the secondary coil thicker than the windings of the primary coil? [1]
  (iii) Why is the core constructed from laminated iron plates? [2]

b) A step-down transformer has a primary coil with 1200 turns and a secondary coil with 60 turns.

  (i) If the primary coil is connected to 240 V a.c. mains, what will the secondary voltage be? [1]
  (ii) The percentage efficiency of the transformer was measured and found to be 80%. If the primary current is not to exceed 0.1 A, what is the maximum current that can be delivered to a 12 V light bulb connected to the secondary coil? [2]

5 a) (i) Why is electrical power transmitted through the grid system at high voltage? [2]

  (ii) Domestic consumers in the UK are supplied with mains electricity at 240 V. In the USA, the mains voltage is 110 V. Which system is safer and why? [2]

b) The cables used to distribute electricity through the grid system are often carried by pylons. Give one advantage and one disadvantage of using pylons rather than underground cables for this purpose. [2]

Well done if you've improved. Don't worry if you haven't. Take a break and try again.

Equations and symbols you should know

Read, learn and inwardly digest the formulas below. To test yourself, cover each equation with a blank card after the first word and see if you can write the rest of the equation on the card.

voltage = current × resistance

electrical power = voltage × current

charge = current × time

energy transferred = potential difference × charge

energy transferred (in J) = power (in W) × time (in seconds)

energy transferred (in kW h) = power (in kW) × time (in hours)

$$\frac{\text{voltage across coil 1}}{\text{voltage across coil 2}} = \frac{\text{number of turns in coil 1}}{\text{number of turns in coil 2}}$$

*pressure = $\frac{\text{force}}{\text{area}}$

speed = $\frac{\text{distance}}{\text{time}}$

acceleration = $\frac{\text{change of velocity}}{\text{time taken}}$

force = mass × acceleration

work done = force × distance moved in direction of force

energy transferred = work done

efficiency = $\frac{\text{useful energy transferred by device}}{\text{total energy supplied to device}}$

power = $\frac{\text{work done}}{\text{time taken}}$

weight = mass × gravitational field strength (g)

change of potential energy = weight × change in height

kinetic energy = $\frac{1}{2}$ × mass × (speed)^2

*moment of a force = force × perpendicular distance to pivot

sum of clockwise moments = sum of anticlockwise moments

wave speed = frequency × wavelength

*pressure × volume = constant

* = not AQA, EDEXCEL or OCR specifications

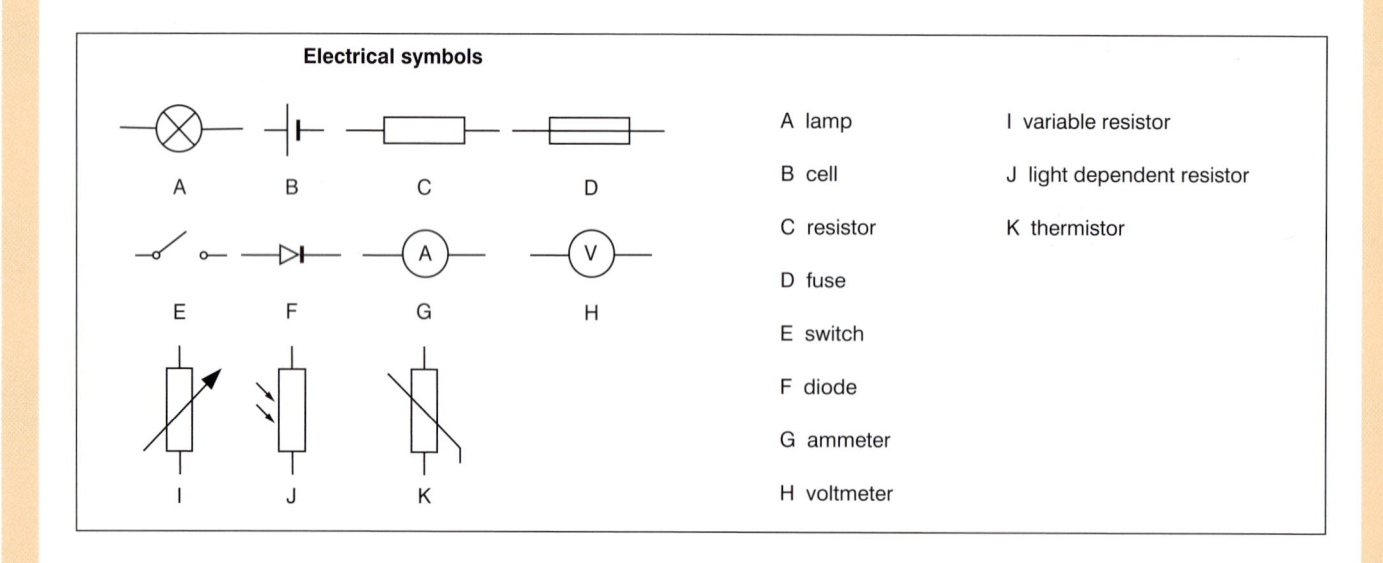

Electrical symbols

A lamp
B cell
C resistor
D fuse
E switch
F diode
G ammeter
H voltmeter
I variable resistor
J light dependent resistor
K thermistor

Answers

1 Test yourself (page 219)

Beyond the Earth

1. VMJUN (✓ for each correct answer)
2. The mass of the planet (✓). The distance from the Sun to the planet (✓).
3. As it orbits the Sun, its distance from Earth changes (✓) and the amount of its sunlit surface we see changes (✓).
4. The stars we see each night are in the opposite direction to the Sun (✓). As the Earth moves round the Sun, the stars we see at night change during the year (✓).
5. a) Mars (✓) b) Jupiter (✓)
6. a) speeding up (✓) b) moving towards the Sun (✓)
7. nuclear fusion (✓)
8. A massive star exploding at the end of its life (✓) releasing an enormous amount of energy in a short time (✓).
9. The light spectrum from the star is shifted towards the red end of the spectrum (✓) due to the star receding (✓).
10. Distant galaxies are moving away from us (✓) at speeds in proportion to their distances away (✓).

Your score: ☐ out of 22

1 Round up (page 226)

Beyond the Earth

1. a) The force of gravity on each planet due to the Sun acts towards the Sun (✓). This force stops each planet leaving the Solar System (✓).
   b) In both cases, a body with relatively small mass orbits a body with much more mass (✓).
2. The Earth spins eastwards (✓), so the constellations appear to move across the sky westwards (✓).
3. a) planets reflect sunlight (✓)
   b) Sketch A is when Venus is in position 2, nearer Earth (✓). Its disc appears larger and crescent shaped (✓).
4. Moon (✓), Sun (✓), Pole star (✓), Andromeda galaxy (✓)
5. a) Jupiter shown in the opposite direction to the Sun (Sun Earth Jupiter) (✓).
   b) (i) Mars is smaller, further from the Sun, has two moons, and has no oxygen in its atmosphere (✓✓✓).
      (ii) Jupiter is larger, not solid, further from the Sun than Earth, and spins faster (✓✓✓).
      (iii) Saturn is larger, not solid, further from the Sun than Earth, and has a ring system (✓✓✓).

6. a) It is close to the Sun (✓) and can therefore only be seen just before sunrise (✓) or just after sunset (✓).
   b) Neptune's orbit is circular (✓) whereas Pluto's orbit is elliptical and partly inside Neptune's orbit (✓).
   c) Neptune (✓)
   d) They become cold and dark when they move away from the Sun (✓), so cannot be seen (✓) until the Sun's gravity pulls them round back near the Sun (✓).
7. a) It is red (✓) and much larger than the Sun (✓).
   b) The Sun will become a red giant (✓) and then collapse to become a white dwarf (✓) before radiating all its energy (✓) and becoming invisible (✓).
   c) A massive star which explodes after the white dwarf stage (✓) because its internal pressure is too great (✓).
8. a) They must acquire sufficient speed to overcome gravity (✓) to gain orbital height (✓) then go into orbit (✓).
   b) Its mass (✓) and density are smaller (✓).
9. See page 225 (✓✓✓).
10. a) The Universe originated in a massive explosion (✓) and has been expanding ever since (✓).
    b) The Universe will continue to expand (✓) at a rate which might decrease or increase (✓).
    c) Four points from: Earth-like planets probably orbit other stars (✓); life might exist or have existed in primitive form (e.g. microbes) on other planets (✓); a meteorite thought to be from Mars contains evidence of microbes on Mars long ago (✓); radio telescopes have not detected communications signals from other planets or stars (✓); intelligent life on a planet may be short-lived in terms of the age of the planet (✓).

Your score: ☐ out of 60

Your improvement index: $\dfrac{\Box/60}{\Box/22} \times 100\% = \Box\%$

2 Test yourself (page 227)

Energy resources and energy transfer

1. B (✓)
2. weight – the newton (✓), power – the watt (✓)
3. 1200 J (✓)
4. a) KE = 6 J (✓), PE = 2 J (✓)
   b) KE = 8 J (✓), PE = 0 (✓)
5. 10 (✓) (= 4 + 6 (✓))
6. PE loss = 2000 J (✓), KE gain = 250 J (✓), therefore required ratio = 8 (✓)

Answers

7 Metals contain electrons which move about freely inside the metal (✓). When the metal is heated, the electrons at the point of heating gain kinetic energy (✓) which they transfer to other parts of the metal (✓).

8 **a** and **b** (✓✓)

9 **c** only (✓)

10 **b)** heat due to friction (✓)   **c)** electrical energy (✓)
    d) sound (✓)   **e)** light (✓)   **f)** heat due to electrical resistance (✓)

Your score: ☐ out of 24

2 Round up (page 234)

Energy resources and energy transfer

1 **a)** chemical energy in the battery → electrical energy → sound energy (✓)
   b) gravitational potential energy → kinetic energy (✓) + work done against air resistance (✓)

2 **a)** (i) 800 J (✓)   (ii) 40 J/s (✓)   **b)** 0.2 (= 20%) (✓)

3 **a)** 2750 J (✓)   **b)** 5.0 m (✓)

4 **a)** 80 MJ (✓)   **b)** 1.6 MW (✓)

5 **a)** 6.75 kWh (✓)   **b)** 40.5p (✓)

6 **a)** 22.5 kJ (✓)   **b)** (i) 16.8 kJ (✓)   (ii) 26 W (✓)

7 **a)** China is a better thermal insulator but shiny metal radiates less (✓). The china teapot is likely to be better unless it has very thin walls (✓).
   b) There is a larger open surface in the wide-brimmed cup so there is more evaporation (✓) and thermal radiation (✓) from the wide-brimmed cup. Hence the tea in it loses thermal energy faster and it cools more quickly (✓).
   c) A double-glazed unit traps a layer of still air between its two panes (✓). This is a good thermal insulator (✓).
   d) (i) Condensation occurs where moist air meets a cold surface (✓). A classroom full of people will be full of moist air and in winter, the windows will be cold enough to cause condensation (✓).
   (ii) The inner glass pane is warmer than the outer pane (✓) so the moist air does not come into contact with a cold surface (✓).

Your score: ☐ out of 26

Your improvement index: $\dfrac{\Box/26}{\Box/24} \times 100\% = \Box\%$

3 Test yourself (page 235)

Radioactivity

1 **a)** negative (✓)   **b)** positive (✓)   **c)** uncharged (✓)
   d) positive (✓)   **e)** negative (✓)

2 **a)** 2 p + 2 n (✓✓)   **b)** 92 p + 143 n (✓✓)

3 positive (✓)

4 alpha, beta and gamma radiation (✓✓✓); Alpha radiation is most easily absorbed (✓).

5 Radioactivity from the surroundings or caused by cosmic radiation (✓).

6 the Geiger counter (✓)

7 Half-life – the time taken for half the atoms of a given radioactive isotope to disintegrate (✓).
   Isotope – atoms of an element with the same number of neutrons and protons (✓).

8 A nucleus of an atom splits (✓) into two approximately equal halves (✓).

9 The waste from the spent fuel rods contains radioactive isotopes with very long half-lives (✓). Radiation released by radioactive isotopes is harmful (✓).

10 See page 240 (✓✓).

Your score: ☐ out of 24

3 Round up (page 243)

Radioactivity

1 **a)** U-238 = 92 p + 146 n (✓✓); U-235 = 92 p + 143 n (✓✓)
   b) isotopes (✓)
   c) The time taken for half the initial number of atoms of a given isotope to decay (✓).

2 **a)** Smoke absorbs alpha radiation (✓) but not beta or gamma radiation (✓).
   b) If the half-life was much shorter than 5 years, the decrease in activity of the source within a year would set the alarm off (✓).

3 **a)** $^{220}_{82}\text{Rn} \rightarrow {}^{216}_{80}\text{Po} + {}^{4}_{2}\alpha$ (✓✓)
   b) (i) 100/s (✓)   (ii) 25/s (✓)

4 **a)** Steel plate stops alpha and beta radiation (✓✓) but not gamma radiation (✓).
   b) (i) 200/s (✓)   (ii) 160/s (✓)
   (iii) It became thicker (✓).

5 **a)** (i) See page 237 (✓).   (ii) It produces ions (✓).
   b) X-rays, radioactive waste (✓✓)
   c) Start the Geiger counter and the stopwatch together. Stop the Geiger counter after, say, exactly 600 seconds (✓). Measure the number of counts recorded by the counter. Divide this number by 600 to give the count rate (✓).

6 Alpha and gamma radiation (✓✓), the tin foil stops alpha radiation (✓) whereas even thick lead is unable to stop the gamma radiation completely (✓).

Answers

7 **a)** The radiation becomes weaker with distance (✓).
   b) **(i)** Electromagnetic radiation of very short wavelength (✓), it penetrates the body (✓).
   (ii) The source is enclosed in a thick-walled lead container with a small hole to let the gamma radiation out in a thin beam (✓). The beam is directed at the tumour from different directions (✓) so as not to damage the surrounding healthy tissue (✓).

Your score: ☐ out of 35

Your improvement index: $\dfrac{\boxed{}/35}{\boxed{}/24} \times 100\% = \boxed{}\%$

4 Test yourself (page 244)

Waves

1 Any four from: sound waves, water waves, waves on a string, seismic waves, electromagnetic waves (radio, microwaves, infrared, visible, ultraviolet, X-rays, gamma rays) (✓✓✓✓).

2 **a)** Longitudinal waves vibrate along the direction in which the wave travels (✓); transverse waves vibrate at 90° to the direction in which they travel (✓).
   b) longitudinal (✓)

3 Any electromagnetic wave can pass through a vacuum (✓); any other type of wave needs a medium (✓).

4 wavelength = 40 mm (✓); amplitude = 15 mm (✓)

5 **a)** Frequency = $\dfrac{\text{speed}}{\text{wavelength}} = \dfrac{20\,\text{mm/s}}{40\,\text{mm}} = 0.50\,\text{Hz}$ (✓)
   b) 30 (✓)

6 **a)** −15 mm below middle (✓) **b)** +15 mm above middle (✓)

7 There is no hard surface to reflect them (✓). The amplitude becomes less and less as they run up the shore (✓).

8 Refraction is the change of direction (✓) due to a change of speed when waves pass across a boundary (✓).

9 **a)** increased (✓) **b)** decreased (✓)

10 **a)** 850 Hz (✓) **b)** 1.0 mm (✓)

Your score: ☐ out of 23

4 Round up (page 248)

Waves

1 **a)** **(i)** sound waves (✓)
   (ii) radio waves (✓), waves on a rope (✓)
   b) (1) Light is transverse; sound is longitudinal (✓).
   (2) Light can travel through a vacuum; sound cannot (or sound requires a medium; light does not) (✓).
   (3) Light travels faster than sound (✓).

2 [diagram: reflection with 40°, 50°, 50° angles; and curved mirror reflection] (✓✓) (✓✓)

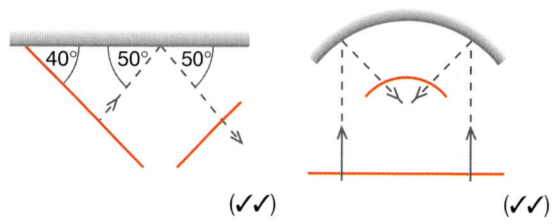

3 **a)** diffraction (✓)
   b) **(i)** increase (✓) **(ii)** decrease (✓) **(iii)** increase (✓)

4 **a)** Its wavelength becomes smaller (✓). Its frequency stays the same (✓).
   b) [diagram: refraction from shallow water to deep water across boundary] (✓✓)

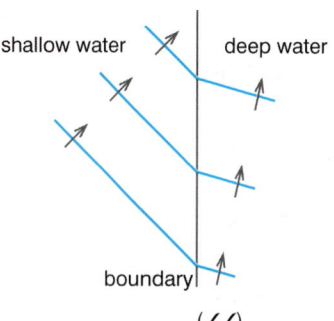

5 **a)** 0.50 m (✓) **b)** **(i)** 0.40 m/s (✓) **(ii)** 2.0 Hz (✓)

6 **a)** diffraction (✓)
   b) The spreading becomes less (✓).

7 **a)** 3.0 m (✓)
   b) The radio waves from the station are polarised (✓). As the aerial is turned, it moves more and more out of line with the plane of polarisation (✓) until it can no longer detect the signal (✓).
   c) The wire mesh reflects radio waves onto the aerial (✓).

8 **a)** The bow waves would form a sharper 'V' at the bow (✓).
   b) The bow waves would form a less sharp 'V' (✓).

Your score: ☐ out of 30

Your improvement index: $\dfrac{\boxed{}/30}{\boxed{}/23} \times 100\% = \boxed{}\%$

Answers

5 Test yourself (page 249)

Sound waves and seismic waves

1. **a)** longitudinal (✓)
   b) Primary waves are longitudinal (✓); secondary waves are transverse (✓).
2. It produces a note at a precise frequency (✓).
3. **a)** (i) increases (✓) (ii) decreases (✓)
   b) The thicker string (✓) because it would produce sound at a lower pitch if it was at the same tension, and the pitch increases if the tension is increased (✓).
4. A reflected sound wave from a hard smooth surface (✓).
5. **a)** The amplitude increases (✓); the wavelength is unchanged (✓).
   b) The amplitude decreases (✓); the wavelength is shorter (✓).
6. diffraction (✓)
7. **a)** C (✓) **b)** B (✓)
   c) They sound deeper (✓) (because the higher frequencies are cut out).
8. **a)** Ultrasonic pulses are directed towards the sea bed (✓). On hitting the sea bed the pulses are reflected back to the surface (✓). Each pulse is timed from when it is emitted to when it is detected after reflection (✓). The time taken t for each pulse to reach the sea bed = $0.5 \times$ the time from when it is emitted to when it is detected (✓). The depth of the sea bed = speed of ultrasound in water $\times$ time t (✓).
   b) Two of: medical imaging; crack detection; cleaning (✓✓).
9. **a)** 0.17 mm (✓) **b)** (i) no change (✓) (ii) increases (✓)
10. **a)** The plates of the Earth's crust press against each other at certain parts (✓). An earthquake occurs when one of the plates gives way (✓).
    b) S waves are transverse (✓); transverse waves cannot pass through a liquid (✓); the outer core is liquid (✓).

Your score: ☐ out of 32

5 Round up (page 253)

Sound waves and seismic waves

1. **a)** 850 m (✓)
   b) Sound the siren briefly every 10 seconds and measure the time between each pulse being emitted and its return (✓). The timing becomes shorter if the ship is approaching the cliffs (✓).
2. **a)** The surface pushes and pulls the air near it back and forth (✓). The air near the speaker pushes and pulls on the air further away (✓).
   b) A small loudspeaker is lighter (✓) and so can vibrate faster (✓).
3. **a)** amplitude less (✓), horizontal spacing the same (✓)
   b) The waves are stretched out horizontally (✓).
4. **a)** 3400 Hz (✓) **b)** 68 mm (✓)
5. The glass panes reflect most of the sound (✓). Some sound penetrates the room because the glass panes vibrate when they reflect the sound waves (✓).
6. **a)** 37.5 mm (✓)
   b) (i) Without the paste, the ultrasound pulses from the probe would be almost completely reflected at the air–body boundary (✓). With the paste, the pulses from the probe travel directly into the body from the paste without passing into the air (✓).
   (ii) Reflection at each internal boundary is partial (✓); the pulses spread out as they move away from the probe (✓).
7. **a)** (i) B = outer core (✓), C = mantle (✓); D = crust (✓).
   (ii) B = molten (✓); A, C, D = solid (✓✓✓).
   b) They are more common where the plates of the Earth's crust meet (✓).
8. **a)** longitudinal (✓)
   b) (i) See page 252 (✓✓✓).
   (ii) The outer core is liquid (✓); S waves are transverse waves and therefore cannot travel through liquid (✓).
   (iii) The speed of a seismic wave increases with depth (✓). The seismic waves not moving directly towards the centre are therefore refracted away from the centre (✓).
   (iv) See page 252. S waves cannot reach the other side of the Earth from the epicentre (✓). Also, P waves cannot reach part of this zone because they refract back to the surface (✓). L waves therefore arrive without being preceded by P or S waves (✓).

Your score: ☐ out of 38

Your improvement index: $\dfrac{\square/38}{\square/32} \times 100\% = \square\%$

6 Test yourself (page 254)

Light

1. **a)** The angle between the reflected ray and the normal = the angle between the incident ray and the normal (✓).
   b) 1.20 m (✓)
2. **a)** towards (✓) **b)** less than 30° (✓).
   c) The light ray is totally internally reflected (✓).
3. (i) reflection (✓) (ii) refraction (✓) (iii) reflection (✓)
4. Non-vertical light rays from any point at the bottom of the pool are refracted at the surface (✓) away from the normal (✓) and therefore appear to come from an image of the bottom of the pool nearer the surface than the bottom (✓).
5. **a)** decrease (✓) **b)** decrease (✓)
6. red, orange, yellow, green, blue, indigo, violet (✓)
7. **a)** red (✓)
   b) The surface absorbs all colours except blue (✓) which it reflects (✓). Therefore in red light, no light is reflected so it appears black (✓).

Answers

8 a) Reflection of a light ray incident in a transparent substance at a boundary with a less refractive substance or air. (✓)
   b) fibre optics used in the endoscope or in communications (✓)
   c) Total internal reflection only happens if the angle of incidence is greater than the critical angle (✓) whereas reflection at a flat mirror happens at any angle of incidence. (✓)

9 communications, to carry light pulses (✓); medicine, to see inside the body (✓)

10 a) more (✓)
   b) The wavelength of blue light is less than that of any other colour (✓); blue light is diffracted less than any other colour when it enters the microscope (✓), therefore separate images seen in blue light can be closer together than seen in any other colour (✓).

Your score: ☐ out of 28

6 Round-up (page 260)

Light

1 a) (✓✓) b) (✓)
   c) Image I_1 is directly opposite O_1 and image I_2 is directly opposite O_2 (✓). Hence distance $I_1 I_2$ is the same as distance $O_1 O_2$ (✓).

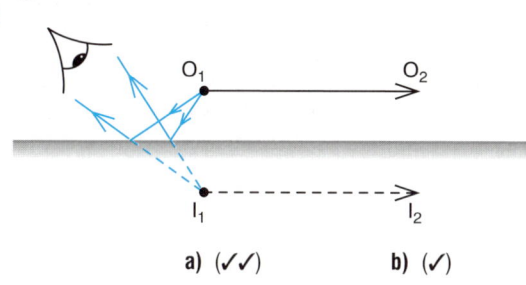

2 a) 2.0 m (✓)
   b) The top of the mirror needs to be just above eye level (✓) to be able to see the head (✓). The bottom of the mirror needs to be opposite the midpoint between the floor and eye level (✓) to be able to see the feet (✓).
   c) Two of: in a periscope; to make a corner cube reflector; to read a scale (✓✓).

3 a) See page 257 (✓✓).
   b) (✓✓) 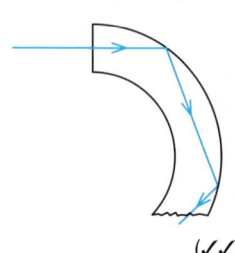
   c) The angle of incidence at the point of incidence becomes less than the critical angle and so light is reflected out, not internally reflected (✓).
   d) communications, to carry light pulses (✓); medicine, to see inside the body (✓)

4 (i) towards (✓) (ii) away (✓) (iii) away (✓)

5 (i) diffraction (✓) (ii) reflection (✓) (iii) total internal reflection (✓) (iv) refraction (✓)

6 See page 258 (✓✓) for correct refraction at each boundary (✓) for correct order of colours.

7 a) less (✓) b) diffraction causes image details to merge (✓) less diffraction with blue light than any other colour (✓) because its wavelength is less (✓).

8 The wider the lens, the less the diffraction of light (✓), giving more detail in the image (✓).

Your score: ☐ out of 35

Your improvement index: $\dfrac{\Box/35}{\Box/28} \times 100\% = \Box \%$

7 Test yourself (page 261)

The electromagnetic spectrum

1 radio (✓), microwaves (✓), infrared (✓), visible (✓), ultraviolet (✓), X-rays and gamma rays (✓)

2 See page 262 (✓✓✓✓✓).

3 visible light (✓) and radio (✓)

4 a) X-rays and gamma radiation (✓✓)
   b) infrared radiation (✓)
   c) ultraviolet light (✓)

5 X-rays or gamma radiation can (✓); radio waves, microwaves, visible light cannot (✓).

6 a) X-rays (✓)
   b) ultraviolet light (✓)

7 a) microwave radiation (✓)
   b) (i) To focus microwave radiation from the satellite onto the dish aerial (✓).
      (ii) Metal reflects microwaves (✓).

8 The pigment in the ink does not absorb visible light (✓). It absorbs ultraviolet light and emits visible light (✓). Under a UV lamp, the ink is therefore visible (✓).

9 a) (i) infrared radiation (✓)
      (ii) X-rays and gamma radiation (✓)
   b) radio waves and microwaves (✓)

10 a) infrared radiation (✓)
   b) visible light and infrared radiation (✓)

Your score: ☐ out of 33

Answers

7 Round up (page 266)

The electromagnetic spectrum

1 a) X-rays and gamma rays (✓), ultraviolet (✓), visible (✓), infrared (✓), microwave (✓), radio (✓)
  b) (i) Any two of: travel at the same speed in a vacuum; transverse waves; do not need a substance/pass through a vacuum; can be reflected or refracted or diffracted; make charged particles vibrate (✓✓).
  (ii) visible (✓), ultraviolet (✓), X-rays and gamma rays (✓)
  (iii) radio (✓), microwaves (✓), infrared (✓), visible (✓)

2 a) cooker 0.12 m (✓), satellite 0.03 m (✓)
  b) faster, uses less energy, cooks the food throughout (✓)

3 a) Long wave radio waves follow the Earth's curvature (✓), medium wave radio waves reflect from the ionosphere (✓).
  b) (i) The frequency of the electromagnetic waves that carry the audio or TV signals (✓).
  (ii) If they broadcast at the same frequency, the broadcasts would interfere with each other where they overlap (✓).
  c) The satellite signals are much weaker (✓); a dish is used to focus them onto an aerial (✓).

4 a) Ultraviolet light in bright sunlight would be absorbed by the powder molecules in the clothing (✓). The molecules would emit visible light, making the clothes seem brighter (✓).
  b) (i) It damages the retinal cells of the eye (✓); it causes sunburn (✓).
  (ii) To absorb ultraviolet light from sunlight (✓), to prevent sunburn (✓).

5 a) Their bodies emit infrared light which can be detected by an infrared camera (✓).
  b) (i) infrared light (✓)
  (ii) A conventional heating element consists of resistance wire surrounded by an electrical insulator in a metal tubing (✓); conduction of heat from the resistance wire to the metal tubing is very slow and so the hob takes much longer to heat up than a ceramic hob (✓).

6 a) (i) To attract electrons from the heated filament (✓).
  (ii) The X-rays need to originate from a small spot on the anode (✓) otherwise the image they produce will be blurred (✓).
  b) (i) X-rays pass through soft tissues and are absorbed by bone (✓). X-rays blacken photographic film (✓).
  (ii) The stomach consists of soft tissues only (✓). The barium meal in the stomach enables the lining of the stomach to be seen because barium absorbs X-rays (✓).

7 a) X, There are more cycles per second of the waveform at the higher frequency (✓). Each pulse needs the same number of cycles per second (✓), so more pulses per second are possible at higher frequencies (✓).
  b) (i) 1000 (✓)
  (ii) They would interfere with mobile phone communications (✓).

8 a) An orbit directly above the equator (✓) with an orbital time of exactly 24 hours (✓).
  b) The satellite is always in the same position over the equator (✓).

Your score: ☐ out of 49

Your improvement index: $\dfrac{\square/49}{\square/33} \times 100\% = \square\%$

8 Test yourself (page 267)

Force and motion

1 a) 5 km/h (✓) **b)** 1.4 m/s (✓)
2 a) the area under the line (✓) **b)** speed (✓)
3 0.5 m/s^2 (✓), 500 N (✓)
4 a) 9.0 m (✓) **b)** −6.0 m/s^2 (✓)
  c) (i) 19 m (✓) **(ii)** 28 m (✓)
5 a) (i) 4000 N (✓), 800 J (✓) **(ii)** 8000 J (✓)
  b) Potential energy is converted into thermal energy (or heat) (✓) by the braking force acting on the lift cable (✓). This force is necessary to prevent the lift from falling freely (✓).
6 The force of air resistance depends on the speed and the shape of the vehicle (✓). The speed increases until the force of air resistance is equal to the engine force (✓). Changing the shape to reduce the force of air resistance enables the car to reach a higher top speed (✓).
7 The force of air resistance increases with speed (✓). As the parachutist falls, his/her speed increases until the force of air resistance is equal and opposite to the weight of the parachutist (✓). The speed therefore becomes constant as the overall force becomes zero (✓).
8 a) 80 000 N (✓), 80 000 N (✓)
  b) 6000 m (✓), 20 MJ (✓)
  c) It is carried away by the air as thermal energy (✓).

Your score: ☐ out of 27

8 Round up (pages 273–4)

Force and motion

1 a) (i) 4320 m (✓) **(ii)** 4.32 km (✓) **b)** 4.3 m/s (✓)
2 a) It was steady (✓) and less than the speed of X for most of the journey (✓). Then the speed of Y was greater than that of X (✓) and Y overtook X (✓).
  b) (i) 10 m/s (✓) **(ii)** 15 m/s (✓)
3 a) Speed is distance travelled per second (✓); velocity is speed in a given direction (✓).
  b) (i) 9 km north (✓) then 24 km south (✓).
  (ii) 15 km south (✓).
4 a) 1.6 m/s^2 (✓), 20 m (✓) **b)** 1120 N (✓)
5 a) 2.5 s (✓)
  b) (i) 63 J (✓) **(ii)** 63 J (✓) **(iii)** 31 m (✓)
6 a) 9.5 m/s (✓) **b)** 2.7 kJ (✓) **c)** 4.5 m (✓)

Answers

d) The pole vaulter uses his or her arm muscles to gain height (✓).

7 a) Graph to show a straight line with a negative gradient (✓) from 10 m/s to 0 in 50 s (✓).
b) (i) 250 m (✓) **(ii)** −0.2 m/s² (✓)
c) −6000 N (✓)
d) 0.02 (✓)

8 a) The car skids if the force of the brakes on the wheels exceeds the frictional force of the road on the tyres (✓).
b) The maximum frictional force of the road on the tyres is less on a wet road (✓). This force is equal and opposite to the force of the road on the car (✓). Hence the maximum braking force for no skidding must be less on a wet road (✓), so it takes longer to stop from a given speed (✓).
c) (i) 22.5 m (✓) **(ii)** −5.0 m/s² (✓), 6000 N (✓)
d) 6 s (✓), 45 m (✓)

Your score: ☐ out of 41

Your improvement index: $\dfrac{☐/41}{☐/27} \times 100\% = ☐\%$

9 Test yourself (page 275)
Forces in balance

1 your weight (✓), the support force from your chair (✓)

2 a) neutral (✓) **b)** unstable (✓) **c)** stable (✓)

3 a) about 1.2 m (✓)
b) The point at which the lift force is exerted is three times further from the pivot than the centre of gravity (✓). Hence the lift force is one-third of the weight (✓).
c) 50 kg (✓)

4 a) (i) The force is applied to a much smaller contact area if the knife is sharp (✓).
(ii) Atmospheric pressure acting on the outer surface is greater than the pressure of the air trapped between the cap and the tile (✓). The pressure difference creates sufficient force to hold the cap on the wall (✓).
b) 6 kPa (✓✓)

5 a) The original shape is regained after the removal of applied forces (✓).
b) The original shape is not regained after the removal of applied forces (✓).

6 a) 20 cm (✓) **b)** 2.5 N (✓)

7 The moment of the applied force is greater with a long spanner than with a short spanner (✓). Hence less force is needed to produce the necessary moment (✓).

8 a) 0.40 N m (✓) **b)** 2.7 N (✓✓)

Your score: ☐ out of 23

9 Round up (page 282)
Forces in balance

1 a) The tyres are wider to create less pressure on the soft ground (✓). Also, the tractor can tilt further with big wheels before it topples over (✓).
b) Your diagram should show a small base and a high centre of gravity (✓). The pin needs to tilt only a little before it falls over because of its high centre of gravity in relation to its small base (✓).

2 a) (i) 200 kPa (✓) **(ii)** 6 kPa (✓) **b)** 0.004 m² (✓)

3 a) The stiffness of the steel spring is constant (✓); the stiffness of the elastic band changes as it is stretched (✓).
b) No (✓), it does not give equal changes in length for equal increases in force (✓).

4 0.4 m (✓), 1.1 N (✓), 10 N (✓), 0.19 m (✓)

5 a) Your graph should show axes labelled correctly and units shown (✓), points plotted correctly (✓), points covering at least half of each scale (✓), a straight line drawn through the points (✓).
b) 1.9 N (✓)

6 a) The molecules rebound repeatedly off the container surface (✓). Each impact exerts a force on the surface (✓). The pressure is caused by the average force of many impacts per second (✓).
b) 10 cm³ (✓✓)

Your score: ☐ out of 25

Your improvement index: $\dfrac{☐/23}{☐/25} \times 100\% = ☐\%$

10 Test yourself (page 283)
Electric charge

1 B and C (✓✓)

2 a) C (✓) **b)** B (✓)

3 a) A metal contains electrons which move about freely inside it (✓). These electrons carry charge and hence transfer charge through the metal when a potential difference is set up across the metal (✓).
b) All the electrons are firmly attached to atoms (✓) and so cannot transfer charge through the material (✓).

4 If the charged rod is negative, it repels electrons from the cap onto the leaf and stem (✓) which then repel each other (✓). If the charged rod is positive, it attracts electrons onto the cap from the leaf and stem (✓). This makes the leaf and stem positive, so the leaf is repelled from the stem (✓).

Answers

5 (i) It leaks away (✓). (ii) The plate retains its charge where it is dark. The charge attracts the particles (✓).

6 The pipe would become charged due to fluid friction, and a spark might be created (✓). This would be dangerous since it might ignite oil vapour (✓).

7 Any two from: electrostatic paint spray; ink jet printer; electrostatic precipitator (✓✓).

8 360 C (✓✓)

9 The liquid in the cell contains hydrogen ions and chloride ions (✓). Hydrogen ions are positive and are discharged at the anode (✓); chloride ions are negative and are discharged at the anode (✓).

10 Any two from: chromium electroplating; tin plating; extraction of aluminium from its ore; purification of copper (✓✓).

Your score: ☐ out of 25

10 Round up (page 289)

Electric charge

1 a) ii, iv, i then iii (✓✓✓) **b)** positive charge (✓) **c)** no (✓)

2 a) Electrons transfer from the electroscope to the rod (✓) so the leaf and stem both become positive (✓). Hence the leaf is repelled by the stem (✓).
 b) No charge can transfer to or from the electroscope once the rod has been removed (✓).
 c) Hold the rod near the electroscope (✓). Earth the electroscope cap (✓). Remove the earth connection (✓). Remove the rod (✓). (See page 285.)
 d) Charge the electroscope with a known charge. Bring the unknown charge near the cap (✓). If the leaf rises, the unknown charge is the same as the charge on the electroscope (✓). If the leaf falls, it is oppositely charged (✓).

3 a) (i) The charge on the metal car body discharges to earth (✓) through a person in contact with the ground who touches the car (✓).
  (ii) The car driver would be charged from the car (✓) and would discharge to earth on setting foot out of the car (✓).
 b) (i) The charge on the car leaks to earth through the trailing conductor (✓).
  (ii) Rainwater conducts electricity (✓) so allows the charge on the car body to transfer to earth (✓).

4 a) 180 C (✓), 1080 C (✓) **b)** 0.06 g (✓) **c)** 0.36 g (✓)
 d) 0.35 A (✓)

5 a) (i) The toner cartridge is nearly empty (✓) so less and less powder reaches the plate (✓) (or the 'lighter/darker' contrast control knob is not set correctly (✓) so not enough powder is attracted on to the plate (✓)).
  (ii) The powder does not dry fast enough (✓) immediately after it has been heated (✓).
 b) (i) No deflection (✓) (ii) reverse deflection (✓).

6 a) Uncharged dust particles are attracted to the live wire grid (✓) where they become charged the same as the grid (✓) and are then attracted on to the earthed tube and stay there (✓).
 b) In the presence of a nearby charged object, touching a pin allows opposite charge to transfer to it from earth (✓). Removing the earth connection leaves the pin charged (✓).

Your score: ☐ out of 40

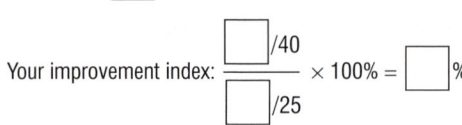

Your improvement index: $\dfrac{\square/40}{\square/25} \times 100\% = \square\%$

11 Test yourself (page 290)

Electric circuits

1 a)

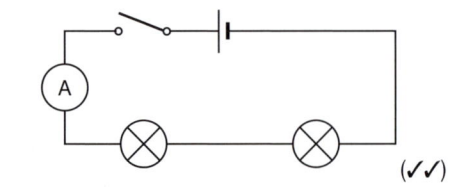

(✓✓)

 b) $0.2 \times 1.5 \times \dfrac{60}{2}$ (✓) = 9 J each (✓)

2 a)

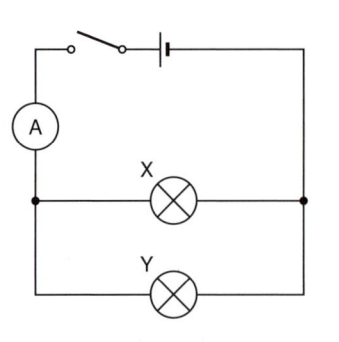

(✓✓)

 b) (i) 0.45 J (✓) (ii) 27 J (✓)

3 a) 0.2 A (✓) **b)** $\dfrac{1.0\,V}{0.2\,A}$ (✓) = 5.0 Ω (✓)

4 a) 15.0 V (✓) **b)** 37.5 W (✓)

5 a)

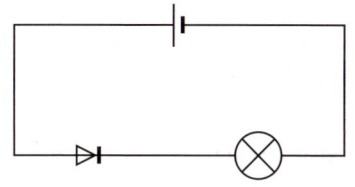

(✓✓)

b) The diode is now reverse biased (✓) so it will not conduct (✓).

6

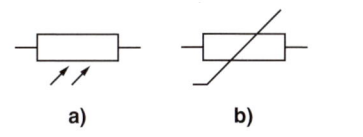

a)   b)   (✓✓)

a) An LDR's resistance depends on the incident light intensity (✓).
b) A thermistor's resistance depends on temperature (✓).

7 a) 300 kJ (✓) **b)** $\frac{1000\,W}{240\,V}$ (✓) = 4.2 A (✓)

8 a) A fuse is intended to protect an appliance or the connecting wires from excessive current (✓).
b) If the current rises above a certain value, the fuse wire overheats and melts (✓) causing a gap in the circuit (✓).

9 a) $\frac{20 \times 6\,W}{240\,V}$ (✓) = 0.5 A (✓) **b)** $\frac{240\,V}{20}$ (✓) = 12 V (✓)

10 a) 0.8 kW × 0.25 h (✓) = 0.2 kWh (✓)
b) 1.2p (✓)

Your score: ☐ out of 34

11 Round up (page 296)

Electric circuits

1 a) 12 Ω (✓)
b) The ammeter reading would double (✓); the voltmeter reading would be unchanged (✓).

2 a) (i) 6.3 A (✓) (ii) 3 kWh (✓)
b) (i) It is used to earth the metal frame of an appliance connected to the ring main (✓). It therefore prevents the frame from becoming live (✓).
(ii) 3 A (✓)
(iii) If the fuse rating is too low, the fuse will blow when the appliance is switched on (✓). If the fuse rating is too large, the fuse will not blow if the current becomes excessive. This would create a risk of fire due to resistance heating (✓).

3 a) (i) 1.5 V (✓) (ii) 0.3 A (✓) **b)** 0.45 W (✓)
c) The current in P becomes less (✓); the current in Q becomes greater (✓).

4 a) 2 A (✓), 6 Ω (✓)
b) $\frac{6\,\Omega}{5\,\Omega/m}$ (✓) = 1.2 m (✓)

c)

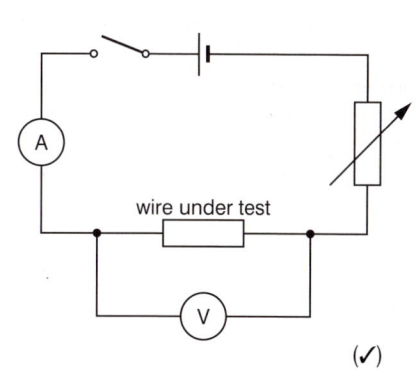

(✓)

Connect an exact length of 1.0 m into the circuit (✓) and measure the current and p.d. using the ammeter and the voltmeter (✓✓). Calculate the resistance from p.d./current (✓).

5 a) (i) 1.2 kWh (✓) (ii) 10 kWh (✓) (iii) 1.0 kWh (✓)
b) 61p (✓)
c) 29 minutes (✓✓)

6 a) Tap water conducts electricity (✓). Water might run into the appliance and provide a conducting path to earth via the user (✓). Also, the contact resistance between the appliance and the user is reduced by water (✓).
b) If the case became live (✓), current leakage to earth via the user might not be enough to blow the fuse (✓). An RCCB would cut the mains supply off if the leakage current exceeds 30 mA (✓).
c) The cable would become warm due to its resistance (✓). If it overheated, the insulation might melt (✓).

Your score: ☐ out of 38

Your improvement index: $\frac{\Box/38}{\Box/34} \times 100\% = \Box\%$

12 Test yourself (page 297)

Electromagnetism

1 a) soft iron (✓) **b)** steel (✓)
2 a) north (✓) **b)** north (✓)
3 a) circles centred on the wire (✓) in a horizontal plane (✓)

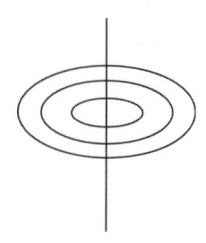

b) field lines loop round from one end to the other (✓) and pass through the solenoid along its axis (✓)

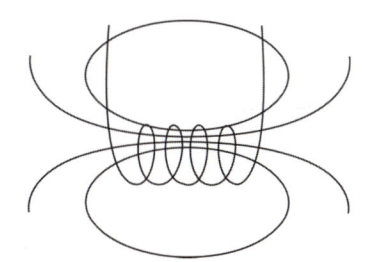

313

Answers

4 a) and c) permanent magnet (✓✓)   b) electromagnet (✓)

5 a) the same (✓)
   b) The turning effect on the coil would reverse each time the current reversed (✓), so the coil would be unable to spin (✓).

6 a) The peak voltage would decrease (✓) and the time for one cycle would increase (✓).
   b) Alternating current can be stepped up to high voltage on the grid system (✓). The same power can then be delivered with smaller currents than would be necessary if the voltage was low (✓). There is less resistance heating in the grid cables and therefore less power is wasted (✓).

7 The electromagnet creates a changing magnetic field through the aluminium plate, which induces alternating current in the plate (✓). Resistance heating therefore occurs in the plate (✓).

8 a) 12 V (✓)   b) 8.3 A (✓)

Your score: ☐ out of 23

12 Round-up (page 303)

Electromagnetism

1 a) See page 298 for diagram (✓✓✓). The electromagnet attracts the iron armature when current passes through the electromagnet coil (✓). The make-or-break switch opens (✓), the current switches off and the electromagnet is no longer attracted to the armature (✓). The armature springs back and closes the switch gap (✓). Current passes again and the process is repeated (✓).
   b) (i) The iron bar is attracted into the solenoid when the switch is closed (✓).
      (ii) To ensure it is pulled into the coil when the switch is closed (✓).
      (iii) It would operate on a.c. (✓) since the bar is attracted into the coil whatever the direction of the current (✓).

2 a) See page 298 for diagram (✓✓✓). Current through the electromagnet coil causes magnetism in its core (✓). The armature is attracted to the core (✓). The switch is closed by the movement of the armature (✓).
   b) The alternating current in the coil of the electromagnet creates an alternating magnetic field (✓). This field induces an alternating current in any conductor it passes through (✓).

3 a) See page 300 for diagram (✓✓✓). The sides of the coil cut the magnetic field lines as the coil turns (✓) so a voltage is induced in the coil (✓). The voltage alternates because the angle between the direction of motion of the coil sides and field lines changes continuously (✓).
   b) (i) See page 300 (✓✓).
      (ii) any maximum or minimum (✓)
   c) The peaks are higher (✓) and nearer to each other (✓).

4 a) (i) A changing primary current causes a changing magnetic field in the core (✓). A changing magnetic field through the secondary coil causes an induced voltage in the secondary coil (✓).
      (ii) The secondary current is greater since the voltage is stepped down (✓).
      (iii) The plates are made of iron to make the magnetic field as strong as possible (✓). The plates are laminated to reduce induced currents in the core (✓).
   b) (i) 12 V (✓)   (ii) 1.6 A (✓✓) (✓ for answer 2.0 A)

5 a) (i) There is less current for the same power (✓) so less heat is produced due to resistance in the cables (✓).
      (ii) UK – the higher voltage in the UK is more dangerous (✓) but smaller currents for the same power in the UK mean less risk of overheating (✓).
   b) Advantages: no underground trenches need to be dug, no waterproof insulating material needed round cable (✓). Disadvantages: liable to lightning strikes, unsightly (✓).

Your score: ☐ out of 45

Your improvement index: $\dfrac{\boxed{}/45}{\boxed{}/23} \times 100\% = \boxed{}\%$

Index

a.c. generator 300–1
acceleration 269
acid rain 160–1, 164
acids 145–7
AIDS 69
alcohol 57, 73, 88
alkanes 197–8, 201
alkenes 202–3, 205
alleles 96, 97
alloys *see* metals
alpha emissions 237, 238, 242
alternating current 300–1
amino acids 40, 59
ammonia 157
animal kingdom 4
argon 239
arteries 65, 67, 72
artificial vegetative reproduction 93
asexual reproduction 94–5
atmosphere 3, 153–4, 163
atmospheric pressure 285
atoms 124–6, 236–7
auxin 50, 51, 54

bacteria 6, 81
balanced forces 276
bases 147–9, 156
beta minus emissions 237, 238, 242
Big Bang 225
binomial system 6
biomass 15
biotechnology 99–100
blood 65–9
   white blood cells 84–5
body temperature 81, 83, 232
bonding 135–9
Boyle's law 281
brain 71, 73
breathing 62–4
Brownian motion 118

capillaries 68
carbohydrates 39–40
carbon dioxide 153, 157–8, 163
carbon monoxide 159, 164
cast iron 183
catalysts 187–8, 189
cells 27
   division 32–3, 34–5
   functions 30
   movement of molecules in 28, 29
   and organ systems 33, 36–7, 38
   structures 30, 31
   surface area to volume ratio 33, 38
   types 30
cellulose 39, 40
centre of gravity 276, 277
change of state 116
chemical reactions *see* reactions
chitin 40
chromatography 116
chromosomes 42
circuit breakers 295
circulatory system 65–70
classification of living things 3–6
classifying elements 140–3
coal 196, 201, 207
colour 278–9
comets 220
communications 258, 264–5
competitive exclusion 17
compounds 119, 121, 123
concentration 187, 189, 193, 195
conductors 284
conservation of Earth's resources 20, 181

constellations 221
continental drift 171, 172
copper-plating 288
corrosion 181, 185
covalent bonding 136–7, 138
cracking 197, 201
critical angle 257
crystals 118, 136
Curie, Marie 235

Darwin, Charles 102, 103
defecation 3
density 117
diet 56–7
diffraction 247, 250
diffusion 28, 29, 118
digital signals 264
digestive system 58–61
disaccharides 39
diseases 81, 84–7, 97
distillation 197
distribution of organisms 16–17
DNA (deoxyribonucleic acid) 41–4
drag 271
drugs 88
dynamo 301

ears 75, 76, 251
Earth 169, 170, 175
   atmosphere 153–4, 163
   plate tectonics 169–72
   raw materials 173–4
   in space 220, 222
   supporting life 2–3
earthing 285, 295
earthquakes 169, 170, 252
echoes 250
ecological pyramids 14–16
ecosystems 9, 10
Einstein, Albert 237
elastic behaviour 278
electric bell 298
electric motor 299
electricity 233
   current and charge 287, 291
   electrical power 230, 291
   mains electricity 294
   resistance 292–3
   safety 295
electrolysis 119, 128–32, 136, 179, 288
   copper (II) chloride 129
   copper (II) sulphate 130, 131
   sodium chloride 130–1
electromagnetic induction 300–10
electromagnetic waves 245, 261–5
electromagnetism 298–302
electrons 124, 125, 126
electroplating 132, 288
electrostatics 284–6
elements 119, 120, 140–9
empirical formula 192, 193
endoscope 258
endothermic reactions 198, 199
energy
   and chemical reactions 198–200, 201
   conservation of 229
   efficiency 230, 233
   food energy 13, 16, 20–1, 57
   forms of 228, 272
   measuring 228
   and power 230
   resources 196, 233
   transferring 228
environment 2, 3, 9–10
   human impact on 19–20, 22–3

enzymes 41, 59, 188
equations for chemical reactions 122
equilibrium 286–7
evolution 101, 102–5, 106
excretion 3
exothermic reactions 198, 199
extinction 106
eyes 75, 76–7

Faraday's law 300
farming 20–1, 24–5
fats 40
fertilisers 24, 157, 167
fibre optics 257–8, 264
fission 242
food chains 11–13, 21
food and diet 56–7
food energy 13, 16, 20–1
food irradiation 240
food webs 13, 14, 18–19
forces
   in balance 276–81
   and motion 268–72
formulas 120–1, 192–3
fossils 104, 105
fractional distillation 197
frequency 246
frequency bands 264
friction 284
fuels 196–8, 201, 233
fungi 6, 10
fuses 295

galaxies 225
gamma radiation 238, 240, 242, 263
gases 117, 118, 281
Geiger counters 237
genetic codes 41, 43
genetic engineering 100
genetics vocabulary 93, 96
glycogen 39, 40, 77
gold leaf electroscope 285
gravitational potential energy (GPE) 229, 272
gravity 220, 269
greenhouse effect 158, 163

haemophilia 69, 84, 97
half-life 239
halogen hobs 262
heart 65, 68, 69–70
heat transfer 231–2
helium 151
hepatic portal vein 59, 67, 68
HIV 69
homeostasis 80–1, 82–3
Hooke's law 278
hormones 77–80
Hubble's law 225
human population 19
   environmental impact of 19–20, 22–3
hydration 203
hydraulics 280
hydrocarbons 161, 164, 197–8
hydrogenation 203

infra-red radiation 262
igneous rocks 172
inheritance 93, 95, 96, 98
   of sex 96–7
ink jet printer 286
insulators 232, 284
intensive farming 24–5
ionic bonding 135–6, 138
ionic compounds 137–9
ionic equations 122

315

Index

ions 129, 130, 238
iron 180, 181, 183
isotopes 125, 236–7

keys 6–7
kidneys 81, 82, 85–6
kilowatt hour (kWh) 230, 286
kinetic energy (KE) 229, 272
kinetic theory 117–8
kingdoms 4–6

lead 161, 164
Lenz's law 300
leukaemia 69
light
   energy 187
   intraspecific competition for 17
   and plant growth 51
   rays and waves 255–9
lime kilns 173, 174
limestone 173, 174, 175
Linnaeus, Carolus 6
lipids 40
liquids 117, 279
liver 59, 61
loudspeakers 300

magnetic fields 298
mains circuits 294
masses of reacting solids 193–5
materials 117
matter 116
meiosis 32, 33, 35, 90
Mendeleev, Dmitri 140
metals 120, 123, 177, 178–9, 185
   conservation 181
   corrosion 181
   extraction 130–1, 180
   reactions 177–8
   uses 182–3
metamorphic rocks 172
microphone 301
microwave cookers 262
mirrors 255
mitosis 32, 33, 34, 90
molar mass 191
molecular formula 192, 193
molecules 119, 236
moment of a force 276–7
monohybrid inheritance 93–8
monosaccharides 39
motion 278–82
motor effect 299
mutations 43, 101

nastic movements 50
natural gas 196
neon 151
nervous system 70–3
neutralisation 122, 149, 151–2, 198
neutrons 124, 125
Newlands, John 140
Newton's laws 271
nitrogen 154, 156–7, 163
noble gases 143, 144, 153, 159
NPK fertilisers 157
nuclear reactors 241, 242
nucleic acids 41

Ohm's law 292
oil (petroleum) 196–7, 201
oils 40
optical fibres 257–8, 264
organ systems 33, 36–7, 38
osmosis 28, 29
oxidation 155–6

oxides 179
oxides of nitrogen 161, 164
oxygen 154–6, 163, 166

pancreas 59, 61, 79
particle size 86
periodic table 140–3, 144, 207
petroleum oil 196–7, 201
phloem 49, 52, 53
photocopier 286
photosynthesis 13, 45–6, 47–8, 198
planets 221–2
plants
   growth 46, 50–1
   kingdom 5
   reproduction 91–3, 94
   response to light 50, 51, 54
   root growth 51
   transpiration 49–50
   transport system 52–3
   see also photosynthesis
plastic behaviour 278
plastics 203–5
plate tectonics 169–72
polarisation 245
pollution 23, 159–61, 164, 166–7, 168
polysaccharides 39–40
populations 18–19
power 230
precipitation 122, 152
predators 12, 17, 18–19
pressure 187, 189, 279–81
properties of materials 117
proteins 40–1
protista 6
protons 124, 125
pulmonary artery 68
pyramids 14–16

radioactive dating 239
radioactive waste 242
radioactivity 235–42, 263
reactions 135, 177–8, 193–195
   and energy 194–5, 197
   equations 122
   heat of 198–9
   speeds 186–9
red shift 225
reduction 155–6
reflection 247, 255
refraction 247, 250, 256
relative atomic mass 125, 190
relative molecular mass 190
renewable energy resources 233
reproduction 90–3
resistance 292–3
respiration 3, 30, 62–5, 198
RNA (ribonucleic acid) 41
rocks 172–3, 175
root growth 51
rusting 181

salts 149–52
satellites 220
scavengers 12
sedimentary rocks 172
seismic waves 252
senses 73–7
SETI 224
sexual characteristics 80
sexual reproduction 90–2
silica 173, 175
skin 74, 83
smell 74, 76
smog 161
smoking 86–7
soil 2, 3

solar system 220, 221–2
solids
   kinetic theory 117, 118
   masses of reacting solids 193–195
   soluble 117, 118
   strength of 278
solutions 117
solvents 88, 117
sound waves 249–51
speed 268
stability 276
starch 39, 40
stars 223–4
steel 181, 186
stomata 47, 49, 50
stopping distances 270
sulphur dioxide 160–1, 164
Sun 220, 222
sweat pores 83
symbols, chemical 120

tape recorders 301
tarnishing 177
taste buds 74, 76
temperature 187, 232
   body temperature 81, 83, 232
terminal velocity 271
thermal conduction 231–2
thermal convection 231
thermal energy 228
thermal radiation 231, 232
thigmotropism 51
tongue 74, 76
total internal reflection 257
transformers 302
transpiration 49–50
trophic levels 14
tropisms 50–1

U-tube manometer 279, 281
ultrasound 251
ultraviolet radiation 262
Universe 225

vapours 116
variation 101–2, 105
vegetative reproduction 92–3
veins 65, 67
velocity 268, 271
visible spectrum 262
volcanoes 170

water 3, 168
   cycle 165
   pollution 166–7, 168
   pure water 168
   underground 168
wavelength 246, 259
waves 244–7, 249–52
weathering 172
weedkillers 54
weight 271
white blood cells 65, 84–5
work and energy 228, 272

X-rays 263
xylem 30